Ford Pick-ups & Bronco Automotive Repair Manual

by Mark Christman, John B Raffa and John H Haynes

Member of the Guild of Motoring Writers

Models covered:

F-100, F-150, F-250, F-350 and Bronco with 300 cu in (4.9L) inline six-cylinder, 232 cu in V6, and 255, 302 (5.0L), 351 (5.8L), 400 and 460 cu in (7.5L) V8 engines

Manual and automatic transmissions

Two-wheel drive and four-wheel drive, 1980 thru 1996, and 1997 F-250HD and F-350

Does not include diesel engine or Super Duty vehicles

(36058 - 9R23)

ABCDE
FGHIJ
KLMNO

4

Haynes Publishing Group
Sparkford Nr Yeovil
Somerset BA22 7JJ England

Haynes North America, Inc
861 Lawrence Drive
Newbury Park
California 91320 USA

About this manual

Its purpose

The purpose of this manual is to help you get the best value from your vehicle. It can do so in several ways. It can help you decide what work must be done, even if you choose to have it done by a dealer service department or a repair shop; it provides information and procedures for routine maintenance and servicing; and it offers diagnostic and repair procedures to follow when trouble occurs.

We hope you use the manual to tackle the work yourself. For many simpler jobs, doing it yourself may be quicker than arranging an appointment to get the vehicle into a shop and making the trips to leave it and pick it up. More importantly, a lot of money can be saved by avoiding the expense the shop must pass on to you to cover its labor and overhead costs. An added benefit is the sense of satisfaction and accomplishment that you feel after doing the job yourself.

Using the manual

The manual is divided into Chapters. Each Chapter is divided into numbered Sections, which are headed in bold type between horizontal lines. Each Section consists of consecutively numbered paragraphs.

At the beginning of each numbered Section you will be referred to any illustrations which apply to the procedures in that Section. The reference numbers used in illustration captions pinpoint the pertinent Section and the Step within that Section. That is, illustration 3.2 means the illustration refers to Section 3 and Step (or paragraph) 2 within that Section.

Procedures, once described in the text, are not normally repeated. When it's necessary to refer to another Chapter, the reference will be given as Chapter and Section number. Cross references given without use of the word "Chapter" apply to Sections and/or paragraphs in the same Chapter. For example, "see Section 8" means in the same Chapter.

References to the left or right side of the vehicle assume you are sitting in the driver's seat, facing forward.

Even though we have prepared this manual with extreme care, neither the publisher nor the author can accept responsibility for any errors in, or omissions from, the information given.

NOTE

A **Note** provides information necessary to properly complete a procedure or information which will make the procedure easier to understand.

CAUTION

A **Caution** provides a special procedure or special steps which must be taken while completing the procedure where the Caution is found. Not heeding a Caution can result in damage to the assembly being worked on.

WARNING

A **Warning** provides a special procedure or special steps which must be taken while completing the procedure where the Warning is found. Not heeding a Warning can result in personal injury.

© Haynes North America, Inc. 1994, 1995, 1996, 2004, 2012
With permission from J.H. Haynes & Co. Ltd.

A book in the Haynes Automotive Repair Manual Series

Printed in the U.S.A.

ISBN: 978-1-62092-010-7

Library of Congress Control Number: 2012948584

Contents

Haynes mechanic, author and photographer with an F250 pick-up

Introduction

The F-series and Bronco models are conventional front-engine, rear-wheel drive vehicles.

Over the years of production covered by this manual, engine options include the 300 cu. in. (4.9L) inline six-cylinder engine, the 232 cu. in. V6 engine and the 255 cu. in., 302 cu. in. (5.0L), 351 cu. in. (5.8L), 400 and 460 (7.5L) V8 engines.

Power is transmitted through either manual or automatic transmission to a driveshaft and solid rear axle on two-wheel drive (2WD) models. On four-wheel drive (4WD) models, a transfer case transfers power to the front axle by way of a driveshaft. Transmissions used include a four-speed manual, two different five-speed overdrive manuals, a three-speed automatic and two different four-speed overdrive automatics. Three different transfer cases are available - two manual shift and one electronic shift.

All 2WD models use twin I-beam independent front suspension with coil springs and radius arms. 4WD models (except F350)

use a similar independent front suspension with a two-piece front driveaxle assembly, coil springs and radius arms (except F250). F250 4WD models use leaf springs instead of coil springs on its independent front suspension. F350 4WD models use a solid front axle and leaf springs. All models use semi-elliptical leaf springs at the rear.

All models are equipped with front disc and rear drum brakes.

Vehicle identification numbers

Modifications are a continuing and unpublicized process in vehicle manufacturing. Since spare parts lists and manuals are compiled on a numerical basis, the individual vehicle numbers are necessary to correctly identify the component required.

Vehicle Identification Number (VIN)

This very important identification number is stamped on a plate attached to the dashboard inside the windshield on the driver's side of the vehicle **(see illustration)**. The VIN also appears on the Vehicle Certificate of Title and Registration. It contains information such as where and when the vehicle was manufactured, the model year and the body style.

Vehicle Certification Label

The Vehicle Certification Label is attached to the driver's side door pillar **(see illustration)**. Information on this label includes the name of the manufacturer, the month and year of production, the Gross Vehicle Weight Rating (GVWR), the Gross Axle Weight Rating (GAWR) and other vehicle specific information. Some of the information is in the form of codes, requiring a conversion chart to obtain the desired information. Included are the conversions for the rear axle ratio and transmission type codes.

Engine number

The engine number is stamped onto a machined pad on the external surface of the engine block. There's also an identification label that's usually on the valve cover **(see illustration)**.

The Vehicle Identification Number (VIN) is visible through the driver's side of the windshield

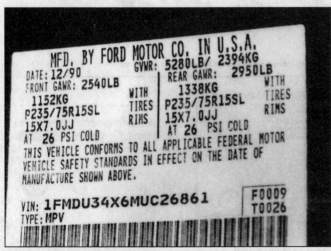

Typical Certification label

The engine identification label can usually be found on the valve cover

Buying parts

Replacement parts are available from many sources, which generally fall into one of two categories - authorized dealer parts departments and independent retail auto parts stores. Our advice concerning these parts is as follows:

Retail auto parts stores: Good auto parts stores will stock frequently needed components which wear out relatively fast, such as clutch components, exhaust systems, brake parts, tune-up parts, etc. These stores often supply new or reconditioned parts on an exchange basis, which can save a considerable amount of money. Discount auto parts stores are often very good places to buy materials and parts needed for general vehicle maintenance such as oil, grease, filters, spark plugs, belts, touch-up paint, bulbs, etc. They also usually sell tools and general accessories, have convenient hours, charge lower prices and can often be found not far from home.

Authorized dealer parts department: This is the best source for parts which are unique to the vehicle and not generally available elsewhere (such as major engine parts, transmission parts, trim pieces, etc.).

Warranty information: If the vehicle is still covered under warranty, be sure that any replacement parts purchased - regardless of the source - do not invalidate the warranty!

To be sure of obtaining the correct parts, have engine and chassis numbers available and, if possible, take the old parts along for positive identification.

Maintenance techniques, tools and working facilities

Maintenance techniques

There are a number of techniques involved in maintenance and repair that will be referred to throughout this manual. Application of these techniques will enable the home mechanic to be more efficient, better organized and capable of performing the various tasks properly, which will ensure that the repair job is thorough and complete.

Fasteners

Fasteners are nuts, bolts, studs and screws used to hold two or more parts together. There are a few things to keep in mind when working with fasteners. Almost all of them use a locking device of some type, either a lockwasher, locknut, locking tab or thread adhesive. All threaded fasteners should be clean and straight, with undamaged threads and undamaged corners on the hex head where the wrench fits. Develop the habit of replacing all damaged nuts and bolts with new ones. Special locknuts with nylon or fiber inserts can only be used once. If they are removed, they lose their locking ability and must be replaced with new ones.

Rusted nuts and bolts should be treated with a penetrating fluid to ease removal and prevent breakage. Some mechanics use turpentine in a spout-type oil can, which works quite well. After applying the rust penetrant, let it work for a few minutes before trying to loosen the nut or bolt. Badly rusted fasteners may have to be chiseled or sawed off or removed with a special nut breaker, available at tool stores.

If a bolt or stud breaks off in an assembly, it can be drilled and removed with a special tool commonly available for this purpose.

Most automotive machine shops can perform this task, as well as other repair procedures, such as the repair of threaded holes that have been stripped out.

Flat washers and lockwashers, when removed from an assembly, should always be replaced exactly as removed. Replace any damaged washers with new ones. Never use a lockwasher on any soft metal surface (such as aluminum), thin sheet metal or plastic.

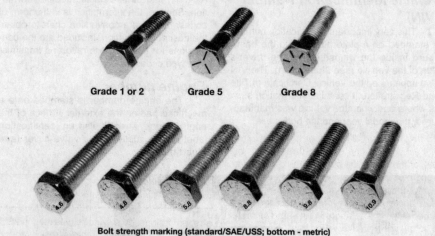

Grade 1 or 2   Grade 5   Grade 8

Bolt strength marking (standard/SAE/USS; bottom - metric)

Grade	Identification	Grade	Identification		
Hex Nut Grade 5	3 Dots	Hex Nut Property Class 9	Arabic 9		
Hex Nut Grade 8	6 Dots	Hex Nut Property Class 10	Arabic 10		

Class 10.9	Class 9.8	Class 8.8

Standard hex nut strength markings   Metric hex nut strength markings   Metric stud strength markings

00-1 HAYNES

Fastener sizes

For a number of reasons, automobile manufacturers are making wider and wider use of metric fasteners. Therefore, it is important to be able to tell the difference between standard (sometimes called U.S. or SAE) and metric hardware, since they cannot be interchanged.

All bolts, whether standard or metric, are sized according to diameter, thread pitch and length. For example, a standard 1/2 - 13 x 1 bolt is 1/2 inch in diameter, has 13 threads per inch and is 1 inch long. An M12 - 1.75 x 25 metric bolt is 12 mm in diameter, has a thread pitch of 1.75 mm (the distance between threads) and is 25 mm long. The two bolts are nearly identical, and easily confused, but they are not interchangeable.

In addition to the differences in diameter, thread pitch and length, metric and standard bolts can also be distinguished by examining the bolt heads. To begin with, the distance across the flats on a standard bolt head is measured in inches, while the same dimension on a metric bolt is sized in millimeters (the same is true for nuts). As a result, a standard wrench should not be used on a metric bolt and a metric wrench should not be used on a standard bolt. Also, most standard bolts have slashes radiating out from the center of the head to denote the grade or strength of the bolt, which is an indication of the amount of torque that can be applied to it. The greater the number of slashes, the greater the strength of the bolt. Grades 0 through 5 are commonly used on automobiles. Metric bolts have a property class (grade) number, rather than a slash, molded into their heads to indicate bolt strength. In this case, the higher the number, the stronger the bolt. Property class numbers 8.8, 9.8 and 10.9 are commonly used on automobiles.

Strength markings can also be used to distinguish standard hex nuts from metric hex nuts. Many standard nuts have dots stamped into one side, while metric nuts are marked with a number. The greater the number of dots, or the higher the number, the greater the strength of the nut.

Metric studs are also marked on their ends according to property class (grade). Larger studs are numbered (the same as metric bolts), while smaller studs carry a geometric code to denote grade.

It should be noted that many fasteners, especially Grades 0 through 2, have no distinguishing marks on them. When such is the case, the only way to determine whether it is standard or metric is to measure the thread pitch or compare it to a known fastener of the same size.

Standard fasteners are often referred to as SAE, as opposed to metric. However, it should be noted that SAE technically refers to a non-metric fine thread fastener only. Coarse thread non-metric fasteners are referred to as USS sizes.

Since fasteners of the same size (both standard and metric) may have different

Metric thread sizes	Ft-lbs	Nm
M-6	6 to 9	9 to 12
M-8	14 to 21	19 to 28
M-10	28 to 40	38 to 54
M-12	50 to 71	68 to 96
M-14	80 to 140	109 to 154

Pipe thread sizes		
1/8	5 to 8	7 to 10
1/4	12 to 18	17 to 24
3/8	22 to 33	30 to 44
1/2	25 to 35	34 to 47

U.S. thread sizes		
1/4 - 20	6 to 9	9 to 12
5/16 - 18	12 to 18	17 to 24
5/16 - 24	14 to 20	19 to 27
3/8 - 16	22 to 32	30 to 43
3/8 - 24	27 to 38	37 to 51
7/16 - 14	40 to 55	55 to 74
7/16 - 20	40 to 60	55 to 81
1/2 - 13	55 to 80	75 to 108

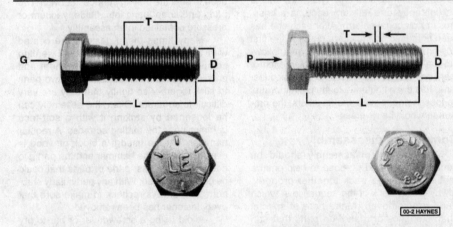

Standard (SAE and USS) bolt dimensions/ grade marks

G   Grade marks (bolt strength)
L   Length (in inches)
T   Thread pitch (number of threads per inch)
D   Nominal diameter (in inches)

Metric bolt dimensions/grade marks

P   Property class (bolt strength)
L   Length (in millimeters)
T   Thread pitch (distance between threads in millimeters)
D   Diameter

strength ratings, be sure to reinstall any bolts, studs or nuts removed from your vehicle in their original locations. Also, when replacing a fastener with a new one, make sure that the new one has a strength rating equal to or greater than the original.

Tightening sequences and procedures

Most threaded fasteners should be tightened to a specific torque value (torque is the twisting force applied to a threaded component such as a nut or bolt). Overtightening the fastener can weaken it and cause it to break, while undertightening can cause it to eventually come loose. Bolts, screws and studs, depending on the material they are made

of and their thread diameters, have specific torque values, many of which are noted in the Specifications at the beginning of each Chapter. Be sure to follow the torque recommendations closely. For fasteners not assigned a specific torque, a general torque value chart is presented here as a guide. These torque values are for dry (unlubricated) fasteners threaded into steel or cast iron (not aluminum). As was previously mentioned, the size and grade of a fastener determine the amount of torque that can safely be applied to it. The figures listed here are approximate for Grade 2 and Grade 3 fasteners. Higher grades can tolerate higher torque values.

Fasteners laid out in a pattern, such as cylinder head bolts, oil pan bolts, differential cover bolts, etc., must be loosened or tight-

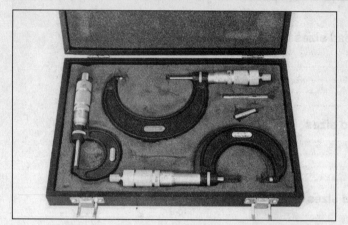

Micrometer set

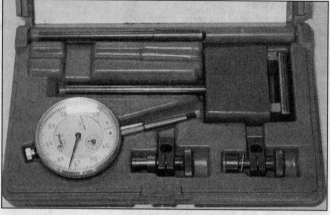

Dial indicator set

ened in sequence to avoid warping the component. This sequence will normally be shown in the appropriate Chapter. If a specific pattern is not given, the following procedures can be used to prevent warping.

Initially, the bolts or nuts should be assembled finger-tight only. Next, they should be tightened one full turn each, in a criss-cross or diagonal pattern. After each one has been tightened one full turn, return to the first one and tighten them all one-half turn, following the same pattern. Finally, tighten each of them one-quarter turn at a time until each fastener has been tightened to the proper torque. To loosen and remove the fasteners, the procedure would be reversed.

Component disassembly

Component disassembly should be done with care and purpose to help ensure that the parts go back together properly. Always keep track of the sequence in which parts are removed. Make note of special characteristics or marks on parts that can be installed more than one way, such as a grooved thrust washer on a shaft. It is a good idea to lay the disassembled parts out on a clean surface in the order that they were removed. It may also be helpful to make sketches or take instant photos of components before removal.

When removing fasteners from a component, keep track of their locations. Sometimes threading a bolt back in a part, or putting the washers and nut back on a stud, can prevent mix-ups later. If nuts and bolts cannot be returned to their original locations, they should be kept in a compartmented box or a series of small boxes. A cupcake or muffin tin is ideal for this purpose, since each cavity can hold the bolts and nuts from a particular area (i.e. oil pan bolts, valve cover bolts, engine mount bolts, etc.). A pan of this type is especially helpful when working on assemblies with very small parts, such as the carburetor, alternator, valve train or interior dash and trim pieces. The cavities can be marked with paint or tape to identify the contents.

Whenever wiring looms, harnesses or connectors are separated, it is a good idea to

identify the two halves with numbered pieces of masking tape so they can be easily reconnected.

Gasket sealing surfaces

Throughout any vehicle, gaskets are used to seal the mating surfaces between two parts and keep lubricants, fluids, vacuum or pressure contained in an assembly.

Many times these gaskets are coated with a liquid or paste-type gasket sealing compound before assembly. Age, heat and pressure can sometimes cause the two parts to stick together so tightly that they are very difficult to separate. Often, the assembly can be loosened by striking it with a soft-face hammer near the mating surfaces. A regular hammer can be used if a block of wood is placed between the hammer and the part. Do not hammer on cast parts or parts that could be easily damaged. With any particularly stubborn part, always recheck to make sure that every fastener has been removed.

Avoid using a screwdriver or bar to pry apart an assembly, as they can easily mar the gasket sealing surfaces of the parts, which must remain smooth. If prying is absolutely necessary, use an old broom handle, but keep in mind that extra clean up will be necessary if the wood splinters.

After the parts are separated, the old gasket must be carefully scraped off and the gasket surfaces cleaned. Stubborn gasket material can be soaked with rust penetrant or treated with a special chemical to soften it so it can be easily scraped off. A scraper can be fashioned from a piece of copper tubing by flattening and sharpening one end. Copper is recommended because it is usually softer than the surfaces to be scraped, which reduces the chance of gouging the part. Some gaskets can be removed with a wire brush, but regardless of the method used, the mating surfaces must be left clean and smooth. If for some reason the gasket surface is gouged, then a gasket sealer thick enough to fill scratches will have to be used during reassembly of the components. For most applications, a non-drying (or semi-drying) gasket sealer should be used.

Hose removal tips

Warning: *If the vehicle is equipped with air conditioning, do not disconnect any of the A/C hoses without first having the system depressurized by a dealer service department or a service station.*

Hose removal precautions closely parallel gasket removal precautions. Avoid scratching or gouging the surface that the hose mates against or the connection may leak. This is especially true for radiator hoses. Because of various chemical reactions, the rubber in hoses can bond itself to the metal spigot that the hose fits over. To remove a hose, first loosen the hose clamps that secure it to the spigot. Then, with slip-joint pliers, grab the hose at the clamp and rotate it around the spigot. Work it back and forth until it is completely free, then pull it off. Silicone or other lubricants will ease removal if they can be applied between the hose and the outside of the spigot. Apply the same lubricant to the inside of the hose and the outside of the spigot to simplify installation.

As a last resort (and if the hose is to be replaced with a new one anyway), the rubber can be slit with a knife and the hose peeled from the spigot. If this must be done, be careful that the metal connection is not damaged.

If a hose clamp is broken or damaged, do not reuse it. Wire-type clamps usually weaken with age, so it is a good idea to replace them with screw-type clamps whenever a hose is removed.

Tools

A selection of good tools is a basic requirement for anyone who plans to maintain and repair his or her own vehicle. For the owner who has few tools, the initial investment might seem high, but when compared to the spiraling costs of professional auto maintenance and repair, it is a wise one.

To help the owner decide which tools are needed to perform the tasks detailed in this manual, the following tool lists are offered: *Maintenance and minor repair, Repair/overhaul* and *Special.*

The newcomer to practical mechanics

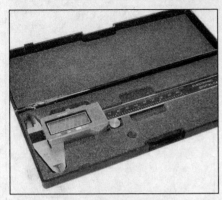

Dial caliper

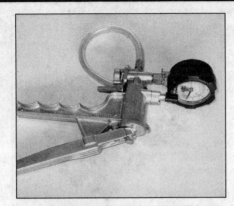

Hand-operated vacuum pump

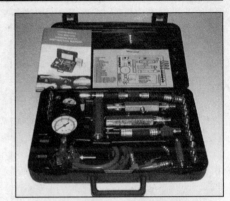

Fuel pressure gauge set

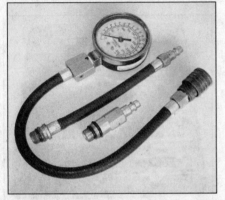

Compression gauge with spark plug hole adapter

Damper/steering wheel puller

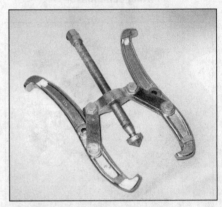

General purpose puller

Hydraulic lifter removal tool

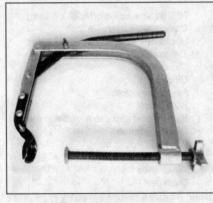

Valve spring compressor

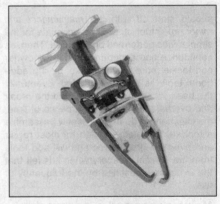

Valve spring compressor

Ridge reamer

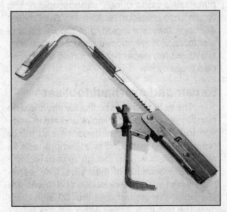

Piston ring groove cleaning tool

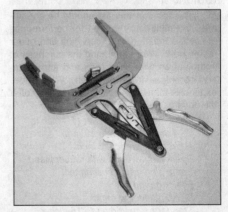

Ring removal/installation tool

Ring compressor

Cylinder hone

Brake hold-down spring tool

Torque angle gauge

Clutch plate alignment tool

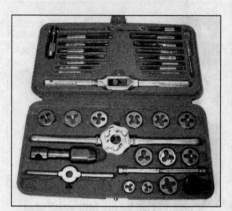

Tap and die set

should start off with the *maintenance and minor repair* tool kit, which is adequate for the simpler jobs performed on a vehicle. Then, as confidence and experience grow, the owner can tackle more difficult tasks, buying additional tools as they are needed. Eventually the basic kit will be expanded into the *repair and overhaul* tool set. Over a period of time, the experienced do-it-yourselfer will assemble a tool set complete enough for most repair and overhaul procedures and will add tools from the special category when it is felt that the expense is justified by the frequency of use.

Maintenance and minor repair tool kit

The tools in this list should be considered the minimum required for performance of routine maintenance, servicing and minor repair work. We recommend the purchase of combination wrenches (box-end and open-end combined in one wrench). While more expensive than open end wrenches, they offer the advantages of both types of wrench.

> *Combination wrench set (1/4-inch to*
> *1 inch or 6 mm to 19 mm)*
> *Adjustable wrench, 8 inch*
> *Spark plug wrench with rubber insert*
> *Spark plug gap adjusting tool*
> *Feeler gauge set*
> *Brake bleeder wrench*
> *Standard screwdriver (5/16-inch x*
> *6 inch)*

> *Phillips screwdriver (No. 2 x 6 inch)*
> *Combination pliers - 6 inch*
> *Hacksaw and assortment of blades*
> *Tire pressure gauge*
> *Grease gun*
> *Oil can*
> *Fine emery cloth*
> *Wire brush*
> *Battery post and cable cleaning tool*
> *Oil filter wrench*
> *Funnel (medium size)*
> *Safety goggles*
> *Jackstands (2)*
> *Drain pan*

Note: *If basic tune-ups are going to be part of routine maintenance, it will be necessary to purchase a good quality stroboscopic timing light and combination tachometer/dwell meter. Although they are included in the list of special tools, it is mentioned here because they are absolutely necessary for tuning most vehicles properly.*

Repair and overhaul tool set

These tools are essential for anyone who plans to perform major repairs and are in addition to those in the maintenance and minor repair tool kit. Included is a comprehensive set of sockets which, though expensive, are invaluable because of their versatility, especially when various extensions and drives are available. We recommend the 1/2-inch drive over the 3/8-inch drive. Although the larger drive is bulky and more expensive, it has the

capacity of accepting a very wide range of large sockets. Ideally, however, the mechanic should have a 3/8-inch drive set and a 1/2-inch drive set.

> *Socket set(s)*
> *Reversible ratchet*
> *Extension - 10 inch*
> *Universal joint*
> *Torque wrench (same size drive as*
> *sockets)*
> *Ball peen hammer - 8 ounce*
> *Soft-face hammer (plastic/rubber)*
> *Standard screwdriver (1/4-inch x 6 inch)*
> *Standard screwdriver (stubby -*
> *5/16-inch)*
> *Phillips screwdriver (No. 3 x 8 inch)*
> *Phillips screwdriver (stubby - No. 2)*
> *Pliers - vise grip*
> *Pliers - lineman's*
> *Pliers - needle nose*
> *Pliers - snap-ring (internal and external)*
> *Cold chisel - 1/2-inch*
> *Scribe*
> *Scraper (made from flattened copper*
> *tubing)*
> *Centerpunch*
> *Pin punches (1/16, 1/8, 3/16-inch)*
> *Steel rule/straightedge - 12 inch*
> *Allen wrench set (1/8 to 3/8-inch or*
> *4 mm to 10 mm)*
> *A selection of files*
> *Wire brush (large)*
> *Jackstands (second set)*
> *Jack (scissor or hydraulic type)*

Note: *Another tool which is often useful is an electric drill with a chuck capacity of 3/8-inch and a set of good quality drill bits.*

Special tools

The tools in this list include those which are not used regularly, are expensive to buy, or which need to be used in accordance with their manufacturer's instructions. Unless these tools will be used frequently, it is not very economical to purchase many of them. A consideration would be to split the cost and use between yourself and a friend or friends. In addition, most of these tools can be obtained from a tool rental shop on a temporary basis.

This list primarily contains only those tools and instruments widely available to the public, and not those special tools produced by the vehicle manufacturer for distribution to dealer service departments. Occasionally, references to the manufacturer's special tools are included in the text of this manual. Generally, an alternative method of doing the job without the special tool is offered. However, sometimes there is no alternative to their use. Where this is the case, and the tool cannot be purchased or borrowed, the work should be turned over to the dealer service department or an automotive repair shop.

> *Valve spring compressor*
> *Piston ring groove cleaning tool*
> *Piston ring compressor*
> *Piston ring installation tool*
> *Cylinder compression gauge*
> *Cylinder ridge reamer*
> *Cylinder surfacing hone*
> *Cylinder bore gauge*
> *Micrometers and/or dial calipers*
> *Hydraulic lifter removal tool*
> *Balljoint separator*
> *Universal-type puller*
> *Impact screwdriver*
> *Dial indicator set*
> *Stroboscopic timing light (inductive pick-up)*
> *Hand operated vacuum/pressure pump*
> *Tachometer/dwell meter*
> *Universal electrical multimeter*
> *Cable hoist*
> *Brake spring removal and installation tools*
> *Floor jack*

Buying tools

For the do-it-yourselfer who is just starting to get involved in vehicle maintenance and repair, there are a number of options available when purchasing tools. If maintenance and minor repair is the extent of the work to be done, the purchase of individual tools is satisfactory. If, on the other hand, extensive work is planned, it would be a good idea to purchase a modest tool set from one of the large retail chain stores. A set can usually be bought at a substantial savings over the individual tool prices, and they often come with a tool box. As additional tools are needed, add-on sets,

individual tools and a larger tool box can be purchased to expand the tool selection. Building a tool set gradually allows the cost of the tools to be spread over a longer period of time and gives the mechanic the freedom to choose only those tools that will actually be used.

Tool stores will often be the only source of some of the special tools that are needed, but regardless of where tools are bought, try to avoid cheap ones, especially when buying screwdrivers and sockets, because they won't last very long. The expense involved in replacing cheap tools will eventually be greater than the initial cost of quality tools.

Care and maintenance of tools

Good tools are expensive, so it makes sense to treat them with respect. Keep them clean and in usable condition and store them properly when not in use. Always wipe off any dirt, grease or metal chips before putting them away. Never leave tools lying around in the work area. Upon completion of a job, always check closely under the hood for tools that may have been left there so they won't get lost during a test drive.

Some tools, such as screwdrivers, pliers, wrenches and sockets, can be hung on a panel mounted on the garage or workshop wall, while others should be kept in a tool box or tray. Measuring instruments, gauges, meters, etc. must be carefully stored where they cannot be damaged by weather or impact from other tools.

When tools are used with care and stored properly, they will last a very long time. Even with the best of care, though, tools will wear out if used frequently. When a tool is damaged or worn out, replace it. Subsequent jobs will be safer and more enjoyable if you do.

How to repair damaged threads

Sometimes, the internal threads of a nut or bolt hole can become stripped, usually from overtightening. Stripping threads is an all-too-common occurrence, especially when working with aluminum parts, because aluminum is so soft that it easily strips out.

Usually, external or internal threads are only partially stripped. After they've been cleaned up with a tap or die, they'll still work. Sometimes, however, threads are badly damaged. When this happens, you've got three choices:

1) *Drill and tap the hole to the next suitable oversize and install a larger diameter bolt, screw or stud.*
2) *Drill and tap the hole to accept a threaded plug, then drill and tap the plug to the original screw size. You can also buy a plug already threaded to the original size. Then you simply drill a hole to the specified size, then run the threaded plug into the hole with a bolt and jam nut.*

Once the plug is fully seated, remove the jam nut and bolt.
3) *The third method uses a patented thread repair kit like Heli-Coil or Slimsert. These easy-to-use kits are designed to repair damaged threads in straight-through holes and blind holes. Both are available as kits which can handle a variety of sizes and thread patterns. Drill the hole, then tap it with the special included tap. Install the Heli-Coil and the hole is back to its original diameter and thread pitch.*

Regardless of which method you use, be sure to proceed calmly and carefully. A little impatience or carelessness during one of these relatively simple procedures can ruin your whole day's work and cost you a bundle if you wreck an expensive part.

Working facilities

Not to be overlooked when discussing tools is the workshop. If anything more than routine maintenance is to be carried out, some sort of suitable work area is essential.

It is understood, and appreciated, that many home mechanics do not have a good workshop or garage available, and end up removing an engine or doing major repairs outside. It is recommended, however, that the overhaul or repair be completed under the cover of a roof.

A clean, flat workbench or table of comfortable working height is an absolute necessity. The workbench should be equipped with a vise that has a jaw opening of at least four inches.

As mentioned previously, some clean, dry storage space is also required for tools, as well as the lubricants, fluids, cleaning solvents, etc. which soon become necessary.

Sometimes waste oil and fluids, drained from the engine or cooling system during normal maintenance or repairs, present a disposal problem. To avoid pouring them on the ground or into a sewage system, pour the used fluids into large containers, seal them with caps and take them to an authorized disposal site or recycling center. Plastic jugs, such as old antifreeze containers, are ideal for this purpose.

Always keep a supply of old newspapers and clean rags available. Old towels are excellent for mopping up spills. Many mechanics use rolls of paper towels for most work because they are readily available and disposable. To help keep the area under the vehicle clean, a large cardboard box can be cut open and flattened to protect the garage or shop floor.

Whenever working over a painted surface, such as when leaning over a fender to service something under the hood, always cover it with an old blanket or bedspread to protect the finish. Vinyl covered pads, made especially for this purpose, are available at auto parts stores.

Jacking and towing

Jacking

The jack supplied with the vehicle should be used for raising the vehicle during a tire change or when placing jackstands under the frame. **Under no circumstances should work be performed beneath the vehicle or the engine started while a jack is being used as the only means of support.**

Wheel removal (all models)

All vehicles are supplied with a screw-type jack (sometimes called a "bottle jack") which is placed under the axle tube or radius arm nearest to the wheel being changed. The vehicle should be on level ground with the wheels blocked and the transmission in Park (automatic) or Reverse (manual). On 4-wheel drive vehicles, the transfer case must be engaged in gear, not neutral. Pry off the hub cap (if equipped) using the tapered end of the lug wrench. Loosen the wheel nuts one-half turn and leave them in place until the wheel is raised off the ground. Place the jack under the axle tube or radius arm **(see illustrations)**. Insert the wrench handle into the jack and turn the jackscrew clockwise until the wheel is raised off the ground. Remove the wheel nuts and pull off the wheel. Remove any corrosion, dirt or foreign material present on the mounting surfaces of the hub, drum or rotor that contacts the wheel. **Warning:** *Installing wheels without proper metal-to-metal contact can cause the wheel lug nuts to loosen and allow the wheel to come off the vehicle while the vehicle is in motion.*

Wheel installation (single rear wheel models)

Position the wheel (or spare) on the hub and rotor or the axle flange and drum assembly. Install the lug nuts, making sure the cone ends of the nuts face inwards and properly seat in the wheel. Tighten the lug nuts until snug. Lower the vehicle by turning the jackscrew counterclockwise. Remove the jack and tighten the nuts in a diagonal pattern to the torque listed in the Chapter 1 Specifications, or securely if using the supplied lug wrench. Install the hubcap by placing it into position and using the heel of your hand or a rubber mallet to seat it. **Warning:** *If replacement is due to a roadside emergency, verify proper torque of the wheel lug nuts using a torque wrench as soon as possible and again after 500 miles.*

Front wheel installation (dual rear wheel models)

Warning: *Later models equipped with dual rear wheels use special two-piece swiveling lug nuts on the front and rear wheels. Do not attempt to use cone-shaped one-piece lug nuts on these models. Do not attempt to use early model wheels on later models, or vice-versa, as the lug nut seats are different. Use of improper lug nuts or wheels can cause the lug nuts to loosen and allow the wheel to come off the vehicle while the vehicle is in motion.*

Mount the front wheel on the hub and align the wheel-to-hub alignment pins. Install the lug nuts and tighten until snug. Lower the vehicle by turning the jackscrew counterclockwise. Remove the jack and tighten the nuts in a diagonal pattern to the torque listed in the Chapter 1 Specifications, or securely if using the supplied lug wrench. Install the hubcap by placing it into position and using the heel of your hand or a rubber mallet to seat it. **Warning:** *If replacement is due to a roadside emergency, verify proper torque of the wheel lug nuts using a torque wrench as soon as possible and again after 500 miles.*

Rear wheel installation (dual rear wheel models)

Warning: *Later models equipped with dual rear wheels use special two-piece swiveling lug nuts on the front and rear wheels. Do not attempt to use cone-shaped one-piece lug nuts on these models. Do not attempt to use early model wheels on later models, or vice-versa, as the lug nut seats are different. Use of improper lug nuts or wheels can cause the wheel lug nuts to loosen and allow the wheel to come off the vehicle while the vehicle is in motion.*

Mount the inner wheel on the rear hub and align the wheel-to-hub alignment pins. Make sure the wheel is flush with the hub mounting surface so there is no gap. Install the outer rear wheel flush against the inner wheel and align the wheel-to-wheel alignment pins. Install the eight lug nuts and tighten them until snug. Lower the vehicle by turning the jackscrew counterclockwise. Remove the jack and tighten the nuts in a

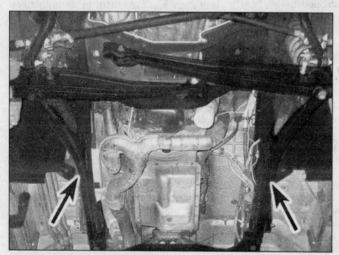

On models with twin I-beam front suspension, place the jack under the radius arm (on models with a solid front axle, place the jack under the axle tube)

When raising the rear of the vehicle, place the jack under the axle tube, nearest the wheel to be changed

diagonal fashion to the torque listed in the Chapter 1 Specifications, or securely if using the supplied lug wrench. Install the hubcap by placing it into position and using the heel of your hand or a rubber mallet to seat it. **Warning:** *If replacement is due to a roadside emergency, verify proper torque of the wheel lug nuts using a torque wrench as soon as possible and again after 500 miles.*

Towing

The vehicle can be towed with all four wheels on the ground provided speeds do not exceed 35 mph and the distance is not over 50 miles, otherwise transmission or transfer case damage can result.

Towing equipment specifically designed for that purpose should be used and should be attached to the main structural members of the vehicle and not the bumper or brackets.

Safety is a major consideration when towing a vehicle and all applicable state and local laws must be obeyed. A safety chain system must be used for all towing.

While towing, the parking brake should be fully released and the transmission should be in Neutral. The steering must be unlocked (ignition switch in the Off position). Remember that power steering and power brakes will not work with the engine off. On 4WD models with a manual transfer case, place the transfer case in Neutral and place the locking hubs in the Free position. On 4WD models with an electronic transfer case, place the transfer case in 2H (2WD High) and make sure the automatic hubs are disengaged.

Booster battery (jump) starting

Observe these precautions when using a booster battery to start a vehicle:

a) *Before connecting the booster battery, make sure the ignition switch is in the Off position.*
b) *Turn off the lights, heater and other electrical loads.*
c) *Your eyes should be shielded. Safety goggles are a good idea.*
d) *Make sure the booster battery is the same voltage as the dead one in the vehicle.*
e) *The two vehicles MUST NOT TOUCH each other!*
f) *Make sure the transaxle is in Neutral (manual) or Park (automatic).*
g) *If the booster battery is not a maintenance-free type, remove the vent caps and lay a cloth over the vent holes.*

Connect the red jumper cable to the positive (+) terminals of each battery **(see illustration)**.

Connect one end of the black jumper cable to the negative (-) terminal of the booster battery. The other end of this cable should be connected to a good ground on the vehicle to be started, such as a bolt or bracket on the body.

Start the engine using the booster battery, then, with the engine running at idle speed, disconnect the jumper cables in the reverse order of connection.

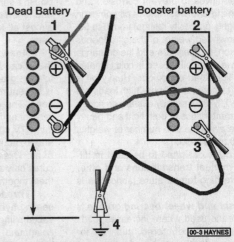

Make the booster battery cable connections in the numerical order shown (note that the negative cable of the booster battery is NOT attached to the negative terminal of the dead battery)

Automotive chemicals and lubricants

A number of automotive chemicals and lubricants are available for use during vehicle maintenance and repair. They include a wide variety of products ranging from cleaning solvents and degreasers to lubricants and protective sprays for rubber, plastic and vinyl.

Cleaners

Carburetor cleaner and choke cleaner is a strong solvent for gum, varnish and carbon. Most carburetor cleaners leave a dry-type lubricant film which will not harden or gum up. Because of this film it is not recommended for use on electrical components.

Brake system cleaner is used to remove brake dust, grease and brake fluid from the brake system, where clean surfaces are absolutely necessary. It leaves no residue and often eliminates brake squeal caused by contaminants.

Electrical cleaner removes oxidation, corrosion and carbon deposits from electrical contacts, restoring full current flow. It can also be used to clean spark plugs, carburetor jets, voltage regulators and other parts where an oil-free surface is desired.

Demoisturants remove water and moisture from electrical components such as alternators, voltage regulators, electrical connectors and fuse blocks. They are non-conductive and non-corrosive.

Degreasers are heavy-duty solvents used to remove grease from the outside of the engine and from chassis components. They can be sprayed or brushed on and, depending on the type, are rinsed off either with water or solvent.

Lubricants

Motor oil is the lubricant formulated for use in engines. It normally contains a wide variety of additives to prevent corrosion and reduce foaming and wear. Motor oil comes in various weights (viscosity ratings) from 0 to 50. The recommended weight of the oil depends on the season, temperature and the demands on the engine. Light oil is used in cold climates and under light load conditions. Heavy oil is used in hot climates and where high loads are encountered. Multi-viscosity oils are designed to have characteristics of both light and heavy oils and are available in a number of weights from 0W-20 to 20W-50.

Gear oil is designed to be used in differentials, manual transmissions and other areas where high-temperature lubrication is required.

Chassis and wheel bearing grease is a heavy grease used where increased loads and friction are encountered, such as for wheel bearings, balljoints, tie-rod ends and universal joints.

High-temperature wheel bearing grease is designed to withstand the extreme temperatures encountered by wheel bearings in disc brake equipped vehicles. It usually contains molybdenum disulfide (moly), which is a dry-type lubricant.

White grease is a heavy grease for metal-to-metal applications where water is a problem. White grease stays soft under both low and high temperatures (usually from -100 to +190-degrees F), and will not wash off or dilute in the presence of water.

Assembly lube is a special extreme pressure lubricant, usually containing moly, used to lubricate high-load parts (such as main and rod bearings and cam lobes) for initial start-up of a new engine. The assembly lube lubricates the parts without being squeezed out or washed away until the engine oiling system begins to function.

Silicone lubricants are used to protect rubber, plastic, vinyl and nylon parts.

Graphite lubricants are used where oils cannot be used due to contamination problems, such as in locks. The dry graphite will lubricate metal parts while remaining uncontaminated by dirt, water, oil or acids. It is electrically conductive and will not foul electrical contacts in locks such as the ignition switch.

Moly penetrants loosen and lubricate frozen, rusted and corroded fasteners and prevent future rusting or freezing.

Heat-sink grease is a special electrically non-conductive grease that is used for mounting electronic ignition modules where it is essential that heat is transferred away from the module.

Sealants

RTV sealant is one of the most widely used gasket compounds. Made from silicone, RTV is air curing, it seals, bonds, waterproofs, fills surface irregularities, remains flexible, doesn't shrink, is relatively easy to remove, and is used as a supplementary sealer with almost all low and medium temperature gaskets.

Anaerobic sealant is much like RTV in that it can be used either to seal gaskets or to form gaskets by itself. It remains flexible, is solvent resistant and fills surface imperfections. The difference between an anaerobic sealant and an RTV-type sealant is in the curing. RTV cures when exposed to air, while an anaerobic sealant cures only in the absence of air. This means that an anaerobic sealant cures only after the assembly of parts, sealing them together.

Thread and pipe sealant is used for sealing hydraulic and pneumatic fittings and vacuum lines. It is usually made from a Teflon compound, and comes in a spray, a paint-on liquid and as a wrap-around tape.

Chemicals

Anti-seize compound prevents seizing, galling, cold welding, rust and corrosion in fasteners. High-temperature ant-seize, usually made with copper and graphite lubricants, is used for exhaust system and exhaust manifold bolts.

Anaerobic locking compounds are used to keep fasteners from vibrating or working loose and cure only after installation, in the absence of air. Medium strength locking compound is used for small nuts, bolts and screws that may be removed later. High-strength locking compound is for large nuts, bolts and studs which aren't removed on a regular basis.

Oil additives range from viscosity index improvers to chemical treatments that claim to reduce internal engine friction. It should be noted that most oil manufacturers caution against using additives with their oils.

Gas additives perform several functions, depending on their chemical makeup. They usually contain solvents that help dissolve gum and varnish that build up on carburetor, fuel injection and intake parts. They also serve to break down carbon deposits that form on the inside surfaces of the combustion chambers. Some additives contain upper cylinder lubricants for valves and piston rings, and others contain chemicals to remove condensation from the gas tank.

Miscellaneous

Brake fluid is specially formulated hydraulic fluid that can withstand the heat and pressure encountered in brake systems. Care must be taken so this fluid does not come in contact with painted surfaces or plastics. An opened container should always be resealed to prevent contamination by water or dirt.

Weatherstrip adhesive is used to bond weatherstripping around doors, windows and trunk lids. It is sometimes used to attach trim pieces.

Undercoating is a petroleum-based, tar-like substance that is designed to protect metal surfaces on the underside of the vehicle from corrosion. It also acts as a sound-deadening agent by insulating the bottom of the vehicle.

Waxes and polishes are used to help protect painted and plated surfaces from the weather. Different types of paint may require the use of different types of wax and polish. Some polishes utilize a chemical or abrasive cleaner to help remove the top layer of oxidized (dull) paint on older vehicles. In recent years many non-wax polishes that contain a wide variety of chemicals such as polymers and silicones have been introduced. These non-wax polishes are usually easier to apply and last longer than conventional waxes and polishes.

Conversion factors

Length (distance)

Inches (in)	X	25.4	= Millimeters (mm)	X 0.0394	= Inches (in)
Feet (ft)	X	0.305	= Meters (m)	X 3.281	= Feet (ft)
Miles	X	1.609	= Kilometers (km)	X 0.621	= Miles

Volume (capacity)

Cubic inches (cu in; in^3)	X	16.387	= Cubic centimeters (cc; cm^3)	X 0.061	= Cubic inches (cu in; in^3)
Imperial pints (Imp pt)	X	0.568	= Liters (l)	X 1.76	= Imperial pints (Imp pt)
Imperial quarts (Imp qt)	X	1.137	= Liters (l)	X 0.88	= Imperial quarts (Imp qt)
Imperial quarts (Imp qt)	X	1.201	= US quarts (US qt)	X 0.833	= Imperial quarts (Imp qt)
US quarts (US qt)	X	0.946	= Liters (l)	X 1.057	= US quarts (US qt)
Imperial gallons (Imp gal)	X	4.546	= Liters (l)	X 0.22	= Imperial gallons (Imp gal)
Imperial gallons (Imp gal)	X	1.201	= US gallons (US gal)	X 0.833	= Imperial gallons (Imp gal)
US gallons (US gal)	X	3.785	= Liters (l)	X 0.264	= US gallons (US gal)

Mass (weight)

Ounces (oz)	X	28.35	= Grams (g)	X 0.035	= Ounces (oz)
Pounds (lb)	X	0.454	= Kilograms (kg)	X 2.205	= Pounds (lb)

Force

Ounces-force (ozf; oz)	X	0.278	= Newtons (N)	X 3.6	= Ounces-force (ozf; oz)
Pounds-force (lbf; lb)	X	4.448	= Newtons (N)	X 0.225	= Pounds-force (lbf; lb)
Newtons (N)	X	0.1	= Kilograms-force (kgf; kg)	X 9.81	= Newtons (N)

Pressure

Pounds-force per square inch (psi; lbf/in^2; lb/in^2)	X	0.070	= Kilograms-force per square centimeter (kgf/cm^2; kg/cm^2)	X 14.223	= Pounds-force per square inch (psi; lbf/in^2; lb/in^2)
Pounds-force per square inch (psi; lbf/in^2; lb/in^2)	X	0.068	= Atmospheres (atm)	X 14.696	= Pounds-force per square inch (psi; lbf/in^2; lb/in^2)
Pounds-force per square inch (psi; lbf/in^2; lb/in^2)	X	0.069	= Bars	X 14.5	= Pounds-force per square inch (psi; lbf/in^2; lb/in^2)
Pounds-force per square inch (psi; lbf/in^2; lb/in^2)	X	6.895	= Kilopascals (kPa)	X 0.145	= Pounds-force per square inch (psi; lbf/in^2; lb/in^2)
Kilopascals (kPa)	X	0.01	= Kilograms-force per square centimeter (kgf/cm^2; kg/cm^2)	X 98.1	= Kilopascals (kPa)

Torque (moment of force)

Pounds-force inches (lbf in; lb in)	X	1.152	= Kilograms-force centimeter (kgf cm; kg cm)	X 0.868	= Pounds-force inches (lbf in; lb in)
Pounds-force inches (lbf in; lb in)	X	0.113	= Newton meters (Nm)	X 8.85	= Pounds-force inches (lbf in; lb in)
Pounds-force inches (lbf in; lb in)	X	0.083	= Pounds-force feet (lbf ft; lb ft)	X 12	= Pounds-force inches (lbf in; lb in)
Pounds-force feet (lbf ft; lb ft)	X	0.138	= Kilograms-force meters (kgf m; kg m)	X 7.233	= Pounds-force feet (lbf ft; lb ft)
Pounds-force feet (lbf ft; lb ft)	X	1.356	= Newton meters (Nm)	X 0.738	= Pounds-force feet (lbf ft; lb ft)
Newton meters (Nm)	X	0.102	= Kilograms-force meters (kgf m; kg m)	X 9.804	= Newton meters (Nm)

Vacuum

Inches mercury (in. Hg)	X	3.377	= Kilopascals (kPa)	X 0.2961	= Inches mercury
Inches mercury (in. Hg)	X	25.4	= Millimeters mercury (mm Hg)	X 0.0394	= Inches mercury

Power

Horsepower (hp)	X	745.7	= Watts (W)	X 0.0013	= Horsepower (hp)

Velocity (speed)

Miles per hour (miles/hr; mph)	X	1.609	= Kilometers per hour (km/hr; kph)	X 0.621	= Miles per hour (miles/hr; mph)

Fuel consumption*

Miles per gallon, Imperial (mpg)	X	0.354	= Kilometers per liter (km/l)	X 2.825	= Miles per gallon, Imperial (mpg)
Miles per gallon, US (mpg)	X	0.425	= Kilometers per liter (km/l)	X 2.352	= Miles per gallon, US (mpg)

Temperature

Degrees Fahrenheit = (°C x 1.8) + 32   Degrees Celsius (Degrees Centigrade; °C) = (°F - 32) x 0.56

*It is common practice to convert from miles per gallon (mpg) to liters/100 kilometers (l/100km),
where mpg (Imperial) x l/100 km = 282 and mpg (US) x l/100 km = 235

Safety first!

Regardless of how enthusiastic you may be about getting on with the job at hand, take the time to ensure that your safety is not jeopardized. A moment's lack of attention can result in an accident, as can failure to observe certain simple safety precautions. The possibility of an accident will always exist, and the following points should not be considered a comprehensive list of all dangers. Rather, they are intended to make you aware of the risks and to encourage a safety conscious approach to all work you carry out on your vehicle.

Essential DOs and DON'Ts

DON'T rely on a jack when working under the vehicle. Always use approved jackstands to support the weight of the vehicle and place them under the recommended lift or support points.

DON'T attempt to loosen extremely tight fasteners (i.e. wheel lug nuts) while the vehicle is on a jack - it may fall.

DON'T start the engine without first making sure that the transmission is in Neutral (or Park where applicable) and the parking brake is set.

DON'T remove the radiator cap from a hot cooling system - let it cool or cover it with a cloth and release the pressure gradually.

DON'T attempt to drain the engine oil until you are sure it has cooled to the point that it will not burn you.

DON'T touch any part of the engine or exhaust system until it has cooled sufficiently to avoid burns.

DON'T siphon toxic liquids such as gasoline, antifreeze and brake fluid by mouth, or allow them to remain on your skin.

DON'T inhale brake lining dust - it is potentially hazardous (see *Asbestos* below).

DON'T allow spilled oil or grease to remain on the floor - wipe it up before someone slips on it.

DON'T use loose fitting wrenches or other tools which may slip and cause injury.

DON'T push on wrenches when loosening or tightening nuts or bolts. Always try to pull the wrench toward you. If the situation calls for pushing the wrench away, push with an open hand to avoid scraped knuckles if the wrench should slip.

DON'T attempt to lift a heavy component alone - get someone to help you.

DON'T *rush or take unsafe shortcuts to finish a job.*

DON'T allow children or animals in or around the vehicle while you are working on it.

DO wear eye protection when using power tools such as a drill, sander, bench grinder, etc. and when working under a vehicle.

DO keep loose clothing and long hair well out of the way of moving parts.

DO make sure that any hoist used has a safe working load rating adequate for the job.

DO get someone to check on you periodically when working alone on a vehicle.

DO carry out work in a logical sequence and make sure that everything is correctly assembled and tightened.

DO keep chemicals and fluids tightly capped and out of the reach of children and pets.

DO remember that your vehicle's safety affects that of yourself and others. If in doubt on any point, get professional advice.

Steering, suspension and brakes

These systems are essential to driving safety, so make sure you have a qualified shop or individual check your work. Also, compressed suspension springs can cause injury if released suddenly - be sure to use a spring compressor.

Airbags

Airbags are explosive devices that can **CAUSE** injury if they deploy while you're working on the vehicle. Follow the manufacturer's instructions to disable the airbag whenever you're working in the vicinity of airbag components.

Asbestos

Certain friction, insulating, sealing, and other products - such as brake linings, brake bands, clutch linings, torque converters, gaskets, etc. - may contain asbestos or other hazardous friction material. Extreme care must be taken to avoid inhalation of dust from such products, since it is hazardous to health. If in doubt, assume that they do contain asbestos.

Fire

Remember at all times that gasoline is highly flammable. Never smoke or have any kind of open flame around when working on a vehicle. But the risk does not end there. A spark caused by an electrical short circuit, by two metal surfaces contacting each other, or even by static electricity built up in your body under certain conditions, can ignite gasoline vapors, which in a confined space are highly explosive. Do not, under any circumstances, use gasoline for cleaning parts. Use an approved safety solvent.

Always disconnect the battery ground (-) cable at the battery before working on any part of the fuel system or electrical system. Never risk spilling fuel on a hot engine or exhaust component. It is strongly recommended that a fire extinguisher suitable for use on fuel and electrical fires be kept handy in the garage or workshop at all times. Never try to extinguish a fuel or electrical fire with water.

Fumes

Certain fumes are highly toxic and can quickly cause unconsciousness and even death if inhaled to any extent. Gasoline vapor falls into this category, as do the vapors from some cleaning solvents. Any draining or pouring of such volatile fluids should be done in a well ventilated area.

When using cleaning fluids and solvents, read the instructions on the container carefully. Never use materials from unmarked containers.

Never run the engine in an enclosed space, such as a garage. Exhaust fumes contain carbon monoxide, which is extremely poisonous. If you need to run the engine, always do so in the open air, or at least have the rear of the vehicle outside the work area.

The battery

Never create a spark or allow a bare light bulb near a battery. They normally give off a certain amount of hydrogen gas, which is highly explosive.

Always disconnect the battery ground (-) cable at the battery before working on the fuel or electrical systems.

If possible, loosen the filler caps or cover when charging the battery from an external source (this does not apply to sealed or maintenance-free batteries). Do not charge at an excessive rate or the battery may burst.

Take care when adding water to a non maintenance-free battery and when carrying a battery. The electrolyte, even when diluted, is very corrosive and should not be allowed to contact clothing or skin.

Always wear eye protection when cleaning the battery to prevent the caustic deposits from entering your eyes.

Household current

When using an electric power tool, inspection light, etc., which operates on household current, always make sure that the tool is correctly connected to its plug and that, where necessary, it is properly grounded. Do not use such items in damp conditions and, again, do not create a spark or apply excessive heat in the vicinity of fuel or fuel vapor.

Secondary ignition system voltage

A severe electric shock can result from touching certain parts of the ignition system (such as the spark plug wires) when the engine is running or being cranked, particularly if components are damp or the insulation is defective. In the case of an electronic ignition system, the secondary system voltage is much higher and could prove fatal.

Hydrofluoric acid

This extremely corrosive acid is formed when certain types of synthetic rubber, found in some O-rings, oil seals, fuel hoses, etc. are exposed to temperatures above 750-degrees F (400-degrees C). The rubber changes into a charred or sticky substance containing the acid. *Once formed, the acid remains dangerous for years. If it gets onto the skin, it may be necessary to amputate the limb concerned.*

When dealing with a vehicle which has suffered a fire, or with components salvaged from such a vehicle, wear protective gloves and discard them after use.

Troubleshooting

Contents

This Section provides an easy reference guide to the more common problems which may occur during the operation of your vehicle. These problems and possible causes are grouped under various components or systems; i.e. Engine, Cooling System, etc., and also refer to the Chapter and/or Section which deals with the problem.

Remember that successful troubleshooting is not a mysterious "black art" practiced only by professional mechanics. It's simply the result of a bit of knowledge combined with an intelligent, systematic approach to the problem. Always work by a process of elimination, starting with the simplest solution and working through to the most complex - and never overlook the obvious. Anyone can forget to fill the gas tank or leave the lights on overnight, so don't assume that you are above such oversights.

Finally, always get clear in your mind why a problem has occurred and take steps to ensure that it doesn't happen again. If the electrical system fails because of a poor connection, check all other connections in the system to make sure that they don't fail as well. If a particular fuse continues to blow, find out why - don't just go on replacing fuses. Remember, failure of a small component can often be indicative of potential failure or incorrect functioning of a more important component or system.

Engine

1 Engine will not rotate when attempting to start

1 Battery terminal connections loose or corroded. Check the cable terminals at the battery. Tighten the cable or remove corrosion as necessary.
2 Battery discharged or faulty. If the cable connections are clean and tight on the battery posts, turn the key to the On position and switch on the headlights and/or windshield wipers. If they fail to function, the battery is discharged.
3 Automatic transmission not completely engaged in Park or Neutral or clutch pedal not completely depressed.
4 Broken, loose or disconnected wiring in the starting circuit. Inspect all wiring and connectors at the battery, starter solenoid and ignition switch.
5 Starter motor pinion jammed in flywheel ring gear. If manual transmission, place transmission in gear and rock the vehicle to manually turn the engine. Remove the starter and inspect the pinion and flywheel at earliest convenience (Chapter 5).
6 Starter solenoid faulty (Chapter 5).
7 Starter motor faulty (Chapter 5).
8 Ignition switch faulty (Chapter 12).

2 Engine rotates but will not start

1 Fuel tank empty.
2 Fault in the carburetor or fuel injection system (Chapter 4).
3 Battery discharged (engine rotates slowly). Check the operation of electrical components as described in the previous Section.
4 Battery terminal connections loose or corroded (see previous Section).
5 Fuel pump faulty or fuel pump inertia switch needs resetting (Chapter 4).
6 Excessive moisture on, or damage to, ignition components (see Chapter 5).
7 Worn, faulty or incorrectly gapped spark plugs (Chapter 1).
8 Broken, loose or disconnected wiring in the starting circuit (see previous Section).
9 Distributor loose, causing ignition timing to change (distributor-equipped models only). Turn the distributor as necessary to start the engine, then set the ignition timing as soon as possible (Chapter 5).
10 Broken, loose or disconnected wires at the ignition coil or faulty coil (Chapter 5).

3 Starter motor operates without rotating engine

1 Starter pinion sticking. Remove the starter (Chapter 5) and inspect.
2 Starter pinion or flywheel teeth worn or broken. Remove the flywheel/driveplate access cover and inspect.

4 Engine hard to start when cold

1 Battery discharged or low. Check as described in Section 1.
2 Fault in the fuel or electrical systems (Chapters 4 and 5).
3 Carburetor (if equipped) in need of overhaul (Chapter 4).
4 Distributor rotor (if equipped) carbon tracked and/or damaged (Chapters 1 and 5).
5 Choke control stuck or inoperative (carbureted models) (Chapters 1 and 4).

5 Engine hard to start when hot

1 Air filter clogged (Chapter 1).
2 Fault in the fuel or electrical systems (Chapters 4 and 5).
3 Fuel not reaching the carburetor or injectors (see Chapter 4).

6 Starter motor noisy or excessively rough in engagement

1 Pinion or flywheel gear teeth worn or broken. Remove the cover at the rear of the engine (if so equipped) and inspect.
2 Starter motor mounting bolts loose or missing.

7 Engine starts but stops immediately

1 Loose or faulty electrical connections at distributor, coil or alternator.
2 Fault in the fuel or electrical systems (Chapters 4 and 5).
3 Insufficient fuel reaching the carburetor (carbureted models). Check the fuel pump (Chapter 4).
4 Vacuum leak at the gasket surfaces of the intake manifold or carburetor/throttle body. Make sure all mounting bolts/nuts are tightened securely and all vacuum hoses connected to the carburetor and manifold are positioned properly and in good condition.

8 Engine lopes while idling or idles erratically

1 Vacuum leakage. Check the mounting bolts/nuts at the carburetor/throttle body and intake manifold for tightness. Make sure all vacuum hoses are connected and in good condition. Use a stethoscope or a length of fuel hose held against your ear to listen for vacuum leaks while the engine is running. A hissing sound will be heard. A soapy water solution will also detect leaks.
2 Fault in the fuel or electrical systems (Chapters 4 and 5).
3 Leaking EGR valve or plugged PCV valve (see Chapters 1 and 6).

4 Air filter clogged (Chapter 1).
5 Fuel pump not delivering sufficient fuel to the carburetor/fuel injectors (see Chapter 4).
6 Carburetor out of adjustment (Chapter 4).
7 Leaking head gasket. Perform a compression check (Chapter 2).
8 Camshaft lobes worn (Chapter 2).

9 Engine misses at idle speed

1 Spark plugs worn, fouled or not gapped properly (Chapter 1).
2 Fault in the fuel or electrical systems (Chapters 4 and 5).
3 Faulty spark plug wires (Chapter 1).
4 Vacuum leaks at intake or hose connections. Check as described in Section 8.
5 Uneven or low cylinder compression. Check compression as described in Chapter 1.

10 Engine misses throughout driving speed range

1 Fuel filter clogged and/or impurities in the fuel system (Chapter 1).
2 Faulty or incorrectly gapped spark plugs (Chapter 1).
3 Fault in the fuel or electrical systems (Chapters 4 and 5).
4 Incorrect ignition timing (Chapter 5).
5 Cracked distributor cap, disconnected distributor wires or damaged distributor components (distributor-equipped models only) (Chapter 1).
6 Defective spark plug wires (Chapter 1).
7 Faulty emissions system components (Chapter 6).
8 Low or uneven cylinder compression pressures. Remove the spark plugs and test the compression with a gauge (Chapter 2).
9 Weak or faulty ignition system (Chapter 5).
10 Vacuum leaks at the carburetor/throttle body, intake manifold or vacuum hoses (see Section 8).

11 Engine stalls

1 Idle speed incorrect. Refer to the VECI label and Chapter 1.
2 Fuel filter clogged and/or water and impurities in the fuel system (Chapter 1).
3 Distributor components damp or damaged (if equipped) (Chapter 5).
4 Fault in the fuel system or sensors (Chapters 4 and 6).
5 Faulty emissions system components (Chapter 6).
6 Faulty or incorrectly gapped spark plugs (Chapter 1). Also check the spark plug wires (Chapter 1).
7 Vacuum leak at the carburetor/throttle body, intake manifold or vacuum hoses. Check as described in Section 8.

12   Engine lacks power

1   Incorrect ignition timing (Chapter 5).
2   Fault in the fuel or electrical systems (Chapters 4 and 5).
3   Excessive play in the distributor shaft (if equipped). At the same time, check for a damaged rotor, faulty distributor cap, wires, etc. (Chapters 1 and 5).
4   Faulty or incorrectly gapped spark plugs (Chapter 1).
5   Carburetor not adjusted properly or excessively worn (carbureted models) (Chapter 4).
6   Faulty coil (Chapter 5).
7   Brakes binding (Chapter 1).
8   Automatic transmission fluid level incorrect (Chapter 1).
9   Clutch slipping (Chapter 8).
10   Fuel filter clogged and/or impurities in the fuel system (Chapter 1).
11   Emissions control system not functioning properly (Chapter 6).
12   Use of substandard fuel. Fill the tank with the proper octane fuel.
13   Low or uneven cylinder compression pressures. Test with a compression tester, which will detect leaking valves and/or a blown head gasket (Chapter 2).

13   Engine backfires

1   Emissions system not functioning properly (Chapter 6).
2   Fault in the fuel or electrical systems (Chapters 4 and 5).
3   Ignition timing incorrect (Chapter 5).
4   Faulty secondary ignition system (cracked spark plug insulator, faulty plug wires, distributor cap and/or rotor if equipped) (Chapters 1 and 5).
5   Carburetor or fuel injection system malfunctioning (Chapter 4).
6   Vacuum leak at the carburetor/throttle body, intake manifold or vacuum hoses. Check as described in Section 8.
7   Valves sticking (Chapter 2).
8   Crossed spark plug wires (Chapter 1).

14   Pinging or knocking engine sounds during acceleration or uphill

1   Incorrect grade of fuel. Fill the tank with fuel of the proper octane rating.
2   Fault in the fuel or electrical systems (Chapters 4 and 5).
3   Ignition timing incorrect (Chapter 5).
4   Carburetor in need of adjustment (carbureted models) (Chapter 4).
5   Improper spark plugs. Check the plug type against the VECI label located in the engine compartment. Also check the plugs and wires for damage (Chapter 1).
6   Worn or damaged distributor components (if equipped) (Chapter 5).
7   Faulty emissions system (Chapter 6).
8   Vacuum leak. Check as described in Section 9.

15   Engine diesels (continues to run) after switching off

1   Idle speed too high. Refer to the VECI label and Chapter 1.
2   Fault in the fuel or electrical systems (Chapters 4 and 5).
3   Ignition timing incorrectly adjusted (Chapter 5).
4   Thermo-controlled air cleaner heat valve not operating properly (Chapter 6).
5   Excessive engine operating temperature. Probable causes of this are a malfunctioning thermostat, clogged radiator, faulty water pump (see Chapter 3).

Engine electrical system

16   Battery will not hold a charge

1   Alternator drivebelt defective or not adjusted properly (Chapter 1).
2   Electrolyte level low or battery discharged (Chapter 1).
3   Battery terminals loose or corroded (Chapter 1).
4   Alternator not charging properly (Chapter 5).
5   Loose, broken or faulty wiring in the charging circuit (Chapter 5).
6   Short in the vehicle wiring causing a continuous drain on battery (refer to Chapter 12 and the Wiring Diagrams).
7   Battery defective internally.

17   Ignition light fails to go out

1   Fault in the alternator or charging circuit (Chapter 5).
2   Alternator drivebelt defective or not properly adjusted (Chapter 1).

18   Ignition light fails to come on when key is turned on

1   Instrument cluster warning light bulb defective (Chapter 12).
2   Alternator faulty (Chapter 5).
3   Fault in the instrument cluster printed circuit, dashboard wiring or bulb holder (Chapter 12).

Fuel system

19   Excessive fuel consumption

1   Dirty or clogged air filter element (Chapter 1).
2   Incorrectly set ignition timing (Chapter 5).
3   Choke sticking or improperly adjusted (carbureted models) (see Chapter 1).
4   Emissions system not functioning properly (Chapter 6).

5   Fault in the fuel or electrical systems (Chapters 4 and 5).
6   Carburetor or fuel injection system malfunctioning (Chapter 4).
7   Low tire pressure or incorrect tire size (Chapter 1).

20   Fuel leakage and/or fuel odor

1   Leak in a fuel feed or vent line (Chapter 4).
2   Tank overfilled. Fill only to automatic shut-off.
3   Evaporative emissions system canister clogged (Chapter 6).
4   Vapor leaks from system lines (Chapter 4).
5   Carburetor or fuel injection system component leaking (Chapter 4).

Cooling system

21   Overheating

1   Insufficient coolant in the system (Chapter 1).
2   Water pump drivebelt defective or not adjusted properly (Chapter 1).
3   Radiator core blocked or radiator grille dirty and restricted (see Chapter 3).
4   Thermostat faulty (Chapter 3).
5   Fan blades broken or cracked (Chapter 3).
6   Radiator cap not maintaining proper pressure. Have the cap pressure tested by a gas station or repair shop.
7   Ignition timing incorrect (Chapter 5).

22   Overcooling

1   Thermostat faulty (Chapter 3).
2   Inaccurate temperature gauge (Chapter 12).

23   External coolant leakage

1   Deteriorated or damaged hoses or loose clamps. Replace hoses and/or tighten the clamps at the hose connections (Chapter 1).
2   Water pump seals defective. If this is the case, water will drip from the weep hole in the water pump body (Chapter 3).
3   Leakage from radiator core or header tank. This will require the radiator to be professionally repaired (see Chapter 3 for removal procedures).
4   Engine drain plug leaking (Chapter 1) or water jacket core plugs leaking (see Chapter 2).

24   Internal coolant leakage

Note: *Internal coolant leaks can usually be detected by examining the oil. Check the dipstick and inside of the valve cover for water deposits and an oil consistency like that of a milkshake.*

1   Leaking cylinder head gasket. Have the cooling system pressure tested.

2   Cracked cylinder bore or cylinder head. Dismantle the engine and inspect (Chapter 2).

25   Coolant loss

1   Too much coolant in the system (Chapter 1).

2   Coolant boiling away due to overheating (see Section 15).

3   External or internal leakage (see Sections 23 and 24).

4   Faulty radiator cap. Have the cap pressure tested.

26   Poor coolant circulation

1   Inoperative water pump (Chapter 3).

2   Restriction in the cooling system. Drain, flush and refill the system (Chapter 1). If necessary, remove the radiator (Chapter 3) and have it reverse flushed.

3   Water pump drivebelt defective or not adjusted properly (Chapter 1).

4   Thermostat sticking (Chapter 3).

Clutch

27   Fails to release (pedal pressed to the floor - shift lever does not move freely in and out of Reverse)

1   Leak in the clutch hydraulic system. Check the master cylinder, slave cylinder and lines (Chapter 8).

2   Clutch fork off ball stud (early models only). Look under the vehicle, on the left side of the transmission.

3   Clutch plate warped or damaged (Chapter 8).

4   Worn or dry clutch release shaft bushing (Chapter 8).

28   Clutch slips (engine speed increases with no increase in vehicle speed)

1   Clutch plate oil soaked or lining worn. Remove the clutch (Chapter 8) and inspect. Correct any leakage source.

2   Clutch plate not seated. It may take 30 or 40 normal starts for a new one to seat.

3   Pressure plate worn (Chapter 8).

29   Grabbing (chattering) as clutch is engaged

1   Oil on clutch plate lining. Remove the (Chapter 8) and inspect. Correct any leakage source.

2   Worn or loose engine or transmission mounts. These units move slightly when the clutch is released. Inspect the mounts and bolts (Chapter 2).

3   Worn splines on clutch plate hub. Remove the clutch components (Chapter 8) and inspect.

4   Warped pressure plate or flywheel. Remove the clutch components and inspect.

30   Squeal or rumble with clutch fully engaged (pedal released)

Release bearing binding on transmission bearing retainer. Remove clutch components (Chapter 8) and check bearing. Remove any burrs or nicks; clean and relubricate bearing retainer before installing.

31   Squeal or rumble with clutch fully disengaged (pedal depressed)

1   Worn, defective or broken release bearing (Chapter 8).

2   Worn or broken pressure plate springs (or diaphragm fingers) (Chapter 8).

32   Clutch pedal stays on floor when disengaged

1   Linkage or release bearing binding. Inspect the linkage or remove the clutch components as necessary.

2   Make sure proper pedal stop (bumper) is installed.

Manual transmission

Note: *All of the following references are in Chapter 7A, unless noted.*

33   Noisy in Neutral with engine running

1   Input shaft bearing worn.

2   Damaged main drive gear bearing.

3   Worn countershaft bearings.

4   Worn or damaged countershaft endplay shims.

34   Noisy in all gears

1   Any of the above causes, and/or:

2   Insufficient lubricant (see the checking procedures in Chapter 1).

35   Noisy in one particular gear

1   Worn, damaged or chipped gear teeth for that particular gear.

2   Worn or damaged synchronizer for that particular gear.

36   Slips out of high gear

1   Transmission loose on clutch housing.

2   Dirt between the transmission case and engine or misalignment of the transmission.

37   Difficulty in engaging gears

1   Clutch not releasing completely (Chapter 8).

2   Loose, damaged or out-of-adjustment shift linkage. Make a thorough inspection, replacing parts as necessary.

38   Oil leakage

1   Excessive amount of lubricant in the transmission (see Chapter 1 for correct checking procedures). Drain lubricant as required.

2   Extension housing oil seal or speedometer oil seal in need of replacement (Chapter 7).

Automatic transmission

Note: *Due to the complexity of the automatic transmission, it's difficult for the home mechanic to properly diagnose and service this component. For problems other than the following, the vehicle should be taken to a dealer service department or a transmission shop. All of the following references are in Chapter 7B, unless noted.*

39   General shift mechanism problems

1   Chapter 7 deals with checking and adjusting the shift linkage on Manual transmission automatic transmissions. Common problems which may be attributed to poorly adjusted linkage are:

a)   *Engine starting in gears other than Park or Neutral.*

b)   *Indicator on shifter pointing to a gear other than the one actually being selected.*

c)   *Vehicle moves when in Park.*

2   Refer to Chapter 7 to adjust the linkage.

40   Transmission will not downshift with accelerator pedal pressed to the floor

Chapter 7, part B deals with adjusting the throttle cable to enable the transmission to downshift properly.

41   Transmission slips, shifts rough, is noisy or has no drive in forward or reverse gears

1   There are many probable causes for the above problems, but the home mechanic

should be concerned with only one possibility - fluid level.

2   Before taking the vehicle to a repair shop, check the level and condition of the fluid as described in Chapter 1. Correct fluid level as necessary or change the fluid and filter if needed. If the problem persists, have a professional diagnose the probable cause.

42   Fluid leakage

1   Automatic transmission fluid is a deep red color. Fluid leaks should not be confused with engine oil, which can easily be blown by air flow to the transmission.

2   To pinpoint a leak, first remove all built-up dirt and grime from around the transmission. Degreasing agents and/or steam cleaning will achieve this. With the underside clean, drive the vehicle at low speeds so air flow will not blow the leak far from its source. Raise the vehicle and determine where the leak is coming from. Common areas of leakage are:

a)   *Pan: Tighten the mounting bolts and/ or replace the pan gasket as necessary (Chapter 1).*
b)   *Filler pipe: Replace the rubber seal where the pipe enters the transmission case.*
c)   *Transmission oil lines: Tighten the connectors where the lines enter the transmission case and/or replace the lines.*
d)   *Vent pipe: Transmission overfilled and/or water in fluid (Chapter 1).*
e)   *Speedometer connector: Replace the O-ring where the speedometer cable enters the transmission case (Chapter 7).*

Transfer case

Note: *All of the following references are in Chapter 7C, unless noted.*

43   Transfer case is difficult to shift into the desired range

1   Speed may be too great to permit engagement. Stop the vehicle and shift into the desired range.

2   Shift linkage loose, bent or binding. Check the linkage for damage or wear and replace or lubricate as necessary.

3   If the vehicle has been driven on a paved surface for some time, the driveline torque can make shifting difficult. Stop and shift into two-wheel drive on paved or hard surfaces.

4   Insufficient or incorrect grade of lubricant. Drain and refill the transfer case with the specified lubricant. (Chapter 1).

5   Worn or damaged internal components. Disassembly and overhaul of the transfer case may be necessary.

44   Transfer case noisy in all gears

Insufficient or incorrect grade of lubricant. Drain and refill (Chapter 1).

45   Noisy or jumps out of 4WD Low range

1   Transfer case not fully engaged. Stop the vehicle, shift into Neutral and then engage 4L.

2   Shift linkage loose, worn or binding. Tighten, repair or lubricate linkage as necessary.

3   Shift fork cracked, inserts worn or fork binding on the rail. Disassemble and repair as necessary.

46   Lubricant leaks from the vent or output shaft seals

1   Transfer case is overfilled. Drain to the proper level (Chapter 1).

2   Vent is clogged or jammed closed. Clear or replace the vent.

3   Output shaft seal incorrectly installed or damaged. Replace the seal and check contact surfaces for nicks and scoring.

Driveshaft

47   Oil leak at front of driveshaft

Defective transmission rear oil seal. See Chapter 7 for replacement procedures. While this is done, check the splined yoke for burrs or a rough condition which may be damaging the seal. Burrs can be removed with crocus cloth or a fine whetstone.

48   Knock or clunk when the transmission is under initial load (just after transmission is put into gear)

1   Loose or disconnected rear suspension components. Check all mounting bolts, nuts and bushings (see Chapter 10).

2   Loose driveshaft bolts. Inspect all bolts and nuts and tighten them to the specified torque (see Chapter 8).

3   Worn or damaged universal joint bearings. Check for wear (see Chapter 8).

49   Metallic grinding sound consistent with vehicle speed

Pronounced wear in the universal joint bearings. Check as described in Chapter 8.

50   Vibration

Note: *Before assuming that the driveshaft is at fault, make sure the tires are perfectly balanced and perform the following test.*

1   Install a tachometer inside the vehicle to monitor engine speed as the vehicle is driven. Drive the vehicle and note the engine speed at which the vibration (roughness) is most pronounced. Now shift the transmission to a different gear and bring the engine speed to the same point.

2   If the vibration occurs at the same engine speed (rpm) regardless of which gear the transmission is in, the driveshaft is NOT at fault since the driveshaft speed varies.

3   If the vibration decreases or is eliminated when the transmission is in a different gear at the same engine speed, refer to the following probable causes.

4   Bent or dented driveshaft. Inspect and replace as necessary (see Chapter 8).

5   Undercoating or built-up dirt, etc. on the driveshaft. Clean the shaft thoroughly and recheck.

6   Worn universal joint bearings. Remove and inspect (see Chapter 8).

7   Driveshaft and/or companion flange out of balance. Check for missing weights on the shaft. Remove the driveshaft (see Chapter 8) and reinstall 180-degrees from original position, then retest. Have the driveshaft professionally balanced if the problem persists.

Axles

51   Noise

1   Road noise. No corrective procedures available.

2   Tire noise. Inspect tires and check tire pressures (Chapter 1).

3   Rear wheel bearings loose, worn or damaged (Chapter 8).

52   Vibration

See probable causes under Driveshaft. Proceed under the guidelines listed for the driveshaft. If the problem persists, check the rear wheel bearings by raising the rear of the vehicle and spinning the wheels by hand. Listen for evidence of rough (noisy) bearings. Remove and inspect (see Chapter 8).

53   Oil leakage

1   Pinion seal damaged (see Chapter 8).

2   Axleshaft oil seals damaged (see Chapter 8).

3   Differential inspection cover leaking. Tighten the bolts or replace the gasket as required (see Chapters 1 and 8).

Brakes

Note: *Before assuming that a brake problem exists, make sure that the tires are in good condition and inflated properly (see Chapter 1), that the front end alignment is correct and that the vehicle is not loaded with weight in an unequal manner.*

54   Vehicle pulls to one side during braking

1   Defective, damaged or oil contaminated

disc brake pads or shoes on one side. Inspect as described in Chapter 9.

2   Excessive wear of brake shoe or pad material or drum/disc on one side. Inspect and correct as necessary.

3   Loose or disconnected front suspension components. Inspect and tighten all bolts to the specified torque (Chapter 10).

4   Defective drum brake or caliper assembly. Remove the drum or caliper and inspect for a stuck piston or other damage (Chapter 9).

55   Noise (high-pitched squeal with the brakes applied)

1   Disc brake pads worn out. The noise comes from the wear sensor rubbing against the disc (does not apply to all vehicles) or the actual pad backing plate (or rivets) if the material is completely worn away. Replace the pads with new ones immediately (Chapter 9). If the pad material has worn completely away, the brake discs should be inspected for damage as described in Chapter 9.

2   Missing or damaged brake pad insulators (disc brakes). Replace pad insulators (see Chapter 9).

3   Linings contaminated with dirt or grease. Replace pads or shoes.

4   Incorrect linings. Replace with correct linings.

56   Excessive brake pedal travel

1   Partial brake system failure. Inspect the entire system (Chapter 9) and correct as required.

2   Insufficient fluid in the master cylinder. Check (Chapter 1), add fluid and bleed the system if necessary (Chapter 9).

3   Rear brakes not adjusting properly. Make a series of starts and stops while the vehicle is in Reverse. If this does not correct the situation, remove the drums and inspect the self-adjusters (Chapter 9).

57   Brake pedal feels spongy when depressed

1   Air in the hydraulic lines. Bleed the brake system (Chapter 9).

2   Faulty flexible hoses. Inspect all system hoses and lines. Replace parts as necessary.

3   Master cylinder mounting bolts/nuts loose.

4   Master cylinder defective (Chapter 9).

58   Excessive effort required to stop vehicle

1   Power brake booster not operating properly (Chapter 9).

2   Excessively worn linings or pads. Inspect and replace if necessary (Chapter 9).

3   One or more caliper pistons or wheel cyl-

inders seized or sticking. Inspect and rebuild as required (Chapter 9).

4   Brake linings or pads contaminated with oil or grease. Inspect and replace as required (Chapter 9).

5   New pads or shoes installed and not yet seated. It will take a while for the new material to seat against the drum (or rotor).

59   Pedal travels to the floor with little resistance

1   Little or no fluid in the master cylinder reservoir caused by leaking wheel cylinder(s), leaking caliper piston(s), loose, damaged or disconnected brake lines. Inspect the entire system and correct as necessary.

2   Worn master cylinder seals (Chapter 9).

60   Brake pedal pulsates during brake application

1   Caliper improperly installed. Remove and inspect (Chapter 9).

2   Disc or drum defective. Remove (Chapter 9) and check for excessive lateral runout and parallelism. Have the discs or drums resurfaced or replace them with new ones.

Suspension and steering systems

61   Vehicle pulls to one side

1   Tire pressures uneven (Chapter 1).

2   Defective tire (Chapter 1).

3   Excessive wear in suspension or steering components (Chapter 10).

4   Front end in need of alignment.

5   Front brakes dragging. Inspect the brakes as described in Chapter 9.

62   Shimmy, shake or vibration

1   Tire or wheel out-of-balance or out-of-round. Have professionally balanced.

2   Loose, worn or out-of-adjustment rear wheel bearings (Chapter 1).

3   Shock absorbers and/or suspension components worn or damaged (Chapter 10).

63   Excessive pitching and/or rolling around corners or during braking

1   Defective shock absorbers. Replace as a set (Chapter 10).

2   Broken or weak springs and/or suspension components. Inspect as described in Chapter 10.

64   Excessively stiff steering

1   Lack of fluid in power steering fluid res-

ervoir (Chapter 1).

2   Incorrect tire pressures (Chapter 1).

3   Lack of lubrication at steering joints (see Chapter 1).

4   Front end out of alignment.

5   Lack of power assistance (see Section 66).

65   Excessive play in steering

1   Loose front wheel bearings (Chapters 1 and 10).

2   Excessive wear in suspension or steering components (Chapter 10).

3   Steering gearbox damaged or out of adjustment (Chapter 10).

66   Lack of power assistance

1   Steering pump drivebelt faulty or not adjusted properly (Chapter 1).

2   Fluid level low (Chapter 1).

3   Hoses or lines restricted. Inspect and replace parts as necessary.

4   Air in power steering system. Bleed the system (Chapter 10).

67   Excessive tire wear (not specific to one area)

1   Incorrect tire pressures (Chapter 1).

2   Tires out-of-balance. Have professionally balanced.

3   Wheels damaged. Inspect and replace as necessary.

4   Suspension or steering components excessively worn (Chapter 10).

68   Excessive tire wear on outside edge

1   Inflation pressures incorrect (Chapter 1).

2   Excessive speed in turns.

3   Front end alignment incorrect (excessive toe-in). Have professionally aligned.

4   Suspension arm bent or twisted (Chapter 10).

69   Excessive tire wear on inside edge

1   Inflation pressures incorrect (Chapter 1).

2   Front end alignment incorrect (toe-out). Have professionally aligned.

3   Loose or damaged steering components (Chapter 10).

70   Tire tread worn in one place

1   Tires out-of-balance.

2   Damaged or buckled wheel. Inspect and replace if necessary.

3   Defective tire (Chapter 1).

Chapter 1
Tune-up and routine maintenance

Contents

Specifications

Recommended lubricants and fluids

Engine oil
  Type .... API certified for gasoline engines
  Viscosity .... See chart

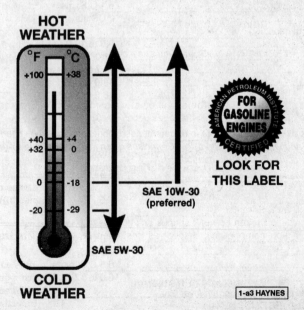

Engine oil viscosity chart - for best fuel economy and cold starting, select the lowest SAE viscosity grade for the expected temperature range

1-a3 HAYNES

Recommended lubricants and fluids (continued)

Automatic transmission fluid type

C4, C6, AOD	
1980	DEXRON II
1981 on	MERCON
C5	Type H
E4OD	MERCON

Manual transmission lubricant

4-speed (1992 and earlier)	SAE 80W gear lube
4-speed (1993 on) and 5-speed	MERCON
Transfer case lubricant	MERCON
Engine coolant	50/50 mixture of Ethylene-glycol based antifreeze and water

Differential lubricant*

Ford rear axles (conventional and limited slip)	Hypoid gear lubricant
Dana rear axles (conventional and limited slip)	Hypoid gear lubricant
Dana front axles	Gear oil
Manual steering gear lubricant	Steering gear grease

Power steering fluid

1995 and earlier	Type F ATF
1996 and later	MERCON
Brake and clutch fluid type	DOT 3 heavy-duty brake fluid

Add friction modifier to limited slip differentials - four ounces for 8.8 inch and Dana limited slip differentials, eight ounces for 10.5 inch differentials.

Capacities*

Engine oil (with new filter)	6.0 qts

Cooling system (U.S. quarts)

Inline six-cylinder engines	14
232 cu in V6 engines	12
255 and 302 cu in engines	14
351 and 400 cu in engines	16
460 cu in engines	17.5

Manual transmission (U.S. pints)

Ford 3-speed	3.5
Ford 4-speed overdrive and single-rail overdrive	4.5
New Process 435 4-speed with extension	7.0
New Process 435 4-speed without extension	6.5
Warner T-18, T18B and T19B 4-speed	7.0
Mazda M5 OD 5-speed	7.6
ZF S5-42 and ZF S5-47 5-speeds	6.8

Transfer case (U.S. pints, unless specified)

New Process 2-speed part-time	6.0 to 6.5
Warner 13-45 full-time	6.0 to 6.5
Borg Warner 13-56 manual and electronic shift	2.0 U.S. qts
Borg Warner 13-56 with PTO	6.1 U.S. qts
Borg Warner 44-07	2 US qts

Automatic transmission (U.S. quarts) (total system capacity)

C4	9.6 to 10.0
C5	11.0
C6	11.7 to 13.5
AOD	12.0
E4OD	16.2 to 17.7

Differential capacities

Note: *Specifications below include any additives as required, see note in* Recommended lubricants and fluids *chart at the beginning of this Section concerning complete refills of Ford Traction-Lok and Dana limited slip axles. Capacities given in the chart below are approximate dry capacities, the fill plug level height should be used to determine actual fluid requirements.*

Ford 8.8 and 9.0	5.5 U.S. pints
Ford 10.25	
1989 and earlier	7.5
1990 and later w/Limited Slip Differential**	6.5
Dana 44 IFS, IFS HD and 50 IFS-front	3.6 to 4.0 U.S. pints
Dana 60 - front	6.0 U.S. pints
Dana 60, 60-5, 61-1, 61-2 and 62	6.0 U.S. pints
Dana 70	6.5 U.S. pints
Dana 70 HD	6.0 to 7.5 U.S. pints

* All capacities approximate. Add as necessary to bring to appropriate level
** Add 8 ounces of friction modifier C8AZ-19B546A (EST M2C118-A)

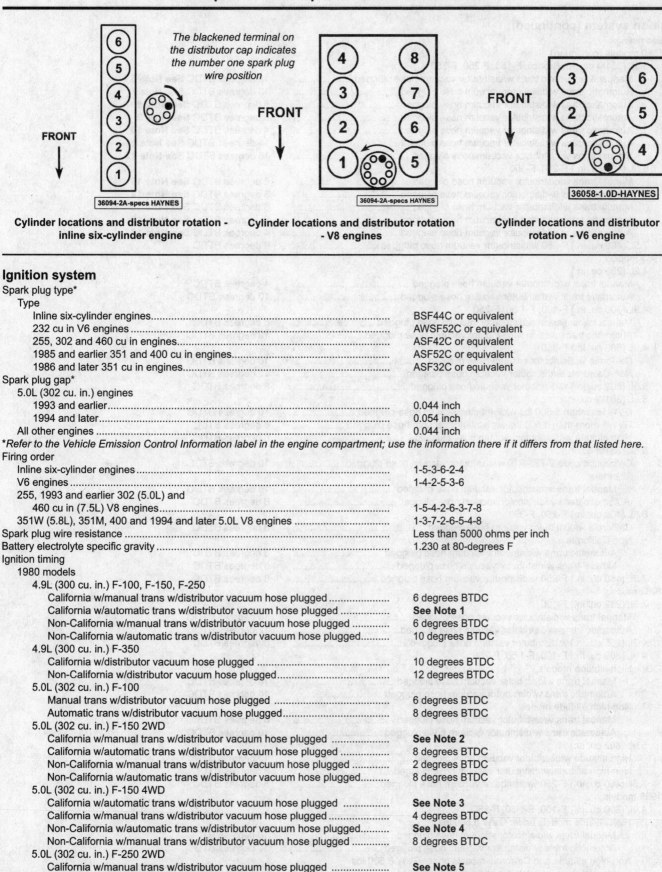

Cylinder locations and distributor rotation - inline six-cylinder engine

The blackened terminal on the distributor cap indicates the number one spark plug wire position

FRONT

36094-2A-specs HAYNES

Cylinder locations and distributor rotation - V8 engines

FRONT

36094-2A-specs HAYNES

Cylinder locations and distributor rotation - V6 engine

FRONT

36058-1.0D-HAYNES

Ignition system

Spark plug type*
  Type
    Inline six-cylinder engines... BSF44C or equivalent
    232 cu in V6 engines .... AWSF52C or equivalent
    255, 302 and 460 cu in engines... ASF42C or equivalent
    1985 and earlier 351 and 400 cu in engines.............................. ASF52C or equivalent
    1986 and later 351 cu in engines.. ASF32C or equivalent
Spark plug gap*
  5.0L (302 cu. in.) engines
    1993 and earlier .... 0.044 inch
    1994 and later .... 0.054 inch
  All other engines .... 0.044 inch
*Refer to the Vehicle Emission Control Information label in the engine compartment; use the information there if it differs from that listed here.
Firing order
  Inline six-cylinder engines 1-5-3-6-2-4
  V6 engines 1-4-2-5-3-6
  255, 1993 and earlier 302 (5.0L) and
  460 cu in (7.5L) V8 engines.. 1-5-4-2-6-3-7-8
  351W (5.8L), 351M, 400 and 1994 and later 5.0L V8 engines 1-3-7-2-6-5-4-8
Spark plug wire resistance .... Less than 5000 ohms per inch
Battery electrolyte specific gravity .... 1.230 at 80-degrees F
Ignition timing
  1980 models
    4.9L (300 cu. in.) F-100, F-150, F-250
      California w/manual trans w/distributor vacuum hose plugged .... 6 degrees BTDC
      California w/automatic trans w/distributor vacuum hose plugged .... **See Note 1**
      Non-California w/manual trans w/distributor vacuum hose plugged .... 6 degrees BTDC
      Non-California w/automatic trans w/distributor vacuum hose plugged.......... 10 degrees BTDC
    4.9L (300 cu. in.) F-350
      California w/distributor vacuum hose plugged .... 10 degrees BTDC
      Non-California w/distributor vacuum hose plugged .... 12 degrees BTDC
    5.0L (302 cu. in.) F-100
      Manual trans w/distributor vacuum hose plugged .... 6 degrees BTDC
      Automatic trans w/distributor vacuum hose plugged .... 8 degrees BTDC
    5.0L (302 cu. in.) F-150 2WD
      California w/manual trans w/distributor vacuum hose plugged .... **See Note 2**
      California w/automatic trans w/distributor vacuum hose plugged .... 8 degrees BTDC
      Non-California w/manual trans w/distributor vacuum hose plugged .... 2 degrees BTDC
      Non-California w/automatic trans w/distributor vacuum hose plugged......... 8 degrees BTDC
    5.0L (302 cu. in.) F-150 4WD
      California w/automatic trans w/distributor vacuum hose plugged .... **See Note 3**
      California w/manual trans w/distributor vacuum hose plugged .... 4 degrees BTDC
      Non-California w/automatic trans w/distributor vacuum hose plugged.......... **See Note 4**
      Non-California w/manual trans w/distributor vacuum hose plugged .... 8 degrees BTDC
    5.0L (302 cu. in.) F-250 2WD
      California w/manual trans w/distributor vacuum hose plugged .... **See Note 5**
      California w/automatic trans w/distributor vacuum hose plugged .... 10 degrees BTDC
      Non-California w/automatic trans w/distributor vacuum hose plugged.......... 8 degrees BTDC
    5.0L (302 cu. in.) F-250 4WD w/distributor vacuum hose plugged.................... 8 degrees BTDC

Ignition system (continued)

Ignition timing
  1980 models (continued)
    5.8L (351M cu. in.) Bronco, F-150, F-250, F-350
      Manual & automatic trans w/distributor vacuum hose plugged .... 10 degrees BTDC **See Note 6**
      Automatic trans w/distributor vacuum hose plugged................................... 12 degrees BTDC **See Note 7**
      Automatic trans w/distributor vacuum hose plugged................................... 8 degrees BTDC **See Note 8**
      Automatic trans w/distributor vacuum hose plugged................................... 6 degrees BTDC **See Note 9**
      Automatic trans w/distributor vacuum hose plugged................................... 4 degrees BTDC **See Note 10**
      Automatic trans w/distributor vacuum hose plugged................................... 14 degrees BTDC **See Note 11**
      Manual trans w/distributor vacuum hose plugged .... 16 degrees BTDC **See Note 12**
    6.6L (400 cu. in.) F-250, F-350
      Manual trans w/distributor vacuum hose plugged .... 6 degrees BTDC **See Note 13**
      Automatic trans w/distributor vacuum hose plugged................................... 3 degrees BTDC **See Note 14**
      Manual trans w/distributor vacuum hose plugged .... 6 degrees BTDC **See Note 15**
      Automatic trans w/distributor vacuum hose plugged................................... 6 degrees BTDC **See Note 16**
      Automatic trans w/distributor vacuum hose plugged................................... 4 degrees BTDC **See Note 17**
    7.5L (460 cu. in.) F-250 w/distributor vacuum hose plugged............................ 8 degrees BTDC
  1981 models
    4.2L (255 cu. in.)
      Manual trans w/distributor vacuum hose plugged .... 4 degrees BTDC
      Automatic trans w/distributor vacuum hose plugged................................... 10 degrees BTDC
    4.9L (300 cu. in.) F-100, F-1-50, F-250
      Manual transmission w/distributor vacuum hose plugged .... 6 degrees BTDC
      Automatic transmission w/distributor vacuum hose plugged....................... 10 degrees BTDC
    4.9L (300 cu. in.) F-350
      California w/distributor vacuum hose plugged .... 10 degrees BTDC
      Non-California w/distributor vacuum hose plugged.................................... 12 degrees BTDC
    5.0L (302 cu. in.) w/distributor vacuum hose plugged .... 8 degrees BTDC
    5.8L (351W cu. in.)
      GVW less than 8,500 lbs w/distributor vacuum hose plugged .... 10 degrees BTDC
      GVW6 more than 8,500 lbs w/distributor vacuum hose plugged .... 6 degrees BTDC
      High altitude w/distributor vacuum hose plugged...................................... 8 degrees BTDC
    5.8L (351M cu. in.)
      Calibration code 9-72J-R10 w/distributor vacuum hose plugged................. 10 degrees BTDC
      All others
        Manual trans w/distributor vacuum hose plugged .... 10 degrees BTDC
        Automatic trans w/distributor vacuum hose plugged............................ 6 degrees BTDC
    6.6L (400 cu. in.) F-250, F-350
      California w/distributor vacuum hose plugged .... 6 degrees BTDC
      Non-California
        Automatic trans w/distributor vacuum hose plugged .... 3 degrees BTDC
        Manual trans w/distributor vacuum hose plugged .... 6 degrees BTDC
    7.5L (460 cu. in.) F-250 w/distributor vacuum hose plugged.......................... 8 degrees BTDC
  1982 models
    3.8L (232 cu. in.) F-100
      Manual trans w/distributor vacuum hose plugged .... 10 degrees BTDC
      Automatic trans w/distributor vacuum hose plugged................................. 12 degrees BTDC
    4.2L (255 cu. in.) w/distributor vacuum hose plugged .... 8 degrees BTDC
    4.9L (300 cu. in.) F-100, F-1-50, F-250
      High altitude models
        Manual trans w/distributor vacuum hose plugged .... 10 degrees BTDC
        Automatic trans w/distributor vacuum hose plugged .... 14 degrees BTDC
      Non-high altitude models
        Manual trans w/distributor vacuum hose plugged .... 6 degrees BTDC
        Automatic trans w/distributor vacuum hose plugged .... 10 degrees BTDC
    5.0L (302 cu. in.)
      High altitude w/distributor vacuum hose plugged..................................... 10 degrees BTDC
      Non-high altitude w/distributor vacuum hose plugged............................... 8 degrees BTDC
    7.5L (460 cu. in.) F-250 w/distributor vacuum hose plugged........................... 8 degrees BTDC
  1983 models
    4.9L (300 cu. in.) F-100, F-1-50, F-250
      High altitude models under GVW 8,500 lbs
        Manual trans w/distributor vacuum hose plugged .... 10 degrees BTDC
        Automatic trans w/distributor vacuum hose plugged .... 14 degrees BTDC
      Non-high altitude and California models under GVW 8,500 lbs
        Manual trans w/distributor vacuum hose plugged .... 6 degrees BTDC
        Automatic trans w/distributor vacuum hose plugged .... 10 degrees BTDC
      Models over GVW 8,500 lbs w/distributor vacuum hose plugged................ 12 degrees BTDC

5.0L (302 cu. in.)
    High altitude w/distributor vacuum hose plugged .... 12 degrees BTDC
    Non-high altitude w/distributor vacuum hose plugged................................... 8 degrees BTDC
    California models w/single wire next to distributor disconnected .... 10 degrees BTDC
5.8L (351W cu. in.)
    GVW less than 8,500 lbs w/single wire next to distributor disconnected ...... 14 degrees BTDC
    GVW more than 8,500 lbs w/distributor vacuum hose plugged .... 8 degrees BTDC
7.5L (460 cu. in.) F-250 w/distributor vacuum hose plugged.......................... **See Note 18**
1984
  4.9L (300 cu. in.)
    GVW less than 8,500 lbs w/distributor vacuum hose plugged .... 10 degrees BTDC
    GVW more than 8,500 lbs w/distributor vacuum hose plugged .... 12 degrees BTDC
  5.0L (302 cu. in.)
    High altitude w/distributor vacuum hose plugged.. 12 degrees BTDC
    Non-high altitude w/distributor vacuum hose plugged................................... 8 degrees BTDC
    California models w/distributor vacuum hose plugged .... 10 degrees BTDC
  5.8L (351W cu. in.)
    GVW less than 8,500 lbs w/distributor vacuum hose plugged .... 10 degrees BTDC
    GVW more than 8,500 lbs w/distributor vacuum hose plugged .... 8 degrees BTDC
  7.5L (460 cu. in.) F-250 w/distributor vacuum hose plugged........................... 8 degrees BTDC
1985
  4.9L (300 cu. in.) w/single wire next to distributor disconnected .... 10 degrees BTDC
  5.0L (302 cu. in.)
    Carbureted models w/single wire next to distributor disconnected .... 10 degrees BTDC
    EFI models w/single wire next to distributor disconnected...........................
      Calibration codes 5-53F-R01 and 5-53H-R01 .... 8 degrees BTDC
      All other models .... 10 degrees BTDC
  5.8L (351W) and 7.5L (460) w/distributor vacuum hose plugged .... 8 degrees BTDC
1986
  4.9L (300 cu. in.)
    Light duty models w/SPOUT disconnected .... 10 degrees BTDC
    Heavy duty models w/SPOUT disconnected
      Manual transmission... 6 degrees BTDC
      Automatic transmission.. 8 degrees BTDC
  5.0L (302) w/SPOUT disconnected .... 10 degrees BTDC
  5.8L (351W) w/distributor vacuum hose plugged .... 8 degrees BTDC
  7.5L (460) w/distributor vacuum hose plugged.. 8 degrees BTDC
1987
  4.9L (300) w/SPOUT disconnected .... 10 degrees BTDC
  5.0L (302) w/SPOUT disconnected .... 10 degrees BTDC
  5.8L (351W) w/distributor vacuum hose plugged
    High altitude model.. 14 degrees BTDC
    Non-high altitude models... 10 degrees BTDC
    GVW more than 8,500 lbs... 8 degrees BTDC
  7.5L (460) w/distributor vacuum hose plugged.. 8 degrees BTDC
1988 through 1996
  4.9L (300) w/SPOUT disconnected .... 10 degrees BTDC
  5.0L (302) w/SPOUT disconnected .... 10 degrees BTDC
  5.8L (351W) w/SPOUT disconnected .... 10 degrees BTDC
  7.5L (460) w/SPOUT disconnected .... 10 degrees BTDC
1997
  5.8L (351W) w/SPOUT disconnected .... 10 degrees BTDC
  7.5L (460) w/SPOUT disconnected .... 10 degrees BTDC

Note 1: *Calibration codes 0-52S-R10, 6 degrees BTDC; except 0-52S-R10-6, 10 degrees BTDC*
Note 2: *Models w/3 speed or 4-speed OD manual trans, 2 degrees BTDC, w/4-speed manual trans, 4 degrees BTDC*
Note 3: *Calibration codes 0-54M-R0, 8 degrees BTDC; 0-54R-R0, 10 degrees BTDC*
Note 4: *Calibration codes 0-54D-R0, 14 degrees BTDC; 0-54D-R11, 12 degrees BTDC; 0-54F-R0 & M-R0, 8 degrees BTDC*
Note 5: *Models w/3 speed or 4 speed OD, 6 degrees BTDC; w/4 speed, 8 degrees BTDC*
Note 6: *Calibration codes manual trans 9-71J-R10 and automatic 9-72J-R11*
Note 7: *Calibration codes 0-60B-R0 and R10, 0-60C-R0 and R10*
Note 8: *Calibration codes 0-60G-R0 and 0, 0-60H-R11 and R13*
Note 9: *Calibration codes 0-60H-R0 and R12, 0-60K-R0,R10,R11,R12 and 0-60J-R0*
Note 10: *Calibration code 0-60L-R10*
Note 11: *Calibration codes 0-60-R0 and R10*
Note 12: *Calibration codes 0-59-RC*
Note 13: *Calibration code 9-73J-R11*
Note 14: *Calibration code 9-74J-R11*
Note 15: *Calibration code 9-73J-R12*
Note 16: *Calibration code 9-74J-R12*

Ignition system (continued)

Note 17: *Calibration code 0-62L-R0*
Note 18: *Calibration codes 3-98S-R00, 6 degrees BTDC; 9-97J-R-13, 8 degrees BTDC*

Drivebelt tension (measured with Burroughs-type gauge)

1/4-inch V-belts
    New (before being rotated more than once) .... 50 to 80 lbs
    Used (less than 10 minutes operation) .... 40 to 80 lbs
    Belts having more than 10 minutes operation.. 40 to 60 lbs
3/8, 15/32 and 1/2-inch V-belts
    New (before being rotated more than once) .... 120 to 160 lbs
    Used (less than 10 minutes operation) .... 90 to 160 lbs
    Belts (more than 10 minutes operation)... 72 to 120 lbs
Serpentine belts
    New .... 150 to 190 lbs
    Used (more than 10 minutes operation)... 140 to 160 lbs

Clutch pedal free play .... 1 to 2 inches

Brakes

Front disc brake pad minimum thickness 1/8-inch
Rear (drum) brake lining thickness... 1/16-inch

Torque specifications   Ft-lbs (unless otherwise indicated)

Note: *One foot-pound (ft-lb) of torque is equivalent to 12 inch-pounds (in-lbs) of torque. Torque values below approximately 15 ft-lbs are expressed in inch-pounds, since most foot-pound torque wrenches are not accurate at these smaller values.*

Spark plug
    4.9L engine .... 17 to 22
    7.5L engine .... 72 to 120 in-lbs
    All others .... 10 to 15
Oil pan drain plug .... 15 to 25
Manual transmission drain and fill plugs
    New Process 435 .... 25 to 35
    Borg-Warner 4-speed (all)... 25 to 40
    Mazda M5 OD 5-speed .... 29 to 43
    ZF S5-42 5-speed 37
    ZF S5-47 5-speed 44
    All others .... 10 to 20
Transfer case drain and fill plugs
    New Process 208 .... 30 to 40
    Borg-Warner 13-45 .... 14 to 22
    Borg-Warner 13-56 .... 14 to 22
    Borg Warner 44-07 .... 7 to 17
Automatic transmission pan bolts .... 120 to 168 in-lbs
Automatic transmission converter drain plug
    C4 .... 15 to 26
    C5 .... 12 to 17
    AOD and C6.. 8 to 28
    E4OD .... 18 to 20
Automatic transmission filter screen-to-main body bolts
    C4 and C6 .... 40 to 55 in-lbs
    C5 .... 25 to 40 in-lbs
    AOD .... 80 to 100 in-lbs
    E4OD .... N/A
Differential fill plug
    Conventional .... 15 to 30
    Dana... 20 to 30
Wheel lug nuts
    1/2-inch nut 100
    9/16-inch nut (single rear wheels).. 145
    9/16-inch nut (dual rear wheels, standard lug nut)... 220
    9/16-inch nut (dual rear wheels, swivel lug nut)... 145

Maintenance schedule

Normal driving conditions

Every 250 miles or weekly, whichever comes first

Fluid level checks (refer to Section 4)
Tire and tire pressure checks (refer to Section 5)

Every 3000 miles or 3 months, whichever comes first

All items listed above plus . . .
Check the power steering fluid level (Section 6)
Check the automatic transmission fluid level (Section 7)
Change the engine oil and oil filter (Section8)

7500 miles or 6 months, whichever comes first

All items listed above plus . . .
Wheel inspection and lug nut torque check (refer to Section 9)
Battery check, maintenance and charging (refer to Section 10)
Underhood hose check and replacement (refer to Section 11)
Drivebelt check, adjustment and replacement (refer to Section 12)
Lubrication - driveline, steering and chassis (refer to Section 13)

Every 15,000 miles or 12 months, whichever comes first

All items listed above plus . . .
Fuel system check (refer to Section 14)
Cooling system check (refer to Section 15)
Wheel removal and tire rotation (refer to Section 16)
Windshield wipers - inspection and blade replacement (refer to Section 17)
Brake check (refer to Section 18)
Suspension and steering - inspection (refer to Section 19)
Exhaust system check (refer to Section 20)
Clutch hydraulic linkage check (refer to Section 21)
Driveline fluid level checks (refer to Section 22)
Replace fuel filter (refer to Section 23)

Clutch linkage adjustment - early models (refer to Section 24)
Automatic transmission - band adjustment (Section 25)

Every 30,000 miles or 30 months, whichever comes first

All items listed above plus . . .
Spark plug replacement (refer to Section 26)
Spark plug wire, distributor cap and rotor check and replacement (refer to Section 27)
Cooling system servicing, draining, flushing and refilling (refer to Section 28)
Air filter - inspection and replacement (refer to Section 29)
PCV valve and filter - inspection and replacement (refer to Section 30)
Wheel bearings - check, repack and adjustment (refer to Section 31)
Front spindle/knuckle needle bearing (4x4) - check and repack (refer to Section 32)
Front locking hubs (4X4) - lubricant check and repack (refer to Section 33)

Every 60,000 miles

Manual transmission - oil change (refer to Section 34)
Transfer case - oil change (refer to Section 35)
Automatic transmission - fluid change (refer to Section 36)
Evaporative emissions system - inspection (refer to Section 37)

Every 100,000 miles

Differential(s) - lubricant change (refer to Section 38)

Unique driving conditions

Every 1000 miles (extreme duty only)

Use this schedule if your vehicle is operated off-road, in mud and/or water.
Lubrication - driveline, steering and chassis (refer to Section 13)
Brake check (refer to Section 18)
Check axle lube for contamination (if submerged in water) (refer to Section 22)
Wheel bearings - check, repack and adjustment (refer to Section 31)

Every 3000 miles or 3 months (extreme duty only)

Use this schedule if your vehicle is used or operated under any of the following conditions:

    a) *Towing or carrying heavy loads.*
    b) *Operated in very hot, cold or dusty environments.*
    c) *Constant stop and go driving or extended idling.*

Change the engine oil and filter (refer to Section 8)
Replace air filter (dusty conditions only) (refer to Section 29)
Change rear axle lubricant (heavy duty axles only) (refer to Section 38)

Every 30,000 miles or 30 months (extreme duty only)

Use this schedule if your vehicle is used or operated under any of the following conditions:

    a) *Towing or carrying heavy loads.*
    b) *Operated in very hot, cold or dusty environments.*
    c) *Constant stop and go driving or extended idling.*

Manual transmission - oil change (refer to Section 34)
Transfer case - oil change (refer to Section 35)
Automatic transmission - fluid change (refer to Section 36)

1   Introduction

This Chapter was designed to help the home mechanic maintain his or her vehicle for peak performance, economy, safety and longevity. On the following pages you will find a maintenance schedule along with Sections which deal specifically with each item on the schedule. Included are visual checks, adjustments and item replacements.

Servicing your vehicle using the time/mileage maintenance schedule and the sequenced Sections involves a planned program of maintenance. Keep in mind that it is a complete plan, and maintaining only a few items at the specified intervals will not produce the same results.

You will find as you service your vehicle that many of the procedures can, and should, be grouped together due to the nature of the job at hand, Examples of this are as follows:

If the vehicle is raised for a chassis lubrication, for example, this is the ideal time for the following checks: manual transmission oil, exhaust system, suspension, steering and the fuel system.

If the tires and wheels are removed, as during a routine tire rotation, go ahead and check the brakes and wheel bearings at the same time.

If you must borrow or rent a torque wrench, it would be advisable to service the spark plugs and repack (or replace) the wheel bearings all in the same day to save time and money.

The first step of this or any maintenance plan is to prepare yourself before the actual work begins. Read through the appropriate Sections for all work that is to be performed before you begin. Gather together all necessary parts and tools. If it appears you could have a problem during a particular job, don't hesitate to ask advice from your local parts man or dealer service department.

2   Routine maintenance intervals

Refer to illustration 2.3

General information

1   The following recommendations are given with the assumption that the vehicle owner will be doing the maintenance or service work (as opposed to a dealer service department). They are based on factory service/maintenance recommendations, but the time and/or mileage intervals have been shortened in most cases, to ensure that the service is thorough and complete. Not all maintenance checks or operations apply to every vehicle.

2   When the vehicle is new, it should be serviced initially by a factory authorized dealer service department to protect the factory warranty. In most cases the initial maintenance check is done at no cost to the owner.

3   The majority of the procedures described are for late model vehicles which are designed for reduced maintenance. Also included are general schedules for extreme duty service, however, review your owners manual for specific items particular to your vehicle. For early models, consult your owners manual for additional direction. For assistance in location of various maintenance check items and components, refer to the engine compartment component layout diagram **(see illustration)**.

2.3 Engine compartment components (typical)

1	Automatic transmission fluid dipstick	6	Windshield washer fluid/coolant
2	PCV valve		reservoir
3	Air filter housing	7	Power steering fluid reservoir
4	Engine oil dipstick	8	Radiator cap
5	Brake fluid reservoir	9	Oil filler cap

10	Distributor
11	Valve cover
12	Spark plugs
13	Upper radiator hose
14	Air cleaner duct
15	Battery

3   Tune-up general information

The term *tune-up* is used in this manual to represent a combination of individual operations rather than one specific procedure. If from the time the vehicle is new the routine maintenance schedule is followed closely and frequent checks are made of fluid levels and high wear items as suggested throughout this manual, the engine will be kept in relatively good running condition and the need for additional work will be minimized.

More likely than not, however, there will be times when the engine is running poorly due to lack of regular maintenance. This is even more likely if a used vehicle which has not received regular and frequent maintenance checks is purchased. In such cases an engine tune-up will be needed outside of the regular routine maintenance intervals.

The first step in any tune-up or diagnostic procedure to help correct a poor running engine is a cylinder compression check. A compression check (see Chapter 2, Part D) will help determine the condition of internal engine components and should be used as a guide for tune-up and repair procedures. If, for instance, a compression check indicates serious internal engine wear, a conventional tune-up will not improve the performance of the engine and would be a waste of time and money.

The following procedures are those most often needed to bring a generally poor running engine back into a proper state of tune.

Minor tune-up

Clean inspect and test the battery (Section 10)
Check all engine related fluids (Sections 4, 6, 7, 22 and 33)
Check and adjust (if adjustable) the idle speed (carbureted models) (Chapter 4)
Check the PCV valve (Section 30)
Check the air filter (Section 29)
Check the cooling system (Section 15)
Check all underhood hoses (Section 11)
Check and adjust the drivebelts (Section 12)
Inspect the distributor cap and rotor (Section 27)
Inspect the spark plug and coil wires (Section 27)
Replace the spark plugs (Section 26)

Major tune-up

All items listed under Minor tune-up, plus . . .

Check the EGR system (Chapter 6)
Check the ignition system and timing (Chapter 5)
Check the charging system (Chapter 5)
Check the fuel system (Section 14)
Check the exhaust heat control valve (carbureted models) (Chapter 6)
Check the curb idle speed (carbureted models) (Chapter 4)
Check the fast idle speed (carbureted models) (Chapter 4)
Check the choke system (carbureted models) (Section 39)

Replace the fuel filter (Section 23)
Replace the air and PCV filters (Sections 29 and 30)
Replace the distributor cap and rotor (Section 27)
Replace the spark plug wires (Section 27)
Drain the chassis-mounted fuel filter (Chapter 4)

4   Fluid level checks (every 250 miles or weekly)

Refer to illustrations 4.4, 4.9, 4.16, 4.17, 4.20 and 4.35

1   Fluids are an essential part of the lubrication, cooling, brake and windshield washer systems. Because the fluids gradually become depleted and/or contaminated during normal operation of the vehicle, they must be periodically replenished. See *Recommended lubricants fluids and capacities* at the beginning of this Chapter before adding fluid to any of the following components. In addition to the illustrations listed, refer to illustrations in Section 2. **Note:** *The vehicle must be on level ground when fluid levels are checked.*

Engine oil

2   The engine oil level is checked with a dipstick located on side of the engine block.
3   The oil level should be checked when the engine is cold or at least 5 minutes after it has been shut off. Make sure that the vehicle is sitting on level ground. Any deviations in level can cause a major variation in the actual fluid level.
4   Pull the dipstick from the tube and wipe all the oil from the end with a clean rag. Insert the dipstick all the way back into the oil pan and pull it out again. Check the dipstick at the end and note the oil level in relationship to the marks on the dipstick. Some dipsticks have an Add mark followed by a number to help indicate how much oil to add to the engine. In any case, the oil should be kept within the safe range on the dipstick **(see illustration)**.
5   Oil is added to the engine by removing the cap located on the rocker arm cover. Use an oil spout or funnel to reduce any chance of oil being poured on the outside of the engine.
6   Checking the oil level can also be an important preventive maintenance step. If the oil level is dropping abnormally, it indicates an oil leak or internal engine wear problems which should be checked and corrected. If there are water droplets in the oil, or if it has a milky-looking color, this also indicates internal engine problems that should be looked into immediately.
7   The condition of the oil is also important and can be observed when checking the level. With the dipstick removed from the engine, take your thumb and index finger and wipe oil from the dipstick onto your fingers. Look for small dirt particles or metal particles which will show up on the dipstick or feel gritty to the touch. This is an indication that the oil should be drained and fresh oil added. If this condition

4.4 The oil level should be in the SAFE range - if it's below the ADD line add enough oil to bring the level into the SAFE range (if the level is between the SAFE range and the circle DO NOT add more oil)

persists, abnormal engine wear is occurring and should be checked and corrected.

Engine coolant

Warning: *Do not allow antifreeze to come in contact with your skin or painted surfaces of the vehicle. Rinse off spills immediately with plenty of water. Antifreeze is highly toxic if ingested. Never leave antifreeze lying around in an open container or in puddles on the floor; children and pets are attracted by it's sweet smell and may drink it. Check with local authorities about disposing of used antifreeze. Many communities have collection centers which will see that antifreeze is disposed of safely.*
8   All vehicles covered by this manual are equipped with a pressurized coolant recovery system. A white plastic coolant reservoir located in the left front corner of the engine compartment is connected by a hose to the radiator filler neck. If the engine overheats, coolant escapes through a valve in the radiator cap and travels through the hose into the reservoir. As the engine cools, the coolant is automatically drawn back into the cooling system to maintain the correct level.
9   The coolant level in the reservoir should be checked regularly. **Warning:** *Do not remove the radiator cap to check the coolant level when the engine is warm.* The level in the reservoir varies with the temperature of the engine. When the engine is cold, the coolant level should be at, or slightly above, the Add mark on the reservoir. **Note:** *The coolant recovery reservoir is combined in a housing which also includes the windshield washer fluid reservoir - make sure the proper level is being checked.* Once the engine has warmed up, the level should be at, or near, the Full Hot mark **(see illustration)**. If it isn't, allow the engine to cool, then slowly remove the cap from the radiator and add a 50/50 mixture of ethylene glycol based antifreeze and water. **Warning:** *When removing the radiator cap, turn the cap to the first stop and listen for a hissing sound, indicating that there is still pressure inside the system. Wait for the hissing to stop, then push down on the cap and turn it the rest of the way and remove it.*
10   Drive the vehicle and recheck the coolant level. Do not use rust inhibitors or additives. If

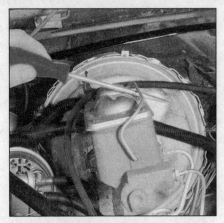

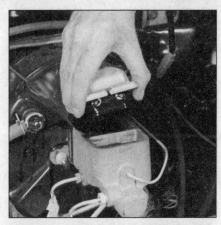

4.9 The coolant level in the reservoir should be at the ADD line when it's cool and between the FULL HOT and ADD lines when the engine is at operating temperature

4.16 Removing the lock clip from the brake master cylinder fluid reservoir - early models

4.17 Removing the brake fluid reservoir cover to check fluid level - early models

only a small amount of coolant is required to bring the system up to the proper level, water can be used. However, repeated additions of water will dilute the antifreeze and water solution. In order to maintain the proper ratio of antifreeze and water, always top up the coolant level with the correct mixture. An empty plastic milk jug or bleach bottle makes an excellent container for mixing coolant.

11   If the coolant level drops consistently, there may be a leak in the system. Inspect the radiator, hoses, filler cap, drain plugs and water pump (see Sections 11 and 15). If no leaks are noted, have the radiator cap pressure tested by a service station.

12   If you have to remove the radiator cap, wait until the engine has cooled completely, then wrap a thick cloth around the cap and turn it to the first stop. If coolant or steam escapes, let the engine cool down longer, then remove the cap.

13   Check the condition of the coolant as well. It should be relatively clear. If it is brown or rust colored, the system should be drained, flushed and refilled. Even if the coolant appears to be normal, the corrosion inhibitors wear out, so it must be replaced at the specified intervals.

Brake fluid

Early models

14   On early models, the brake fluid reservoir is an integral part of the brake master cylinder, which is attached to either the firewall at the left of the engine or to the power brake booster in that same location.

15   Remove any accumulation of dirt or loose particles from the cover.

16   Snap the retaining clip to the side to release the cover from the master cylinder reservoir **(see illustration)**.

17   Remove the cover being very careful not to let any type of contamination enter the reservoir **(see illustration)**.

18   Observe the fluid level inside the dual chambers. Check that it is within 1/2-inch of the top of the reservoir.

Later models

19   On later models, the brake fluid level is checked by looking through the plastic reservoir mounted on the master cylinder. The master cylinder is mounted on the front of the power booster unit in the left rear corner of the engine compartment.

20   The fluid level should be between the Max and Min lines on the side of the reservoir **(see illustration)**.

21   If the fluid level is low, wipe the top of the reservoir and the cap with a clean rag to prevent contamination of the system as the cap is unscrewed.

All models

22   Add only the specified brake fluid to the reservoir (refer to *Recommended lubricants and fluids* at the front of this Chapter or to your owner's manual). Mixing different types of brake fluid can damage the system. Fill the reservoir to the Max line. **Warning:** *Brake fluid can harm your eyes and damage painted surfaces, so use extreme caution when handling or pouring it. Do not use brake fluid that has been standing open or is more than one year old. Brake fluid absorbs moisture from the air. Moisture in the system can cause a dangerous loss of braking effectiveness.*

23   While the reservoir cap is off, check the master cylinder reservoir for contamination. If rust deposits, dirt particles or water droplets are present, the system should be drained, refilled and the system bled of air (see Chapter 9).

24   After filling the reservoir to the proper level, make sure the cap is securely installed to prevent fluid leakage and/or contamination.

25   The fluid level in the master cylinder will drop slightly as the brake shoes or pads at each wheel wear down during normal operation. If the brake fluid level drops consistently, check the entire system for leaks immediately. Examine all brake lines, hoses and connections, along with the calipers, wheel cylinders and master cylinder (see Section 18).

26   When checking the fluid level, if you

4.20 The brake fluid level should be between the MAX and MIN lines on the master cylinder reservoir - late model master cylinder shown

discover one or both reservoirs empty or nearly empty, the brake system should be bled (see Chapter 9).

Clutch fluid (manual transmission models only)

27   Clutch fluid level is checked by looking through the plastic reservoir mounted on the clutch master cylinder. The clutch master cylinder is mounted on the firewall at the rear of the engine compartment adjacent to the brake master cylinder.

28   The fluid level should be between the Max and Min lines on the side of the reservoir.

29   If the fluid level is low, wipe the top of the reservoir and the cap with a clean rag to prevent contamination of the system as the cap is unscrewed.

30   Add only the specified brake fluid to the clutch reservoir (refer to *Recommended lubricants and fluids* at the front of this Chapter or to your owner's manual). Mixing different

4.35 The windshield washer reservoir is combined with the coolant reservoir (there are separate compartments for the two fluids)

5.2 A tire tread depth indicator should be used to monitor tire wear - they're available at auto parts stores and service stations and cost very little

windshield washer fluid reservoir is combined in a housing which also includes the coolant recovery reservoir - make sure the proper level is being checked.

36   In milder climates, plain water can be used in the reservoir, but it should be kept no more than 2/3 full to allow for expansion if the water freezes. In colder climates, use windshield washer system antifreeze, available at any auto parts store, to lower the freezing point of the fluid. Mix the antifreeze with water in accordance with the manufacturer's directions on the container. **Caution**: *Do not use cooling system antifreeze - it will damage the vehicle's paint.*

types of brake fluid can damage the system. Fill the reservoir to the Max line. **Warning:** *Brake fluid can harm your eyes and damage painted surfaces, so use extreme caution when handling or pouring it.*

31   After filling the reservoir to the proper level, make sure the cap is securely installed to prevent fluid leakage and/or contamination.

32   The fluid level in the clutch master cylinder will drop slightly as the clutch plate wears down during normal operation. If the fluid level drops consistently, check the entire system for leaks immediately. Examine all lines, hoses

and connections, along with the slave cylinder and clutch master cylinder (see Chapter 7, Part A).

33   When checking the fluid level, if you discover it empty or nearly empty, the system should be bled (see Chapter 7, Part A).

Windshield washer fluid

34   Fluid for the windshield washer system is stored in a plastic reservoir located at the left front corner of the engine compartment.

35   Check the translucent reservoir for the proper fluid level **(see illustration)**. **Note:** *The*

5   Tire and tire pressure checks (every 250 miles or weekly)

Refer to illustrations 5.2, 5.3, 5.4a, 5.4b and 5.8

1   Periodic inspection of the tires may spare you the inconvenience of being stranded with a flat tire. It can also provide you with vital information regarding possible problems in the steering and suspension systems before major damage occurs.

2   Tread wear can be monitored with a simple, inexpensive device known as a tread depth indicator **(see illustration)**. Tread depth should not be less than 1/16 inch.

3   Note any abnormal tread wear **(see illustration)**. Tread pattern irregularities such as cupping, flat spots and more wear on one

UNDERINFLATION

CUPPING

Cupping may be caused by:
• Underinflation and/or mechanical irregularities such as out-of-balance condition of wheel and/or tire, and bent or damaged wheel.
• Loose or worn steering tie-rod or steering idler arm.
• Loose, damaged or worn front suspension parts.

OVERINFLATION

INCORRECT TOE-IN OR EXTREME CAMBER

FEATHERING DUE TO MISALIGNMENT

5.3 This chart will help you determine the condition of your tires, the probable cause(s) of abnormal wear and the corrective action necessary

5.4a If a tire continually loses pressure over and over again at a slow rate, check the valve stem core first to make sure that it's snug

5.4b If the valve stem core is tight, raise the corner of the vehicle with the low tire and spray the tire with a solution of soapy water - slow leaks will cause small bubbles to appear

5.8 Check the pressure of all four tires at least once a week with an accurate tire pressure gauge

side than the other are indications of front end alignment and/or balance problems. If any of these conditions are noted, take the vehicle to a tire shop or service station to correct the problem.

4　Look closely for cuts, punctures and embedded nails or tacks. Sometimes a tire will hold air pressure for a short time or leak down very slowly after a nail has embedded itself in the tread. If a slow leak persists, check the valve stem core to make sure it is tight **(see illustration)**. Examine the tread for an object that may have embedded itself in the tire or for a 'plug' that may have begun to leak (radial tire punctures are repaired with a plug that is installed in a puncture). If a puncture is suspected, it can be easily verified by spraying a solution of soapy water onto the puncture area **(see illustration)**. The soapy solution will bubble if there is a leak. Unless the puncture is unusually large, a tire shop or service station can usually repair the tire.

5　Carefully inspect the inner sidewall of each tire for evidence of brake fluid leakage. If you see any, inspect the brakes immediately.

6　Correct air pressure adds miles to the life span of the tires, improves mileage and enhances overall ride quality. Tire pressure cannot be accurately estimated by looking at a tire, especially if it's a radial. A tire pressure gauge is essential. Keep an accurate gauge in the glove box. The pressure gauges attached to the nozzles of air hoses at gas stations are often inaccurate.

7　Always check tire pressure when the tires are cold. Cold, in this case, means the vehicle has not been driven over a mile in the three hours preceding a tire pressure check. A pressure rise of four to eight pounds is not uncommon once the tires are warm.

8　Unscrew the valve cap protruding from the wheel or hubcap and push the gauge firmly onto the valve stem **(see illustration)**. Note the reading on the gauge and compare the figure to the recommended tire pressure shown on the tire placard on the driver's side door. Be sure to set the pressure in accordance with both the size of tire on your particular vehicle and with the load you are planning to carry with it. These specifications will

vary widely so be careful when looking them up. Overloaded and/or under inflated tires on a truck are one of the most common areas of breakdown as well as being potentially dangerous. Be sure to reinstall the valve cap to keep dirt and moisture out of the valve stem mechanism. Check all four tires and, if necessary, add enough air to bring them up to the recommended pressure.

9　Don't forget to keep the spare tire inflated to the specified pressure (refer to your owner's manual or the tire sidewall). Note that the pressure recommended for the compact spare is higher than for the tires on vehicles so equipped.

6　Power steering fluid level check (every 3000 miles or 3 months)

Refer to illustrations 6.2 and 6.5

1　Check the power steering fluid level periodically to avoid steering system problems, such as damage to the pump. **Caution: DO NOT** *hold the steering wheel against either stop (extreme left or right turn) for more than five seconds. If you do, the power steering pump could be damaged.*

2　The power steering pump, located at the lower left front corner of the engine, utilizes a built-in reservoir and is equipped with a twist-off cap with an integral fluid level dipstick for verifying fluid level **(see illustration)**.

3　Park the vehicle on level ground and apply the parking brake.

4　Run the engine until it has reached normal operating temperature. With the engine at idle, turn the steering wheel back-and-forth several times to get any air out of the steering system. Shut the engine off.

5　Remove the cap and wipe the dipstick. Install, then remove the cap again and note the fluid level. It must be between the two lines designating the Full Hot range **(see illustration)** (be sure to use the proper temperature range on the dipstick when checking the fluid level, the Full Cold lines on the reverse side of the dipstick are only usable when the engine is cold).

6.2 The power steering fluid filler cap/dipstick is located in front of the engine oil dipstick

6　Add small amounts of fluid until the level is correct. **Caution:** *Do not overfill. If too much fluid is added, remove the excess with a clean syringe or suction pump.*

7　Check the power steering hoses and connections for leaks and wear (see Section 11).

8　Check the condition and tension of the power steering pump drivebelt (see Section 12).

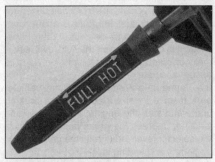

6.5 Once the engine is warmed up and the wheel has been turned back-and-forth a few times to rid the system of air bubbles, pull the dipstick out and wipe it off, reinsert it and verify that the fluid level is in the FULL HOT range. If it isn't, add enough fluid to bring the level between the two lines

7.4 The automatic transmission fluid dipstick is near the firewall, to the right of the engine

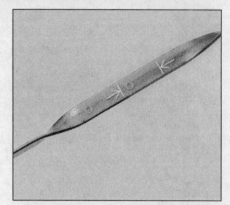

7.6 If the automatic transmission fluid is cold, the level should be between the two circles - if it's at operating temperature, the level should be between the two lines

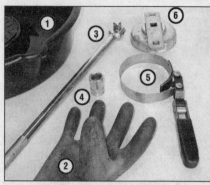

8.2 These tools are required when changing the engine oil and filter

1   **Drain pan** - *It should be fairly shallow in depth, but wide in order to prevent spills*
2   **Rubber gloves** - *When removing the drain plug and filter it is inevitable that you will get oil on your hands - the gloves will prevent burns!*
3   **Breaker bar** - *Sometimes the oil drain plug is pretty tight and a long breaker bar is needed to loosen it*
4   **Socket** - *To be used with the breaker bar or a ratchet (must be the correct size to fit the drain plug)*
5   **Filter wrench** - *This is a metal band-type wrench, which requires clearance around the filter to be effective*
6   **Filter wrench** - *This type fits on the bottom of the filter and can be turned with a ratchet or breaker bar - different size wrenches are available for different types of filters)*

7   Automatic transmission fluid level check (every 3000 miles or 6 months)

Refer to illustrations 7.4 and 7.6

1   The automatic transmission fluid level should be carefully maintained. Low fluid level can lead to slipping or loss of drive, while overfilling can cause foaming and loss of fluid. Either condition can cause transmission damage.
2   Since transmission fluid expands as it heats up, the fluid level should only be checked when the transmission is warm (at normal operating temperature). If the vehicle has just been driven over 20 miles (32 km), the transmission can be considered warm. **Caution:** *If the vehicle has just been driven for a long time at high speed or in city traffic in hot weather, or if it has been pulling a trailer, an accurate fluid level reading cannot be obtained. Allow the transmission to cool down for about 30 minutes.* You can also check the transmission fluid level when the transmission is cold. If the vehicle has not been driven for over five hours and the fluid is about room temperature (70 to 95-degrees F), the transmission is cold. However, the fluid level is normally checked with the transmission warm to ensure accurate results.
3   Immediately after driving the vehicle, park it on a level surface, set the parking brake and start the engine. While the engine is idling, depress the brake pedal and move the selector lever through all the gear ranges, beginning and ending in PARK.
4   Locate the automatic transmission dipstick tube at the right (passenger's) side of the engine compartment **(see illustration)**.
5   With the engine still idling, pull the dipstick from the tube, wipe it off with a clean rag, push it all the way back into the tube and withdraw it again, then note the fluid level.
6   If the transmission is cold, the level

should be in the room temperature range on the dipstick (between the two circles); if it's warm, the fluid level should be in the operating temperature range (between the two lines) **(see illustration)**. If the level is low, add the specified automatic transmission fluid through the dipstick tube. Use a funnel to prevent spills.
7   Add just enough of the recommended fluid to fill the transmission to the proper level. It takes about one pint to raise the level from the low mark to the high mark when the fluid is hot, so add the fluid a little at a time and keep checking the level until it's correct. Use only transmission fluid specified by the manufacturer. This information can be found in the *Recommended lubricants and fluids* Section of the Specifications.
8   The condition of the fluid should also be checked along with the level. If the fluid is black or a dark reddish-brown color, or if it smells burned, it should be changed (refer to Section 36). If you are in doubt about its condition, purchase some new fluid and compare the two for color and smell.

8   Engine oil and filter change (every 3000 miles or 3 months)

Refer to illustrations 8.2, 8.11, 8.12 and 8.16

1   Frequent oil changes are the most important preventive maintenance procedures that can be done by the home mechanic. As engine oil ages, it becomes diluted and contaminated, which leads to premature engine wear. Although some sources recommend oil filter changes every other oil change, we feel that the minimal cost of an oil filter and the relative ease with which it is installed dictate that a new filter be used whenever the oil is changed.
2   Make sure that you have all the necessary tools before you begin this procedure **(see illustration)**. You should also have

plenty of rags or newspapers handy for mopping up oil spills.
3   Access to the oil drain plug and filter will be improved if the vehicle can be lifted on a hoist, driven onto ramps or supported by jackstands. **Warning:** *Do not work under a vehicle supported only by a bumper, hydraulic or scissors-type jack - always use jackstands!*
4   If you haven't changed the oil on this vehicle before, get under it and locate the oil drain plug in the oil pan and the oil filter on the left side of the engine. The exhaust components will be warm as you work, so note how they are routed to avoid touching them when you are under the vehicle.
5   Start the engine and allow it to reach normal operating temperature - oil and sludge will flow out more easily when warm. If new oil, a filter or tools are needed, use the vehicle to go get them and warm up the engine/oil at the same time. Park on a level surface and shut off the engine when it's warmed up. Remove the oil filler cap from the rocker arm cover.
6   Raise the vehicle and support it securely on jackstands.
7   Being careful not to touch the hot exhaust components, position a drain pan under the plug in the bottom of the engine, then remove the plug. **Caution:** *It's a good*

8.11 Location of oil filter on left side of V8 engines -
early model shown

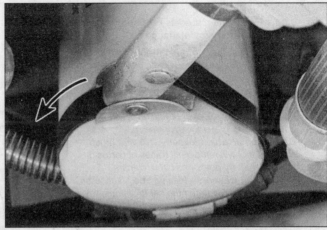

8.12 The oil filter is usually on very tight, and will require a
special wrench for removal - do not use the wrench
to tighten the new filter

idea to wear an old glove while unscrewing the plug the final few turns to avoid being scalded by hot oil.

8   It may be necessary to move the drain pan slightly as oil flow slows to a trickle. Inspect the old oil for the presence of metal particles.

9   After all the oil has drained, wipe off the drain plug with a clean rag. Any small metal particles clinging to the plug would immediately contaminate the new oil.

10   Clean the area around the drain plug opening, reinstall the plug and tighten it securely, but don't strip the threads.

11   Move the drain pan into position under the oil filter, located on the left side of the engine block **(see illustration)**.

12   Loosen the oil filter by turning it counterclockwise with a filter wrench **(see illustration)**. Any standard filter wrench will work.

13   Sometimes the oil filter is screwed on so tightly that it cannot be loosened. If it is, punch a metal bar or long screwdriver directly through it and use it as a T-bar to turn the filter. Be prepared for oil to spurt out of the canister as it is punctured.

14   Once the filter is loose, use your hands to unscrew it from the block. Just as the filter is detached from the block, immediately tilt the open end up to prevent the oil inside the filter from spilling out. **Warning:** *The engine exhaust manifold may still be hot, so be careful.*

15   Using a clean rag, wipe off the mounting surface on the block. Also, make sure that none of the old gasket remains stuck to the mounting surface. It can be removed with a scraper, if necessary.

16   Compare the old filter with the new one to make sure they are the same type. Smear some engine oil on the rubber gasket of the new filter and screw it into place **(see illustration)**. Over-tightening the filter will damage the gasket, so don't use a filter wrench. Most filter manufacturers recommend tightening the filter by hand only. Normally they should be tightened 1/2 to 3/4-turn after the gasket contacts the block, but be sure to follow the

directions on the filter or container.

17   Remove all tools and materials from under the vehicle, being careful not to spill the oil in the drain pan, then lower the vehicle.

18   Add 5 quarts of new oil to the engine through the oil filler cap in the rocker arm cover. Use a funnel to prevent oil from spilling onto the top of the engine. Wait a few minutes to allow the oil to drain into the pan, then check the level on the dipstick (see Section 4, if necessary). If the oil level is in the SAFE range, install the filler cap. If not, add oil until it is.

19   Start the engine and run it for about a minute. **Warning:** *Observe the oil warning light or pressure gauge - it should indicate normal oil pressure a few seconds after start-up.* While the engine is running, look under the vehicle and check for leaks at the oil pan drain plug and around the oil filter. If either one is leaking, stop the engine and tighten the plug or filter slightly.

20   Wait a few minutes, turn off the engine, then recheck the level on the dipstick. Add oil as necessary to bring the level into the SAFE range.

8.16 Lubricate the oil filter gasket with
clean engine oil before installing
the filter on the engine

21   During the first few trips after an oil change, make it a point to check frequently for leaks and proper oil level.

22   The old oil drained from the engine cannot be reused in its present state and should be disposed of. Check with your local auto parts store, disposal facility or environmental agency to see if they will accept the oil for recycling. After the oil has cooled it can be drained into a container (capped plastic jugs, topped bottles, milk cartons, etc.) for transport to one of these disposal sites. Don't dispose of the oil by pouring it on the ground or down a drain!

9   Wheel inspection and lug nut torque check (every 7500 miles or 6 months)

1   Carefully inspect the wheels for damage and signs of deterioration. Wheels that have been scraped or hit against a curb are especially susceptible to cracking or bending, If a wheel is damaged in any way it is a good idea to replace it with a new one.

2   Some F-250 and F-350 model trucks will have two-piece or "split-rim" type wheels. Check these types of wheels very carefully for any signs of incorrect seating between the outer ring and the main center of the wheel. This type of wheel can come apart with the power of a small explosion and has been known to cause injury and even death. If you have a wheel of this type that appears to be incorrectly assembled or is coming apart, take it immediately to a truck-tire service facility. **Warning:** *Do not attempt to do any type of work on these wheels, as they require a safety cage as well as other special equipment to be handled properly.*

3   Remove the hub cap if equipped.

4   Check the wheel lug nuts for tightness. Wheel nuts should be tightened to the torque value listed in this Chapter's Specifications with a torque wrench. If the bolt holes have become elongated or flattened, replace the wheel.

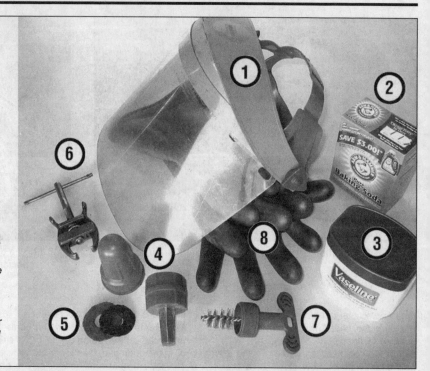

10.1 Tools and materials required for battery maintenance

1 *Face shield/safety goggles - When removing corrosion with a brush, the acidic particles can easily fly up into your eyes*
2 *Baking soda - A solution of baking soda and water can be used to neutralize corrosion*
3 *Petroleum jelly - A layer of this on the battery posts will help prevent corrosion*
4 *Battery post/cable cleaner - This wire brush cleaning tool will remove all traces of corrosion from the battery posts and cable clamps*
5 *Treated felt washers - Placing one of these on each post, directly under the cable clamps, will help prevent corrosion*
6 *Puller - Sometimes the cable clamps are very difficult to pull off the posts, even after the nut/bolt has been completely loosened. This tool pulls the clamp straight up and off the post without damage*
7 *Battery post/cable cleaner - Here is another cleaning tool which is a slightly different version of number 4 above, but it does the same thing*
8 *Rubber gloves - Another safety item to consider when servicing the battery; remember that's acid inside the battery!*

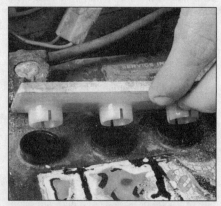

10.4 Checking the electrolyte level in a non-maintenance-free battery

10.8a Battery terminal corrosion usually appears as light, fluffy powder

10.8b Removing the cable from a battery post with a wrench - sometimes special battery pliers are required for this procedure if corrosion has caused deterioration of the nut hex (always remove the ground cable first and hook it up last!)

10   Battery check, maintenance and charging (every 7500 miles or 6 months)

Refer to illustrations 10.1, 10.4, 10.8a, 10.8b, 10.8c and 10.8d

Warning: *Certain precautions must be followed when checking and servicing the battery. Hydrogen gas, which is highly flammable, is always present in the battery cells, so keep lighted tobacco and all other open flames and sparks away from the battery. The electrolyte inside the battery is actually dilute sulfuric acid, which will cause injury if splashed on your skin or in your eyes. It will also ruin clothes and painted surfaces. When removing the battery cables, always detach the negative cable first and hook it up last!*

1   Battery maintenance is an important procedure which will help ensure that you are

not stranded because of a dead battery. Several tools are required for this procedure **(see illustration).**
2   Before servicing the battery, always turn the engine and all accessories off and disconnect the cable from the negative terminal of the battery.
3   A sealed (sometimes called maintenance-free) battery is now standard equipment. The cell caps cannot be removed, no electrolyte checks are required and water cannot be added to the cells. However, if an aftermarket battery has been installed and it is a type that requires regular maintenance, the following procedure can be used.
4   Check the electrolyte level in each of the battery cells **(see illustration).** It must be above the plates. There's usually a split-ring indicator in each cell to indicate the correct level. If the level is low, add distilled water only, then install the cell caps. **Caution:** *Overfilling the cells may cause electrolyte to spill*

over during periods of heavy charging, causing corrosion and damage to nearby components.
5   If the positive terminal and cable clamp on your vehicle's battery is equipped with a rubber protector, make sure that it's not torn or damaged. It should completely cover the terminal.
6   The external condition of the battery should be checked periodically. Look for damage such as a cracked case.
7   Check the tightness of the battery cable clamps to ensure good electrical connections and inspect the entire length of each cable, looking for cracked or abraded insulation and frayed conductors.
8   If corrosion (visible as white, fluffy deposits) is evident, remove the cables from the terminals, clean them with a battery brush

10.8c Regardless of the type of tool used to clean the battery posts, a clean, shiny surface should be the result

10.8d When cleaning the cable clamps, all corrosion must be removed (the inside of the clamp is tapered to match the taper on the post, so don't remove too much material)

and reinstall them **(see illustrations)**. Corrosion can be kept to a minimum by installing specially treated washers available at auto parts stores or by applying a coat of petroleum jelly or grease to the terminals and cable clamps after they are assembled.

9   Make sure that the battery carrier is in good condition and that the hold-down clamp bolt is tight. If the battery is removed (see Chapter 5 for the removal and installation procedure), make sure that no parts remain in the bottom of the carrier when it's reinstalled. When reinstalling the hold-down clamp, don't over-tighten the bolt.

10   Corrosion on the carrier, battery case and surrounding areas can be removed with a solution of water and baking soda. Apply the mixture with a small brush, let it work, then rinse it off with plenty of clean water.

11   Any metal parts of the vehicle damaged by corrosion should be coated with a zinc-based primer, then painted.

12   Additional information on the battery can be found in Chapter 5 and at the front of this manual.

Charging

13   If the battery's specific gravity is below the specified amount, the battery must be recharged.

14   If the battery is to remain in the vehicle during charging, disconnect the cables from the battery to prevent damage to the electrical system.

15   **Warning:** *When batteries are being charged, hydrogen gas (which is very explosive and flammable) is produced. Do not smoke or allow an open flame near a charging or a recently charged battery. Also, do not plug in the battery charger until the connections have been made at the battery posts.*

16   The average time necessary to charge a battery at the normal rate is from 12 to 16 hours (sometimes longer). Always charge the battery slowly. A quick charge or boost charge is hard on a battery and will shorten its life. Use a battery charger that is rated at no more than three amperes.

17   Remove all of the vent caps and cover

the vent holes with a clean cloth to prevent the spattering of electrolyte. Hook the battery charger leads to the battery posts (positive to positive, negative to negative), then plug in the charger. Make sure it is set at 12-volts if it has a selector switch.

18   Check the battery often during charging to make sure that it does not overheat.

19   The battery can be considered fully charged when it is gassing freely and there is no increase in specific gravity during three successive readings taken at hourly intervals.

20   Overheating of the battery during charging at normal charging rates, excessive gassing and continual low specific gravity readings are an indication that the battery should be replaced with a new one.

11   Underhood hose check and replacement (every 7500 miles or 6 months)

Warning: *Replacement of air conditioning hoses must be left to a dealer service department or air conditioning shop that has the equipment to depressurize the system safely. Never remove air conditioning components or hoses until the system has been depressurized.*

General

1   High temperatures under the hood can cause the deterioration of the rubber and plastic hoses used for engine, accessory and emission systems operation. Periodic inspection should be made for cracks, loose clamps, material hardening and leaks.

2   Information specific to the cooling system hoses can be found in Section 15.

3   Most (but not all) hoses are secured to the fittings with clamps. Where clamps are used, check to be sure they haven't lost their tension, allowing the hose to leak. If clamps aren't used, make sure the hose has not expanded and/or hardened where it slips over the fitting, allowing it to leak.

PCV system hose

4   To reduce hydrocarbon emissions, crankcase blow-by gas must be vented into the intake manifold for combustion. This is accomplished through the PCV system. Air flow is introduced into the crankcase through a hose between the air cleaner housing and the valve cover. A small filter, either in the air housing or in the valve cover provides the crankcase with clean air. Engine vacuum from the intake manifold through a rubber hose to the rocker arm cover mounted PCV valve draws this air and the blow-by gasses into the intake manifold. The blow-by gas mixes with incoming air before being burned in the combustion chambers.

5   Check the PCV hose for cracks, leaks and other damage. Disconnect it from the rocker arm cover (refer to Chapter 6) and the intake manifold and check the inside for obstructions. If it's clogged, clean it out with solvent.

Vacuum hoses

6   It is quite common for vacuum hoses, especially those in the emissions system, to be color coded or identified by colored stripes molded into each hose. Various systems require hoses with different wall thicknesses, collapse resistance and temperature resistance. When replacing hoses, be sure the new ones are made of the same material.

7   Often the only effective way to check a hose is to remove it completely from the vehicle. If more than one hose is removed, be sure to label the hoses and fittings to ensure correct installation.

8   When checking vacuum hoses, be sure to include any plastic fittings in the check. Inspect the fittings for cracks and the hose where it fits over each fitting for distortion, which could cause leakage.

9   A small piece of vacuum hose (1/4-inch inside diameter) can be used as a stethoscope to detect vacuum leaks. Hold one end of the hose to your ear and probe around vacuum hoses and fittings, listening for the "hissing" sound characteristic of a vacuum leak. **Warning:** *When probing with the vacuum hose stethoscope, be careful not to allow your body or the hose to come into contact with moving engine components such as drivebelts, the cooling fan, etc.*

Fuel hose

Warning: *There are certain precautions which must be taken when inspecting or servicing fuel system components. Work in a well ventilated area and do not allow open flames/cigarettes, appliance pilot lights, etc. or bare light bulbs near the work area. Mop up any spills immediately and do not store fuel-soaked rags where they could ignite.*

10   If it is necessary to disconnect any fuel lines, refer to Chapter 4 for the fuel pressure relief procedure.

11   Check all rubber fuel lines for deterioration and chafing. Check especially for cracks in areas where the hose bends and just before fittings, such as where a hose

attaches to the fuel pump, fuel filter and car-buretor or fuel injection unit.

12   High quality fuel line, usually identified by the word *Fluroelastomer* printed on the hose, should be used for fuel line replace-ment. Never, under any circumstances, use unreinforced vacuum line, clear plastic tubing or water hose for fuel lines. **Warning**: *When replacing hose on fuel-injected models, make sure it is designed for high pressure applica-tions.*

13   Spring-type clamps are commonly used on fuel lines. These clamps often lose their ten-sion over a period of time, and can be "sprung" during the removal process. As a result, it is recommended that all spring-type clamps be replaced with screw clamps whenever a hose is replaced. **Note**: *Fuel-injected models utilize special high pressure fittings and couplings (see Chapter 4). These cannot be substituted for.*

Metal lines

14   Sections of metal line are often used for fuel line between the fuel pump and carbure-tor or fuel injection unit. Check carefully to be sure the line has not been bent and crimped and that cracks have not started in the line,

particularly where bends occur.

15   If a section of metal fuel line must be replaced, use original equipment line only, since copper and aluminum tubing do not have the strength necessary to withstand vibration caused by the engine.

16   Check the metal brake lines where they enter the master cylinder and brake propor-tioning unit (if used) for cracks in the lines and loose fittings. Any sign of brake fluid leakage calls for an immediate thorough inspection of the brake system.

---

12   Drivebelt check, adjustment and replacement (every 7500 miles or 6 months)

Refer to illustrations 12.3a, 12.3b, 12.5 and 12.6

Description

1   The accessory drivebelts, also referred to as V-belts or simply fan belts, are located at the front of the engine. The condition and tension of the drivebelts are critical to the operation of the engine and accessories. Excessive tension causes bearing wear, while insufficient tension produces slippage, noise, component vibration and belt failure. Because of their composition and the high stresses to which they are subjected, drive-belts stretch and deteriorate as they get older. As a result, they must be periodically checked and adjusted.

2   The number and type of belts used on a particular vehicle depends on the accesso-ries installed. On early models, conventional V-belts are used and manual tension adjust-ment is required for all belts. Later models utilize one (4.9L, 5.0L and 5.8L) or two (7.5L) V-ribbed belt(s) to operate all systems and an automatic tensioner to eliminate all manual belt

adjustments (except for the alternator belt on 7.5L models). **Note**: *Belt condition must be still be checked as described below.*

Check

3   With the engine off, open the hood and locate the drivebelt(s) at the front of the engine. With a flashlight, check each belt for separation of the rubber plies from each side of the core, a severed core, separation of the ribs from the rubber, cracks, torn or worn ribs and cracks in the inner ridges of the ribs **(see illustration)**. Also check for fraying and glaz-ing, which gives the belt a shiny appearance **(see illustration)**. Both sides of each belt should be inspected, which means you'll have to twist them to check the undersides. Use your fingers to feel a belt where you can't see it. If any of the above conditions are evident, replace the belt as described below.

4   To check the tension on manually adjust-able V-belts in accordance with factory recom-mendations, install a drivebelt tension gauge. Measure the tension in accordance with the tension gauge instructions and compare your measurement to the specified drivebelt ten-sion for either a used or new belt. **Note**: *A "new" belt is defined as any belt which has not been run - a "used" belt is one that has been run for more than ten minutes.*

5   The special gauge is the most accu-rate way to check belt tension. However, if you don't have a gauge, and cannot borrow one, the following "rule-of-thumb" method is rec-ommended as an alternative. Lay a straightedge across the longest free span (the distance between two pulleys) of the belt. Push down firmly on the belt at a point half way between the pulleys and see how much the belt moves (deflects). Measure the deflec-tion with a ruler **(see illustration)**. The belt should deflect 1/8 to 1/4-inch if the distance from pulley center-to-pulley center is less than 12-inches; it should deflect from 1/8 to 3/8-inch

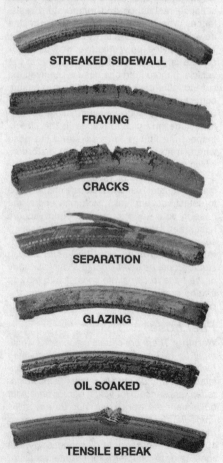

STREAKED SIDEWALL

FRAYING

CRACKS

SEPARATION

GLAZING

OIL SOAKED

TENSILE BREAK

12.3a Here are some of the more common problems associated with drivebelts (check the belts very carefully to prevent an untimely breakdown)

12.3b Small cracks in the underside of a V-ribbed belt are acceptable - lengthwise cracks, or missing pieces that cause the belt to make noise, are cause for replacement

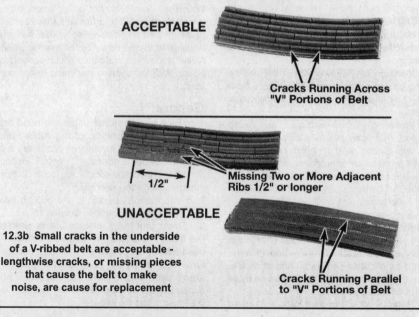

ACCEPTABLE

Cracks Running Across "V" Portions of Belt

1/2"

Missing Two or More Adjacent Ribs 1/2" or longer

UNACCEPTABLE

Cracks Running Parallel to "V" Portions of Belt

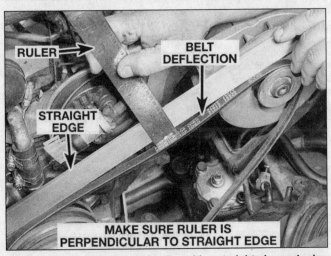

12.5 **Measuring drivebelt deflection with a straightedge and ruler**

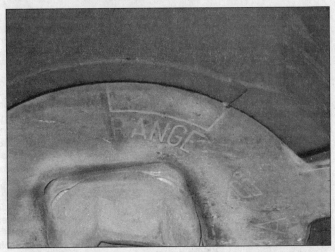

12.6 **Automatic tensioner with wear indicator as used on 5.0 and 5.8L engines - wear indicator must be between the limit marks or the belt is excessively stretched**

if the distance from pulley center-to-pulley center is over 12 inches.

6 On models with an automatic tensioner, belt stretch is determined by inspecting the wear indicator marks on the tensioner assembly **(see illustration)**. If the indicator mark is beyond the MAX mark, the belt is worn and must be replaced.

Adjustment (non auto-tensioned belts)

7 If it is necessary to adjust the belt tension, either to make the belt tighter or looser, it is done by moving the belt-driven accessory on its bracket.

8 For each component there will be an adjustment or strap bolt and a pivot bolt. Both bolts must be loosened slightly to enable you to move the component.

9 After the two bolts have been loosened, move the component away from the engine (to tighten the belt) or toward the engine (to loosen the belt). Hold the accessory in this position and check the belt tension. If it is correct, tighten the two bolts until snug, the recheck the tension. If it is all right tighten the

two bolts completely.

10 It will often be necessary to use some sort of prybar to move the accessory while the belt is adjusted. If this must be done to gain the proper leverage, be very careful not to damage the component being moved, or the part being pried against.

11 On some engines, loosen the two idler bracket bolts and turn the adjusting bolt until the belt is adjusted properly. Turning the wrench to the right tightens the belt and turning the wrench to the left loosens the belt.

12 Tighten the two idler pulley bolts and recheck the belt tension.

13 If the belt tension is still incorrect, repeat procedure as required.

Adjustment (auto-tensioned belts)

14 Belt tension on these models is controlled automatically by the belt tensioner. There is no provision for manual adjustment.

Replacement (all belts)

15 On non auto-tensioned applications, to replace a belt, follow the above procedures

for drivebelt adjustment but slip the belt off the pulleys and remove it. In some cases, several belts must be removed to access the one belt requiring replacement. Since belts tend to wear out more or less at the same time, it is a good idea to replace all of them at the same time. Mark each belt and the corresponding pulley grooves so the replacement belts can be installed properly.

16 On belts with automatic tensioners, to remove the belt, use a breaker bar and appropriately sized socket over the tensioner's idle wheel retaining bolt and rotate the tensioner against spring tension while simultaneously removing the belt from the tensioner idler wheel. Remove the belt from the remaining pulleys noting the exact routing for reinstallation. If necessary, make a sketch of the pulleys and belt routing. There should be a belt routing diagram sticker under the hood somewhere **(see illustration)**. **Note:** *If the same belt will be re-used, mark the direction of rotation on the belt to make sure the belt is installed the same way.*

17 Take the old belts with you when purchasing new ones in order to make a direct comparison for length, width and design.

18 When replacing a V-ribbed drivebelt, make sure it fits properly into the pulley grooves - it must be completely engaged.

19 Installation is the reverse of removal.

20 Adjust the belts, if necessary, as described earlier in this Section.

13 Chassis lubrication (every 7500 miles or 6 months)

Refer to illustration 13.1 and 13.6

Driveline and steering

1 A grease gun filled with the proper grease (see *Recommended lubricants* at the front of this Chapter) and some rags are the main pieces of equipment necessary to lubricate the chassis and steering components

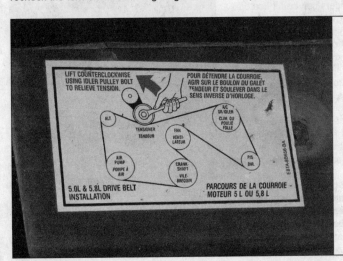

12.16 **Typical drivebelt routing decal (this one's on a 5.8L Bronco)**

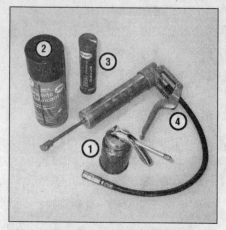

13.1 Materials required for driveline and chassis lubrication

1　*Engine oil - Light engine oil in a can be used for door and hood hinges*

2　*Graphite spray - Used to lube lock cylinders*

3　*Grease - Grease, in a variety of types and weights, is available for use in a grease gun. Check the Specifications for your requirements.*

4　*Grease gun - A common grease gun, shown here with a detachable hose and nozzle, is needed for driveline and chassis lubrication.*

(see illustration). Notice that different components require different types of grease, so a grease gun with changeable cartridges or several grease guns will be necessary to correctly perform the lubrication process. **Note:** *Some universal joints, particularly those found on 4WD models, will require the use of a special 'needle' lubrication adapter for your grease gun.*

2　Locate the lubrication fittings (if equipped) on the driveline and steering linkage. Depending on the year and model, special grease fittings can be factory or aftermarket installed on the following components:

　　Driveshaft(s) slip joints and universal joints (see Chapter 8)
　　Right side front axle shaft slip joint (4WD models only) (see Chapter 8)
　　Steering system linkage and tie rods (see Chapter 11)
　　Front knuckle/spindle balljoints (see Chapter 11)
　　Front axle kingpins (see Chapter 11)

3　Easier access to some of these fittings will require raising and supporting the vehicle with a jack and jackstands. Be sure the vehicle is firmly supported with jackstands and read the information on jacking instructions at the front of this book if you are unfamiliar with the correct procedures.

4　Before you do any greasing, force a little of the grease out the nozzle to remove any dirt from the end of the gun. Wipe the nozzle

clean with a rag.

5　With the grease gun, plenty of clean rags and the location diagram, go under the vehicle to begin lubricating the components.

6　Wipe the grease fitting nipple clean and push the nozzle firmly over the fitting nipple **(see illustration)**. Squeeze the trigger on the grease gun to force grease into the component. **Note:** *When lubricating the steering linkage joints, pump only enough lubricant to fill the rubber cup to a firm-to-the-touch capacity.* If you pump in too much grease, the cups can rupture allowing grease to leak out and dirt to enter the joint. For all other suspension and steering fittings, continue pumping grease into the nipple until grease seeps out of the joint between the two components. If the grease seeps out around the grease gun nozzle, the nipple is clogged or the nozzle is not fully seated around the fitting nipple. Resecure the gun nozzle to the fitting and try again. If necessary, replace the fitting. Make sure the king pins have plenty of grease of the correct type.

7　Wipe the excess grease from the components and the grease fitting.

Chassis

8　While you are under the vehicle, clean and lubricate the parking brake cable along with its cable guides and levers. This can be done by smearing some of the chassis grease onto the cable and its related parts with your fingers. Place a few drops of light engine oil on the standard transmission and transfer case shifting linkage rods and swivels. Lubricate automatic transmission linkages with the lubricants specified at the beginning of this Chapter.

9　Lower the vehicle to the ground for the remaining body lubrication process.

10　Open the hood and smear a little chassis grease on the hood latch mechanism. If the hood has an inside release, have an assistant pull the release knob from inside the vehicle as you lubricate the cable at the latch.

11　Lubricate all the hinges (door, hood, tailgate) with a few drops of light engine oil to keep them in proper working order.

12　The key lock cylinders can be lubricated with spray-on graphite which is available at auto parts stores.

13　Spray silicone lubricant on the door seals to keep them pliable and effective.

14　Lubricate the accelerator linkage pivots with a multi-purpose lubricant, usually available in small spray cans.

15　Lubricate the clutch linkage (if the vehicle is equipped) with the grease gun through the fitting provided on the cross-shaft linkage.

16　Use a rust penetrant and inhibitor on the manifold exhaust heat control valve if the vehicle is so equipped.

17　Spray some multi-purpose lubricant on the brake pedal (and clutch pedal) pivot shafts under the dash area for smooth, quiet operation of these pedal(s). Be sure to wipe off any excess so that the operator's shoes and clothing do not pick up any extra lubricant.

14　Fuel system check (every 15,000 miles or 12 months)

Warning: *Gasoline is extremely flammable, so take extra precautions when you work on any part of the fuel system. Don't smoke or allow open flames or bare light bulbs near the work area, and don't work in a garage where a gas-type appliance (such as a water heater or clothes dryer) is present. If you spill any fuel on your skin, rinse it off immediately with soap and water. When you perform any kind of work on the fuel system, wear safety glasses and have a Class B type fire extinguisher on hand.*

1　If you smell gasoline while driving or after the vehicle has been sitting in the sun, inspect the fuel system immediately.

2　Remove the gas filler cap and inspect if for damage and corrosion. The gasket should have an unbroken sealing imprint. If the gasket is damaged or corroded, install a new cap.

3　Inspect the fuel feed and return lines for cracks. Make sure that the connections between the fuel lines and the carburetor or fuel injection system and between the fuel lines and the in-line fuel filter are tight. **Warning:** *If your vehicle is fuel-injected, you must relieve the fuel system pressure before servicing fuel system components. The fuel system pressure relief procedure is outlined in Chapter 4.*

4　Since some components of the fuel system (the fuel tank and part of the fuel feed and return lines, for example) are underneath the vehicle, they can be inspected more easily with the vehicle raised on a hoist. If that is not possible, raise the vehicle and support it on jackstands.

5　With the vehicle raised and safely supported, inspect the gas tank and filler neck for punctures, cracks and other damage. The connection between the filler neck and

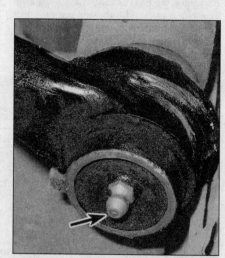

13.6 Be sure to clean the grease fittings before connecting the grease gun to them, to prevent forcing grit into the balljoint

Check for a chafed area that could fail prematurely.

Check for a soft area indicating the hose has deteriorated inside.

Overtightening the clamp on a hardened hose will damage the hose and cause a leak.

Check each hose for swelling and oil-soaked ends. Cracks and breaks can be located by squeezing the hose.

15.4 Hoses, like drivebelts, have a habit of failing at the worst possible time - to prevent the inconvenience of a blown radiator or heater hose, inspect them carefully as shown here

the tank is particularly critical. Sometimes a rubber filler neck will leak because of loose clamps or deteriorated rubber. Inspect all fuel tank mounting brackets and straps to be sure that the tank is securely attached to the vehicle. **Warning:** *Do not, under any circumstances, try to repair a fuel tank (except rubber components). A welding torch or any open flame can easily cause fuel vapors inside the tank to explode.*

6   Carefully check all rubber hoses and metal lines leading away from the fuel tank. Check for loose connections, deteriorated hoses, crimped lines and other damage. Repair or replace damaged sections as necessary (see Chapter 4).

15 Cooling system check (every 15,000 miles or 12 months)

Refer to illustration 15.4

1   Many major engine failures can be attributed to a faulty cooling system. If the vehicle is equipped with an automatic transmission, the cooling system also plays an important role in prolonging transmission life because it cools the transmission fluid.

2   The engine should be cold for the cooling system check, so perform the following procedure before the vehicle is driven for the day or after it has been shut off for at least three hours.

3   Remove the radiator cap and clean it thoroughly, inside and out, with clean water. Also clean the filler neck on the radiator. The presence of rust or corrosion in the filler neck means the coolant should be changed (see Section 28). The coolant inside the radiator should be relatively clean and transparent. If it's rust colored, drain the system and refill it with new coolant.

4   Carefully check the radiator hoses and the smaller diameter heater hoses **(see illustration)**. Inspect each coolant hose along its entire length, replacing any hose which is

cracked, swollen or deteriorated. Cracks will show up better if the hose is squeezed. Pay close attention to hose clamps that secure the hoses to cooling system components. Hose clamps can pinch and puncture hoses, resulting in coolant leaks.

5   Make sure that all hose connections are tight. A leak in the cooling system will usually show up as white or rust colored deposits on the area adjoining the leak. If wire-type clamps are used on the hoses, it is a good idea to replace them with screw-type clamps.

6   Clean the front of the radiator and air conditioning condenser with compressed air, if available, or a soft brush. Remove all bugs, leaves, etc. embedded in the radiator fins. Be extremely careful not to damage the cooling fins or cut your fingers on them.

7   If the coolant level has been dropping consistently and no leaks are detectable, have the radiator cap and cooling system pressure checked at a service station.

16 Tire rotation (every 15,000 miles or 12 months)

Refer to illustrations 16.2a, 16.2b and 16.2c

1   The tires should be rotated at the specified intervals and whenever uneven wear is noticed. Since the vehicle will be raised and the tires removed anyway, check the brakes also (see Section 18).

2   Since most trucks are equipped with bias-ply based tires, many different rotation patterns are possible. However, it is advisable to be consistent after choosing a pattern. Typical rotation patterns are shown **(see illustrations)**. **Note:** *If the vehicle is equipped with radial tires, they must be rotated in a specific pattern.* **Warning:** *Vehicles with A/S front and A/T rear tires can only be rotated*

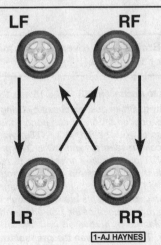

16.2a Tire rotation diagram for bias-ply tires

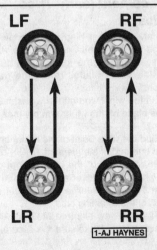

16.2b Tire rotation diagram for radial tires

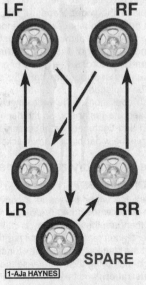

16.2c Tire rotation diagram, including spare

side-to-side and vehicles with dual rear wheels should only have their front tires rotated side-to-side. Do not include special space saver or temporary spare tires in the rotation schedule, they are for emergency use only. Consult your owner's manual if further clarification is necessary.

3   Refer to the information on *Jacking and towing* at the front of this manual for the proper procedure to follow when raising the vehicle and changing a tire (wheel removal). If the brakes are to be checked, do not apply the parking brake as stated.

4   The vehicle must be raised on a hoist or supported on jackstands to get all four wheels off the ground. Make sure the vehicle is safely supported!

5   After the rotation procedure is finished, check and adjust the tire pressures as necessary and be sure to check the lug nut tightness as specified in the *Jacking and towing* section.

---

17   Windshield wiper blade check and replacement (every 15,000 miles or 12 months)

Refer to illustrations 17.6 and 17.15

1   Use the illustrations in this Section to help identify the type of wiper blades used on your vehicle.

2   Road film can build up on the wiper blades and affect their efficiency, so they should be washed regularly with a mild detergent solution.

Check

3   The windshield wiper and blade assembly should be inspected periodically. Even if you don't use your wipers, the sun and elements will dry out the rubber portions, causing them to crack and break apart. If inspection reveals hardened or cracked rubber, replace the wiper blades. If inspection reveals nothing unusual, wet the windshield, turn the wipers on, allow them to cycle several times, then shut them off. An uneven wiper pattern across the glass or streaks over clean glass indicate that the blades should be replaced.

4   The operation of the wiper mechanism can loosen the fasteners, so they should be checked and tightened, as necessary, at the same time the wiper blades are checked.

Blade assembly replacement (Tridon blades)

5   Park the wiper blades in a convenient position to be worked on. To do this, run the wipers, then turn the ignition key to OFF when the wiper blades reach the desired position.

6   Lift the blade slightly from the windshield. Press on the spring lock to release the blade **(see illustration)** and take the blade off. **Caution:** *Do not press too hard on the spring lock or it could be distorted.*

7   Push the new blade assembly onto

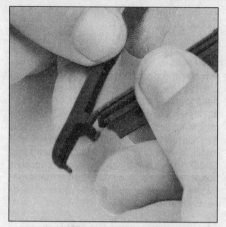

17.6 Wiper blade and element replacement (Tridon type)

the arm pivot pin. Make sure the spring lock secures the blade to the pin.

Blade element replacement (Tridon blades)

8   Remove the wiper blade from the arm (see Step 5).

9   Locate the name TRIDON stamped in the blade assembly **(see illustration 17.6)**. Insert a coin or screwdriver at that point, pry the blade element downward from the blade frame and slide the blade element out.

10   Find the rectangular slot in one end of the new blade element. This end will be installed first.

11   At the end of the blade frame without the word TRIDON, find the first retaining claw.

12   Install the slotted end of the blade element into the first retaining claw, then through all the other claws. The element will snap into place when it's been pulled all the way in.

13   Check to make sure the element is securely retained in all of the claws and that the locking nib is positioned correctly.

Blade assembly and element replacement (early Trico blades)

14   Park the wiper blades in a convenient position to be worked on. To do this, run the wipers, then turn the ignition key to OFF when the wiper blades reach the desired position.

15   Lift the wiper arm off the windshield and pull the blade off the wiper arm pin **(see illustration)**.

16   Find the wide point of the metal backing strip at one end of the element.

17   Pry one end of the element out of the blade with a screwdriver as shown **(see illustration 17.15)**, then slide the element out of the rest of the retaining tabs.

18   Slide the new element into the four sets of retaining tabs. Make sure it is securely fastened.

19   Push the wiper blade firmly onto the wiper arm and make sure it is securely engaged.

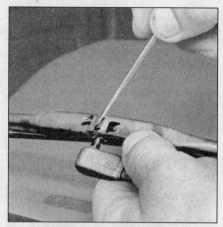

17.15 Wiper blade and element replacement (early Trico type).

Blade assembly and element replacement (later Trico blades)

20   Park the wiper blades in a convenient position to be worked on. To do this, run the wipers, then turn the ignition key to OFF when the wiper blades reach the desired position.

21   Let the blade assembly rest on the windshield and insert a small flat-bladed screwdriver into the release hole **(see illustration 7.15)**. Push down on the coil spring inside the hole and pull the wiper blade from the arm.

22   Insert a flat-bladed screwdriver 1/8-inch or less into the space between the element and rubber backing strip. While pressing the screwdriver down and inward, twist it clockwise to separate the element from the retaining tab.

23   Slide the element out of the other retaining tabs.

24   Slide the new element into four of the five retaining tabs. Twist the element into the fifth retaining tab to secure it.

25   Make sure the new element is secured by all five tabs, then push the blade onto the pivot pin until it locks.

---

18   Brake check (every 15,000 miles or 12 months)

Refer to illustrations 18.11, 18.15 and 18.17
Warning: *Brake dust produced by lining wear and deposited on brake components is hazardous to your health. DO NOT blow it out with compressed air and DO NOT inhale it! DO NOT use gasoline or solvents to remove the dust. Brake system cleaner should be used to flush the dust into a drain pan. After the brake components are wiped clean with a damp rag, dispose of the contaminated rags and cleaner in a covered and labeled container. Try to use non-asbestos replacement parts whenever possible.*
Note: *In addition to the specified intervals, the brake system should be inspected each*

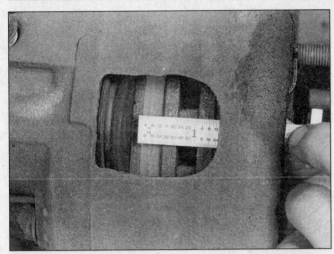

18.11 The front disc brake pads can be checked easily through the inspection hole in each caliper - position a steel rule against the pads and measure the lining thickness

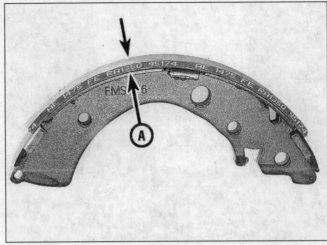

18.15 The rear brake shoe lining thickness (A) is measured from the outer surface of the lining to the metal shoe

time the wheels are removed or a malfunction is indicated. Because of the obvious safety considerations, the following brake system checks are some of the most important maintenance procedures you can perform on your vehicle.

Symptoms of brake system problems

1   The disc brake pads have built-in wear indicators which should make a high pitched squealing or scraping noise when they are worn to the replacement point. When you hear this noise, replace the pads immediately or expensive damage to the discs could result.
2   Any of the following symptoms could indicate a potential brake system defect. The vehicle pulls to one side when the brake pedal is depressed, the brakes make squealing or dragging noises when applied, brake travel is excessive, the pedal pulsates and brake fluid leaks are noted (usually on the inner side of the tire or wheel). If any of these conditions are noted, inspect the brake system immediately.

Brake lines and hoses

Note: Steel tubing is used throughout the brake system, with the exception of flexible, reinforced hoses at the front wheels and as connectors at the rear axle. Periodic inspection of these lines is very important.
3   Park the vehicle on level ground and turn the engine off.
4   Remove the wheel covers. Loosen, but do not remove, the lug nuts on all four wheels.
5   Raise the vehicle and support it securely on jackstands.
6   Remove the wheels (see Jacking and towing at the front of this book, or refer to your owner's manual, if necessary).
7   Check all brake hoses and lines for cracks, chafing of the outer cover, leaks, blisters and distortion. Check all threaded fit-

tings for leaks and make sure the brake hose mounting bolts and clips are secure.
8   If leaks or damage are discovered, they must be fixed immediately. Refer to Chapter 9 for detailed information on brake system repair procedures.

Front disc brakes

9   If it hasn't already been done, raise the front of the vehicle and support it securely on jackstands. Apply the parking brake and remove the front wheels (see Jacking and towing at the front of this book, or refer to your owner's manual, if necessary).
10   The disc brake calipers, which contain the pads, are now visible. Each caliper has an outer and an inner pad all pads should be checked.
11   Note the pad thickness by looking through the inspection hole in the caliper **(see illustration)**. The inspection hole is an oval-shaped window squarely in the center of the brake caliper bracket. If the lining material is 1/8-inch thick or less (above rivet heads if used), or if it is tapered from end-to-end, the pads should be replaced (see Chapter 9). Keep in mind that the lining material is riveted or bonded to a metal plate or shoe - the metal portion is not included in this measurement.
12   Check the condition of the brake disc. Look for score marks, deep scratches and overheated areas (they will appear blue or discolored). If damage or wear is noted, the disc can be removed and resurfaced by an automotive machine shop or replaced with a new one. Refer to Chapter 9 for more detailed inspection and repair procedures.
13   Remove the caliper slide rails or retainers and lubricate as required (see Chapter 9).

Rear drum brakes

14   Refer to Chapter 9 and remove the rear brake drums.
15   Note the thickness of the lining material on the rear brake shoes **(see illustra-**

tion) and look for signs of contamination by brake fluid and grease. If the lining material is within 1/16-inch of the recessed rivets or metal shoes, replace the brake shoes with new ones. The shoes should also be replaced if they are cracked, glazed (shiny lining surfaces) or contaminated with brake fluid or grease. See Chapter 9 for the replacement procedure.
16   Check the shoe return and hold-down springs and the adjusting mechanism to make sure they are installed correctly and in good condition. Deteriorated or distorted springs, if not replaced, could allow the linings to drag and wear prematurely.
17   Check the wheel cylinders for leakage by carefully peeling back the rubber boots **(see illustration)**. If brake fluid is noted behind the boots, the wheel cylinders must be replaced (see Chapter 9).
18   Check the drums for cracks, score marks, deep scratches and hard spots, which will appear as small discolored areas. If imper-

18.17 Carefully peel back the rubber boots on each end of the wheel cylinder - if the exposed area is covered with brake fluid, the wheel cylinder is leaking and must be replaced

19.7a To check the suspension balljoints, try to move the lower edge of each front tire in-and-out while watching/feeling for movement at the top of the tire and balljoints

19.7b To check the steering gear mounts and tie-rod ends for play, grasp each front tire like this and try to move it back-and-forth - if play is noted, check the steering gear mounts and make sure that they're tight; if either tie-rod is worn or bent, replace it

fections cannot be removed with emery cloth, the drums must be resurfaced by an automotive machine shop (see Chapter 9 for more detailed information).

19   Refer to Chapter 9 and install the brake drums.

20   Install the wheels (see *Jacking and towing* at the front of this book, or refer to your owner's manual, if necessary) but do not lower the vehicle yet.

Parking brake

21   The parking brake cable and linkage should be periodically checked and lubricated. This maintenance procedure helps prevent the parking brake cable adjuster or the linkage from binding and adversely affecting the operation or adjustment of the parking brake.

Lubrication

22   Set the parking brake.

23   Apply multi-purpose grease to the parking brake linkage, adjuster assembly, connectors and the areas of the parking brake cable that come in contact with the other parts of the vehicle.

24   Release the parking brake and repeat the lubrication procedure.

25   Remove the jackstands and lower the vehicle.

26   Tighten the wheel lug nuts to the torque listed in this Chapter's Specifications and install the wheel covers, if equipped.

Check

27   The easiest, and perhaps most obvious, method of checking the parking brake is to park the vehicle on a steep hill with the parking brake set and the transmission in NEUTRAL (be sure to stay in the vehicle during this check). If the parking brake cannot prevent the vehicle from rolling, refer to Chapter 9 and adjust it.

19   Suspension and steering check (every 15,000 miles or 12 months)

Refer to illustration 19.7a and 19.7b

1   Whenever the front of the vehicle is raised for service it is a good idea to visually check the suspension and steering components for wear.

2   Indications of a fault in these systems are excessive play in the steering wheel before the front wheels react, excessive sway around corners or body movement over rough roads and binding at some point as the steering wheel is turned.

3   Before the vehicle is raised for inspection, test the shock absorbers by pushing down to rock the vehicle at each corner. If you push the vehicle down and it does not come to a stop within one or two bounces, the shocks are worn and need to be replaced. As this is done, check for squeaks and strange noises from the suspension components. Information on shock absorber and suspension components can be found in Chapter 11.

4   Now raise the front end of the vehicle and support it securely on jackstands placed under the frame rails.

5   Grab the top and bottom of the front tire with your hands and rock the tire/wheel on its spindle or balljoints. If there is any play or looseness, the wheel bearings should be serviced (see Section 31).

6   Crawl under the vehicle and check for loose bolts, broken or disconnected parts and deteriorated rubber bushings on all suspension and steering components. Look for grease or fluid leaking from around the steering box. Check the power steering hoses and connections for leaks.

7   If the wheel bearings have been adjusted or determined to be adjusted properly, again grasp the wheel assembly and move it up and down and side-to-side to check the spindle or balljoints and steering tie-rods for looseness **(see illustrations)**. Any play or looseness in these components requires disassembly and usually replacement (refer to Chapter 11). Improper lubrication usually causes failure of these components. If they are loose, steering control, shimmying at the steering wheel and other problems often crop up. Do not ignore these components, as they are the major connecting points of the wheel/spindle assembly to the suspension of the vehicle.

20   Exhaust system check (every 15,000 miles or 12 months)

1   With the engine cold (at least three hours after the vehicle has been driven), check the complete exhaust system from the engine to the end of the tailpipe. Ideally, the inspection should be done with the vehicle on a hoist to permit unrestricted access. If a hoist is not available, raise the vehicle and support it securely on jackstands.

2   Check the exhaust pipes and connections for evidence of leaks, severe corrosion and damage. Make sure that all brackets and hangers are in good condition and tight.

3   Remove any trapped foreign material or debris from the exhaust systems heat shield(s).

4   At the same time, inspect the underside of the body for holes, corrosion, open seams, etc. which may allow exhaust gases to enter the passenger compartment. Seal all body openings with silicone or body putty.

5   Rattles and other noises can often be traced to the exhaust system, especially the mounts and hangers. Try to move the pipes, muffler and catalytic converter. If the components can come in contact with the body or suspension parts, secure the exhaust system with new mounts.

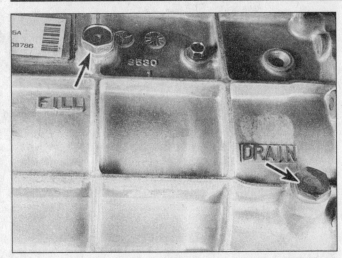

22.2 The manual transmission fill plug and drain plug are located on the side of the transmission case

22.5 The transfer case fill plug (A) and drain plug (B) are located on the rear of the transfer case

6 Check the running condition of the engine by inspecting inside the end of the tail-pipe. The exhaust deposits here are an indication of engine state-of-tune. If the pipe is black and sooty or coated with white deposits, the engine is in need of a tune-up, including a thorough fuel system inspection and adjustment.

21 Clutch hydraulic linkage check (every 15,000 miles or 12 months)

1 Check the line running from the clutch master cylinder to the slave cylinder for leaks. Replace the line and bleed the system if there is any sign of leakage (see Chapter 8).
2 On external slave cylinders, pull back the rubber boot from the slave cylinder and check for fluid leaks. Slight moisture inside the boot is acceptable, but if fluid runs out, refer to Chapter 8 and overhaul or replace the slave cylinder.

22 Driveline lubricant level checks (every 15,000 miles or 12 months)

Refer to illustrations 22.2, 22.5, 22.7a and 22.7b

Manual transmission lubricant

1 Raise the vehicle and support it securely on jackstands.
2 Locate the fill plug at the side of the transmission case **(see illustration)**. Clean all dirt from the area adjacent to the plug. Slowly withdraw the plug. If oil starts to come out as the plug is withdrawn, immediately reinsert it into the transmission, as the level is correct.
3 Remove the fill plug if the oil does not run out, and check to see if the level is up to the bottom of the plug hole. If it is not, fill the transmission through this hole until it is.
4 Visually check the transmission for any signs of leakage at either the front or rear seal or near such components as the speedometer drive.

Transfer case lubricant (4x4 models only)

5 To check the oil level in the transfer case (if so equipped), locate the fill plug on the side of the transfer case (usually on the rear driveshaft side) **(see illustration)**.
6 Check the transfer case oil level in the same manner as the manual transmission.

Differential lubricant

7 Differentials are checked by withdrawing the fill plug from either the rear cover or from the side of the differential assembly **(see illustrations)**. Use the same procedure as was used to check the oil level in the manual transmission.

23 Fuel filter replacement (every 15,000 miles or 12 months)

Refer to illustrations 23.7 and 23.9
Warning: *Gasoline is extremely flammable, so take extra precautions when you work on*

22.7a Typical location for cover-mounted differential check/fill plug (4WD front axle housing shown)

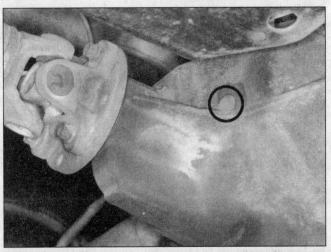

22.7b Typical location for side-mounted differential check/fill plug

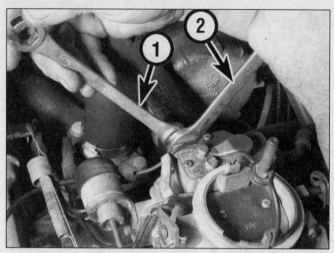

23.7 When unscrewing the fuel line from the carburetor, use a flare-nut wrench (1) on the tube nut, and a "back-up" wrench (2) on the inlet fitting nut to keep it from turning (which could cause the fuel line to twist)

23.9 Typical layout of a fuel filter inside the carburetor inlet

any part of the fuel system. Don't smoke or allow open flames or bare light bulbs near the work area, and don't work in a garage where a gas-type appliance (such as a water heater or clothes dryer) is present. Since gasoline is carcinogenic, wear latex gloves when there's a possibility of being exposed to fuel, and, if you spill any fuel on your skin, rinse it off immediately with soap and water. Mop up any spills immediately and do not store fuel-soaked rags where they could ignite. The fuel system on fuel-injected models is under constant pressure, so, if any fuel lines are to be disconnected, the fuel pressure in the system must be relieved first (see Chapter 4 for more information). When you perform any kind of work on the fuel system, wear safety glasses and have a Class B type fire extinguisher on hand.

Carbureted models

1   Fuel filters must be replaced according to the maintenance interval suggestions as well as when a blockage in the fuel line occurs due to excessive foreign material in the fuel.
2   Considering the volatile nature of gasoline, precautions should be exercised when a fuel filter is replaced. This work should be done on a cool engine. Never smoke or have any open flames around the work area. Do not work within an enclosed area. When removing a fuel system component, take care to clean up any spills which will inevitably occur when gasoline under pressure is released. Make sure that gasoline does not puddle or stand anywhere in the engine compartment or work area. Clean any spilled gasoline off the vehicle as well as yourself, as it can burn your skin.
3   Fuel filters are located in a number of different places depending on the year, engine size and weight rating of the vehicle. Most fuel filters can be found in-line somewhere between the fuel pump and the carburetor.
4   If a fuel filter is located in-line between the carburetor and the fuel pump, it is usually connected with rubber hoses. Release

the clamps on the rubber hoses and slowly remove the filter from the system. Use caution, as gasoline will be under pressure at this point. It's a good idea to wrap a rag around the filter and hose to catch the escaping fuel.
5   After removing the filter, drain it and discard it in a non-incendiary refuse container. Replace the filter with an exact duplicate replacement and push it into new rubber connecting hoses which should be provided with the filter. Also replace the clamps if they appear weak.
6   Tighten all clamps. Start the vehicle and check for leaks.
7   If the filter is the type located in the inlet of the carburetor, first detach the line leading to the inlet by unthreading it, if it has a fitting, or by removing the clamp and hose if it is so equipped **(see illustration)**.
8   Carefully unscrew the carburetor inlet/filter unit from the carburetor. To reinstall, simply thread a new filter into the carburetor and tighten securely. Be careful not to damage the threads in the carburetor.
9   If an internal filter is located inside the carburetor inlet, the spring, gasket and filter must be removed after the inlet is unscrewed **(see illustration)**.
10   Assemble the new filter, seal and spring in the reverse order of their removal.
11   Carefully screw in the inlet connector using caution not to damage the threads in the carburetor.
12   Some fuel filters are located in the bottom of the fuel pump. To remove this type of filter, unscrew the canister from the bottom of the fuel pump in the same way that an oil filter is removed.
13   Slowly lower the canister and filter assembly off the bottom of the fuel pump, being careful not to spill the gasoline contained within it.
14   Empty the fuel into an approved gasoline container, then remove the filter and gasket assembly.

15   Insert a new filter and gasket assembly.
16   Screw the filter and filter housing assembly back on to the base of the fuel pump.
17   Start the vehicle and check the filter and surrounding area for leaks.

Fuel-injected models

18   Refer to the procedure outlined in Chapter 4.

24 Clutch linkage adjustment (early models) (every 15,000 miles or 12 months)

Note: *Late model hydraulic clutch systems are self adjusting and have no provision for manual adjustment.*
1   Clutch pedal freeplay will change over time due to normal clutch plate and linkage wear.
2   Clutch pedal freeplay adjustment is an important maintenance item. Excessive pedal freeplay can result in gear clashing and excessive transmission wear. Insufficient freeplay can result in clutch slippage and premature clutch wear.
3   For check and adjustment, refer to the procedure outlined in Chapter 8.

25 Automatic transmission band adjustment (every 15,000 miles or 12 months)

1   Automatic transmission band wear is a normal consequence of transmission operation.
2   Band check and adjustment can be performed at regular intervals or whenever performance related symptoms are noted. Normal wear can cause sluggish shifts, delayed shifts, slipping, and in extreme cases, no drive.
3   For adjustment, refer to the procedure outlined in Chapter 7, Part B.

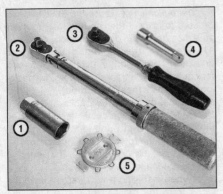

26.2 Tools required for changing spark plugs

1   **Spark plug socket** - This will have special padding inside to protect the spark plug porcelain insulator

2   **Torque wrench** - Although not mandatory, use of this tool is the best way to ensure that the plugs are tightened properly

3   **Ratchet** - Standard hand tool to fit the plug socket

4   **Extension** - Depending on model and accessories, you may need special extensions and universal joints to reach one or more of the plugs

5   **Spark plug gap gauge** - This gauge for checking the gap comes in a variety of styles. Make sure the gap for your engine is included

26.5a Spark plug manufacturers recommend using a wire-type gauge when checking the gap - if the wire does not slide between the electrodes with a slight drag, adjustment is required

26.5b To change the gap, bend the side electrode only, as indicated by the arrows and be very careful not to crack or chip the porcelain insulator surrounding the center electrode

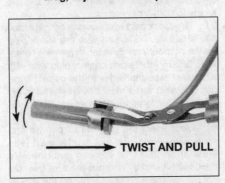

TWIST AND PULL

26.6 When removing the spark plug wires, pull only on the boot and use a twisting/ pulling motion

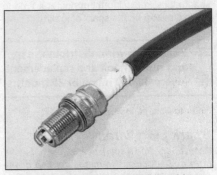

26.10 A length of snug-fitting rubber hose will save time and prevent damaged threads when installing the spark plugs

26 Spark plug replacement (every 30,000 miles or 30 months)

Refer to illustrations 26.2, 26.5a, 26.5b, 26.6 and 26.10

Note: *Every time a spark plug wire is disconnected from a plug, the distributor cap or coil, silicone dielectric compound (available at most auto parts stores) should be applied to the inside of the spark plug boot or terminal before reconnecting.*

1   The spark plugs are located on the left side of the engine (4.9L) and on both sides of the engine on V6s and V8s.

2   In most cases, the tools necessary for spark plug replacement include a spark plug socket which fits onto a ratchet (spark plug sockets are padded inside to prevent damage to the porcelain insulators on the new plugs), various extensions and a gap gauge to check and adjust the gaps on the new plugs **(see illustration)**. A special plug wire removal tool is available for separating the wire boots from the spark plugs, but it isn't absolutely necessary. A torque wrench should be used to tighten the new plugs.

3   The best approach when replacing the spark plugs is to purchase the new ones in advance, adjust them to the proper gap and replace the plugs one at a time. When buying the new spark plugs, be sure to obtain the correct plug type for your particular engine. This

information can be found on the *Vehicle Emission Control Information* (VECI) label located under the hood and in the owner's manual. If differences exist between the plug specified on the emissions label and in the owner's manual, assume that the emissions label is correct.

4   Allow the engine to cool completely before attempting to remove any of the plugs. While you are waiting for the engine to cool, check the new plugs for defects and adjust the gaps.

5   The gap is checked by inserting the proper thickness gauge between the electrodes at the tip of the plug **(see illustration)**. The gap between the electrodes should be the same as the one specified on the VECI label. The wire should just slide between the electrodes with a slight amount of drag. If the gap is incorrect, use the adjuster on the gauge body to bend the curved side electrode slightly until the proper gap is obtained **(see illustration)**. If the side electrode is not exactly over the center electrode, bend it with the adjuster until it is. Check for cracks in the porcelain insulator (if any are found, the plug should not be used).

6   With the engine cool, remove the spark plug wire from one spark plug. Pull only on the

boot at the end of the wire, do not pull on the wire. A plug wire removal tool should be used if available **(see illustration)**.

7   If compressed air is available, use it to blow any dirt or foreign material away from the spark plug hole. A common bicycle pump will also work. The idea here is to eliminate the possibility of debris falling into the cylinder as the spark plug is removed.

8   Place the spark plug socket over the plug and remove it from the engine by turning it in a counterclockwise direction.

9   Compare the spark plug to those shown on the inside back cover of this manual to get an indication of the general running condition of the engine.

10   Thread one of the new plugs into the hole until you can no longer turn it with your fingers, then tighten it with a torque wrench (if available) or the ratchet. It is a good idea to slip a short length of rubber hose over the end of the plug to use as a tool to thread it into place **(see illustration)**. The hose will grip the plug well enough to turn it, but will start to slip if the plug begins to cross-thread in the hole. This will prevent damaged threads and the accompanying repair costs.

11   Before pushing the spark plug wire onto the end of the plug, inspect it following the

27.11 Shown here are some of the common defects to look for when inspecting the distributor cap (if in doubt about its condition, install a new one)

procedures outlined in Section 27.

12 Attach the plug wire to the new spark plug, again using a twisting motion on the boot until it is seated on the spark plug.

13 Repeat the procedure for the remaining spark plugs, replacing them one at a time to prevent mixing up the spark plug wires.

27 Spark plug wire, distributor cap and rotor check and replacement (every 30,000 miles or 30 months)

Refer to illustrations 27.11 and 27.12

Spark plug wires

Note: *Every time a spark plug wire is detached from a spark plug, the distributor cap or the coil, silicone dielectric compound (available at most auto parts stores) should be applied to the inside of each boot before reconnection.*

1 The spark plug wires should be checked and, if necessary, replaced at the same time new spark plugs are installed.

2 The easiest way to identify bad wires is to make a visual check while the engine is running. In a dark, well-ventilated garage,

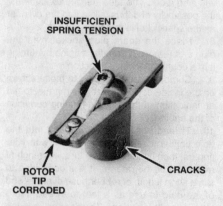

27.12 Check the rotor for cracks and carbon tracks and make sure the center terminal spring tension is adequate - if the rotor tip is burned or corroded, a new rotor should be installed

start the engine and look at each plug wire. Be careful not to come into contact with any moving engine parts. If there is a break in the wire, you will see arcing or a small spark at the damaged area. If arcing is noticed, make a note to obtain new wires.

3 The spark plug wires should be inspected one at a time, beginning with the spark plug for the number one cylinder to prevent confusion. Clearly label each original plug wire with a piece of tape marked with the correct number. The plug wires must be reinstalled in the correct order to ensure proper engine operation.

4 Disconnect the plug wire from the first spark plug. A removal tool can be used **(see illustration 26.6)**, or you can grab the wire boot, twist it slightly and pull the wire free. Do not pull on the wire itself, only on the rubber boot.

5 Push the wire and boot back onto the end of the spark plug. It should fit snugly. If it doesn't, detach the wire and boot once more and use a pair of pliers to carefully crimp the metal connector inside the wire boot until it does.

6 Using a clean rag, wipe the entire length of the wire to remove built-up dirt and grease.

7 Once the wire is clean, check for burns, cracks and other damage. Do not bend the wire sharply or you might break the conductor.

8 Disconnect the wire from the distributor. Again, pull only on the rubber boot. Check for corrosion and a tight fit. Replace the wire in the distributor.

9 Inspect each of the remaining spark plug wires, making sure that each one is securely fastened at the distributor and spark plug when the check is complete.

10 If new spark plug wires are required, purchase a set for your specific engine model. Precut wire sets with the boots already installed are available. Remove and replace the wires one at a time to avoid mix-ups in the firing order.

Distributor cap and rotor

Note: *it is common practice to install a new distributor cap and rotor each time new spark plug wires are installed. If you're planning to install new wires, install a new cap and rotor also. But*

if you are planning to reuse the existing wires, be sure to inspect the cap and rotor to make sure that they are in good condition.

11 Remove the mounting screws and detach the cap from the distributor. Check it for cracks, carbon tracks and worn, burned or loose terminals **(see illustration)**.

12 Check the rotor for cracks and carbon tracks. Make sure the center terminal spring tension is adequate and look for corrosion and wear on the rotor tip **(see illustration)**.

13 Replace the cap and rotor if damage or defects are found.

14 When installing a new cap, remove the wires from the old cap one at a time and attach them to the new cap in the exact same location. Do not simultaneously remove all the wires from the old cap or firing order mix-ups may occur.

28 Cooling system servicing (draining, flushing and refilling) (every 30,000 miles or 30 months)

Refer to illustrations 28.4 and 28.5

Warning: *Do not allow antifreeze to come in contact with your skin or painted surfaces of the vehicle. Rinse off spills immediately with plenty of water. Antifreeze is highly toxic if ingested. Never leave antifreeze lying around in an open container or in puddles on the floor; children and pets are attracted by it's sweet smell and may drink it. Check with local authorities about disposing of used antifreeze. Many communities have collection centers which will see that antifreeze is disposed of safely.*

1 Periodically, the cooling system should be drained, flushed and refilled to replenish the antifreeze mixture and prevent formation of rust and corrosion, which can impair the performance of the cooling system and cause engine damage. When the cooling system is serviced, all hoses and the radiator cap should be checked and replaced, if necessary.

Draining

2 Apply the parking brake and block the wheels. If the vehicle has just been driven, wait several hours to allow the engine to cool down before beginning this procedure.

3 Once the engine is completely cool, remove the radiator cap.

4 Move a large container under the radiator drain to catch the coolant. Attach a 3/8-inch diameter hose to the drain fitting to direct the coolant into the container, then open the drain fitting (a pair of pliers may be required to turn it) **(see illustration)**.

5 After the coolant stops flowing out of the radiator, move the container under the engine block drain plug(s), if equipped. Remove the plug(s) and allow the coolant in the block to drain **(see illustration)**. **Note:** *On some models with V8 engines, the right side drain plug is hidden behind the starter, making starter removal necessary (see Chapter 5).*

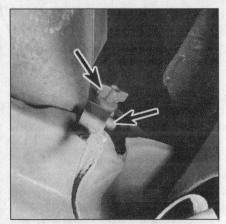

28.4 Attach a 3/8-inch diameter hose to the drain fitting (right arrow) then turn the valve (left arrow)

6   While the coolant is draining, check the condition of the radiator hoses, heater hoses and clamps (see Section 15, if necessary).

7   Replace any damaged clamps or hoses.

Flushing

8   Once the system is completely drained, flush the radiator with fresh water from a garden hose until water runs clear at the drain. The flushing action of the water will remove sediments from the radiator but will not remove rust and scale from the engine and cooling tube surfaces.

9   These deposits can be removed by the chemical action of a cooling system cleaner. Follow the procedure outlined in the manufacturer's instructions. If the radiator is severely corroded, damaged or leaking, it should be removed (see Chapter 3) and taken to a radiator repair shop. **Caution:** *If the vehicle is equipped with an aluminum radiator, make sure any chemical flush used is compatible with aluminum.*

10   Remove the overflow hose from the coolant recovery reservoir. Drain the reservoir and flush it with clean water, then reconnect the hose.

Refilling

11   Close and tighten the radiator drain. Install and tighten the block drain plug if removed.

12   Place the heater temperature control in the maximum heat position.

13   Slowly add new coolant (a 50/50 mixture of water and antifreeze) to the radiator until it is full. Add coolant to the reservoir up to the lower mark.

14   Leave the radiator cap off and run the engine in a well ventilated area until the thermostat opens (coolant will begin flowing through the radiator and the upper radiator hose will become hot).

15   Turn the engine off and let it cool. Add more coolant mixture to bring the level back up to the lip on the radiator filler neck.

16   Squeeze the upper radiator hose to expel air, then add more coolant mixture, if necessary. Replace the radiator cap.

17   Start the engine, allow it to reach normal operating temperature and check for leaks.

29   Air filter check and replacement (every 30,000 miles or 30 months)

Refer to illustration 29.4

Carbureted models

1   At the specified intervals, the air filter should be replaced with a new one. A thorough program of preventative maintenance would call for the filter to be inspected periodically between changes.

2   The air filter is located inside the air cleaner housing on the top of the engine. To remove the filter, unscrew the wing nut at the top of the air cleaner and lift off the top plate. If the top plate is connected to emissions control devices, tilt it back far enough to allow access to the filter element.

3   While the top plate is off, be careful not to drop anything down into the carburetor.

4   Lift the air filter out of the housing **(see illustration)**.

5   To check the filter, hold it up to strong sunlight, or place a flashlight or droplight on the inside of the ring-shaped filter. If you can see light coming through the paper element, the filter is all right. Check all the way around the filter.

6   Wipe the inside of the air cleaner housing with a rag. Be careful not to drop any debris down the carburetor.

7   Place the old filter (if in good condition) or the new filter (if specified interval has elapsed) back into the air cleaner housing. Make sure it seats properly in the bottom of the housing.

8   Reinstall the top plate with the wing nut.

Fuel-injected models

9   See Chapter 4, Section 20.

30   Positive Crankcase Ventilation (PCV) valve and filter check and replacement (every 30,000 miles or 30 months)

Refer to illustrations 30.5a and 30.5b

Note: *To maintain efficient operation of the PCV system, clean the hoses and check the PCV valve and filter at the intervals recommended in the maintenance schedule. For additional information on the PCV system, refer to Chapter 6.*

1   Locate the PCV valve on the rocker arm cover or rear of intake manifold (refer to Chapter 6).

2   Check the PCV valve rubber grommet in the rocker arm cover for cracks and distortion. If it's damaged, replace it.

3   To check the valve, first pull it out of the rocker arm cover and shake it - if it rattles, reinstall it in the cover. If the valve doesn't rattle, it is probably clogged with deposits, install a new PCV valve. **Note**: *If utilized, a new PCV valve will not include the elbow. The original must be transferred to the new valve. If a new elbow is purchased, it may be necessary to soak it in warm water for up to an hour to slip it*

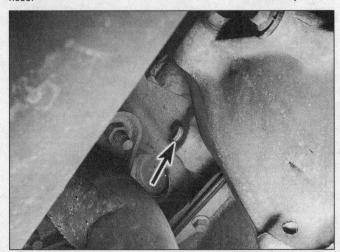

28.5 Location of the left side engine block drain plug (arrow) on a V8 engine (the plug on the right side is obscured by the starter)

29.4 Lifting the air filter out of the housing (early model shown)

onto the new valve. Do not attempt to force the elbow onto the valve or it will break.

4   If the valve is clogged, the hoses may also be plugged. Remove the hose between the valve and the intake manifold and the hose between the rocker arm cover and the clean air source and inspect them.

5   Remove and check the PCV system filter. On some vehicles, the filter is integral with the oil filler cap, on other vehicles, the filter assembly is located inside the air cleaner housing **(see illustrations)**, still others have both. If the filter (or filter assembly) appears to be restrictive or dirty, replace it. Reconnect the hoses to the system.

31 Wheel bearing check, repack and adjustment (every 30,000 miles or 30 months)

30.5a Location of the crankcase ventilation filter inside the air filter housing (early models)

30.5b Typical late model PCV filter mounted in the air cleaner housing

Refer to illustrations 31.6, 31.9, 31.15 and 31.16

Front wheel bearings - 2WD models

1   In most cases, the front wheel bearings will not need servicing until the brake pads are changed. However, these bearings should be checked whenever the front wheels are raised for any reason.

2   With the vehicle securely supported on jackstands, spin the wheel and check for noise, rolling resistance and freeplay. Now grab the top of the tire with one hand and the bottom of the tire with the other. Move the tire in and out on the spindle. If it moves more than 0.005 inch, the bearings should be checked, then repacked with grease or replaced, if necessary.

3   To remove the bearings for replacing or repacking, begin by removing the hub cap and wheel.

4   Remove the brake caliper as described in Chapter 9.

5   Use wire to hang the caliper assembly out of the way. Be careful not to kink or damage the brake hose.

6   Pry the grease cap off the hub using a screwdriver. This cap is located at the center of the hub **(see illustration)**.

7   Straighten the bent ends of the cotter pin and pull the cotter pin out of the locking nut. Discard the cotter pin, as a new one should be used on reassembly.

8   Remove the nut and washer from the end of the spindle.

9   Pull the hub assembly out slightly and then push it back into its original position. This should force the outer bearing off the spindle enough so that it can be removed with your fingers **(see illustration)**. Remove the outer

bearing, noting how it is installed on the end of the spindle.

10   The hub assembly can now be pulled off the spindle.

11   Use a screwdriver to pry out the inner bearing lip seal on the rear side of the hub. As this is done, note the direction in which the seal is installed.

12   The inner bearing can now be removed from the hub, again noting how it is installed.

13   Use clean solvent to remove all traces of the old grease from the bearings, hub and spindle. A small brush may prove useful; however, make sure no bristles from the brush embed themselves inside the bearing rollers. Allow the parts to air dry.

14   Carefully inspect the bearings for cracks, heat discoloration, bent rollers, etc. Check the bearing races inside the hub for cracks, scoring, and uneven surfaces. If the bearing races are in need of replacement, this

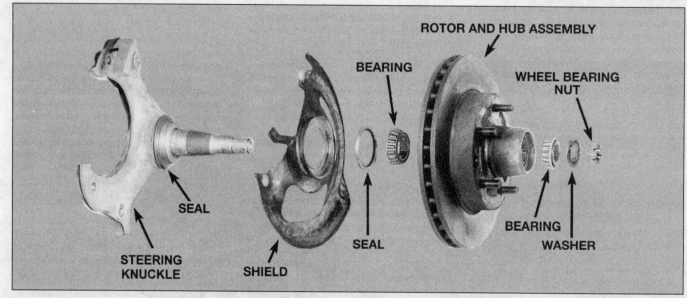

31.6 Exploded view of a typical front wheel bearing assembly (2WD models)

31.9 Pull out the hub/disc assembly to dislodge the outer bearing

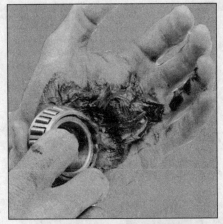

31.15 Pack each wheel bearing by working the grease into the rollers from the back side

31.16 Apply a thin coat of grease to the spindle, particularly where the seal rides

job is best left to a repair shop which can press the new races into position.

15 Use an approved high-temperature wheel bearing grease to pack the bearings. Work the grease fully into the bearings, forcing it between the rollers, cone and cage **(see illustration)**.

16 Apply a thin coat of grease to the spindle at the outer bearing seat, inner bearing seat, shoulder and seal seat area **(see illustration)**.

17 Put a small quantity of grease inboard of each bearing race inside the hub. Using your fingers, form a dam at these points to provide extra grease availability and to keep thinned grease from flowing out of the bearing.

18 Place the grease-packed inner bearing into the rear of the hub and put a little more grease outboard of the bearings.

19 Place a new seal over the inner bearing and tap the seal with a seal driver or a flat plate and a hammer until it is flush with the hub.

20 Carefully place the hub assembly onto the spindle and push the grease-packed outer bearing into position.

21 Put a little grease outboard of the outer bearing to provide extra grease availability.

22 Install the washer and spindle nut. Tighten the nut only slightly (22 to 25 ft-lbs of torque).

23 Spin the hub in a forward direction to seat the bearings and remove any grease or burrs which would cause excessive bearing play later.

24 Now check that the spindle nut is still tight (22 to 25 ft-lbs).

25 Loosen the spindle nut 1/8-turn.

26 Using your hand (not a wrench of any kind), tighten the nut until it is snug. Install a new cotter pin through the hole in the spindle and spindle nut. If the nut slits do not line up, loosen the nut slightly until they do. From the hand-tight position the nut should not be loosened any more than one-half flat to install the cotter pin.

27 Bend the ends of the new cotter pin until

they are flat against the nut. Cut off any extra length which could interfere with the dust cap.

28 Install the dust cap, tapping it into place with a rubber mallet.

29 Reinstall the brake caliper as described in Chapter 9.

30 Install the wheel and tighten the lug nuts.

31 Grab the top and bottom of the tire and check the bearings in the same manner as described at the beginning of this Section.

32 Lower the vehicle to the ground and tighten the lug nuts to the torque listed in this Chapter's Specifications. Install the hub cap, using a rubber mallet to fully seat it.

Front wheel bearings - 4WD models

33 Refer to procedure outlined in Chapter 8. **Note:** *If the specified maintenance interval has elapsed, perform this operation after checking/repacking the spindle/knuckle needle bearings (see Section 32).*

Rear wheel bearings - models with full floating axles

34 Refer to the procedure in Chapter 8.

32 Front spindle/knuckle needle bearing (4WD models) check and repack (every 30,000 miles or 30 months)

1 The front driveaxle needle bearings located within the knuckle spindle assemblies are an often forgotten item. Because of its location, it is exposed to more environmental contaminants then the wheel bearings. Therefore, it is important that they are inspected and serviced as scheduled, especially if the vehicle is used off-road or in wet conditions.

2 For removal, repack and installation, refer to the procedure outlined in Chapter 8. **Note:** *Perform this operation prior to front wheel bearing check/repack (see Section 31).*

33 Front locking hub (4WD models) lubricant check and repack (every 30,000 miles or 30 months)

1 The front drive locking hub assemblies are an often forgotten item. Their function is essential to proper 4WD operation. Therefore, it is important that they are inspected and serviced as scheduled, especially if the vehicle is used off-road or in wet conditions.

2 For removal, repack and installation, refer to the procedure outlined in Chapter 8.

34 Manual transmission lubricant change (every 60,000 miles or 60 months)

1 Drive the vehicle for at least 15 minutes in stop-and-go traffic to warm the oil in the transmission.

2 If necessary, raise the vehicle to a level position using either a suitable lift or four jackstands (see *Jacking and towing* at the front of this book). Remove the drain plug from the transmission. Allow plenty of time for the lubricant to drain.

3 After all of the lubricant has been drained, install and tighten the drain plug securely.

4 Using a small hand pump dispenser available at most auto parts stores, refill the transmission case with the specified lubricant until the fluid reaches the filler hole level (see Section 22).

5 Install the filler plug and tighten it securely. Drive the vehicle for a short distance and recheck the oil level. In some cases a small amount of additional fluid will have to be added.

6 After driving the vehicle, recheck the drain and filler plugs for any signs of leakage.

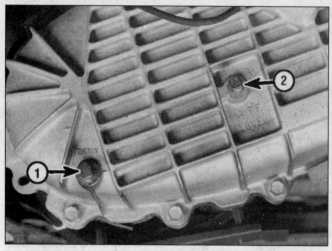

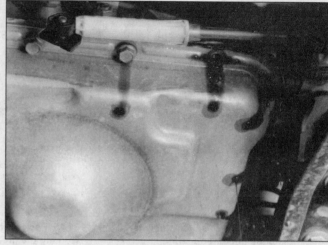

35.4 Typical location of transfer case drain and fill plugs

1   Drain plug   *2   Filler plug*

36.8 Allow the pan to hang down so the fluid can drain

35   Transfer case lubricant change (every 60,000 miles or 60 months)

Refer to illustration 35.4

1   Drive the vehicle for at least 15 minutes in stop-and-go traffic to warm the oil in the case.

2   If necessary, raise the vehicle to a level position using either a suitable lift or four jackstands (see *Jacking and towing* at the front of this book).

3   Remove the filler plug from the rear top case half.

4   Remove the drain plug from the rear bottom case half and allow the old lubricant to drain completely **(see illustration)**.

5   Carefully clean and install the drain plug after the case is completely drained. Tighten the drain plug securely.

6   Using a small hand pump dispenser available at most auto parts stores, fill the case with the specified lubricant until it is level with the lower edge of the filler hole (see Section 22).

7   Install the filler plug and tighten it securely.

8   Drive the vehicle for a short distance and recheck the oil level. In some cases a small amount of additional oil will have to be added.

9   After driving the vehicle, recheck the drain and filler plugs for any signs of leakage.

36   Automatic transmission fluid and filter change (every 60,000 miles or 60 months)

Refer to illustration 36.8

1   At the specified time intervals, the transmission fluid should be changed and the filter replaced with a new one. Since there is no drain plug, the transmission oil pan must be removed from the bottom of the transmission to drain the fluid.

2   Before any draining, purchase the specified transmission fluid (see *Recommended*

lubricants near the front of this Chapter) a new filter and all necessary gaskets. **Note:** *Due to the susceptibility of automatic transmissions to contamination, under no circumstances should the old filter or gaskets be reused.*

3   Other tools necessary for this job include jackstands to support the vehicle in a raised position, a wrench to remove the oil pan bolts, a standard screwdriver, a drain pan capable of holding at least 30 pints, newspapers and clean rags.

4   The fluid should be drained immediately after the vehicle has been driven. This will remove any built-up sediment better than if the fluid were cold. Because of this, it's a good idea to wear protective gloves (fluid temperature can exceed 350-degrees F in a hot transmission).

5   After the vehicle has been driven to warm up the fluid, raise it and place it on jackstands for access underneath. Make sure it is firmly supported by the four stands placed under the frame rails.

6   Move the necessary equipment under the vehicle, being careful not to touch any of the hot exhaust components.

7   Place the drain pan under the transmission oil pan and remove the oil pan bolts along the rear and sides of the pan. Loosen, but do not remove, the bolts at the front of the pan.

8   Carefully pry the pan down at the rear, allowing the hot fluid to drain into the drain pan **(see illustration)**. If necessary, use a screwdriver to break the gasket seal at the rear of the pan; however, do not damage the pan or transmission in the process.

9   Support the pan and remove the remaining bolts at the front of the pan. Lower the pan and drain the remaining fluid into the drain receptacle. As this is done, check the fluid for metal particles which may be an indication of transmission failure.

10   Now visible on the bottom of the transmission is the filter/strainer held in place by screws (except on E4OD transmissions).

11   Remove the screws, the filter and the gasket.

12   On E4OD transmissions, remove the filter by carefully pulling and rotating it as necessary. **Note:** *Make sure the O-ring seal is not in the filter pick-up bore. If it is, remove and discard it.*

13   Thoroughly clean the transmission oil pan with solvent. Inspect for metal particles and foreign matter. Dry with compressed air, if available. It is important that all remaining gasket material be removed from the oil pan mounting flange. Use a gasket scraper or putty knife for this.

14   Clean the filter mounting surface on the valve body. Again, this surface should be smooth and free of old gasket material.

15   Place the new filter into position with a new gasket between it and the transmission valve body. Install the mounting screws and tighten them to the torque value listed in this Chapter's Specifications.

16   On E4OD transmissions, lubricate the new filter O-ring with transmission fluid and press the filter and seal assembly into the transmission bore.

17   Apply a bead of RTV sealant around the oil pan mounting surface, with the sealant to the inside of the bolt holes. Press the new gasket into place on the pan, making sure all bolt holes line up.

18   Lift the pan up to the bottom of the transmission and install the mounting bolts. Tighten the bolts in a diagonal fashion, working around the pan. Using a torque wrench, tighten the bolts to the torque listed in this Chapter's Specifications.

19   Lower the vehicle off the jackstands.

20   Open the hood and remove the transmission fluid dipstick from its guide tube.

21   Since fluid capacities vary between the various transmission types, it is best to add a little fluid at a time, continually checking the level with the dipstick. Allow the fluid time to drain into the pan. Add fluid until the level just registers on the end of the dipstick. In most cases, a good starting point will be 3 to 4 quarts (depending on model) added to the transmission through the filler tube (use a

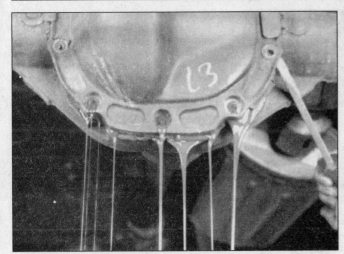

38.4 On differentials without a drain plug, remove all of the bolts but one, then pry the cover off and let the fluid drain

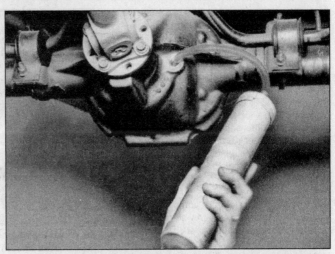

38.5 A small hand pump can be used to remove the old lubricant from the differentials - it's the only method for some types of differentials that don't have drain plugs or covers (and would require extensive disassembly otherwise)

funnel to prevent spills).

22   With the selector lever in PARK apply the parking brake and start the engine without depressing the accelerator pedal (if possible). Do not race the engine at a high speed; run at a slow idle only, for at least two minutes.

23   Depress the brake pedal and shift the transmission through each gear. Place the selector in the NEUTRAL position and (with the engine still idling) check the level on the dipstick. Look under the vehicle for leaks around the transmission oil pan mating surface.

24   Add more fluid through the dipstick tube until the level on the dipstick is just above the middle hole. Do not add any more fluid at this time.

25   Push the dipstick firmly back into its tube and drive the vehicle to reach normal operating temperature (15 minutes of driving should be adequate). Park on a level surface and check the fluid level on the dipstick with the engine idling and the transmission in NEUTRAL. The level should now be at or just below the DON'T ADD mark on the dipstick. If not, add more fluid as necessary to bring the level up to this point. Again, do not overfill.

37   Evaporative emissions system check (every 60,000 miles or 60 months)

Note: *See illustrations in Chapter 6 for component location and identification.*

1   The evaporative emissions system consists of the charcoal carbon canister, the lines connecting the canister to the carburetor, air cleaner and the fuel tank, and the fuel tank filler cap.

2   Inspect the fuel filler cap(s) and make sure the gasket sealing the cap is in good condition. It should not be cracked, broken or show signs of leakage.

3   Inspect the lines leading to the charcoal

canister from the fuel tank. They should be in good shape and the rubber should not show signs of cracking or leakage.

4   Check all of the clamps and make sure they are sealing the system. Check the carbon-filled canister for any signs of leakage or damage. In most cases, a carbon canister will last the lifetime of the vehicle; however, certain situations will require replacement. If the carbon canister shows signs of leakage or damage, replace it, as it is not a serviceable unit.

5   Check all the lines leading from the carbon canister to the air cleaner. In some cases there will be two lines, one leading from the carburetor fuel bowl to vent it, and one line leading from the carbon canister to the air cleaner for burning of the accumulated vapors.

6   Replace any lines in questionable condition and exercise the same precautions as are necessary when dealing with fuel lines or the fuel filter.

38   Differential lubricant change (every 100,000 miles)

Refer to illustrations 38.4, 38.5 and 38.7

Note: *Carefully read through this and the specifications Section before undertaking this procedure. You will need to purchase the correct type and amount of differential lubricant before draining the old oil out of the vehicle. In some cases you will also need a differential cover gasket and an additive (for models with a limited slip differential)*

1   The vehicle should be driven for several minutes before draining the differential oil. This practice will warm up the oil and ensure complete drainage.

2   Move a drain pan, rags, newspapers, and tools under the vehicle. Place the drain pan under the differential.

3   If equipped with a cover-mounted drain plug, remove the drain plug from the bottom

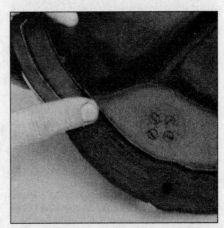

38.7 If you drain the differential by removing the cover, apply RTV sealant to the cover just before installation (this only applies to differentials without cover gaskets)

of the housing and drain the lubricant into the pan. Remove the inspection/fill plug to help vent this type differential to aid in draining.

4   On some differentials, no drain plug is provided which necessitates that the differential cover be removed. To remove the cover, unscrew the cover attaching screws leaving one upper screw loose but still attached. Pry the cover loose and allow the lubricant to drain before removing the cover completely **(see illustration)**.

5   Another alternative on some differentials, is to suck the old lubricant out of the housing by using a small hand-operated pump and hose inserted through the fill plug **(see illustration)**.

6   On differentials with drain plugs, after the oil has completely drained, wipe the area around the drain hole with a clean rag and install the drain plug.

7   If cover was removed, reinstall the differential cover with a new gasket (if originally

issued) or apply a bead of RTV sealant to the cover as shown **(see illustration)** on differentials with machined sealing surfaces. Tighten the cover retaining bolts to the torque value listed in the Chapter's Specifications.

8   Check the manufacturer's tag on the driver's door latch post or the tag attached to the differential to determine if your vehicle is equipped with a locking or equal-lock (limited-slip) type of differential. These differentials require the use of an additive to supplement the normal differential lubricant (see *Recommended lubricants* at the beginning of this Chapter). Add the prescribed amount of the additive at this time.

9   Using a small hand pump dispenser available at most auto parts stores, fill the housing (through the inspection hole) with the recommended lubricant until the level is even with the bottom of the inspection hole (see Section 22). Install the inspection plug after cleaning it and the threads in the case or cover.

10   After driving the vehicle, check for leaks at the drain and inspection plugs.

11   When the job is complete, check for metal particles or chips in the drained oil, which indicate that the differential should be thoroughly inspected and repaired (see Chapter 8 for more information).

39   Carburetor and choke system - inspection

Refer to illustration 39.19

Carburetor check

1   The first step in inspection of the carburetor is the removal of the air cleaner. The following instructions will apply to most vehicles; however, some variations may be encountered.

2   Remove the wing nut in the center of the top cover.

3   Remove the clamp and rubber fresh air inlet hose from the air cleaner duct and valve assembly.

4   Remove the hose clamp and flexible hot air tube from the bottom of the duct and valve assembly. Be careful in this step, if the engine is warm, as this hose is used to duct hot air from the exhaust manifold area up to the carburetor.

5   Remove any vacuum hoses attached to the bottom of the air cleaner assembly. Mark them carefully so they may be reattached in the correct positions. Plug these hoses with a golf tee, pencil, or similar item to prevent vacuum leaks.

6   Remove the valve cover vent hose from the side of the air cleaner (at the elbow). This is a rubber hose leading from the valve cover and PCV valve.

7   Remove the flexible air purge hose leading from the charcoal canister to the air cleaner.

8   Lift the air cleaner assembly off of the carburetor. **Note:** *Make sure that the gasket at the base of the air cleaner assembly either*

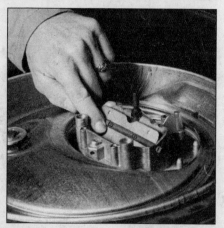

39.19 As the engine warms up, the choke plate should gradually open

remains with the air cleaner or stays on the inlet flange of the carburetor. It sometimes can come loose and fall into the carburetor intake as the air cleaner is removed.

9   The air cleaner cover may be set to the side of the engine compartment if it is connected to one or two vacuum hoses (optional). If you do this, place the cover where it will not be damaged or contact hot engine parts.

10   Once the air cleaner has been removed, a visible inspection of the carburetor is possible. The main item to look for is decaying and/or leaking hoses. It is not necessary to remove any hoses to check their condition, but flexing them with the fingers will usually reveal telltale cracks or splits. Check the carburetor body itself for any signs of leakage and/or built-up sludge which could hamper the operation of any moving parts. Take care not to knock loose any large pieces of residue which will fall down into the carburetor inlet and finally end up in the engine. If excessively dirty, the carburetor should be removed and thoroughly cleaned (see Chapter 4).

11   While looking for leaks, check the carburetor top plate hold-down screws for tightness. Often, over a period of time, vibration will cause these screws to loosen, creating a major source of gasoline and vacuum leakage. If a leak is suspected at any other point in the carburetor system, but it is not readily identifiable, clean the entire area and then prepare to run the vehicle without the air cleaner. **Note:** *Do not drive the vehicle with the air filter removed. This is a test procedure and should be performed only long enough to pinpoint any leaks which may occur under pressure or with the engine running.* Before starting the engine, disconnect and plug the small vacuum hose(s) which connect to the base of the air cleaner. Place these hoses out of the way from any heat sources or from the drivebelts and pulleys.

12   Check the accelerator linkage or the cable that connects the carburetor to the accelerator pedal. A helper working the throttle from the driver's seat will allow you to make close observation of the moving components of the accelerator system. Perform this procedure with the engine off.

13   Have an assistant slowly depress the accelerator to its full travel, then allow it to return while observing the cable or linkage and attending moving parts. Lubrication of these parts can be accomplished at the same time. Use a lightweight penetrating oil for the cable and pivot points.

14   If any major leaks or problems are noticed in the carburetor, refer to Chapter 4 for further information. **Caution:** *Always make sure that nothing is dropped into the carburetor air intake, as it will eventually end up in the engine and cause serious damage.*

Choke system check

15   The choke operates only when the engine is cold, so this check should be performed before the engine has been started for the day. The vehicle should be allowed to sit at least four hours at a temperature under 68-degrees F since the last time it was run.

16   The air cleaner need not be removed for this check, but the top cover must be opened up. Take the top off by removing the wing nut and washer. Set the top cover aside, making sure you place it in a position where it is out of the way of any moving parts and is not in contact with any heat sources.

17   Look at the top of the carburetor at the center of the air cleaner housing. You will notice a flat plate at the carburetor opening.

18   Have an assistant press the accelerator pedal to the floor. The plate should close off the inlet fully. (On four-barrel carburetors, the plate covers only the front two barrels of the carburetor). Start the engine while you observe the plate at the carburetor inlet. Do not position your face directly over the carburetor, as the engine could backfire, causing serious burns. When the engine starts, the choke plate should open slightly.

19   Allow the engine to continue running at a fast idle speed. As the engine warms up to operating temperature, the plate should slowly open, allowing more air to enter through the top of the carburetor **(see illustration)**. Some vehicles will not fully open the plate unless the accelerator pedal is once again quickly pushed to more than its half-way position and released. If, after a few moments, you notice that the plate is not moving, try this quick depression of the accelerator pedal to see if it does release the choke linkage.

20   After a few minutes of operation, the choke plate should be fully opened to the vertical position once the engine has warmed up to operating temperature. You will notice that the engine speed corresponds with the plate opening. With the plate fully closed, the engine should run at a fast idle speed. As the plate opens, the engine speed should decrease and eventually arrive at its normal curb idle operation level.

21   If a fault is detected during the above checks, refer to Chapter 4 for specific information on adjusting and servicing the choke components. Chapter 6 also contains information on emissions control systems related to the carburetor.

Chapter 2 Part A
Inline six-cylinder engine

Contents

Specifications

Camshaft lobe lift

Intake
F100 and F150 2WD with 2.47:1 or 2.75:1 axle ratio and manual transmission	0.247 inch
All others	0.249 inch

Exhaust
F100 and F150 2WD with 2.47:1 or 2.75:1 axle ratio and manual transmission	0.247 inch
All others	0.249 inch

Torque specifications

Ft-lb (unless otherwise indicated)

Note: One foot-pound (ft-lb) of torque is equivalent to 12 inch-pounds (in-lbs) of torque. Torque values below approximately 15 ft-lbs are expressed in inch-pounds, since most foot-pound torque wrenches are not accurate at these smaller values.

Timing cover bolts	12 to 18
Cylinder head bolts	
Step 1	55
Step 2	65
Step 3	85
Crankshaft vibration damper bolt	130 to 150
Flywheel/flexplate-to-crankshaft bolts	75 to 85
Intake manifold-to-cylinder head bolts	22 to 32
Intake manifold-to-exhaust manifold nuts	28 to 32
Exhaust manifold-to-cylinder head bolts	
1980 and 1981	28 to 33
1982 on	22 to 32
Oil filter insert-to-cylinder block/adapter	20 to 30
Oil filter adapter-to-cylinder block	40 to 50
Oil pump pick-up tube-to-pump bolts	10 to 15
Oil pan drain plug	15 to 25
Oil pan-to-cylinder block bolts	
1990 and earlier	10 to 15
1991 on	15 to 18
Oil pump-to-cylinder block bolts	10 to 15
Oil inlet tube-to-main bearing cap	22 to 32
Pulley-to-damper bolt	35 to 50
Rocker arm stud nut or bolt	17 to 23
Valve cover bolts	72 to 108 in-lbs
Pushrod cover bolts	18 to 27 in-lbs
Camshaft thrust plate bolts	12 to 18
Engine mount to chassis bracket	70 to 93
Engine mount to engine bracket	70 to 93
Engine mount bracket to block bolts	60 to 80

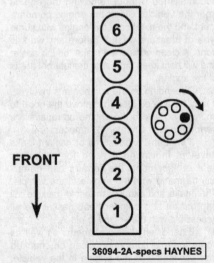

36094-2A-specs HAYNES

Cylinder locations and distributor rotation - inline six-cylinder engine

The blackened terminal on the distributor cap indicates the number one spark plug wire position

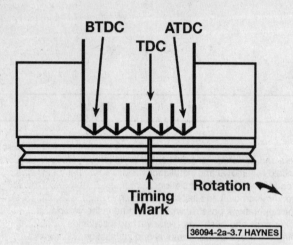

3.7 Details of the timing scale and timing mark on the crankshaft vibration damper

4.4 To measure cam lobe lift, secure a dial indicator to the head next to the valve (one at a time) and position the indicator plunger tip against the rocker arm directly above and in line with the pushrod - rotate crankshaft and measure lift

1   General information

The in-line six-cylinder engine block is made of cast iron. The crankshaft, which is supported by seven main bearings, is cast of nodular iron and the pistons are of aluminum alloy with integral steel struts. The rocker arms are of the ball pivot, stud-mounted design, employing positive-stop studs. The lifters (tappets) are hydraulic and self-adjusting. Rotators are employed on the exhaust valves and timing gears are of the helical type.

2   Repair operations possible with the engine in the vehicle

1   Many major repair operations can be accomplished without removing the engine from the vehicle. Clean the engine compartment and the exterior of the engine with some type of pressure washer before any work is done. A clean engine will make the job easier and will help keep dirt out of the internal areas of the engine.

2   Depending on the components involved, it may be a good idea to remove the hood to improve access to the engine as repairs are performed (see Chapter 12, if necessary).

3   If vacuum, exhaust, oil or coolant leaks develop, indicating a need for gasket or seal replacement, the repairs can generally be made with the engine in the vehicle. The intake and exhaust manifold gaskets, oil pan gasket and cylinder head gasket are all accessible with the engine in place.

4   Exterior engine components as well as some internal components can be checked and serviced with the engine in the vehicle. Refer to this Chapters table of contents for these operations and components. In addition, the water pump (refer to Chapter 3), the starter motor, the alternator, the distributor (refer to Chapter 5) and the fuel injection system (refer to Chapter 4) can be removed for

repair with the engine in place.

5   Some component checks such as camshaft lobe lift measurement, timing gear wear, and piston ring/cylinder head condition (compression check) can also be performed while the engine is installed.

6   Since the cylinder head can be removed without pulling the engine, valve component servicing can also be accomplished with the engine in the vehicle.

7   In extreme cases caused by a lack of necessary equipment, repair or replacement of piston rings, pistons, connecting rods and rod bearings is possible with the engine in the vehicle. However, this practice is not recommended because of the cleaning and preparation work that must be done to the components involved.

3   Top Dead Center (TDC) for number 1 piston - locating

Refer to illustration 3.7

1   Top Dead Center (TDC) is the highest point in the cylinder that each piston reaches as it travels up-and-down when the crankshaft turns. Each piston reaches TDC on the compression stroke and again on the exhaust stroke, but TDC generally refers to piston position on the compression stroke.

2   Positioning the piston(s) at TDC is an essential part of many procedures such as rocker arm removal, timing chain and sprocket replacement and distributor removal.

3   Before beginning this procedure, be sure to disconnect the coil wire from the distributor cap and ground it to prevent damage to the coil (see Chapter 5).

4   In order to bring any piston to TDC, the crankshaft must be turned using one of the following methods. When looking at the front of the engine, normal crankshaft rotation is *clockwise*. **Warning:** *Before beginning this procedure, be sure to place the transmission in Neutral (manual transmission) or*

Park (automatic transmission).

a)   *The preferred method is to turn the crankshaft with a large socket and breaker bar attached to the pulley bolt threaded into the front of the crankshaft.*

b)   *A remote starter switch, which may save some time, can also be used. Attach the switch leads to the small ignition switch terminal and the positive (red) battery cable terminal on the starter solenoid (mounted near the battery). Once the piston is close to TDC, use a socket and breaker bar as described above.*

c)   *If an assistant is available to turn the ignition switch to the START position in short bursts, you can get the piston close to TDC without a remote starter switch. Use a socket and breaker bar as described in Paragraph a) to complete the procedure.*

5   Note the position of the terminal for the number one spark plug wire on the distributor cap (it's marked with a 1). Use a scribe or chalk to make a mark on the distributor directly under the terminal. Remove the screws, detach the cap from the distributor and set it aside.

6   Rotate the crankshaft until the rotor is pointing directly to the chalk mark.

7   The timing marks are located on the crankshaft pulley and the scale on the timing chain cover. The timing mark line should indicate close to 0-degrees (TDC) **(see illustration)**. If not, turn the crankshaft until it does.

8   When the rotor is pointing at the number one spark plug wire terminal in the distributor cap and the 0-degree timing marks are aligned, the number one piston is at TDC on the compression stroke.

9   After the number one piston has been positioned at TDC on the compression stroke, TDC for any of the remaining cylinders can be located by turning the crankshaft clockwise 120-degrees at a time and following the firing order of the engine.

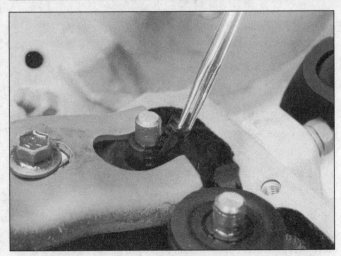

5.8 Compress the valve spring and remove the keepers with a small magnet, a pair of needle-nose pliers or tweezers

5.9 It doesn't really matter how you remove the old valve stem seals, since they will be replaced - be sure that you don't scratch, nick or otherwise damage the valve stems

---

4 Camshaft lobe lift - check

Refer to illustration 4.4

1   To determine the extent of cam lobe wear, the lobe lift should be checked prior to camshaft removal.

2   Remove the valve cover (see Section 6).

3   Position the number one piston at TDC on the compression stroke (see Section 3).

4   Beginning with the valves for the number one cylinder, mount a dial indicator on the engine and position the plunger against the top surface of the first rocker arm. The plunger should be directly above and in line with the pushrod **(see illustration)**.

5   Zero the dial indicator, then very slowly turn the crankshaft in the normal direction of rotation. The dial indicator needle will begin to move as the cam ramps up. Continue rotating until the indicator needle stops and begins to move in the opposite direction. The point at which the highest reading is noted indicates maximum cam lobe lift. Record the indicator reading.

6   After recording the first rocker arm measurement, again reposition the piston at TDC on the compression stroke for the same cylinder.

7   Move the dial indicator to the other number one cylinder rocker arm and repeat the check. Be sure to record the results for each valve.

8   Repeat the same check for the remaining valves. Since each piston must be at TDC on the compression stroke for this procedure, work from cylinder-to-cylinder following the firing order sequence.

9   After the check is complete, compare the results to the values listed in this Chapter's Specifications. If camshaft lobe lift is less than specified, cam lobe wear has occurred and a new camshaft should be installed.

---

5 Valve springs, retainers and seals - replacement

Refer to illustrations 5.8, 5.9, 5.14 and 5.16

Note: *Broken valve springs and defective valve stem seals can be replaced without removing the cylinder head. Two special tools and a compressed air source are normally required to perform this operation, so read through this Section carefully and rent or buy the tools before beginning the job. If compressed air is not available, a length of nylon rope can be used to keep the valves from falling into the cylinder during this procedure.*

Removal

1   Remove the valve cover from the cylinder head (see Section 6).

2   Remove the spark plug from the cylinder with the defective valve component. If all of the valve stem seals are being replaced, remove all of the spark plugs.

3   Turn the crankshaft until the piston in the affected cylinder is at top dead center on the compression stroke (refer to Section 3 for instructions). If you're replacing all of the valve stem seals, begin with cylinder number one and work on the valves for one cylinder at a time. Move from cylinder-to-cylinder following the firing order sequence.

4   Thread an adapter into the spark plug hole and connect an air hose from a compressed air source to it. Most auto parts stores can supply the air hose adapter. **Note:** *Many cylinder compression gauges utilize a screw-in fitting that may work with your air hose quick-disconnect fitting.*

5   Remove the rocker arm mounting nut or bolt, the rocker arm/fulcrum and the pushrod (see Section 7) for the valve with the defective part. If all of the valve stem seals are being replaced, all of the rocker arms and pushrods should be removed (be sure to keep them in order).

6   Apply compressed air to the cylinder.

Warning: *The piston may be forced down by compressed air, causing the crankshaft to turn suddenly. If the wrench used when positioning the number one piston at TDC is still attached to the bolt in the crankshaft nose, it could cause damage or injury when the crankshaft moves. The valves should be held in place by the air pressure. If the valve faces or seats are in poor condition, leaks may prevent the air pressure from retaining the valves. Refer to the alternative procedure below.*

7   If you don't have access to compressed air, an alternative method can be used. Position the piston at a point approximately 45-degrees before TDC on the compression stroke, then feed a long piece of nylon rope through the spark plug hole until it fills the combustion chamber. Be sure to leave the end of the rope hanging out of the engine so it can be removed easily. Use a large breaker bar and socket to turn the crankshaft in the normal direction of rotation until *slight* resistance is felt.

8   Stuff shop rags into the cylinder head oil return holes to prevent parts from falling into the engine, then use a valve spring compressor to compress the spring. **Note:** *A couple of different types of tools are available for compressing the valve springs with the head in place. One type grips the lower spring coils and presses on the retainer as the knob is turned, while the other type, used in this procedure, utilizes the rocker arm mounting stud or bolt for leverage. Both types work well, but the lever type is less expensive.* Remove the keepers with a small pair of needle-nose pliers, a magnet or forceps **(see illustration)**.

9   Remove the spring retainer and valve spring and set them aside. Using a pair of pliers, remove the valve stem seal **(see illustration)** and discard it. **Note:** *Watch for the presence of a spring shim(s) under the spring or on the spring seat and make sure it is installed prior to retainer re-installation. Also, if air pressure fails to hold the valve in the closed position during this operation, the*

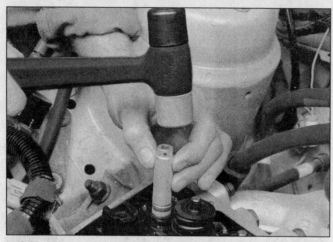

5.14 A deep socket and hammer can be used to seat the new seals on the valve guides

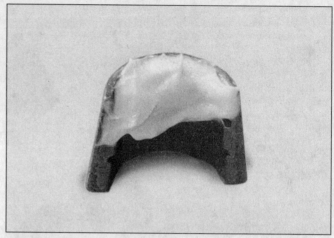

5.16 Keepers don't always want to stay in place, so apply a small dab of grease as shown to help hold them in place during valve spring retainer installation

valve face or seat is probably damaged. If so, the cylinder head will have to be removed for additional repair operations.

10   Wrap a rubber band or tape around the top of the valve stem so the valve won't fall into the combustion chamber, then release the air pressure. **Note**: *If a rope was used instead of air pressure, turn the crankshaft slightly in the direction opposite normal rotation.*

11   Inspect the valve stem for damage. Rotate the valve in the guide and check the end for eccentric movement, which would indicate that the valve is bent.

12   Move the valve up-and-down in the guide and make sure it doesn't bind. If the valve stem binds, the valve is bent or the guide is damaged. In either case, the head will have to be removed for repair.

13   Reapply air pressure to the cylinder to retain the valve in the closed position, then remove the tape or rubber band from the valve stem. If a rope was used instead of air pressure, rotate the crankshaft in the normal direction of rotation until slight resistance is felt.

Installation

14   Lubricate the valve stem with engine oil and install a new valve stem seal. Use a 5/8 inch deep socket and a hammer to seat the seal squarely on the valve guide **(see illustration)**.

15   Place the valve spring in position, then install the retainer.

16   Compress the valve spring assembly and carefully install the keepers in the grooves in the valve stem. Apply a small dab of grease to the inside of each keeper to hold it in place, if necessary **(see illustration)**.

17   Remove the pressure from the spring tool and make sure the keepers are seated.

18   Disconnect the air hose and remove the adapter from the spark plug hole. If a rope was used in place of air pressure, pull it out of the cylinder.

19   Refer to Section 7 and install the rocker arm and pushrod.

20   If you are replacing all of the seals,

repeat the procedure for each valve assembly. Remember, the piston for each cylinder must be positioned at TDC before removing the valve keepers.

21   Install the spark plug(s) and hook up the wire(s).

22   Install the valve cover (Section 7).

23   Start and run the engine, then check for oil leaks and unusual sounds coming from the valve cover area.

6   Valve cover and pushrod cover - removal and installation

Removal

Valve cover

1   Remove the PCV valve from the top of the valve cover (see Chapter 6).

2   Disconnect the clean air vent tube from the valve cover mounted oil filler cap or filter assembly (see Chapter 6).

3   On carbureted models, disconnect the fuel supply hose at the fuel pump and at the carburetor (see Chapter 4).

4   On fuel-injected models, remove the upper intake manifold (see Chapter 4).

5   Remove the retaining screws holding the valve cover to the cylinder head. On fuel-injected models, inspect bolts for worn or damaged seals under the head of the bolts and replace, if necessary.

6   Remove the valve cover from the cylinder head and clean the old gasket from the mating surfaces.

Pushrod cover

7   Remove the distributor cap from the distributor.

8   Remove the ignition coil and bracket from the side of the engine (see Chapter 5).

9   Remove the retaining bolts for the pushrod cover on left side of the engine.

10   Remove the pushrod cover from the side of the engine and clean the old gasket from the cover and engine block.

Installation

Valve cover

11   On carbureted models, install a new valve cover gasket in the valve cover. RTV sealant will hold it in place, if necessary.

12   On Fuel-injected models, place a new gasket on the cylinder head making sure the tabs of the gasket face down, towards the head. No sealant is required.

13   Install the valve cover on the cylinder head, making sure that the bolt holes line up and the gasket seals evenly all around the head.

14   Install the valve cover retaining bolts and tighten them to the torque listed in this Chapter's Specifications.

15   The remainder of installation is the reverse of removal.

Pushrod cover

16   Install a new gasket on the pushrod cover. Use RTV sealant on the gasket to keep it positioned, if necessary.

17   Place the pushrod cover on the engine and tighten the retaining bolts to the torque listed in this Chapter's Specifications.

18   The remainder of installation is the reverse of removal.

Either cover

19   After the engine has been started, run it until it reaches normal operating temperature. Check the pushrod cover and/or valve cover for leaks.

7   Rocker arms and pushrods - removal and installation

Refer to illustrations 7.2, 7.3 and 7.4

Removal

1   Remove the valve cover (see Section 6).

2   Remove the rocker arm stud nut (early models) or bolt (later models) **(see illustration)**, fulcrum seat and rocker arm from each cylinder. Keep them in order or mark them, if

they are to be re-installed, so they can be replaced in their original positions.

3   Inspect the rocker arms for wear **(see illustration)**.

4   To remove the pushrods, pull them straight up through the cylinder head and out of the lifter pocket. Keep them in order or mark them, if they are to be re-installed, so that they can be replaced in their original positions **(see illustration)**.

5   Inspect the pushrods as described in Chapter 2, Part D.

Installation

6   Apply engine oil or assembly lube to the top of the valve stem.

7   Apply assembly lube to the rocker arm fulcrum seat and the fulcrum seat socket in the rocker arm.

8   Install the pushrod (with lubricant applied to both ends).

9   Install the fulcrum guide (if equipped), rocker arm, fulcrum seat and stud nut or bolt. Tighten the bolt or nut to the torque listed in this Chapter's Specifications.

10   If components were replaced, check the valve clearance (see Chapter 2, Part D). If necessary, install a longer or shorter pushrod.

11   Replace the valve cover and gasket (see Section 6).

---

8   Timing cover and gears - removal and installation

Refer to illustrations 8.7, 8.17 and 8.31

Note: *The following procedure requires the use of a gear puller and gear installation tools.*

Removal

Cover

1   Drain the cooling system (see Chapter 3).

2   Remove the fan shroud and the radiator (see Chapter 3).

3   Remove the fan and pulley (see Chapter 3).

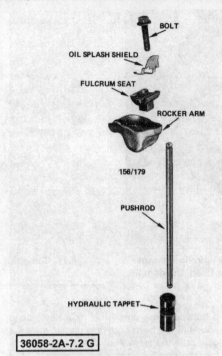

36058-2A-7.2 G

7.2 Exploded view of the rocker arm, pushrod and related components

4   Remove the power steering pump (see Chapter 10) and air conditioning compressor (see Chapter 3) from the engine bracket and position to side of engine compartment. **Note:** *Don't disconnect the hoses from these accessories.* Remove the bracket from the engine to gain access to the timing cover bolts.

5   Remove any alternator support brackets from the timing cover, if necessary, to gain access to timing cover bolts (see Chapter 5).

6   Remove the pulley from the crankshaft damper, then remove the large bolt and washer from the crankshaft nose. It may be necessary to prevent the crankshaft from rotating by putting the transmission in gear (if the engine is still in the vehicle) or by holding

the flywheel or crankshaft flange with a suitable tool if the engine is out of the vehicle.

7   Remove the vibration damper using a vibration damper puller **(see illustration)**.

8   Remove the front oil pan attaching bolts and loosen the first six pan bolts on each side of the pan to allow the pan to droop slightly under a light downward force.

9   Remove the timing cover attaching bolts.

10   Remove the cover and scrape the old gasket from the mating surfaces of the cover and the engine block.

11   Remove the crankshaft oil seal by pushing it out of the front cover with a suitably sized drift. Be careful not to damage the front cover while performing this operation.

12   Remove any chemical sealants from the seal bore of the cover. Check the bore carefully for anything that would prevent the new seal from seating properly in the cover.

Timing gears

13   Before removing the gears, the camshaft endplay, timing gear backlash and timing gear runout should be inspected (see Chapter 2, Part D). If measurements indicate worn components, replace as required during reassembly.

14   Turn the crankshaft and/or camshaft until the timing marks of both gears can be aligned.

15   Use a two-jaw puller to remove the gear from the camshaft. **Note**: *This operation can also be done with camshaft out of engine as during camshaft removal (see section 9).* **Caution:** *If the head, valves and pistons remain in the engine while the gears are being installed, do not turn either the crankshaft or camshaft prior to gear installation. Serious internal engine damage can result from rotating either assembly independent of the other. If the camshaft begins to turn by itself, remove the valve cover and loosen the rocker arm nuts or bolts two or three turns.*

16   Using a bolt-type puller, remove the timing gear from the crankshaft. **Note:** *Most steering wheel pullers can be used.*

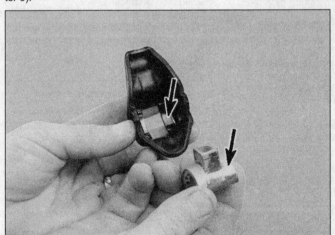

7.3 Check the rockers arm and fulcrums for wear in the points indicated (and also where the rocker arm contacts the valve and pushrod)

7.4 Keep the pushrods in order or mark them if they are to be re-installed so that they can be replaced in their original positions - a cardboard box such as the one shown can be used to identify and store pushrods in order

8.7 Use the recommended puller to remove the vibration damper - if a puller that applies force to the outer edge is used, the damper will be damaged

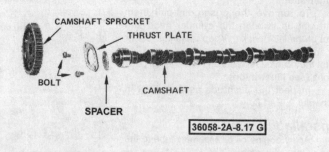

8.17 Camshaft and related components - exploded view

Installation

Timing gears

17   Align the key, spacer and thrust plate before installing the camshaft drive gear onto the camshaft **(see illustration)**. **Note**: *If camshaft endplay was excessive during the wear checks, install an appropriately sized thrust plate prior to gear installation. If backlash was excessive, be sure to install new timing gears.*

18   Install the gear on the camshaft using a drawbolt-type press tool **(see illustration)**. **Note**: *If the crankshaft gear is still installed, make sure the timing marks are correctly aligned prior to gear engagement.* An alternative is to use a bolt that will fit the threaded hole in the end of the camshaft. Put a nut and large flat washer on the bolt. Thread the bolt into the camshaft with the gear in place. Hold the bolt stationary and turn the nut down the bolt to push the gear into place on the camshaft. Remove the bolt and nut combination after the cam gear is in place.

19   Install the crankshaft key and gear using

8.31 Align the damper keyway with the key on the crankshaft and install the damper using installation tool as shown

a drawbolt-type press tool or a large deep socket (if you have access to one) to drive the gear onto the crankshaft. Make sure the timing marks on both gears are correctly aligned prior to gear engagement. Adjust camshaft **slightly** if necessary to align. **Caution:** *If the head, valves and pistons remain in the engine while the gears are being installed, do not turn either the crankshaft or camshaft prior to gear installation. Serious internal engine damage can result from rotating either assembly independent of the other.* **Note:** *If the rocker arm nuts or bolts were loosened, tighten them to the torque listed in this Chapter's Specifications, then install the valve cover.*

20   Install the crankshaft oil slinger in front of the crankshaft drive gear. Note that the cupped side faces away from the engine.

Cover

21   Coat the outside edge of the new crankshaft oil seal with grease and install the seal in the cover using an appropriate drive tool. Make sure the seal is seated completely in the bore.

22   If the oil pan is still on the engine, cut the old front oil pan seal flush at the cylinder block-to-pan junction. Remove the old seal.

23   Clean all gasket surfaces on the timing cover, block and oil pan.

24   If the oil pan is in place, cut and install a new pan seal so that it is flush with the engine block-to-oil pan junction.

25   Align the pan seal locating tabs with the holes in the oil pan. Make sure the seal tabs pull all the way through so that the seal is completely seated. Apply RTV sealant to the block and pan mating surfaces (particularly to the corner junctions of the block, oil pan and cover).

26   Position the cover over the end of the crankshaft and onto the cylinder block. Start the cover and pan retaining screws by hand.

27   Slide an alignment tool over the end of the crankshaft to make sure the cover is located correctly before tightening the retaining bolts.

If no alignment tool is available, temporarily install the crankshaft vibration damper to serve as a guide.

28   Tighten the retaining bolts for the cover first and then the oil pan to the torque values listed in this Chapter's Specifications. Remove the alignment tool if used.

29   Lubricate the nose of the crankshaft, the inner hub of the vibration damper and the seal surface with engine oil.

30   Apply RTV sealant to the inside keyway of the damper hub.

31   Align the damper keyway with the key on the crankshaft and install the damper using a damper installation tool **(see illustration)**.

32   Install the bolt and washer retaining the damper and tighten it to the torque listed in this Chapter's Specifications. Install the pulley on the damper and tighten the bolts to the torque listed in this Chapter's Specifications.

33   The remainder of installation is reverse of removal.

34   Fill the engine with oil if the oil has been drained (see Chapter 1).

35   Start the engine and allow it to reach normal operating temperature. Check for leaks of any type. Check the ignition timing (see Chapter 5).

9   Lifters and camshaft - removal and installation

Refer to illustrations 9.3a, 9.3b, 9.9, 9.10 and 9.15

Removal

Lifters

1   Remove the valve cover and pushrod cover (see Section 6).

2   Remove the applicable rocker arm(s) and pushrod(s) for the lifter(s) to be removed (see Section 7). If the camshaft is to be removed, remove all of the lifters.

3   Remove the valve lifter(s) with a retrieval

9.3a The lifters in an engine that has accumulated many miles may have to be removed with a special tool

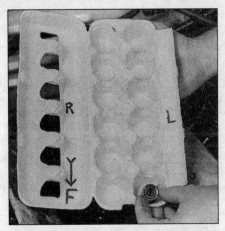

9.3b Keep the lifters in order or mark them if they are to be re-installed so they can be installed in their original positions - an old egg carton works well

9.9 Proper alignment of the camshaft and crankshaft gear timing marks

tool **(see illustration)**. Keep them in order or mark them, if they are to be re-installed, so they can be replaced in their original positions **(see illustration)**.

4   Inspect the lifters as described in Chapter 2, Part D). If no further disassembly is required, proceed to Step 21.

Camshaft

5   Position the engine at TDC compression for the number one cylinder (see Section 3) and remove the distributor (see Chapter 5).

6   Remove the valve lifters as described in this Section.

7   Remove the timing cover (see Section 8).

8   Prior to removing camshaft, check camshaft endplay and timing gears for wear (see Chapter 2, Part D). If measurements indicate worn components, replace as required during reassembly.

9   Check the timing marks - they should be directly adjacent to each other **(see illustration)**. If not, turn the crankshaft until they are.

10   Remove the camshaft thrust plate retaining bolts **(see illustration)**.

11   Pull the camshaft from the engine block, being careful that the lobes do not catch on the camshaft bearings (they can scrape and damage them easily). **Caution:** *Do not rotate the engine until re-installation is complete.*

12   Inspect the camshaft and bearings as described in Chapter 2, Part D. If your measurements indicate worn components, replace parts as required during reassembly.

13   If required for gear or camshaft replacement, remove the gear from the camshaft (see Section 8).

Installation
Camshaft

14   If removed, install the camshaft gear onto the camshaft (see Section 8). If a new timing gear is installed, replacement of the corresponding crankshaft timing gear is also recommended (see Section 9). **Note:** *If camshaft endplay was excessive during wear checks, install an appropriately sized thrust plate prior to gear installation.*

15   Apply camshaft installation lubricant to

all of the camshaft lobes and journals **(see illustration)**.

16   Install the camshaft into the engine making sure the mark on the camshaft gear is aligned with the mark on the crankshaft gear **(see illustration 9.9)**. Be careful not to nick or damage the camshaft bearings. Install the thrust plate bolts.

17   Tighten the camshaft thrust plate bolts to the torque listed in this Chapter's Specifications.

18   The remainder of installation is reverse of removal.

19   Start the engine and check for leaks.

20   Adjust the ignition timing as described in Chapter 5.

Lifters

21   Lubricate the bottom of the lifters with engine assembly lube and install them. If the original lifters are to be used, install them in their original bores.

22   The remainder of installation is reverse of removal.

---

10   Manifolds - removal and installation

Refer to illustrations 10.18a and 10.18b.

Warning: *Gasoline is extremely flammable, so take extra precautions when you work on any part of the fuel system. Don't smoke or allow open flames or bare light bulbs near the work area, and don't work in a garage where a gas-type appliance (such as a water heater or clothes dryer) is present. Since gasoline is carcinogenic, wear latex gloves when there's a possibility of being exposed to fuel, and, if you spill any fuel on your skin, rinse it off immediately with soap and water. Mop up any spills immediately and do not store fuel-soaked rags where they could ignite. The fuel system on fuel-injected models is under constant pressure, so if any fuel lines are to be disconnected, the fuel pressure in the system must be relieved first (see Chapter 4 for more infor-*

9.10   The camshaft thrust plate retaining bolts are accessible through the two openings in the camshaft gear

9.15   Be sure to apply moly-based grease or camshaft installation lube to the cam lobes and bearing journals before installing the camshaft

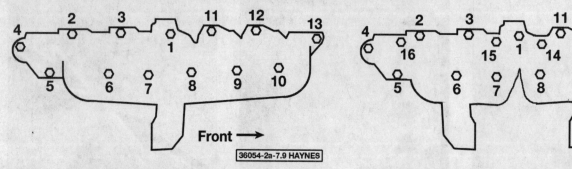

10.18a Intake and exhaust manifold bolt tightening sequence (early models)

10.18b Intake and exhaust manifold bolt tightening sequence (later models)

mation). When you perform any kind of work on the fuel system, wear safety glasses and have a Class B type fire extinguisher on hand.

Removal
Carbureted models

1   Remove the air cleaner and related air cleaner attachments.
2   Disconnect the choke cable at the carburetor.
3   Disconnect the accelerator cable or linkage at the carburetor. Remove the accelerator return spring.
4   Remove the kick-down rod return spring and the kick-down rod from its linkage at the carburetor.
5   Disconnect the fuel inlet line from the carburetor.
6   Disconnect all vacuum lines from the carburetor.
7   Disconnect the power brake booster vacuum line from the intake manifold.

Fuel-injected models

8   Remove the upper intake manifold and throttle body (see Chapter 4).
9   Remove the lines from the fuel rail (see Chapter 4).
10   Remove the fuel rail and injectors from the lower intake manifold (see Chapter 4).
11   Label and disconnect the lower intake manifold vacuum hoses, thermactor bypass valve and tube assembly, and any other electrical connectors that may be present.

All models

12   Disconnect the exhaust pipe from the exhaust manifold and support it out of the way.
13   Remove the bolts (and nuts if equipped) retaining the intake and exhaust manifolds to the cylinder head. Lift the manifold assemblies away from the engine.
14   Clean all traces of old gasket material from the mating surfaces of the manifolds and cylinder head. If new manifolds are to be installed, remove the nuts connecting the intake manifold to the exhaust manifold.

Installation

15   Install new studs in the exhaust manifold for the inlet pipe. **Note:** This step is not absolutely necessary if the studs are in good con-

dition, however, it is recommended in order to prevent future problems.
16   If the intake and the exhaust manifolds have been separated, coat the mating surfaces with graphite grease. Place the exhaust manifold over the studs on the intake manifold. Connect the two with the lock washers and nuts. Tighten the nuts finger tight.
17   Install a new intake manifold-to-head gasket.
18   Coat the mating surfaces lightly with graphite grease. Place the manifold assemblies against the mating surface of the cylinder head, making sure that the gaskets are positioned correctly. Install the attaching washers, bolts and nuts finger tight and make sure everything is positioned and aligned correctly. Tighten the nuts and bolts to the torque values listed in this Chapter's Specifications in the order shown **(see illustrations)**. Tighten the exhaust-to-intake manifold nuts to the torque values listed in this Chapter's Specifications (if they were removed).
19   Attach a new gasket to the exhaust pipe and fasten the pipe to the exhaust manifold. Tighten the nuts securely.
20   The remainder of installation is reverse of removal.

11   Cylinder head - removal and installation

Refer to illustration 11.19

Removal

1   Disconnect the negative cable from the battery.
2   Drain the cooling system (see Chapter 3).
3   Disconnect the upper radiator hose from the thermostat outlet (see Chapter 3).
4   Remove the heater hose at the coolant outlet elbow (see Chapter 3).
5   Mark the wires leading to the coil and disconnect them. Remove the coil bracket attaching bolt. Secure the coil and bracket out of the way (see Chapter 5).
6   Remove any power accessory brackets attached to the cylinder head. **Note:** It is not necessary to disconnect refrigerant hoses or power steering hoses.
7   Remove the manifolds (see Section 10).
8   Remove the valve cover (see Section 6).

9   Loosen the rocker arm bolts or stud nuts so the rocker arms can be rotated to one side.
10   Remove the pushrods (see Section 7). A numbered box or rack will keep them properly organized.
11   Disconnect the spark plug wires at the spark plugs (see Chapter 1) and any sensor electrical connectors that would interfere with removal.
12   Remove the cylinder head retaining bolts, in sequence, using the reverse order of the tightening sequence. If you have an engine hoist or similar device handy, attach eyelet bolts at the two ends of the cylinder head in the holes provided and lift the cylinder head off of the engine block. If equipment of this nature is not available, use a helper and pry the cylinder head up off of the engine block. **Caution:** Do not wedge any tools between the cylinder head and block gasket mating surfaces - pry only on casting protrusions.
13   Secure the head on a workbench or cylinder head holding device.
14   Inspect the cylinder head as outlined in Chapter 2, Part D. **Note:** New and rebuilt cylinder heads are commonly available for engines at dealer parts departments and auto parts stores. Due to the fact that some specialized tools are necessary for the dismantling and inspection of the head, and replacement parts may not be readily available, it may be more practical and economical for the home mechanic to purchase a replacement head and install it. Another alternative, at this point, is to take the cylinder head to an automotive machine shop or shop specializing in cylinder heads and exchange it or leave your head for the overhaul process.
15   Replace or service the cylinder head as required (see Chapter 2D).

Installation

16   Make sure the cylinder head and cylinder block mating surfaces are clean, flat and prepared for the new cylinder head gasket (see Chapter 2 Part D for the inspection procedures). Clean the exhaust manifold and exhaust pipe gasket surfaces.
17   Position the gasket over the dowel pins on the cylinder block, making sure that it is facing the right direction and that the correct surface is exposed. Gaskets are often marked 'front' and 'this side up' to aid in installation.

18   Using the previously installed lifting hooks (or two people) carefully lower the cylinder head into place on the block. Take care not to move the head sideways or to scrape it across the surface as it can dislodge the gasket and/or damage the mating surfaces.

19   Coat the cylinder head retaining bolts with a light coat of engine oil and thread the bolts into the block. Tighten the bolts using the tightening sequence shown in the accompanying illustration **(see illustration)**. Work up to the final torque in three steps to avoid warping the head.

20   The remaining steps are the reverse of the removal procedure.

21   Refill radiator with coolant (see Chapter 3).

22   Start the engine and allow it to reach operating temperature. Check for leaks. **Note:** *Some gasket manufacturers recommend retightening the cylinder head bolts after the engine has cooled down. Check the instructions furnished with the gasket kit to determine if this is necessary.*

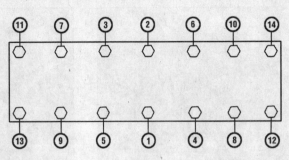

11.19 Cylinder head bolt TIGHTENING sequence

 Front

36094-2A-11.19 HAYNES

12   Oil pan - removal and installation

Note: *This procedure is for removal and installation of the oil pan with the engine in the vehicle only. If the engine has been removed for an overhaul, use only Step 10 and Steps 14 through 26.*

Removal

1   Disconnect the negative battery cable from the battery (see Chapter 1).

2   Drain the cooling system (see Chapter 3) and engine oil (see Chapter 1).

3   Remove the radiator (see Chapter 3). **Note:** *This operation is required so that the radiator is not damaged by the engine when it is raised form its mounts.*

4   Raise the vehicle and support it securely on jackstands. Disconnect the starter cable at the starter (see Chapter 5).

5   Remove the starter (see Chapter 5).

6   Remove the engine front insulator-to-support bracket retaining nuts and washers (see Section 16).

7   Raise the front of the engine with a jack. Place a thick wooden block between the jack and the oil pan to serve as a cushion.

8   Place one inch wood blocks between the front support insulators and the support brackets.

9   Lower the engine onto the spacer blocks and remove the jack.

10   Remove the oil pan attaching bolts.

11   Lower the pan to the crossmember.

12   Remove the two oil pump pick-up tube-to-oil pump retaining bolts and washers.

13   Remove the oil pump pick-up tube and allow it to rest in the oil pan.

14   Remove the oil pan from the vehicle. It may be necessary to rotate the crankshaft so the counterweights clear the pan.

15   Clean all gaskets from the mating surfaces of the engine block and the pan.

16   Remove the rear main bearing cap-to-oil pan seal.

17   Remove the timing cover-to-oil pan seal.

Installation

18   Clean all mating surfaces and seal grooves.

19   Install new oil pan-to-front cover oil seals (early models).

20   Install a new rear main bearing cap-to-oil pan seal (early models).

21   Install new oil pan side gaskets (early models) on the block. Later models use a one-piece gasket. Apply a thin, even coat of RTV sealant to both sides of the gaskets.

22   Make sure the tabs of the front and rear seal fit properly into the mating slots on the oil pan side seals (early models). A small amount of RTV sealant at each mating junction will help prevent any leaks from these critical spots.

23   Clean the pick-up tube and screen assembly and place it in the oil pan.

24   Position the oil pan underneath the engine.

25   Lift the pick-up tube and screen assembly from the oil pan and secure it to the oil pump with a new gasket. Tighten the two retaining bolts to the torque listed in this Chapter's Specifications.

26   Attach the oil pan to the engine block and install the retaining bolts. Tighten the bolts to the torque listed in this Chapter's Specifications, starting from the center and working out in each direction.

27   Raise the engine with a jack and a block of wood underneath the oil pan and remove the wood spacers previously installed under the support brackets.

28   Lower the engine to the correct installed position and install the washers and nuts on the insulator studs. Tighten the nuts to the torque listed in this Chapter's Specifications.

29   Install the starter (see Chapter 5).

30   Lower the vehicle.

31   Install the radiator (see Chapter 3).

32   Fill the cooling system with coolant (see Chapter 1) and check for leaks.

33   Fill the engine crankcase with oil (see Chapter 1) and hook up the negative battery cable.

34   Start the engine and check carefully for leaks at the oil pan gasket sealing surfaces.

13   Oil pump - removal and installation

1   Remove the oil pan as described in Section 12.

2   Remove the bolts retaining the oil pump to the block.

3   Remove the oil pump assembly.

4   Clean the mating surfaces of the oil pump and the block.

5   Inspect the oil pump as described in Chapter 2, Part D.

6   Before installation, prime the pump by filling the inlet opening with oil and rotating the pump shaft until the oil spurts out of the outlet.

7   Attach the oil pump to the engine block using the two retaining bolts.

8   Tighten the bolts to the torque listed in this Chapter's Specifications.

9   Install the oil pan (see Section 12).

14   Crankshaft oil seals - replacement

Refer to illustrations 14.6 and 14.8

Crankshaft front oil seal

Note: *The following operation requires a special tool for proper seal installation.*

1   Drain the cooling system (see Chapter 3).

2   Remove the fan shroud and the radiator (see Chapter 3).

3   Remove the fan and pulley (see Chapter 3).

4   Remove the large bolt and washer from the crankshaft nose. It may be necessary to prevent the crankshaft from rotating by putting the transmission in gear (if the engine is still in the vehicle) or by holding the flywheel or crankshaft flange with a suitable tool (if the engine is out of the vehicle).

5   Remove the vibration damper **(see illustration 8.7)**.

6   Using a seal remover tool (available at most auto parts stores), remove the seal from

14.6 Using a seal removal tool, remove the seal from the timing cover

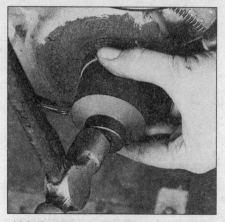

14.8 If you're very careful, you can use a large socket to drive the new seal into the timing cover

the timing cover (see illustration).

7   Clean out the recess in the cover.

8   Coat the outer edge of the new seal with engine oil and install it using a seal driver (available at most auto parts stores). As an alternative, a large socket or piece of pipe can be used to push the new seal in (see illustration). However, use extreme caution as the seal can be damaged easily with this method. Drive in the seal until it is fully seated in the recess. Make sure the spring is properly positioned within the seal.

9   Lubricate the nose of the crankshaft, the inner hub of the vibration damper and the seal surface with engine oil.

10   Apply RTV sealant to the inside keyway of the damper hub.

11   Align the damper keyway with the key on the crankshaft and install the damper using an installation tool (available at most auto parts stores).

12   Install the bolt and washer retaining the damper and tighten it to the torque listed in this Chapter's Specifications.

13   The remainder of installation is the reverse of removal.

14   Fill the engine with oil, if the oil has been drained (see Chapter 1).

15   Start and operate the engine at a fast idle and check for leaks of any type.

Rear main oil seal

16   Disconnect the negative battery cable from the battery, then remove the starter (see Chapter 5).

17   Remove the transmission (Chapter 7).

18   On manual transmission equipped vehicles, remove the clutch assembly (see Chapter 8). On automatic transmission equipped vehicles, remove the driveplate (see Chapter 7, Part A).

19   Remove the flywheel attaching bolts and remove the flywheel and engine rear cover plate (see Section 15).

20   Use an awl to punch two holes in the oil seal. Punch the holes on opposite sides of the crankshaft, just above the bearing cap-to-engine block junction.

21   Thread a sheet metal screw into each punched hole.

22   Use two large screwdrivers or small prybars and pry against both screws at the same time to remove the seal. A block or blocks of wood placed against the engine will provide additional leverage. **Caution:** *Be very careful when performing this operation that you do not damage the oil seal contact surfaces on the crankshaft.*

23   Clean the oil recess in the rear of the engine block and the main bearing cap surface of the crankshaft.

24   Inspect, clean and, using crocus cloth, polish the oil seal contact surfaces of the crankshaft. If the area in which the seal rides is grooved or otherwise damaged, the new seal will leak.

25   Coat the outer diameter of the new seal with a light film of engine oil.

26   Coat the crankshaft surface with a light film of engine oil.

27   Start the seal into the cavity in the back of the engine with the seal lip facing the engine and install it with a special seal driver tool. Make sure that the tool stays in alignment with the crankshaft until the tool contacts the block.

28   Make sure the seal has been installed correctly after removing the tool.

29   The remainder of installation is the reverse of removal. If the engine oil was drained, refill the crankcase (see Chapter 1). Start the engine and check for leaks.

15   Flywheel/driveplate - removal, inspection and installation

1   Remove the transmission (see Chapter 7) and, on models with a manual transmission, remove the clutch housing (see Chapter 8).

2   Mark the relationship of the flywheel/driveplate to the crankshaft to ensure installation in the same position.

3   To keep the crankshaft from turning, wedge a large screwdriver or prybar between the ring gear teeth and the engine block (it must be positioned so that as the crankshaft moves, the tool bears against the block). Make sure that the tool is not pushing against the oil pan.

4   Remove the flywheel/driveplate retaining bolts from the crankshaft flange. **Warning:** *The flywheel is heavy. Leave one bolt in place until you are ready to detach the flywheel from the crankshaft.*

5   Remove the flywheel/driveplate from the crankshaft by it pulling straight back. If it's stuck, wiggle it from side-to-side.

6   Inspect the flywheel surface for scoring, heat marks, cracks and warpage (see Chapter 8). If any of these conditions exist, the flywheel should be taken to an automotive machine shop to be resurfaced (or replaced with a new one). If the flywheel is cracked, it must be replaced with a new one.

7   Installation is the reverse of removal. The retaining bolts should be coated with a thread-locking compound and tightened in a criss-cross pattern to the torque listed in this Chapter's Specifications.

16   Engine mounts - check and replacement

1   Engine mounts seldom require attention, but broken or deteriorated mounts should be replaced immediately or the added strain placed on the driveline components may cause damage.

Check

2   During the check, the engine must be raised slightly to remove the weight from the mounts.

3   Raise the vehicle and support it securely on jackstands, then position the jack under the engine oil pan. Place a large block of wood between the jack head and the oil pan, then carefully raise the engine just enough to take the weight off the mounts.

4   Check the mounts to see if the rubber is cracked, hardened or separated from the metal plates. Sometimes the rubber will split right down the center.

5   Check for relative movement between the mount plates and the engine, transmission or frame/body (use a large screwdriver or prybar to attempt to move the mounts). If excess movement is noted, new mount isolators will be required.

Replacement (front mounts)

6   Raise the vehicle and place it securely on jackstands.

7   Place a wood block and a jack under the engine.

8   Remove the upper and lower nut and washer assemblies from the insulator assembly.

9   Raise the engine just enough to allow clearance for the removal of the mount insulator and heat shield if equipped. **Warning:** *DO NOT place any part of your body under the engine when it's supported only by a jack.*

10   Installation is reverse of removal.

Replacement (rear mount)

11   For the rear (transmission) mount replacement procedure, see Chapter 7.

Chapter 2 Part B
V8 engines

Contents

Specifications

Camshaft lobe lift

302 (5.0L), 351W (5.8L) and 5.8L Lightning engines

Intake
302	0.2375 inch
351W (carbureted)	0.2600 inch
351W (fuel injected)	
1996 and earlier	0.2780 inch
1997	0.2637 inch
5.8L Lightning	0.2600 inch

Exhaust
302 1980 and 1981	0.2470 inch
1982 on	0.2474 inch
351W (carbureted)	0.2600 inch
351W (fuel injected)	
1996 and earlier	0.2830 inch
1997	0.2801 inch
5.8L Lightning	0.2780 inch
Maximum allowable lift loss	0.0050 inch

460 (7.5L) engine
Intake	0.2520 inch
Exhaust	0.2780 inch
Maximum allowable lift loss	0.0050 inch

Torque specifications
Ft-lb (unless otherwise indicated)

Note: *One foot pound (ft-lb) of torque is equivalent to 12 inch-pounds (in-lbs) of torque. Torque values below approximately 15 ft-lbs are expressed in inch-pounds, since most foot pound torque wrenches are not accurate at these smaller values.*

Camshaft sprocket bolt	40 to 45
Camshaft thrust plate screws	108 to 144 in-lbs
Timing cover bolts	15 to 21
Cylinder head bolts	
5.0L engine with flanged head bolts	
1st step	25 to 35
2nd step	45 to 55
3rd step	Turn an additional 85 to 95-degrees rotation
255 cu. in. and 5.0L engine with hex head bolts	
1st step	55 to 65
2nd step	65 to 72
351W (5.8L) engine	
1st step	95 to 105
2nd step	105 to 112
351M and 400 engines	
1st step	75
2nd step	95 to 105
7.5L engine	
1st step	70 to 80
2nd step	100 to 110
3rd step	130 to 140

Torque specifications (continued)

Ft-lb (unless otherwise indicated)

Note: *One foot-pound (ft-lb) of torque is equivalent to 12 inch-pounds (in-lbs) of torque. Torque values below approximately 15 ft-lbs are expressed in inch-pounds, since most foot-pound torque wrenches are not accurate at these smaller values.*

Crankshaft vibration damper bolt	70 to 90
Flywheel/driveplate bolts	75 to 85
Intake manifold bolts	
Small block engines	
Lower intake manifold	
3/8-inch bolts	22 to 30
5/16-inch bolts	19 to 25
Upper intake manifold	12 to 18
Big block (7.5L) engine	
Lower intake manifold	
Step 1	96 to 132 in-lbs
Step 2	12 to 22
Step 3	22 to 35
Upper intake manifold	12 to 18
Exhaust manifold bolts	
Small block engines	
1995 and earlier	18 to 24
1996 and later	26 to 32
Big block (7.5L) engine	24 to 30
Oil pick-up tube-to-oil pump bolts	12 to 18
Oil pick-up tube-to-main bearing cap bolt	22 to 32
Oil pump-to-block bolt	22 to 32
Oil pan bolts	
1/4-inch bolts	84 to 108 in-lbs
5/16-inch bolts	108 to 132 in-lbs
Crankshaft pulley-to-damper bolts	35 to 50
Rocker arm bolts	18 to 25
Valve cover bolts	
Small block engines	132 to 168 in-lbs
Big block (7.5L) engine	
1993 and earlier	72 to 108 in-lbs
1994 and later	108 to 132 in-lbs

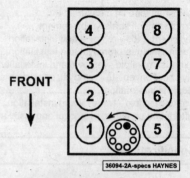

36094-2A-specs HAYNES

**Cylinder locations and distributor
rotation - V8 engines**

*The blackened terminal on the distributor cap
indicates the number one spark plug
wire position*

1   General information

Several V8s of various displacements are covered by this manual. All are gasoline fueled with overhead valves actuated by hydraulic lifters and have crankshafts supported by five main bearings.

'Family' engine groupings include the 255 cubic inch and 302 cubic inch (5.0L) models, the 351W cubic inch (5.8L) and 5.8L Lightning, the 351M and 400 cubic inch models, and the 460 cubic inch (7.5L) model.

All of these engines are three-point mounted, with two side mounts at the front and one crossmember mount underneath the transmission. The engines can be removed from the vehicle with a normal amount of preparatory work when overhaul or other major operations are necessary.

2   Repair operations possible with the engine in the vehicle

Many major repair operations can be accomplished without removing the engine from the vehicle. Clean the engine compartment and the exterior of the engine with some type of pressure washer before any work is done. A clean engine will make the job easier and will help keep dirt out of the internal areas of the engine.

Depending on the components involved, it may be a good idea to remove the hood to improve access to the engine as repairs are performed (see Chapter 11, if necessary).

If vacuum, exhaust, oil or coolant leaks develop, indicating a need for gasket or seal replacement, the repairs can generally be made with the engine in the vehicle. The intake and exhaust manifold gaskets, oil pan gasket and cylinder head gasket are all accessible with the engine in place.

Exterior engine components as well as some internal components can be checked and serviced with the engine in the vehicle. Refer to this Chapter's Table of Contents for these operations and components. In addition, the water pump (see Chapter 3), the starter motor, the alternator, the distributor (see Chapter 5) and the fuel injection system (see Chapter 4) can be removed for repair with the engine in place.

Some component checks such as camshaft lobe lift measurement, timing chain wear, and piston ring/cylinder head condition (compression check) can also be performed while the engine is installed.

Since the cylinder head can be removed without pulling the engine, valve component servicing can also be accomplished with the engine in the vehicle.

In extreme cases caused by a lack of necessary equipment, repair or replacement of piston rings, pistons, connecting rods and rod bearings is possible with the engine in the vehicle. However, this practice is not recommended because of the cleaning and preparation work that must be done to the components involved.

3   Top Dead Center (TDC) for number 1 piston - locating

Refer to illustration 3.1

Follow the procedure described in Chapter 2, Part A, but use the timing marks as shown in the accompanying illustration **(see illustration)**.

4   Camshaft lobe lift measurement

Follow the procedure described in Chapter 2, Part A, but note that it will be necessary to remove both valve covers as described in Section 7 of this Chapter and use the specifications listed at the front of this Chapter.

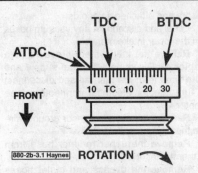

3.1 Details of the timing marks and stationary pointer

5 Valve springs, retainers and seals - replacement

Procedure is described in Chapter 2, Part A. **Note:** *On the 7.5L engine, intake and exhaust valve seals are different and are not interchangeable. Intake seals are identified by the marking IN and exhaust seals by the marking EX.*

6 Timing chain wear - quick check

1   Using a breaker bar and a socket on the crankshaft vibration damper bolt, rotate the crankshaft until the timing marks on the pulley indicate TDC (see Section 3).
2   Rotate the crankshaft counterclockwise about 30-degrees, then slowly and smoothly bring the crank back up to TDC. Do not pass the 0-degree mark. If TDC is passed, repeat steps 1 and 2.
3   Remove the distributor cap from the distributor (if not already done) (see Chapter 5). **Note:** *It is not necessary to remove the spark plug wires for this operation.*
4   While observing the distributor rotor for movement, slowly rotate the crankshaft counterclockwise again, stopping as soon as any rotor movement is noted.
5   Check the timing marks and record the number of degrees before TDC.
6   If the check indicates that over five

degrees of crankshaft movement is required before any rotor movement is noted, the timing chain is probably stretched and requires replacement.
7   Replace the timing chain and sprockets as required (see Section 12).

7 Valve covers - removal and installation

Refer to illustrations 7.9 and 7.11

Removal

1   Remove the air cleaner and intake duct assembly.
2   Remove the crankcase ventilation hoses and lines where applicable. Make sure that all lines and hoses have been removed from the valve covers and position them out of the way.
3   On the 5.8L Lightning engine only, remove the upper intake manifold assembly (see Chapter 4). **Note:** *Only perform this step if you're removing the right side valve cover.*
4   Disconnect the spark plug wires. Mark them so they can be installed in their original locations.
5   Remove the left or right side engine lifting eyes if necessary for clearance.
6   If necessary, remove the air injection valves and hoses and position them out of the way (see Chapter 6).
7   On some models it is necessary to remove the air conditioning compressor for clearance. If this is the case, refer to Chapter 3 and unbolt the air conditioning compressor and position it aside. **Warning:** *The air conditioning system is under pressure. Don't disconnect the hoses.*
8   Mark and detach any vacuum hoses, electrical connectors or wiring harnesses that would interfere with removal of the valve cover(s).
9   Remove the valve cover retaining bolts **(see illustration)**.
10   Remove the valve cover(s). If the cover sticks, knock it loose with a hammer and a block of wood. If it is still stuck, carefully pry the cover off, but be very careful not to distort the sealing surface of the cover.

11   Remove all old gasket material and sealant from the valve cover and cylinder head gasket surfaces **(see illustration)**.

Installation

12   Make sure the gasket surfaces of the valve covers are flat and smooth, particularly around the bolt holes. Use a hammer and a block of wood to flatten them out if they are deformed.
13   Attach a new valve cover gasket to the cover. Notice that there are tabs provided in the cover to retain the gasket. It may be necessary to apply RTV sealant to the corners of the cover to retain the gasket there.
14   Install the valve cover onto the cylinder head, making sure that the bolt holes are aligned correctly.
15   Install the valve cover retaining bolts finger tight.
16   Tighten the retaining bolts, a little at a time, to the torque listed in this Chapter's Specifications. **Caution:** *Do not overtighten the bolts or the valve covers will warp and the gaskets will be pushed out of position, resulting in leaks.*
17   The remainder of the installation procedure is the reverse of removal.
18   Start the engine and run it until it reaches normal operating temperature, then check for leaks.

8 Rocker arms and pushrods - removal and installation

Refer to illustration 8.4

Removal

1   Remove the valve covers as described in Section 7.
2   If you're removing the rocker arms, remove the rocker arm fulcrum bolts.
3   Remove the oil deflectors (if equipped), fulcrums, fulcrum guides (if equipped) and the rocker arms. Keep the rocker arms and fulcrums in order so that they may be installed in their original positions and orientation.
4   If only the pushrods are being removed,

7.9 The valve cover is held in place with several bolts (arrows)

7.11 Being careful not to damage the mating surface of the head, carefully remove the valve cover gasket with a gasket scraper or putty knife

loosen the fulcrum retaining bolts and rotate the rocker arms out of the way of the pushrods. Simply lift the pushrods from their holes in the cylinder head **(see illustration)**. Keep the pushrods in order so that they may be installed in their original positions and orientation **(see illustration 7.4 in Chapter 2, Part A)**.

5　Inspect the rocker arms and pushrods as described in Chapter 2, Part D.

Installation

6　Apply engine oil or assembly lube to the top of the valve stem and the pushrod guide in the cylinder head.

7　Apply engine oil to the rocker arm fulcrum seat and the fulcrum seat socket in the rocker arm.

8　Install the pushrods in the correct positions, with lubricant applied to both ends.

9　Install the fulcrum guides (if equipped), rocker arms, fulcrums, oil deflectors (if equipped) and fulcrum bolts.

10　Tighten the fulcrum bolts to the torque listed in this Chapter's Specifications.

11　If components were replaced, check the valve clearances (see Chapter 2, Part D). If necessary, install a longer or shorter pushrod.

12　Install the valve covers as described in Section 7.

13　Start the engine and check for oil leaks.

9　Intake manifold - removal and installation

Refer to illustrations 9.37, 9.38, 9.43a and 9.43b

Removal

Carbureted models

1　Drain the cooling system (see Chapter 1).

2　Remove the air cleaner and intake duct assemblies (see Chapter 4).

3　Carefully mark and detach any emissions control connections at the air cleaner.

4　Disconnect the upper radiator hose from the thermostat housing (see Chapter 3).

5　Disconnect the heater hose and the water pump by-pass hose at the intake mani-

fold connections (see Chapter 3).

6　If you're working on a 7.5L engine, remove the right valve cover (see Section 7).

7　Mark and disconnect the spark plug wires at the spark plugs. Remove the distributor cap together with the spark plug wires.

8　Disconnect the primary (low voltage) wires from the coil and mark them so they can be reinstalled correctly (see Chapter 5).

9　Remove the coil mounting bracket and mounting bolt (see Chapter 5).

10　Remove the carburetor fuel inlet line from the carburetor and position it out of the way. It may be necessary to disconnect the line or loosen it at the fuel pump in order to perform this operation if the line is constructed of steel (see Chapter 4).

11　Disconnect the vacuum advance hose(s) from the distributor and mark them for proper installation (see Chapter 5).

12　Remove the distributor (see Chapter 5).

13　Remove the wire(s) from any sensors mounted in the intake manifold and/or the upper thermostat housing.

14　Remove the accelerator cable or linkage connection at the carburetor (see Chapter 4).

15　Remove the kickdown cable at the carburetor if the vehicle is equipped with an automatic transmission (see Chapter 7).

16　Remove the pull cable and activating unit from the intake manifold if the vehicle is equipped with cruise control.

17　Remove the vacuum hose leading to the power brake booster from the intake manifold. Secure this hose to the firewall out of the way.

18　Remove the carburetor from the intake manifold if the carburetor is to be serviced separately (see Chapter 4).

19　Remove any wiring leading to components located on the intake manifold. Locate the wires where they won't be damaged.

20　Disconnect the crankcase vent hose leading from the manifold to the valve cover.

Fuel-injected models

21　Remove the upper intake manifold (see Chapter 4).

22　Drain the cooling system (see Chapter 3).

23　Remove the distributor (see Chapter 5).

24　Label and disconnect all electrical harness connectors from lower intake manifold

sensors and attached solenoids.

25　Label and disconnect any vacuum hoses from the lower intake manifold.

26　Relieve the fuel system pressure (see Chapter 4). Disconnect the fuel supply and return lines from the fuel rail and disconnect the fuel injector electrical connectors (see Chapter 4).

27　Remove the oxygen sensor ground wire from the intake manifold stud.

28　Remove the upper radiator hose from the thermostat housing.

29　Remove the bypass and outlet hoses from the intake manifold.

30　Remove the coil/solenoid bracket assembly and position it out of the way (see Chapter 5).

All engines

31　Remove the bolts retaining the intake manifold to the cylinder heads.

32　Attach the lifting hooks at opposite corners and lift the intake manifold from the engine using an engine hoist. If a hoist isn't available, have an assistant help you lift the manifold off. **Note:** *It may be necessary to pry the intake manifold away from the cylinder heads but be careful to avoid damaging the mating surfaces.*

33　Clean the mating surfaces of the intake manifold and cylinder heads. Take care not to get any material down into the intake ports.

34　Remove the end gaskets from the top of the engine block.

35　Remove the oil gallery splash pan from the engine (if so equipped).

Installation

36　If the manifold was disassembled, reassemble it by reversing the disassembly procedure. When installing the temperature sending unit, coat the threads with electrical conductive sealant and coat the thermostat gasket with a thin film of RTV sealant.

37　Apply a 1/8 inch diameter bead of RTV sealant to the mating points at the junctions of the cylinder heads and engine block **(see illustration)**.

38　Position the new manifold end seals (sometimes called *ridge* seals) carefully on the engine block **(see illustration)**. If necessary, use a small amount of sealant to hold in place.

39　Position the intake manifold gaskets on the cylinder heads with the interlocking alignment tabs engaged correctly into the end seals. Be sure that all of the holes in the gasket are aligned with the corresponding holes in the cylinder heads. Some gaskets will be marked "FRONT" or "THIS SIDE UP." Gaskets manufactured by Ford may only have a small Ford emblem on them. If this is the case, install the gaskets with the emblem facing the cylinder head. Some models use a combination valley cover/gasket assembly.

40　Apply a 1/16-inch diameter bead of RTV sealant again to the interlocking corners of the intake manifold gasket and end seal.

41　If necessary, install locating pins into opposite corners to aid in manifold installation).

8.4　Loosen the nut or bolt (arrow) and pivot the rocker arm to the side to remove the pushrod

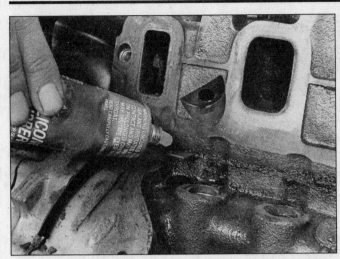

9.37 Apply RTV sealant to the areas where the cylinder heads meet the ridges at the front and rear of the block

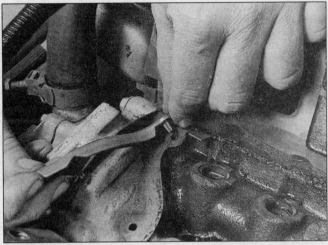

9.38 Install the end seals, pushing the locating pins into the corresponding holes, then apply a dab of RTV sealant to the ends where they meet the heads

42   Lower the intake manifold into position using either a lift or an assistant, being careful not to disturb the gaskets. After the manifold is in place, run a finger around the seal area to make sure that the seals are in place. If the seals are not in place, remove the manifold and reposition the seals.

43   Install the intake manifold retaining bolts. Tighten the bolts in the sequence shown **(see illustrations)** in three steps, to the torque listed in this Chapter's Specifications.

44   Install the remaining components in the reverse order of removal.

45   Refill the cooling system (see Chapter 1).

46   Start and run the engine and allow it to reach operating temperature. After it has reached operating temperature, check carefully for leaks.

47   Check the ignition timing and adjust it, if necessary (see Chapter 5).

10   Exhaust manifold - removal and installation

Refer to illustration 10.13

Removal
Carbureted models

1   If the right side exhaust manifold is being removed, remove the air cleaner, intake duct and heat duct.

2   If the left side exhaust manifold is being removed from a 351M or 400 engine, remove the engine oil filter. Remove the cruise control bracket (if so equipped), and, on all engines except the 460 (7.5L), remove the oil dipstick and tube assembly.

3   On vehicles equipped with a column selector and automatic transmission, disconnect the cross lever shaft for the automatic transmission selector to provide the clearance necessary to remove the manifold.

EFI models

4   If you're removing the right side manifold, remove the air cleaner and intake duct.

5   On the right side manifold, remove the upper intake manifold-to-exhaust manifold support bracket (5.0L and 5.8L engines only).

6   On the right side manifold, remove the engine and/or transmission dipstick tube bracket(s) as applicable.

7   Also on the right side manifold, remove the EGR tube (5.8L engine only).

8   On the left side manifold, remove the EGR tube (7.5L engine only).

9   On the left side manifold, remove the engine oil dipstick tube bracket if equipped.

10   On either manifold, remove the thermal reactor manifold, if equipped.

All models

11   Disconnect the retaining bolts holding the exhaust pipe(s) to the exhaust manifold(s) (see Chapter 4).

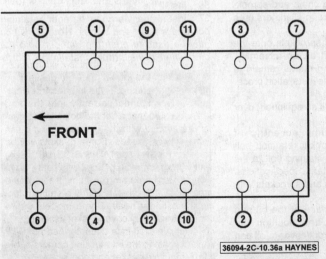

9.43a Intake manifold bolt tightening sequence - small block engines

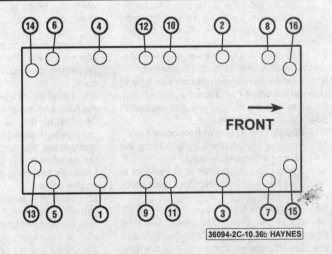

9.43b Intake manifold bolt tightening sequence - big block (7.5L) engine

12   Remove the spark plug wires and heat shields if so equipped.

13   Remove the exhaust manifold retaining bolts, lifting eyes and nuts **(see illustration)**. Note: *Keep track of parts location and bolt lengths so they may be reinstalled in their original positions.*

14   Remove the exhaust manifold.

15   Clean the mating surfaces of the exhaust manifold and the cylinder head.

16   Clean the mounting flange of the exhaust manifold and the exhaust pipe.

Installation

17   Apply graphite grease to the mating surface of the exhaust manifold and cylinder head (all except 5.8L Lightning engines).

18   On the 5.8L Lightning, install a new exhaust manifold gasket.

19   Position the exhaust manifold on the head and install the attaching bolts. Tighten the bolts to the torque listed in this Chapter's Specifications in three steps, working from the center to the ends.

20   If so equipped, install the spark plug heat shields and lifting eyes.

21   The remainder of installation is the reverse of removal.

22   Start the engine and check for exhaust leaks.

11   Timing cover and chain - removal and installation

Refer to illustrations 11.15 and 11.17

Removal

Carbureted models only

1   Remove and plug the fuel inlet line at the fuel pump.

2   Disconnect the fuel line at the carburetor. Remove the fuel feed line from the fuel pump.

3   Remove the fuel pump (see Chapter 4).

All models

4   Remove the radiator (see Chapter 3).

5   Remove the water pump (see Chapter 3).

6   Remove the bolts and washers retaining the crankshaft pulley to the vibration damper. Remove the crankshaft pulley.

7   Remove the large bolt and washer retaining the vibration damper to the crankshaft.

8   Remove the vibration damper with a puller **(see illustration 8.7** in Chapter 2, Part A).

9   Remove the damper key and crankshaft pulley spacer if equipped.

10   Remove the oil pan-to-front cover bolts.

11   Remove the retaining bolts holding the timing cover to the engine block.

12   Use a thin bladed knife or similar tool to cut the oil pan seal flush with the engine block mating surface.

13   Remove the timing cover.

14   Check the timing chain deflection (see Chapter 2, Part D). If the deflection exceeds the Specifications, the timing chain and sprockets will need replacement with new parts.

15   If the timing chain and sprockets are

10.13 Some models are equipped with manifold bolt locking tabs (arrows) - bend these down before removing the bolts (use new locking tabs on installation, bending the tabs up to lock the bolts in place

being removed, turn the engine until the timing marks are aligned **(see illustration)**.

16   Remove the camshaft sprocket retaining bolt, washer, fuel pump eccentric (two-piece on early 460 [7.5L] engines) if equipped and front oil slinger (if present) from the crankshaft.

17   Slide the timing chain and sprockets forward and off of the camshaft and crankshaft as an assembly **(see illustration)**. **Warning:** *Do not rotate the crankshaft or the camshaft while the timing chain is removed or damage to valvetrain or pistons may result.*

18   Remove the timing cover gasket and oil pan seal. Clean all residual gasket material from the cover, oil pan and block.

19   Remove the crankshaft front oil seal from the timing cover.

Installation

20   Coat the outside edge of the new crankshaft oil seal with engine oil and install the seal in the cover using an appropriate drive tool. Make sure the seal is seated completely in the bore.

21   Assemble the timing chain and sprockets so the timing marks are in alignment **(see illustration 11.15)**.

22   Install the chain and sprockets onto the camshaft and crankshaft as an assembly. Make sure that the timing marks remain in proper alignment during the installation procedure.

23   Install the oil slinger (if so equipped) over the nose of the crankshaft.

24   Install the fuel pump eccentric (if equipped), camshaft sprocket retaining bolt and washer. Tighten the retaining bolt to the torque listed in this Chapter's Specifications. Lubricate the timing chain and sprockets with engine oil.

25   Coat the gasket surface of the oil pan with RTV sealant. Cut and position the required sections of new front cover-to-oil pan seal on the oil pan.

26   Apply sealant at the corners of the mating surfaces.

27   Coat the gasket surfaces of the cover

11.15 Correct alignment of the crankshaft and the camshaft sprocket timing marks (arrows)

with sealant and install a new gasket. Coat the mating surface on the block with sealant.

28   Position the timing cover on the block. Use care when installing the cover to avoid damaging the front seal or dislocating any gaskets.

29   Install the cover alignment tool. If no alignment tool is available, you will have to use the harmonic balancer to position the seal. It may be necessary to force the cover down slightly to compress the oil pan seal. This can be done by inserting a punch through the bolt holes.

30   Coat the threads of the bolts with RTV sealant and install the bolts.

31   While holding the cover in alignment, tighten the cover bolts and then the oil pan-to-front cover retaining bolts to the torque values listed in this Chapter's Specifications.

32   Remove the alignment tool or punch.

33   Apply a thin coat of grease to the vibration damper seal contact surface.

34   Install the crankshaft spacer if equipped.

35   Install the Woodruff key onto the crankshaft and slide the vibration damper into position.

36   Install the damper.

37   Install the vibration damper retaining bolt and washer and torque. **Note:** *This bolt may be used to push the damper onto the crankshaft if the proper installation tool is*

11.17 Once the camshaft sprocket bolt has been removed, pull both sprockets and the chain from their shafts

12.4a On models with roller lifters, remove the bolts securing the lifter guide retainer . . .

12.4b . . . remove the lifter retainer . . .

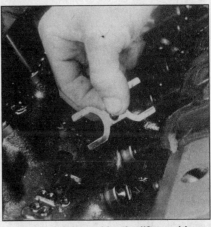

12.4c . . . followed by the lifter guides and lifters

not available.

38   Attach the crankshaft pulley to the damper and install the pulley retaining bolts.

39   The remainder of the installation procedure is the reverse of removal. Make sure that all bolts are tightened securely.

40   If any coolant entered the oil pan when separating the timing chain cover from the block, the crankcase oil should be drained and the oil filter removed. Install a new oil filter and refill the crankcase with the proper grade and amount of oil (see Chapter 1).

41   Start and run the engine at a fast idle and check for coolant and oil leaks.

42   Check the engine idle speed and ignition timing (see Chapter 5).

12   Lifters and camshaft - removal and installation

Refer to illustrations 12.4a, 12.4b, 12.4c, 12.6, 12.14 and 12.17

Removal

Lifters

1   Remove the intake manifold (see Section 9).

2   Remove the valve covers (see Section 7).

3   Loosen the rocker arm nuts and rotate the rocker arms to the side (see Section 8). Remove the pushrods (see Section 8).

4   If the engine is equipped with roller lifters, remove the lifter guide retainer and lifter guides (see illustrations). Mark the location of each lifter guide so they can be returned to their original locations.

5   Remove the valve lifters from the engine with a magnet if there is no varnish build up or wear on them. Keep the lifters in order so they can be returned to their original bores.

6   If the lifters are stuck in their bores, you will have to obtain a special tool designed for grasping lifters internally and work them out (see illustration).

7   Inspect the lifters as described in Chapter 2, Part D. If no further disassembly is required, proceed to Step 22.

Camshaft

8   Rotate engine to TDC compression for the number one cylinder (see Section 3) and remove the distributor (see Chapter 5).

9   Remove the valve lifters as described in this Section.

10   Remove the radiator and condenser (if equipped) (see Chapter 3).

11   Remove the timing cover (see Section 11).

12   Prior to removing camshaft, check camshaft endplay and timing chain for wear (see Chapter 2, Part D). If measurements indicate worn components, replace as required during reassembly.

13   Remove the timing chain and sprockets (see Section 11).

14   Remove the bolts securing the camshaft thrust plate to the engine block (see illustration).

15   Carefully withdraw the camshaft from the engine block, being careful that the lobes do not catch on the camshaft bearings (they can scrape and damage them easily). **Note:** *Do not rotate the engine until re-installation is complete.*

16   Perform camshaft and bearing inspections (see Chapter 2, Part D). If measurements indicate worn components, replace as required during reassembly.

12.6   The lifters in an engine that has accumulated many miles may have to be removed with a special tool - be sure to store the lifters in an organized manner to make sure they're reinstalled in their original locations

Installation

Camshaft

17   Lubricate the camshaft journals and lobes with camshaft installation lube (see illustration).

18   Slide the camshaft into position, being careful not to scrape or nick the bearings.

19   Install the camshaft thrust plate. Tighten the thrust plate bolts to the torque listed in

12.14   Some models use T-30 Torx screws to retain the camshaft thrust plate (arrows)

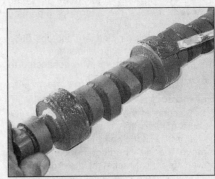

12.17   Be sure to apply camshaft installation lube or engine assembly lube to the lobes and journals prior to installation

this Chapter's Specifications. **Note:** *If camshaft endplay was excessive during wear checks, install an appropriately sized thrust plate prior to sprocket installation.*

20   Check the camshaft endplay (see Chapter 2, Part D).

21   If the endplay is excessive, check the spacer for correct installation before it is removed. If the spacer is installed correctly, replace the thrust plate. Notice that the thrust plate has a groove on it; it should face in on all engines.

Lifters

22   Lubricate the bottom of the lifters with engine assembly lube and install them into their original bores (if the same lifters are being installed).

23   The remainder of installation is the reverse of removal.

24   Start the engine and check for oil and fuel leaks.

25   Adjust the ignition timing as described in Chapter 5.

13   Cylinder heads - removal and installation

Refer to illustration 13.23

Caution: *The engine must be completely cool before beginning this operation.*

Removal

Carbureted models

1   Disconnect the cable from the negative terminal of the battery.

2   If the left cylinder head is being removed on a vehicle equipped with air conditioning, remove the compressor and support it securely to the side of the engine compartment. **Warning:** *The air conditioning system is under high pressure. Do not disconnect the hoses, as serious injury or damage to the system will result.*

3   If the left cylinder head is being removed and the vehicle is equipped with power steering, remove the power steering bracket retaining bolt from the left cylinder head. Position the power steering pump out of the way so it will not leak fluid.

4   If the right cylinder head is being removed, remove the alternator mounting bracket through-bolt.

5   Remove the air cleaner inlet tube (if so equipped) from the right cylinder head.

6   Remove the ground wire connected to the rear of the cylinder head.

EFI models

7   Disconnect the cable from the negative terminal of the battery.

8   If left cylinder head is being removed, remove the air conditioning compressor/power steering bracket at the front of the engine, complete with accessories. If necessary, remove compressor from bracket. **Warning:** *The air conditioning system is under high pressure. Do not disconnect the hoses, as serious injury or damage to the system will result.*

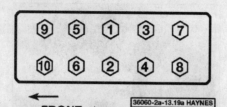

FRONT

`36060-2a-13.19a HAYNES`

13.23 Cylinder head bolt TIGHTENING sequence

9   If left cylinder head is being removed, remove oil dipstick and tube assembly and speed control bracket, if equipped.

10   If right cylinder head is being removed, disconnect the alternator wiring harness and air pump hoses. Remove alternator/air pump bracket at front of engine, complete with accessories.

All Models

11   Remove the intake manifold (see Section 9).

12   Remove the valve cover(s) (see Section 7).

13   Remove the rocker arms and pushrods (see Section 8).

14   Remove exhaust manifold(s) (see Section 10).

15   If equipped, disconnect thermactor air supply tubes from rear of head.

16   Loosen the cylinder head retaining bolts by reversing the order shown in the tightening sequence diagram **(see illustration 13.23)**, then remove the bolts from the heads. Keep them in order so they can be installed in their original locations.

17   Using a hoist (or an assistant), carefully remove the cylinder head from the block, using care to avoid damaging the gasket mating surfaces.

18   If necessary, inspect the cylinder head and components. Be sure to check the cylinder head and block deck for flatness (see Chapter 2, Part D).

Installation

19   Make sure the cylinder head and engine block mating surfaces are clean, flat and prepared properly for the new cylinder head gasket.

20   Position the head gasket over the dowel pins on the block. Make sure that the head gasket is facing the right direction and that the correct surface is exposed. Gaskets are sometimes marked 'front' and 'top' to help clarify their installation position.

21   Using a hoist (or an assistant), carefully lower the cylinder head(s) into place on the block in the correct position. Take care not to move the head sideways or scrape it across the block as it can dislodge the gasket and/or damage the gasket surfaces.

22   Coat the cylinder head retaining bolts with light engine oil and thread the bolts into the engine block through the head.

23   Tighten the bolts in the sequence shown **(see illustration)**, in two or three steps, to the

torque listed in this Chapter's Specifications.

24   The remainder of the installation procedure is the reverse of removal.

25   Start and run the engine and check it carefully for leaks and unusual noises.

26   Check and adjust the ignition timing (see Chapter 5).

14   Oil pan - removal and installation

Refer to illustration 14.24

Removal

7.5L models only

1   Remove the oil dipstick tube and bracket.

2   Disconnect the throttle body linkages, wiring and vacuum hoses to allow the engine to be raised (see Chapter 4).

3   Remove the fuel supply and return lines from fuel rail (see Chapter 4).

4   Remove the power steering pump and air conditioning compressor from bracket to allow the engine to be raised (see Chapter 3).

5   Remove the manual shift and kickdown linkage from automatic transmission to allow the engine to be raised (see Chapter 7).

6   Remove the driveshaft from the transmission to allow the engine to be raised (see Chapter 8).

All models

7   Disconnect the negative battery cable from the battery.

8   If you're working in a 5.0L or 5.8L engine with fuel-injection, remove the upper intake manifold (plenum) (see Chapter 4).

9   Drain the engine oil (see Chapter 1). Drain the cooling system (see Chapter 3).

10   Remove the radiator (as described in Chapter 3). **Note:** *This operation is required so that the radiator is not damaged by the engine when it is raised form its mounts.*

11   Raise the vehicle and support it securely on jack stands.

12   Remove the engine front insulator-to-support bracket retaining nuts and washers (see Section 19).

13   Disconnect the exhaust pipes from exhaust manifolds to allow the engine to be raised (see Chapter 4).

14   Place a thick wooden block between the jack and the oil pan and raise the front of the engine with a jack. **Caution:** *Verify that all cables, wiring and hoses between engine and vehicle have enough service slack to avoid damage.*

15   On all engines except 7.5L, raise engine only far enough to facilitate pan removal.

16   On 7.5L engine, raise engine until the transmission bellhousing contacts the floor pan (minimum of four inches).

17   Place wood blocks between the front support insulators and the support brackets to maintain the engine in the raised position.

18   Lower the engine onto the spacer blocks and remove the jack.

19   Remove the oil pan attaching bolts.

14.24 Scrape away all traces of gasket material and sealant, then clean the gasket surfaces with lacquer thinner or acetone

15.2a Remove the nut from the brace . . .

15.2b . . . and the two bolts from the oil pick-up tube

20   Lower the pan to the crossmember.
21   On 5.0 and 5.8L engines, remove the two oil pump inlet tube-to-oil pump retaining bolts and washers and inlet tube support brace fastener (see Section 16). Let inlet tube drop into pan.
22   On 7.5L engine, remove entire pump from block (see Section 16). Let pump and pickup drop into pan.
23   Remove the oil pan from the vehicle. It may be necessary to rotate the crankshaft so the counterweights clear the pan.
24   Clean all gasket material from the mating surfaces of the engine block and the pan **(see illustration)**.

Installation

25   Apply a thin, even coat of RTV sealant to both sides of the gasket(s). A small amount of RTV sealant at each mating junction will help prevent any leaks from these critical spots. Install the gaskets and seals on the pan. **Note:** *Later models use one-piece gaskets.*
26   On 5.0 and 5.8L engines, clean the oil pump pick-up tube and screen assembly and place it in the oil pan.
27   On the 7.5L engine, clean the inlet tube screen and prime the oil pump (see Section 15). Place the primed pump and pick-up tube in oil pan.
28   Position the oil pan underneath the engine.
29   On 5.0 and 5.8L engines, lift the inlet tube and screen assembly from the oil pan and secure it to the oil pump with a new gasket. Tighten the two retaining bolts to the proper torque.
30   On the 7.5L engine, install the pump and pickup tube to the block (see Section 15).
31   Attach the oil pan to the engine block and install the retaining bolts. Tighten the bolts to the torque listed in this Chapter's Specifications, starting from the center and working out in each direction.
32   Raise the engine with a jack and a block of wood underneath the oil pan and remove the wood spacers previously installed under the support brackets.

33   Lower the engine to the correct installed position and connect the engine mounts (see Section 18).
34   The remainder of installation is the reverse of removal.
35   Fill the cooling system with coolant and check for leaks.
36   Fill the engine with oil (see Chapter 1) and connect the negative battery cable.
37   Start the engine and check carefully for leaks at the oil pan gasket sealing surfaces.

15   Oil pump - removal and installation

Refer to illustrations 15.2a and 15.2b

1   Remove the oil pan as described in Section 14.
2   Remove the bolts retaining the oil pump and support brace to the block **(see illustrations)**.
3   Remove the oil pump and pick-up tube assembly.
4   Clean the mating surfaces of the oil pump and the block.
5   Inspect the oil pump as described in Chapter 2, Part D.
6   Before installation, prime the pump by filling the inlet opening with oil and rotating the pump shaft until the oil spurts out of the outlet.

7   Attach the oil pump to the engine block using the two retaining bolts.
8   Tighten the bolts to the torque listed in this Chapter's Specifications.
9   Install the oil pan (see Section 15).

16   Crankshaft oil seals - replacement

Refer to illustrations 16.7 and 16.9

Front oil seal

1   Drain the cooling system (see Chapter 1).
2   Remove the fan shroud and the radiator (see Chapter 3).
3   Remove the fan and pulley (see Chapter 3).
4   On 7.5L engines, remove remaining drivebelt.
5   Remove the large bolt and washer from the crankshaft nose. It may be necessary to prevent the crankshaft from rotating by putting the transmission in gear (if the engine is still in the vehicle) or by holding the flywheel or crankshaft flange with a suitable tool (if the engine is out of the vehicle).
6   Remove the vibration damper using a suitable puller **(see illustration 8.7** in Chapter 2, Part A).
7   Remove the seal from the timing cover by carefully tapping it out with a chisel and hammer **(see illustration)**.

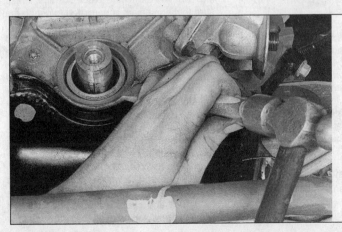

16.7 A chisel and hammer must be used to work the seal out of the timing chain cover - be very careful not to damage the cover or nick the crankshaft!

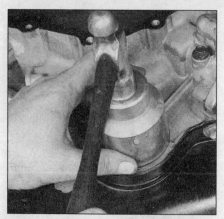

16.9 Clean the bore, then apply a small amount of oil to the outer edge of the new seal and drive it squarely into the opening with a large socket and a hammer - don't damage the seal in the process and make sure it's completely seated

16.23 Correct installation of the crankshaft rear oil seal for the two-piece seal

8   Clean out the recess in the cover.
9   Coat the outer edge of the new seal with motor oil and install it using a seal driver. As an alternative, a large socket or piece of pipe can be used to push the new seal in **(see illustration)**. However, use extreme caution as the seal can be damaged easily with this method. Drive in the seal until it is fully seated in the recess. Make sure that the spring is properly positioned within the seal.
10   Lubricate the nose of the crankshaft, the inner hub of the vibration damper and the seal surface with engine oil.
11   Apply RTV sealant to the inside keyway of the damper hub.
12   Align the damper keyway with the key on the crankshaft and install the damper using an installation tool **(see illustration 8.31 in Chapter 2A)**.
13   Install the bolt and washer retaining the damper and tighten it to the torque listed in this Chapter's Specifications.
14   The remainder of installation is the reverse of removal.
15   Fill the engine with oil (if the oil has been drained) and coolant (see Chapter 1).
16   Start and operate the engine at a fast idle and check for leaks of any type.

Rear main oil seal

Note: *All V8 engines through 1983 used a two-piece rear main oil seal. In 1984, a one-piece seal was used on all models, except the 7.5L engine, which continues to use a two-piece seal. If you're unsure which type you have, check with an auto parts store.*

One-piece rear main oil seal

17   See Chapter 2, Part A for the procedure, but use the flywheel torque specifications listed in this Chapter.

Two-piece rear main oil seal

18   Remove the oil pan to gain access to the seal (see Section 14).
19   Loosen the main bearing cap bolts

slightly to allow the crankshaft to drop no more than 1/32-inch.
20   Remove the rear main bearing cap and detach the oil seal from the cap. To remove the portion of the rear main seal housed in the block, install a small sheet metal screw in one end of the seal and pull on the screw to rotate the seal out of the groove. Exercise extreme caution during this procedure to prevent scratching or damaging the crankshaft seal surfaces.
21   Carefully clean the seal grooves in the cap and block with a brush dipped in solvent.
22   Dip both new seal halves in clean engine oil.
23   Carefully install the upper seal (engine block) into the groove with the lip of the seal toward the front of the engine. It will be necessary to rotate it into the seal seat. Make sure that 3/8 inch of the seal protrudes on one side below the parting surface of the bearing cap.
24   Tighten all but the rear main bearing cap bolts to the torque listed in the Chapter 2, Part D Specifications.
25   Install the lower seal into the rear bearing cap with the undercut side of the seal towards the front of the engine, allow the seal to protrude 3/8 inch above the parting surface on the opposite side of the upper protruding seal to properly mate with the upper seal.
26   Apply a thin coat of RTV sealant to the rear main bearing cap at the top of the mating surface and to the block surface. Make sure that no sealant is permitted to get on the inside of the split lip seal.
27   Install the rear main bearing cap and make sure that the parting surfaces of the seals meet each other as shown.
28   Tighten the cap bolts to the torque listed in the Chapter 2, Part D Specifications, making sure that no sealant has worked its way forward of the seal side groove.
29   Install the oil pan and oil pump (see Sections 14 and 15).
30   The remainder of the installation procedure is the reverse of removal.
31   Fill the engine with oil and coolant (see Chapter 1).
32   Start and operate the engine at a fast idle and check for leaks of any type.

17   Flywheel/driveplate - removal, inspection and installation

Refer to the procedure described in Chapter 2, Part A, but use the torque values listed in this Chapter's Specifications.

18   Engine mounts - removal and installation

1   Engine mounts seldom require attention, but broken or deteriorated mounts should be replaced immediately or the added strain placed on the driveline components may cause damage.
2   For the check and replacement procedure, refer to Chapter 2, Part A.

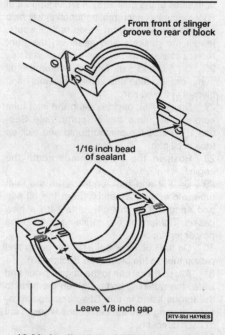

16.26 Application of RTV sealant to the main bearing cap and block during rear seal installation (two-piece seal)

Chapter 2 Part C
V6 engine

Contents

Specifications

General
Camshaft lobe lift
Intake	0.240 inch
Exhaust	0.241 inch
Allowable lobe lift loss	0.005 inch

FRONT

Cylinder locations and distributor rotation - V6 engine

The blackened terminal on the distributor cap indicates the number one spark plug wire position

36058-1.0D-HAYNES

Torque specifications

Ft-lbs (unless otherwise indicated)

Note: *One foot-pound (ft-lb) of torque is equivalent to 12 inch-pounds (in-lbs) of torque. Torque values below approximately 15 ft-lbs are expressed in inch-pounds, since most foot-pound torque wrenches are not accurate at these smaller values.*

Camshaft sprocket-to-camshaft bolts	15 to 22
Timing cover-to-cylinder block bolts	15 to 22
Oil pick-up tube-to-main bearing cap nuts	30 to 40
Oil pick-up tube bolts	15 to 22
Oil pan bolts	80 to 106 in-lbs
Oil filter adapter-to-timing cover bolts	18 to 22
Cylinder head bolts	
Step 1	47
Step 2	55
Step 3	63
Step 4	74
Step 5	Back off all bolts 2 to 3 turns
Step 6	Repeat Steps 1 through 4
Rocker arm fulcrum-to-cylinder head bolt	
Step 1	60 to 132 in-lbs
Step 2	18 to 26
Intake manifold bolts	18
Valve cover bolts	36 to 61 in-lbs
Flywheel-to-crankshaft bolts	54 to 64
Crankshaft pulley-to-damper bolts	20 to 28
Crankshaft damper-to-crankshaft bolts	93 to 121
Exhaust manifold bolts	15 to 22
Engine mount-to-crossmember bolts	25 to 35

1   General information

The 232 cubic inch V6 is similar to the V8s in construction and components used. However, important differences do exist. In the following paragraphs, similarities and differences between the V6 and V8 will be noted.

Fuel is delivered by a mechanical fuel pump mounted on the right side of the front (timing) cover assembly. The carburetor is mounted on an aluminum manifold which is bolted to aluminum alloy cylinder heads. Service procedures related to these components remain similar to those for the V8. However, a spark plug thread service procedure is provided in the event damage should occur to these threads (see Section 6).

The crankshaft is supported by four main bearings, with the number three bearing designated as the thrust bearing. The crankpins are positioned to provide a power impulse every 120-degrees of crankshaft rotation. This spacing, along with the necessary changes to camshaft lobe and distributor timing, provides smoothness of operation and quietness comparable to a V8.

The camshaft is also supported by four bearings. Thrust loads and endplay are limited by a thrust button and spring installed in the front of the camshaft. The spring-loaded button bears against the inside surface of the timing cover with lubrication supplied by oil splash from the timing chain. Immediately behind the thrust button bore are the distributor drive gear and the fuel pump actuating eccentric. These are not separate components installed on the cam, but, like the lobes, are part of the camshaft casting.

The configuration of the valve train is identical to that employed in the V8 and service procedures are the same.

The rotary gear type oil pump, which develops the oil pressure necessary to force-feed the lubrication system, is located in the timing cover assembly. The pump driven gear is rotated by the distributor shaft through an intermediate shaft.

Many of the component mating surfaces which are sealed with a gasket in V8 engines are sealed in the V6 with silicone rubber, or RTV (room temperature vulcanizing) sealant. The surfaces sealed in this manner in the V6 include the oil pan sides and front where they mate to the cylinder block and timing cover: the thermostat housing-to-the intake manifold; the valve covers-to-the cylinder head: both ends of the intake manifold-to-the cylinder block: along the rear main bearing cap and cylinder block parting line; and the thermactor air injection secondary cover-to-the intake manifold. When applying this sealant, always use the bead size specified and join the components within 15 minutes of application. After that time, the sealant begins to "set-up" and its sealing effectiveness may be reduced.

Because this engine is equipped with aluminum cylinder heads, a special corrosion inhibited coolant formulation is required to avoid radiator damage.

2   Intake manifold - removal and installation

Refer to illustration 2.13

1   Drain the cooling system (see Chapter 1) and disconnect the cable from the negative battery terminal.

2   Remove the carburetor (see Chapter 4).
3   Remove the attaching bolts from the accelerator cable mounting bracket and position the cable so it will not interfere with manifold removal.
4   If equipped with cruise control, disconnect the chain at the carburetor and remove the servo bracket assembly attaching nuts. Position the assembly so it will not interfere with manifold removal.
5   Disconnect the upper radiator hose at the thermostat housing.
6   Disconnect the coolant bypass hose at the manifold.
7   Disconnect the heater tube at the intake manifold and remove the tube support bracket attaching nut.
8   Disconnect the necessary electrical connectors.
9   If equipped with air conditioning, remove the air compressor support bracket attached to the left front intake manifold attaching bolt.
10   Remove the EGR tube. Remove the three EGR spacer attaching screws from the manifold.
11   With the EGR adapter and valve attached, work the EGR spacer loose from the manifold and remove the spacer and gasket.
12   Remove the PCV line.
13   Remove the intake manifold attaching bolts in the reverse order of the tightening sequence **(see illustration)**.
14   Remove the intake manifold. **Note:** *The manifold is sealed at each end with RTV sealant. To break the seal, it may be necessary to pry on the front of the manifold with a prybar. If so, use care to prevent damage to the machined surfaces.*
15   Remove the manifold side gaskets.
16   If the manifold is to be disassembled,

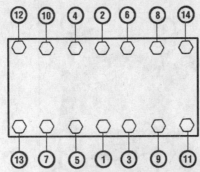

FRONT
OF
ENGINE
←

2.13 Intake manifold bolt tightening sequence

36086-2A-7.23a HAYNES

remove the thermostat housing and thermostat, water temperature sending unit, thermactor check valve and all vacuum fittings.

17   The heater outlet and water bypass tubes are pressed in and are not serviceable. If they are damaged, replace the manifold with a new one.

18   If the intake manifold was disassembled, apply a coat of pipe sealant to the temperature sending unit, all vacuum fittings, the spark knock sensor/adapter (if so equipped) and the electric PVS (if so equipped) and install them in the manifold.

19   Install the thermostat in the manifold with the outlet side up.

20   Apply a 1/8-inch bead of RTV sealant to the thermostat housing and tighten it to the torque listed in the Chapter 3 Specifications.

21   Install the thermactor check valve, using a new gasket in the manifold.

22   Apply a dab of RTV sealant to each cylinder head mating surface in the indicated areas **(see illustrations 9.37 and 9.38 in** Chapter 2B**)** and press new intake manifold gaskets into place, using the locating pins.

23   Apply a 1/8-inch bead of RTV sealant at each corner where the cylinder head joins the cylinder block and a 3/4-inch bead at each end of the cylinder block where the manifold seats against the block.

24   Carefully lower the manifold into position on the cylinder block and cylinder heads. Use the locating pins to prevent smearing the sealant and causing gasket voids.

25   Apply a thin coat of pipe sealant to the manifold attaching bolt threads and to the underside of the bolt heads.

26   Install the 12 bolts and two stud bolts and tighten them in the numerical sequence shown in **illustration 2.13**. The bolts should be tightened to the torque listed in this Chapter's Specifications in three steps.

27   Install the remaining components in the reverse order of removal.

28   Fill the cooling system with the specified coolant (see Chapter 1).

29   Start and run the engine and allow it to reach operating temperature, checking carefully for leaks.

30   Shut the engine off and retighten the manifold bolts while the engine is still warm.

---

3   Exhaust manifold(s) - removal and installation

Left (driver's) side

1   Remove the oil level dipstick tube support bracket.

2   If equipped with a speed control, remove the air cleaner assembly and disconnect the servo chain at the carburetor.

3   Remove the servo bracket attaching bolts and nuts and position the servo/bracket assembly out of the way.

4   If so equipped, disconnect the oxygen sensor at the electrical connector.

5   Disconnect the spark plug wires.

6   Raise the front of the vehicle and place it securely on jackstands.

7   Remove the manifold-to-exhaust pipe attaching nuts.

8   Remove the jackstands and lower the vehicle.

9   Remove the exhaust manifold attaching bolts and the manifold.

10   Installation is the reverse of removal. **Note**: *When installing the attaching bolts, install the pilot bolt (lower front bolt on no. 5 cylinder) first.*

11   A slight warpage in the exhaust manifold may cause a misalignment between the bolt holes in the head and manifold. If so, elongate the holes in the exhaust manifold as necessary to correct the misalignment, but do not elongate the pilot hole.

Right (passenger's) side

12   Remove the air cleaner assembly and heat tube.

13   Disconnect the thermactor hose from the downstream air tube check valve.

14   Remove the downstream air tube bracket attaching bolt at the rear of the right cylinder head.

15   Disconnect the coil secondary wire from the coil and the wires from the spark plugs.

16   Remove the spark plugs and the outer heat shroud.

17   Raise the front of the vehicle and place it securely on jackstands.

18   Remove the transmission dipstick tube, if so equipped.

19   Remove the manifold-to-exhaust pipe attaching nuts.

20   Remove the jackstands and lower the vehicle.

21   Remove the exhaust manifold attaching bolts, then remove the manifold, inner heat shroud and EGR tube as an assembly.

22   Installation is the reverse of removal. If the bolt holes are misaligned, see Step 11, but do not elongate the pilot hole (lower rear bolt hole on no. 2 cylinder).

---

4   Valve covers - removal and installation

1   Disconnect the spark plug wires.

2   Remove the spark plug wire routing clips from the valve cover attaching studs.

3   If the left valve cover is being removed, remove the oil filler cap. If equipped with cruise control, reposition the air cleaner assembly and disconnect the servo chain at the carburetor. Remove the servo bracket attaching bolts and nuts, and position the servo/bracket assembly aside.

4   If the right valve cover is being removed, reposition the air cleaner assembly and heat tube, remove the PCV valve, then disconnect and remove the thermactor diverter valve and hose assembly at the bypass valve downstream air tube and the engine mounted check valve.

5   Remove the valve cover attaching screws.

6   Loosen the RTV sealant by inserting a putty knife under the cover flange. Work the cover loose and remove it. **Caution**: *Pry carefully, as the plastic valve covers will break if excessive force is applied.*

7   Installation is the reverse of removal. Apply a 1/8 to 3/16-inch bead of RTV sealant to the valve cover before placing it on the head. Make sure the sealant fills the channel in the cover flange and make sure the installation is made within 15 minutes of the sealant application.

---

5   Cylinder head(s) - removal, inspection and installation

Refer to illustrations 5.28

Removal

1   Drain the engine coolant (see Chapter 1).

2   Disconnect the cable from the negative battery terminal.

3   Remove the air cleaner assembly, including the air intake duct and heat tube.

4   Loosen the accessory drivebelt idler, then remove the drivebelt.

5   If the left cylinder head is being removed, refer to Steps 6 through 9 and Steps 17 through 30.

6   If equipped with power steering, remove the pump mounting bracket attaching bolts.

7   Leaving the hoses connected, place the pump/bracket assembly aside, making sure that it is in a position to prevent the fluid from leaking out.

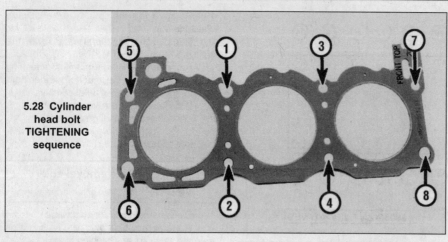

5.28 Cylinder head bolt TIGHTENING sequence

8   If equipped with air conditioning, remove the mounting bracket attaching bolts.

9   Leaving the hoses connected, position the compressor aside. **Warning:** *Under no circumstances should the air conditioning hoses be disconnected except by an authorized air conditioning service technician, as personal injury and equipment damage may result.*

10   If the right cylinder head is being removed, refer to Steps 11 through 23.

11   Disconnect the thermactor diverter valve and hose assembly at the bypass valve and downstream air tube, then remove the assembly.

12   Remove the accessory drive idler.

13   Remove the alternator.

14   Remove the thermactor pump pulley and pump.

15   Remove the alternator bracket.

16   Remove the PCV valve.

17   Remove the intake manifold (see Section 2).

18   Remove the valve cover(s) (see Section 4).

19   Remove the exhaust manifold(s) (see Section 3).

20   Remove the pushrods (see Chapter 2, Part B), making sure to note the position of each rod.

21   Remove the cylinder head attaching bolts, then remove the cylinder head(s). Discard the bolts, since new ones must be installed upon installation.

22   Remove and discard the old cylinder head gasket(s).

23   See Chapter 2, Part D for the cylinder head disassembly and inspection procedures.

Installation

24   Position new head gasket(s) on the cylinder block using the dowels for alignment.

25   Position the head(s) on the block.

26   Apply a thin coat of pipe sealant to the threads of the short cylinder head bolts (nearest to the exhaust manifold). Do not apply sealant to the long bolts.

27   Lightly oil the cylinder head bolt flat washers and install the flat washers and cylinder head bolts. **Caution:** *Always use new cylinder head bolts.*

28   Tighten the attaching bolts in the proper

sequence **(see illustration)**, following the torque values listed in this Chapter's Specifications.

29   The remaining installation steps are the reverse of those for removal. Make sure to use the proper coolant (see Chapter 3) when refilling the cooling system.

30   Change the engine oil and filter (see Chapter 1).

31   Start the engine and check for leaks.

6   Spark plug thread repair

A thread repair kit is required for this procedure and the cylinder head with the damaged threads must be removed from the engine, as the procedure involves the cutting of new threads (a process which produces metal chips). Performing this procedure with the cylinder head on the engine will cause metal chips to fall into the cylinder, resulting in damage to the cylinder wall when the engine is started. This procedure is best performed by an automotive machine shop.

7   Timing chain wear - check

Refer to Chapter 2B, Section 6, for the timing chain wear check procedure.

8   Timing cover and timing chain - removal and installation

Removal

1   Disconnect the cable from the negative battery terminal. Position the engine at TDC compression for the number one cylinder (see Chapter 2, Part B).

2   Drain the cooling system and the engine oil (see Chapter 1).

3   Remove the air cleaner assembly and air intake duct.

4   Remove the fan shroud attaching screws.

5   Remove the fan/clutch assembly attaching bolts.

6   Remove the fan/clutch assembly and shroud (see Chapter 3).

7   Loosen the accessory drivebelt idler pulley.

8   Remove the drivebelt.

9   Remove the water pump pulley (see Chapter 3).

10   If equipped with power steering, remove the pump mounting bracket attaching bolts.

11   Leaving the hoses connected, place the pump bracket assembly aside, making sure that it is in a position that prevents the fluid from leaking out.

12   If equipped with air conditioning, remove the compressor front support bracket, leaving the compressor in place. **Warning:** *Do not attempt to disconnect the air conditioning hoses, as personal injury and/or equipment damage may result.*

13   Disconnect the engine coolant bypass hose at the water pump.

14   Disconnect the heater hose at the water pump.

15   Disconnect the radiator upper hose at the thermostat housing.

16   Disconnect the coil wire from the distributor cap, then remove the cap with the spark plug wires attached.

17   Remove the distributor hold-down clamp and lift the distributor out of the timing cover.

18   Raise the vehicle and place it securely on jackstands.

19   Remove the crankshaft damper, using a puller that bears on the hub of the damper.

20   Remove the fuel pump shield, if so equipped.

21   Disconnect the fuel pump-to-carburetor fuel line at the fuel pump.

22   Remove the fuel pump attaching bolts, pull the pump out of the timing cover and lay the pump aside with the flexible line attached.

23   Remove the oil filter.

24   Disconnect the radiator lower hose at the water pump.

25   Remove the oil pan (see Section 10). **Note:** *The timing cover cannot be removed without lowering the oil pan.*

26   Remove the jackstands and lower the vehicle.

27   Remove the timing cover attaching bolts. It is not necessary to remove the water pump. **Note:** *Do not overlook the cover attaching bolt located behind the oil filter adapter. The timing cover will break if pried upon and all attaching bolts have not been removed.*

28   Remove the ignition timing indicator from the timing cover.

29   Remove the timing cover and water pump as an assembly.

30   Remove the camshaft thrust button and spring from the end of the camshaft.

31   Remove the camshaft sprocket attaching bolts.

32   Remove the camshaft sprocket, crankshaft sprocket and timing chain. If the crankshaft sprocket is difficult to remove, pry the sprocket off the shaft using a pair of large screwdrivers positioned on the sides of the sprocket.

33   The timing cover contains the oil pump

and oil pump intermediate shaft. If a new timing cover is being installed, remove the water pump, oil pump, oil filter adapter and the oil pump intermediate shaft from the old cover.

34 See Section 9 for procedures involving the oil pump assembly. See Chapter 3 for procedures involving the water pump.

Installation

35 If re-using the timing cover, replace the crankshaft front oil seal (see Chapter 2, Part A).

36 If a new timing cover is being used, install the oil pump, oil filter adapter, oil pump intermediate shaft and the water pump.

37 If not already done, rotate the crankshaft as necessary to position piston no. 1 at TDC and the crankshaft keyway at the 12 o'clock position (this will be necessary if the timing chain broke, for example).

38 Lubricate the timing chain with clean engine oil.

39 Install the camshaft sprocket, crankshaft sprocket and timing chain, making sure the timing marks are exactly opposite each other **(see illustration 11.15 in Chapter 2, Part B)**.

40 Install the camshaft sprocket attaching bolts and tighten them to the torque listed in this Chapter's Specifications.

41 Lubricate the camshaft thrust button with polyethylene grease and install the thrust button and spring in the front of the camshaft. **Note**: *The thrust button and spring must be bottomed in the camshaft seat. Make sure that the thrust button and spring do not fall out during the installation of the timing cover.*

42 Lubricate the crankshaft front oil seal with clean engine oil.

43 Position a new cover gasket on the cylinder block and install the timing cover/water pump assembly, using the dowels for proper alignment. Contact adhesive may be used to hold the gasket in position while the timing cover is installed.

44 Attach the ignition timing indicator to the timing cover.

45 Coat the timing cover attaching bolts with pipe sealant and install the timing cover, tightening the bolts to the torque listed in this Chapter's Specifications.

46 Raise the vehicle and position it securely on jackstands.

47 Install the oil pan (see Section 10).

48 Connect the lower radiator hose and tighten the clamp securely.

49 Install the oil filter.

50 Turn the crankshaft clockwise 180-degrees to position the fuel pump eccentric away from the fuel pump actuating arm. **Note**: *Failure to turn the crankshaft can result in the threads being stripped out of the timing cover when the fuel pump attaching bolts are installed.*

51 Position a new gasket on the fuel pump and install the pump.

52 Connect the fuel line to the fuel pump.

53 Coat the crankshaft damper sealing surface with clean engine oil.

54 Position the crankshaft pulley key in the

crankshaft keyway.

55 Install the crankshaft damper.

56 Install the damper washer and bolt and tighten the bolt to the torque listed in this Chapter's Specifications. **Note**: *This bolt may be used to push the damper onto the crankshaft if the proper installation tool is unavailable.*

57 Install the crankshaft pulley and tighten the bolts to the torque listed in this Chapter's Specifications.

58 Turn the crankshaft 180-degrees counterclockwise to bring piston no. 1 back to TDC.

59 Remove the jackstands and lower the vehicle.

60 The remaining installation procedures are the reverse of those for removal. When installing the distributor, make sure the rotor is pointing at the no. 1 distributor cap tower (see Chapter 5).

61 Start the engine and check for coolant, oil or fuel leaks.

62 Check the ignition timing and idle speed and adjust as required (see Chapters 5 and 4, respectively).

9 Oil pump - removal, inspection and installation

1 Remove the timing cover assembly (see Section 8).

2 Remove the oil pump cover attaching bolts, then remove the cover.

3 Lift the pump gears out of the pocket in the timing cover.

4 See Chapter 2, Part D for the oil pump inspection procedures.

5 To assemble the oil pump, lightly pack the gear pocket with petroleum jelly or heavy oil. **Note**: *Do not use chassis lubricants.*

6 Install the gears in the cover pocket, making sure that the petroleum jelly fills all the voids between the gears and the pocket. **Note**: *Failure to properly coat the oil pump gears may result in failure of the pump to prime when the engine is started, leading to severe engine damage.*

7 Position the cover gasket and install the pump cover.

8 Tighten the pump cover attaching bolts to the torque listed in this Chapter's Specifications.

9 Using an electric drill, drill a small hole through the center of the relief valve plug.

10 Remove the plug with a sheet metal screw and slide hammer or by prying it out with an ice pick or similar tool.

11 Remove the spring and valve from the bore.

12 Thoroughly clean the valve bore and valve to remove any metal chips which may have entered the bore as a result of drilling the plug.

13 See Chapter 2, Part D for further relief valve inspection procedures.

14 Lubricate the relief valve with engine oil and install it in its bore.

15 Position the spring in the bore.

16 Tap a new plug into the bore using a soft-faced hammer. Make sure the plug is flush with the machined surface.

17 Remove the clip from the intermediate shaft and slide the shaft out of the cover.

18 Before installing the shaft, measure and mark the shaft one inch from the end.

19 Position the shaft in the cover, making sure that it is seated in the oil pump drive gear.

20 Install the clip on the shaft so the top of the clip is just below the mark made in Step 18. Use a screwdriver blade to snap the clip onto the shaft.

21 Install the timing cover assembly (see Section 8).

10 Oil pan - removal, inspection and installation

1 Disconnect the cable from the negative battery terminal.

2 Remove the air cleaner assembly.

3 Remove the bolts attaching the fan shroud to the radiator and position the shroud over the fan.

4 Remove the engine oil dipstick.

5 Raise the vehicle and place it securely on jackstands.

6 Remove the oil filter.

7 Disconnect the exhaust pipes from the exhaust manifolds.

8 Remove the clamp attaching the exhaust pipe to the catalytic converter pipe and remove the inlet pipe from the vehicle.

9 Disconnect the transmission shift linkage at the transmission (see Chapter 7, if necessary).

10 If so equipped, disconnect the transmission cooler lines at the radiator.

11 Remove the nuts attaching the engine mounts to the chassis brackets (see Chapter 2A, if necessary).

12 Using a jack with a block of wood placed on top of the lifting pad, lift the engine and place wood blocks between the engine mounts and the chassis brackets. then remove the jack.

13 Remove the oil pan attaching bolts and lower the oil pan. Unbolt the oil pick-up tube assembly and let it lay in the pan, then remove the pan from the vehicle. Remove the old gaskets and rear pan seal.

14 Clean the oil pan and sealing surfaces. Inspect the gasket sealing surfaces for damage and distortion due to overtightening of the bolts. Repair and straighten as required.

15 Trial fit the pan to the cylinder block. Make sure enough clearance exists to allow the pan to be installed without the sealant scraping off when the pan is positioned for final installation.

16 Lower the oil pan and let it rest on the frame crossmember.

17 Using a new gasket, install the oil pick-up tube assembly. Make sure that the support bracket engages the stud on the no. 2 main bearing cap attaching bolt.

18   Tighten the pick-up tube assembly nuts and bolts to the torque listed in this Chapter's Specifications.

19   Install a new rear pan seal in the seal groove in the rear main cap. working it into place with a small screwdriver.

20   Apply an 1/8-inch bead of RTV sealant to the seam where the timing cover and cylinder block join, to each end of the rear seal where the rear main cap and cylinder block join, and along the oil pan rails on the cylinder block. Where the bead crosses the timing cover, increase the bead width to 1/4-inch.

21   Position the oil pan on the bottom of the engine and install the bolts. Tighten the bolts to the torque listed in this Chapter's Specifications.

22   Raise the engine and remove the wood blocks.

23   The remaining installation procedures are the reverse of those for removal.

11   Camshaft and lifters - removal, inspection and installation

Note: *To determine the extent of cam lobe wear, the lobe lift should be checked prior to camshaft removal. Follow the procedure described in Chapter 2, Part A, but note that it will be necessary to remove both valve covers as described in Section 4 of this Chapter and use the specifications listed at the front of this Chapter.*

Removal

Warning: *If the vehicle is equipped with air conditioning, the condenser must be removed. This requires discharging of the air conditioning system by an authorized air conditioning system technician. Under no circumstances should the home mechanic attempt to discharge the system or disconnect any of the air conditioning system lines while they are still pressurized, as this can cause serious personal injury as well as damage to the air conditioning system.*

1   Disconnect the cable from the negative battery terminal.

2   Drain the engine coolant (see Chapter 1).

3   Remove the radiator (see Chapter 3).

4   Remove the grille (see Chapter 11).

5   Remove the intake manifold (see Section 2).

6   Remove the valve covers (see Section 4).

7   Loosen the rocker arm nuts and rotate the rocker arms to the side.

8   Remove the pushrods (see Chapter 2B).

9   Remove the valve lifters from the engine using a special tool designed for this purpose. Sometimes they can be removed with a magnet if there is no varnish build-up or wear on them. If they are stuck in their bores, you will have to obtain a special tool designed for grasping lifters internally and work them out.

10   Remove the timing cover, chain and gears (see Section 9).

11   Remove the oil pan (see Section 10).

12   Remove the camshaft from the front of the engine by slowly withdrawing it, being careful not to damage the bearings with the cam lobes.

Inspection

13   Inspect the lifters as described in Chapter 2, Part D.

14   Inspect the camshaft following the procedures outlined in Chapter 2, Part D.

15   Check the camshaft bearings in the engine block for signs of excessive wear. If new bearings are required, take the engine to an automotive machine shop, as special tools and expertise are required to replace them.

Installation

16   Lubricate the cam lobes and bearing surfaces with camshaft installation lube.

17   Carefully guide the camshaft into place, taking care not to damage the bearings with the cam lobes.

18   The remaining installation procedures are the reverse of those for removal.

19   Change the engine oil and filter and add the specified type and amount of coolant (see Chapter 1).

20   Run the engine and check for leaks and proper operation. Set the ignition timing and idle speed (see Chapters 5 and 4).

Chapter 2 Part D
General engine overhaul procedures

Contents

Specifications

Inline six-cylinder engine (4.9L)

General

Displacement	300 cubic inches
Bore and stroke	4.00 x 3.98 inches
Compression pressure	Lowest cylinder must be within 75-percent of highest cylinder
Oil pressure (at 2000 rpm, normal operating temperature)	40 to 60 psi

Engine block

Cylinder bore
Diameter	4.000 to 4.0048 inches
Taper limit	0.010 inch
Out-of-round limit	0.005 inch
Deck warpage limit	0.003 inch per 6 inches, or 0.006 inch overall

Pistons and rings

Piston diameter
Coded red	3.9982 to 3.9988 inches
Coded blue	3.9994 to 4.0000 inches
Oversize available	0.003 inch

Piston-to-cylinder bore clearance
Selection fit	0.0010 to 0.0018 inch

Piston ring-to-groove side clearance

Standard
Top ring	0.0019 to 0.0036 inch
2nd ring	0.002 to 0.004 inch
Oil ring	Snug fit in groove
Service limit	0.002 inch maximum increase in clearance

Piston ring end gap
Top ring	0.010 to 0.020 inch
2nd ring	0.010 to 0.020 inch
Oil ring	0.015 to 0.055 inch
Piston pin diameter (standard)	0.9749 to 0.9754 inch
Piston pin-to-piston clearance	0.0002 to 0.0004 inch; under 8500 GVW - 0.0003 to 0.0005 inch
Piston pin-to-connecting rod clearance	Interference fit

Inline six-cylinder engine (4.9L) (continued)

Crankshaft and flywheel

Main journal
    Diameter.. 2.3982 to 2.3990 inches
    Taper limit... 0.0005 inch per inch
    Out-of-round limit .... 0.0006 inch
    Runout limit .... 0.002 inch
Main bearing oil clearance
    Standard.. 0.0008 to 0.0015 inch
    Service limit.. 0.0028 inch
Connecting rod journal
    Diameter.. 2.1228 to 2.1236 inches
    Taper limit... 0.0006 inch per inch
    Out-of-round limit .... 0.0006 inch
Connecting rod bearing oil clearance
    Standard.. 0.0008 to 0.0015 inch
    Service limit.. 0.0024 inch
Connecting rod side clearance
    Standard.. 0.006 to 0.013 inch
    Service limit.. 0.018 inch
Crankshaft endplay
    Standard.. 0.004 to 0.008 inch
    Service limit.. 0.012 inch
Flywheel clutch face runout limit.. 0.010 inch
Flywheel/driveplate ring gear lateral runout limit
    Manual transmission .... 0.040 inch
    Automatic transmission .... 0.060 inch

Camshaft

Bearing journal
    Diameter.. 2.017 to 2.018 inches
    Journal runout .... 0.008 inch max
Bearing oil clearance
    Standard.. 0.001 to 0.003 inch
    Service limit.. 0.006 inch
Lobe lift
    Intake
        F100 and F150 4x2 with 2.47:1 or 2.75:1 axle ratio
            and manual transmission .... 0.247 inch
        All others... 0.249 inch
    Exhaust
        F100 and F150 4x2 with 2.47:1 or 2.75:1 axle ratio and
            manual transmission .... 0.247 inch
        All others... 0.249 inch
Runout limit.. 0.008 inch
Endplay
    Standard.. 0.001 to 0.007 inch
    Service limit.. 0.009 inch
Cam gear-to-crankshaft gear backlash .... 0.004 to 0.100 inch
Cam gear runout limit (assembled) .... 0.005 inch
Crankshaft gear runout limit (assembled).............................. 0.005 inch

Cylinder head and valve train

Head warpage limit.. 0.006 inch per 6 inches or 0.007 in overall
Valve seat angle 45-degrees
Valve seat width
    Intake .... 0.060 to 0.080 inch
    Exhaust .... 0.070 to 0.090 inch
Valve seat runout limit .... 0.002 inch
Valve face angle 44-degrees
Valve face runout limit .... 0.002 inch
Valve margin width .... 1/32 inch min
Valve stem diameter - standard
    Intake .... 0.3416 to 0.3423 inch
    Exhaust .... 0.3416 to 0.3423 inch
Valve guide diameter
    Intake .... 0.3433 to 0.3443 inch
    Exhaust .... 0.3433 to 0.3443 inch

Valve stem-to-guide clearance
  Intake
    Standard .... 0.0010 to 0.0027 inch
    Service limit .... 0.0055 inch
  Exhaust
    Standard .... 0.0010 to 0.0027 inch
    Service limit .... 0.0055 inch
Valve spring free length
  Intake .... 1.96 inches
  Exhaust .... 1.78 inches
Valve spring pressure (lbs. at specified length)
  Intake (1st check)
    Standard .... 66 to 74 at 1.64 inches
    Service limit .... 10-percent loss of pressure
  Intake (2nd check)
    Standard .... 166 to 184 at 1.24 inches
    Service limit .... 10-percent loss of pressure
  Exhaust (1st check)
    Standard .... 66 to 74 at 1.47 inches
    Service limit .... 10-percent loss of pressure
  Exhaust (2nd check)
    Standard .... 166 to 184 at 1.07 inches
    Service limit .... 10-percent loss of pressure
Valve spring installed height
  Intake .... 1.61 to 1.67 inches
  Exhaust .... 1.44 to 1.5 inches
Valve spring out-of-square limit .... 0.078 inch
Collapsed lifter gap .... 0.125 to 0.175 inch
Lifter diameter... 0.8740 to 0.8745 inch
Lifter bore diameter .... 0.8752 to 0.8767 inch
Lifter-to-bore clearance
  Standard.. 0.007 to 0.0027 inch
  Service limit... 0.005 inch
Pushrod runout limit... 0.015 inch

Oil pump

Outer race-to-housing clearance .... 0.001 to 0.013 inch
Rotor assembly end clearance .... 0.004 inch max
Driveshaft-to-housing bearing clearance... 0.0015 to 0.0030 inch
Relief spring tension .... 20.6 to 22.6 lbs. at 2.49 inches
Relief valve clearance .... 0.0015 to 0.0030 inch

Torque specifications

                                                                                                    Ft-lbs
Connecting rod nuts .... 40 to 45
Main bearing cap bolts .... 60 to 70

V6 engine

General

Displacement... 232 cubic inches
Bore and stroke .... 3.81 x 3.39 inches
Oil pressure (hot @ 2500 rpm)... 54 to 59 psi
Compression pressure .... Lowest cylinder must be within 75-percent of highest cylinder

Engine block

Cylinder bore
  Diameter.. 3.81 inches
  Taper service limit .... 0.002 inch
  Out-of-round service limit .... 0.002 inch
Deck warpage limit.. 0.003 inch per 6 inches

Pistons and rings

Piston
  Diameter
    Coded red.. 3.8095 to 3.8101 inches
    Coded blue... 3.8107 to 3.8113 inches
  Oversizes available.. 0.004 inch
Piston-to-cylinder bore clearance... 0.0014 to 0.0022 inch

V6 engine (continued)

Pistons and rings (continued)

Piston ring-to-groove clearance

Top compression	0.0016 to 0.0037 inch
Bottom compression	0.0016 to 0.0037 inch
Oil ring	Snug fit in groove

Piston ring end gap

Top compression	0.010 to 0.020 inch
Bottom compression	0.010 to 0.020 inch
Oil ring	0.0150 to 0.0583 inch
Piston pin diameter	0.9119 to 0.914 inch
Piston pin-to-piston clearance	0.0002 to 0.0005 inch
Piston pin-to-connecting rod clearance	Press fit at 1800 lbs

Crankshaft and flywheel

Main journal

Diameter	2.5190 to 2.5198 inches
Taper limit	0.0003 inch per 1 inch
Out-of-round limit	0.0003 inch per 45-degrees or 0.0006 inch total
Journal runout limit	0.002 inch*

Main bearing oil clearance

Desired	0.0010 to 0.0014 inch
Allowable	0.0005 to 0.0023 inch

Connecting rod journal

Diameter	2.3103 to 2.3111 inch
Taper limit	0.0003 inch per 1 inch
Out-of-round limit	0.0003 inch per 45-degrees or 0.0006 inch total

Connecting rod bearing oil clearance

Desired	0.0010 to 0.0014 inch
Allowable	0.0008 to 0.0027 inch

Connecting rod side clearance

Standard	0.0047 to 0.0114 inch
Service limit	0.014 inch max
Crankshaft endplay	0.004 to 0.008 inch
Flywheel clutch face runout limit	0.005 inch

Flywheel/driveplate ring gear lateral runout

Standard transmission	0.025 inch
Automatic transmission	0.070 inch

Runout of journal numbers 2 and 3 to journal numbers 1 and 4, and runout of adjacent journals to each other.

Camshaft

Bearing journal diameter	2.0505 to 2.0515 inches
Endplay	None (camshaft is restrained by spring)
Bearing oil clearance	0.001 to 0.003 inch
Lobe lift	See Chapter 2, Part C
Runout limit	0.020 inch (runout of no. 2 or no. 3 relative to no. 1 and no. 4)

Camshaft drive - assembled gear face runout

Crankshaft	0.002 inch
Camshaft	0.018 inch

Cylinder heads and valve train

Head warpage limit	0.007 inch
Valve seat angle	45-degrees
Valve seat width (intake and exhaust)	0.060 to 0.080 inch
Valve seat runout limit	0.003 inch
Valve face angle	44-degrees
Valve face runout limit	0.002 inch
Valve margin width	1/32-inch min

Valve stem diameter (standard)

Intake	0.3416 to 0.3423 inch
Exhaust	0.3411 to 0.3418 inch
Valve guide diameter (intake and exhaust)	0.3433 to 0.3443 inch

Valve stem-to-guide clearance

Intake	0.0010 to 0.0027 inch
Exhaust	0.0015 to 0.0032 inch
Valve spring free length	1.70 to 1.78 inches

Valve spring pressure (lbs @ specified length)

Loaded (without damper)	215 @ 1.40 inches
Unloaded (without damper)	75 @ 1.70 inches
Service limit	10-percent loss of pressure

Collapsed lifter gap	0.088 to 0.189 inch
Lifter diameter	0.874 inch
Lifter bore diameter	0.8752 to 0.8767 inch
Lifter-to-bore clearance	
Standard	0.0007 to 0.0027 inch
Service limit	0.005 inch

Oil pump

Relief valve spring tension (force @ length)	15.2 to 17.1 lbs @ 1.20 inches
Relief valve-to-bore clearance	0.0017 to 0.0029 inch
Oil pump gear backlash	0.008 to 0.012 inch
Oil pump gear radial clearance (idler and driver	0.0020 to 0.0055 inch
Oil pump gear and height (extends beyond housing)	0.0005 to 0.0055 inch
Idler shaft-to-idler gear clearance	0.0005 to 0.0017 inch
Driver shaft-to-housing clearance	0.0015 to 0.0030 inch

Torque specifications*

	Ft-lbs
Main bearing cap bolts	65 to 81
Connecting rod nuts	31 to 36

* Additional torque specifications can be found in Chapter 2, Part C.

255, 302 (5.0L), 351W (5.8L) and 5.8L Lightning engines

General

Bore and stroke	
255	3.68 x 3.00 inches
302	4.00 x 3.00 inches
351W and Lightning	4.00 x 3.50 inches
Compression pressure	Lowest cylinder must be at least 75-percent of highest cylinder
Oil pressure (at 2000 rpm, normal operating temperature)	
255 and 302	40 to 60 psi
351W and Lightning	40 to 65 psi

Engine block

Cylinder bore	
Diameter	
255	3.6800 to 3.6835 inches
302	4.0004 to 4.0052 inches
351W and Lightning	4.0000 to 4.0048 inches
Taper limit	0.010 inch
Out-of-round limit	0.005 inch
Deck warpage limit	0.003 inch per 6 inch or 0.006 inch overall

Pistons and rings

Piston diameter	
255	
Coded red	3.6784 to 3.6790 inches
Coded blue	3.6798 to 3.6804 inches
302	
1986 and earlier	
Coded red	3.9984 to 3.9990 inches
Coded blue	3.9960 to 4.0000 inches
1987 through 1990	
Coded red	3.9991 to 3.9985 inches
Coded blue	3.9990 to 4.0000 inches
1991 on	
Coded red	3.9989 to 3.9995 inches
Coded blue	4.0001 to 4.0007 inches
351W	
Coded red	3.9978 to 3.9984 inches
Coded blue	3.9990 to 3.9996 inches
351 Lightning	
Coded red	3.9984 to 3.9990 inches
Coded blue	3.9996 to 4.0002 inches
Oversizes available	0.003 inch
Piston-to-bore clearance	
255 and 302	
1986 and earlier	0.0018 to 0.0026 inch
1987 through 1990	0.0013 to 0.0030 inch
1991 on	0.0014 to 0.0022 inch

255, 302 (5.0L), 351W (5.8L) and 5.8L Lightning engines (continued)

Pistons and rings (continued)

351W	
1990 and earlier	0.0018 to 0.0026 inch
1991 on	0.0015 to 0.0023 inch
351 Lightning	0.0015 to 0.0023 inch
Piston ring-to-groove clearance	
Top and bottom compression	
255 and 302	0.0013 to 0.0033 inch
351W	0.0020 to 0.0040 inch
Lightning	0.0013 to 0.0033 inch
Oil	Snug fit in groove
Service limit	0.002 inch max increase in clearance
Piston ring end gap	
Top compression	0.010 to 0.020 inch
Bottom compression	
255 and 302	0.018 to 0.028 inch
351W	
1993 and earlier	0.010 to 0.020 inch
1994 and later	0.018 to 0.028 inch
Lightning	0.018 to 0.028 inch
Oil	0.010 to 0.040 inch
Piston pin diameter (standard)	
1996 and earlier	0.9119 to 0.9124 inch
1997	0.9121 to 0.9122 inch
Piston pin-to-piston clearance	
255 and 302	0.0002 to 0.0004 inch
351W and Lightning	0.0003 to 0.0005 inch
Piston pin-to-connecting rod bushing clearance	Interference fit

Crankshaft and flywheel

Main journal	
Diameter	
255 and 302	2.2482 to 2.2490 inches
351W and Lightning	2.9994 to 3.0002 inches
Taper limit - max per inch	0.0005 inch
Out-of-round limit	0.0006 inch
Runout	0.002 inch TIR
Service limit	0.005 inch
Main bearing oil clearance	
Standard	
No. 1 bearing	0.0001 to 0.0015 inch
All other bearings	0.0005 to 0.0015 inch
Service limit	
No. 1 bearing	0.0001 to 0.0020 inch
All other bearings	0.0005 to 0.0024 inch
Connecting rod journal	
Diameter	
255 and 302	2.1228 to 2.1236 inches
351W and Lightning	2.3103 to 2.3111 inches
Taper limit - max per inch	0.0006 inch
Out-of-round limit	0.0006 inch
Connecting rod bearing oil clearance	
Standard	0.0008 to 0.0015 inch
Service limit	
255 and 302	0.0007 to 0.0024 inch
351W and Lightning	0.0008 to 0.0025 inch
Connecting rod side clearance	
Standard	0.010 to 0.020 inch
Service limit	0.023 inch
Crankshaft endplay	
Standard	0.004 to 0.008 inch
Service limit	0.012 inch
Flywheel clutch face runout limit	0.010 inch

Camshaft

Bearing journal diameter

255 and 302

No. 1	2.0805 to 2.0815 inches
No. 2	2.0655 to 2.0665 inches
No. 3	2.0505 to 2.0515 inches
No. 4	2.0355 to 2.0365 inches
No. 5	2.0205 to 2.0215 inches

351W and Lightning

No. 1	2.0815 inches
No. 2	2.0665 inches
No. 3	2.0515 inches
No. 4	2.0365 inches
No. 5	2.0215 inches

Bearing oil clearance

Standard	0.001 to 0.003 inch
Service limit	0.006 inch
Front bearing location	0.005 to 0.020 inch (distance that front edge of the bearing is located below the front face of the cylinder block)

Lobe lift

Intake

255 and 302	0.2375 inch

351W

Carbureted	0.2600 inch

Fuel injected

1996 and earlier	0.2780 inch
1997	0.2637 inch
Lightning	0.2600 inch

Exhaust

255 and 302

1980 and 1981	0.2470 inch
1982 on	0.2474 inch

351W

Carbureted	0.2600 inch

Fuel injected

1996 and earlier	0.2830 inch
1997	0.2801 inch
Lightning	0.2780 inch
Maximum allowable lift loss	0.005 inch

Endplay

Standard	0.001 to 0.007 inch
Service limit	0.009 inch
Timing chain deflection limit	1/2 inch

Cylinder heads and valve train

Head warpage limit	0.003 inch per 6 inches or 0.006 inch total
Valve seat angle	45-degrees
Valve seat width	0.060 to 0.080 inch
Valve seat runout limit	0.002 inch
Valve face angle	44-degrees
Valve face runout limit	0.002 inch
Valve margin width	1/32 inch min.

Valve stem diameter

Intake	0.3416 to 0.3423 inch
Exhaust	0.3411 to 0.3418 inch
Valve guide diameter	0.3433 to 0.3443 inch

Valve stem-to-guide clearance

Intake

Standard	0.0010 to 0.0027 inch
Service limit	0.0055 inch

Exhaust

Standard	0.0015 to 0.0032 inch
Service limit	0.0055 inch

Valve spring free length

Intake	2.06 inches
Exhaust	1.88 inches

255, 302 (5.0L), 351W (5.8L) and 5.8L Lightning engines (continued)

Cylinder heads and valve train (continued)

Valve spring pressure (lbs at specified length)	
Intake (1st check)..	74 to 82 at 1.78 inches
Intake (2nd check)	
255 and 302	196 to 212 at 1.36 inches
351W and Lightning...	190 to 210 at 1.20 inches
Exhaust (1st check)..	76 to 84 at 1.60 inches
Exhaust (2nd check)	190 to 219 at 1.20 inches
Service limit...	10-percent loss of pressure
Valve spring installed height	
Intake	1.78 to 1.81 inches
Exhaust	1.58 to 1.64 inches
Valve spring out-of-square limit	0.078 inch
Collapsed lifter gap	
255 and 302	0.091 to 0.151 inch
351W and Lightning...	0.112 to 0.172 inch
Lifter diameter..	0.8740 to 0.8745 inch
Lifter bore diameter	0.8752 to 0.8767 inch
Lifter-to-bore clearance	
Standard..	0.0007 to 0.0027 inch
Service limit	0.005 inch
Pushrod runout limit...	0.015 inch

Oil pump

Outer race-to-housing clearance	
255 and 302	0.001 to 0.013 inch
351W and Lightning...	0.001 to 0.003 inch
Rotor assembly end clearance.................................	0.004 inch max
Driveshaft-to-housing clearance..............................	0.0015 to 0.0030 inch
Relief spring tension (lbs at specified length)	
255 and 302	10.6 to 12.2 lbs at 1.74 inches
351W and Lightning...	18.2 to 20.2 at 2.49 inches

Torque specifications

	Ft-lbs
Connecting rod nuts	
255 and 302	19 to 24
351W and Lightning...	40 to 45
Main bearing cap bolts	
255 and 302	60 to 70
351W and Lightning...	95 to 105

351M and 400 engines

General

Bore and stroke	
351M...	4.00 x 3.50 inches
400	4.00 x 4.00 inches
Compression pressure	Lowest cylinder must be at least 75-percent of highest cylinder
Oil pressure (at 2000 rpm, normal operating temperature)....................	50 to 75 psi

Engine block

Cylinder bore	
Diameter..	4.0000 to 4.0048 inches
Taper limit..	0.010 inch
Out-of-round limit	0.005 inch
Deck warpage limit	0.003 inch per 6 inches or 0.006 inch overall

Pistons and rings

Piston diameter	
Coded red	3.9982 to 3.9998 inches
Coded blue...	3.9994 to 4.0000 inches
Oversize available..	0.003 inch
Piston-to-cylinder bore clearance - selective fit......................	0.0014 to 0.0022 inch
Piston ring-to-groove clearance	
Top compression	0.0019 to 0.0036 inch
Bottom compression	0.002 to 0.004 inch
Oil	Snug fit in groove
Service limit...	0.002 inch max increase in clearance

Piston ring end gap

Top compression	0.010 to 0.020 inch
Bottom compression	0.010 to 0.020 inch
Oil	0.010 to 0.035 inch
Piston pin diameter (standard)	0.9749 to 0.9754 inch
Piston pin-to-piston clearance	0.0003 to 0.0005 inch
Piston pin-to-connecting rod bushing clearance	Interference fit

Crankshaft and flywheel

Main journal

Diameter	2.9994 to 3.0002 inches
Taper limit - max per inch	0.0005 inch
Out-of-round limit	0.0006 inch

Runout limit

Standard	0.002 inch
Service limit	0.005 inch

Main bearing oil clearance

Desired	0.0008 to 0.0015 inch
Allowable	0.0008 to 0.0026 inch

Connecting rod journal

Diameter	2.3103 to 2.3111 inches
Taper limit - max per inch	0.0006 inch
Out-of-round limit	0.0006 inch

Connecting rod bearing oil clearance

Desired	0.0008 to 0.0015 inch
Allowable	0.0008 to 0.0025 inch

Connecting rod side clearance

Standard	0.010 to 0.020 inch
Service limit	0.023 inch

Crankshaft endplay

Standard	0.004 to 0.008 inch
Service limit	0.012 inch

Camshaft

Bearing journal diameter

No. 1	2.1238 to 2.1248 inches
No. 2	2.0655 to 2.0665 inches
No. 3	2.0505 to 2.0515 inches
No. 4	2.0355 to 2.0365 inches
No. 5	2.0205 to 2.0215 inches

Bearing oil clearance

Standard	0.001 to 0.003 inch
Service limit	0.006 inch
Front bearing location	0.040 to 0.060 inch (distance that front edge of the bearing is located from the front face of the cylinder block)

Lobe lift

Intake	0.250 inch
Exhaust	0.250 inch
Maximum allowable lift loss	0.005 inch

Endplay

Standard	0.001 to 0.006 inch
Service limit	0.009 inch
Timing chain defection limit	1/2 inch

Cylinder heads and valve train

Head warpage limit	0.003 inch per 6 inches or 0.006 inch overall
Valve seat angle	45-degrees

Valve seat width

Intake	0.060 to 0.080 inch
Exhaust	0.070 to 0.090 inch
Valve seat runout limit	0.002 inch
Valve face angle	44-degrees
Valve face runout limit	0.002 inch
Valve margin width	1/32 inch min

Valve stem diameter

Intake	0.3416 to 0.3423 inch
Exhaust	0.3411 to 0.3418 inch

351M and 400 engines (continued)

Cylinder heads and valve train (continued)

Valve guide diameter	0.3433 to 0.3443 inch
Valve stem-to-guide clearance	
Intake	
Standard	0.0010 to 0.0027 inch
Service limit	0.005 inch max
Exhaust	
Standard	0.0015 to 0.0032 inch
Service limit	0.005 inch max
Valve spring free length	
Intake	2.06 inches
Exhaust	1.93 inches
Valve spring pressure (lbs at specified length)	
Intake	
1st check	76 to 84 at 1.82 inches
2nd check	215 to 237 at 1.39 inches
Exhaust	
1st check	79 to 87 at 1.68 inches
2nd check	215 to 237 at 1.39 inches
Service limit	10-percent loss of pressure
Valve spring installed height	
Intake	1.79 to 1.84 inches
Exhaust	1.66 to 1.71 inches
Valve spring out-of-square limit	0.078 inch
Collapsed lifter gap clearance	
Allowable	0.100 to 0.200 inch
Desired	0.125 to 0.175 inch
Lifter diameter	0.8740 to 0.8745 inch
Lifter bore diameter	0.8752 to 0.8767 inch
Lifter-to-bore clearance	
Standard	0.007 to 0.027 inch
Service limit	0.005 inch
Pushrod runout limit	0.015 inch

Oil pump

Outer race-to-housing clearance	0.001 to 0.003 inch
Rotor assembly end clearance	0.004 inch max
Driveshaft-to-housing clearance	0.0015 to 0.0030 inch
Relief spring tension (lbs at desired length)	20.6 to 22.6 at 2.49 inches

Torque specifications

	Ft-lbs
Connecting rod nut	40 to 45
Main bearing cap bolts	95 to 105

460 engine (7.5L)

General

Bore and stroke	4.36 x 3.85 inches
Compression pressure	Lowest cylinder must be at least 75-percent of highest cylinder
Oil pressure (at 2000 rpm, normal operating temperature)	40 to 88 psi

Engine block

Cylinder bore	
Diameter	4.3600 to 4.3636 inches
Taper limit	0.10 inch
Out-of-round	
Maximum	0.0015 inch
Service limit	0.005 inch
Deck warpage limit	0.003 inch per 6 inches or 0.006 inch overall

Pistons and rings

Piston diameter	
Coded red	
1996 and earlier	4.3577 to 4.3583 inches
1997	4.3585 to 4.3595 inches

Coded blue

1996 and earlier... 4.3589 to 4.3595 inches

1997 .... 4.3595 to 4.3605 inches

Oversize available .... 0.003 inch

Piston to bore clearance - selective fit

1996 and earlier... 0.0022 to 0.0030 inch

1997 .... 0.0014 to 0.0022 inch

Piston ring-to-groove clearance

Compression - top and bottom... 0.0025 to 0.0045 inch

Oil .... Snug fit in groove

Service limit.. 0.002 inch max increase in clearance

Piston ring end gap

Compression - top and bottom... 0.010 to 0.020 inch

Oil .... 0.010 to 0.035 inch

Piston pin diameter (standard) .... 1.0398 to 1.0403 inches

Piston pin-to-piston clearance .... 0.0002 to 0.0005 inch

Piston pin-to-connecting rod bushing clearance...................... Interference fit

Crankshaft and flywheel

Main journal

Diameter.. 2.9994 to 3.0002 inches

Taper limit - max per inch... 0.0005 inch

Out of round limit.. 0.0006 inch

Runout limit

Standard .... 0.002 inch

Service limit .... 0.005 inch

Main bearing oil clearance

Standard.. 0.0008 to 0.0015 inch

Service limit .... 0.0008 to 0.0026 inch

Connecting rod journal

Diameter.. 2.4992 to 2.5000 inches

Taper limit - max per inch... 0.0006 inch

Out-of-round limit .... 0.0006 inch

Connecting rod bearing oil clearance

Desired.. 0.0008 to 0.0015 inch

Allowable... 0.0008 to 0.0025 inch

Connecting rod side clearance

Standard.. 0.010 to 0.020 inch

Service limit .... 0.023 inch

Crankshaft endplay

Standard.. 0.004 to 0.008 inch

Service limit .... 0.012 inch

Camshaft

Bearing journal diameter (all) .... 2.1238 to 2.1248 inches

Bearing oil clearance

Standard.. 0.001 to 0.003 inch

Service limit .... 0.006 inch

Front bearing location... 0.040 to 0.060 inch (distance that front edge of the bearing is located from the front face of the cylinder block)

Lobe lift

Intake .... 0.252 inch

Exhaust .... 0.278 inch

Maximum allowable lift loss... 0.005 inch

Endplay

Standard.. 0.001 to 0.006 inch

Service limit .... 0.009 inch

Timing chain deflection limit .... 0.500 inch

Cylinder heads and valve train

Head warpage limit... 0.003 inch per 6 inches or 0.006 inch overall

Valve seat angle.. 45-degrees

Valve seat width.. 0.060 to 0.080 inch

Valve seat runout limit .... 0.002 inch

Valve face angle 44-degrees

Valve face runout limit .... 0.002 inch

Valve margin width .... 1/32 inch

Valve stem diameter .... 0.3416 to 0.3423 inch

Valve guide diameter .... 0.3433 to 0.3443 inch

460 engine (7.5L) (continued)

Cylinder heads and valve train (continued)

Valve stem-to-guide clearance
    Standard... 0.0010 to 0.0027 inch
    Service limit.. 0.0055 inch
Valve spring free length .... 2.06 inches
Valve spring pressure (lbs at specified length)
    1st check... 76 to 84 at 1.81 inches
    2nd check.. 218 to 240 at 1.33 inches
    Service limit.. 10-percent loss of pressure
Valve spring installed height .... 1.77 to 1.82 inches
Valve spring out-of-square limit .... 0.078 inch
Collapsed lifter gap clearance
    Allowable.. 0.075 to 0.175 inch
    Desired... 0.100 to 0.150 inch
Lifter diameter... 0.8740 to 0.8745 inch
Lifter bore diameter .... 0.8752 to 0.8767 inch
Lifter-to-bore clearance
    Standard... 0.0007 to 0.0027 inch
    Service limit.. 0.005 inch
Pushrod runout limit.. 0.015 inch

Oil pump

Outer race-to-housing clearance .... 0.001 to 0.013 inch
Rotor assembly end clearance... 0.004 inch max
Driveshaft-to-housing clearance...................................... 0.0015 to 0.0030 inch
Relief spring tension (lbs at specified length).................. 20.6 to 22.6 at 2.49 inches

Torque specifications

                                                                       Ft-lbs
Connecting rod nuts
    1990 and earlier .... 45 to 50
    1991 through 1993 .... 41 to 45
    1994 and later .... 45 to 50
Main bearing cap bolts .... 95 to 105

---

1 General information

Included in this portion of Chapter 2 are the general overhaul procedures for the cylinder head and internal engine components. The information ranges from advice concerning preparation for an overhaul and the purchase of replacement parts to detailed, step-by-step procedures covering removal and installation of internal engine components and the inspection of parts.

The following Sections have been written based on the assumption that the engine has been removed from the vehicle. For information concerning in-vehicle engine repair, as well as removal and installation of the external components necessary for the overhaul, see Part A, B or C of this Chapter.

The Specifications included here in Part C are only those necessary for the inspection and overhaul procedures which follow. Refer to Part A, B or C for additional Specifications.

2 Engine overhaul - general information

Refer to illustration 2.4

It's not always easy to determine when, or if, an engine should be completely overhauled, as a number of factors must be considered.

High mileage is not necessarily an indication that an overhaul is needed, while low mileage does not preclude the need for an overhaul. Frequency of servicing is probably the most important consideration. An engine that has had regular and frequent oil and filter changes, as well as other required maintenance, will most likely give many thousands of miles of reliable service. Conversely, a neglected engine may require an overhaul very early in its life.

Excessive oil consumption is an indication that piston rings and/or valve guides are in need of attention. Make sure that oil leaks are not responsible before deciding that the rings and/or guides are bad.

If the engine is making obvious knocking or rumbling noises, the connecting rod and/or main bearings are probably at fault. Check the oil pressure with a gauge installed in place of the oil pressure sending unit **(see illustration)**. On small block V8 engines and inline six-cylinder engines, the sending unit is located next to the oil filter. On V6 engines, it's located behind the power steering pump and air conditioning compressor. On big block V8 engines, it's located at the rear of the engine block behind the intake manifold. Compare the reading on the gauge to the Specifications at the front of this Chapter. If it's extremely low, the bearings and/or oil pump are probably worn out. As a general rule, engines should have about 10

psi oil pressure for every 1,000 rpm.

Loss of power, rough running, excessive valve train noise and high fuel consumption rates may also point to the need for an overhaul, especially if they are all present at the same time. If a complete tune-up doesn't remedy the situation, major mechanical work is the only solution. A compression check which indicates bad rings is also a good indicator (see Section 3).

2.4 Location of the oil pressure sending unit on the V6 engine

An engine overhaul involves restoring the internal parts to the specifications of a new engine. During an overhaul, the piston rings are replaced and the cylinder walls are reconditioned (rebored and/or honed). If a rebore is done, new pistons are required. The main bearings, connecting rod bearings and camshaft bearings are generally replaced with new ones and, if necessary, the crankshaft may be reground to restore the journals. Generally, the valves are serviced as well, since they are usually in less-than-perfect condition at this point. While the engine is being overhauled, other components, such as the distributor, starter and alternator, can be rebuilt as well. The end result should be a like new engine that will give many trouble free miles. **Note:** *Critical cooling system components such as the hoses, the drivebelts, the thermostat and the water pump MUST be replaced with new parts when an engine is overhauled. The radiator should be checked carefully to ensure that it isn't clogged or leaking; if in doubt, replace it with a new one. Also, we do not recommend overhauling the oil pump - always install a new one when an engine is rebuilt.*

Before beginning the engine overhaul, read through the entire procedure to familiarize yourself with the scope and requirements of the job. Overhauling an engine is not difficult, but it is time consuming. Plan on the vehicle being tied up for a minimum of two weeks, especially if parts must be taken to an automotive machine shop for repair or reconditioning. Check on availability of parts and make sure that any necessary special tools and equipment are obtained in advance. Most work can be done with typical hand tools, although a number of precision measuring tools are required for inspecting parts to determine if they must be replaced. Often an automotive machine shop will handle the inspection of parts and offer advice concerning reconditioning and replacement. **Note:** *Always wait until the engine has been completely disassembled and all components, especially the engine block, have been inspected before deciding what service and repair operations must be performed by an automotive machine shop.* Since the block's condition will be the major factor to consider when determining whether to overhaul the original engine or buy a rebuilt one, never purchase parts or have machine work done on other components until the block has been thoroughly inspected. As a general rule, time is the primary cost of an overhaul, so it doesn't pay to install worn or substandard parts.

As a final note, to ensure maximum life and minimum trouble from a rebuilt engine, everything must be assembled with care in a spotlessly clean environment.

3 Cylinder compression check

Refer to illustration 3.6

1   A compression check will tell you what mechanical condition the upper end (pistons, rings, valves, head gasket[s]) of your engine is in. Specifically, it can tell you if the compression is down due to leakage caused by worn piston rings, defective valves and seats or a blown head gasket. **Note:** *The engine must be at normal operating temperature and the battery must be fully charged for this check.*

2   Begin by cleaning the area around the spark plugs before you remove them (compressed air should be used, if available, otherwise a small brush or even a bicycle tire pump will work). The idea is to prevent dirt from getting into the cylinders as the compression check is being done.

3   Remove all of the spark plugs from the engine (see Chapter 1).

4   Block the throttle wide open.

5   Detach the primary (low voltage) wiring from the coil (see Chapter 5). On fuel-injected models the fuel pump circuit should also be disabled (see Chapter 4).

6   Install the compression gauge in the spark plug hole **(see illustration)**.

7   Crank the engine over at least seven compression strokes and watch the gauge. The compression should build up quickly in a healthy engine. Low compression on the first stroke, followed by gradually increasing pressure on successive strokes, indicates worn piston rings. A low compression reading on the first stroke, which doesn't build up during successive strokes, indicates leaking valves or a blown head gasket (a cracked head could also be the cause). Deposits on the undersides of the valve heads can also cause low compression. Record the highest gauge reading obtained.

8   Repeat the procedure for the remaining cylinders and compare the results to this Chapter's Specifications

9   Add some engine oil (about three squirts from a plunger-type oil can) to each cylinder, through the spark plug holes, and repeat the test.

10   If the compression increases after the oil is added, the piston rings are definitely worn. If the compression doesn't increase significantly, the leakage is occurring at the valves or head gasket. Leakage past the valves may be caused by burned valve seats and/or faces or warped, cracked or bent valves.

11   If two adjacent cylinders have equally low compression, there's a strong possibility that the head gasket between them is blown. The appearance of coolant in the combustion chambers or the crankcase would verify this condition.

12   If one cylinder is 20-percent lower than the others, and the engine has a slightly rough idle, a worn exhaust lobe on the camshaft could be the cause.

13   If the compression is unusually high, the combustion chambers are probably coated with carbon deposits. If that's the case, the cylinder head(s) should be removed and decarbonized.

14   If compression is way down or varies greatly between cylinders, it would be a good idea to have a leak-down test performed by an automotive repair shop. This test will pin-

3.6 A gauge with a threaded fitting for the spark plug hole is preferred over the type that requires hand pressure to maintain the seal during the compression check

point exactly where the leakage is occurring and how severe it is.

4 Engine rebuilding alternatives

1   The do-it-yourselfer is faced with a number of options when performing an engine overhaul. The decision to replace the engine block, piston/connecting rod assemblies and crankshaft depends on a number of factors, with the number one consideration being the condition of the block. Other considerations are cost, access to machine shop facilities, parts availability, time required to complete the project and the extent of prior mechanical experience on the part of the do-it-yourselfer.

2   Some of the rebuilding alternatives include:

3   **Individual parts** - If the inspection procedures reveal that the engine block and most engine components are within specifications, purchasing individual parts may be the most economical alternative. The block, crankshaft and piston/connecting rod assemblies should all be inspected carefully. Even if the block shows little wear, the cylinder bores should be surface honed.

4   **Crankshaft kit** - This rebuild package consists of a reground crankshaft and a matched set of pistons and connecting rods. The pistons will already be installed on the connecting rods. Piston rings and the necessary bearings will be included in the kit. These kits are commonly available for standard cylinder bores, as well as for engine blocks which have been bored to a regular oversize.

5   **Short block** - A short block consists of an engine block with a crankshaft and piston/connecting rod assemblies already installed. All new bearings are incorporated and all clearances will be correct. The existing camshaft, valve train components, cylinder head and external parts can be bolted to the short block with little or no machine shop work necessary.

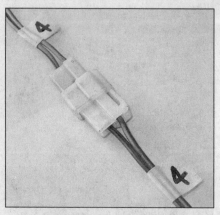

6.5 Label each wire before unplugging the connector

6   Long block - A long block consists of a short block plus an oil pump, oil pan, cylinder head, valve cover, camshaft and valve train components, timing sprockets and chain and front cover. All components are installed with new bearings, seals and gaskets incorporated throughout. The installation of manifolds and external parts is all that is necessary.

7   Give careful thought to which alternative is best for you and discuss the situation with local automotive machine shops, auto parts dealers and experienced rebuilders before ordering or purchasing replacement parts.

5   Engine removal - methods and precautions

1   If it has been decided that an engine needs to be removed for overhaul or major repair work, certain preliminary steps should be taken.
2   Locating a suitable work area is of greatest importance. A shop is, of course, the most desirable place to work. Adequate work space along with storage space for the vehicle is very important. If a shop or garage is not available, at the very least a flat, level, clean work surface made of concrete or asphalt is required.
3   Cleaning of the engine compartment and engine prior to removal will help you keep tools clean and organized.
4   A hoist such as an engine A-frame will also be necessary. Make sure that the equipment is rated in excess of the combined weight of the engine and its accessories. Safety is of primary importance, considering the potential hazards involved in lifting the engine out of the vehicle.
5   If the engine is being removed by a novice, a helper should be available. Advice and aid from someone more experienced would also be helpful. There are many instances when one person cannot simultaneously perform all of the operations which will be required when lifting the engine out of the vehicle.
6   Plan the operation ahead of time. Arrange for or obtain all of the tools and equip-

ment you will need prior to beginning the job. Some of the equipment necessary to perform engine removal and installation safely and with relative ease are (in addition to an engine hoist) a heavy duty floor jack, complete sets of wrenches and sockets as described in the front of this book, wooden blocks and plenty of rags and cleaning solvent for mopping up the inevitable spills. If the hoist is to be rented, make sure that you arrange for it in advance and perform all of the operations possible without it beforehand. This will save you money and time.
7   Always use extreme caution when removing and installing the engine; serious injury can result from careless actions. Plan ahead. Take your time and a job of this nature, although major, can be accomplished successfully.

6   Engine - removal and installation

Refer to illustration 6.5

Warning 1: *Gasoline is extremely flammable, so take extra precautions when you work on any part of the fuel system. Don't smoke or allow open flames or bare light bulbs near the work area, and don't work in a garage where a gas-type appliance (such as a water heater or clothes dryer) is present. Since gasoline is carcinogenic, wear latex gloves when there's a possibility of being exposed to fuel, and, if you spill any fuel on your skin, rinse it off immediately with soap and water. Mop up any spills immediately and do not store fuel-soaked rags where they could ignite. The fuel system on fuel-injected models is under constant pressure, so, if any fuel lines are to be disconnected, the fuel pressure in the system must be relieved first (see Chapter 4 for more information). When you perform any kind of work on the fuel system, wear safety glasses and have a Class B type fire extinguisher on hand.*
Warning 2: *The air conditioning system is under high pressure. DO NOT loosen any hose or line fittings or remove any components until after the system has been discharged by a dealer service department or service station. Always wear eye protection when disconnecting air conditioning system fittings.*
Note: *The engine must be removed alone, with the transmission left in the vehicle or removed beforehand. Also, due to the wide range of vehicle models and engines covered by this manual, the following instructions are of a general nature and may cover some steps not applicable to your vehicle. If a step doesn't apply to your vehicle, move on to the next one.*

Removal

1   Refer to Chapter 4 and relieve the fuel system pressure (fuel-injected models only), then disconnect the negative cable from the battery.
2   Cover the fenders and cowl and remove the hood (see Chapter 11). Special pads are available to protect the fenders, but an old bedspread or blanket will also work.

3   Remove the air cleaner assembly.
4   Drain the cooling system (see Chapter 1).
5   Label the vacuum lines, emissions system hoses, wiring connectors, ground straps and fuel lines, to ensure correct reinstallation, then detach them. Pieces of masking tape with numbers or letters written on them work well **(see illustration)**. If there's any possibility of confusion, make a sketch of the engine compartment and clearly label the lines, hoses and wires. Plug or cap all open fittings or lines.
6   Label and detach all coolant hoses from the engine.
7   Remove the cooling fan, shroud and radiator (see Chapter 3). If the vehicle is equipped with air conditioning, remove the condenser also (see Chapter 3).
8   Remove the drivebelts (see Chapter 1).
9   Disconnect the throttle linkage or cable (and TV linkage/cruise control cable, if equipped) from the engine (see Chapter 4).
10   On power steering equipped vehicles, unbolt the power steering pump (see Chapter 10). Leave the lines/hoses attached and make sure the pump is kept in an upright position in the engine compartment (use wire or rope to restrain it out of the way).
11   On air-conditioned models, unbolt the compressor (see Chapter 3) and set it aside. Do not disconnect the hoses.
12   Drain the engine oil (see Chapter 1) and remove the filter.
13   Remove the starter motor (see Chapter 5).
14   Remove the alternator (see Chapter 5).
15   Unbolt the exhaust system from the engine (see Chapter 4).
16   If you're working on a vehicle with an automatic transmission, refer to Chapter 7, Part B and remove the driveplate-to-torque converter fasteners.
17   Support the transmission with a jack. Position a block of wood between them to prevent damage to the transmission. Special transmission jacks with safety chains are available - use one if possible.
18   Attach an engine sling or a length of chain to the lifting brackets on the engine.
19   Roll the hoist into position and connect the sling to it. Take up the slack in the sling or chain, but don't lift the engine. **Warning:** *DO NOT place any part of your body under the engine when it's supported only by a hoist or other lifting device.*
20   Remove the transmission-to-engine block bolts.
21   Remove the engine mount-to-frame bolts.
22   Recheck to be sure nothing is still connecting the engine to the transmission or vehicle. Disconnect anything still remaining.
23   Raise the engine slightly. Carefully work it forward to separate it from the transmission. If you're working on a vehicle with an automatic transmission, be sure the torque converter stays in the transmission (clamp a pair of vise-grips to the housing to keep the converter from sliding out). If you're working on a vehicle with a manual transmission, the input shaft must be completely disengaged

from the clutch. Slowly raise the engine out of the engine compartment. Check carefully to make sure nothing is hanging up.

24 Remove the flywheel/driveplate and mount the engine on an engine stand.

Installation

25 Check the engine and transmission mounts. If they're worn or damaged, replace them.

26 If you're working on a manual transmission equipped vehicle, install the clutch and pressure plate (see Chapter 8). Now is a good time to install a new clutch.

27 Carefully lower the engine into the engine compartment - make sure the engine mounts line up.

28 If you're working on a manual transmission equipped vehicle, apply a dab of high-temperature grease to the input shaft and guide it into the crankshaft pilot bearing until the bellhousing is flush with the engine block.

29 Install the transmission-to-engine bolts and tighten them securely. **Caution:** *DO NOT use the bolts to force the transmission and engine together!*

30 If you're working on an automatic transmission equipped vehicle, slide the torque converter up to the driveplate and install the driveplate-to-torque converter bolts (see Chapter 7, Part B).

31 Reinstall the remaining components in the reverse order of removal.

32 Add coolant, oil, power steering and transmission fluid as needed (see Chapter 1).

33 Run the engine and check for leaks and proper operation of all accessories, then install the hood and test drive the vehicle.

34 Have the air conditioning system recharged and leak tested.

7 Engine overhaul - disassembly sequence

Note: *When removing the external components from the engine, pay close attention to details that may be helpful or important during installation. Note the installed position of gaskets, seals, spacers, pins, washers, bolts and other small items.*

1 Before beginning the disassembly and overhaul procedures, make sure the following items are available:

> Crankshaft vibration damper puller
> Common hand tools
> Small cardboard boxes or plastic bag
>   for storing parts
> Gasket scraper
> Ridge reamer
> Vibration damper installation tool
> Micrometers
> Telescoping gauges
> Dial indicator set
> Valve spring compressor
> Cylinder surfacing hone
> Piston ring groove cleaning tool
> Electric drill motor
> Tap and die set
> Wire brushes

> Oil gallery brushes
> Cleaning solvent

2 It's much easier to disassemble and work on the engine if it's mounted on a portable engine stand. These stands can often be rented quite cheaply from an equipment rental yard. Before the engine is mounted on a stand, the flywheel/driveplate should be removed from the crankshaft.

3 If a stand is not available, it's possible to disassemble the engine with it blocked up on a sturdy workbench or on the floor. Be extra careful not to tip or drop the engine when working without a stand.

4 Begin disassembly with the removal of external components as follows:

> Alternator, if not already removed (see
>   Chapter 5)
> Accessory drivebelts and pulleys (if not
>   previously removed, see Chapter 1)
> Water pump and related hoses (see
>   Chapter 3)
> On carbureted models, fuel pump and
>   filter assembly (see Chapter 4)
> Distributor and coil (see Chapter 5)
> Carburetor and fuel lines or, on fuel-in-
>   jected models, the upper intake mani-
>   fold and fuel rail (see Chapter 4)
> Clutch assembly (see Chapter 8)
> Oil dipstick and dipstick tube
> Spark plugs (see Chapter 1)

5 With these components removed, the engine sub-assemblies can be removed in the following order:

> Valve cover(s) and lifter cover (4.9L only)
>   (see Chapter 2A, B or C)
> Exhaust manifold(s) (see Chapter 2A, B
>   or C)
> Intake manifold (see Chapter 2A, B or C)
> Rocker arms and pushrods (see Chapter
>   2A, B or C)
> Lifters (see Chapter 2A, B or C)
> Cylinder head assembly (see Chapter 2A,
>   B or C)
> Crankshaft vibration damper assembly
>   (see Chapter 2A, B or C)
> Timing cover, timing chain/sprockets or
>   gears (Chapter 2A, B or C). Note:
>   Perform timing chain/gear wear check
>   before removing components (see
>   Section 8)
> Camshaft (see Chapter 2A, B or C)
> Oil pan (see Chapter 2A, B or C)
> Oil pump and pickup assembly (see
>   Chapter 2A, B or C)
> Piston and rod assemblies (see Section 9)
> Crankshaft and bearings (see Section 10)
> Cylinder head disassembly (see Section 11)

8 Timing chain/sprockets or gears - wear checks

Refer to illustration 8.4

Timing chain check - all engines (except 4.9L)

Note: *This procedure requires that the timing*

8.4 Check timing chain and sprocket wear by taking up all chain slack on one side and measuring total chain deflection on the other side

cover be removed.

1 Turn the crankshaft in a counterclockwise direction (viewed from the front of the engine) to take up the slack on the left side of the chain.

2 At the approximate mid-point of the right side chain run, force the chain out with your finger while holding a graduated scale against chain to establish initial measurement. The centerline of one link pin makes a good reference point.

3 Force the chain in the opposite direction and measure the amount of total deflection from the initial starting point.

4 Compare the total deflection measurement **(see illustration)** to the figure listed in this Chapter's Specifications. If chain deflection is excessive, replace the chain and both sprockets with new ones. **Note:** *It is recommended to replace the timing chain and sprockets during a major overhaul regardless of condition since the investment is small in comparison to the time and effort required to replace them later.*

Endplay check - all engines

Note: *The following checking procedures require the use of a magnetic base dial indicator.*

5 Check the camshaft endplay by pushing the camshaft all the way to the rear of its travel in the block.

6 Install a dial indicator so the indicator stem is on the camshaft gear/sprocket retaining bolt. Zero the dial indicator in this position.

7 Using a large screwdriver between the camshaft gear/sprocket and the block, pull the camshaft forward and release it. The reading on the dial indicator will give you the endplay measurement. Compare it to the value listed in this Chapter's Specifications. If the endplay is excessive, check the spacer for correct installation. If the spacer is correctly installed, and the endplay is too great, the thrust plate must be replaced with a new one.

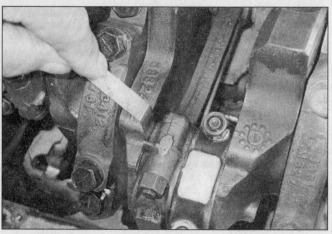

9.1 A ridge reamer is required to remove the ridge from the top of the cylinder - do this *before* removing the pistons!

9.3 Checking the connecting rod endplay with a feeler gauge

Timing gear check - 4.9L engine

8 Check the timing gear backlash by installing a dial indicator on the cylinder block and positioning the stem against the timing gear.

9 Zero the pointer on the dial indicator.

10 While holding the crankshaft still, move the camshaft timing gear until all slack is taken up.

11 Read the dial indicator to obtain the gear backlash.

12 Compare the results to the value listed in this Chapter's Specifications.

13 If the backlash is excessive, replace the timing gear and the crankshaft gear with new ones.

14 To check the timing gear runout, install a dial indicator on the engine block with the stem touching the face of the timing gear.

15 Hold the camshaft gear against the camshaft thrust plate and zero the indicator.

16 Rotate the crankshaft to turn the camshaft while holding the camshaft gear against the thrust plate.

9.5 To prevent damage to the crankshaft journals and cylinder walls, slip sections of hose over the rod bolts before removing the pistons

17 Rotate the gear through one complete revolution of the camshaft. Observe the reading on the dial indicator during this revolution.

18 If the runout exceeds the Specifications, remove the camshaft gear and check for foreign objects or burrs between the camshaft and gear flanges. If this condition does not exist and the runout is excessive, the gears must be replaced with new ones.

19 Use a similar procedure to check the crankshaft gear runout. Make sure that the crankshaft is situated against one end of the thrust bearing (this will prevent you from obtaining a crankshaft endplay measurement as opposed to the actual runout of the crankshaft gear).

9 Piston/connecting rod assembly - removal

Refer to Illustrations 9.1, 9.3 and 9.5

Note: *Prior to removing the piston/connecting rod assemblies, remove the cylinder head, the oil pan and the oil pump by referring to the appropriate Sections in Chapter 2, Part A, B or C.*

1 Completely remove the ridge at the top of each cylinder with a ridge reaming tool **(see illustration)**. Follow the manufacturer's instructions provided with the tool. Failure to remove the ridges before attempting to remove the piston/connecting rod assemblies will result in piston breakage.

2 After the cylinder ridges have been removed, turn the engine upside-down so the crankshaft is facing up.

3 Before the connecting rods are removed, check the endplay with feeler gauges. Slide them between the first connecting rod and the crankshaft throw until the play is removed **(see illustration)**. The endplay is equal to the thickness of the feeler gauge(s). If the endplay exceeds the service limit, new connecting rods will be required. If new rods (or a new crankshaft) are installed, the endplay may fall under the specified minimum (if it does,

the rods will have to be machined to restore it - consult an automotive machine shop for advice if necessary). Repeat the procedure for the remaining connecting rods.

4 Check the connecting rods and caps for identification marks. If they aren't plainly marked, use a small center-punch to make the appropriate number of indentations on each rod and cap (1, 2, 3 etc., depending on the cylinder they are associated with).

5 Loosen each of the connecting rod cap nuts 1/2-turn at a time until they can be removed by hand. Remove the number one connecting rod cap and bearing insert. Don't drop the bearing insert out of the cap. While supporting the connecting rod, slip a short length of plastic or rubber hose over each connecting rod cap bolt to protect the crankshaft journal and cylinder wall when the piston is removed **(see illustration)**. Push the connecting rod/piston assembly out through the top of the engine. Use a wooden or plastic hammer handle to push on the upper bearing insert in the connecting rod. If resistance is felt, double-check to make sure that all of the ridge was removed from the cylinder.

6 Repeat the procedure for the remaining cylinders. After removal, reassemble the connecting rod caps and bearing inserts in their respective connecting rods and install the cap nuts finger tight. Leaving the old bearing inserts in place until reassembly will help prevent the connecting rod bearing surfaces from being accidentally nicked or gouged.

10 Crankshaft - removal

Refer to illustrations 10.1, 10.3, 10.4a, 10.4b and 10.4c

Note: *The crankshaft can be removed only after the engine has been removed from the vehicle. It is assumed that the flywheel or driveplate, front crankshaft pulley, timing chain and sprockets, oil pan, oil pump and piston/connecting rod assemblies have already been removed.*

10.1 Checking crankshaft endplay with a dial indicator

10.3 Checking crankshaft endplay with a feeler gauge

1   Before the crankshaft is removed, check the endplay. Mount a dial indicator with the stem in line with and just touching one of the crank throws **(see illustration)**.

2   Push the crankshaft all the way to the rear and zero the dial indicator. Next, pry the crankshaft to the front as far as possible and note the reading on the dial indicator. The distance that it moves is the endplay. If it's greater than specified, check the crankshaft thrust surfaces for wear. If no wear is evident, a new thrust bearing should correct the endplay. If the endplay is less than the minimum, check the thrust bearing surfaces for deep scratches, burrs, nicks and dirt.

3   If a dial indicator is not available, feeler gauges can be used. Gently pry or push the crankshaft all the way to the front of the engine. Slip feeler gauges between the crankshaft and the front face of the thrust main bearing to determine the clearance **(see illustration)**. The thrust bearing is the number 5

bearing saddle on 4.9L engines and in the number three bearing saddle on V6 and V8 engines.

4   Check the main bearing caps to see if they are marked to indicate their locations. They should be numbered consecutively from the front of the engine to the rear. If they aren't, mark them with number stamping dies or a center-punch **(see illustrations)**. Main bearing caps generally have a cast-in arrow, which points to the front of the engine **(see illustration)**. Loosen the main bearing cap bolts 1/4-turn at a time each, until they can be removed by hand.

5   Gently tap the caps with a soft-face hammer, then separate them from the engine block. If necessary, use the bolts as levers to remove the caps. Try not to drop the bearing inserts if they come out with the caps.

6   Carefully lift the crankshaft out of the engine. It's a good idea to have an assistant available, since the crankshaft is quite heavy.

With the bearing inserts in place in the engine block and main bearing caps, return the caps to their respective locations on the block and tighten the bolts finger tight.

7   Remove the Woodruff key from the crankshaft nose so it doesn't get lost. If it's hard to remove, just leave it in place.

11   Cylinder head - disassembly

Refer to illustrations 11.2, 11.3a and 11.3b

Note: *New and rebuilt cylinder heads are commonly available for most engines at dealerships and auto parts stores. Due to the fact that some specialized tools are necessary for the disassembly and inspection procedures, and replacement parts may not be readily available, it may be more practical and economical for the home mechanic to purchase a replacement head rather than taking the time to disassemble, inspect and recondition the original.*

1   Cylinder head disassembly involves

10.4a If necessary, use a center-punch or number stamping dies to mark the main bearing caps to ensure that they are reinstalled in their original locations on the block (make the punch marks near one of the bolt heads)

10.4b Mark the caps in order from the front of the engine to the rear (one mark for the front cap, two for the second one and so on)

10.4c The arrow on each main bearing cap indicates the front of the engine

11.2 A small plastic bag, with an appropriate label, can be used to store the valve train components so they can be kept together and reinstalled in the correct guide

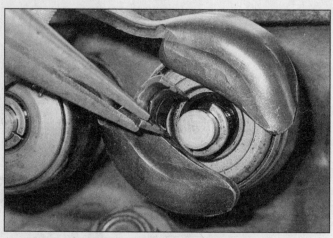

11.3a Use a valve spring compressor to compress the spring, then remove the keepers from the valve stem

11.3b If the valve won't pull through the guide, deburr the edge of the stem end and the area around the keeper grooves with a file or whetstone

removal of the intake and exhaust valves and related components. Remove the rocker arms and fulcrums from the cylinder heads (see Chapter 2A or 2B). Label the parts and store them separately so they can be reinstalled in their original locations.

2   Before the valves are removed, arrange to label and store them, along with their related components, so they can be kept separate and reinstalled in the same valve guides they are removed from **(see illustration)**.

3   Compress the springs on the first valve with a spring compressor and remove the keepers **(see illustration)**. Carefully release the valve spring compressor and remove the retainer, the valve spring, the valve spring damper, the valve stem seal and the valve. Store the components together and discard the seal. If the valve binds in the guide (won't pull through), push it back into the head and deburr the area around the keeper groove with a fine file or whetstone **(see illustration)**.

4   Repeat the above procedure for the remaining valves. Remember to keep all the parts for each valve together so they can be reinstalled in the same locations.

5   Once the valves and related components have been removed and stored in an organized manner, the head should be thoroughly cleaned and inspected. If a complete engine overhaul is being done, finish the engine disassembly procedures before beginning the cylinder head cleaning and inspection process.

12 Component inspection

1   Perform inspections and check procedures as outlined in the following sections to determine component replacement and machining requirements:
   a) *Cylinder head (see Section 13).*
   b) *Valve lifters and pushrods (see Section 14).*
   c) *Camshaft and bearings (see Section 15).*
   d) *Engine block (see Sections 16 and 17).*
   e) *Piston/connecting rod assembly (see Section 18).*
   f) *Crankshaft (see Section 19).*
   g) *Main and connecting rod bearings (see Section 20).*
   h) *Oil pump (see Section 21).*

13 Cylinder head - cleaning and inspection

Refer to illustrations 13.12, 13.14, 13.15, 13.16, 13.17, 13.18, 13.20a, 13.20b and 13.20c.

Note: *Decarbonizing chemicals are available and may prove very useful when cleaning the cylinder head and valve train components. They are very caustic and should be used with caution. Be sure to follow the instructions on the container.*

1   Thorough cleaning of the cylinder head and related valve train components, followed by a detailed inspection, will enable you to decide how much valve service work must be done during the engine overhaul.

Cleaning

2   Scrape away all traces of old gasket material and sealing compound from the head gasket, intake manifold and exhaust manifold sealing surfaces. Be very careful not to gouge the cylinder head. Special gasket removal solvents, which soften gaskets and make removal much easier, are available at auto parts stores.

3   Remove any built up scale from the coolant passages.

4   Run a stiff wire brush through the various holes to remove any deposits that may have formed in them.

5   Run an appropriate size tap into each of the threaded holes to remove any corrosion and thread sealant that may be present. If compressed air is available, use it to clear the holes of debris produced by this operation. **Warning:** *Wear eye protection!*

6   Clean the rocker arm bolt threads with a wire brush.

7   Clean the cylinder head with solvent and dry it thoroughly. Compressed air will speed the drying process and ensure that all holes and recessed areas are clean.

8   Clean the rocker arms, fulcrums and pushrods with solvent and dry them thoroughly (don't mix them up during cleaning). Compressed air will speed the drying process and can be used to clean out the oil passages.

9   Clean all the valve springs, keepers and retainers with solvent and dry them thoroughly. Do the components from one valve at a time to avoid mixing up the parts.

10   Scrape off any heavy deposits that may have formed on the valves, then use a motorized wire brush to remove deposits from the valve heads and stems. Again, make sure the valves do not get mixed up.

13.12 Check the cylinder head gasket surface for warpage by trying to slip a feeler gauge under the straightedge (see the Specifications for the maximum warpage allowed and use a feeler gauge of that thickness)

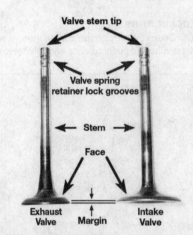

13.14 A dial indicator can be used to determine the valve stem-to-guide clearance (move the valve stem as indicated by the arrows)

Inspection

Cylinder head

11   Inspect the head very carefully for cracks, evidence of coolant leakage and other damage. If cracks are found, a new cylinder head should be obtained.

12   Using a straightedge and feeler gauge, check the head gasket mating surface for warpage **(see illustration)**. If the warpage exceeds the specified limit, the head can be resurfaced at an automotive machine shop.

13   Examine the valve seats in each of the combustion chambers. If they are pitted, cracked or burned, the head will require valve service that is beyond the scope of the home mechanic.

14   Check the valve stem-to-guide clearance by measuring the lateral movement of the valve stem with a dial indicator attached securely to the head **(see illustration)**. The valve must be in the guide and approximately 1/16-inch off the seat. The total valve stem movement indicated by the gauge needle must be divided by two to obtain the actual clearance. After this is done, if there is still some doubt regarding the condition of the valve guides they should be checked by an automotive machine shop (the cost should be minimal).

Valves

15   Carefully inspect each valve face for uneven wear, deformation, cracks, pits and burned spots **(see illustration)**. Check the valve stem for scuffing and galling and the neck for cracks. Rotate the valve and check for any obvious indication that it's bent. Look for pits and excessive wear on the end of the stem. The presence of any of these conditions indicates the need for valve service by an automotive machine shop.

16   Measure the margin width on each valve **(see illustration)**. Any valve with a margin narrower than 1/32-inch will have to be replaced with a new one.

Valve springs

17   Check each valve spring for wear (on the ends) and pits. Measure the free length and compare it to this Chapter's Specifications **(see illustration)**. Any springs that are shorter than specified have sagged and should not be reused. The tension of all springs should be checked with a special fixture before deciding that they are suitable for use in a rebuilt engine (take the springs to an automotive machine shop for this check).

18   Stand each spring on a flat surface and check it for squareness **(see illustration)**. If **any of the springs** are distorted or sagged, replace all of them with new parts.

13.15 Check for valve wear at the points shown here

19   Check the spring retainers and keepers for obvious wear and cracks. Any questionable parts should be replaced with new ones, as extensive damage will occur if they fail during engine operation.

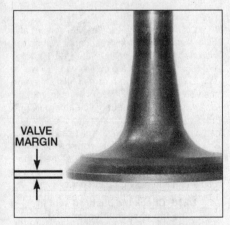

13.16 The margin width on each valve must be as specified (if no margin exists, the valve cannot be reused)

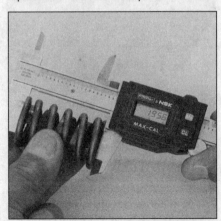

13.17 Measure the free length of each valve spring with a dial or vernier caliper

13.18 Check each valve spring for squareness

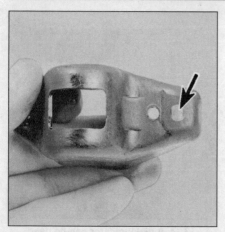

13.20a Check the rocker arm surfaces that contact the valve stem and pushrod (arrows) . . .

13.20b . . . the fulcrum seats in the rocker arm . . .

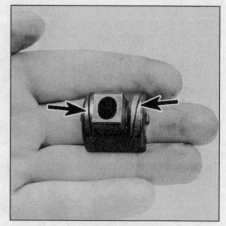

13.20c . . . and the fulcrums themselves for wear and galling

Rocker arms

20   Check the rocker arm faces (the areas that contact the pushrod ends and valve stems)

14.3a If the lifters are pitted or rough, they shouldn't be re-used

for pits, wear, galling, score marks and rough spots. Check the rocker arm fulcrum contact areas and fulcrums as well **(see illustrations)**. Look for cracks in each rocker arm.

21   Check the rocker arm bolts or studs for damaged threads.

22   Any damaged or excessively worn parts must be replaced with new ones.

General

23   If the inspection process indicates that the valve components are in generally poor condition and worn beyond the limits specified, which is usually the case in an engine that is being overhauled, reassemble the valves in the cylinder head and see Section 23 for valve servicing recommendations.

24   If the inspection turns up no excessively worn parts, and if the valve faces and seats are in good condition, the valve train components can be reinstalled in the cylinder head without major servicing. Refer to the appropriate Section for the cylinder head reassembly procedure.

14   Valve lifters and pushrods - inspection

Refer to illustrations 14.3a, 14.3b, 14.3c, 14.3d and 14.5

Lifters (non-roller)

1   Remove the lifters (refer to the appropriate engine Chapter).

2   Once the lifters have been removed, clean them with solvent and dry them thoroughly without mixing them up. Remember that the lifters must be reinstalled in their original bores in the block.

3   Check each lifter wall, pushrod seat and foot for scuffing, score marks and uneven wear **(see illustrations)**. Each lifter foot (the surface that rides on the cam lobe) must be slightly convex, although this can be difficult to determine by eye. If the base of the lifter is concave, the lifters and camshaft must be replaced. If the lifter walls are damaged or worn, inspect the lifter bores in the engine

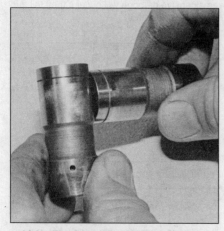

14.3b The foot of each lifter should be slightly convex - the side of another lifter can be used as a straightedge to check it; if it appears flat, it is worn and must not be used

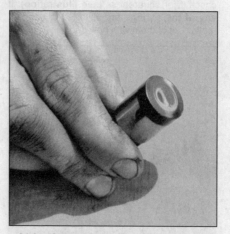

14.3c If the bottom of any lifter is worn concave, scratched or galled, replace the entire set with new lifters

14.3d Check the pushrod seat in the top of each lifter for wear

14.5 The roller on roller lifters must turn freely - check for wear and excessive play as well

15.2 Check the diameter of each camshaft bearing journal to pinpoint excessive wear and out-of-round conditions

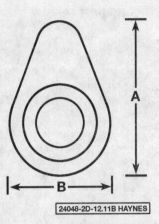

15.4 To verify camshaft lobe lift, measure the major (A) and minor (B) diameters of each lobe with a micrometer - subtract each minor diameter from the major diameter to arrive at the lobe lift

block as well. If the pushrod seats are worn, check the pushrod ends.

4   If new lifters are being installed, a new camshaft must also be installed. If a new camshaft is installed, then use new lifters as well. Never install used lifters unless the original camshaft is used and the lifters can be installed in their original locations.

Roller lifters

5   Some late model engines are equipped with roller lifters. Check each lifter wall and pushrod seat for scuffing, score marks, and uneven wear. Check rollers for score marks, ease of rotation and flat spots **(see illustration)**. If the lifters show signs of excessive wear, check the camshaft carefully. If the cam lobes aren't worn excessively, the camshaft can be re-used. If the lifter walls are damaged or worn (which is not very likely), inspect the lifter bores in the engine block as well. If the push-rod seats are worn, check the pushrod ends.

6   Used roller lifters can be installed with a new camshaft, provided they are in good condition. They must be installed in their original bores, however.

Pushrods

7   Inspect the pushrod ends for scuffing, cracks and excessive wear. Roll each push-rod on a flat surface, such as a piece of plate glass, to determine if it's bent. Replace any bent pushrods.

8   Check pushrod oil passage for possible blockage, clean as required.

---

15   Camshaft and bearings - inspection

Refer to illustrations 15.2 and 15.4

Inspection

1   After the camshaft has been removed from the engine, cleaned with solvent and dried, inspect the bearing journals for uneven wear, pitting and evidence of seizure. If the journals are damaged, the bearing inserts in the block are probably damaged as well. Both the cam-shaft and the bearings will have to be replaced.

2   If they're in good condition, measure the bearing journals with a micrometer **(see illus-tration)** to determine their size and whether or

not they're out-of-round. The inside diameter of each bearing can be measured with a tele-scoping gauge and micrometer. Subtract each cam journal diameter from the corresponding bearing inside diameter to obtain the bearing oil clearance. Compare the clearance for each bearing to the Specifications. If it's excessive for any of the bearings, have new bearings installed by an automotive machine shop.

3   Check the camshaft lobes for heat dis-coloration, score marks, chipped areas, pit-ting and uneven wear. If the lobes are in good condition and the lobe lift measurements are within the specified limits, the camshaft can be reinstalled (assuming that the bearing jour-nals are in acceptable condition).

4   Camshaft lobe lift can be checked with the camshaft installed in the engine (see Chapter 2A, B or C) or after it has been removed using the following procedure. Mea-sure the major (A) and minor (B) diameters of each lobe with a micrometer and record the results **(see illustration)**. The difference between the two is the lobe lift. If the mea-sured lift for any lobe is less than specified, replace the camshaft.

Bearing replacement

5   Camshaft bearing replacement requires special tools and expertise that place it out-side the scope of the home mechanic. Take the block to an automotive machine shop to ensure that the job is done correctly.

---

16   Engine block - cleaning

Refer to illustrations 16.1a, 16.1b, 16.8 and 16.10

1   Using a hammer and punch, tap the core plug on one side to rotate it within its bore, then remove it from the block with pliers **(see illustrations)**. **Caution:** *The core plugs may be difficult or impossible to remove if driven into the cooling passages.*

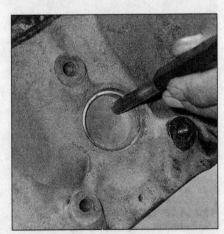

16.1a A hammer and large punch can be used to knock the core plugs sideways in their bores

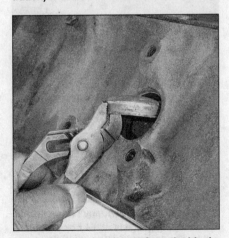

16.1b Pull the core plugs from the block with pliers

16.8 All bolt holes in the block - particularly the main bearing cap and head bolt holes - should be cleaned and restored with a tap (be sure to remove debris from the holes after this is done)

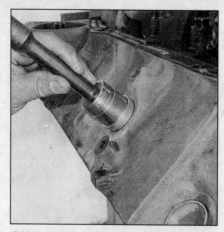

16.10 A large socket on an extension can be used to drive the new core plugs into the block

2   Using a gasket scraper, remove all traces of gasket material from the engine block. Be very careful not to nick or gouge the gasket sealing surfaces.

3   Remove the main bearing caps and separate the bearing inserts from the caps and the engine block. Tag the bearings, indicating which cylinder they were removed from and whether they were in the cap or the block, then set them aside.

4   Remove all of the threaded oil gallery plugs from the block. Discard the plugs and use new ones when the engine is reassembled.

5   If the engine is extremely dirty it should be taken to an automotive machine shop for cleaning.

6   After the block is returned, clean all oil holes and oil galleries one more time. Brushes specifically designed for this purpose

are available at most auto parts stores. Flush the passages with warm water until the water runs clear, dry the block thoroughly and wipe all machined surfaces with a light, rust preventive oil. If you have access to compressed air, use it to speed the drying process and to blow out all the oil holes and galleries. **Warning:** *Wear eye protection!*

7   If the block isn't extremely dirty or sludged up, you can do an adequate cleaning job with warm soapy water and a stiff brush. Take plenty of time and do a thorough job. Regardless of the cleaning method used, be sure to clean all oil holes and galleries very thoroughly, dry the block completely and coat all machined surfaces with light oil.

8   The threaded holes in the block must be clean to ensure accurate torque readings during reassembly. Run the proper size tap into each of the holes to remove any rust, corrosion, thread sealant or sludge and to restore any damaged threads **(see illustration)**. If possible, use compressed air to clear the holes of debris produced by this operation. **Warning:** *Wear eye protection!* Now is a good

time to clean the threads on the head bolts and the main bearing cap bolts as well.

9   Reinstall the main bearing caps and tighten the bolts finger tight.

10   After coating the sealing surfaces of the new core plugs with core plug sealant, install them in the engine block **(see illustration)**. Make sure they are driven in straight and seated properly or leakage could result. Special tools are available for this purpose, but a large socket, with an outside diameter that will just slip into the core plug, and a hammer will work just as well.

11   Apply non-hardening sealant (such as Permatex number 2 or Teflon tape) to the new oil gallery plugs and thread them into the holes in the block. Make sure they're tightened securely.

12   If the engine isn't going to be reassembled right away, cover it with a large plastic trash bag to keep it clean.

17   Engine block - inspection

Refer to illustrations 17.4a, 17.4b and 17.4c

1   Before the block is inspected, it should be cleaned (see Section 16). Double-check to make sure that the ridge at the top of each cylinder has been completely removed.

2   Visually check the block for cracks, rust and corrosion. Look for stripped threads in the threaded holes. It's also a good idea to have the block checked for hidden cracks by an automotive machine shop that has the special equipment to do this type of work. If defects are found, have the block repaired, if possible, or replaced.

3   Check the cylinder bores for scuffing and scoring.

4   Measure the diameter of each cylinder at the top (just under the ridge area), center and bottom of the cylinder bore, parallel to the crankshaft axis **(see illustrations)**. **Note:** *These measurements should not be made*

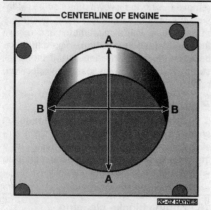

17.4a Measure the diameter of each cylinder at a right angle to the engine centerline (A), and parallel to engine centerline (B) - out-of-round is the difference between A and B; taper is the difference between A and B at the top of the cylinder and A and B at the bottom of the cylinder

17.4b The ability to "feel" when the telescoping gauge is at the correct point will be developed over time, so work slowly and repeat the check until you are satisfied that the bore measurement is accurate

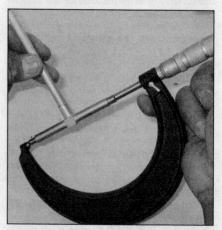

17.4c The gauge is then measured with a micrometer to determine the bore size

18.4a The piston ring grooves can be cleaned with a special tool, as shown here . . .

18.4b . . . or a section of a broken ring

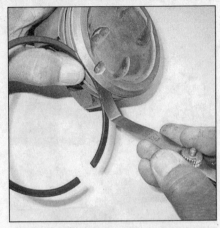

18.10 Check the ring side clearance with a feeler gauge at several points around the groove

with the bare block mounted on an engine stand - the cylinders will be distorted and the measurements will be inaccurate.

5   Next, measure each cylinder's diameter at the same three locations across the crankshaft axis. To calculate an out-of-round condition, subtract each measurement (A, B and C) taken parallel to the crankshaft axis from the ones taken across the crankshaft axis. The difference is the out-of-round reading. To determine cylinder taper, subtract measurement C from measurement A. Compare your results to this Chapter's Specifications.

6   If the required precision measuring tools aren't available, the piston-to-cylinder clearances can be obtained, though not quite as accurately, using feeler gauge stock. Feeler gauge stock comes in 12-inch lengths and various thicknesses and is generally available at auto parts stores.

7   To check the clearance, select a feeler gauge and slip it into the cylinder along with the matching piston. The piston must be positioned exactly as it normally would be. The feeler gauge must be between the piston and cylinder on one of the thrust faces (90-degrees to the piston pin bore).

8   The piston should slip through the cylinder (with the feeler gauge in place) with moderate pressure.

9   If it falls through or slides through easily, the clearance is excessive and a new piston will be required. If the piston binds at the lower end of the cylinder and is loose toward the top, the cylinder is tapered. If tight spots are encountered as the piston/feeler gauge is rotated in the cylinder, the cylinder is out-of-round.

10   Repeat the procedure for the remaining pistons and cylinders.

11   If the cylinder walls are badly scuffed or scored, or if they're out-of-round or tapered beyond the limits given in this Chapter's Specifications, have the engine block rebored and honed at an automotive machine shop. If

a rebore is done, oversize pistons and rings will be required.

12   If the cylinders are in reasonably good condition and not worn to the outside of the limits, and if the piston-to-cylinder clearances can be maintained properly, they don't have to be rebored. Honing is all that's necessary (see Section 25).

18   Piston/connecting rod assembly - inspection

Refer to illustrations 18.4a, 18.4b, 18.10 and 18.11

1   Before the inspection process can be carried out, the piston/connecting rod assemblies must be cleaned and the original piston rings removed from the pistons. **Note:** *Always use new piston rings when the engine is reassembled.*

2   Using a piston ring expander, carefully remove the rings from the pistons. Be careful not to nick or gouge the pistons in the process.

3   Scrape all traces of carbon from the crown (top) of the piston. A hand-held wire brush or a piece of fine emery cloth can be used once the majority of the deposits have been scraped away. Do not, under any circumstances, use a wire brush mounted in a drill motor to remove deposits from the pistons. The piston material is soft and will be eroded away by the wire brush.

4   Use a piston ring groove cleaning tool to remove carbon deposits from the ring grooves **(see illustration)**. If a ring groove cleaning tool isn't available, use a broken piece from one of the old rings **(see illustration)**. Be very careful to remove only the carbon deposits-don't remove any metal and do not nick or scratch the sides of the ring grooves.

5   Once the deposits have been removed, clean the piston/rod assemblies with solvent and dry them with compressed air (if available). Make sure that the oil return holes in

the back sides of the ring grooves are clear.

6   If the pistons aren't damaged or worn excessively, and if the engine block isn't rebored, new pistons won't be necessary. Normal piston wear appears as even vertical wear on the piston thrust surfaces and slight looseness of the top ring in its groove. New piston rings, on the other hand, should always be used when an engine is rebuilt.

7   Carefully inspect each piston for cracks around the skirt, at the pin bosses and at the ring lands.

8   Look for scoring and scuffing on the thrust faces of the skirt, holes in the piston crown and burned areas at the edge of the crown. If the skirt is scored or scuffed, the engine may have been suffering from overheating and/or abnormal combustion, which caused excessively high operating temperatures. The cooling and lubrication systems should be checked thoroughly. A hole in the piston crown is an indication that abnormal combustion (preignition) was occurring. Burned areas at the edge of the piston crown are usually evidence of spark knock (detonation). If any of the above conditions are noted, the causes must be corrected or the damage will occur again.

9   Corrosion of the piston, in the form of small pits, indicates that coolant is leaking into the combustion chamber and/or the crankcase. Again, the cause must be corrected or the problem may persist in the rebuilt engine.

10   Measure the piston ring side clearance by laying a new piston ring in each ring groove and slipping a feeler gauge in beside it **(see illustration)**. Check the clearance at three or four locations around each groove. Be sure to use the correct ring for each groove - they are different. If the side clearance is greater than specified, new pistons will have to be used.

11   Check the piston-to-bore clearance by measuring the bore (see Section 17) and the piston diameter. Make sure that the pistons and bores are correctly matched. Measure

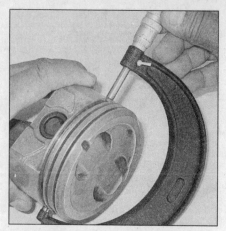

18.11 Measure the piston diameter at a 90-degree angle to the piston pin, at the centerline of the piston pin hole

19.1 The oil holes should be chamfered so sharp edges don't gouge or scratch the new bearings

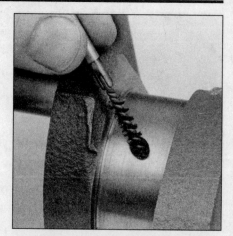

19.2 Use a wire or stiff plastic bristle brush to clean the oil passages in the crankshaft

the piston across the skirt, at a 90-degree angle to and in line with the piston pin **(see illustration)**. Subtract the piston diameter from the bore diameter to obtain the clearance. If it's greater than specified, the block will have to be rebored and new pistons and rings installed.

12   Check the piston-to-rod clearance by twisting the piston and rod in opposite directions. Any noticeable play indicates that there is excessive wear, which must be corrected. The piston/connecting rod assemblies should be taken to an automotive machine shop to have the pistons and rods rebored and new pins installed.

13   If the pistons must be removed from the connecting rods for any reason, they should be taken to an automotive machine shop. While they are there, have the connecting rods checked for bend and twist, since automotive machine shops have special equipment for this purpose. **Note:** *Unless new pistons and/or connecting rods must be installed, do not disassemble the pistons and connecting rods.*

14   Check the connecting rods for cracks and other damage. Temporarily remove the rod caps, lift out the old bearing inserts, wipe

the rod and cap bearing surfaces clean and inspect them for nicks, gouges and scratches. After checking the rods, replace the old bearings, slip the caps into place and tighten the nuts finger tight.

19 Crankshaft - inspection

Refer to illustrations 19.1, 19.2, 19.4, 19.6 and 19.8

1   Remove all burrs from the crankshaft oil holes with a stone, file or scraper **(see illustration)**.

2   Clean the crankshaft with solvent and dry it with compressed air (if available). Be sure to clean the oil holes with a stiff brush and flush them with solvent **(see illustration)**.

3   Check the main and connecting rod bearing journals for uneven wear, scoring, pits and cracks.

4   Rub a penny across each journal several times **(see illustration)**. If a journal picks up copper from the penny, it's too rough and must be reground.

5   Check the rest of the crankshaft for cracks and other damage. It should be magnafluxed to reveal hidden cracks - an automotive machine shop will handle the procedure.

6   Using a micrometer, measure the diameter of the main and connecting rod journals and compare the results to the Specifications **(see illustration)**. By measuring the diameter at a number of points around each journal's circumference, you'll be able to determine whether or not the journal is out-of-round. Take the measurement at each end of the journal, near the crank throws, to determine if the journal is tapered. Crankshaft runout should be checked also, but large V-blocks and a dial indicator are needed to do it correctly. If you don't have the equipment, have a machine shop check the runout.

7   If the crankshaft journals are damaged, tapered, out-of-round or worn beyond the limits given in the Specifications, have the crankshaft reground by an automotive machine shop. Be sure to use the correct size bearing inserts if the crankshaft is reconditioned.

8   Check the oil seal journals at each end of the crankshaft for wear and damage **(see illus-**

19.4 Rubbing a penny lengthwise on each journal will reveal its condition - if copper rubs off and is embedded in the crankshaft, the journals should be reground

19.6 Measure the diameter of each crankshaft journal at several points to detect taper and out-of-round conditions

19.8 If the seals have worn grooves in the crankshaft journals, or if the seal contact surfaces are nicked or scratched, the new seals will leak

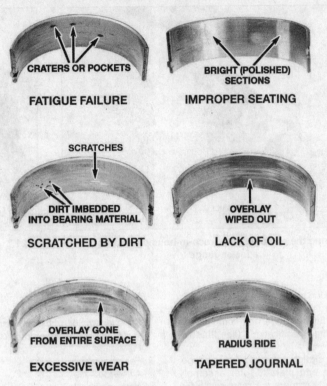

20.1 Typical bearing failures

tration). If the seal has worn a groove in the journal, or if it's nicked or scratched, the new seal may leak when the engine is reassembled. In some cases, an automotive machine shop may be able to repair the journal by pressing on a thin sleeve. If repair isn't feasible, a new or different crankshaft should be installed.

9   Examine the main and rod bearing inserts (see Section 20).

20 Main and connecting rod bearings - inspection

Refer to illustration 20.1

1   Even though the main and connecting rod bearings should be replaced with new ones during the engine overhaul, the old bearings should be retained for close examination, as they may reveal valuable information about the condition of the engine **(see illustration)**.

2   Bearing failure occurs because of lack of lubrication, the presence of dirt or other foreign particles, overloading the engine and corrosion. Regardless of the cause of bearing failure, it must be corrected before the engine is reassembled to prevent it from happening again.

3   When examining the bearings, remove them from the engine block, the main bearing caps, the connecting rods and the rod caps and lay them out on a clean surface in the same general position as their location in the engine. This will enable you to match any bearing problems with the corresponding crankshaft journal.

4   Dirt and other foreign particles get into the engine in a variety of ways. It may be left in the engine during assembly, or it may pass through filters or the PCV system. It may get into the oil, and from there into the bearings. Metal chips from machining operations and normal engine wear are often present. Abrasives are sometimes left in engine components after reconditioning, especially when parts are not thoroughly cleaned using the proper cleaning methods. Whatever the

source, these foreign objects often end up embedded in the soft bearing material and are easily recognized. Large particles will not embed in the bearing and will score or gouge the bearing and journal. The best prevention for this cause of bearing failure is to clean all parts thoroughly and keep everything spotlessly clean during engine assembly. Frequent and regular engine oil and filter changes are also recommended.

5   Lack of lubrication (or lubrication breakdown) has a number of interrelated causes. Excessive heat (which thins the oil), overloading (which squeezes the oil from the bearing face) and oil leakage or throw off (from excessive bearing clearances, worn oil pump or high engine speeds) all contribute to lubrication breakdown. Blocked oil passages, which usually are the result of misaligned oil holes in a bearing shell, will also oil starve a bearing and destroy it. When lack of lubrication is the cause of bearing failure, the bearing material is wiped or extruded from the steel backing of the bearing. Temperatures may increase to the point where the steel backing turns blue from overheating.

6   Driving habits can have a definite effect on bearing life. Full throttle, low speed operation (lugging the engine) puts very high loads on bearings, which tends to squeeze out the oil film. These loads cause the bearings to flex, which produces fine cracks in the bearing face (fatigue failure). Eventually the bearing material will loosen in pieces and tear away from the steel backing. Short trip driving leads to corrosion of bearings because insufficient engine heat is produced to drive off the condensed

water and corrosive gases. These products collect in the engine oil, forming acid and sludge. As the oil is carried to the engine bearings, the acid attacks and corrodes the bearing material.

7   Incorrect bearing installation during engine assembly will lead to bearing failure as well. Tight fitting bearings leave insufficient bearing oil clearance and will result in oil starvation. Dirt or foreign particles trapped behind a bearing insert result in high spots on the bearing which lead to failure.

21 Oil pump - inspection

Refer to illustrations 21.6 and 21.7

Note: *The oil pump must be removed from the engine prior to this procedure (see Chapter 2A, 2B or 2C).*

1   Remove the two bolts securing the pick-up tube to the oil pump, then remove the pick-up.

2   Clean the oil pump with solvent and dry it thoroughly with compressed air. **Warning:** *Wear eye protection.*

3   Remove the oil pump housing cover. It is retained by four bolts.

4   Use solvent and a brush to clean the inside of the pump housing and the pressure relief valve chamber. Make sure that the interior of the oil pump is clean.

5   Visually check the inside of the pump housing and the outer race and rotor for excessive wear, scoring or damage. Check the mating surface of the pump cover for wear, grooves or damage. If any of these conditions

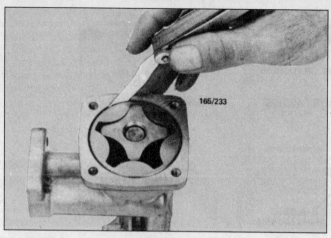

21.6 Measuring the oil pump outer race-to-housing clearance with a feeler gauge

21.7 Checking the oil pump rotor endplay with a feeler gauge and straightedge

exist, replace the pump with a new one.

6   Measure the outer race-to-housing clearance with a feeler gauge and compare the results with the Specifications **(see illustration)**.

7   Using a straightedge and feeler gauge, measure the end plate-to-rotor assembly clearance and compare the results with the Specifications **(see illustration)**.

8   Check the driveshaft-to-housing bearing clearance by measuring the inside diameter of the housing bearing and subtracting that figure from the outside diameter of the driveshaft. Compare the results with the Specifications.

9   If any components fail the checks mentioned, replace the entire oil pump, as the components are not serviced as separate parts.

10   Inspect the relief valve spring for wear or a collapsed condition.

11   Check the relief valve piston for scoring, damage and free operation within its bore.

12   If the relief valve fails any of the above tests, replace the entire relief valve assembly with a new one.

13   Install the rotor, outer housing and race in the oil pump. Pack the pump cavities with petroleum jelly (this will prime the pump and ensure good suction when the engine is started).

14   Install the cover and the four retaining bolts and tighten them to the torque listed in this Chapter's Specifications.

15   Attach the pick-up tube to the oil pump body using a new gasket. Tighten the bolts to the torque listed in the Chapter 2A, B or C Specifications.

22   Engine overhaul - reassembly sequence

1   Before beginning engine reassembly, make sure you have all the necessary new parts, gaskets and seals as well as the following items on hand:

Common hand tools
Crankshaft damper removal/installation tool
1/2-inch drive torque wrench
Piston ring installation tool
Piston ring compressor
Short lengths of rubber or plastic hose to fit over connecting rod bolts
Plastigage
Feeler gauges
A fine-tooth file
New engine oil
Engine assembly lube or moly-base grease
RTV gasket sealant
Thread locking compound

2   In order to save time and avoid problems, engine tolerance checks and reassembly should be done in the suggested order:

If necessary, have the cylinder head and valves serviced (see Section 23)
If necessary, reassemble cylinder head (see Section 24)
If necessary, hone the cylinder walls in block (see Section 25)
Crankshaft and main bearings (see Section 26)
Piston/connecting rod assemblies (see Sections 27 and 28)
Camshaft (see Chapter 2A, B or C)
Timing chain and sprockets (see Chapter 2B or 2C)
Timing cover (see Chapter 2A, B or C)
Cylinder head(s) (see Chapter 2A, B or C)
Oil pump (see Chapter 2A, B or C)
Rear main oil seal (see Chapter 2A or 2B)
Oil pan (see Chapter 2A, B or C)
Valve lifters (see Chapter 2A, B or C)
Rocker arms and pushrods (see Chapter 2A, B or C)
Intake manifold (see Chapter 2A, B or C)
Exhaust manifolds (see Chapter 2A, B or C)
Check, and if necessary, adjust the valve clearances (see Section 29)
Valve cover(s) and (on the 4.9L engine) pushrod cover (see Chapter 2A, B or C)
Front pulley and vibration damper assembly (see Chapter 2A, B or C)

3   Remaining engine build operations are reverse of removal operations.

4   Prior to engine start-up, perform engine initial start-up checks (see Section 30).

23   Valves - servicing

1   Because of the complex nature of the job and the special tools and equipment needed, servicing of the valves, the valve seats and the valve guides, commonly known as a valve job, is best left to a professional.

2   The home mechanic can remove and disassemble the head, do the initial cleaning and inspection, then reassemble and deliver the head to a dealer service department or an automotive machine shop for the actual valve servicing.

3   The dealer service department, or automotive machine shop, will remove the valves and springs, recondition or replace the valves and valve seats, recondition the valve guides, check and replace the valve springs, spring retainers and keepers as required, replace the valve seals with new ones, reassemble the valve components and make sure the installed spring height is correct. The cylinder head gasket surface will also be resurfaced if it's warped.

4   After the valve job has been performed by a professional. the head will be in like new condition. When the head is returned, be sure to clean it again before installation on the engine to remove any metal particles and abrasive grit that may still be present from the valve service or head resurfacing operations. Use compressed air, if available, to blow out all the oil holes and passages. **Warning:** *Wear eye protection.*

24   Cylinder head - reassembly

Refer to illustrations 24.6 and 24.8

1   Regardless of whether or not the head was sent to an automotive repair shop for valve servicing, make sure it's clean before beginning reassembly .

2   If the head was sent out for valve servicing, the valves and related components will already be in place. Refer to Step 8.

24.6 Apply a small dab of grease to each keeper as shown here before installation - it will hold them in place on the valve stem as the spring is released

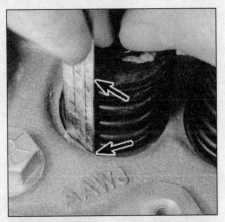

24.8 Be sure to check the valve spring installed height (the distance from the bottom of the spring/shield to the underside of the retainer

3   Beginning at one end of the head, lubricate and install the first valve. Apply moly-base grease or clean engine oil to the valve stem.

4   Slide a new valve stem seal over the valve and seat it on the guide with a deep socket and hammer (gently tap the seal until it's completely seated on the guide, see Chapter 2A or 2B). Be very careful not to deform or cock the seal during installation. **Note:** *On some engines the intake and exhaust valve seals may be different - refer to the appropriate engine Chapter.*

5   Install the valve spring seats or shims if any, then set the valve spring, damper and retainer in place.

6   Compress the springs with a valve spring compressor. Position the keepers in the valve stem grooves, then slowly release the compressor and make sure the keepers seat properly. Apply a small dab of grease to each keeper to hold it in place if necessary **(see illustration)**.

7   Repeat the same procedure for each valve. Be sure to return the components to their original locations - don't mix them up!

8   Check the installed valve spring height with a ruler graduated in 1/64-inch increments

or a dial caliper. If the head was sent out for service work, the installed height should be correct (but don't automatically assume that it is). The measurement is taken from the underside of the spring damper to the underside of the spring retainer **(see illustration)**. If the height is greater than specified, shims can be added under the springs to correct it. **Caution:** *Do not, under any circumstances, shim the springs to the point where the installed height is less than specified.*

25   Cylinder honing

Refer to illustrations 25.3a and 25.3b

Note: *If you don't have the tools or don't want to tackle the honing operation, most automotive machine shops will do it for a reasonable fee.*

1   Prior to engine reassembly, the cylinder bores must be honed so the new piston rings will seat correctly and provide the best possible combustion chamber seal.

2   Before honing the cylinders. install the main bearing caps and tighten the bolts to the torque listed in this Chapter's Specifications.

3   Two types of cylinder hones are commonly available - the flex hone or "bottle brush" type and the more traditional surfacing hone with spring-loaded stones. Both will do the job, but for the less experienced mechanic the "bottle brush" hone will probably be easier to use. You'll also need plenty of light oil or honing oil, some rags and an electric drill motor. Proceed as follows:

a) *Mount the hone in the drill motor, compress the stones and slip it into the first cylinder* **(see illustration)**.

b) *Lubricate the cylinder with plenty of oil, turn on the drill and move the hone up-and-down in the cylinder at a pace which will produce a fine crosshatch pattern on the cylinder walls. Ideally, the crosshatch lines should intersect at approximately a 60° angle* **(see illustration)**. *Be sure to use plenty of lubricant and don't take off any more material than is absolutely necessary to produce the desired finish.* **Note:** *Piston ring manufacturers may specify a smaller crosshatch angle than the traditional 60-degrees - read and follow any instructions printed on the piston ring packages.*

c) *Don't withdraw the hone from the cylinder while it's running. Instead, shut off the drill and continue moving the hone up-and-down in the cylinder until it comes to a complete stop, then compress the stones and withdraw the hone. If you're using a "bottle brush" type hone, stop the drill motor, then turn the chuck in the normal direction of rotation while withdrawing the hone from the cylinder.*

d) *Wipe the oil out of the cylinder and repeat the procedure for the remaining cylinders.*

4   After the honing job is complete, chamfer the top edges of the cylinder bores with a small file so the rings won't catch when the pistons are installed. Be very careful not to nick the cylinder walls with the end of the file.

5   The entire engine block must be washed

25.3a A "bottle brush" hone is the easiest type of hone to use

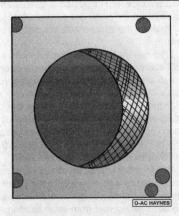

25.3b The cylinder hone should leave a smooth, cross-hatch pattern with the lines intersecting at approximately a 60-degree angle

26.10 Lay the Plastigage strips on the main bearing journals, parallel to the crankshaft centerline

26.14 Compare the width of the crushed Plastigage to the scale on the container to determine the main bearing oil clearance (always take the measurement at the widest point of the Plastigage); be sure to use the correct scale - standard and metric scales are included

again very thoroughly with warm, soapy water to remove all traces of the abrasive grit produced during the honing operation. **Note:** *The bores can be considered clean when a white cloth-dampened with clean engine oil-used to wipe down the bores doesn't pick up any more honing residue, which will show up as gray areas on the cloth. Be sure to run a brush through all oil holes and galleries and flush them with running water.*

6   After rinsing, dry the block and apply a coat of light rust preventive oil to all machined surfaces. Wrap the block in a plastic trash bag to keep it clean and set it aside until reassembly.

26 Crankshaft - installation and main bearing oil clearance check

Refer to illustrations 26.10 and 26.14

1   Crankshaft installation is the first step in engine reassembly. It's assumed at this point that the engine block and crankshaft have been cleaned, inspected and repaired or reconditioned.
2   Position the engine with the bottom facing up.
3   Remove the main bearing cap bolts and lift out the caps. Lay them out in the proper order to ensure that they are installed correctly.
4   If they're still in place, remove the old bearing inserts from the block and the main bearing caps. Wipe the main bearing surfaces of the block and caps with a clean, lint free cloth. They must be kept spotlessly clean.
5   Clean the back sides of the new main bearing inserts and lay one bearing half in each main bearing saddle in the block. Lay the other bearing half from each bearing set in the corresponding main bearing cap. Make sure the tab on the bearing insert fits into the recess in the block or cap. Also, the oil holes in the block must line up with the oil holes in the bearing insert. Do not hammer the bearing

into place and don't nick or gouge the bearing faces. No lubrication should be used at this time.
6   The flanged thrust bearing must be installed in the number five bearing saddle on the inline six-cylinder engine and in the number three bearing saddle on V6 and V8 engines.
7   Clean the faces of the bearings in the block and the crankshaft main bearing journals with a clean, lint free cloth. Check or clean the oil holes in the crankshaft, as any dirt here can only go one way - straight through the new bearings!
8   Once you're certain that the crankshaft is clean, carefully lay it in position (an assistant would be very helpful here) in the main bearings.
9   Before the crankshaft can be permanently installed, the main bearing oil clearance must be checked.
10   Trim several pieces of the appropriate size Plastigage - they must be slightly shorter than the width of the main bearings - and place one piece on each crankshaft main bearing journal, parallel with the journal axis **(see illustration).**
11   Clean the faces of the bearings in the caps and install the caps in their respective positions - don't mix them up with the arrows pointing toward the front of the engine. Do not disturb the Plastigage!
12   Starting with the center main and working out toward the ends, tighten the main bearing cap bolts, in three steps, to the specified torque. DO NOT rotate the crankshaft at any time during this operation!
13   Remove the bolts and carefully lift off the main bearing caps. Keep them in order. Don't disturb the Plastigage or rotate the crankshaft. If any of the main bearing caps are difficult to remove, tap them gently from side-to-side with a soft-face hammer to loosen them.

14   Compare the width of the crushed Plastigage on each journal to the scale printed on the Plastigage container to obtain the main bearing oil clearance **(see illustration).** Check the Specifications to make sure it's correct.
15   If the clearance is not as specified. the bearing inserts may be the wrong size (which means different ones will be required). Before deciding that different inserts are needed, make sure that no dirt or oil was between the bearing inserts and the caps or block when the clearance was measured. If the Plastigage was wider at one end than the other, the journal may be tapered.
16   Carefully scrape all traces of the Plastigage material off the main bearing journals and/or the bearing faces. Don't nick or scratch the bearing faces.
17   Carefully lift the crankshaft out of the engine. Clean the bearing faces in the block, then apply a thin, uniform layer of clean moly-base grease or engine assembly lube to each of the bearing surfaces. Be sure to coat the thrust faces as well as the journal face of the center bearing. On engines equipped with a two-piece rear main oil seal, install the upper half of the rear main seal (see Chapter 2B).
18   Make sure the crankshaft journals are clean, then lay the crankshaft back in place in the block. Clean the faces of the bearings in the caps, then apply lubricant to them. Install the caps in their respective positions with the arrows pointing toward the front of the engine and tighten bolts finger tight. On engines equipped with a two-piece rear main oil seal, install the lower half of the rear main oil seal prior to installing the rear bearing cap (see Chapter 2B).
19   Tighten all except the thrust bearing cap bolts to the torque listed in this Chapter's Specifications. Pry the crankshaft forward against the thrust surface of the bearing. Hold the crankshaft in this position, then pry the thrust bearing cap to the rear. Maintain the forward pressure on the crankshaft and tighten the thrust bearing cap bolts to the specified torque. Recheck the torque on all of the cap bolts.
20   On manual transmission equipped models, install a new pilot bearing in the end of the crankshaft (see Chapter 8).
21   Rotate the crankshaft a number of times by hand to check for any obvious binding. The effort required to turn the crankshaft should not be excessive.
22   The final step is to check the crankshaft endplay with a feeler gauge or a dial indicator as described in Section 10. The endplay should be correct if the crankshaft thrust faces are not worn or damaged and new bearings have been installed.
23   Install a new one-piece rear main oil seal if equipped (see Chapter 2A or 2B).
24   If it was removed, install the Woodruff key in the front of the crankshaft. Fill the keyway chamfer cavity with Loctite 518 or equivalent, up to where the front face of the sprocket will fall.

27.3 When checking the piston ring end gap, the ring must be square in the cylinder bore. This is done by pushing the ring down with the top of the piston as shown

27.4 With the ring square in the cylinder, measure the end gap with a feeler gauge

27 Piston rings - installation

Refer to illustrations 27.3, 27.4, 27.5, 27.9a, 27.9b, 27.10 and 27.12

1   Before installing the new piston rings, the ring end gaps must be checked. It's assumed that the piston ring side clearance has been checked and verified correct (see Section 18).

2   Lay out the piston/connecting rod assemblies and the new rings so the ring sets will be matched with the same piston and cylinder during the end gap measurement and engine assembly.

3   Insert the top (number one) ring into the first cylinder and square it up with the cylinder walls by pushing it in with the top of the piston **(see illustration)**. The ring should be near the bottom of the cylinder, at the lower limit of ring travel.

4   To measure the end gap, slip feeler gauges between the ends of the ring until a gauge equal to the gap width is found **(see illustration)**. The feeler gauge should slide between the ring ends with a slight amount of drag. Compare the measurement to the Specifications. If the gap is larger or smaller than specified, double-check to make sure that you

have the correct rings before proceeding.

5   If the gap is too small, it must be enlarged or the ring ends may come in contact with each other during engine operation, which can cause serious damage. The end gap can be increased by filing the ring ends very carefully with a fine file. Mount the file in a vise equipped with soft jaws, slip the ring over the file with the ends contacting the file face and slowly move the ring to remove material from the ends - file only from the outside in **(see illustration)**.

6   End gap should not exceed the value listed in this Chapter's Specifications.

7   Repeat the procedure for each ring that will be installed in the first cylinder and for each ring in the remaining cylinders. Remember to keep rings, pistons and cylinders matched up.

8   Once the ring end gaps have been checked/corrected, the rings can be installed on the pistons.

9   The oil control ring (lowest one on the piston) is installed first. It's composed of three separate components. Slip the spacer/ expander into the groove **(see illustration)**. Next, install the lower side rail. Don't use a piston ring installation tool on the oil ring

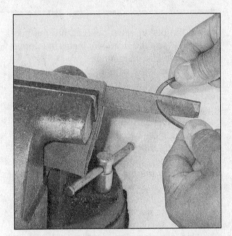

27.5 If the end gap is too small, clamp a file in a vise and file the ring ends (from the outside in only) to enlarge the gap slightly

side rails, as they may be damaged. Instead, place one end of the side rail into the groove between the spacer/expander and the ring land, hold it firmly in place and slide a finger

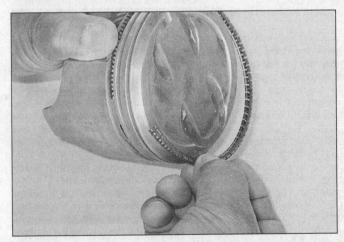

27.9a Installing the spacer/expander in the oil control ring groove

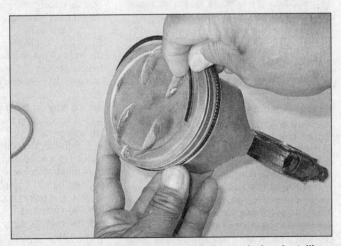

27.9b DO NOT use a piston ring installation tool when installing the oil ring side rails

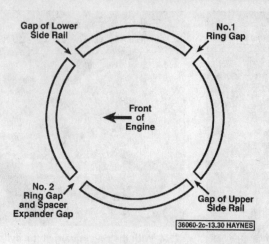

27.10 Ring end gap positions

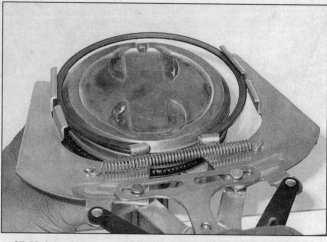

27.12 Installing the compression rings with a ring expander - the mark (arrow) must face up

around the piston while pushing the rail into the groove **(see illustration)**. Install the upper side rail in the same manner.

10   After the three oil ring components have been installed, check to make sure that both the upper and lower side rails can be turned smoothly in the ring groove and stagger the gaps **(see illustration)**.

11   The number two (middle) ring is installed next. It's stamped with a mark which must face up, toward the top of the piston. **Note:** *Always follow the instructions printed on the ring package or box-different manufacturers may require different approaches. Don't mix up the top and middle rings, as they have different cross sections.*

12   Use a piston ring installation tool and make sure that the identification mark is facing the top of the piston, then slip the ring into the middle groove on the piston **(see illustration)**. Don't expand the ring any more than necessary to slide it over the piston.

13   Install the number one (top) ring in the same manner. Make sure the mark is facing up. Be careful not to confuse the number one and number two rings.

14   Repeat the procedure for the remaining pistons and rings.

28   Piston/connecting rod assembly - installation and rod bearing oil clearance check

Refer to illustrations 28.9, 28.11 and 28.13

1   Before installing the piston/connecting rod assemblies, the cylinder walls must be perfectly clean, the top edge of each cylinder must be chamfered (to remove the sharp edge) and the crankshaft must be in place.

2   Remove the connecting rod cap from the end of the number one connecting rod. Remove the old bearing inserts and wipe the bearing surfaces of the connecting rod and cap with a clean, lint free cloth. They must be kept spotlessly clean.

3   Clean the back side of the new upper

bearing half, then lay it in place in the connecting rod. Make sure that the tang on the bearing fits into the appropriate slot in the rod. Do not hammer the bearing insert into place and be very careful not to nick or gouge the bearing face. Do not lubricate the bearing at this time.

4   Clean the back side of the other bearing insert and install it in the rod cap. Again, make sure the tang on the bearing fits into the slot in the cap, and do not apply any lubricant. It is critically important that the mating surfaces of the bearing and connecting rod are perfectly clean and oil free when they are assembled.

5   Position the piston ring gaps at intervals around the piston **(see illustration 27.10)**, then slip a section of plastic or rubber hose over each connecting rod cap bolt.

6   Lubricate the piston and rings with clean engine oil and attach a piston ring compressor to the piston. Leave the skirt protruding about 1/4-inch to guide the piston into the cylinder. The rings must be compressed until they are flush with the piston.

7   Rotate the crankshaft until the number one connecting rod journal is at BDC (bottom dead center) and apply a coat of engine oil to the cylinder walls.

8   With the notch on top of the piston facing the front of the engine, gently insert the piston/connecting rod assembly into the number one cylinder bore and rest the bottom edge of the ring compressor on the engine block. Tap the top edge of the ring compressor to make sure it's contacting the block around its entire circumference.

9   Carefully tap on the top of the piston with the end of a wooden or plastic hammer handle **(see illustration)** while guiding the end of the connecting rod into place on the crankshaft journal. The piston rings may try to pop out of the ring compressor just before entering the cylinder bore, so keep some downward pressure on the ring compressor. Work slowly, and if any resistance is felt as the piston enters the cylinder. stop immediately! Find out what's

hanging up and fix it before proceeding. DO NOT, for any reason, force the piston into the cylinder - you'll break a ring and/or the piston!

10   Once the piston/connecting rod assembly is installed, the connecting rod bearing oil clearance must be checked before the rod cap is permanently bolted in place.

11   Cut a piece of the appropriate size Plastigage slightly shorter than the width of the connecting rod bearing and lay it in place on the number one connecting rod journal, parallel with the journal axis **(see illustration)**.

12   Clean the connecting rod cap bearing face. remove the protective hoses from the connecting rod bolts and install the rod cap. Make sure the mating mark on the cap is on the same side as the mark on the connecting rod. Install the nuts and tighten them to the specified torque, working up to it in three steps. **Note:** *Use a thin-wall socket to avoid erroneous torque readings that can result if the socket becomes wedged between the rod cap and nut. Do not rotate the crankshaft at any time during this operation.*

13   Remove the rod cap, being very careful not to disturb the Plastigage. Compare the

28.9 The piston can be driven (gently) into the cylinder bore with the end of a wooden or plastic hammer handle

28.11 Lay the Plastigage strips on each rod bearing journal, parallel to the crankshaft centerline

28.13 Measuring the width of the crushed Plastigage to determine the rod bearing oil clearance (be sure to use the correct scale - standard and metric scales are included)

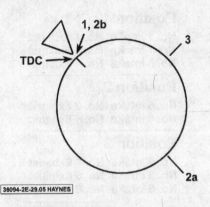

29.5 Vibration damper markings for valve adjustment on 1996 and earlier V6 and V8 engines

1   Position 1 (TDC), all engines
2a   Position 2, all except V6 and 7.5L V8 engine
2b   Position 2, V6 and 7.5L V8 engine
3   Position 3, all except V6 and 7.5L V8 engine

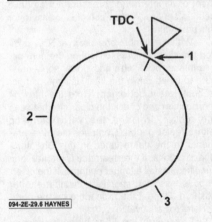

29.6 Vibration damper markings for valve adjustment on the inline six-cylinder engine

width of the crushed Plastigage to the scale printed on the Plastigage container to obtain the oil clearance **(see illustration)**. Compare it to the value listed in this Chapter's Specifications to make sure the clearance is correct. If the clearance is not as specified, the bearing inserts may be the wrong size (which means different ones will be required). Before deciding that different inserts are needed, make sure that no dirt or oil was between the bearing inserts and the connecting rod or cap when the clearance was measured. Also, recheck the journal diameter. If the Plastigage was wider at one end than the other, the journal may be tapered.

14   Carefully scrape all traces of the Plastigage material off the rod journal and/or bearing face. Be very careful not to scratch the bearing - use your fingernail or a piece of hardwood. Make sure the bearing faces are perfectly clean, then apply a uniform layer of clean moly-base grease or engine assembly lube to both of them. You'll have to push the piston into the cylinder to expose the face of the bearing insert in the connecting rod - be sure to slip the protective hoses over the rod bolts first.

15   Slide the connecting rod back into place on the journal, remove the protective hoses from the rod cap bolts, install the rod cap and tighten the nuts to the torque listed in this Chapter's Specifications. Again, work up to the final torque in three steps.

16   Repeat the above procedure for each of the remaining piston/connecting rod assemblies. Keep the back sides of the bearing inserts and the inside of each connecting rod and cap perfectly clean during reassembly. Make sure that you have the correct piston for each cylinder and the notch on the piston faces the front (timing chain end) of the engine when the piston is installed. Remember, use plenty of oil to lubricate the piston before installing the ring compressor. Also, when installing the rod caps for the final time, be sure to lubricate the bearing faces adequately.

17   After all the piston/connecting rod assemblies have been properly installed,

rotate the crankshaft a number of times by hand to check for any obvious binding.

18   As a final step, the connecting rod end-play must be checked. See Section 9 for this procedure. Compare the measured endplay to the Specifications to make sure it's correct. If it was correct before disassembly and the original crankshaft and rods were reinstalled, it should still be right. If new rods or a new crankshaft were installed, the endplay may be too small. If so, the rods will have to be removed and taken to an automotive machine shop for recessing.

29 Valve adjustment

Refer to illustrations 29.5, 29.6, 29.14, 29.17 and 29.20.

1   On V8 engines, the valve arrangement on the left bank is E-I-E-I-E-I-E-I and on the right bank is I-E-I-E-I-E-I-E. For the inline six-cylinder engine, the valve arrangement is E-I-E-I-E-I-E-I-E-I-E-I. On V6 engines, the valve arrangement is I-E-I-E-I-E on the right bank and E-I-E-I-E-I on the left bank.

2   Normally these engines do not need any valve adjustments because the lash is accounted for by the hydraulic lifter. If you have a running engine that has symptoms of valve clearance problems (such as excessive noise from a lifter), check for a defective part. Normally an engine will not reach a point at which it needs a valve adjustment unless a component malfunction has occurred. Hydraulic lifter failure and excessive rocker arm wear are two examples of likely component failure. Also, if major engine work is done, such as a valve job, which alters the relationship among valve train components, a means of compensating for the dimensional changes must be provided. Shorter and longer pushrods are available for this purpose. To determine whether a shorter or longer pushrod is necessary, proceed as follows.

3   Connect an auxiliary starter switch to the starter solenoid. If this is not used, the crankshaft will have to rotated with a socket and breaker bar.

4   Position the piston in the number one cylinder at Top Dead Center (TDC) on the compression stroke (see Chapter 2A or 2B).

5   On V6 and V8 engines with the crank-shaft in the TDC position, make a mark at 0-degrees TDC. On V8 engines, mark a line from the zero mark across the pulley (at 180-degrees), and except on V6 engines and the 460 (7.5L) V8 engine, mark another line 90-degrees from the timing mark **(see illustration)**.

6   On inline six-cylinder engines, mark the pulley with two chalk marks spaced 120-degrees on either side of the zero timing mark **(see illustration)**.

7   Remove the valve cover(s) (see the appropriate Chapter for your engine).

Position 1

No. 1 intake No. 1 Exhaust
No. 7 intake No. 5 Exhaust
No. 8 intake No. 4 Exhaust

Position 2

No. 5 intake No. 2 Exhaust
No. 4 intake No. 6 Exhaust

Position 3

No. 2 intake No. 7 Exhaust
No. 3 intake No. 3 Exhaust
No. 6 intake No. 8 Exhaust

36054-2c-5.2c HAYNES

29.14 Vibration damper position and valve adjustment order for 255 and 302 (5.0L) engines

Position 1

No. 1 intake No. 1 Exhaust
No. 4 intake No. 3 Exhaust
No. 8 intake No. 7 Exhaust

Position 2

No. 3 intake No. 2 Exhaust
No. 7 intake No. 6 Exhaust

Position 3

No. 2 intake No. 4 Exhaust
No. 5 intake No. 5 Exhaust
No. 6 intake No. 8 Exhaust

36054-2c-5.2d HAYNES

29.17 Vibration damper position and valve adjustment order for 351 (5.8L) and 400 engines

Position 1

No. 1 intake No. 1 Exhaust
No. 3 intake No. 8 Exhaust
No. 7 intake No. 5 Exhaust
No. 8 intake No. 4 Exhaust

Position 2

No. 2 intake No. 2 Exhaust
No. 4 intake No. 3 Exhaust
No. 5 intake No. 6 Exhaust
No. 6 intake No. 7 Exhaust

36058-2D-29.20 HAYNES

29.20 Vibration damper position and valve adjustment order for the 460 (7.5L) engine

8   Make sure the lifters are compressed (not pumped up with oil). This is accomplished during engine assembly by installing new lifters, or by compressing the lifters and relieving them of all internal oil pressure if they have been in service. A special tool is available for this procedure.

9   With the number one piston at TDC, position the lifter compressor tool on the num-ber one intake rocker arm and slowly apply pressure to bleed down the lifter until the plunger is completely bottomed. Hold the lifter in this position and check the clearance between the rocker arm and the valve stem tip with a feeler gauge. Compare the measurements to the value listed in this Chapter's Specifications. If the clearance is greater than specified, install a longer pushrod. If the clearance is less than specified, install a shorter pushrod. Repeat the procedure on the number one exhaust valve.

10   Employing the lifter bleed down and measuring procedures stated in Step 9, complete the valve clearance check as follows.

Inline six-cylinder engines

11   Rotate the crankshaft with the auxiliary starter, one-third revolution at a time, and adjust both intake and exhaust valves at each position in the remaining firing order sequence, 5-3-6-2-4.

V6 engines

12   After checking the clearances on both number one cylinder valves, check number 3 intake and number 2 exhaust, then number 6 intake and number 4 exhaust without rotating the crankshaft.

13   Rotate the crankshaft 360-degrees with the auxiliary starter switch and check, in order, number 2 intake and number 3 exhaust, number 4 intake and number 5 exhaust, and number 5 intake and number 6 exhaust.

255 and 302 (5.0L) V8 engines

14   After checking the clearances on both number one cylinder valves, check the remain-

ing valves as shown **(see illustration)**.
15   Rotate the engine 180-degrees with the auxiliary starter switch to Position 2 and check the valves as indicated.
16   Rotate the engine 270-degrees to Position 3 and check the remaining valves as indicated.

351 (5.8L) and 400 V8 engines

17   After checking the clearances on both number one cylinder valves, check the remaining valves as shown **(see illustration)**.
18   Rotate the engine 180-degrees with the auxiliary starter switch to Position 2 and check the valves as indicated.
19   Rotate the engine 270-degrees to Position 3 and check the remaining valves as indicated.

460 (7.5L) V8 engine

20   After checking the clearances on both number one cylinder valves, check the remaining valves as shown **(see illustration)**.
21   Rotate the crankshaft 360-degrees with the auxiliary starter switch to Position 2 and check the remaining valves as indicated.

All engines

22   After completion of the entire valve clearance checking/adjustment procedure, install the remaining engine components and run the engine. It may be necessary for an engine to run several minutes for the clearance in the valve train to be taken up completely by the hydraulic lifter(s), particularly if new lifters were installed.
23   If the components are all in good shape and a valve lash problem is indicated by excessive noise or rough engine idling, use the special service tool to compress the lifter to recheck the valve clearance.

30   Initial start-up and break-in after overhaul

Warning: *Have a fire extinguisher handy when starting the engine for the first time.*

1   Once the engine has been installed in the vehicle, double-check the engine oil and coolant levels.
2   With the spark plugs out of the engine and the primary wires disconnected from the ignition coil, crank the engine until oil pressure registers on the gauge or until the oil light goes out. .
3   Install the spark plugs, hook up the plug wires and reconnect the primary wires to the coil.
4   Start the engine. It may take a few moments for the gasoline to reach the carburetor or fuel-injectors, but the engine should start without a great deal of effort. **Note:** *If the engine keeps backfiring, recheck the ignition timing and spark plug wire routing.*
5   After the engine starts, it should be allowed to warm up to normal operating temperature. Try to keep the engine speed at approximately 2000 rpm. While the engine is warming up, make a thorough check for oil and coolant leaks.
6   Shut the engine off and recheck the engine oil and coolant levels.
7   Drive the vehicle to an area with minimum traffic, accelerate at full throttle from 30 to 50 mph, then allow the vehicle to slow to 30 mph with the throttle closed. Repeat the procedure 10 or 12 times. This will load the piston rings and cause them to seat properly against the cylinder walls. Check again for oil and coolant leaks.
8   Drive the vehicle gently for the first 500 miles (no sustained high speeds) and keep a constant check on the oil level. It's not unusual for an engine to use oil during the break-in period.
9   At approximately 500 to 600 miles, change the oil and filter.
10   For the next few hundred miles, drive the vehicle normally. Don't pamper it or abuse it.
11   After 2000 miles, change the oil and filter again and consider the engine fully broken in.

COMMON ENGINE OVERHAUL TERMS

B

Backlash - The amount of play between two parts. Usually refers to how much one gear can be moved back and forth without moving gear with which it's meshed.

Bearing Caps - The caps held in place by nuts or bolts which, in turn, hold the bearing surface. This space is for lubricating oil to enter.

Bearing clearance - The amount of space left between shaft and bearing surface. This space is for lubricating oil to enter.

Bearing crush - The additional height which is purposely manufactured into each bearing half to ensure complete contact of the bearing back with the housing bore when the engine is assembled.

Bearing knock - The noise created by movement of a part in a loose or worn bearing.

Blueprinting - Dismantling an engine and reassembling it to EXACT specifications.

Bore - An engine cylinder, or any cylindrical hole; also used to describe the process of enlarging or accurately refinishing a hole with a cutting tool, as to bore an engine cylinder. The bore size is the diameter of the hole.

Boring - Renewing the cylinders by cutting them out to a specified size. A boring bar is used to make the cut.

Bottom end - A term which refers collectively to the engine block, crankshaft, main bearings and the big ends of the connecting rods.

Break-in - The period of operation between installation of new or rebuilt parts and time in which parts are worn to the correct fit. Driving at reduced and varying speed for a specified mileage to permit parts to wear to the correct fit.

Bushing - A one-piece sleeve placed in a bore to serve as a bearing surface for shaft, piston pin, etc. Usually replaceable.

C

Camshaft - The shaft in the engine, on which a series of lobes are located for operating the valve mechanisms. The camshaft is driven by gears or sprockets and a timing chain. Usually referred to simply as the cam.

Carbon - Hard, or soft, black deposits found in combustion chamber, on plugs, under rings, on and under valve heads.

Cast iron - An alloy of iron and more than two percent carbon, used for engine blocks and heads because it's relatively inexpensive and easy to mold into complex shapes.

Chamfer - To bevel across (or a bevel on) the sharp edge of an object.

Chase - To repair damaged threads with a tap or die.

Combustion chamber - The space between the piston and the cylinder head, with the piston at top dead center, in which air-fuel mixture is burned.

Compression ratio - The relationship between cylinder volume (clearance volume) when the piston is at top dead center and cylinder volume when the piston is at bottom dead center.

Connecting rod - The rod that connects the crank on the crankshaft with the piston. Sometimes called a con rod.

Connecting rod cap - The part of the connecting rod assembly that attaches the rod to the crankpin.

Core plug - Soft metal plug used to plug the casting holes for the coolant passages in the block.

Crankcase - The lower part of the engine in which the crankshaft rotates; includes the lower section of the cylinder block and the oil pan.

Crank kit - A reground or reconditioned crankshaft and new main and connecting rod bearings.

Crankpin - The part of a crankshaft to which a connecting rod is attached.

Crankshaft - The main rotating member, or shaft, running the length of the crankcase, with offset throws to which the connecting rods are attached; changes the reciprocating motion of the pistons into rotating motion.

Cylinder sleeve - A replaceable sleeve, or liner, pressed into the cylinder block to form the cylinder bore.

D

Deburring - Removing the burrs (rough edges or areas) from a bearing.

Deglazer - A tool, rotated by an electric motor, used to remove glaze from cylinder walls so a new set of rings will seat.

E

Endplay - The amount of lengthwise movement between two parts. As applied to a crankshaft, the distance that the crankshaft can move forward and back in the cylinder block.

F

Face - A machinist's term that refers to removing metal from the end of a shaft or the face of a larger part, such as a flywheel.

Fatigue - A breakdown of material through a large number of loading and unloading cycles. The first signs are cracks followed shortly by breaks.

Feeler gauge - A thin strip of hardened steel, ground to an exact thickness, used to check clearances between parts.

Free height - The unloaded length or height of a spring.

Freeplay - The looseness in a linkage, or an assembly of parts, between the initial application of force and actual movement. Usually perceived as slop or slight delay.

Freeze plug - See Core plug.

G

Gallery - A large passage in the block that forms a reservoir for engine oil pressure.

Glaze - The very smooth, glassy finish that develops on cylinder walls while an engine is in service.

H

Heli-Coil - A rethreading device used when threads are worn or damaged. The device is installed in a retapped hole to reduce the thread size to the original size.

I

Installed height - The spring's measured length or height, as installed on the cylinder head. Installed height is measured from the spring seat to the underside of the spring retainer.

J

Journal - The surface of a rotating shaft which turns in a bearing.

K

Keeper - The split lock that holds the valve spring retainer in position on the valve stem.

Key - A small piece of metal inserted into matching grooves machined into two parts fitted together - such as a gear pressed onto a shaft - which prevents slippage between the two parts.

Knock - The heavy metallic engine sound, produced in the combustion chamber as a result of abnormal combustion - usually detonation. Knock is usually caused by a loose or worn bearing. Also referred to as detonation, pinging and spark knock. Connecting rod or main bearing knocks are created by too much oil clearance or insufficient lubrication.

L

Lands - The portions of metal between the piston ring grooves.

Lapping the valves - Grinding a valve face and its seat together with lapping compound.

Lash - The amount of free motion in a gear train, between gears, or in a mechanical assembly, that occurs before movement can begin. Usually refers to the lash in a valve train.

Lifter - The part that rides against the cam to transfer motion to the rest of the valve train.

M

Machining - The process of using a machine to remove metal from a metal part.

Main bearings - The plain, or babbit, bearings that support the crankshaft.

Main bearing caps - The cast iron caps, bolted to the bottom of the block, that support the main bearings.

O

O.D. - Outside diameter.

Oil gallery - A pipe or drilled passageway in the engine used to carry engine oil from one area to another.

Oil ring - The lower ring, or rings, of a piston; designed to prevent excessive amounts of oil from working up the cylinder walls and into the combustion chamber. Also called an oil-control ring.

Oil seal - A seal which keeps oil from leaking out of a compartment. Usually refers to a dynamic seal around a rotating shaft or other moving part.

O-ring - A type of sealing ring made of a special rubberlike material; in use, the O-ring is compressed into a groove to provide the sealing action.

Overhaul - To completely disassemble a unit, clean and inspect all parts, reassemble it with the original or new parts and make all adjustments necessary for proper operation.

P

Pilot bearing - A small bearing installed in the center of the flywheel (or the rear end of the crankshaft) to support the front end of the input shaft of the transmission.

Pip mark - A little dot or indentation which indicates the top side of a compression ring.

Piston - The cylindrical part, attached to the connecting rod, that moves up and down in the cylinder as the crankshaft rotates. When the fuel charge is fired, the piston transfers the force of the explosion to the connecting rod, then to the crankshaft.

Piston pin (or wrist pin) - The cylindrical and usually hollow steel pin that passes through the piston. The piston pin fastens the piston to the upper end of the connecting rod.

Piston ring - The split ring fitted to the groove in a piston. The ring contacts the sides of the ring groove and also rubs against the cylinder wall, thus sealing space between piston and wall. There are two types of rings: Compression rings seal the compression pressure in the combustion chamber; oil rings scrape excessive oil off the cylinder wall.

Piston ring groove - The slots or grooves cut in piston heads to hold piston rings in position.

Piston skirt - The portion of the piston below the rings and the piston pin hole.

Plastigage - A thin strip of plastic thread, available in different sizes, used for measuring clearances. For example, a strip of plastigage is laid across a bearing journal and mashed as parts are assembled. Then parts are disassembled and the width of the strip is measured to determine clearance between journal and bearing. Commonly used to measure crankshaft main-bearing and connecting rod bearing clearances.

Press-fit - A tight fit between two parts that requires pressure to force the parts together. Also referred to as drive, or force, fit.

Prussian blue - A blue pigment; in solution, useful in determining the area of contact between two surfaces. Prussian blue is commonly used to determine the width and location of the contact area between the valve face and the valve seat.

R

Race (bearing) - The inner or outer ring that provides a contact surface for balls or rollers in bearing.

Ream - To size, enlarge or smooth a hole by using a round cutting tool with fluted edges.

Ring job - The process of reconditioning the cylinders and installing new rings.

Runout - Wobble. The amount a shaft rotates out-of-true.

S

Saddle - The upper main bearing seat.

Scored - Scratched or grooved, as a cylinder wall may be scored by abrasive particles moved up and down by the piston rings.

Scuffing - A type of wear in which there's a transfer of material between parts moving against each other; shows up as pits or grooves in the mating surfaces.

Seat - The surface upon which another part rests or seats. For example, the valve seat is the matched surface upon which the valve face rests. Also used to refer to wearing into a good fit; for example, piston rings seat after a few miles of driving.

Short block - An engine block complete with crankshaft and piston and, usually, camshaft assemblies.

Static balance - The balance of an object while it's stationary.

Step - The wear on the lower portion of a ring land caused by excessive side and back-clearance. The height of the step indicates the ring's extra side clearance and the length of the step projecting from the back wall of the groove represents the ring's back clearance.

Stroke - The distance the piston moves when traveling from top dead center to bottom dead center, or from bottom dead center to top dead center.

Stud - A metal rod with threads on both ends.

T

Tang - A lip on the end of a plain bearing used to align the bearing during assembly.

Tap - To cut threads in a hole. Also refers to the fluted tool used to cut threads.

Taper - A gradual reduction in the width of a shaft or hole; in an engine cylinder, taper usually takes the form of uneven wear, more pronounced at the top than at the bottom.

Throws - The offset portions of the crankshaft to which the connecting rods are affixed.

Thrust bearing - The main bearing that has thrust faces to prevent excessive endplay, or forward and backward movement of the crankshaft.

Thrust washer - A bronze or hardened steel washer placed between two moving parts. The washer prevents longitudinal movement and provides a bearing surface for thrust surfaces of parts.

Tolerance - The amount of variation permitted from an exact size of measurement. Actual amount from smallest acceptable dimension to largest acceptable dimension.

U

Umbrella - An oil deflector placed near the valve tip to throw oil from the valve stem area.

Undercut - A machined groove below the normal surface.

Undersize bearings - Smaller diameter bearings used with re-ground crankshaft journals.

V

Valve grinding - Refacing a valve in a valve-refacing machine.

Valve train - The valve-operating mechanism of an engine; includes all components from the camshaft to the valve.

Vibration damper - A cylindrical weight attached to the front of the crankshaft to minimize torsional vibration (the twist-untwist actions of the crankshaft caused by the cylinder firing impulses). Also called a harmonic balancer.

W

Water jacket - The spaces around the cylinders, between the inner and outer shells of the cylinder block or head, through which coolant circulates.

Web - A supporting structure across a cavity.

Woodruff key - A key with a radiused backside (viewed from the side).

Chapter 3
Cooling, heating and air conditioning systems

Contents

Specifications

Torque specifications

	Ft-lbs
Fan-to-water pump fasteners	12 to 18
Fan-to-clutch fasteners	12 to 18
Fan clutch-to-water pump bolts	12 to 18
Fan clutch-to-water pump (threaded)	30 to 100
Oil cooler adapter bolt (7.5L)	40 to 65
Oil filter/cooler mounting bolt (5.8L Lightning)	20 to 30
Thermostat housing bolts	12 to 18
Water pump bolts	12 to 21

1 General information

Engine cooling system

1 The models covered by this manual have a cooling system consisting of a horizontal flow radiator, a thermostat for temperature control and an impeller-type water pump driven by a belt from the crankshaft pulley.

2 The radiator cooling fan is mounted on the front of the water pump and shares the same accessory drive pulley. Some early and all later vehicles incorporate an automatic clutch which disengages the fan at high speeds or when the outside temperature is sufficient to maintain a low radiator temperature. A fan shroud is mounted to the rear face of the radiator to increase cooling efficiency.

3 A poppet type thermostat is located in a housing near the front of the engine. During warm up, the closed thermostat prevents coolant from circulating through the radiator. As the engine nears normal operating temperature, the thermostat opens and allows hot coolant to travel through the radiator, where it's cooled before returning to the engine.

4 The cooling system is sealed by a pressure type radiator cap, which raises the boiling point of the coolant and increases the cooling efficiency of the radiator. If the system pressure exceeds the cap pressure relief value, the excess pressure in the system forces the spring loaded valve inside the cap off its seat and allows the coolant to escape through the overflow tube into a coolant reservoir. When the system cools the excess coolant is automatically drawn from the reservoir back into the radiator.

5 The coolant reservoir serves as both the point at which fresh coolant is added to the cooling system to maintain the proper fluid level and as a holding tank for overheated coolant.

6 This type of cooling system is known as a closed design because coolant that escapes past the pressure cap is saved and reused.

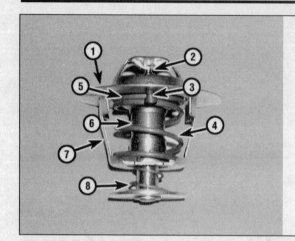

3.6 A typical thermostat

1 *Flange*
2 *Piston*
3 *Jiggle valve*
4 *Main coil spring*
5 *Valve seat*
6 *Valve*
7 *Frame*
8 *Secondary coil spring*

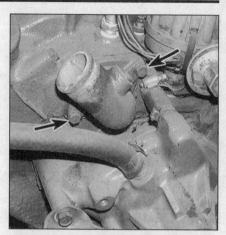

3.10a The thermostat housing is located at the front of the intake manifold

Oil cooling system

7   On some models, in addition to conventional engine cooling as described above, engine heat is also dissipated through the lubrication system. Oil coolers on vehicles equipped with 7.5L engines and the 5.8L Lightning engine help keep engine and oil temperatures within design limits under extreme load conditions. Early 7.5L engines utilized oil-to-air type radiators while later models use an oil-to-engine coolant type heat exchanger. The 5.8L Lightning engine also uses an oil-to-engine coolant type heat exchanger.

Heating system

8   The heating system consists of an engine compartment mounted heater blower assembly (which houses the blower motor, blower resistor and on early non-A/C models, the heater core), the cab mounted heater plenum assembly (which houses the ducting/mix doors and on early A/C and all later models, the heater core), the hoses connecting the heater core to the engine cooling system and the heater/air conditioning control assembly on the dashboard. Hot engine coolant is circulated through the heater core. When the heater mode is activated, a flap door opens to expose the heater box to the passenger compartment. A fan switch on the control assembly activates the blower motor, which forces air through the core, heating the air.

Air conditioning system

9   The air conditioning system consists of a condenser mounted in front of the radiator, an engine compartment mounted evaporator case assembly (which houses the evaporator core, blower motor and resistor, accumulator/drier and duct door), a compressor mounted on the engine, and the plumbing connecting all of the above components. The evaporator case replaces the heater blower assembly normally found in non-air conditioned models.
10   A blower fan forces the warmer air of the passenger compartment through the evaporator core (sort of a radiator-in-reverse), transferring the heat from the air to the refrigerant.

The liquid refrigerant boils off into low pressure vapor, taking the heat with it when it leaves the evaporator.

2   Antifreeze - general information

Warning: *Do not allow antifreeze to come in contact with your skin or painted surfaces of the vehicle. Rinse off spills immediately with plenty of water. Antifreeze is highly toxic if ingested. Never leave antifreeze lying around in an open container or in puddles on the floor; children and pets are attracted by it's sweet smell and may drink it. Check with local authorities about disposing of used antifreeze. Many communities have collection centers which will see that antifreeze is disposed of safely.*

1   The cooling system should be filled with a 50/50 water/ethylene glycol based antifreeze solution, which will prevent freezing down to at least -20 degrees F, or lower if local climate requires it. It also provides protection against corrosion and increases the coolant boiling point. Don't use a lower concentration of antifreeze, even if the temperature never gets below freezing.
2   The cooling system should be drained, flushed and refilled at the specified intervals (see Chapter 1). Old or contaminated antifreeze solutions are likely to cause damage and encourage the formation of rust and scale in the system. Use distilled water with the antifreeze.
3   Before adding antifreeze, check all hose connections, because antifreeze tends to leak through very minute openings. Engines don't normally consume coolant, so if the level goes down, find the cause and correct it.
4   The exact mixture of antifreeze-to-water which you should use depends on the relative weather conditions. The mixture should contain at least 50-percent antifreeze, but should never contain more than 70-percent antifreeze. Consult the mixture ratio chart on the antifreeze container before adding coolant. Hydrometers are available at most auto parts stores to test the coolant. Use antifreeze which meets the vehicle manufacturer's specifications.

3   Thermostat - check and replacement

Refer to illustrations 3.6, 3.10a and 3.10b
Warning: *Do not remove the radiator cap, drain the coolant or replace the thermostat until the engine has cooled completely.*

Check

1   Before assuming the thermostat is to blame for a cooling system problem, check the coolant level (see Chapter 1), fan operation (see Section 4) and temperature gauge (or light) operation.
2   If the engine seems to be taking a long time to warm up (based on heater output or temperature gauge operation), the thermostat is probably stuck open. Replace the thermostat with a new one.
3   If the engine runs hot, use your hand to check the temperature of the upper radiator hose. If the hose isn't hot, but the engine is, the thermostat is probably stuck closed, preventing the coolant inside the engine from escaping to the radiator. Replace the thermostat. **Caution:** *Don't drive the vehicle without a thermostat. The computer may stay in open loop and emissions and fuel economy will suffer.*
4   If the upper radiator hose is hot, it means that the coolant is flowing and the thermostat is open. Consult the *Troubleshooting* section at the front of this manual for cooling system diagnosis.

Removal

5   Drain the radiator so that the coolant level is below the thermostat,

Inline six-cylinder engine

6   Remove the coolant outlet elbow attaching bolts, then pull the elbow away from the cylinder head sufficiently to provide access to the thermostat (**see illustration**).
7   Remove the thermostat and gasket, noting the top and bottom to assure proper installation.

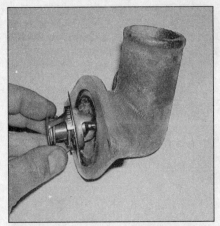

3.10b Be sure to install the thermostat facing the proper direction

V6 and V8 engines

8   Disconnect the bypass hoses at the water pump and intake manifold.
9   Remove the bypass tube, then remove the water outlet housing attaching bolts.
10 Bend the radiator upper hose upward and remove the thermostat and gasket, taking note of the top and bottom to assure proper installation **(see illustrations)**.

Installation

Inline six-cylinder engine

11 After cleaning the coolant outlet elbow and cylinder head gasket surfaces, coat a new gasket with water-resistant sealer and position the gasket on the cylinder head opening. **Note:** *The gasket must be positioned on the cylinder head before the thermostat is installed.*
12 The coolant elbow contains a locking recess into which the thermostat is turned and locked. Install the thermostat with the bridge section in the outlet elbow.
13 Turn the thermostat clockwise to lock it in position on the flats cast into the elbow.
14 Position the elbow against the cylinder head and tighten the attaching bolts to the torque listed in this Chapter's Specifications.

V6 and V8 engines

15 After cleaning the water outlet gasket surfaces, coat a new water outlet gasket with water-resistant sealer.
16 Position the gasket on the intake manifold opening.
17 Install the thermostat in the intake manifold with the copper element toward the engine and the thermostat flange positioned in the recess.
18 Position the water outlet housing against the intake manifold and install and tighten the attaching bolts to the torque listed in this Chapter's Specifications.
19 Install the water bypass line and tighten the hose connections.

All engines

20 Fill the cooling system with the proper amount and type of coolant (see Chapter 1).
21 Start and run the engine until it reaches normal operating temperature, then check the coolant level and look for leaks.

---

4   Cooling fan and clutch - check, removal and installation

Refer to illustrations 4.7a, 4.7b, 4.9, 4.12a, 4.12b, 4.14 and 4.17
Warning: *To avoid possible injury or damage, do not operate the engine with a damaged fan. Do not attempt to repair fan blades - replace a damaged fan with a new one.*

Fan clutch check (vehicles so equipped)

1   With the engine cold (not run for at least one hour) and stopped, rotate fan by hand and feel motion. The fan should have some viscous drag and move smoothly through a full rotation. If the fan is not smooth, has no resistance, or does not turn at all, replace the fan clutch.
2   Cut a piece of cardboard large enough to cover the front of the radiator (or condenser) and cut a six-inch diameter hole in line with the fan clutch. Do not place it on the vehicle until called for in procedure.
3   Open the hood and start the engine. Hold the engine at approximately 2,000 rpm and listen to the fan. Initially, the fan should be engaged and make a distinctive "roaring" sound until the clutch disengages. Fan noise should decline to inaudible levels after no more than five minutes, indicating that the clutch has disengaged. If the fan fails to slow (clutch still engaged and fan "roaring") after five minutes, replace the fan clutch. If clutch disengages, proceed to the next step.
4   **Note:** *This operation will require an assistant to watch the engine temperature gauge - do not overheat engine.* Stop the engine. While the engine cools, place the cut cardboard in front of the radiator (condenser). Start the engine and hold it above 2,500 rpm while listening for fan engagement ("roaring") and watching the engine temperature. As engine temperature climbs and prior to exceeding recommended maximum temperature, the fan should begin to speed up ("roar") as the clutch warms and begins to engage. If the clutch does not engage before the maximum safe operating temperature is reached, replace the fan clutch. If the clutch engages, proceed to the next step.
5   Shut engine off and remove the cardboard. Start the engine and hold it above 2,500 rpm. As the engine cools, the fan should slow (clutch disengaging) and return to a reduced noise level. If the clutch remains engaged even after five minutes of operation at normal temperature, replace fan clutch. If the fan slows, clutch is operational.

Fan clutch removal and installation (vehicles so equipped)

Bolt-on fan clutch

6   Remove the radiator shroud.
7   Remove the four screws retaining the clutch to the water pump **(see illustrations)**.

4.7a Unbolt the fan clutch from the water pump hub

4.7b When storing the fan clutch after removal, always place it with this side down to prevent silicone fluid from leaking out or into the bearing

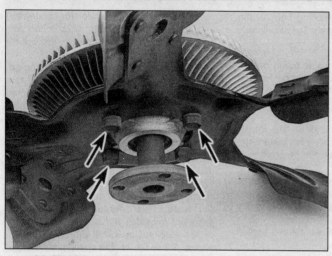

4.9 The fan is attached to the fan clutch with four bolts

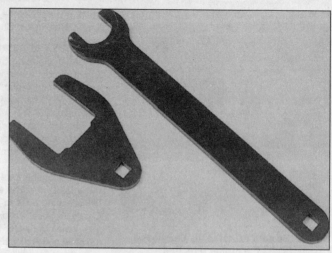

4.12a Hold the water pump pulley with the large wrench (attached to a breaker bar) and turn the fan clutch nut with the long wrench

8   Pull the clutch and fan assembly off the water pump pilot and remove it from the vehicle.

9   If necessary, remove the four bolts and separate the clutch from the fan **(see illustration)**.

10   Installation is the reverse of removal.

Threaded fan clutch

11   Remove the radiator shroud.

12   Using special tools designed for fan clutch removal (available at most auto parts stores) hold the pulley while turning the large nut to remove the clutch **(see illustrations)**. **Note:** *On some models the nut is turned counterclockwise to loosen, but on others it's turned clockwise to loosen.*

13   Remove the clutch and fan assembly from the vehicle.

14   If necessary, remove the four bolts and separate the clutch from the fan **(see illustration)**.

15   Installation is the reverse of removal.

Non-clutch fan removal and installation

16   Remove the radiator shroud.

17   Remove the fan retaining bolts from the water pump **(see illustration)**.

18   Remove the fan and fan spacer, if equipped.

19   Installation is the reverse of removal.

5   Radiator - removal and installation

Refer to illustration 5.4, 5.6a, 5.6b and 5.7

Warning: *Wait until the engine is completely cold before beginning this procedure.*

Removal

1   Drain the radiator using the draincock located near the bottom of the radiator. See the information given in Chapter 1 pertaining to this.

2   Remove the lower radiator hose and clamp from the radiator. Be careful not to put excess pressure on the outlet tube, as it can easily break away.

3   Remove the upper radiator hose and coolant reservoir tube from the radiator filler neck.

4   If equipped with an automatic transmission, remove the transmission cooler lines from the side of the radiator, taking care not to twist the lines or damage the fittings **(see illustration)**. It is best to use a flare-nut wrench for this particular job. Plug the ends of the disconnected lines to prevent leakage and stop dirt from entering the system.

5   Remove the bolts which attach the fan shroud to the radiator support. Place the shroud over the fan, allowing space for radiator removal. In some cases the fan itself will have to be removed (see Section 4).

6   On early models, remove the two upper radiator retaining brackets and pads **(see illustration)**. On later models, remove the

4.12b Use the long wrench to unscrew the fan clutch nut; the large wrench spans the bolts on the water pump hub to prevent it from turning

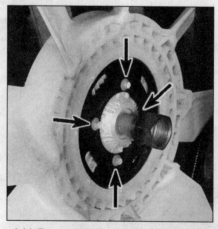

4.14 To separate the fan clutch from the fan blades, remove these four bolts

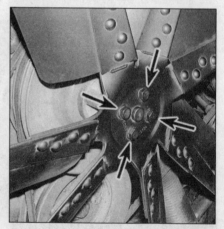

4.17 Fan mounting bolts (models without a fan clutch)

5.4 On automatic transmission models, hold the cooler line fitting with a wrench while loosening the tube nut (this will prevent the line from twisting)

5.6a Remove the bolts from the radiator retaining brackets (early models)

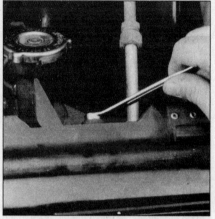

5.6b On later models, remove the mounting bolts from the upper corners of the radiator

two upper radiator-to-cowling screws (see illustration).

7   Lift the radiator straight up from the lower pads support (early models) or bracket support (late models) and remove it from the vehicle (see illustration).

Installation

8   Installation is the reverse of removal. Take care to install the radiator into the vehicle with caution as the cooling fins along with the radiator itself are fragile and can be damaged easily by mishandling or contact with the fan or radiator support. Make sure that the radiator is mounted properly into the lower retaining pads or brackets and securely with the proper retaining brackets and bolts. Check the radiator hoses for possible replacement (refer to Chapter 1) prior to clamping to the radiator (see Chapter 1).

9   After remounting all components related to the radiator, fill it with the proper type and amount of coolant.

10   Start the engine and allow it to reach normal operating temperature, then check for leaks.

5.7 When lifting the radiator out, be very careful not to damage the fins or the core tubes

6   Aluminum core radiator - repair

1   The cross flow fin-and-tube design radiator used on later model F-Series and Bronco vehicles is constructed with a vacuum-brazed aluminum core and nylon end tanks. The nylon side tanks are attached to the aluminum core by bending tabs on the core over the edge of the nylon tank. An O-ring gasket is placed between the nylon tank and the radiator core to achieve a seal between the tank and the core. The nylon tanks are a molded one-piece design with the mounting brackets part of each tank. It is possible for the home mechanic to replace these tanks or correct a leak between the tank and the core.

Radiator side tank - removal and installation

2   When removing a nylon tank, a screwdriver or one of the various special tools available can be used to open the tabs. Some of these tools, including a screwdriver, may cause a small section of the header side to bend with the tabs as they are opened. This slight deformation is permissible, provided the tabs are opened only enough for tank removal. The header sides will usually return to the normal position when the tabs are crimped during tank installation.

3   Procedures are given for tank removal using a screwdriver. Follow the manufacturer's instructions for other radiator tab opening and closing tools.

4   Insert the end of a medium screwdriver between the end of the header tab and the tank. Press the screwdriver blade against the tank to bend the tab away from the tank edge. Repeat this procedure for each tab. Note: Bend the tabs only enough for tank removal.

5   Lift the tank from the core when all of the tabs are bent away from the tank edge.

6   Remove the O-ring gasket from the core.

Note: If any header tabs are missing from the aluminum core, the core should be replaced.

7   Inspect the seal surface of the radiator core to be sure it is clean and free of foreign material or damage.

8   Check the new O-ring to be sure it is not twisted.

9   Dip the new O-ring in glycol or silicone lubricant, and place the gasket in the header groove.

10   If the outlet tank is being replaced and is equipped with an oil cooler, transfer the oil cooler from the replaced tank to the new tank (see step 18).

11   Position the tank on the core using care not to scratch the tank sealing surfaces with the header tabs.

12   Clamp the tank in position on the core with two clamps. Tighten the header clamps to compress the O-ring gasket.

13   If locking type pliers are used to squeeze the header tabs against the tank, install a locking nut on the adjusting screw.

14   With the jaws of the pliers closed and locked, turn the adjusting screw to position the jaws against the shank of a 13/32-inch drill bit. Tighten the nut on the adjusting screw against the handle to lock the adjustment in place.

15   Squeeze the header tabs down against the lip of the tank base with the locking-type pliers while rotating the pliers toward the tank. Caution: It is important that the assembled height of the crimp be 13/32-inch when measured from the bottom of the header to the top of the tab.

16   Remove the header clamps and squeeze the header tabs down that were behind the clamps.

17   Leak test the radiator at 21 psi. Most minor leaks at the header to tank seal can be corrected by again squeezing the header tabs down against the tank lip in the area of the leak.

Transmission oil cooler - transfer or replacement

18   Remove the outlet tank from the radiator as described in the previous Steps.

19   Remove the nuts and washers from the oil cooler inlet and outlet connections. Lift the oil cooler from the radiator outlet tank.

20   Remove the rubber gaskets from the oil cooler inlet and outlet connections if the oil cooler is to be reused.

21   Install new rubber gaskets on the oil cooler inlet and outlet connections.

22   Position the oil cooler in the radiator outlet tank and insert the inlet and outlet connections through the holes in the outlet tank.

23   Install the flat washer and nut on each oil cooler connection to retain the oil cooler in the radiator outlet tank.

24   Install the outlet tank on the radiator core as described in the previous Steps.

Aluminum core radiator - cleaning

External

25   The aluminum core can be cleaned externally with a soft bristle brush, warm water and a mild liquid detergent.

26   If the radiator is equipped with an oil cooler, install plugs in the inlet and outlet fittings.

Internal

Caution: *Do not use caustic cleaning solutions or copper/brass radiator cleaning agents on aluminum radiators.*

27   Internal cleaning of the aluminum tubes can be accomplished with sonic cleaning equipment or by removing one end tank to gain access to tubes.

28   Clean the tubes with a mild liquid detergent. Rinse the core with clean water when completed. Do not use a metal brush to clean an aluminum core. Use only horsehair, bristle or nylon bushes.

7   Water pump - check

1   A water pump that is in need of replacement will usually give indications through noise from the bearing and/or leakage.

2   Visually check the water pump for leakage. Pay special attention to the area around the front pump seal at the outlet of the driveshaft and at the drain hole.

3   The front bearing in the water pump can be checked for roughness or excessive looseness by first removing the drivebelt and grasping the fan by hand to check for movement. Attempt to move the fan up and down as well as rotationally to test for a loose bearing.

4   Visually check the sealing surfaces where the water pump mates to the front cover (or to the cylinder block on inline six-cylinder engines) for signs of leakage.

5   If any of the above indications are present, the water pump will have to be replaced.

8   Water pump - removal and installation

Warning: *Wait until the engine is completely cold before beginning this procedure.*

Removal

Early carbureted models

1   With the engine cold, drain the cooling system by removing the radiator drain plug.

2   On V6-equipped models, remove the air cleaner assembly and air intake duct.

3   Remove the fan or fan clutch assembly (refer to Section 4).

4   On V6-equipped models, loosen the accessory drivebelt idler and remove the drivebelt and water pump pulley. **Note:** *In the Steps which follow, further references to drivebelt removal should be ignored if your vehicle is equipped with a V6 engine.*

5   If equipped, loosen the power steering pump attaching bolt(s). Loosen the power steering pump drivebelt by releasing the adjustment bolt and allowing the power steering pump to move toward the engine. If the power steering pump bracket is retained at the water pump, the power steering pump should be completely removed and laid to one side to facilitate removal of the bracket.

6   If equipped with air conditioning, do not disconnect any of the hoses or lines. The following procedures can be performed by moving, not disconnecting, the air conditioning compressor. Loosen the air conditioning compressor top bracket retaining bolts. Remove the bracket on engines that have it secured to the pump.

7   Remove the air conditioning compressor and power steering pump drivebelt. Remove the compressor drivebelt idler arm assembly.

8   If equipped, remove the air pump pulley hub bolts and remove the bolt and pulley. Remove the air pump pivot bolt, bypass hose and air pump.

9   Loosen the alternator pivot bolt.

10   Remove the retaining bolt and spacer for the alternator.

11   Remove the adjustment arm bolt, pivot bolt and alternator drivebelt.

12   Remove the alternator bracket if it is retained at the water pump.

Fuel-injected models

13   With the engine cold, drain the cooling system by removing the radiator drain plug.

14   Remove the fan or fan clutch assembly (see Section 4).

15   Release the accessory drivebelt from the water pump pulley. On 7.5L engines, release tension on both accessory belts (refer to Chapter 1).

16   On 5.0L, 5.8L and 7.5L engines, remove the bolts retaining the air conditioning compressor/power steering pump bracket to the front of the engine. Move the bracket and attached

accessories off of the water pump studs and away from the water pump enough to gain access to the water pump attaching bolts.

17   On 7.5L engines, remove the bolt securing the alternator adjusting bracket to the water pump, then remove the bolts retaining the air pump/alternator bracket to the front of the engine. Move the bracket and attached accessories away from the water pump enough to gain access to the water pump attaching bolts.

18   On 5.8L Lightning engines, remove the oil cooler adapter tube from the water pump inlet.

All models

Refer to illustrations 8.21a, 8.21b and 8.22

19   Disconnect the lower radiator hose from the water pump inlet.

20   Disconnect the heater and bypass hoses from the water pump.

21   Remove the water pump retaining bolts and remove the water pump from the front cover or the engine block (depending on engine type) **(see illustrations)**. **Note:** *Take note of the installed positions of the various-sized bolts and studs.*

22   Remove the gaskets from the mating faces of the water pump and from the front cover or cylinder block **(see illustration)**.

23   Before installing, remove and clean all gasket material from the water pump, front cover, separator plate mating surfaces and/or cylinder block as applicable.

24   If necessary, transfer hose ports and/or fittings from the old pump if you are replacing it with a new pump. Use sealer on the threads of the fittings.

Installation

25   Apply a thin film of RTV sealant to both sides of the new water pump gaskets, then position new gaskets onto the water pump.

26   Carefully install the water pump.

27   Install the retaining bolts finger-tight and make sure that all gaskets are in place and that the hoses line up in the correct position.

28   Tighten the water pump retaining bolts to the torque listed in this Chapter's Specifications.

29   Connect the radiator lower hose and clamp.

30   Connect the heater return hose and clamp.

31   Connect the bypass hose to the water pump.

32   Attach the remaining components to the water pump and engine in the reverse order of removal.

33   Install all of the accessory drivebelts and adjust, if required (see Chapter 1).

34   Fill the cooling system with the proper coolant mixture (see Chapter 1).

35   Start the engine and make sure there are no leaks. Check the level frequently during the first few weeks of operation.

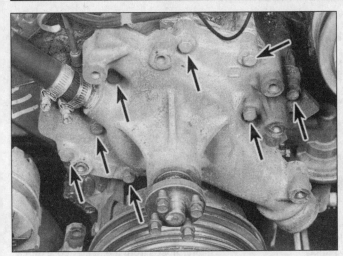

8.21a Water pump mounting bolts (not all are visible in this photo) - small-block V8

8.21b If the water pump won't come off by hand, you can use a block of wood and a hammer to break the seal

9 Coolant temperature sending unit - check and replacement

Refer to illustration 9.4

Check

1   The coolant temperature indicator system is composed of a temperature gauge mounted in the instrument panel and a coolant temperature sending unit mounted on the engine. Some vehicles have more than one sending unit, but only one is used for the indicator system.

2   If an overheating indication occurs, check the coolant level in the system and then make sure the wiring between the gauge and the sending unit is secure and all fuses are intact.

3   When the engine is first started, the gauge should be in the Cold position and gradually move to the Normal range.

4   With the engine off, disconnect the wire from the temperature sending unit (see illustration). **Note:** *On the inline six-cylinder engine, the coolant temperature sending unit is located at the right rear corner of the engine block, just below the cylinder head.*

5   Switch on the ignition without starting the engine - the gauge pointer should be at the Cold mark. Using a jumper wire, ground the sending unit wire. The needle on the gauge should now be pointing to (or past) the Hot mark. **Caution:** *Don't leave the jumper wire connected any longer than necessary.*

a) *If the gauge doesn't perform as described, the problem may be in the gauge or wiring.*

b) *If the gauge does perform as described, the sending unit is defective.*

Replacement

Warning: *Wait until the engine is completely cool before beginning this procedure.*

6   Prepare the new sending unit by wrapping its threads with Teflon tape. Remove the radiator cap to relieve any residual pressure, then reinstall the cap.

7   Unscrew the old sending unit and install the new one as quickly as possible to minimize coolant loss. Tighten the sending unit securely and attach the wire.

8   Check the coolant level (see Chapter 1) and add, if necessary, to bring to the appropriate level.

10 Heater blower motor - removal and installation

Refer to illustrations 10.3 and 10.5

1   Disconnect the cable from the negative battery terminal.

2   Working in the engine compartment, disconnect the wires or wiring harness connector from the rear of the blower motor.

3   Remove the screws retaining the blower motor to the heater case **(see illustration)**.

4   Remove the blower motor and wheel from the heater case.

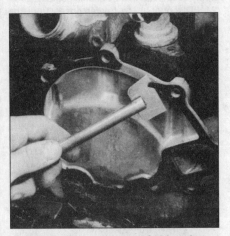

8.22 Remove all traces of old gasket material from the pump mating surfaces

9.4 On the small block V8 engine, the coolant temperature sending unit is located in the intake manifold, near the distributor (other V8 engines similar)

10.3 Typical blower motor mounting details (not all screws are visible in this photo)

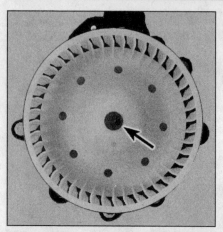

10.5 Squeeze the clamp to loosen it and remove it from the shaft, then slide the blower wheel off the shaft

11.4 Typical blower motor resistor assembly

12.5 Loosen the clamps and detach the heater hoses from the heater core tubes

5   Remove the blower wheel hub clamp and washer from the motor shaft, then pull the blower wheel from the motor shaft (see illustration).
6   Installation is the reverse of the removal procedures.

11   Blower motor resistor - replacement

Refer to illustration 11.4

1   In the engine compartment, locate the resistor on the heater or evaporator housing.
2   Disconnect the negative cable from the battery.
3   Disconnect the resistor electrical connector.
4   Remove the resistor screws and remove the resistor from the housing (see illustration).
5   Installation is the reverse of removal.

12   Heater core - removal and installation

Early non-air conditioned models (engine compartment-mounted heater cores)
Removal

Refer to illustrations 12.5, 12.11a and 12.11b

1   Disconnect the cable from the negative battery terminal.
2   From inside the engine compartment, disconnect the temperature control cable from the temperature blend door and the mounting bracket from the top of the heater case.
3   From inside the engine compartment, disconnect the wires from the blower motor resistor and the blower motor.
4   With the engine cool, drain the coolant from the radiator into a suitable container (see Chapter 1).

5   Disconnect the heater hoses from the heater core tubes on the engine side of the firewall (see illustration).
6   Working in the passenger compartment, remove the nuts retaining the left end of the heater case and the right end of the plenum to the dash panel.
7   Working in the engine compartment, remove the screw retaining the top center of the heater case to the dash panel.
8   From the engine compartment, remove the screws retaining the right end of the heater case to the dash panel and remove the heater case assembly from the vehicle.
9   Remove the screws, nuts and bolts retaining the heater housing plate to the heater case, then remove the heater housing plate.
10   If so equipped, remove the screws attaching the heater core frame to the heater case and remove the frame.
11   Remove the heater core and seal from the heater case (see illustrations).

Installation
12   Installation is reverse of removal except for the following:

13   Slide the self-adjusting clip on the temperature control cable to a position approximately one inch from the cable end loop.
14   Snap the temperature control cable onto the cable mounting bracket of the heater case, then position the self-adjusting clip on the temperature blend door crank arm.
15   Adjust the temperature control cable (refer to Section 14).
16   Fill the radiator with the proper type and amount of coolant (see Chapter 1).
17   Attach the cable to the negative battery terminal.
18   Start the engine and check for leaks.

All other models (cab-mounted heater cores)
Removal

Refer to illustrations 12.22, 12.23 and 12.25

19   Disconnect the cable from the negative battery terminal.
20   With the engine cool, drain the coolant from the radiator into a suitable container.
21   Disconnect the heater hoses from the heater core on the engine side of the firewall.

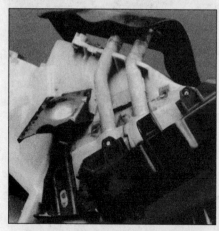

12.11a Remove the cover from the heater core . . .

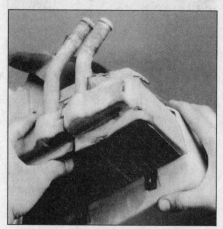

12.11b . . . then pull the core from the case

12.22 Remove the glove box

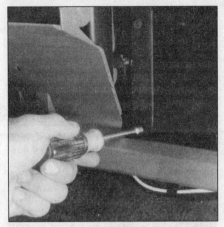

12.23 Remove the heater core access cover from the plenum chamber

12.25 Remove the heater core from the plenum chamber

22   Working in the passenger compartment, remove the glove box for better access **(see illustration)**.
23   Working in the passenger compartment, remove the seven screws which attach the heater core cover to the plenum assembly **(see illustration)**.
24   Disconnect the vacuum source, but leave the vacuum harness attached to the cover. Remove the cover.
25   Remove the heater core from the plenum chamber **(see illustration)**.

Installation
26   Installation is reverse of removal except for the following:
27   Fill the radiator with the proper type and amount of coolant (see Chapter 1).
28   Start the engine and check for leaks.

13   Heater control assembly - removal and installation

1991 and earlier models
Removal
1   Disconnect the cable from the negative battery terminal.
2   If so equipped, pull the control knobs off the radio shafts.
3   Remove the screws retaining the top of the instrument panel center finish panel to the instrument panel pad and remove the finish panel.
4   Remove the knobs from the control assembly by placing a small screwdriver between the knob and the control assembly face plate. While applying pressure to the spring retainer behind the knob, pull the knob off. Repeat for each knob.
5   Remove the ashtray and the ashtray bracket.
6   Remove the four instrument panel-to-control assembly retaining screws.
7   Disconnect the wiring harness connectors from the blower switch, the panel illumination light and the auxiliary fuel tank switch or rear window switch (if so equipped).

8   On 1980 through 1982 vehicles, remove the screw retaining each control cable (function and temperature) to the control assembly.
9   On 1983 and later vehicles, remove the function and temperature control cables from the control assembly by disengaging the cable end retainer tab with a screwdriver while pulling on the cable.
10   Remove the spring nut retaining each control cable pigtail to the control lever arms, then remove the control assembly.

Installation
11   If a new control assembly is being installed, transfer the panel illumination light, the blower switch and the rear window switch or auxiliary fuel tank switch (if so equipped) to the new control panel.
12   Install the control cables to the control lever arms (open coil of each pigtail away from the control lever) and install new spring nuts. **Note:** *The cable with the black flag connects to the temperature (upper) lever and the cable with the white flag connects to the function (lower) lever.*
13   The remaining installation procedures are the reverse of removal.

1992 and later models
Removal
14   Disconnect the cable from the negative battery terminal.
15   Remove the trim strip located above the control assembly and glove box door.
16   Pull the center finish panel away from the instrument panel and remove the four screws that attach the control assembly to the instrument panel.
17   Pull the control assembly out far enough through the opening in the panel to allow disengagement of the electrical connectors for the blower switch, vacuum selector valve and illumination lamp. Disconnect connectors.
18   Remove the vacuum harness connector from the notch in the lower edge of the floor distribution duct and disconnect the vacuum harness from the connector on the plenum.
19   Using a screwdriver, carefully release

the temperature control snap-in flange from the underside of the control assembly.
20   Rotate the assembly and disconnect the temperature control cable from the tab on the gear rack.
21   Remove the control assembly.

Installation
22   Installation is the reverse of removal. Proceed to Section 14 for the cable adjustment procedure.

14   Heater function and temperature control cables - adjustment

1980 and 1981 models
1   The function and temperature control cables are self-adjusting with the movement of the respective control levers to the right ends of the slots (Warm and Defrost). To prevent kinking of the control cable and wires, a pre-set adjustment should be made before attempting to perform the self-adjustment procedure. The pre-set adjustment may be made either with the cables installed in the vehicle or before installation of the cables.

Before installation
2   Insert the blade of a small screwdriver in the end loop of the respective function or temperature cable.
3   Grip the self-adjusting clip with pliers and slide it down the control cable wire until it is approximately one inch away from the end loop.
4   Repeat Steps 2 and 3 for the other cable.
5   Install the cable assembly (refer to Section 13).
6   Move the control levers to the right ends of the slots (function to Defrost, temperature to Warm) to position the self-adjusting clips.
7   Check the system for proper control operation.

After installation
8   Move the control levers to the left ends of the control assembly slots (function to Off,

temperature to Cool).

9   Working on one control at a time, hold the crank arm firmly in position, then insert the blade of a small screwdriver into the wire loop and pull the cable wire through the self-adjusting clip until a space of approximately one inch exists between the clip and the wire end loop.

10   Move the control levers to the right ends of the slots to position the self-adjusting clips.

11   Check the system for proper control operation.

1982 through 1991 models

Function cable

12   Refer to and perform the appropriate procedures in Steps 2 through 11.

Heater temperature cable

13   The temperature control cable does not normally require adjustment; however, proper cable operation may be checked as follows.

14   Move the temperature control lever all the way to the left and then all the way to the right. When released, the lever should bounce back slightly from both extremes of travel, indicating that the blend door is sealing properly.

15   If the temperature control lever moves to either end of the slot without bouncing back, maximum or minimum heat cannot be obtained and the control cable should be adjusted, following Steps 16 through 18 for 1982 vehicles, or Steps 16, 17 and 19 for 1983 to 1991 vehicles.

16   Remove the screw attaching the cable to the heater case assembly in the engine compartment.

17   Move the instrument panel temperature control lever all the way to the left.

18   On 1982 vehicles, move the heater door crank and cable coil all the way toward the rear of the vehicle, making sure not to move or push on the cable housing or slotted flag while doing this, then tighten the cable mounting screw in the engine compartment.

19   On 1983 to 1991 vehicles, two drill dimples can be seen on the cable mounting flange. If maximum heat can not be obtained, drill an 11/64-inch hole in the dimple closest to the heater case crank. If minimum heat cannot be obtained, drill the hole in the dimple farthest from the heater case. Install the cable using the newly drilled hole and tighten the cable mounting screw in the engine compartment.

1992 and later models (temp control only)

20   Remove the glove box.

21   Remove the cable jacket from the metal attaching clip on the top of the plenum by depressing the clip tab and pulling the cable up.

22   Set the temperature control knob to COOL and hold firmly.

23   With the cable end attached to the temperature door cam, push on the cable jacket to seat the blend door until resistance is felt.

Install the cable onto the clip by pushing the cable jacket into the clip from the top until it snaps into place.

24   Operate the system to check temperature control.

15   Air conditioning system - check and maintenance

Warning: *The air conditioning system is under high pressure. Do not loosen any hose fittings or remove any components until after the refrigerant has been recovered by an authorized air conditioning technician. As a precaution, always wear eye protection when disconnecting air conditioning system fittings.*
Note: *The air conditioning system on 1995 and later models uses the non-ozone depleting refrigerant, referred to as R-134a. The R-134a refrigerant and its lubricating oil are not compatible with the R-12 system, and under no circumstances should the two types of refrigerant and lubricating oils be intermixed. If mixed, it could result in costly compressor failure due to improper lubrication.*

1   The following maintenance checks should be performed on a regular basis to ensure that the air conditioner continues to operate at peak efficiency.

a) *Check the compressor drivebelt. If it's worn or deteriorated, replace it (see Chapter 1).*

b) *Check the drivebelt tension and, if necessary, adjust it (see Chapter 1).*

c) *Check the system hoses. Look for cracks, bubbles, hard spots and deterioration. Inspect the hoses and all fittings for oil bubbles and seepage. If there's any evidence of wear, damage or leaks, replace the hose(s).*

d) *Inspect the condenser fins for leaves, bugs and other debris. Use a "fin comb" or compressed air to clean the condenser.*

e) *Make sure the system has the correct refrigerant charge.*

2   It's a good idea to operate the system for about 10 minutes at least once a month, particularly during the winter. Long term non-use can cause hardening, and subsequent failure, of the seals.

3   Because of the complexity of the air conditioning system and the special equipment necessary to service it, in-depth troubleshooting and repairs are not included in this manual. However, simple checks and component replacement procedures are provided in this Chapter. For more complete information on the air conditioning system, refer to the *Haynes Automotive Heating and Air Conditioning Manual.*

4   The most common cause of poor cooling is simply a low system refrigerant charge. If a noticeable drop in cool air output occurs, the following check will help you determine if the refrigerant level is low.

5   Warm the engine up to normal operating temperature.

6   Place the air conditioning temperature selector at the coldest setting and put the blower at the highest setting. Open the doors (to make sure the air conditioning system doesn't cycle off as soon as it cools the passenger compartment).

7   With the compressor engaged - the clutch will make an audible click and the center of the clutch will rotate - feel the evaporator inlet pipe between the orifice tube and the accumulator with one hand while placing your other hand on the surface of the accumulator housing.

8   If both surfaces feel about the same temperature and if both feel a little cooler than the surrounding air, the refrigerant level is probably okay. Further inspection of the system is beyond the scope of the home mechanic and should be left to a professional.

9   If the inlet pipe has frost accumulation or feels cooler than the accumulator surface, the refrigerant charge is low. Add refrigerant.

Adding refrigerant

Note: *Because of Federal regulations implemented by the Environmental Protection Agency, 14-ounce cans of refrigerant may not be available in your area. If this is the case, it will be necessary to take your vehicle to a licensed air conditioning technician for charging. If you decide to add refrigerant yourself from one of the large 30 pound bottles still available, you will need a manifold gauge set, all the necessary fittings, adapters and hoses and a copy of the* Haynes Automotive Heating and Air Conditioning Manual *before beginning.*

16   Air conditioning accumulator - removal and installation

Refer to illustration 16.3
Warning: *The air conditioning system is under high pressure. DO NOT disassemble any part of the system (hoses, compressor, line fittings, etc.) until after the refrigerant has been recovered by an authorized air conditioning technician. As a precaution, always wear eye protection when disconnecting air conditioning system fittings.*

1   Have the air conditioning system discharged (see **Warning** above).

2   Disconnect the cable from the negative battery terminal.

3   Unplug the electrical connector from the pressure switch near the top of the accumulator **(see illustration)**.

4   Disconnect the refrigerant lines from the accumulator using two wrenches to prevent component damage. Cap the lines to prevent contamination.

5   Remove the screws securing the accumulator to the evaporator case and remove accumulator.

6   Installation is the reverse of removal. Replace all O-rings with new ones specifically

16.3 The air conditioning accumulator is located near the firewall on the passenger's side; the pressure switch is threaded into the side of it

designed for air conditioning system use and lubricate them with refrigerant oil.
7   Take the vehicle to the shop that discharged it and have the system evacuated and recharged.

17 Air conditioning compressor - removal and installation

Refer to illustrations 17.3
Warning: *The air conditioning system is under high pressure. DO NOT disassemble any part of the system (hoses, compressor, line fittings, etc.) until after the refrigerant has been recovered by an authorized air conditioning technician. As a precaution, always wear eye protection when disconnecting air conditioning system fittings.*
Note: *The accumulator should be replaced whenever the compressor is replaced.*
1   Have the air conditioning system discharged (see **Warning** above).

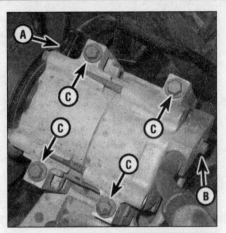

17.3 Air conditioning compressor mounting details

A   *Compressor clutch electrical connector*
B   *Refrigerant line manifold bolt*
C   *Compressor mounting bolts*

2   Disconnect the cable from the negative battery terminal.
3   Disconnect the compressor clutch wiring harness **(see illustration)**.
4   Remove the drivebelt (see Chapter 1).
5   Unbolt the refrigerant line manifold from the compressor. Plug the open fittings to prevent entry of dirt and moisture.
6   Unbolt the compressor from the mounting brackets and lift it out of the vehicle.
7   If a new compressor is being installed, follow the directions with the compressor regarding the draining of excess oil prior to installation.
8   The clutch may have to be transferred from the original to the new compressor.
9   Installation is the reverse of removal. Replace all O-rings with new ones specifically designed for air conditioning system use and lubricate them with refrigerant oil. Position the O-rings in the manifold.
10   Have the system evacuated, recharged and leak tested by the shop that discharged it.

18 Air conditioning condenser - removal and installation

Refer to illustrations 18.4a, 18.4b and 18.4c
Warning: *The air conditioning system is under high pressure. DO NOT disassemble any part of the system (hoses, compressor, line fittings, etc.) until after the refrigerant has been recovered by an authorized air conditioning technician. As a precaution, wear eye protection when disconnecting air conditioning system fittings.*
1   Have the air conditioning system discharged (see **Warning** above).
2   Drain the cooling system (see Chapter 1).
3   Remove the upper radiator hose.
4   Disconnect the refrigerant lines from the condenser. Some models may use wrench type fittings and others may use a quick-connect spring lock coupling. On wrench fittings, use a back-up wrench to prevent twisting of the hard lines. A spring lock coupling tool will be required on quick connect type fittings **(see illustrations)**. Plug the lines to keep dirt and moisture out.
5   Remove the two lower screws attaching the condenser to the front radiator supports.
6   Remove the two upper radiator attaching screws and tilt the top of the radiator rearwards to gain access to the two top condenser attaching screws.
7   Remove the attaching screws and lift the condenser out of the vehicle.
8   If the original condenser will be reinstalled, store it with the line fittings on top to prevent oil from draining out.
9   If a new condenser is being installed, pour one ounce of refrigerant oil into it prior to installation.
10   Reinstall the components in the reverse order of removal.
11   Have the system evacuated, recharged and leak tested by the shop that discharged it.

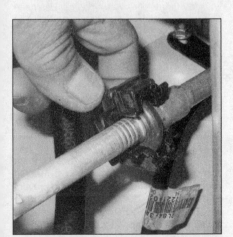

18.4a If equipped, remove the protective cover from the spring-lock coupling . . .

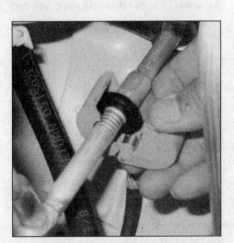

18.4b . . . install the spring-lock coupling tool . . .

18.4c . . . and release the coupling by pressing the tool into the spring

19   Oil cooler - removal and installation

Warning: *Wait until the engine is completely cool before beginning this procedure.*

Early model 7.5L engine

1   Raise vehicle and support it securely on jackstands.
2   Remove the front grille (refer to Chapter 11).
3   From under the vehicle, disconnect the oil cooler lines at the filter adapter. A back-up wrench on the line fitting must be used when disconnecting this line. **Warning:** *Be prepared for oil to spill from the lines and the adapter.* **Caution:** *Do not attempt to disconnect the lines at the cooler fittings. The fittings or the cooler could be damaged.*
4   Pull the lines out toward the front of the vehicle.
5   Remove the six oil cooler bolts and lift out the oil cooler.
6   If the oil filter adapter must be removed, remove the through bolt at the center of the adapter.
7   When reinstalling the filter adapter use a new O-ring between the engine block and the adapter.
8   Position the oil cooler on the radiator support and install the six bolts.
9   Install the oil cooler lines in their original positions.
10   Put sealing compound on the threads of the line fittings and reinstall the lines on the filter adapter. Use a back-up wrench on the adapter fittings.
11   Check the oil level and correct if necessary.
12   Start the engine and check for oil leaks.
13   Remove the vehicle from the jackstands.

Late model 7.5L engine

14   Drain the radiator of coolant.
15   Remove the lower radiator to oil cooler hose.
16   Disconnect the oil cooler to water pump hose.
17   Remove the oil cooler adapter to engine

block bolt and remove the oil cooler assembly. **Note:** *Some loss of oil will result from residual oil in the filter and cooler.*
18   Prior to reinstallation, verify that the oil cooler-to-engine block seal is present and in good condition.
19   To install, push the oil cooler onto the water pump hose and align the arrow on the hose with the ridge on the inlet of the oil cooler.
20   Place the oil cooler assembly against the engine block and center it over the threaded insert in the block.
21   Install the oil cooler adapter bolt into the block and tighten it only hand tight at this time. **Warning:** *This is a special hollow bolt which allows oil to flow - do not replace it with a standard fastener.*
22   Rotate the oil cooler assembly until the adapter housing flange rests against the machined boss on the engine block.
23   Tighten the oil filter adapter-to-engine block bolt to the torque listed in this Chapter's Specifications.
24   Install the lower radiator hose to the oil cooler and tighten all hose clamps securely.
25   Install a new oil filter and add approximately 1/2-quart of engine oil to the crankcase.
26   Refill the radiator and check for leaks. Check the engine oil level and coolant level and fill as required (refer to Chapter 1).

5.8L Lightning engine

27   Drain the radiator of coolant (see Chapter 1).
28   Remove the oil filter (refer to Chapter 1).
29   Remove the two coolant hoses from the oil cooler assembly.
30   Note the orientation of the coolant inlet and outlet spigots, remove the oil cooler mounting bolt (threaded tube the filter spins onto) and remove the oil cooler assembly.
31   Prior to installation, verify that the oil cooler-to-adapter seal is present and in good condition.
32   Center the oil cooler assembly against the adapter housing.
33   Install the oil cooler mounting bolt and

hand tighten it. **Warning:** *This is a special hollow bolt which allows oil to flow - do not replace it with a standard fastener.*
34   Rotate the cooler assembly until the coolant hose spigots are properly oriented.
35   Tighten the oil cooler mounting bolt to the torque listed in this Chapter's Specifications.
36   Install the two coolant hoses to the oil cooler and tighten all hose clamps securely.
37   Install a new oil filter and add approximately 1/2-quart of engine oil to the crankcase.
38   Refill the radiator and check for leaks. Check the engine oil level and coolant level and fill as required (refer to Chapter 1).

20   Transmission oil cooler (auxiliary) - removal and installation

Warning: *Wait until the engine and transmission are completely cold before beginning this procedure.*

1   Place a drain pan under the transmission oil cooler.
2   Disconnect the fluid cooler tubes from the transmission oil cooler. Take care not to twist the lines or damage the fittings. It is best to use a flare-nut wrench for this particular job. Plug the ends of the disconnected lines to prevent leakage and stop dirt from entering the system.
3   Remove the transmission oil cooler mounting bolts and nuts and lift out the cooler.
4   Position the transmission oil cooler on the support bracket and install the bolts and nuts.
5   Install the transmission oil cooler lines and hoses in their original positions.
6   Put sealing compound on the threads of the line fittings and reinstall the lines on the transmission oil cooler fittings. Use a back-up wrench on the fittings.
7   Check the transmission oil level and correct if necessary.
8   Start the engine and check for leaks.

Chapter 4
Fuel and exhaust systems

Contents

Specifications

Mechanical fuel pump
Pressure
    All except in-line six-cylinder engine ... 6 to 8 psi
    In-line six-cylinder engine ... 5 to 7 psi
Volume (at idle rpm) ... 1 pint in 20 seconds

Electric fuel pump
Fuel system pressure
    Engine off
        4.9L EFI (except 1987 models) ... 50 to 60 psi
        All other EFI engines ... 35 to 45 psi
    Engine running (vacuum hose connected to regulator)
        4.9L EFI (except 1987 models) ... 45 to 60 psi
        All other EFI engines ... 30 to 45 psi
    Engine running (vacuum hose disconnected) ... Pressure should increase 5 to 10 psi
Low pressure pump (pressure)
    Carbureted 7.5L with "Hot Fuel" option ... 6 to 8 psi
Low pressure pumps (volume)
    Early EFI models ... 6 oz min in 5 seconds
    7.5L "Hot Fuel" option ... 6 oz min in 5 seconds
Fuel injector resistance ... 11 to 18 ohms

Torque specifications
Ft-lbs (unless otherwise indicated)

Note: *One foot-pound (ft-lb) of torque is equivalent to 12 inch-pounds (in-lbs) of torque. Torque values below approximately 15 ft-lbs are expressed in inch-pounds, since most foot-pound torque wrenches are not accurate at these smaller values.*

Carbureted fuel system
Carburetor retaining nuts ... 144 to 180 in-lbs

EFI systems
4.9L engine
Air bypass valve-to-throttle body ... 71 to 102 in-lbs
Fuel rail mounting bolts ... 70 to 105 in-lbs
Throttle body-to-upper intake manifold ... 12 to 16
Upper intake manifold-to-lower intake manifold bolts ... 12 to 18

Torque specifications (continued)

Ft-lbs (unless otherwise indicated)

Note: *One foot-pound (ft-lb) of torque is equivalent to 12 inch-pounds (in-lbs) of torque. Torque values below approximately 15 ft-lbs are expressed in inch-pounds, since most foot-pound torque wrenches are not accurate at these smaller values.*

5.0L and 5.8L engines
Air bypass valve-to-throttle body .... 71 to 102 in-lbs
Fuel rail mounting bolts .... 70 to 105 in-lbs
Throttle body-to-upper intake manifold.. 12 to 18
Upper intake manifold-to-lower intake manifold .... 15 to 22

7.5L engine
Air bypass valve to-lower manifold .... 70 to 100 in-lbs
Fuel rail mounting bolts .... 70 to 105 in-lbs
Throttle body-to-upper intake manifold.. 12 to 16
Upper intake manifold-to-lower intake manifold bolts............................. 12 to 18

1 Carburetor systems - general information

1   During the years prior to electronic fuel injection, F-series trucks and Bronco vehicles saw no less than four carburetor-based fuel control systems:

a) *Stand alone conventional carburetors.*

b) *MCU (Microprocessor Control Unit) controlled feedback carburetors.*

c) *EEC-III (Electronic Engine Control - design three) controlled feedback carburetors.*

d) *EEC-IV (Electronic Engine Control - design four) controlled feedback carburetors.*

2   Early carburetors were of conventional design relying simply on the proper sizing of the various jets, needles and air bleeds to provide a combustible air fuel mixture to the engine.These early carburetors were of single, dual or four-venturi, downdraft type, depending on the engine displacement and year of production.

3   As demands for more precise control over air/fuel mixtures grew, closed loop feedback controlled carburetors and their associated engine control sensors and control electronics were introduced. The fuel metering systems of these carburetors is influenced by the operation of the feedback control solenoid, which when cycled by the control electronics, causes the air/fuel mixture to be altered. The MCU system used only one sensor; an Exhaust Gas Oxygen sensor (EGO) to determine fuel rich or lean conditions. The MCU would then send a varying signal to the feedback solenoid to move the mixture back to optimum. The MCU system was fairly simple by today's standards, and operated only when the vehicle was at operating temperature and at steady part throttle cruise conditions.

4   The EEC-III system was much more advanced and operated in a closed-loop mode in all conditions. In operation, the electronic engine control computer (EEC-III) would measure various engine operating conditions such as manifold pressure (MAP sensor), throttle position (TP sensor), engine coolant temperature (ECT sensor) and unburned oxygen in the exhaust manifold or pipe (oxygen sensor) and compute mixture correction commands which are sent to the carburetors feedback control solenoid.

5   The EEC-IV system was the next step up in sophistication and was the prelude to electronic fuel injection systems. While offering the same basic fuel control as the EEC-III system, the EEC-IV control module was packaged to accommodate the additional control circuits required by the impending switch to EFI and to support other new systems such as the new TFI-IV ignition system.

6   All fuel systems consists of a fuel tank (or tanks) mounted in a variety of locations on the chassis, a mechanically-operated fuel pump and an air cleaner for filtering purposes. Vehicles equipped with 7.5L engine with "Hot Fuel" option utilize an in-tank low pressure electric fuel pump (two pumps, one each in dual tank options) with associated fuel return line. All models used various vacuum and electro-mechanical actuators, dash-pots and solenoids to control idle speed and throttle return speed.

7   Ultimately, the feedback control systems were only a temporary stopgap between traditional carburetors and fuel injection. Because of their limited usage (select years and/or states) the electronic control systems will not be addressed in this manual. If a problem is suspected in the electronics portion of the feedback carburetor system, consult your local dealer.

2 Carburetor - servicing and overhaul

Refer to illustration 2.7

1   A thorough road test and check of carburetor adjustments should be done before any major carburetor service. Specifications for some adjustments are listed on the Vehicle Emissions Control Information label found in the engine compartment.

2   Some performance complaints directed at the carburetor are actually a result of loose, misadjusted or malfunctioning engine or electrical components. Others develop when vacuum hoses leak, are disconnected or are incorrectly routed. The proper approach to analyzing carburetor problems should include a routine check as follows:

a) *Inspect all vacuum hoses and actuators for leaks and proper installation (see Chapter 6, Emissions control systems).*

b) *Tighten the intake manifold nuts and carburetor mounting nuts evenly and securely (see Section 17 and Chapter 2).*

c) *Perform a cylinder compression test (see Chapter 2).*

d) *Clean or replace the spark plugs as necessary (see Chapter 1).*

e) *Test the spark plug wires (see Chapter 5).*

f) *Inspect the ignition primary wires and check the vacuum advance operation. Replace any defective parts (see Chapter 5).*

g) *Check the ignition timing according to the instructions listed on the Emissions Control Information label (see Chapter 5).*

h) *Set the carburetor idle mixture (see Section 4).*

i) *Check the fuel pump pressure (see Section 7).*

j) *Inspect the heat control valve in the air cleaner for proper operation (see Chapter 6).*

k) *Remove the carburetor air filter element and blow out any dirt with compressed air. If the filter is extremely dirty, replace it with a new one (see Chapter 1).*

l) *Inspect the crankcase ventilation system (see Chapter 6).*

3   Carburetor problems usually show up as flooding, hard starting, stalling, severe backfiring, poor acceleration and lack of response to idle mixture screw adjustments. A carburetor that is leaking fuel and/or covered with wet-looking deposits needs attention.

4   Diagnosing carburetor problems may require that the engine be started and run with the air cleaner removed. While running the engine without the air cleaner it is possible that it could backfire. A backfiring situation is likely to occur if the carburetor is malfunctioning, but removal of the air cleaner alone can lean the air/fuel mixture enough to produce an engine backfire. Perform this type of testing for as short a time as possible and be especially watchful for the potential of backfire and the possibility of starting a fire. Do not position your face or any portions of your body directly over the carburetor during inspection or servicing procedures.

5   Once it is determined that the carburetor is in need of work or an overhaul, several alternatives should be considered. If you are going to attempt to overhaul the carburetor yourself, first obtain a good quality carburetor rebuild kit which will include all necessary gaskets, internal pans, instructions and a parts list. You will also need carburetor cleaning solvent and some means of blowing out the internal passages of the carburetor with air.

6   Due to the many configurations and variations of carburetors offered on the range of vehicles covered in this book, it is not feasible for us to do a step-by-step overhaul of each type. However, you will find a good, detailed instruction list and illustrations with any quality carburetor overhaul kit and it will apply in a more specific manner to the carburetor you have.

7   Another alternative is to obtain a new or rebuilt carburetor. These are readily available from dealers and auto parts stores for all engines covered in this manual. The important fact when purchasing one of these units is to make sure the exchange carburetor is identical to the original. Often times a tag is attached to the top plate of your carburetor and will aid the parts man in determining the exact type of carburetor you have **(see illustration)**. When obtaining a rebuilt carburetor or a rebuild kit, take time to ascertain that the kit or carburetor matches your application exactly. Seemingly insignificant differences can make a considerable difference in the overall running condition of your engine.

8   If you choose to overhaul your own carburetor, allow enough time to disassemble the carburetor carefully, soak the necessary parts in the cleaning solvent (usually for at least one half day or according to the instructions listed on the carburetor cleaner) and reassemble it, which will usually take you much longer than disassembly. When you are disassembling a carburetor, take care to match each part with the illustration in your carburetor kit and lay the parts out in order on a clean work surface to help you reassemble the carburetor. Overhauls by amateurs sometimes result in a vehicle which runs poorly, or not at all, compared to the original condition. To avoid this happening to you, use care and patience when disassembling your carburetor so you can reassemble it correctly.

3   Carburetor - removal and installation

Warning: *Gasoline is extremely flammable, so take extra precautions when you work on any part of the fuel system. Don't smoke or allow open flames or bare light bulbs near the work area, and don't work in a garage where a gas-type appliance (such as a water heater or clothes dryer) is present. Since gasoline is carcinogenic, wear fuel-resistant gloves when there's a possibility of being exposed to fuel, and, if you spill any fuel on your skin, rinse it off immediately with soap and water. Mop up*

2.7 Typical carburetor identification tag

any spills immediately and do not store fuel-soaked rags where they could ignite. The fuel system on fuel-injected models is under constant pressure, so, if any fuel lines are to be disconnected, the fuel pressure in the system must be relieved first (see Section 8). When you perform any kind of work on the fuel system, wear safety glasses and have a Class B type fire extinguisher on hand.

1   Disconnect the negative battery cable. Remove the hose connections leading to the air cleaner. Mark these with coded pieces of tape to help in reassembly.

2   Remove the air cleaner assembly.

3   Use a small catch-can and disconnect the fuel feed line from the carburetor. Plug the end of this hose to prevent further leakage.

4   Disconnect any electrical leads from the emissions control devices connected to the carburetor. Mark these connections so they can be installed in the proper position.

5   Remove any vacuum lines from the carburetor. Mark them for installation purposes.

6   If equipped, disconnect the kick-down lever or cable from the carburetor (see Chapter 7C).

7   Disconnect the throttle cable or linkage from the carburetor.

8   Disconnect any under-carburetor heater hoses that may be connected to the carburetor.

9   Disconnect any coolant transfer hoses that may be connected to the choke system.

10   Remove the carburetor retaining nuts from the studs in the intake manifold.

11   Lift off the carburetor, spacer plate (if equipped), and gasket(s). Place a piece of cardboard over the intake manifold surface to prevent debris from falling into the engine while the carburetor is removed.

12   Before installation, carefully clean the mating surfaces of the intake manifold, spacer plate (if equipped), and the base of the carburetor of any old gasket material. These surfaces must be perfectly clean and smooth to prevent vacuum leaks.

13   Install a new gasket(s).

14   Install the carburetor and spacer plate (if equipped) over the studs on the intake manifold.

15   Install the retaining nuts and tighten them to the torque listed in this Chapter's Specifications. Be careful not to over-torque these retaining nuts as they can warp the base plate of the carburetor.

4   Carburetor - external adjustments

Note: *All carburetors on U.S. vehicles come equipped with adjustment limiters or limiter stops on the carburetor idle mixture screws. All adjustments to these mixture screws are to be made only within the range provided by the limiter devices. In addition, the following procedures are intended for general use only. The information given on the Emissions Control Information label located under the hood is specific for your engine and should be followed.*

Note: *The instructions given below should be regarded only as temporary adjustments. The vehicle should be taken to an auto facility equipped with the necessary instruments for adjusting the idle mixture as soon as possible after the vehicle is running. At the same time the idle mixture is set, the idle speed will also be reset, so your carburetor is operating within the range specified on the Emissions Control Information label.*

Note: *All necessary adjustments and/or inspection procedures discussed in Section 2 of this Chapter should be performed before carburetor servicing begins.*

Idle speed (preliminary)

1   Set the fuel mixture screws to the full counterclockwise position allowed by the limiter caps.

2   Back off the idle speed adjusting screw until the throttle bore plates are seated in the throttle bore. Some vehicles are equipped with either a dashpot or a solenoid-type idle valve to hold the linkage open. Make sure these devices are not holding the idle up when making this adjustment.

3   Turn the idle adjusting screw inward until it initially contacts the throttle stop. Turn the screw an additional 1-1/2 turns to establish a preliminary idle speed adjustment.

4.11 Location of the idle speed screw - four-barrel carburetor

5.4 To adjust a choke controlled by a thermostatic spring housing, loosen the three screws (lower screw not visible here) and turn the housing in the required direction

Idle speed (engine running)

Refer to illustration 4.11

4   Apply the parking brake and block the wheels to prevent movement. If equipped with an automatic transmission, have an assistant apply the brakes as a further safety precaution during the following procedures.

5   Start the engine and allow the engine to achieve normal operating temperature.

6   Ensure that the ignition timing is adjusted properly as described in Chapter 5.

7   On a vehicle with a manual shift transmission, the idle should be adjusted with the transmission in Neutral. On vehicles with automatic transmissions, the idle adjustment is made with the transmission in DRIVE.

8   Make sure the choke plate is fully opened.

9   Make sure the air conditioning is turned off.

10   Use a tachometer of known accuracy and connect it to the vehicle according to the manufacturer's instructions.

11   Adjust the engine curb idle rpm to the specifications given on the *Emissions Control Information label* **(see illustration)**. Make sure the air cleaner is installed for this adjustment.

12   If so equipped, turn the solenoid assembly to obtain the specified curb idle rpm with the solenoid activated.

13   Shift the automatic transmission to NEUTRAL.

14   Disconnect the power to the solenoid lead wire at the electrical connector.

15   Adjust the carburetor throttle stop screw to obtain 500 rpm in NEUTRAL.

16   Connect the solenoid power wire and open the throttle slightly by hand. The solenoid plunger should hold the throttle lever in the extended position and move the rpm range up.

Fast idle adjustment

17   The fast idle adjusting screw is provided to maintain engine idle rpm while the choke is operating and the engine has a limited air supply during its cold running cycle. As the choke plate moves through its range of travel from the closed to the open position, the fast idle cam rotates to allow decreasingly slower idle speeds until the normal operating temperature and correct curb idle rpm is reached.

18   Before adjusting the fast idle make sure the curb idle speed is adjusted as previously discussed.

19   With the engine at normal operating temperature and the tachometer attached, manually rotate the fast idle cam until the fast idle adjusting screw rests on the specific step of the cam (see *Emissions Control Information label* for proper step).

20   Turn the fast idle adjusting screw inward or outward to obtain the specified fast idle rpm.

5   Automatic choke (carburetor) - inspection and adjustment

Refer to illustration 5.4

Note: *Choke checking procedures can be found in Chapter 1.*

1   Remove the air cleaner with the engine cold and not running.

2   Rotate the throttle (or have an assistant depress the gas accelerator to the open position and see if the choke plate shuts tightly in the opening of the upper body air horn. With the accelerator held open, make sure that the choke plate can be moved freely and that it is not hanging up due to deposits of varnish. If the choke plate has excessive deposits of varnish, it will have to be either cleaned with a commercial spray-on carburetor cleaner or the carburetor will need to be dismantled and overhauled or replaced (see Section 2). A spray-on type carburetor cleaner will remove any surface varnish which may be causing sticky or erratic choke plate action. However, care must be used to prevent sediment from entering the throttle bores.

3   Start the vehicle. If equipped with an electric choke, use a voltmeter to check that the electric assist on the side of the choke thermostat housing has voltage. Voltage should be constantly supplied to the temperature sensing switch as long as the engine is running. If no voltage is present, check the system circuit to determine the problem.

4   Some automatic chokes will come equipped with a thermostatic spring housing which controls the choke action. To adjust this type of housing, loosen the three clamp screws that attach the thermostatic spring housing to the choke housing. The spring housing can now be turned to vary the setting on the choke **(see illustration)**. Set the spring housing to the specified mark (see the Emissions Control Information label in the engine compartment) and tighten the retaining screws. Do not try to compensate for poor choke operation by varying the index setting from the specified spot. If the choke is not operating properly, the spring inside the housing may be worn or broken or other problems may exist in the choke system. If this situation exists, the spring housing will need to be replaced.

5   Allow the vehicle to completely cool (at least four hours - preferably overnight) and check for proper operation as described in Chapter 1.

6   Fuel lines and fittings - replacement

Refer to illustrations 6.5, 6.10, 6.14, 6.26a, 6.26b and 6.26c

Warning: *The fuel system pressure must be relieved before disconnecting fuel lines and fittings on fuel-injected models (see Section 8). Gasoline is extremely flammable, so extra precautions must be taken when working on any part of the fuel system. DO NOT smoke or allow open flames or bare light bulbs near the work area. Also, don't work in a garage where a gas appliance such as a water heater or clothes dryer is present.*

6.5 A hairpin clip-type push-connect fitting - the clip is being
pointed to with a screwdriver

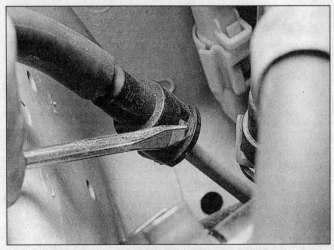

6.10 A push connect fitting with a duck bill clip

Push connect fittings - disassembly and reassembly

1   There are two different push connect fitting designs. Fittings used with 3/8 and 5/16-inch diameter lines have a "hairpin" type clip; fittings used with 1/4-inch diameter lines have a "duck bill" type clip. The procedure used for releasing each type of fitting is different. The clips should be replaced whenever a connector is disassembled.

2   Disconnect all push connect fittings from fuel system components such as the fuel filter, the carburetor/fuel charging assembly, the fuel tank, etc. before removing the assembly.

3/8 and 5/16-inch fittings (hairpin clip)

3   Inspect the internal portion of the fitting for accumulations of dirt. If more than a light coating of dust is present, clean the fitting before disassembly.

4   Some adhesion between the seals in the fitting and the line will occur over a period of time. Twist the fitting on the line, then push and pull the fitting until it moves freely.

5   Remove the hairpin clip from the fitting by bending the shipping tab down until it clears the body **(see illustration)**. Then, using nothing but your hands, spread each leg about 1/8-inch to disengage the body and push the legs through the fitting. Finally, pull lightly on the triangular end of the clip and work it clear of the line and fitting. Remember, don't use any tools to perform this part of the procedure.

6   Grasp the fitting and hose and pull it straight off the line.

7   Do not reuse the original clip in the fitting. A new clip must be used.

8   Before reinstalling the fitting on the line, wipe the line end with a clean cloth. Inspect the inside of the fitting to ensure that it's free of dirt and/or obstructions.

9   To reinstall the fitting on the line, align them and push the fitting into place. When the fitting is engaged, a definite click will be heard. Pull on the fitting to ensure that it's completely engaged. To install the new clip, insert it into any two adjacent openings in the fitting with the triangular portion of the clip pointing away from the fitting opening. Using your index finger, push the clip in until the legs are locked on the outside of the fitting.

1/4-inch fittings (duck bill clip)

10   The duck bill clip type fitting consists of a body, spacers, O-rings and the retaining clip **(see illustration)**. The clip holds the fitting securely in place on the line. One of the two following methods must be used to disconnect this type of fitting.

11   Before attempting to disconnect the fitting, check the visible internal portion of the fitting for accumulations of dirt. If more than a light coating of dust is evident, clean the fitting before disassembly.

12   Some adhesion between the seals in the fitting and line will occur over a period of time. Twist the fitting on the line, then push and pull the fitting until it moves freely.

13   The preferred method used to disconnect the fitting requires a special tool, available at most auto parts stores. To disengage the line from the fitting, align the slot in the push connect disassembly tool with either tab on the clip (90-degrees from the slots on the side of the fitting) and insert the tool. This disengages the duck bill from the line. **Note:** *Some fuel lines have a secondary bead which aligns with the outer surface of the clip. The bead can make tool insertion difficult. If necessary, use the alternative disassembly method described in Steps 16 through 19.*

14   Holding the tool and the line with one hand, pull the fitting off **(see illustration)**. **Note:** *Only moderate effort is necessary if the clip is properly disengaged. The use of anything other than your hands should not be required.*

15   After disassembly, inspect and clean the line sealing surface. Also inspect the inside of the fitting and the line for any internal parts

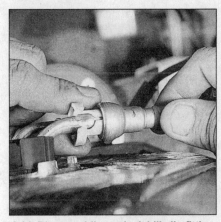

6.14 Disassembling a duck bill clip fitting
using the special tool

that may have been dislodged from the fitting. Any loose internal parts should be immediately reinstalled (use the line to insert the parts).

16   The alternative disassembly procedure requires a pair of small adjustable pliers. The pliers must have a jaw width of 3/16-inch or less.

17   Align the jaws of the pliers with the openings in the side of the fitting and compress the portion of the retaining clip that engages the body. This disengages the retaining clip from the body (often one side of the clip will disengage before the other - both sides must be disengaged).

18   Pull the fitting off the line. **Note:** *Only moderate effort is required if the retaining clip has been properly disengaged. Do not use any tools for this procedure.*

19   Once the fitting is removed from the line end, check the fitting and line for any internal parts that may have been dislodged from the fitting. Any loose internal parts should be immediately reinstalled (use the line to insert the parts).

20   The retaining clip will remain on the line. Disengage the clip from the line bead to remove it. Do not reuse the retaining clip - install a new one!

6.26a If the spring lock couplings are equipped with safety clips, pry them off with a small screwdriver

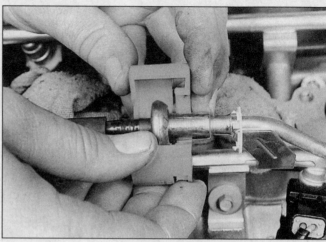

6.26b Open the spring-loaded halves of the spring lock coupling tool and place it in position around the coupling, then close it

21 Before reinstalling the fitting, wipe the line end with a clean cloth. Check the inside of the fitting to make sure that it's free of dirt and/or obstructions.

22 To reinstall the fitting, align it with the line and push it into place. When the fitting is engaged, a definite click will be heard. Pull on the fitting to ensure that it's fully engaged.

23 Install the new replacement clip by inserting one of the serrated edges on the duck bill portion into one of the openings. Push on the other side until the clip snaps into place.

Spring lock couplings - disassembly and reassembly

24 The fuel supply and return lines used on EFI engines utilize spring lock couplings at the engine fuel rail end instead of plastic push connect fittings. The male end of the spring lock coupling, which is girded by two O-rings, is inserted into a female flared end engine fitting. The coupling is secured by a garter spring which prevents disengagement by gripping the flared end of the female fitting.

On later models, a cup-tether assembly provides additional security.

25 To disconnect the 1/2-inch (12.7mm) spring lock coupling supply fitting, you will need to obtain a spring lock coupling tool kit, available at most auto parts stores that carry specialty tools.

26 Study the accompanying illustrations carefully before detaching either spring lock coupling fitting (see illustration).

---

7 Fuel pump (mechanical) - general information and check

Refer to illustrations 7.1a and 7.1b

Warning: *Gasoline is extremely flammable, so take extra precautions when you work on any part of the fuel system. Don't smoke or allow open flames or bare light bulbs near the work area, and don't work in a garage where a gas-type appliance (such as a water heater or clothes dryer) is present. Since gasoline is carcinogenic, wear fuel-resistant gloves when*

there's a possibility of being exposed to fuel, and, if you spill any fuel on your skin, rinse it off immediately with soap and water. Mop up any spills immediately and do not store fuel-soaked rags where they could ignite. When you perform any kind of work on the fuel system, wear safety glasses and have a Class B type fire extinguisher on hand.

General information

1 The fuel pump is bolted to the left front side of the block or timing chain cover (see illustrations). It is operated by an eccentric cam on the camshaft which provides the up and down movement of the pumps rocker arm. The pumps rocker arm pulls the internal diaphragm against its internal spring while drawing fuel into the pump chamber. The pumps internal spring then applies its pressure against the diaphragm which raises the pressure of the fuel in the pump chamber. The fuel exits the pump under pressure. Check valves in the pump prevent reverse flow. If a problem occurs in the fuel pump itself, it will normally either deliver no fuel at all or not enough to

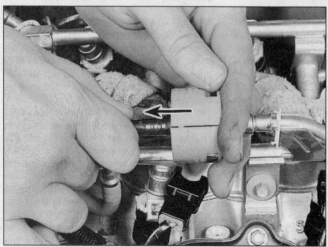

6.26c To disconnect the coupling, push the tool into the cage opening to expand the garter spring and release the female fitting, then pull the male and female fittings apart

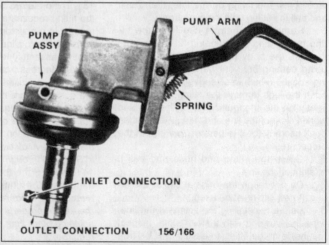

7.1a The mechanical fuel pump is operated by a pump arm, which is actuated by an eccentric on the camshaft

7.1b On V8 models, the fuel pump is mounted on the left front of the engine

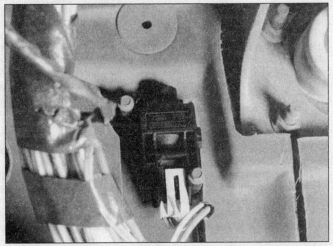

8.2 The inertia switch is located on the driver's side of the firewall, to the left of the brake pedal or behind the right kick panel

sustain high engine speeds or loads. **Note:** *When an engine develops a lean (fuel starved) condition, the fuel pump is often to blame, but the same symptoms will be evident if the carburetor float bowl filter is clogged. A lean condition will also occur if the carburetor is malfunctioning, the fuel lines and hoses are leaking, kinked or restricted or the electrical system is shorting out or malfunctioning.*

General check

2   To be considered operational, the fuel pump must pass both capacity and pressure tests. However, before removing a potentially defective fuel pump verify the following:
a) *Be sure the tank has fuel in it.*
b) *Be sure the fuel filter is not plugged. If it hasn't been changed recently, install a new one (see Chapter 1).*
c) *Inspect all mechanical connections and rubber hoses from the fuel pump to the fuel tank for leaks, kinks and cracks. Repair as required.*
d) *Inspect the fuel pump diaphragm crimp (the area where the stamped steel section is attached to the casting) and the breather hole(s) in the casting for evidence of fuel or oil leakage. Replace the pump if it's leaking.*

Output (capacity) test

3   Remove the air cleaner assembly.
4   Carefully disconnect the fuel line at the fuel filter inlet. The fuel line is pressurized so it's a good idea to shield your eyes with goggles or wrap a shop rag around the fitting when breaking it loose.
5   Attach a section of rubber fuel hose to the end of the disconnected line with hose clamps and route the end of the hose into an approved gasoline container. Disconnect the primary wires from the coil to disable the ignition system. Crank the engine over for ten seconds. The fuel pump should deliver 1/3-pint of fuel in ten seconds.
6   If the output is as specified, perform the pressure test below (see Step 10).

7   If the output is less than specified, repeat the test with a remote fuel supply. Detach the hose from the fuel pump inlet line and attach a separate section of fuel hose to the line with a hose clamp. Route the end of the hose into the remote fuel supply (an approved gasoline container at least half full of fuel) and repeat the procedure in Step 5.
8   If the output is now as specified, the problem is in the fuel supply system. This can be a plugged intake filter (part of the fuel gauge sending unit assembly) or a kinked or blocked fuel supply line from the tank. Make the necessary repairs. In addition, on dual tank models, verify proper operation of the tank selector valve and switching circuits (see Section 11).
9   If the output is still low, remove the fuel pump and inspect the fuel pump lobe on the camshaft and pump operating lever. If in acceptable operating condition, replace the fuel pump (see Section 18).

Pressure test

10   Connect a fuel pressure gauge (0 to 15 psi) to the carburetor end of the line.
11   Reconnect the wires to the coil and start the engine (it should be able to run for over 30 seconds on the fuel in the carburetor bowl). Read the pressure after ten seconds. Compare your reading to the specified pressure listed in this Chapter's Specifications.
12   If pump pressure is not as specified, install a new fuel pump (see Section 18).
13   Reconnect the fuel line and install the air cleaner.

8   Fuel pressure relief procedure (EFI models)

Refer to illustration 8.2
Warning 1: *The fuel supply lines will remain pressurized for long periods of time after the engine is shut down. The pressure within the fuel system must be relieved before servicing the fuel system.*

Warning 2: *Gasoline is extremely flammable, so take extra precautions when you work on any part of the fuel system. Don't smoke or allow open flames or bare light bulbs near the work area, and don't work in a garage where a gas-type appliance (such as a water heater or clothes dryer) is present. Since gasoline is carcinogenic, wear fuel-resistant gloves when there's a possibility of being exposed to fuel, and, if you spill any fuel on your skin, rinse it off immediately with soap and water. Mop up any spills immediately and do not store fuel-soaked rags where they could ignite. When you perform any kind of work on the fuel system, wear safety glasses and have a Class B type fire extinguisher on hand.*
1   The "inertia switch," which shuts off fuel to the engine in the event of a collision, affords a simple and convenient means by which fuel pressure can be relieved before servicing fuel injection components.
2   The inertia switch is located under the dash on the firewall, to the left of the brake pedal or behind the right kick panel **(see illustration)**.
3   Once you've found the switch, start the engine.
4   With the engine idling, insert a small screwdriver into the slot provided and pry the red button up. If there's no button provided, disconnect the electrical connector from the inertia switch.
5   Let the engine run until it stalls. Crank the engine for a few seconds after it stalls (to make sure there's no residual pressure). The fuel pressure is now relieved. **Warning** *Although there's no pressure in the fuel system, there is still fuel in the lines, so some fuel may still flow out when you disconnect fittings. Observe the fuel Warning at the beginning of this procedure and wrap shop rags around the connection point before disconnecting the lines.*
6   Before beginning work on the fuel system, disconnect the cable from the negative terminal of the battery.
7   After repairs are completed, depress the

red button on the inertia switch or reconnect the electrical connector. Reconnect the cable to the negative terminal of the battery. The fuel pump is now enabled, but it may take several seconds of cranking before the engine starts.

9   Electric fuel pump - general information and check

Warning *The fuel system pressure on EFI models must be relieved before disconnecting fuel lines and fittings (see Section 8). Gasoline is extremely flammable, so take extra precautions when you work on any part of the fuel system. Don't smoke or allow open flames or bare light bulbs near the work area, and don't work in a garage where a gas-type appliance (such as a water heater or clothes dryer) is present. Since gasoline is carcinogenic, wear fuel-resistant gloves when there's a possibility of being exposed to fuel, and, if you spill any fuel on your skin, rinse it off immediately with soap and water. Mop up any spills immediately and do not store fuel-soaked rags where they could ignite. When you perform any kind of work on the fuel system, wear safety glasses and have a Class B type fire extinguisher on hand.*
Note: *Always make sure there is fuel in the tank before assuming the fuel pump is defective.*

General information

1   Three electric fuel pump configurations are possible on F-series and Bronco vehicles: Early carbureted models equipped with 7.5L engines and the "Hot Fuel" option and two different electronic fuel injection systems depending on the model year.
2   Carbureted 7.5L engines with the "Hot Fuel" option use an in-tank low pressure fuel pump. A fuel pump relay is controlled by an engine oil pressure switch and supplies power through an inertia switch directly to the pump only when the engine is running. The pump is energized by a separate START circuit during engine cranking. On dual tank models, a dash-mounted tank selection switch is required to route pump relay power to one or the other in-tank low pressure pump. Fuel pressure is maintained by the engine mounted vapor separator.
3   Early (prior to 1990) EFI models use a low pressure in-tank mounted pump and an externally mounted (on the left side frame rail) high pressure in-line pump. The low pressure electric fuel pump provides pressurized fuel to the inlet of the high pressure pump. The externally mounted fuel pump is a high pressure unit which increases the fuel pressure to operating pressure. The pump has an internal relief valve to provide overpressure protection in the event the fuel flow becomes restricted (clogged filter, damaged fuel lines, etc.). The system pressure is controlled by a pressure regulator on the fuel rail. The main fuel pump relay is controlled by the electronic engine control (EEC) system power relay (powers

the fuel pump relay control circuit) and the EEC computer (energizes the fuel pump relay switch circuit by grounding control circuit). When energized, the fuel pump relay provides power through an inertia switch directly to the high and low pressure fuel pumps on single tank models. Dual tank models require three pumps (one high, two low pressure) plus a dash-mounted tank selection switch to route pump relay power to one or the other in-tank low pressure pumps. Power to the high pressure pump is routed identically to the single tank models.
4   Later models (1990 on) utilize an in-tank mounted fuel delivery module (FDM). The FDM unit includes a high pressure fuel pump, venturi jet pump, relief check valves, and a shuttle selector valve all housed inside a canister reservoir body. The FDM is mounted at the fuel level sender mounting flange with the sending unit and wiring attached to the pump reservoir body. The system pressure is controlled by a pressure regulator on the fuel rail. The main fuel pump relay is controlled by the electronic engine control (EEC) system power relay (powers the fuel pump relay control circuit) and the EEC computer (energizes the fuel pump relay switch circuit by grounding the control circuit). When energized, the fuel pump relay provides power through an inertia switch directly to the fuel pump. Dual tank models require a FDM in each tank plus a dash mounted tank selection switch to route pump relay power to one or the other in-tank fuel pump.

Operational checks (all models)

5   An electric fuel pump malfunction will usually result in a loss of fuel flow and/or pressure that is often reflected by a corresponding drop in performance (or a no-run condition).
6   Verify pump operation in Start Up mode as follows:
a)   *On EFI models, turn the ignition key to ON, but don't start the engine. You should hear a brief whirring sound from the pump(s) and pressure return noise from the fuel pressure regulator under the hood as the fuel pump(s) comes on to pressurize the system (it normally lasts about a second). If no sound is noted, proceed to Step 7.*
b)   *On 7.5L non-EFI models with "Hot Fuel" option, disconnect start wire at starter relay (see Chapter 5) and have an assistant hold the key in the START position. The in-tank fuel pump should be heard running. Reconnect START wire at start relay. If no sound is noted, repair the circuit (see Chapter 12).*
7   Power up the fuel pump(s) to run continuously for the engine off pressure tests as follows:
a)   *On EFI models, locate the diagnostic Data Link Connector (DLC) under the hood (see Section 14). Ground the fuel pump terminal of the connector. Now the pump noise should be constant. Listen specifically for the following:*

1)   *External high and in-tank low pressure pumps on early EFI models.*
2)   *In-tank FDM pump on late model EFI vehicles.*
3)   *On dual tank models, switch tanks (key on) and verify operation of alternate in-tank pump.*
b)   *On 7.5L non-EFI models with the "Hot Fuel" option, locate the oil pressure switch on the engine and disconnect the electrical connector. Jumper both red/yellow wires together at the electrical connector. Turn the ignition key to the RUN position. Now the pump noise should be constant. Listen specifically for the following:*
1)   *In-tank low pressure pump.*
2)   *On dual tank models, switch tanks (key on) and verify operation of alternate in-tank pump.*
8   On EFI models, if troubleshooting a no-run condition and Start Up mode test fails to power the pump, but the pump works when powered as described in Step 7, suspect faulty circuitry from the fuel pump relay to the EEC-IV module or a bad EEC module (see Section 16). If the pump is still non-functional, perform the following precheck operations:
a)   *Make sure the inertia switch is in the fuel-pump-enabled position (see Section 8).*
b)   *Check the fuel pump fuse and relay, replace them if unsure or their condition (see Section 17).*
c)   *Check for power at the pump terminals as follows:*
1)   *On an externally mounted pump, remove the electrical connector and place voltmeter probes between electrical connector pins. Ground DLC and check for voltage.*
2)   *On in-tank pumps, if accessible, remove harness electrical connector at the tank. If not accessible, locate harness as close to the tank as possible and carefully breakout harness wires by removing external protective shielding to reveal wires.*
3)   *Locate pink/black wire on single tank models or red (front tank) or brown/white (rear tank) wires on dual tank models as applicable.*
4)   *Place voltmeter probes between indicated colored wires and black (GRD) wire. Use electrical connector pins if accessible, if not, use probes to penetrate wire insulation at harness breakout. Ground DLC (EFI models) or jumper oil pressure switch with key on (Hot Fuel) and check for voltage. Don't forget to switch to the applicable tank on dual tank vehicles.*
9   If no voltage is present at the pump, perform circuit checks (see Section 16).
10   If battery voltage is present, replace the pump (see Section 18). **Note:** *Some low pressure pump systems use a resistor in the pump circuit - voltage in these circuits will be less than battery voltage (about 11-volts).*

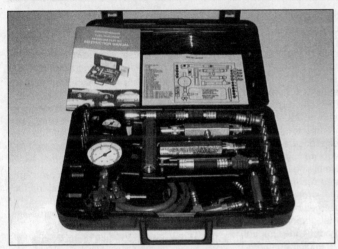

9.12a This fuel pressure testing kit contains all the necessary fittings and adapters, along with the fuel pressure gauge, to test most automotive fuel systems

9.12b Fuel pressure gauge connected to the Schrader valve on the fuel rail

Engine off pressure check (EFI models)

Refer to illustrations 9.12a and 9.12b

11   Relieve the fuel pressure (see Section 8).

12   Connect a fuel pressure gauge (it must be designed for use with fuel injection systems and be capable of indicating 100 psi) to the Schrader valve on the fuel rail following the instructions included with the gauge **(see illustrations)**. **Note:** *The Schrader valve is a small valve, covered by a screw-on cap, that operates the same way as a valve core for a tire.*

13   Locate the diagnostic Data Link Connector (DLC) under the hood and ground the fuel pump test terminal (see Step 20).

14   Turn the key to ON, but do not start the engine. The fuel pump should run. If it does not, there's a problem in the fuel pump circuit, or the pump is bad.

15   Observe the reading on the fuel pressure gauge and compare it to the Specifications listed in this Chapter.

16   If the pressure is within Specification, proceed to Step 19.

17   If the pressure is higher than specified, perform regulator overpressure tests (see Section 10).

18   If the pressure is lower than specified, proceed as follows:

a) *If the vehicle is an early model EFI (prior to 1990), first check the operation of the low pressure pump. If the pump passes the test, perform the regulator underpressure tests (see Section 10).*

b) *If the vehicle is a later model (1990 and later) perform the regulator underpressure tests (see Section 10).*

Engine running pressure check (EFI models)

19   Disconnect the jumper wire from the DLC connector. Start the engine and allow it to idle. Compare the fuel pressure to this Chapter's Specifications. If pressure is within specifica-

tions, proceed to Step 22.

20   If the fuel pressure was OK during the engine off pressure check, but is now too high, perform the following:

a) *With the engine idling, disconnect and plug the vacuum hose from the fuel pressure regulator.* **Warning:** *Stay away from rotating engine components! The pressure should rise. Unplug and reconnect the hose - the pressure should drop, returning to about where it was before the hose was disconnected. If there is no change in pressure when the hose is disconnected, perform the demand regulating test (see Section 10).*

21   If the fuel pressure was OK during the engine off pressure check, but is now too low, the supply system is probably marginal. Perform engine off, regulator underpressure tests with the engine running (see Section 10).

Static pressure leakage check (EFI models)

22   Turn the ignition key to OFF. Verify that the fuel pressure remains within 5 psi of the Specifications for 1 minute after shutting off the engine. If not, perform the regulator check valve function test (see Section 10).

23   After all testing is done, relieve the fuel system pressure (see Section 8) and remove the fuel pressure gauge.

In-tank low pressure pump(s) check (EFI models through 1989)

24   Perform this check when low fuel pressure is observed in engine off pressure check (see checks in this Section).

25   Although not entirely necessary, as a safety precaution, relieve fuel pump pressure (see Section 8).

26   Raise the vehicle and support it securely on jackstands (front end slightly higher than rear).

27   Locate the single or dual function res-

ervoirs (see Section 18). Place a catch pan under the reservoir.

28   Remove fuel tank supply line from the reservoir (see Section 6). **Note:** *On dual tank models, select line of tank that was in use during fuel pressure check.*

29   Place the end of the line into a calibrated one quart container. **Note:** *If fuel begins to siphon, plug the end until you're ready for the test.*

30   Locate the diagnostic Data Link Connector (DLC) under the hood (see Section 14). Ground the fuel pump terminal of the electrical connector. Don't forget to reset the inertia switch, if required. **Note:** *Fuel will begin to pump. Be ready!*

31   Run the pump for five seconds and measure the volume of fuel delivered. If within the values listed in this Chapter's Specifications, the pump is operating as it should. If the volume is significantly low, check for restrictions in the supply line from the tank. If none can be found, replace the pump (see Section 18). **Note:** *Pump speed and resulting volume is very sensitive to voltage. Verify that all connections are clean and tight.*

32   On dual tank models, switch tanks (key on) and repeat test on the second tank pump and supply line.

Pressure check (non-EFI 7.5L vehicles with "Hot Fuel" option)

33   Perform and successfully pass operational checks (see checks in this Section).

34   Remove the air cleaner housing, if not already done (see Section 21).

35   Detach the fuel line from the carburetor and install a zero to 15 psi fuel pressure gauge to the fuel line.

36   If not already done, locate the oil pressure switch on the engine, disconnect the electrical connector and jumper the red/yellow wires together. Turn the key to the RUN position and observe the pressure gauge.

Compare your results to this Chapter's Specifications.

37   If the pressure is correct, turn the key off, remove the jumper wire and reconnect the oil pressure switch. Remove the fuel pressure gauge and connect the fuel line.

38   If the pressure is high, perform the following:

a) *Check the fuel vapor separator for restriction.*

b) *Check for a pinched or clogged fuel return hose or pipe (see Section 6).*

c) *Check for a restricted or faulty selector valve (dual tanks only). Perform the 6-port selector valve return line mechanical test (see Section 11).*

d) *Repair restriction and retest. Remove the jumper and reconnect the oil pressure switch. Remove the fuel pressure gauge and reinstall the fuel line.*

39   If the pressure is low, perform the following:

a) *Check for a pinched or clogged fuel supply hose or pipe (see Section 6).*

b) *Check for a clogged fuel filter, replace it if you're unsure of its condition (see Chapter 1).*

c) *Check for a restricted or faulty selector valve (dual tanks only). Perform the 6-port selector valve supply line mechanical test (see Section 11).*

d) *Repair restriction. If no restriction can be found, replace the fuel pump. Retest to verify the repair. Remove the jumper and reconnect the oil pressure switch. Remove the fuel pressure gauge and connect the fuel line.*

10   Fuel pressure regulator (EFI) - general information and check

Warning: *Gasoline is extremely flammable, so take extra precautions when you work on any part of the fuel system. Don't smoke or allow open flames or bare light bulbs near the work area, and don't work in a garage where a gas-type appliance (such as a water heater or clothes dryer) is present. Since gasoline is carcinogenic, wear fuel-resistant gloves when there's a possibility of being exposed to fuel, and, if you spill any fuel on your skin, rinse it off immediately with soap and water. Mop up any spills immediately and do not store fuel-soaked rags where they could ignite. The fuel system on fuel-injected models is under constant pressure, so, if any fuel lines are to be disconnected, the fuel pressure in the system must be relieved first (see Section 8). When you perform any kind of work on the fuel system, wear safety glasses and have a Class B type fire extinguisher on hand.*

General information

1   The purpose of the fuel pressure regulator on EFI models is to maintain a desired fuel pressure under varying engine demands. The fuel pump is designed to provide a constant volume of fuel at a rate much greater than the engine can use under the highest demand conditions. The regulator simply adds a calibrated restriction downstream of the injectors which allows a given portion of the fuel supplied by the pump to return to the tank. The remaining flow provided by the pump has no place to go and therefore builds up pressure to the desired levels. The injectors, when opened, cause the pressure to fall in direct relation to engine demand (injector on time). To compensate, the fuel pressure regulator (actually a fuel flow regulator), will further reduce the amount of fuel returning to the tank by increasing the calibrated restriction, thus maintaining a constant fuel pressure at the injectors. The regulator uses engine vacuum working against an internal diaphragm and spring to set, sense and adjust the amount of restriction in response to engine demands. In addition, the regulator also acts as a check valve. When pump flow is stopped (vehicle shut off), the regulator will close the restriction path completely, cutting off the fuel path back to the tank. This traps pressurized fuel between the regulator and the fuel pump reverse flow check valve allowing for quick restarts of the engine.

2   To operate correctly, the fuel pressure regulator requires an unrestricted flow of fuel from the fuel pump at the designed volume, an equally unrestricted path back to the fuel tank and a good vacuum supply signal from the intake manifold. Restrictions in fuel delivery or volume will result in underpressure situations. Restrictions in return lines downstream of the regulator that are greater than the internal restriction of the regulator will cause an overpressure situation. Lack of a good vacuum signal will result in an overpressure situation.

3   The regulator itself is not immune to failure. Contamination can clog the regulator (overpressure), the vacuum diaphragm can leak (usually overpressure) or the valve may fail to properly restrict flow (underpressure). Although sometimes difficult to diagnose, the following tests should help to find a defective fuel pressure regulator.

Overpressure test

4   Perform this procedure if an engine off fuel pressure test (see Section 9) indicates an overpressure situation. If the pressure is higher than specified, then the pump is supplying adequate flow but there is unwanted restriction being created somewhere between the pressure regulator (including the regulator) and the fuel tank (return side).

5   Relieve fuel line pressure (see Section 8). Don't forget to reset the inertia switch afterwards.

6   If not already done, install a fuel pressure gauge and prepare the vehicle for a fuel pressure test (see Section 9).

7   Disconnect the fuel return line from the fuel rail on the engine (see Section 6).

8   Install a suitable hose over the end of the fuel rail return line quick connect housing and route other end into a suitable fuel catch container.

9   Activate the fuel pump using the diagnostic link connector (DLC) (see Section 14).

10   Observe the pressure gauge.

11   If pressure is now within specifications, the problem is a restriction downstream of the pressure regulator. Check the following:

a) *All EFI models for pinched or clogged fuel return hose or pipe (see Section 6).*

b) *Early EFI models for blocked single or dual function reservoir return ports (see Section 12).*

c) *Late EFI models for malfunctioning FDM shuttle valve (see Section 11).*

12   Repair restrictions and retest pressure. Remove the catch hose and connect the fuel return line to the fuel rail. Retest pressure, relieve fuel pressure and remove pressure check equipment (see Section 9).

13   If the pressure is still high, replace the pressure regulator (see Section 16) and retest. Remove the catch hose and reinstall the fuel return line. Retest pressure, relieve pressure and remove the pressure check equipment (see Section 9).

Underpressure test

14   Perform this procedure if an engine off fuel pressure test (see Section 9) indicates an underpressure situation. If the pressure is lower than specified, then either the pump is not supplying adequate flow, there is a restriction somewhere between the fuel tank (supply side) and the fuel rail, or the fuel pressure regulator is faulty. **Note:** *This test assumes that the pump(s) operate electrically. If in doubt, perform the operational checks (see Section 9).*

15   If not already done, install a fuel pressure gauge and prepare the vehicle for the fuel pressure test (see Section 9).

16   Activate the fuel pump using the diagnostic link connector (DLC) (see Section 14).

17   Pinch off the fuel return line downstream of the pressure regulator and observe the pressure gauge (use a C-clamp over the rubber section of fuel line).

18   If pressure rises substantially, replace the pressure regulator (see Section 16) and retest. Relieve pressure and remove the pressure check equipment (see Section 9). **Note:** *Release the clamp quickly after observing substantial pressure rise to avoid damage to the lines or pump.*

19   If the pressure is still low, the problem is either bad pump(s) or supply line restrictions, check the following:

a) *All EFI models for a pinched or clogged fuel supply hose or pipe (see Section 6).*

b) *All EFI models for a clogged fuel filter, replace it if you're unsure of its condition (see Section 19).*

c) *Early EFI models for a restricted single or dual function reservoir supply ports (see Section 12).*

d) *Late EFI models, for a FDM reverse flow check valve stuck open (dual tanks only). To check, perform regulator check valve function test as described in this section.*

e) *Leaking fuel injectors. To check, perform regulator check valve function test as described later in this Section.*

20   Repair restrictions and retest pressure. If no restrictions are found replace the pump(s) (see Section 18) and retest. Relieve the fuel pressure and remove the pressure check equipment (see Section 9).

Demand regulating test

21   Perform this procedure if an engine running fuel pressure test (see Section 9) indicates an overpressure condition, a non-responding condition or if the engine exhibits signs of a fuel rich condition (black smoke, fouled plugs, poor mileage).

22   Remove the vacuum line from the regulator and apply vacuum with a hand-held vacuum pump. If vacuum holds, continue the test. If vacuum leaks, replace the fuel pressure regulator (see Section 17) and perform the fuel pressure test (see Section 9) to verify the repair. Relieve fuel pressure and remove pressure check equipment (see Section 9).

23   Install a vacuum gauge on the fuel pressure regulator vacuum hose (from the engine).

24   Start the engine and observe the gauge for presence of vacuum.

25   If no vacuum signal is received, trace the hose back to the intake manifold and repair as required. **Note:** *Some vehicles may be equipped with devices which delay vacuum to the regulator during cold start conditions until the engine is warm. Retest to verify presence of vacuum.* If not already done, install the fuel pressure gauge and perform the fuel pressure test (see Section 9) to verify the repair. Relieve the fuel pressure and remove the pressure check equipment (see Section 9).

26   If a vacuum signal is received, replace the regulator (see Section 17) and perform the fuel pressure test (see Section 9) to verify the repair. Relieve the fuel pressure and remove the pressure check equipment (see Section 9).

Regulator check valve function test

27   Perform this procedure if an engine off static pressure test fails (see Section 9). This condition can be caused by several items. A faulty fuel pressure regulator, leaking fuel injectors or a stuck-open fuel pump reverse check valve (or valves in dual tank models equipped with FDMs). Isolate the component as follows:

28   During static leakage test (see Section 9), completely pinch off the return line downstream of the regulator (use a C-clamp over a rubber section of fuel line). Observe the leakage rate. **Note:** *Pinch the hose after the pump has been turned off.*

29   If leakage slows significantly, replace the regulator (see Section 17) and repeat the static test (see Section 9) to verify the repair. Relieve the fuel pressure and remove the pressure check equipment (see Section 9).

30   If the leakage rate is still high, during static leakage test (see Section 9) pinch off the supply line on the engine side of the fuel pump(s) (use C-clamp over rubber hose). Observe the leakage rate. **Note:** *Pinch hose after pump has been turned off.*

31   If leakage slows significantly, replace the pump. **Note:** *This would be the external high-pressure pump on early EFI models or the in-tank FDM on later EFI models (see Section 18).* On later models with dual tanks with FDM(s), pinch or plug off the supply line on the individual tanks between the tank and the intersecting "T" fitting one at a time to isolate which pump is leaking.

32   If the leakage rate is still high, the problem is probably leaking fuel injectors. Specific tests for leaking injectors is beyond the scope of this manual, however, a spark plug which indicates a rich mixture after extended idle may be an indicator of a leaky injector for that cylinder. For fuel rail removal and injector replacement, see Section 17.

11   Dual tank selection valve systems - general information

Warning: *Gasoline is extremely flammable, so take extra precautions when you work on any part of the fuel system. Don't smoke or allow open flames or bare light bulbs near the work area, and don't work in a garage where a gas-type appliance (such as a water heater or clothes dryer) is present. Since gasoline is carcinogenic, wear fuel-resistant gloves when there's a possibility of being exposed to fuel, and, if you spill any fuel on your skin, rinse it off immediately with soap and water. Mop up any spills immediately and do not store fuel-soaked rags where they could ignite. The fuel system on fuel-injected models is under constant pressure, so, if any fuel lines are to be disconnected, the fuel pressure in the system must be relieved first (see Section 8). When you perform any kind of work on the fuel system, wear safety glasses and have a Class B type fire extinguisher on hand.*

Selector valve - general operation

1   F-series trucks have several unique and specialized fuel supply components not typically encountered on standard passenger cars. Due to the need to travel extended distances carrying or pulling heavy loads, some of the vehicles covered by this manual have options for dual fuel tanks. The addition of a second fuel tank requires both a fuel tank selector valve to physically switch tank supply lines (and return lines on EFI and some carbureted models) and associated selector valve control switch and circuitry for the driver to operate depending on fuel level conditions. In response to the physical switching of the fuel tank supply lines, vehicles with electric fuel pumps (one per tank) require a corresponding switching of the fuel pump power circuits. In addition, fuel level gauge circuits must also be switched so the selected tank fuel level is always shown. The selection mechanisms and control circuits covered by this manual include the three-port selector valve (mechanical fuel pumps with no fuel return line), the six-port selector valve (mechanical fuel pumps with fuel return line and 7.5L carbureted models with electric pump), the dual function reservoir assembly (early EFI models) and the shuttle selector valve (late EFI models).

Three-port selector valve

2   The three-port selector valve is used on carbureted models equipped with mechanical fuel pumps with no fuel return line. As its name implies, the valve has three ports; two inlet (one each for both tank supplies) and one outlet (to the fuel pump). The internal port switching is electro-mechanically actuated by voltage supplied by the dash mounted control switch. The valve is spring loaded so that without a voltage supply from the selector switch, the valve will remain in the normally open to the primary (rear) fuel tank position and closed to the front tank. When the secondary (front) tank is selected with ignition in RUN, voltage is supplied by the valve selector switch to the valve. A solenoid within the selector valve energizes and pulls the switching valve to open the front tank fuel supply port and close the rear. The selector valve is located between the fuel tanks and the mechanical fuel pump along the left side frame rail. The selector control switch also switches the fuel level gauge circuits to correspond with the tank in use. Tank switching versus gauge conflicts can occur under certain failure mode conditions.

Six-port selector valve

3   The six-port selector valve is used on carbureted models equipped with mechanical or electric fuel pumps with a separate fuel return-to-tank line. The use of return line systems helps maintain constant pressure at the carburetor and due to the continual circulation, reduces fuel temperature buildup which leads to unwanted fuel vaporization upon entry to the carburetor float bowl.

4   Due to the requirement to return unused fuel back to the tank, the valve uses six ports, two supply inputs (one from each tank), one supply outlet (to engine), one return inlet (from engine) and two return outlets (one to each tank). The internal port switching is of rotary design and is driven by a small motor inside the valve assembly. Switching tanks is accomplished by supplying the motor voltage through the dash-mounted selector control switch. Switching to an alternate tank reverses voltage polarity to the motor which causes the motor to rotate to the opposite position, switching the tank supply and return lines in the process.

5   Due to potential problems associated with the fuel level gauge switching being accomplished by the selector control switch, six port valves utilize internal switching of the gauge circuits. This arrangement guarantees that gauge switching can only occur upon successful switching of the tank ports.

Dual function reservoir

6   The dual function reservoir is used on early EFI vehicles using in-tank low pressure and external high pressure fuel pumps and

optional dual tanks. Special internal valving within the unit provides mechanical (non-electrical) switching of fuel tank supply and return lines. The unit uses six ports, two supply inputs (one from each tank), one supply outlet (to high pressure fuel pump), one return inlet (from fuel pressure regulator) and two return outlets (one to each tank). The unit is located between the low pressure and high pressure pumps against the left side frame rail. The pressure created by the selected in-tank pump is sensed by the internal valve mechanism which responds by automatically switching to provide the proper supply and return port connections within the reservoir.

7   Operation of the dual function reservoir is totally mechanical in nature with no electrical circuitry involved. Tank switching is completely dependent on proper low pressure pump selection and pressure (one pump in each tank) to operate the switch valving. Tank (actually low pressure pump) selection is accomplished by the dash-mounted tank selection switch. Since the unit is non-serviceable, if a tank switching problem is found, the reservoir assembly must be replaced.

8   Gauge switching is accomplished by the tank (actually the pump) selection switch. Tank switching versus gauge conflicts can occur under certain failure mode conditions.

Shuttle selector valve

9   Late model EFI vehicles incorporate an in-tank Fuel Delivery Module (FDM). In dual tank applications, each tank receives an FDM. The Module combines the functions of several previously separate components into a single unit, including the shuttle selector valve. The shuttle selector valve in each FDM normally prevents return of unused fuel to its tank unless its FDM pump is energized. The pressure created by the selected pump opens the shuttle valve allowing fuel to return back to the tank. This system guarantees that unused fuel always returns to the tank from which it was pumped, thus avoiding tank overfill conditions. The new design allows for a much more simplified external fuel delivery system.

10   Tank selection is determined by which in-tank FDM is energized by the dash mounted tank (actually pump) selection switch. Since the FDM is non-serviceable, if a fuel return problem is found, the applicable FDM must be replaced.

11   Gauge switching is accomplished by the tank (actually the pump) selection switch. Tank switching versus gauge conflicts can occur under certain failure mode conditions.

Checks

12   There is no specific test for the shuttle selector valve portion of the FDM. If tank overfilling or cross filling is experienced, the overfilled tank's FDM probably has a stuck open shuttle valve. If excessively high fuel pressure is experienced, suspect a stuck-closed shuttle valve in the selected FDM exhibiting the symptom. For FDM replacement, see Section 18.

12   Fuel supply reservoirs (EFI models only) - general information and check

Warning: *Gasoline is extremely flammable, so take extra precautions when you work on any part of the fuel system. Don't smoke or allow open flames or bare light bulbs near the work area, and don't work in a garage where a gas-type appliance (such as a water heater or clothes dryer) is present. Since gasoline is carcinogenic, wear fuel-resistant gloves when there's a possibility of being exposed to fuel, and, if you spill any fuel on your skin, rinse it off immediately with soap and water. Mop up any spills immediately and do not store fuel-soaked rags where they could ignite. The fuel system on fuel-injected models is under constant pressure, so, if any fuel lines are to be disconnected, the fuel pressure in the system must be relieved first (see Section 8). When you perform any kind of work on the fuel system, wear safety glasses and have a Class B type fire extinguisher on hand.*

The models covered by this manual have several unique and specialized fuel supply components not typically encountered on standard passenger cars. They are often subjected to extreme maneuvers and steep attitudes with low tank fill levels. On carbureted models, fuel in the bowl can sustain engine requirements if the fuel pick-up in the tank becomes temporarily uncovered (draws air instead of fuel). On the other hand, fuel-injected models cannot tolerate this condition. Therefore, fuel-injected models are equipped with a fuel reservoir system to guarantee a constant supply of fuel to the high pressure pump under any condition. This avoids a potentially dangerous stall condition during precarious maneuvers. Three such systems have been used: The single and dual function reservoir (early fuel-injected models) and the Fuel Delivery Module (later fuel-injected models).

Single function reservoir

1   The single function reservoir is used on early fuel-injected models equipped with low and high pressure fuel pumps and a single fuel tank. The reservoir is mounted on the inboard side of the right side frame rail approximately mid-vehicle. The reservoir is inserted between the in-tank low pressure pump fuel supply and return lines and the high pressure pump inlet and return lines. Under normal conditions, fuel flows from the low pressure pump through the reservoir to the high pressure pump then to the EFI system. Excess fuel not required by the engine enters the fuel return line and flows back through the reservoir to the fuel tank. If the low pressure pump cannot supply a sufficient quantity of fuel (such as when fuel pick-up in the tank becomes temporarily uncovered), the high pressure pump draws fuel from the reservoir supply and continues to supply the engine with an uninterrupted flow of pressurized fuel.

2   The single function reservoir is a relatively simple component and is not service-

able. Most attention to the unit will be as a result of troubleshooting a fuel pressure (high or low) problem or volume problem as outlined in Section 9. Therefore, only those checks necessary to absolve the reservoir of any related fuel supply problems will be addressed. If a problem is found, the reservoir assembly must be replaced.

Fuel blockage check

3   Raise the vehicle and place securely on jackstands. **Note:** *Adjust the stands so the front end is slightly higher than the rear to reduce the tendency for fuel to siphon after lines are disconnected.*

4   Verify the low pressure pump is operational and adequate fuel is in the tank (see Section 9).

5   Relieve the fuel system pressure (see Section 8). Remove the outlet lines from the reservoir (the lines going forward to the high pressure pump) and the rear return line (small diameter line going back to tank). Place a suitable container under the lines to catch fuel.

6   Connect the outlet ports together using a short piece of fuel hose and small clamps (do not kink the hose). Connect a second hose over the reservoir rear return line port and place the loose end into a calibrated one quart container.

7   Disconnect the high pressure pump electrical connector.

8   Run the low pressure pump for 5 seconds (see Section 9) and measure the volume of fuel that is expelled from the reservoir.

9   If the volume is six ounces or more, the reservoir is not restricting flow and can be considered operational - no further diagnosis is required.

10   If the volume is low, unscrew the reservoir lower housing and clean the filter. Replace the housing and repeat the test.

11   If the volume is still low, perform the low pressure pump tests to verify adequate supply to the reservoir and repair any problems before continuing (see Section 9). If pump repair was required, repeat the reservoir output volume test.

12   If the low pressure pump test passes and the reservoir output volume test is low, the reservoir is blocked and must be replaced (see Section 17).

Dual function reservoir

13   The dual function reservoir is used on early EFI vehicles with low and high pressure fuel pumps and optional dual tanks. As its name implies, the reservoir has two distinct functions. The dual reservoir performs the same functions as the single function unit described above. In addition, special internal valving within the unit provides mechanical (non-electrical) switching of fuel tank supply and return lines. Due to the switching capability, problems associated with the dual function reservoir can be more difficult to diagnose. However, most attention to the unit will probably be as a result of troubleshooting a fuel pressure (high or low) problem or volume problem as outlined in Section 9. Therefore,

only those checks necessary to absolve the reservoir of any related fuel pressure problems will be addressed in this section. As with the single reservoir, if a problem is found, the reservoir assembly must be replaced.

Fuel blockage test

14   Perform operations as described for single function reservoirs with the following exceptions:

a) *Make sure both tanks have an adequate supply of fuel.*

b) *Remove both rear return lines (small diameter lines going back to tank) (see Section 6).*

c) *Connect hoses over both reservoir rear return line ports and place loose ends into separate calibrated one quart containers.*

d) *Check the volume through both reservoir passages by switching the tanks at the dash switch and repeating the test.*

e) *If necessary, perform the low pressure pump tests for both in-tank pumps (see Section 9).*

Fuel Delivery Module

15   Later fuel-injected models incorporate an in-tank Fuel Delivery Module. The Module combines the functions of several previously separate components into a single unit. Included is an integral reservoir and venturi jet system which performs the same function as the externally mounted reservoir units. The new design allows for a much more simplified external fuel delivery system.

Fuel blockage test

16   There is no specific test for the reservoir portion of the FDM. Acceptable performance during fuel pump pressure tests is sufficient evidence of reservoir operation (see Section 9).

13   Electronic Fuel Injection (EFI) systems - general information

The EFI system used on F-series and Bronco vehicles is a multiport, fuel injection system. Fuel is metered into the intake air stream in accordance with engine demand through individual (one for each cylinder) injectors mounted on an intake manifold. An on-board computer accepts information from various engine sensors to determine the required fuel flow rate necessary to maintain a prescribed fuel/air mixture throughout the entire engine operational range. The computer then sends a command to the injectors to meter the required amount of fuel.

Early EFI fuel delivery subsystem consists of a low pressure in-tank fuel pump, a fuel filter/reservoir, and a high pressure chassis mounted electric fuel pump, which delivers fuel from the tank through a 20 micron filter to the fuel charging manifold assembly. Beginning in 1990, a single high-pressure pump mounted in the fuel tank (FDM) was incorporated and is now standard. The fuel charging manifold supplies the pressurized

fuel directly to the electrically actuated fuel injectors mounted directly above each of the intake ports. The fuel charging manifold also incorporates a fuel pressure regulator which maintains a constant fuel pressure to the injectors in response to engine demand (fuel delivery). The pressure regulator uses the engine manifold vacuum to sense engine demand. Excess fuel supplied by the pump, but not required by the engine, passes through the regulator and returns to the tank through a fuel return line.

These models are equipped with on-board computers that are capable of self-diagnosis of the EFI system and component failures. While early on-board diagnostic computers simply lit a "CHECK ENGINE" light on the dash, present systems must monitor complex interactive emission control systems, and provide enough data to the technician to successfully isolate a malfunction.

The computer's role in self-diagnosing emission control problems has become so important that such computers are now required by Federal law. The requirements of the "first generation" system, later named OBD I (On Board Diagnostics I), are incorporated in 1985 through 1995 models with EEC-IV emission control systems. OBD II, a "second generation" system is incorporated in 1996 and later models with EEC-V emission control systems.

The purpose of On Board Diagnostics (OBD) is to ensure that emission related components and systems are functioning properly to reduce emission levels of several pollutants emitted by auto and truck engines. The first step is to detect that a malfunction has occurred which may cause increased emissions. The next step is for the system to notify the driver so that the vehicle can be serviced. The final step is to store enough information about the malfunction so that it can be identified and repaired.

Many of the self-diagnostic tests performed by early OBD systems are retained in OBD II systems, however, they are more sensitive in detecting malfunctions. OBD II systems perform many additional tests not required under the earlier OBD. These include monitoring for engine misfires and detecting deterioration of the catalytic converter.

14   Electronic Engine Control (EEC-IV, EEC-V) system and trouble codes

Refer to illustrations 14.20a, 14.20b and 14.20c

General description

1   1985 through 1995 models use the Electronic Engine Control (EEC-IV) system. 1996 and later models use the EEC-V system. Both systems consist of an onboard computer, known as the Powertrain Control Module (PCM), and information sensors, which monitor various functions of the engine and send data to the PCM. Based on the data and the

information programmed into the computer's memory, the PCM generates output signals to control various engine functions via control relays, solenoids and other output actuators.

2   The PCM, located under the instrument panel, is the "brain" of the EEC system. It receives data from a number of sensors and other electronic components (switches, relays, etc.). Based on the information it receives, the PCM generates output signals to control various relays, solenoids and other actuators. The PCM is specifically calibrated to optimize the emissions, fuel economy and driveability of the vehicle.

3   Because of a Federally mandated extended warranty which covers the EEC system components and because any owner-induced damage to the PCM, the sensors and/or the control devices may void the warranty, it isn't a good idea to attempt diagnosis or replacement of the PCM at home while the vehicle is under warranty. Take the vehicle to a dealer service department if the PCM or a system component malfunctions.

Information sensors

4   When the air-conditioning compressor clutch operates, a signal is sent to the PCM indicating that the compressor has added a load to the engine. The PCM responds by increasing engine idle speed accordingly to compensate.

5   The Intake Air Temperature (IAT) sensor, threaded into a runner of the intake manifold (see Section 16), provides the PCM with fuel/air mixture temperature information. The PCM uses this information to control fuel flow, ignition timing and EGR system operation.

6   The Engine Coolant Temperature (ECT) sensor, which is threaded into a coolant passage in the thermostat housing, monitors engine coolant temperature. The ECT sends the PCM a constantly varying voltage signal which influences PCM control of the fuel mixture, ignition timing and EGR operation.

7   The Heated Exhaust Gas Oxygen (HEGO) sensors, which are threaded into the exhaust manifolds, provide a constant signal to the PCM indicating oxygen content of the exhaust gases as an indication of emissions level. The PCM converts this exhaust gas oxygen content signal to the fuel/air ratio, compares it to the ideal ratio for current engine operating conditions and alters the signal to the injectors accordingly.

8   The Throttle Position Sensor (TPS), which is mounted on the side of the throttle body (see Section 16) and connected directly to the throttle shaft, senses throttle movement and position, then transmits an electrical signal to the PCM that is proportional to throttle position.

9   The Mass Air Flow (MAF) sensor, which is mounted in the air cleaner intake passage, measures the mass of the air entering the engine (see Section 16). Because air mass varies with air temperature (cold air is denser than warm air), measuring air mass provides the PCM with a very accurate way of determining the correct amount of fuel to obtain the ideal fuel/air mixture.

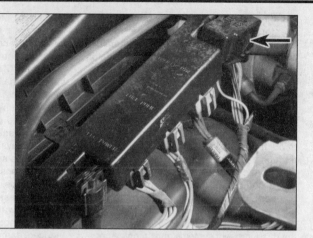

14.20a On early fuel-injected models, the EEC-IV self-test (STI) connector (arrow) is on the driver's side of the engine compartment, behind the air cleaner housing (1989 model shown)

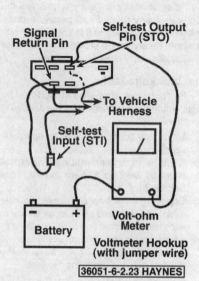

36051-6-2.23 HAYNES

14.20b To read any stored trouble codes, connect a voltmeter to the self-test connector as shown, then connect a jumper wire between the self-test input and pin 2 on the larger connector - turn the ignition On and watch the voltmeter needle

Output devices

10   The EEC power relay, which is activated by the ignition switch, supplies battery voltage to the EEC-IV system components when the switch is the Start or Run position.

11   The canister purge solenoid (CANP) switches manifold vacuum to operate the canister purge valve when a signal is received from the PCM. Vacuum opens the purge valve when the solenoid is energized allowing fuel vapor to flow from the canister to the intake manifold.

12   The solenoid-operated fuel injectors are located above the intake ports (see Section 17). The PCM controls the length of time the injector is open. The "open" time of the injector determines the amount of fuel delivered. For information regarding injector replacement, refer to Chapter 4.

13   The fuel pump relay is activated by the PCM with the ignition switch in the On position. When the ignition switch is turned to the On position, the relay is activated to supply initial line pressure to the system. For information regarding fuel pump check and replacement, refer to Section 9.

14   The PCM uses a signal from the Profile Ignition Pick-Up (PIP) to determine crankshaft position. Ignition timing is determined by the PCM, which then signals the module to fire the coil.

Obtaining codes (1985 through 1995 models)

Note: *On 1996 and later models, a scan tool is the only way to obtain codes from an EEC-V system. Diagnostic trouble codes for the EEC-V system are listed in Section 15.*

15   The diagnostic codes for the EEC systems are arranged in such a way that a series of tests must be completed in order to extract ALL the codes from the system. If one portion of the test is performed without the others, there may be a chance the trouble code that will pinpoint a problem in your particular vehicle will remain stored in the PCM without detection. The tests start first with a Key On, Engine Off (KOEO) test followed by a computed timing test then finally an Engine Running (ER) test.

16   Codes on EEC-IV systems (1985 through 1995 models) can be read with an analog voltmeter, by observing the "Check Engine" light on the dash or by using a scan tool if one is available.

Here is a brief overview of the code-extracting procedures of the EEC-IV system followed by the actual test:

Note: *Before attempting to repair or replace a component, always check vacuum lines and electrical connectors first, as a majority of problems are simple connections and leaking vacuum lines.*

Quick Test - Key On Engine Off (KOEO)

17   The following codes are generated with the key on, engine off "quick test":

Self test codes - These codes are accessed on the test connector by using a jumper wire and an analog voltmeter or the factory diagnostic tool called the Star tester. These codes are also called *Hard Codes.*

Separator pulse codes - After the initial Hard Codes, the system will flash a code 111 and then will flash a series of Soft Codes.

Continuous Memory Codes - These codes indicate a fault that may or may not be present at the time of testing. These codes usually indicate an intermittent failure. Continuous Memory codes are stored in the system and they will flash after the normal Hard Codes. These codes are three digit codes. These codes can indicate chronic or intermittent problems. Also called Soft Codes.

Fast codes - These codes are transmitted 100 times faster than normal codes and can only be read by a Star Tester from the manufacturer or an equivalent SCAN tool.

Engine running codes (KOER) or (ER)

18   **Running tests** - These tests make it possible for the PCM to pick-up a diagnostic trouble code that cannot be set while the engine is in KOEO. These problems usually occur during driving conditions. Some codes are detected by cold or warm running conditions, some are detected at low rpm or high

rpm and some are detected at closed throttle or WOT.

ID Pulse codes - These codes indicate the type of engine (6 or 8 cylinder) or the correct module and Self Test mode access.

Computed engine timing test - This engine running test determines base timing for the engine and starts the process of allowing the engine to store running codes.

Wiggle test - This engine running test checks the wiring system to the sensors and output actuators as the engine performs.

Cylinder balance test - This engine running test determines injector balance as well as cylinder compression balance. **Note:** *This test should be performed by a dealer service department or other qualified repair shop.*

Beginning the test

19   Apply the parking brake. Position the shift lever in PARK and block the drive wheels. Turn off all electrical loads - air conditioning, radio, heater fan blower etc. Make sure the engine is warmed to operating temperatures (if possible).

20   **Perform the KOEO tests:**

a) *Turn the ignition key off for at least 10 seconds*

b) *Locate the Diagnostic Test connector inside the engine compartment* **(see illustration)** *Connect the positive voltmeter lead onto the positive battery terminal and the negative voltmeter lead onto pin number 4 (STO) of the test connector* **(see illustration).** *Connect a jumper wire from the test terminal (STI) to pin number 2 of the Diagnostic Test terminal* **(see illustration).**

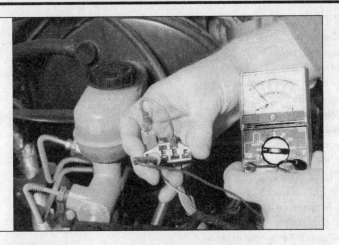

14.20c Here's what the self-test looks like in action

c) Turn the ignition key ON (engine not running) and observe the needle sweeps on the voltmeter. For example, for code 224, the voltmeter will sweep twice indicating the first digit of the code (2). There will be a two second pause, then there will be two more distinct sweeps of the needle to indicate the second digit of the code number (2). After another two second pause, there will be four distinct sweeps to indicate the third digit in the code (4). Additional three-digit codes will be separated by a four second pause and then the indicated sweeps on the voltmeter. Be aware that the code sequence may continue into the continuous memory codes (read further). **Note:** Early models will flash only two digit codes.

d) The CHECK ENGINE light on the dash can be used in place of the voltmeter. The number of flashes indicates each digit instead of needle sweeps.

21   Interpreting the continuous memory codes:

a) After the KOEO codes are reported, there will be a short pause and any stored Continuous Memory codes will appear in order. Remember that the "Separator" code is 111. The computer will not enter the Continuous Memory mode without flashing the separator pulse code. The Continuous Memory codes are read the same as the initial codes or "Hard Codes." Record these codes onto a piece of paper and continue the test.

22   Perform the Engine Running (ER) tests:

a) Remove the jumper wires from the Diagnostic Test connector to start the test.

b) Run the engine until it reaches normal operating temperature.

c) Turn the engine OFF for at least 10 seconds.

d) Install the jumper wire onto the Diagnostic Test connector (**see illustration 14.20b**) and start the engine.

e) Observe that the voltmeter or CHECK

ENGINE light will flash the engine identification code. This code indicates 1/2 the number of cylinders of the engine. For example, 3 flashes represent a 6-cylinder engine, or 4 flashes represent an eight-cylinder engine.

f) Within 1 to 2 seconds of the ID code, turn the steering wheel at least 1/2 turn and release. This will store any power steering pressure switch trouble codes.

g) Depress the brake pedal and release. **Note:** Perform the steering wheel and brake pedal procedure in succession immediately (1 to 2 seconds) after the ID codes are flashed.

h) Observe all the codes and record them on a piece of paper. Be sure to count the sweeps or flashes very carefully as you jot them down.

23   On some models the PCM will request a Dynamic Response check. This test quickly checks the operation of the TPS, MAF or MAP sensors in action. This will be indicated by a code 1 or a single sweep of the voltmeter needle (one flash on CHECK ENGINE light). This test will require the operator to simply full throttle ("goose") the accelerator pedal for one second. DO NOT throttle the accelerator pedal unless it is requested.

24   The next part of this test makes sure the system can advance the timing. This is called the Computed Timing test. After the last ER code has been displayed, the PCM will advance the ignition timing a fixed amount and hold it there for approximately 2 minutes. Use a timing light to check the amount of advance. The computed timing should equal the base timing plus 20 BTDC. The total advance should equal 27 to 33 degrees advance. If the timing is out of specification, have the system checked at a dealer service department. **Note:** If it's necessary to adjust the base timing on (1985 through 1995) engines, remember to remove the SPOUT from the connector as described in the ignition timing procedure in Chapter 5. This will remove the computer from the loop and give base timing. Base timing is not adjustable on most models.

25   **Finally, perform the Wiggle Test.** This test can be used to recreate a possible intermittent fault in the harness wiring system:

a) Use a jumper wire to ground the STI lead on the Diagnostic Test connector (**see illustration 14.20b**).

b) Turn the ignition key ON (engine not running).

c) Now deactivate the self-test mode (remove the jumper wire) and then immediately reactivate self test mode. Now the system has entered Continuous Monitor Test Mode.

d) Carefully wiggle, tap or remove any suspect wiring to a sensor or output actuator. If a problem exists, a trouble code will be stored that indicates a problem with the circuit that governs the particular component. Record the codes that are indicated.

e) Next, enter Engine Running Continuous Monitor Test Mode to check for wiring problems only when the engine is running. Start first by deactivating the Diagnostic Test connector and turning the ignition key OFF. Now start the engine and allow it to idle.

f) Use a jumper wire to ground the STI lead on the Diagnostic Test connector (**see illustration 14.20b**). Wait ten seconds, disconnect the jumper wire, then reconnect it again. This will enter Engine Running Continuous Monitor Test Mode.

g) Carefully wiggle, tap or remove any suspect wiring to a sensor or output actuator. If a problem exists, a trouble code will be stored that indicates a problem with the circuit that governs the particular component. Record the codes that are indicated.

26   If necessary, perform the Cylinder Balance Test. This test must be performed by a dealer service department.

Clearing codes

To clear the codes from the PCM memory, start the KOEO self test diagnostic procedure (**see illustrations 14.20a and 14.20b**) and install the jumper wire into the Diagnostic Test connector. When the codes start to display themselves on the voltmeter or CHECK ENGINE light, remove the jumper wire from the Diagnostic Test connector. This will erase any stored codes within the system. **Note:** You can also clear the codes by disconnecting the negative battery cable. However, this will erase stored operating parameters from the KAM (Keep Alive Memory) and cause the engine to run rough for a period of time (several miles) while the computer relearns the information. **Caution:** Do not disconnect the positive terminal to clear the codes from memory. If a spark should occur when reconnecting the battery, the PCM could be damaged.

2 digit Diagnostic Trouble Codes (EEC-IV)

Code	Test Condition*	Probable Cause
11	O,C,R	Pass (separator code)
12	R	RPM not within Self-test upper limit
13	R	RPM not within Self-test lower limit
14	C	Profile Ignition Pick-up circuit fault
15	O	Read Only Memory test failed
15	C	Keep Alive Memory test failed
16	R	RPM too low to perform Oxygen Sensor/fuel test
18	C	Loss of TACH input to PCM; SPOUT circuit grounded
18	R	SPOUT circuit open
19	O	Failure in EEC reference voltage
21	O,R	Coolant Temperature Sensor out of range
22	O,C	Manifold Absolute/Baro Pressure Sensor out of range
23	O,R	Throttle Position Sensor out of range
24	O,R	Intake Air Temperature sensor out of range
26	O,R	Mass Air Flow Sensor out of range
29	C	No input from Vehicle Speed Sensor
31	O,C,R	EGR Valve Position (EVP) Sensor out of range (low)
32	O,C,R	EGR valve not seated; closed voltage low
33	C,R	EGR valve not opening; Insufficient flow detected
34	O,C,R	EGR Valve Pressure Transducer/Position Sensor voltage above closed limit
35	O,C,R	EGR Valve Pressure Transducer/Position Sensor voltage out of range (high)
41	R	Heated Oxygen Sensor circuit indicates system lean, right side
41	C	No Heated Oxygen Sensor switch detected, right side
42	R	Heated Oxygen Sensor circuit indicates system rich, right side
44	R	Thermactor Air system inoperative, right side
45	R	Thermactor Air upstream during Self-test
46	R	Thermactor Air not by-passed during Self-test
51	O,C	Coolant Temperature sensor circuit open
52	O,C	Power steering pressure switch open circuit
53	O,C	Throttle Position sensor out of range (high)
54	O,C	Intake Air Temperature sensor circuit open
56	O,C	Mass Air Flow sensor out of range (high)
61	O,C	Coolant Temperature sensor circuit grounded
63	O,C	Throttle Position sensor circuit out of range (low)
64	O,C	Intake Air Temperature sensor circuit grounded
66	C	Mass Air Flow sensor circuit out-of-range (low)
67	O	Neutral Drive Switch circuit open
72	R	Insufficient Mass Air Flow change during Dynamic Response Test
73	R	Insufficient Throttle Position output during Dynamic Response Test
74	R	Brake On/Off switch failure
75	R	Brake On/Off circuit failure
77	R	Wide Open Throttle not sensed during Self-test
79	O	Air conditioning on during self-test
81	O	Speed control vent circuit failure
82	O	Speed control vent circuit failure
84	O	EGR Vacuum Regulator circuit failure
85	O	Canister Purge circuit failure
87	O,C	Primary Fuel Pump circuit failure
91	R	Heated oxygen sensor indicates system lean, left side
91	C	No heated oxygen sensor switching indicated, left side
92	R	Heated oxygen sensor indicates system rich, left side
94	R	Thermactor Air system inoperative, left side (5.0L only)
95	O,C	Fuel Pump circuit open, PCM to motor
96	O,C	Fuel Pump circuit open, Battery to PCM
98	R	Hard Fault present

*O = Key On, Engine Off;   C = Continuous Memory;   R = Engine Running

3 digit Diagnostic Trouble Codes (EEC-IV)

Code	Test Condition*	Probable Cause
102	O,C,R	MAF sensor circuits open or sensor defective
103	O,C,R	MAF sensor screen blocked or sensor defective
104	C	MAF sensor circuit erratic
106	O,C,R	BARO sensor slow responding
107	O,C,R	BARO sensor low voltage, open sensor circuits or defective sensor.
108	O,C,R	BARO sensor high voltage detected. BARO circuit shorted to power or defective sensor.
109	O,C,R	BARO sensor intermittent. Check for loose connections.
111	O,C,R	Pass
112	O,C,R	Intake Air Temperature sensor circuit indicates circuit grounded/above 245 degrees F
113	O,C,R	Intake Air Temperature sensor circuit indicates open circuit/below -40 degrees F
114	O,C,R	Intake Air Temperature sensor out of self-test range
116	O,R	Coolant Temperature sensor out of self-test range
117	O,C	Coolant Temperature circuit below minimum voltage or indicates above 245 degrees F
118	O,C	Coolant Temperature sensor circuit above maximum voltage or indicates below -40 degrees F
119	C	Coolant Temperature sensor circuit erratic
121	O,C,R	Throttle Position sensor out of self-test range
121	C	Electronic Throttle Control circuit performance problem
122	O,C	Throttle Position sensor below minimum voltage
122	C	Electronic Throttle Control circuit low input
123	O,C	Throttle Position sensor above maximum voltage
123	C	Electronic Throttle Control circuit high input
124	C	Throttle Position Sensor voltage higher than expected
125	C	Throttle Position Sensor voltage lower than expected
126	O,C,R	MAP/BARO sensor higher than expected
128	C	MAP sensor vacuum hose damaged or disconnected
129	R	Insufficient Manifold Absolute Pressure/Mass Air Flow change during Dynamic Response Check
131	O,C,R	Heated oxygen sensor out of range
133	O,C,R	Heated oxygen sensor slow response
135	O,C,R	Heated oxygen sensor circuits open, shorted or grounded
137	R	Heated oxygen sensor indicates rich condition, left side
139	C	No heated oxygen sensor switching detected, left side
141	O,C,R	Heated oxygen sensor circuits open shorted or grounded
144	C	No heated oxygen sensor switching detected, right side
151	O,C,R	Heated oxygen sensor out of range
153	O,C,R	Heated oxygen sensor slow response
155	O,C,R	Heated oxygen sensor circuits open, shorted or grounded
156	O,C,R	Heated oxygen sensor circuits open, shorted or have corroded connections
157	R	Mass Air Flow Sensor below minimum voltage
158	R	Mass Air Flow Sensor above maximum voltage
159	C, R	Mass Air Flow Sensor out of self-test range
161	O,C,R	Heated oxygen sensor circuits open shorted or grounded
167	R	Insufficient Throttle Position Sensor change during Dynamic Response Check
171	C	Heated oxygen sensor unable to switch, right side
172	C,R	Heated oxygen sensor indicates lean condition, right side
173	C,R	Heated oxygen sensor indicates rich condition, right side
174	C	Heated oxygen sensor switching slow, right side
175	C	Heated oxygen sensor unable to switch, left side
176	C	Heated oxygen sensor indicates lean condition, left side
177	C	Heated oxygen sensor indicates rich condition, left side
178	C	Heated oxygen sensor switching slow, left side
179	C	Adaptive Fuel lean limit reached at part throttle, system rich, right side
181	C	Adaptive Fuel rich limit reached at part throttle, right side
182	C	Adaptive Fuel lean limit reached at idle, right side
183	C	Adaptive Fuel rich limit reached at idle, right side
184	C	Mass Air Flow higher than expected

*O = Key On, Engine Off; C = Continuous Memory; R = Engine Running

3 Digit Trouble Codes (continued)

Code	Test Condition*	Probable Cause
185	C	Mass Air Flow lower than expected
186	C	Injector Pulse-width higher than expected
187	C	Injector Pulse-width lower than expected
188	C	Adaptive Fuel lean limit reached, left side
189	C	Adaptive Fuel rich limit reached, left side
191	C	Adaptive Fuel lean limit reached at idle, left side
192	C	Adaptive Fuel rich limit reached at idle, left side
201	C	Injector number 1 circuit malfunction
202	C	Injector number 2 circuit malfunction
203	C	Injector number 3 circuit malfunction
204	C	Injector number 4 circuit malfunction
205	C	Injector number 5 circuit malfunction
206	C	Injector number 6 circuit malfunction
207	C	Injector number 7 circuit malfunction
208	C	Injector number 8 circuit malfunction
211	C	Profile Ignition Pick-up circuit fault
212	C	Ignition module circuit failure/SPOUT circuit grounded
213	R	SPOUT circuit open
214	C	Cylinder identification (CID) circuit failure
217	C	Engine coolant over-temperature condition
218	C	Transmission Fluid Temperature (TFT) over-temperature condition
219	C	Spark timing defaulted to 10 degrees SPOUT circuit open (EI)
221	C	Throttle Position (TP) sensor 2 circuit, range performance problem
222	C	Throttle Position (TP) sensor 2 circuit, low input
223	C	Throttle Position (TP) sensor 2 circuit, high input
311	R	Thermactor Air System inoperative, right side
313	R	Thermactor Air not by-passed
314	R	Thermactor Air inoperative, left side
326	C,R	EGR circuit voltage lower than expected
327	O,C,R	EGR Valve Pressure Transducer/Position Sensor circuit below minimum voltage
328	O,C,R	EGR Valve Position Sensor voltage below closed limit
332	C,R	EGR valve opening not detected
334	O,C,R	EGR valve position sensor voltage above closed limit
335	O	EGR Sensor voltage out-of-range
336	R	EGR circuit higher than expected
337	O,C,R	EGR Valve Pressure Transducer/Position Sensor circuit above maximum voltage
340	O,C,R	Camshaft position sensor circuit. Check wiring for opens, shorts and grounds
350	O,C,R	Ignition coil primary circuit malfunction. Check each coil primary circuit
405	C	Differential Pressure Feedback (DPF) circuit low voltage detected
406	C	Differential Pressure Feedback (DPF) circuit high voltage detected
411	R	Unable to control RPM during Low RPM Self-test
412	R	Unable to control RPM during High RPM Self-test
415	R	Idle Air Control (IAC) system at maximum adaptive lower limit
416	C	Idle Air Control (IAC) system at upper adaptive learning limit
420	O,C,R	Catalyst system low efficiency, left bank
430	O,C,R	Catalyst system low efficiency, right bank
511	C	Idle Air Control (IAC) circuit malfunction
511	O	Read Only Memory test failed - replace PCM
512	C	Keep Alive Memory test failed
513	O	Internal voltage failure in PCM
522	O	Manual Lever Position (MLP) sensor circuit open/vehicle in gear
525	O	Indicates vehicle in gear, air conditioning on
538	R	Insufficient change in RPM/operator error in Dynamic Response Check
539	O	Air conditioning on during Self-test
542	O,C	Fuel Pump circuit open; PCM to motor

*O = Key On, Engine Off; C = Continuous Memory; R = Engine Running

Code	Test Condition*	Probable Cause
543	O,C	Fuel Pump circuit open; Battery to PCM
551	O	Idle Air Control (IAC) circuit failure KOEO
552	O	Secondary Air Injection Bypass (AIRB) circuit failure
553	O	Secondary Air Injection Diverter (AIRB) circuit failure
554	O	Fuel Pressure Regulator Control (FPRC) circuit failure
556	O,C	Primary Fuel Pump circuit failure
558	O	EGR Vacuum Regulator circuit failure
565	O	Canister Purge circuit failure
569	O	Auxiliary Canister Purge (CANP2) circuit failure KOEO
571	O	EGRA solenoid circuit failure KOEO
572	O	EGRV solenoid circuit failure KOEO
578	C	A/C pressure sensor circuit shorted
579	C	Insufficient AIR CONDITIONING pressure change
581	C	Power to Fan circuit over current
582	O	Fan circuit open
583	C	Power to Fuel pump over current
584	C	VCRM Power ground circuit open (VCRM Pin 1)
585	C	Power to A / C clutch over current
586	C	A/C clutch circuit open
587	O,C	Variable Control Relay Module (VCRM) communication failure
602	O,C,R	Control module programming error
603	O,C,R	Powertrain control module test error
605	C	Powertrain control module read only memory PCM error
606	C	Powertrain control module internal communication error
617	C	1-2 shift error
618	C	2-3 shift error
619	C	3-4 shift error
621	O,C	Shift Solenoid 1 (SS 1) circuit failure KOEO
622	O	Shift Solenoid 2 (SS2) circuit failure KOEO
623	O	Transmission Control Indicator Light (TCIL) circuit failure
624	O,C	Electronic Pressure Control (EPC) circuit failure
625	O,C	Electronic Pressure Control (EPC) driver open in PCM
626	O	Coast Clutch Solenoid (CCS) circuit failure KOEO
627	O	Torque Converter Clutch (TCC) solenoid circuit failure
628	C	Excessive converter clutch slippage
629	O,C	Torque Converter Clutch (TCC) solenoid circuit failure
631	O	Transmission Control Indicator Lamp (TCIL) circuit failure KOEO
632	R	Transmission Control Switch (TCS) circuit did not change states during KOER
634	O,C,R	Manual Lever Position (MLP) sensor voltage higher or lower than expected
636	O,C,R	Transmission Fluid Temp (TFT) higher or lower than expected
637	O,C,R	Transmission Fluid Temp (TFT) sensor circuit above maximum voltage/ -40°F (-40°C) indicated / circuit open
638	O,C,R	Transmission Fluid Temp (TFT) sensor circuit below minimum voltage/ 290°F (143°C) indicated / circuit shorted
639	R,C	Insufficient input from Transmission Speed Sensor (TSS)
641	O,C	Shift Solenoid 3 (SS3) circuit failure
643	O,C	Torque Converter Clutch (TCC) circuit failure
645	C	Incorrect gear ratio obtained for first gear
646	C	Incorrect gear ratio obtained for second gear
647	C	Incorrect gear ratio obtained for third gear
648	C	Incorrect gear ratio obtained for fourth gear
649	C	Electronic Pressure Control (EPC) higher or lower than expected
651	C	Electronic Pressure Control (EPC) circuit failure
652	O	Torque Converter Clutch (TCC) solenoid circuit failure
653	R	Transmission Control Switch (TCS) did not change states during KOER
654	O	Transmission Range (TR) sensor not indicating PARK during KOEO

*O = Key On, Engine Off; C = Continuous Memory; R = Engine Running

3 Digit Trouble Codes (continued)

Code	Test Condition*	Probable Cause
656	C	Torque Converter Clutch continuous slip error
657	C	Transmission over temperature condition occurred
659	C	High vehicle speed in park indicated
667	C	Transmission Range sensor circuit voltage below minimum
668	C	Transmission Range circuit voltage above maximum
675	C	Transmission Range sensor circuit voltage out of range
998	O	Hard fault present

O = Key On, Engine Off; C = Continuous Memory; R = Engine Running

---

15   On-Board Diagnostic (OBD-II) system and trouble codes

Scan tool information

Refer to illustrations 15.1 and 15.2

1   Hand-held scanners are the most powerful and versatile tools for analyzing engine management systems used on later model vehicles **(see illustration)**. Note: *An aftermarket generic scanner should work with any model covered by this manual. However, some early OBD-II models, although technically classified as OBD-II compliant by the manufacturer and by the Federal government, might not be fully compliant with all SAE standards for OBD-II. Some generic scanners are unable to extract all the codes from these early OBD-II models. Before purchasing a generic scan tool, contact the manufacturer of the scanner you're planning to buy and verify that it will work properly with the OBD-II system you want to scan. If necessary, of course, you can always have the codes extracted by a dealer service department or an independent repair shop with a professional scan tool.*

Note: *OBD-I models that did not get updated to the OBD-II system are late model 49 State 5.8L trucks over 8,500 lbs. and 7.5L trucks over 14,000 lbs.*

2   With the arrival of the Federally mandated emission control system (OBD-II), a specially designed scanner has been developed. Several tool manufacturers have released OBD-II scan tools for the home mechanic **(see illustration)**.

OBD-II system general description

3   All 1996 and later models are equipped with the second generation OBD-II system. This system consists of an on-board computer known as the Powertrain Control Module (PCM), and information sensors, which monitor various functions of the engine and send data to the PCM. This system incorporates a series of diagnostic monitors that detect and identify fuel injection and emissions control systems faults and store the information in the computer memory. This updated system also tests sensors and output actuators, diagnoses drive cycles, freezes data and clears codes.

4   This powerful diagnostic computer must be accessed using an OBD-II scan tool and 16-pin Data Link Connector (DLC) located under the driver's dash area. The PCM is mounted at the right end of the firewall, in the engine compartment. The PCM is the brain of the electronically-controlled fuel and emissions system. It receives data from a number of sensors and other electronic components (switches, relays, etc.). Based on the information it receives, the PCM generates output signals to control various relays, solenoids (fuel injectors) and other actuators. The PCM is specifically calibrated to optimize the emissions, fuel economy and driveability of the vehicle.

5   It isn't a good idea to attempt diagnosis or replacement of the PCM or emission control components at home while the vehicle is under warranty. Because of a Federally mandated warranty that covers the emissions system components, and because any owner-induced damage to the PCM, sensors and/or control devices may void this warranty, take the vehicle to a dealer service department if the PCM or a system component malfunctions.

15.1 Simple code readers are an economical way to extract trouble codes when the CHECK ENGINE light comes on

15.2 Scanners like these from Actron and AutoXray are powerful diagnostic aids - they can tell you just about anything that you want to know about your engine management system

Information sensors (OBD-II)

6   Brake Pedal Position (BPP) switch - The BPP switch is located at the top of the brake pedal. It's a normally open switch that closes when the brake pedal is applied and sends a signal to the PCM, which interprets this signal as its cue to disengage the torque converter clutch. The BPP switch is also used to disengage the brake shift interlock.

7   Differential pressure feedback EGR (DPFE) system sensor - The differential pressure feedback EGR system sensor is located near the EGR valve. This sensor is a pressure transducer that monitors the pressure differential across a metering orifice located in the sensor. A transducer is a device that receives a signal from one system and transfers that signal to another system, often in a different form. The differential pressure feedback EGR system sensor outputs a voltage signal that's proportional to the pressure drop across its metering orifice. The PCM uses this data to calculate the EGR flow rate.

8   Manual Lever Position (MLP) sensor - The MLP sensor is located at the manual lever on the left side of the E4OD automatic transmission. The MLP sensor functions like a conventional Park/Neutral Position (PNP) switch: it prevents the engine from starting in any gear other than Park or Neutral, and it closes the circuit for the back-up lights when the shift lever is moved to Reverse. The PCM also sends a voltage signal to the MLP sensor, which uses a series of step-down resistors that act as a voltage divider. The PCM monitors the sensor's voltage output, which corresponds to the position of the manual lever. Thus the PCM is able to determine the gear selected and is able to determine the correct pressure for the electronic pressure control system of the transaxle.

9   Engine Coolant Temperature (ECT) sensor - The ECT sensor is a thermistor (temperature-sensitive variable resistor) that sends a voltage signal to the PCM, which uses this data to determine the temperature of the engine coolant. The ECT sensor helps the PCM control the air/fuel mixture ratio and ignition timing, and it also helps the PCM determine when to turn the Exhaust Gas Recirculation (EGR) system on and off. The ECT sensor is located in the thermostat housing, directly behind the upper radiator hose.

10   Intake Air Temperature (IAT) sensor - The IAT sensor, which is an integral component of the Mass Air Flow (MAF) sensor, monitors the temperature of the air entering the engine and sends a signal to the PCM. The IAT sensor cannot be replaced by itself. If it's defective, you'll have to replace the MAF sensor.

11   Knock sensor - The knock sensor is a piezoelectric crystal that oscillates in proportion to engine vibration. The term *piezoelectric* refers to the property of certain crystals that produce a voltage when subjected to a mechanical stress. The oscillation of the piezoelectric crystal produces a voltage output that is monitored by the PCM, which retards the ignition timing when the oscillation exceeds a certain threshold. When the engine is operating normally, the knock sensor oscillates consistently and its voltage signal is steady. When detonation occurs, engine vibration increases, and the oscillation of the knock sensor exceeds a design threshold. Detonation is an uncontrolled explosion, after the spark occurs at the spark plug, which spontaneously combusts the remaining air/fuel mixture, resulting in a pinging or slapping sound. If allowed to continue, engine performance is diminished and damage to the pistons can result. The knock sensor is located below the intake manifold, in the valley between the cylinder heads.

12   Mass Air Flow (MAF) sensor - The MAF sensor is secured by screws to an opening in the air filter housing just before the intake duct. The MAF sensor is the principal means by which the Powertrain Control Module (PCM) monitors intake airflow. It uses a hot-wire sensing element to measure the amount of air entering the engine. The wire is maintained at a temperature of 392 degrees F (200 degrees C) above the ambient temperature by electrical current. As intake air passes through the MAF sensor and over the hot wire, it cools the wire, and the control system immediately corrects the temperature back to its constant value. The current required to maintain the constant value is used by the PCM as an indicator of airflow.

13   Output Shaft Speed (OSS) sensor - The OSS sensor is a magnetic pick-up coil. The OSS sensor provides the Powertrain Control Module (PCM) with information about the rotational speed of the output shaft in the transmission. The PCM uses this information to control the torque converter and to calculate speed scheduling and the correct pressure for the Electronic Pressure Control system.

14   Oxygen sensors - An oxygen sensor is a galvanic battery that generates a small variable voltage signal in proportion to the difference between the oxygen content in the exhaust stream and the oxygen content in the ambient air. The PCM uses the voltage signal from the upstream oxygen sensor to maintain a "stoichiometric" air/fuel ratio of 14.7:1 by constantly adjusting the on-time of the fuel injectors. There are three oxygen sensors, two upstream and one downstream sensor.

15   Throttle Position (TP) sensor - The TP sensor, which is located on the throttle body, on the end of the throttle valve shaft, is a potentiometer that produces a variable voltage signal in accordance with the opening angle of the throttle valve. This voltage signal tells the PCM when the throttle is closed, in a cruise position, or wide open, or anywhere in between. The PCM uses this information, along with data from a number of other sensors, to calculate injector on-time.

Output actuators

Note: *Based on the information it receives from the information sensors described above,* *the PCM adjusts fuel injector pulse width, idle speed, ignition spark advance, ignition coil dwell and EVAP canister purge operation. It does so by controlling the output actuators. The following list provides a brief description of the function, location and operation of each of the important output actuators.*

16   EVAP canister purge valve - The EVAP canister purge valve, which is located in the engine compartment near the firewall, is normally closed. But when ordered to do so by the PCM, under certain operating conditions, it allows fuel vapors from the EVAP canister to be drawn into the intake manifold for combustion.

17   Exhaust Gas Recirculation (EGR) vacuum regulator solenoid and valve - When the engine is put under a load (hard acceleration, passing, going up a steep hill, pulling a trailer, etc.), combustion chamber temperature increases. When combustion chamber temperature exceeds 2,500 degrees, excessive amounts of oxides of nitrogen (NOx) are produced. NOx is a precursor of photochemical smog. When combined with hydrocarbons (HC), other reactive organic compounds (ROCs) and sun light, it forms ozone, nitrogen dioxide, nitrogen nitrate and other nasty stuff. The vacuum-controlled EGR valve allows exhaust gases to be recirculated back to the intake manifold, where they dilute the incoming air/fuel mixture, which lowers the combustion chamber temperature and decreases the amount of NOx produced during high-load conditions. The amount of exhaust gases recirculated to the intake is determined by the strength of the vacuum signal delivered to the EGR valve. The PCM-controlled EGR vacuum regulator solenoid is the electromagnetic device that regulates the supply of vacuum to the EGR valve.

The EGR valve is located at the right front of the intake manifold, with the solenoid nearby, and the differential pressure feedback (DPF) sensor mounted on the EGR pipe between the right exhaust manifold and the EGR valve.

18   Fuel injectors - The fuel injectors, which spray a fine mist of fuel into the intake ports, where it is mixed with incoming air, are inductive coils under PCM control. For more information about the injectors, see Section 17.

19   Idle Air Control (IAC) valve - The IAC valve controls the amount of air allowed to bypass the throttle valve when the throttle valve is at its (nearly closed) idle position. The IAC valve is controlled by the PCM. When the engine is placed under an additional load at idle (low-speed maneuvers or the air conditioning compressor, for example), the engine can run roughly, stumble and even stall. To prevent this from happening, the PCM opens the IAC valve, to increase the idle speed enough to overcome the extra load imposed on the engine.

20   The Clutch Pedal Position (CPP) switch (manual transmission models) - The CPP switch allows activation of the starter by monitoring the movement of the clutch pedal. The CPP switch is mounted to the top portion of the clutch pedal.

Obtaining and clearing OBD-II Diagnostic Trouble Codes (DTCs)

21   When the PCM recognizes a malfunction in a monitored emission control system, component or circuit, it turns on the Malfunction Indicator Light (MIL) on the dash. The PCM will continue to display the MIL until the problem is fixed and the Diagnostic Trouble Code (DTC) is cleared from the PCM's memory.

22   To test the critical emission control components, circuit and systems on an OBD-II vehicle, the PCM runs a series of *monitors* during each vehicle *trip*. The monitors are a series of testing protocols used by the PCM to determine whether each monitored component, circuit or system is functioning satisfactorily. The monitors must be run in a certain order. For example, the oxygen sensor monitor cannot run until the engine, the catalytic converter and the oxygen sensors are all warmed up. Another example, the misfire monitor cannot run until the engine is in closed-loop operation. For a good overview of the OBD-II monitors, see the Haynes *OBD-II and Electronic Engine Management Systems Techbook*. An OBD-II *trip* consists of operating the vehicle (after an engine-off period) and driving it in such a manner that the PCM's monitors test all of the monitored components, circuits and systems at least once.

23   If the PCM recognizes a fault in some component, circuit or system while it's running the monitors, it stores a Diagnostic Trouble Code (DTC) and turns on the Malfunction Indicator Light (MIL) on the instrument cluster. A DTC can self-erase, but only after the MIL has been extinguished. For example, the MIL might be extinguished for a misfire or fuel system malfunction if the fault doesn't recur when monitored during the next three subsequent sequential driving cycles in which the conditions are similar to those under which the malfunction was first identified. (For other types of malfunctions, the criteria for extinguishing the MIL can vary.)

24   Once the MIL has been extinguished, the PCM must pass the diagnostic test for the most recent DTC for 40 *warm-up cycles* (80 warm-up cycles for the fuel system monitor and the misfire monitor). A warm-up cycle consists of the following chain of events:

   The engine has been started and is running

   The engine temperature rises by at least 40-degrees above its temperature when it was started

   The engine coolant temperature crosses the 160-degree F mark

   The engine is turned off after meeting the above criteria

Obtaining DTCs

25   Before outputting any DTCs stored in the PCM, thoroughly inspect ALL electrical connectors and hoses. Make sure that all electrical connections are tight, clean and free of corrosion. And make sure that all hoses are correctly connected, fit tightly and are in good condition (no cracks or tears). Also, make sure that the engine is tuned up. A poorly running engine is probably one of the biggest causes of emission-related malfunctions. Often, simply giving the engine a good tune-up will correct the problem.

26   Of course, if the MIL does NOT go out after several driving cycles, it's probably an indication that something must be repaired or replaced before the DTC can be erased and the MIL extinguished. This means that you will need to extract the DTC(s) from the PCM, make the necessary repair or replace a component, then erase the DTC yourself.

27   1996 and later models are equipped with On-Board Diagnostic II (OBD-II) systems, the Diagnostic Trouble Codes (DTCs) can only be accessed with a scan tool. Professional scan tools are expensive, but relatively inexpensive generic scan tools **(see illustrations 15.1 and 15.2)** are available at most automotive parts stores. Simply plug the connector of the scan tool into the diagnostic connector, which is located under the left side of the dash, and then follow the instructions included with the scan tool to extract the DTCs.

28   Once you have outputted all of the stored DTCs, look them up on the accompanying DTC chart.

29   After troubleshooting the source of each DTC, make any necessary repairs or replace the defective component(s).

Clearing the DTCs

30   Clear the DTCs with the scan tool in accordance with the instructions provided by the scan tool's manufacturer.

Diagnostic Trouble Codes

31   The accompanying tables are a list of the Diagnostic Trouble Codes (DTCs) that can be accessed by a do-it-yourselfer working at home (there are many more DTCs available to dealerships with proprietary scan tools and software, but those codes cannot be accessed by a generic scan tool). If, after you have checked and repaired the connectors, wire harness and vacuum hoses (if applicable) for an emission-related system, component or circuit, the problem persists, have the vehicle checked by an automotive service technician.

OBD-II trouble codes

Code	Probable cause
P0102	Mass Air Flow (MAF) sensor circuit, low input
P0103	Mass Air Flow (MAF) sensor circuit, high input
P0104	Mass Air Flow (MAF) sensor circuit, intermittent failure
P0106	Barometric (BARO) pressure sensor circuit, performance problem
P0107	Barometric (BARO) pressure sensor/MAP sensor circuit, low voltage
P0108	Barometric (BARO) pressure sensor/MAP sensor circuit, high voltage
P0109	BARO/MAP sensor circuit intermittent
P0111	Intake Air Temperature (IAT) sensor 1 circuit, range/performance problem
P0112	Intake Air Temperature (IAT) sensor 1 circuit, low input
P0113	Intake Air Temperature (IAT) sensor circuit, high input
P0117	Engine Coolant Temperature (ECT) sensor circuit, low input
P0118	Engine Coolant Temperature (ECT) sensor circuit, high input
P0119	Engine Coolant Temperature (ECT) sensor circuit, intermittent failure
P0121	Throttle Position (TP) circuit out of range or performance problem
P0122	Throttle Position (TP) sensor circuit, low input
P0123	Throttle Position (TP) sensor circuit, high input
P0125	Insufficient coolant temperature for closed loop fuel control
P0131	Upstream oxygen sensor circuit problem (right cylinder bank)
P0133	Upstream oxygen sensor circuit, slow response (right cylinder bank)
P0135	Upstream oxygen sensor circuit problem (right cylinder bank)
P0136	Downstream oxygen sensor circuit problem (right cylinder bank)

Code	Probable cause
P0138	Downstream oxygen sensor circuit, high voltage (right cylinder bank)
P0139	Upstream oxygen sensor heater circuit, slow response, Bank 1, sensor 2
P0141	Downstream oxygen sensor heater circuit problem , Bank 1, sensor 2
P0151	Upstream oxygen sensor circuit, low voltage (left cylinder bank)
P0152	Upstream oxygen sensor circuit, high voltage (left cylinder bank)
P0153	Heated oxygen sensor circuit, slow response (left cylinder bank)
P0154	Upstream oxygen sensor heater circuit problem, Bank 2, sensor 1
P0156	Downstream oxygen sensor circuit problem (left cylinder bank)
P0158	Downstream oxygen sensor circuit, high voltage (left cylinder bank)
P0159	Downstream oxygen sensor circuit, slow response, Bank 2, sensor 2
P0161	Downstream oxygen sensor heater circuit problem, Bank 2, sensor 2
P0171	System too lean (right cylinder bank)
P0172	System too rich (right cylinder bank)
P0174	System too lean (left cylinder bank)
P0175	System too rich (left cylinder bank)
P0221	Throttle Position (TP) sensor B circuit range/performance problem
P0222	Throttle Position (TP) sensor B circuit, low input
P0223	Throttle Position (TP) sensor B circuit, high input
P0230	Fuel pump primary circuit malfunction
P0231	Fuel pump secondary circuit low
P0232	Fuel pump secondary circuit high
P0297	Vehicle overspeed condition
P0300	Random misfire detected
P0301	Cylinder no. 1 misfire detected
P0302	Cylinder no. 2 misfire detected
P0303	Cylinder no. 3 misfire detected
P0304	Cylinder no. 4 misfire detected
P0305	Cylinder no. 5 misfire detected
P0306	Cylinder no. 6 misfire detected
P0307	Cylinder no. 7 misfire detected
P0308	Cylinder no. 8 misfire detected
P0320	Ignition engine speed input circuit malfunction
P0325	Knock sensor 1 circuit malfunction (right cylinder head)
P0326	Knock sensor 1 circuit range/performance (right cylinder bank)
P0330	Knock sensor 2 circuit malfunction (left cylinder bank)
P0331	Knock sensor 2 circuit range/performance (left cylinder bank)
P0350	Ignition coil primary or secondary circuit malfunction
P0400	EGR flow failure (outside the minimum or maximum limits)
P0401	Exhaust Gas Recirculation (EGR) valve, insufficient flow detected
P0402	Exhaust Gas Recirculation (EGR) valve, excessive flow detected
P0410	Secondary Air Injection (AIR) system, low flow
P0411	Secondary Air Injection (AIR) system, upstream flow
P0412	Secondary Air Injection (AIR) system, circuit malfunction
P0420	Catalyst system efficiency below threshold (right cylinder bank)
P0430	Catalyst system efficiency below threshold (left cylinder bank)
P0442	EVAP control system, small leak detected
P0443	EVAP control system, canister purge valve circuit malfunction
P0446	EVAP control system, canister vent solenoid circuit malfunction
P0455	EVAP control system, big leak detected
P0500	Vehicle Speed Sensor (VSS), circuit malfunction
P0503	Vehicle Speed Sensor (VSS), intermittent malfunction
P0505	Idle Air Control (IAC) system malfunction
P0506	Idle Air Control (IAC) rpm lower than expected
P0507	Idle Air Control (IAC) rpm higher than expected
P0511	Idle Air Control (IAC) circuit malfunction
P0552	Power Steering Pressure (PSP) sensor circuit malfunction
P0553	Power Steering Pressure (PSP) sensor circuit malfunction
P0602	Control module programming error
P0603	Powertrain Control Module (PCM) Keep-Alive-Memory (KAM) test error
P0605	Powertrain Control Module (PCM) Read-Only-Memory (ROM) error
P0703	Brake Pedal Position (BPP) switch circuit input malfunction
P0704	Clutch pedal position switch malfunction
P0707	Transmission range sensor, A circuit , low
P0708	Transmission range sensor, A circuit, high
P0720	Insufficient input from Output Shaft Speed (OSS) sensor
P0721	Noise interference on Output Shaft Speed (OSS) sensor signal
P0722	No signal from Output Shaft Speed (OSS) sensor
P0723	Output Shaft Speed (OSS) sensor circuit, intermittent failure

GENERAL EEC-IV POWER AND GROUND CHECKS

COMPONENT	TYPE	CHECK	EXP VALVE	ACTION if not expected value
CHECK 1	BATTERY VOLTAGE	Batt(+) - Batt(-)	> 11.5 Volts	Charge or service battery
CHECK 2	EEC PWR IN Relay operation *1	EECc(37) - GRD	> 10.5 Volts	Perform Checks 2a (1992 on)
		EECc(57) - GRD		Perform Checks 2b (others)
CHECK 3	EEC Module PWR GRD	EEC (40) - Batt(-)	< 5 ohms	Service harness open GRD circuit or
		EEC (60) - Batt(-)		replace EEC (internal open)
CHECK 4	EEC Signal Return Harness cont	EECc (46) - DLC(1)	< 5 ohms	Service open in harness Signal Return
CHECK 5	EEC Module SIG RTN GRD	EEC(46) - EEC(40)	< 5 ohms	Replace EEC (internal open)
		EEC(46) - EEC(60)		
CHECK 6	EEC Reference Voltage Out *1	TPc(1) - TPc(3)	4 to 6 Volts	Check TP harness cont (see sensors), if
				good, possible EEC failure (no VREF).
CHECK 2a	EEC Relay PWR IN	EECpb(47) - GRD	>10.5 Volts	Service harn open from Batt or diode assy
	EEC Relay RUN PWR IN *1	EECpb(IGN) - GRD	>10.5 Volts	Service harness open from IGN
	EEC Relay GRD	EECpb(45) - Batt(-)	< 5 ohms	Service harness open to Batt (-)
	EEC Relay PWR OUT	EECpb(46) - EECc(37)	< 5 ohms	Service harness open
		EECpb(46) - EECc(57)		
	Other	All checks pass		Replace EEC Power Relay
CHECK 2b	EEC Relay PWR IN	EECrb(4) - GRD	>10.5 Volts	Service harness open from Batt
	EEC Relay RUN PWR IN *1	EECrb(2) - GRD	>10.5 Volts	Service harness open from IGN
	EEC Relay GRD	EECrb(1) - Batt(-)	< 5 ohms	Service harness open to Batt (-)
	EEC Relay PWR OUT	EECrb(3) - EECc(37)	< 5 ohms	Service harness open
		EECrb(3) - EECc(57)		
	Other	All checks pass		Replace EEC Power Relay

*1 = key on
(x) = Connector pin number
EECc = EEC-IV module vehicle harness connector
EEC = EEC-IV module
TPc = Throttle Position sensor vehicle harness connector
EECpb = EEC relay power box in engine compartment (1992 on)
EECrb = EEC relay box in engine compartment (1991 and earlier)

16.1 General EEC-IV Power and Ground component and circuit check table

16 EFI system components - description, check and sensor/output actuator replacement

Warning: *The following code description and troubleshooting charts represent a streamlined version of the manufacturer's diagnostic procedure which has been tailored for the home mechanic with average tools. By no means is this version as comprehensive or detailed as the manufacturer's. In addition, even the manufacturer's manual states that in the event that no problems can be detected "after all diagnostic steps have been completed and wiring verified, replace the PCM". Therefore, it is recommended that this procedure be used to better inform the owner and facilitate better communication between the owner and dealer service department. If you elect to replace expensive components based on this procedure, remember to ask if the component can be returned if the problem is not resolved - this may be a deciding factor.*

Caution: *When working with the PCM (also known as the EEC-IV module) or associated harness still attached to the module, avoid direct contact with the electrical connector terminals. Static electricity generated by normal activity and stored on the surface of the skin can discharge and damage delicate electronic components inside the PCM. It is best to always wear a static discharging wrist strap (available at electronic stores) and avoid working on electronics when the relative humidity is under 25-percent.*

General EEC-IV power relay and ground checks

Refer to illustration 16.1

1   To prevent confusion and inaccurate diagnosis, it is a good idea to begin all checks with the general EEC-IV power and ground checks outlined in the accompanying chart **(see illustration)**. The EEC relay and associated circuits provide the battery power (VPWR) to all fuel injection and electric fuel pump related components requiring 10.5 volts or greater.

2   The PCM (EEC-IV) reduces the 10.5 or greater input voltage to four-to-six volts for output to sensors requiring a specific reference voltage (VREF).

Fuel delivery component and circuit checks

Refer to illustrations 16.3

3   For fuel delivery (pumps) circuit and component checks, refer to the accompanying chart **(see illustration)**. These checks verify proper electrical operation of the fuel pump relay, inertia switch, fuel pump(s), fuel injectors, and fuel tank selector switch on dual tank models.

Information sensors and output actuators

Engine coolant temperature sensor

Refer to illustrations 16.5 and 16.6

Note: *The check procedure applies only to 1995 and earlier models. The OBD-II system on 1996 and later models requires special diagnostic tools. Refer to the Haynes OBD-II and Electronic Engine Management System manual for diagnosing the information sensors and the output actuators.*

CIRCUIT AND COMPONENT CHECKS - EFI FUEL DELIVERY SYSTEM

COMPONENT	TYPE	CHECK	EXP VALVE	ACTION if not expected value
FP Relay (87 to 91)	Relay control PWR IN *1	FPRb(2) - GRD	> 10.5 Volts	Service EEC PWR Relay (see gen checks)
	Harness, relay control GRD	FPRb(1) - EECc(22)	< 5 ohms	Service open in harness
	Relay Control PWR out *2	EECc(22) - GRD	> 10.5 volts	Replace FP Relay
	Relay switch PWR in	FPRb(4) - GRD	> 10.5 Volts	Service harness to Batt (Fuse Link)
	Harn, relay switch PWR out	FPRb(3) - ISc(1)	< 5 ohms	Service open in harness
	Relay, switch PWR out *2, *3	ISc(1) - GRD	> 10.5 Volts	Replace FP relay
	EEC module elects check *4	FPRb(3) - Batt (-)	Continuity for 1 - 2 sec	Possible EEC failure (see dealer)
FP Relay (92 on)	Relay control PWR IN *1	FPRpb(PWR) - GRD	> 10.5 Volts	Service EEC PWR Relay (see gen checks)
	Harness, relay control GRD	FPRpb(50) - EECc(22)	< 5 ohms	Service open in harness
	Relay Control PWR out *2	EECc(22) - GRD	> 10.5 Volts	Replace FP Relay
	Relay switch PWR in	FPRpb(52) - GRD	> 10.5 Volts	Service harness to Batt (Fuse Link)
	Harn, relay switch PWR out	FPRpb(51) - ISc(1)	< 5 ohms	Service open in harness
	Relay, switch PWR out *2, *3	ISc(1) - GRD	> 10.5 Volts	Replace FP relay
	EEC module elects check *4	FPRpb(50) - Batt (-)	Continuity for 1 - 2 sec	Possible EEC failure (see dealer)
Inertia Switch *5	Inertia switch cont	IS(1) - IS(2)	< 5 ohms	Reset switch/recheck or replace
	Inertia switch short	IS(1) - IS case	> 10,000 ohms	Replace switch
High Press Pump Low Press Pump (87 to 89 only) or FDM (Single Tank) *6	Harness cont , pump	ISc(1) - Pc(2, PK/BK)	< 5 ohms	Service open in harness
	Harness short , pump, *7	ISc(2) - GRD	> 10,000 ohms	Service short in harness
	PWR to pump *2, *3	Pc(2, PK/BK) - GRD	> 10.5 Volts	Perform FP relay and Inertia switch checks
	Pump harn GRD	Pc(1, BK) - GRD	< 5 ohms	Service open in harness GRD
	Pump PWR test	Jump Batt(+) -P(2, PK/BK) Jump Batt(-) - P(1, BK)	Pump should run	Replace pump
	Other	All checks pass	N/A	Possible EEC failure (see dealer)
Tank (pump) Selection Switch (Dual Tanks) *6	Sel Switch PWR in *2, *3	SSc(2) - GRD	> 10.5 Volts	Service harness open
	Sel Switch PWR out (front)*8	SSc(1) - GRD	> 10.5 Volts	Replace switch
	Sel Switch PWR out (rear) *9	SSc(3) - GRD	> 10.5 Volts	Replace switch
	Sel switch short	SS(1) - SS(3)	> 10,000 ohms	Replace switch
LOW PRESS PUMPs (87 to 89) or FDMs (Dual Tanks) *10	Harness cont, pump (front)	SSc(1) - Pc(2, R)	< 5 ohms	
	Harness, pump GRD (front)	Pc(1, Or) - GRD	> 10,000 ohms	
	Harness cont, pump (rear)	SSc(3) - Pc(2, BR/W)	< 5 ohms	
	Harness, pump GRD (rear)	Pc(1, Or) - GRD	> 10,000 ohms	
	Pump PWR test (front) Jump Batt(-) - P(1, Or)	Jump Batt(+) - P(2, R) Pump should run	Replace pump	
	Pump PWR test (rear) Jump Batt(-) - P(1, Or)	Jump Batt(+) - P(2, BR/W) Pump should run	Replace pump	
	Other	All checks pass	N/A	Replace pump
Injectors	Harness cont, bank 1, *11	EECc(58) -each INJc(2)	< 5 ohms	Service open in harness
	Harness short, bank 1, *12	EECc(58) - GRD	> 10,000	Service short in harness
	Harness cont, bank 2, *13	EECc(59) -each INJc(2)	< 5 ohms	Service open in harness
	Harness short, bank 2, *12	EECc(59) - GRD	> 10,000	Service short in harness
	Injector resistance	INJ(1) - INJ(2)	11 to 18 ohms	Replace Injector
	Harness, INJ PWR in *1	INJc (1) - GRD	> 10.5 Volts	Service EEC PWR Relay (see gen checks)

*1 = Key on.
*2 = FP relay installed, key on.
*3 = Ground DLC(1) with jumper to energize fuel pump control circuit.
*4 = EEC connector installed, Circuit should briefly complete (one to two sec) immediately after key is turned to RUN.
*5 = Assumes fuel pump relay checks passed.
*6 = Assumes inertia switch checks passed.
*7 = On 87 through 89 models, both pump connectors must be disconnected (external and in-tank).
*8 = Tank switch in front position, connector mated with meter probes in backshell of connector, plus *3 and *2.
*9 = Tank switch in rear position, connector mated with meter probes in backshell of connector, plus *3 and *2.
*10 = Assumes Tank Selection Switch checks passed.
*11 = Disconnect injector connectors. Bank 1 consists of injectors at cylinders.
*12 = Injector connectors must be disconnected.
*13 = Disconnect injector connectors. Bank 2 consists of injectors at cylinders 2-4-6 (six cyl) or 2-3-6-7 (eight cyl).
FPRb = Fuel pump relay box
EECc = EEC-IV vehicle harness connector.
ISc = Inertia switch vehicle harness connector.
FPRpb = Fuel pump relay power distribution box.
IS = Inertia switch.
Pc = Fuel pump connector vehicle harness connector
P = Fuel pump.
SSc = Selector switch vehicle harness connector.
SS = Selector switch.
INJc = Injector vehicle harness connector.
INJ = Injector.
(X) = Connector pin number or color.

16.3 EFI fuel delivery system component and circuit check table

General description

4   The coolant sensor is a thermistor (a resistor which varies the value of its voltage output in accordance with temperature changes). The change in the resistance values will directly affect the voltage signal from the coolant sensor. As the sensor temperature DECREASES, the resistance values will INCREASE. As the sensor temperature INCREASES, the resistance values will DECREASE. A failure in the coolant sensor circuit should set a Code 21, 51 or 61 for the two-digit code system or 116, 117 or 118 for the three digit code system. These codes indicate a failure in the coolant temperature circuit, so in most cases the appropriate solution to the problem will be either repair of a wire or replacement of the sensor.

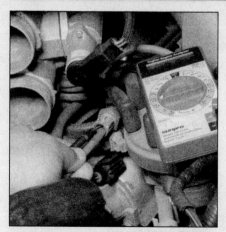

16.5 Check the resistance of the coolant temperature sensor with the engine completely cold and then with the engine at operating temperature - resistance should decrease as temperature increases

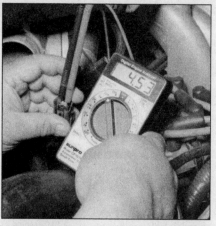

16.6 Working on the harness side, check the voltage from the PCM to the coolant temperature sensor with the ignition key ON and the engine not running. It should be approximately 5.0 volts

16.9 The MAP sensor is mounted against the firewall in the engine compartment, next to the evaporator housing

Check

5   To check the sensor, check the resistance value of the coolant temperature sensor while it is completely cold (50 to 65-degrees F = 58,750 to 40,500 ohms). Next, start the engine and warm it up until it reaches operating temperature **(see illustration)**. The resistance should be lower (180 to 220-degrees F = 3,600 to 1,840 ohms).

6   If the resistance values on the sensor are correct, check the signal voltage to the sensor from the PCM **(see illustration)**. It should be approximately 5.0 volts.

Replacement

7   Before installing the new sensor, wrap the threads with Teflon sealing tape to prevent leakage and thread corrosion.

8   To remove the sensor, unplug the electrical connector, then carefully unscrew the sensor. **Caution:** *Handle the coolant sensor with care. Damage to this sensor will affect the operation of the entire fuel injection system.* Installation is the reverse of removal. Check the coolant level and add some, if necessary, to bring it to the proper level.

Manifold Absolute Pressure (MAP) sensor

Refer to illustrations 16.9, 16.12 and 16.13

Note: *The check procedure applies only to 1995 and earlier models. The OBD-II system on 1996 and later models requires special diagnostic tools. Refer to the Haynes OBD-II and Electronic Engine Management System manual for diagnosing the information sensors and the output actuators.*

General description

9   The Manifold Absolute Pressure (MAP) sensor **(see illustration)** monitors the intake manifold pressure changes resulting from changes in engine load and speed and converts the information into a voltage output. The PCM uses the MAP sensor to control

fuel delivery and ignition timing. There are two different types of MAP sensors; a voltage varying type (early models) and a frequency varying type (late models). The PCM will receive information as a DC voltage signal or a frequency generated voltage signal (mHz). This signal can be detected using a tachometer. The former type will vary the voltage between 1 and 5 volts while the latter will vary the frequency from 310 rpm at closed throttle (high vacuum) to 200 rpm at wide open throttle (low vacuum).

10   A failure in the MAP sensor circuit should set a Code 22, 72 or 81 for the two digit code system or 126, 128 or 129 for the three digit code system.

Check and replacement

11   Disconnect the electrical connector from the MAP sensor. Using a voltmeter, check for reference voltage to the MAP sensor on the VREF wire. With the ignition key ON (engine not running), the reference voltage should be approximately 4.0 to 6.0 volts.

12   Connect the electrical connector onto the MAP sensor and backprobe the harness. If you do not know which type of MAP sensor is installed on your particular year and model, perform the voltage check first. If the MAP sensor does not respond, check the sensor with a tachometer. Set the tachometer selection to the 6-cylinder scale. With the ignition key ON (engine not running) check the signal from the MAP/BP Signal wire (middle terminal) to the signal return wire (ground) **(see illustration)**. **Note:** *Probe the same wire (MAP/BP Signal) to obtain either the voltage signal (voltage varying type) or frequency (frequency varying type) on the MAP sensor electrical sensor.*

13   Without vacuum, the voltmeter should read about 5.0 volts (voltage varying type) or the tachometer should read approximately 310 rpm (frequency varying type). Use a hand-held vacuum pump and apply 20 inches of Hg

to the MAP sensor and observe the voltmeter or the tachometer readings **(see illustration)**. With 20 in. Hg of vacuum applied, the voltmeter should read about 1.0 volt or the tachometer should read about 200 rpm. Look for a smooth transition between these two readings.

14   If the test results are incorrect, replace the MAP sensor.

Oxygen sensor

Refer to illustrations 16.15 and 16.19

Note: *The check procedure applies only to 1995 and earlier models. The OBD-II system on 1996 and later models requires special diagnostic tools. Refer to the Haynes OBD-II and Electronic Engine Management System manual for diagnosing the information sensors and the output actuators.*

General description and check

15   The heated oxygen sensor (HEGO or HO2S), which is located in the exhaust system **(see illustration)**, monitors the oxygen content of the exhaust gas stream. The oxygen content in the exhaust reacts with the oxygen sensor to produce a voltage output which varies from 0.1-volt (high oxygen, lean mixture) to 0.9-volts (low oxygen, rich mixture). The PCM constantly monitors this variable voltage output to determine the ratio of oxygen to fuel in the mixture. The PCM alters the air/fuel mixture ratio by controlling the pulse width (open time) of the fuel injectors. A mixture ratio of 14.7 parts air to 1 part fuel is the ideal mixture ratio for minimizing exhaust emissions, thus allowing the catalytic converter to operate at maximum efficiency. It is this ratio of 14.7 to 1 which the PCM and the oxygen sensor attempt to maintain at all times.

16   The oxygen sensor produces no voltage when it is below its normal operating temperature of about 600-degrees F. During this initial period before warm-up, the PCM operates in open loop mode.

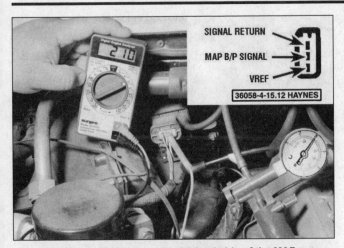

16.12 Using a tachometer, probe the backside of the MAP sensor MAP/BP SIGNAL wire and SIGNAL RETURN (ground wire) and check for frequency voltage. It should be between 300 and 320 rpm depending on the altitude. It is possible to place the negative probe of the voltmeter onto another more convenient ground (valve cover bolt). Be sure the meter is set on 6-cylinder scale

16.13 Now apply 20 inches Hg. of vacuum to the sensor and confirm that the frequency decreases to about 200 to 230 rpm

17   Allow the engine to reach normal operating temperature and check that the oxygen sensor is producing a steady signal voltage between 0.35 and 0.55-volts.

18   A delay of two minutes or more between engine start-up and normal operation of the sensor, followed by a low or a high voltage signal or a short in the sensor circuit, will cause the PCM to also set a code. Codes that indicate problems in the oxygen sensor system are 41, 42, 91 and 92 for the two digit code system and 136, 137, 139, 144 and 171 through 178 for the three digit code system.

19   Also check to make sure the oxygen sensor heater is supplied with battery voltage **(see illustration)**.

20   When any of the above codes occur, the PCM operates in the open loop mode - that is, it controls fuel delivery in accordance with a programmed default value instead of feed-back information from the oxygen sensor.

21   The proper operation of the oxygen sensor depends on four conditions:

a) *Electrical - The low voltages generated by the sensor depend upon good, clean connections which should be checked whenever a malfunction of the sensor is suspected or indicated.*

b) *Outside air supply - The sensor is designed to allow air circulation to the internal portion of the sensor. Whenever the sensor is removed and installed or replaced, make sure the air passages are not restricted.*

c) *Proper operating temperature - The PCM will not react to the sensor signal until the sensor reaches approximately 600-degrees F. This factor must be taken into consideration when evaluating the performance of the sensor.*

d) *Unleaded fuel - The use of unleaded fuel is essential for proper operation of the sensor. Make sure the fuel you are using is of this type.*

22   In addition to observing the above conditions, special care must be taken whenever the sensor is serviced.

a) *The oxygen sensor has a permanently attached pigtail and electrical connector which should not be removed from the sensor. Damage or removal of the pigtail or electrical connector can adversely affect operation of the sensor.*

b) *Grease, dirt and other contaminants should be kept away from the electrical connector and the louvered end of the sensor.*

c) *Do not use cleaning solvents of any kind on the oxygen sensor.*

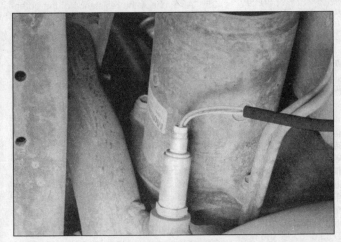

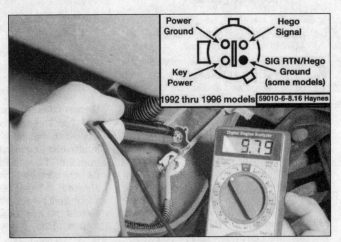

16.15 The oxygen sensor on this Bronco is mounted in the exhaust pipe, near the starter

16.19 The oxygen sensor heater can be checked by probing the KEY POWER terminal and the POWER GROUND and test for battery voltage with the ignition key ON (engine not running). The electrical connector for the oxygen sensor is located under the engine on Bronco models

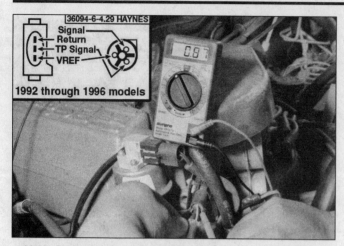

16.32 Check the signal voltage from the TPS with a voltmeter. Backprobe terminal TP SIG with the positive (+) probe of the voltmeter and SIG RTN with the negative probe (-) of the voltmeter and with the throttle closed, the voltage should read 0.5 to 1.0 volts

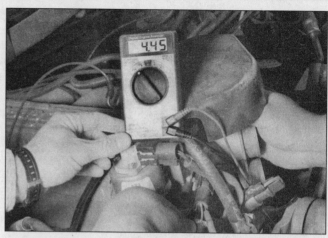

16.33 Backprobe terminal TP SIG with the positive (+) probe of the voltmeter and SIG RTN with the negative probe (-) of the voltmeter and with the throttle completely open (WOT), the voltage should read 4.0 to 5.0 volts

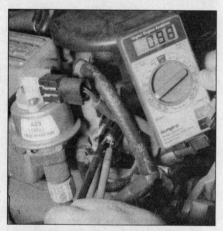

16.35 With the TPS electrical connector disconnected, check the resistance of the TPS with the throttle completely closed . . .

d) Do not drop or roughly handle the sensor.

e) The silicone boot must be installed in the correct position to prevent the boot from being melted and to allow the sensor to operate properly.

Replacement

Note: *Because it is installed in the exhaust manifold or pipe, which contracts when cool, the oxygen sensor may be very difficult to loosen when the engine is cold. Rather than risk damage to the sensor (assuming you are planning to reuse it in another manifold or pipe), start and run the engine for a minute or two, then shut it off. Be careful not to burn yourself during the following procedure.*

23 Disconnect the cable from the negative terminal of the battery.

24 Raise the vehicle and place it securely on jackstands.

25 Carefully disconnect the electrical con-

nector from the sensor.

26 Carefully unscrew the sensor from the exhaust manifold. **Caution:** *Excessive force may damage the threads.*

27 Anti-seize compound must be used on the threads of the sensor to facilitate future removal. The threads of new sensors will already be coated with this compound, but if an old sensor is removed and reinstalled, recoat the threads.

28 Install the sensor and tighten it securely.

29 Reconnect the electrical connector of the pigtail lead to the wiring harness.

30 Lower the vehicle and reconnect the cable to the negative terminal of the battery.

Throttle Position Sensor (TPS)

Refer to illustrations 16.32, 16.33, 16.35 and 16.36

Note: *The check procedure applies only to 1995 and earlier models. The OBD-II system on 1996 and later models requires special diagnostic tools. Refer to the Haynes OBD-II and Electronic Engine Management System manual for diagnosing the information sensors and the output actuators.*

Note: *On some models, the throttle body must be removed for access to the TP sensor.*

General description

31 The Throttle Position Sensor (TPS) is located on the end of the throttle shaft on the throttle body. By monitoring the output voltage from the TPS, the PCM can determine fuel delivery based on throttle valve angle (driver demand). A broken or loose TPS can cause intermittent bursts of fuel from the injector and an unstable idle because the PCM thinks the throttle is moving. Any problems in the TPS or circuit will set a code 23, 53 or 63 for the two digit code system or 122 through 125 for the three digit code system.

Check

32 To check the TPS, turn the ignition switch

to ON (engine not running) and install the probes of the volt-ohmmeter into the ground wire and signal wire on the backside of the electrical connector. This test checks for the proper signal voltage from the TPS **(see illustration)**. **Note:** *Be careful when backprobing the electrical connector. Do not damage the wiring harness or pull on any connectors to make contact.*

33 The sensor should read 0.50 to 1.0-volts at idle. Rotate the throttle to the full-open position and the sensor should increase voltage to 4.0 to 5.0-volts **(see illustration)**. If the TPS voltage readings are incorrect, replace it with a new unit.

34 Also, check the TPS reference voltage. With the ignition key ON (engine not running), install the positive (+) probe of the voltmeter onto the voltage reference wire. There should be approximately 5.0 volts sent from the PCM to the TPS.

35 Also, check the resistance of the potentiometer within the TPS. Disconnect the TPS electrical connector and working on the sensor side, connect the probes of the ohmmeter onto the ground wire and the TPS signal wire. With the throttle valve fully closed, the TPS should read between 3.0 and 4.0 K-ohms **(see illustration)**

36 Now open the throttle with one hand and check the resistance again. Slowly advance the throttle until fully open. The resistance should be approximately 350 ohms **(see illustration)**. The potentiometer should exhibit a smooth change in resistance as it travels from fully closed to wide open throttle. Any deviations indicate a possible worn or damaged TPS.

Replacement

37 If the same sensor is to be reinstalled, scribe a reference mark across the edge of the sensor and the throttle body. Remove the screws and detach the sensor. To install the sensor, position it with the wiring harness

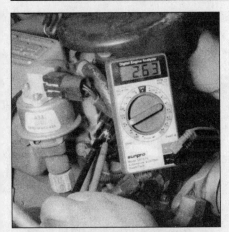

16.36 . . . then with the throttle completely open - the resistance should decrease

16.39 Location of the Intake Air Temperature sensor in the intake manifold

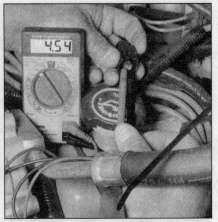

16.41 Disconnect the electrical connector from the IAT sensor and check for reference voltage from the computer with the ignition key ON (engine not running)

(or connector side, on models without a pig-tail) pointing away from the idle air control valve, engage the tangs of the sensor with the throttle shaft blade, then rotate it clockwise to align the reference marks before installing the screws.

38   Adjustment is not necessary on 4.9L models. All other models must be adjusted. If you're working on a 1990 or earlier model, connect the negative probe of a digital volt-meter to the terminal of the TP sensor with the black/white wire, and the positive probe to the terminal with the the dark green/light green wire. **Note:** *You may have to insert small stick pins into the back of the connector where the wires go in, and connect the probes to the pins.* If you're working on a 1991 or later model, connect the negative probe to the terminal with the grey/red wire and the posi-tive probe to the terminal with the grey/white wire (the above note pertains to these mod-els, too). Loosen the TP sensor screws, if not already done. With the ignition key turned On, rotate the TP sensor until the output voltage reads 1.0 volt. Tighten the sensor screws and recheck the voltage.

Intake Air Temperature (IAT) sensor (also called the Air Charge Temperature [ACT] sensor)

Refer to illustrations 16.39, 16.41 and 16.43

Note: *The check procedure applies only to 1995 and earlier models. The OBD-II system on 1996 and later models requires special diagnostic tools. Refer to the Haynes OBD-II and Electronic Engine Management System manual for diagnosing the information sen-sors and the output actuators.*

General description

39   The Intake Air Temperature (IAT) sensor is located in the intake manifold **(see illustra-tion).** This sensor acts as a resistor which changes value according to the temperature of the air entering the engine. Low tempera-tures produce a high resistance value (for

example, at 68 degrees F the resistance is 37.3 K-ohms) while high temperatures pro-duce low resistance values (at 212-degrees F, the resistance is 2.07 K-ohms). The PCM supplies approximately 5-volts (reference voltage) to the IAT sensor. The voltage will change according to the temperature of the incoming air. The voltage will be high when the air temperature is cold and low when the air temperature is warm. Any problems with the IAT sensor will usually set a code 24, 54 or 64 on the two digit code system or 112, 113 or 114 on the three digit code system.

Check

40   To check the IAT sensor, disconnect the two prong electrical connector and turn the ignition key ON but do not start the engine.
41   Measure the voltage (reference voltage) **(see illustration).** The meter should read approximately 5-volts.
42   If the voltage signal is not correct, have the PCM diagnosed by a dealer service department or other repair shop.
43   Measure the resistance across the sen-sor terminals **(see illustration).** The resistance should be HIGH when the air temperature is LOW. Next, start the engine and let it idle (cold). Wait awhile and let the engine reach operating temperature. Turn the ignition OFF, disconnect the IAT sensor and measure the resistance across the terminals. The resistance should be LOW when the air temperature is HIGH. If the sensor does not exhibit this change in resis-tance, replace it with a new part.

Power steering pressure switch

44   Turning the steering wheel increases power steering fluid pressure and engine load. The pressure switch will close before the load can cause an idle problem. A problem in the power steering pressure switch circuit will set a code 52 (two digit code system only).
45   A pressure switch that will not open or an open circuit from the PCM will cause timing to retard at idle and this will affect idle quality.

16.43 Check the resistance of the IAT sensor cold and warm - the resistance of the IAT should be high when the temperature is low, and the resistance should be low when the air temperature is high

46   A pressure switch that will not close or an open circuit may cause the engine to die when the power steering system is used heavily.
47   Any problems with the power steering pressure switch or circuit should be repaired by a dealer service department or other repair shop.

Brake On/Off (BOO) switch

General Information

48   The brake On/Off switch (BOO) tells the PCM when the brakes are being applied. The switch closes when brakes are applied and opens when the brakes are released. The BOO switch is located on the brake pedal assembly.
49   The brake light circuit and bulbs are wired into the BOO circuit so it is important in diagnosing any driveability problems to

16.54 With the ignition key ON (engine not running), probe terminals VREF and SIG-RTN with a voltmeter and check for reference voltage from the computer - it should be about 5.0 volts

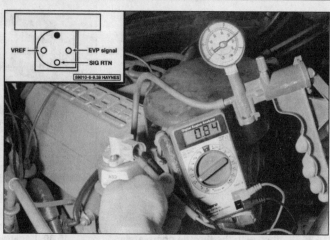

16.56 Check the resistance across terminals EVP and VREF on the sensor - without vacuum it should be about 5,000 ohms and with 20 in. Hg of vacuum about 100 ohms (watch for a smooth transition between the two values)

make sure all the brake light bulbs are working properly (not burned out) or the driver may feel poor idle quality.

Check

50   Disconnect the electrical connector from the BOO switch and using a 12 volt test light, check for battery voltage to the BOO switch.
51   Also, check continuity from the BOO switch to the brake light bulbs. Change any burned out bulbs or damaged wire harnesses.

Replacement

52   Refer to Chapter 9 for the replacement procedure (it's similar to the brake light switch, and located next to it).

EGR Valve Position (EVP) sensor

Refer to illustrations 16.54 and 16.56

53   The EGR valve position sensor is attached to the EGR valve to produce a signal indicating to the EEC-IV system the exact position of the EGR valve.

Check

54   Disconnect the electrical connector on the EVP sensor and check for reference voltage from the computer with the ignition key ON (engine not running). There should be approximately 5.0 volts **(see illustration)**.
55   Next check the resistance of the EVP sensor. Working on the sensor side, check the resistance between EVP and VREF. It should be approximately 5,000 ohms.
56   Now apply 10 in.Hg. of vacuum and check the resistance **(see illustration)**. It should be approximately 100 ohms. Watch for a decrease in resistance as vacuum is applied.

Replacement

57   Disconnect the electrical connector from the sensor.
58   Remove the bolts from the sensor body and lift the EVP sensor from the EGR valve.
59   Installation is the reverse of removal.

Knock Sensor (KS)

60   The knock sensor is a sensor that detects engine detonation (spark knock). When knock occurs, a voltage signal is sent to the computer which in turn retards spark timing. The knock sensor is color coded and must be replaced with one of the same color. Before checking the knock sensor, be sure to test for problems with the fuel for contamination, ignition timing and altitude.

Check

61   A quick check for the knock sensor is to simulate operating conditions. With the engine running and the timing light hooked up, tap the engine manifold next to the knock sensor with a hammer and observe that the timing retards momentarily. If there is no response, check for reference voltage. Disconnect the electrical connector from the knock sensor and with the ignition key ON (engine not running), check for reference voltage from the computer. There should be approximately 5.0 volts.
62   To replace the sensor, simply unscrew it. Install the new sensor, tightening it securely.

Idle Air Control (IAC) or Bypass Air Idle Speed Control (BPA-ISC) solenoid

Refer to illustration 15.66

Check

63   The bypass air valve (BPA-ISC), sometimes referred to as the Idle Air Control valve, controls the amount of air that bypasses the throttle body assembly throttle valve and consequently controls the engine idle speed. This output actuator is mounted on the throttle body and is controlled by voltage pulses sent from the PCM (computer). The BPA-ISC valve body moves in or out allowing more or less intake air into the system according to the engine conditions. To increase idle speed, the PCM extends

the BPA-ISC valve body from the seat and allows more air to bypass the throttle bore. To decrease idle speed, the PCM retracts the BPA-ISC valve body towards the seat, reducing the air flow.
64   To check the system, first check for the voltage signal from the PCM. Turn the ignition key On (engine not running) and with a voltmeter, probe the wires of the terminals of the BPA-ISC valve electrical connector. It should be approximately 10.5 volts. This indicates that the BPA-ISC valve is receiving the proper signal from the PCM.
65   Next, remove the valve and inspect it:

a)   *Check the pintle for excessive carbon deposits. If necessary, clean it with carburetor cleaner spray. Also clean the IAC valve housing to remove any deposits.*

66   Next, check the resistance of the BPA-ISC valve. With the electrical connector disconnected, check the resistance of the valve **(see illustration)**. It should be between 7 and 13 ohms.

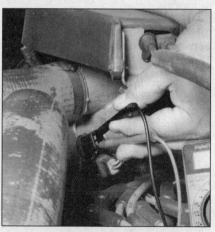

16.66 The resistance of the BPA-ISC solenoid should be approximately 7 to 13 ohms

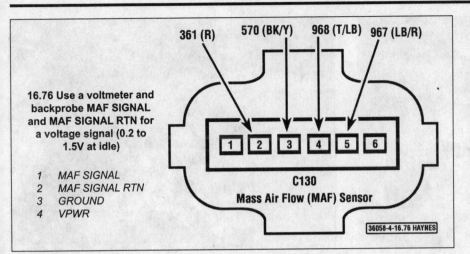

361 (R)   570 (BK/Y)   968 (T/LB)   967 (LB/R)

16.76 Use a voltmeter and backprobe MAF SIGNAL and MAF SIGNAL RTN for a voltage signal (0.2 to 1.5V at idle)

1   MAF SIGNAL
2   MAF SIGNAL RTN
3   GROUND
4   VPWR

**C130
Mass Air Flow (MAF) Sensor**

36058-4-16.76 HAYNES

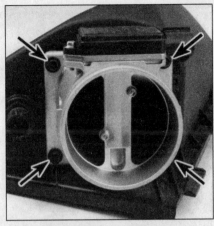

16.82 Remove the four bolts and separate the MAF sensor from the air cleaner housing

Removal

67   Unplug the electrical connector from the BPA-ISC valve.
68   Remove the two valve attaching screws and withdraw the assembly.
69   Check the condition of the rubber O-ring. If it's hardened or deteriorated, replace it.
70   Clean the sealing surface and the bore of the throttle body assembly to ensure a good seal. **Caution:** *The BPA-ISC valve itself is an electrical component and must not be soaked in any liquid cleaner, as damage may result.*

Installation

71   Position the new O-ring on the BPA-ISC valve. Lubricate the O-ring with a light film of engine oil.
72   Install the BPA-ISC valve and tighten the screws securely.
73   Plug in the electrical connector at the BPA-ISC valve assembly.

Mass Airflow (MAF) sensor

Refer to illustrations 16.76 and 16.82

Note: *The check procedure applies only to 1995 and earlier models. The OBD-II system on 1996and later models requires special diagnostic tools. Refer to the Haynes OBD-II and Electronic Engine Management Systems manual for diagnosing the information sensors and the output actuators.*

General information

74   The Mass Airflow (MAF) sensor is located in the air intake duct. This sensor uses a hotwire sensing element to measure the amount of air entering the engine. The air passing over the hotwire causes it to cool. Consequently, this change in temperature can be converted into an analog voltage signal to the PCM which in turn calculates the required fuel injector pulse width.

Check

75   Check for power to the MAF sensor. With the MAF sensor connected, backprobe terminal number 4 on the harness side to check for battery voltage. Use the VPWR terminal indicated in **illustration 16.76**.
76   Move the pin(s) and backprobe terminals

number 1 and 2 MAF SIGNAL and MAF SIGNAL RTN **(see illustration)** with the voltmeter and check for voltage. The voltage should be 0.2 to 1.5 volts at idle.
77   Raise the engine rpm. The signal from the MAF sensor should increase to about 2.0 volts at 60 mph. It is impossible to simulate these conditions in the driveway at home but it is necessary to observe the voltmeter for a fluctuation in voltage as the engine speed is raised. The vehicle will not be under load but it should manage to vary slightly, indicating operational condition.
78   Turn the engine off and disconnect the MAF harness connector and using an ohmmeter, probe the terminals on the MAF sensor MAF SIGNAL and MAF SIGNAL RTN. If the hot wire element inside the MAF sensor has been damaged, it will be indicated by an open circuit (infinite resistance).
79   If the voltage readings are correct, check the wiring harness, for open circuits or damaged harness (see Chapter 12).

Replacement

80   Disconnect the electrical connector from the MAF sensor.
81   Remove the upper section of the air cleaner assembly (see Section 21).
82   Remove the four bolts **(see illustration)** and remove the MAF sensor from the engine compartment.
83   Installation is the reverse of removal.

Manual Lever Position (MLP) sensor

Note: *The check procedure applies only to 1995 and earlier models. The OBD-II system on 1996 and later models requires special diagnostic tools. Refer to the Haynes OBD-II and Electronic Engine Management Systems manual for diagnosing the information sensors and the output actuators.*

General information

Refer to illustration 16.86

84   The Manual Lever Position (MLP) sensor on the transmission indicates to the PCM when the transmission is in Park, Neutral, Drive or Reverse. This information is used for starting, Transmission Converter Clutch (TCC), Exhaust Gas Recirculation (EGR) and Idle Speed Control (ISC) valve operation. For example, if the signal wires become grounded, it may be difficult to start the engine in Park or Neutral.
85   In the event there is a problem with the Manual Lever Position (MLP) sensor, first check the terminal connections for proper attachment.
86   Using a voltmeter, with the ignition key on (engine not running), check for power to each of the signal wires **(see illustration)** of the switch. There should be voltage present.
87   Check the adjustment of the switch (see

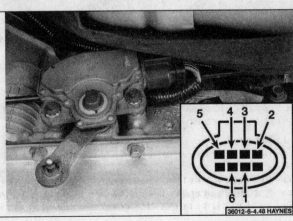

16.86 Manual Lever Position (MLP) sensor terminal designation - 1995 and earlier models

1   PCM signal return
2   Start
3   Back-up lamps
4   Accessory feed
5   Start
6   Sensor signal to PCM

36012-6-4.48 HAYNES

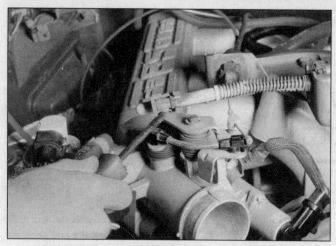

17.3a Pry the accelerator cable from the throttle lever

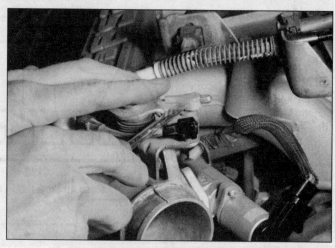

17.3b Detach the TV cable from the throttle lever

Chapter 7B). If the switch is out of adjustment, perform the procedure and clear the codes. Recheck the system for any other problems.
88   Any further diagnostics of the Manual Lever Position (MLP) sensor must be performed by a dealer service department or other repair shop because this system requires a special scan tool to access the working parameters from the PCM.

Adjustment

89   To adjust the Manual Lever Position (MLP) sensor or replace the switch, refer to Chapter 7.

17   EFI system components - removal and installation

Upper intake manifold (with throttle body)

Refer to illustrations 17.3a, 17.3b, 17.4, 17.9 and 17.11

Warning: *Wait until the engine is completely cool before beginning this procedure.*

1   Disconnect the cable from the negative battery terminal. Disconnect the electrical connectors from all electrical components mounted on the upper intake manifold and throttle body. Mark them with pieces of numbered tape, if necessary, to simplify installation.
2   Remove accelerator cable shield, if equipped.
3   Detach the accelerator cable from the throttle lever **(see illustration)**. Remove the automatic transmission throttle valve (TV) cable **(see illustration)** from the throttle body on models so equipped (see Chapter 7B). On vehicles equipped with cruise control, remove the control cable from throttle body.
4   Mark and detach the vacuum hoses from the vacuum tree **(see illustration)**, and any other vacuum hoses that would interfere with removal of the upper intake manifold.
5   Disconnect the PCV system hose from the fitting on the upper manifold. On 5.8L Lightning models, remove the hose at the PCV valve and remove the PCV fresh air hose to the oil fill tube at throttle body.
6   Detach the air cleaner-to-throttle body tubes from the throttle body (see Section 21).

On 7.5L engines, remove the clean air hose to idle air control valve port.
7   Remove the two canister purge lines from the fittings on the throttle body if equipped.
8   If equipped, disconnect the coolant lines at the throttle body (EGR spacer plate on 5.8L Lightning). Prepare to lose some coolant.
9   Unscrew the tube nut and detach the tube from the EGR valve **(see illustration)**. Also remove the nut or bolt from the upper end of the support bracket. Pull the bracket out of the way.
10   Remove the upper intake manifold retaining bolts.
11   Carefully separate the upper manifold and throttle body, as an assembly, from the lower manifold **(see illustration)**. On 5.8L Lightning engines, it may be necessary to partially lift the manifold to remove the additional vacuum lines attached to underside of the manifold prior to complete removal.
12   Clean the mating surfaces of the upper and lower intake manifolds. Be careful not to gouge the soft aluminum or let any old gasket material fall into the intake manifold. Position a new gasket on the lower manifold mounting surface.

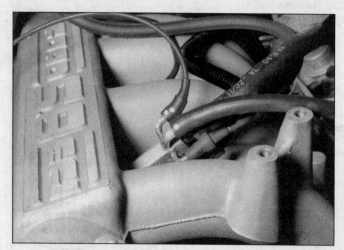

17.4 Mark and disconnect the hoses from the vacuum tree

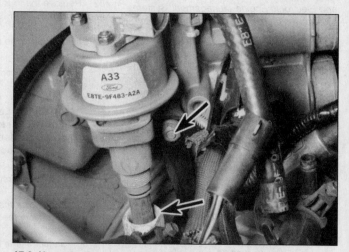

17.9 Unscrew the tube nut from the EGR valve (left arrow) and the nut from the support bracket (right arrow)

17.11 After everything is disconnected and the bolts are removed, carefully lift the upper intake manifold off

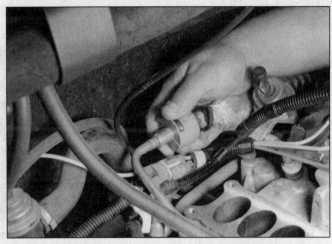

17.27 Using a special tool to disconnect the fuel line-to-fuel rail spring lock coupling

13 Carefully lower the upper manifold into place. Don't disturb the gasket in the process. Install the upper manifold retaining bolts and tighten them to the torque listed in this Chapter's Specifications. Install and tighten the support bracket-to-upper manifold bolt.

14 The remaining steps are the reverse of removal. Make sure the vacuum lines and wires are routed and attached correctly.

Throttle body

Warning: *Wait until the engine is completely cool before beginning this procedure.*

15 Detach the air intake duct from the throttle body (see Section 21).

16 Disconnect the wires from the air bypass valve (except 7.5L) and throttle position sensor.

17 Remove the two canister purge lines from the fittings on the throttle body, if equipped.

18 On 5.8L Lightning models, remove the PCV fresh air hose at the throttle body.

19 On 5.8L Lightning models, remove the EGR solenoid bracket and move it out of the way.

20 If equipped, disconnect the coolant lines at throttle body. Prepare to lose some coolant.

21 Remove the accelerator cable shield if equipped.

22 Detach the accelerator cable from the throttle lever **(see illustration 17.3a)**. Remove the automatic transmission throttle valve (TV) cable **(see illustration 17.3b)** from the throttle body on models so equipped (see Chapter 7B). On vehicles equipped with cruise control, remove the control cable from throttle body.

23 Remove the four throttle body bolts and detach the throttle body (and cable bracket on 4.9L engines) from the upper intake manifold. Be prepared for some coolant loss when removing the throttle body on 5.8L Lightning models.

24 Remove and discard the gasket. Make sure the gasket surfaces of the manifold and throttle body are clean and smooth. If scraping is necessary, do not scratch or nick the manifold or throttle body and do not allow material to fall into the intake manifold.

25 Installation is the reverse of removal.

Fuel rail assembly

Refer to illustrations 17.27 and 17.29

26 Relieve the fuel pump pressure (see Section 8).

27 Remove the upper intake manifold assembly. Remove the fuel supply and return lines from fuel rail **(see illustration)**.

28 Unplug the electrical connectors from the fuel injectors.

29 Remove the fuel rail retaining bolts, then carefully remove the fuel rail and injectors **(see illustration)**.

30 Installation is the reverse of removal. Tighten the fasteners to the torque listed in this Chapter's Specifications. Make sure the injector caps are clean before installing the fuel rail and that the injectors are seated properly. The fuel lines are connected by pushing the sections together carefully. Make sure they are locked (see Section 6).

Fuel pressure regulator

Refer to illustrations 17.32, 17.33a and 17.33b

31 Relieve the fuel system pressure, if not already done (see Section 8), and remove the fuel tank cap.

32 The regulator is located on the fuel rail. On some models, the fuel rail must be removed for access to the regulator screws. Detach the vacuum line from the regulator and remove the three retaining screws from the regulator housing **(see illustration)**.

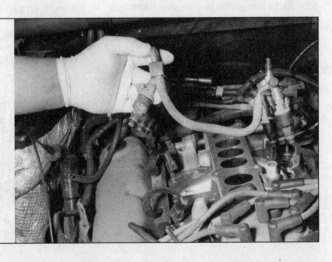

17.29 When removing the fuel rail, be careful not to damage the injectors or distort the rail

17.32 Removing the screws from the fuel pressure regulator

17.33a Replace the O-ring on the fuel pressure regulator . . .

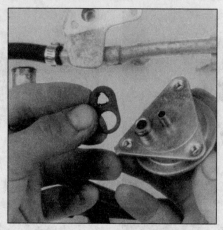

17.33b . . . and the gasket, too

17.39 A firm pull will disengage the fuel injector from the fuel rail

33 Remove the regulator, gasket and O-ring. Discard the gasket and O-ring **(see illustrations)**.

34 Make sure the gasket surfaces are clean and smooth. If scraping is necessary, do not damage the regulator or fuel supply line surfaces.

35 Installation is the reverse of removal. Tighten the screws securely. Lubricate the O-ring with light oil, but do not use silicone grease, as the injectors may clog.

36 Turn the ignition switch On and Off several times without starting the engine to check for fuel leaks.

Fuel injectors

Refer to illustrations 17.39 and 17.40

37 Relieve the fuel system pressure (see Section 8).

38 Remove the upper intake manifold and the fuel rail as described previously.

39 Grasp the injector body and pull it from the rail while gently rocking the injector from side-to-side **(see illustration)**.

40 Check the injector O-rings (two each) for damage and deterioration. Replace them with new ones, if necessary **(see illustration)**.

41 Check the plastic hat covering the pintle for damage and deterioration. If it is missing, look for it in the intake manifold.

42 Installation is the reverse of removal. Lubricate the O-rings with light oil, but do not use silicone grease, as the injector will clog.

43 Start the engine and check for fuel leaks.

3-port and 6-port tank selector valves

44 Relieve the fuel system pressure (see Section 8). Disconnect the cable from the negative terminal of the battery.

45 Raise the vehicle and support it securely on jackstands (front slightly higher than rear).

46 Locate the tank selector valve along the left-side frame rail.

47 Disconnect the electrical connector.

48 Identify each fuel line by location and detach the lines (see Section 6).

49 Remove the mounting bolts and detach the valve from the frame rail.

50 Installation is the reverse of removal.

Single or dual function reservoir

51 Relieve fuel system pressure (see Section 8).

52 Raise the vehicle and support it securely

on jackstands (front slightly higher than rear).

53 Locate the reservoir along the left-side frame rail.

54 Identify each fuel line by location and remove the lines (see Section 6).

55 Remove the reservoir mounting bolts and detach the reservoir from the frame rail.

56 Installation is the reverse of removal.

Powertrain Control Module (EEC-IV)

Refer to illustration 17.58

57 Detach the cable from the negative terminal of the battery. Locate PCM connector in the engine compartment on the driver's side of the firewall. Remove the connector retaining screw and unplug the connector.

58 From within the cab, locate the module under the left-side kick panel **(see illustration)**. Remove the retaining screws and remove the module. **Caution:** *To avoid damage to the internal circuitry caused by static electricity, be sure to ground yourself to a metal component before handling the PCM.*

59 Installation is the reverse of removal.

EEC Power and Fuel Pump relays

60 Locate the relay box in the engine compartment, on the left-side fender apron.

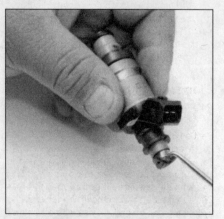

17.40 Remove the injector O-rings by prying them off with a small screwdriver

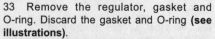

17.58 The PCM (EEC-IV) is located in the cab behind the left-side kick panel (arrow) - prior to removal, the 60-pin connector must be removed from inside the engine compartment

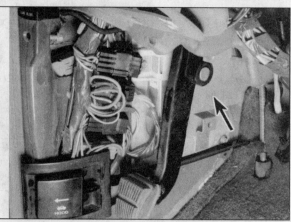

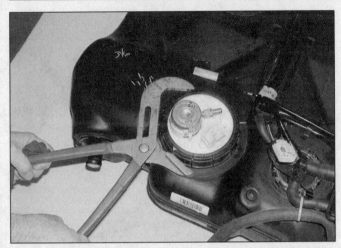

18.26 On plastic fuel tanks, if a special tool is not available, use a pair of large locking pliers to remove the threaded locking ring

18.27 Be sure to use a brass punch or wood dowel when loosening the locking ring on the fuel pump/sending unit

61 Lift the cover to expose the relays. The locations of the various relays are marked on the cover.

62 To remove a relay, simply pull it straight out of the relay box.

18 Fuel pump - removal and installation

Warning: *Gasoline is extremely flammable, so take extra precautions when you work on any part of the fuel system. Don't smoke or allow open flames or bare light bulbs near the work area, and don't work in a garage where a gas-type appliance (such as a water heater or clothes dryer) is present. Since gasoline is carcinogenic, wear fuel-resistant gloves when there's a possibility of being exposed to fuel, and, if you spill any fuel on your skin, rinse it off immediately with soap and water. Mop up any spills immediately and do not store fuel-soaked rags where they could ignite. The fuel system on fuel-injected models is under constant pressure, so, if any fuel lines are to be disconnected, the fuel pressure in the system must be relieved first (see Section 8). When you perform any kind of work on the fuel system, wear safety glasses and have a Class B type fire extinguisher on hand.*

Mechanical fuel pump (carbureted models)

Removal

1 Disconnect the cable from the negative terminal of the battery. Place a drain pan underneath the fuel pump.

2 Remove the outlet pipe at the fuel pump and allow it to drain into the drain pan.

3 Remove the inlet line at the fuel pump. Plug the end of the line to prevent further leakage and possible contamination from dirt.

4 Remove the two bolts and washers securing the fuel pump to the timing cover or engine block.

5 Remove the fuel pump and gasket (on some models a spacer plate may be positioned for heat insulation properties).

6 Clean the mating surfaces of the fuel pump, timing cover or cylinder block, and spacer (if so equipped). The mating surfaces must be perfectly smooth for a good gasket seal upon reinstallation.

Installation

7 Install a new gasket on the fuel pump mating surface. Coat both sides of the gasket with RTV sealant.

8 Lubricate the contact surface of the fuel pump rocker arm with multi-purpose grease or engine assembly lube.

9 Place the fuel pump against the block or timing cover, making sure the pump rocker arm is positioned correctly in relation to the eccentric on the camshaft. It may be necessary to rotate the engine until the eccentric is at its lowest position to ease installation.

10 Holding the fuel pump tightly against its mounting surface, install the retaining bolts and new lock washers.

11 Tighten the retaining bolts to the torque listed in this Chapter's Specifications.

12 Remove the plug from the inlet line and connect the inlet line to the fuel pump.

13 Connect the outlet line to the fuel pump.

14 Connect the cable to the negative battery terminal.

15 Start the engine and check it for fuel and/or oil leaks.

Electric fuel pump (externally mounted) - fuel-injected models, 1987 to 1989

16 Relieve fuel system pressure (see Section 8).

17 Disconnect the cable from the negative terminal of the battery.

18 If necessary, raise the vehicle and support it securely on jackstands (front end slightly higher).

19 Locate the fuel pump along the inboard side of the left-side frame rail.

20 Disconnect the electrical connector from the pump.

21 Detach the fuel lines from the pump (see Section 6).

22 Remove the mounting bolts and remove the pump.

23 Installation is reverse of removal except for the following. Don't forget to reset the inertia switch.

a) *If a new pump is required, the pump fittings may have to be removed from the old pump and installed on the new one. Make sure the fittings on the pump have gaskets in place, are properly positioned and that the fittings have been tightened securely. Check the wiring harness boots to make sure they are pushed onto the pump terminals far enough to seal and that the wire terminals are fully seated onto the pump terminals.*

b) *After wrapping the isolator around the fuel pump, locate the slot in the isolator so it faces the bracket base and push the pump and isolator assembly into the bracket. Make sure the tab of the isolator contacts the tab of the bracket and that the bracket tabs do not contact the pump case.*

c) *Reconnect the battery cable, start the vehicle and check for proper operation of the pump and for leaks.*

Electric fuel pump (in-tank)

Refer to illustration 18.26 and 18.27

24 Relieve the fuel system pressure (see Section 8).

25 Remove the fuel tank (see Section 22).

26 On plastic tanks, unscrew the threaded locking ring and remove the pump/sending unit from the tank **(see illustration)**.

27 On metal tanks, remove the locking ring by tapping it counterclockwise with a hammer and a brass punch (do not use a steel tool, as sparks may occur) and remove the pump/sending unit from the tank **(see illustration)**.

19.6a Remove the clips from the fuel line fittings . . .

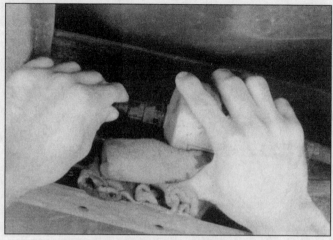

19.6b . . . and detach the lines from the fuel filter. Be sure to place a rag under the fittings to catch any spilling fuel

28   Installation is reverse of removal except for the following:

a) *Lightly coat the new sealing ring with grease to hold it in place during reassembly.*

b) *Do not damage the filter during installation.*

c) *Be sure the tabs in the pump/sending unit match the slots in the tank flange.*

d) *Reconnect the battery cable, start the vehicle and check for proper operation of the pump and for leaks.*

19 In-line fuel filter (fuel-injected models) - removal and installation

Refer to illustrations 19.6a and 19.6b

1   Relieve fuel system pressure (see Section 8) and loosen the fuel filler cap.

2   Disconnect the cable from the negative terminal of the battery.

3   If necessary, raise the vehicle and support it securely on jackstands (front end slightly higher than rear).

4   Locate the fuel filter on the inside of the left-side frame rail.

5   Remove the filter-to-fuel line retainer clips (if equipped).

6   Remove the fuel lines from the filter **(see illustrations)**.

7   Remove the nuts retaining the filter bracket to the frame rail and remove the filter.

8   Installation is the reverse of removal.

9   Turn the key on and off several times to pressurize system. Check the filter for leaks. Don't forget to reset the inertia switch.

20 Fuel pump inertia switch - removal and installation

1   The fuel pump inertia switch is electrically located in the circuit between the fuel

pump relay and the electric fuel pump(s). All power for the pump(s) must go through the switch. In the event of a significant impact (collision) the mechanism inside the switch will cause the switch to open the electrical circuit, shutting off power to the fuel pump as a safety precaution.

2   Locate the inertia switch in the cab on the drivers side, up against the firewall, to the left of the brake pedal or behind the right kick panel **(see illustration 8.2)**.

3   Detach the electrical connector.

4   Remove the mounting screws and remove the switch.

5   Installation is the reverse of removal. Don't forget to push the reset button on the top of the switch to compete the circuit.

21 Air cleaner housing and filter (fuel-injected models) - removal and installation

Air filter replacement

1   Remove the air cleaner cover attaching screws or unclip the cover. Lift the cover up and remove the air filter, noting how it's installed. Clean out the air cleaner housing and install the new filter element.

Air cleaner housing removal and installation

2   Remove the hose clamp(s) securing the air intake tube(s) at the air cleaner cover. Pull the tube(s) free of the air cleaner cover.

3   Remove the crankcase fresh air hose, if equipped, from the air cleaner housing.

4   Detach the fresh air intake duct from the air cleaner housing.

5   Remove the fasteners securing the air cleaner housing to its mounting bracket and remove the housing.

6   Installation is the reverse of removal.

22 Fuel tank - description, removal and installation

Warning: *Gasoline is extremely flammable, so take extra precautions when you work on any part of the fuel system. Don't smoke or allow open flames or bare light bulbs near the work area, and don't work in a garage where a gas-type appliance (such as a water heater or clothes dryer) is present. Since gasoline is carcinogenic, wear fuel-resistant gloves when there's a possibility of being exposed to fuel, and, if you spill any fuel on your skin, rinse it off immediately with soap and water. Mop up any spills immediately and do not store fuel-soaked rags where they could ignite. The fuel system on fuel-injected models is under constant pressure, so, if any fuel lines are to be disconnected, the fuel pressure in the system must be relieved first (see Section 8). When you perform any kind of work on the fuel system, wear safety glasses and have a Class B type fire extinguisher on hand.*

General description

1   The fuel tank on these vehicles is made of either metal or plastic. The main tank may be located either midship, between the driveline and frame rail, or between the frame rails and behind the rear axle.

2   An auxiliary tank is offered as an option on most models, usually located in the alternative midship position.

3   A plastic tank is usually non-repairable and, if damaged, should be replaced with a new one.

Midship tanks

4   On fuel-injected models, relieve the fuel system pressure (see Section 8).

5   Disconnect the cable from the negative battery terminal.

6   If necessary, raise the vehicle and support it securely on jackstands.

7   Drain the fuel into an approved fuel container by siphoning through the fuel hose at the fuel pump-to-fuel tube connection. **Warning:** *Don't start the siphoning action by mouth - use a siphoning pump (available at most auto parts stores).*

8   If equipped, remove the skid plate assembly.

9   Remove the clamps and remove the fuel filler and overflow hoses attached to the fuel tank, labeling the hoses for ease of installation.

10   Place a floor jack and a wood block under the fuel tank and remove the nuts and bolts from the tank restraining straps.

11   Lower the tank enough to detach the fuel lines and electrical connector (see Section 6). On vehicles with an EVAP system, disconnect the vapor hose from the emissions control valve.

12   Remove the tank from under vehicle.

13   If the tank is being replaced with a new one, remove the fuel level sending unit/fuel pump and vapor control valve by turning their respective retaining rings counterclockwise and pulling the units from the tank. On metal tanks, use a brass punch to turn the retaining rings - steel tools could cause a spark.

14   If the same tank is to be installed, scrape away the old gasket material from the gauge and valve mounting surfaces on the tank.

15   Installation is the reverse of the removal procedures. On fuel-injected models, don't forget to reset inertia switch.

Aft-axle tanks

Refer to illustrations 22.21 and 22.22

16   On fuel-injected models, relieve fuel system pressure (see Section 8).

17   Disconnect the cable from the negative battery terminal.

18   Raise the rear of the vehicle and place it securely on jackstands.

19   Drain the fuel into an approved fuel container by siphoning through the fuel hose at the fuel pump-to-fuel line connection. **Warning:** *Don't start the siphoning action by mouth - use a siphoning pump (available at most auto parts stores).*

20   Remove the fuel line hoses and electrical connector (see Section 6).

21   Loosen the clamps on the fuel filler pipe and disconnect the filler pipe hose and vent hose from the tank **(see illustration)**. It may not be possible to completely remove the filler pipe and filler pipe vent hose in this position.

22   If removing a metal tank, support the tank with a floor jack and wood block and remove the bolts attaching the tank supports to the frame **(see illustration)**.

23   Carefully lower the tank and disconnect the vent tube from the vapor emissions control valve in the top of the tank.

24   Finish removing the filler pipe and filler pipe vent hose, if this was not possible in Step 21.

25   Remove the tank from under the vehicle.

26   If removing the plastic type tank, support

22.21 Loosen the clamps and detach the fuel tank filler hose and vent hose from the filler neck

the tank and remove the bolts attaching the combination skid plate and tank support to the frame.

27   Carefully lower the tank and disconnect the vent tube from the vapor emissions control valve in the top of the tank.

28   Finish removing the filler pipe and filler pipe vent hose, if this was not possible in Step 21.

29   Remove the skid plate and tank from under the vehicle, then disassemble the skid plate from the tank.

30   If the fuel tank is being replaced with a new one, remove the vapor emissions control valve by turning its retaining ring counterclockwise and pulling the unit from the tank. On metal tanks, use a brass punch to turn the retaining rings - steel tools could cause a spark.

31   Install the vapor emissions control valve in the tank.

32   Install new support strap insulation as required.

33   If installing the plastic type tank, preassemble the skid plate and support straps to the tank.

34   Raise the tank skid plate and support assembly and attach the vent hose to the vapor emissions control valve.

35   Start the tank neck into the filler hose.

36   Position the tank assembly against the top straps or frame and install the retaining nuts and bolts. **Note:** *Care must be taken not to kink or twist the fuel lines.*

37   The remaining installation procedures are the reverse of those for removal. On fuel-injected models, don't forget to reset inertia switch.

Bronco models

38   On fuel-injected models, relieve the fuel system pressure (see Section 8).

39   Disconnect the cable from the negative battery terminal.

40   Drain the fuel into an approved fuel container by siphoning through the fuel hose at the fuel pump-to-fuel line connection. **Warn-**

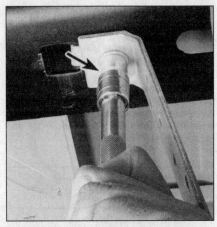

22.22 Remove the bolts from the fuel tank supports

ing: *Don't start the siphoning action by mouth - use a siphoning pump (available at most auto parts stores).*

41   Raise the rear of the vehicle and place it securely on jackstands.

42   Loosen the clamp on the fuel filler hose at the filler pipe and disconnect the hose from the pipe.

43   Remove the fuel lines and electrical connector (see Section 6).

44   Support the tank with a floor jack and wood block and remove the lower support bracket bolts or skid plate bolts (if equipped).

45   Remove the support assembly or skid plate (if equipped) attaching nut at each tank mounting strap, lower the support assemblies, and lower the tank enough to gain access to the tank vent hose.

46   Disconnect the fuel tank vent hose at the top of the tank.

47   Disconnect the fuel tank-to-fuel separator lines at the fuel tank, then remove the fuel tank from under the vehicle.

48   If the fuel tank is being replaced with a new one, remove the vapor emissions control valve by turning its retaining ring counterclockwise and pulling the unit from the tank. On metal tanks, use a brass punch to turn the retaining rings - steel tools could cause a spark.

49   Installation is the reverse of the removal procedure. On fuel-injected models, don't forget to reset the inertia switch.

23 Fuel tank - cleaning and repair

1   If a fuel tank has a build-up of sediment or rust in the bottom, it must be removed and cleaned.

2   When the tank is removed it should be flushed out with hot water and detergent or, preferably, sent to a radiator shop for chemical flushing.

3   **Warning:** *Never attempt to weld, solder or make any type of repairs on an empty fuel tank. Leave this work to a qualified repair shop.*

4   Plastic fuel tanks are not repairable - they must be replaced with new ones in the event of damage.

5   The use of a chemical type sealant for on-vehicle repairs is advised only in case of emergency; the tank should be removed and sent to a shop for more permanent repairs as soon as possible.

6   Never store a gas tank in an enclosed area where gas fumes could build up and cause an explosion and/or fire.

24 Exhaust system - general information

1   The exhaust systems employed on the vehicles covered in this manual vary according to the engine, wheelbase, gross vehicle weight and emissions systems incorporated. Most vehicles employ a catalytic converter in their emissions control system (see Chapter 6), and all vehicles employ a single muffler and tailpipe.

2   Retention and alignment of the exhaust system is maintained through a series of metal and rubber clamps and metal brackets and some systems, those in which excessive

exhaust temperatures are created as a result of the insulation of emissions control equipment, are equipped with heat shields.

3   Due to the high temperatures inherent in exhaust system operation, any attempt to inspect or repair it should be done only after the entire system has cooled, a process which may take several hours.

25 Exhaust system - component replacement

1   See and perform the operations outlined in Chapter 1, *Exhaust system - inspection.*

2   If your inspection reveals the exhaust system, or portions of it need to be replaced, first secure the proper parts needed to repair the system. The components of the exhaust system can generally be split at their major divisions such as the inlet pipe from the muffler or the muffler from the tailpipe. However, if corrosion is the cause for replacement, it will probably be necessary to replace the entire exhaust system, as follows:

3   Raise the vehicle and support it securely on jackstands.

4   Make sure the exhaust system is cool.

5   Apply some rust penetrant to the retainer bolts for the exhaust inlet pipe flange.

6   Remove the exhaust inlet pipe flange retaining nuts.

7   Remove the shields from the catalytic converter, if equipped.

8   Remove the clamps retaining the muffler or converter to the inlet pipe(s).

9   Remove the hanger supporting the muffler and/or catalytic converter from the vehicle.

10   Remove the clamps retaining the rear of the muffler to the tailpipe.

11   Remove the section(s) necessary for replacement. It may be necessary to allow the axle to hang free from the rear frame in order to get the curved section of the tailpipe over the rear axle housing. Be sure to support the vehicle's frame securely before removing the support from the axle.

12   Installation is the reverse of removal. Always use new gaskets and retaining nuts whenever the system is being replaced. It is also a good idea to use new hangers and/or retaining brackets when replacing the exhaust system.

13   Start the vehicle and check for exhaust leaks and/or rattles caused by misalignment.

Chapter 5
Engine electrical systems

Contents

Specifications

Distributor direction of rotation
Inline six-cylinder engine	Clockwise
V6 engines	Counterclockwise
V8 engines	Counterclockwise

Firing order
Inline six-cylinder inline engine	1-5-3-6-2-4
V6 engine	1-4-2-5-3-6
255, 1994 and earlier 302 (5.0L) and 460 (7.5L) cu in V8 engines	1-5-4-2-6-3-7-8
351 (5.8L), 1995 5.0L and 400 cu in V8 engines	1-3-7-2-6-5-4-8
Spark plug wire resistance	Less than 5000 ohms per inch
Ignition timing	See Chapter 1

Ignition system
Duraspark II
Coil primary resistance	0.8 to 1.6 ohms
Coil secondary resistance	7,700 to 10,500 ohms
Ballast resistor	0.8 to 1.6 ohms
Stator assembly and harness	400 to 1,300 ohms
Stator assembly	400 to 1,000 ohms

TFI-IV (DI)
Coil primary resistance	0.3 to 1.0 ohms
Coil secondary resistance	8,000 to 11,500 ohms

Charging system
Battery voltage (engine off)	12 volts
Battery voltage (engine running)	14 to 15 volts
Alternator brush length	
EVR alternator	
New	0.5 inch
Wear limit	0.25 inch
IAR (external & internal fan type)	
New	0.7 inch
Wear limit	0.17 inch

1   General information

1   The engine electrical systems include the ignition, charging and starting components. They are considered separately from the rest of the electrical system (lighting, etc.) because of their proximity and importance to the engine and its prime function in the vehicle.

2   Exercise caution when working around any of these components for several reasons. The components are easily damaged if tested, connected or stressed incorrectly. The alternator is driven by an engine drivebelt which could cause serious injury if your fingers or hands become entangled in it with the engine running. Both the starter and alternator are sources of direct battery voltage which could arc or even cause a fire if overloaded or shorted.

3   Never leave the ignition switch on for long periods of time with the engine not running. Do not disconnect the battery cable(s) while the engine is running. Be especially careful not to cross-connect battery cables from another source such as another vehicle when jump-starting.

4   Don't ground either of the ignition coil terminals, even momentarily. When hooking up a test tachometer/dwell meter to the terminal(s) of the coil, make sure it is compatible with the type of ignition system on the vehicle.

5   Additional safety-related information on the engine electrical system can be found in *Safety first* near the front of this manual. It should be referred to before beginning any operation included in this Chapter.

2   Ignition systems - description

Refer to illustrations 2.2, 2.4 and 2.6

1   In the years covered by this manual, continuing design evolution has seen three different ignition systems utilized on F-series and Bronco vehicles, each with two basic versions. In order of introduction, they are:

a) *Duraspark II and Duraspark II with MCU (Microprocessor Control Unit).*

b) *Duraspark III with remote Crankshaft Position Sensor (CPS) and Duraspark III with distributor mounted CPS (V6 engines only).*

c) *TFI-IV with distributor mounted ICM module or TFI-IV with remote mounted ICM module.*

2   The Duraspark II system is a conventional "breakerless" or "transistorized" ignition system used on all early carbureted models. This system operation was similar to an old style points and condenser system but featured lower maintenance and greater reliability. The distributor uses a stator assembly and armature for signaling the ignition electronic control module (Duraspark II module) when to open the primary coil circuit and fire the ignition. The Duraspark II system incorporates normal centrifugal and vacuum advance mechanisms in the distributor body for control of timing advance and retard under various operating conditions. The presence of a vacuum advance diaphragm on the distributor is a distinguishing characteristic of this system.

3   The Duraspark II with MCU was the first attempt at limited electronic control of ignition spark timing as used on select 4.9L engines with an early feedback control carburetor system. Under most conditions, normal centrifugal and vacuum advance mechanisms in the distributor body controlled timing advance and retard. However, under certain conditions, the MCU will exercise additional control over the ignition control module (Universal Ignition Module, UIM) and delay (retard) timing as programmed. The standard Duraspark II ignition module and the UIM are similar in appearance, but can be distinguished by the number of electrical connectors and the color of the rubber grommets used to seal the holes where the wires enter each module. The Duraspark II module has two connectors and a blue grommet while the UIM module has three connectors with a yellow grommet.

4   The Duraspark III system is an advanced electronically controlled ignition system as used on a limited basis on certain models with feedback control carburetors. The spark advance function in the Duraspark III system is entirely dependent upon the Electronic Engine Control (EEC-III) system which controls the actual primary circuit switching being done by the ignition control module (Duraspark III module). The EEC controls spark advance in response to various engine sensors, therefore, centrifugal and vacuum advance mechanisms are no longer required. On all Duraspark III systems (except the Duraspark III unit for the V6 engine) the typical "breakerless ignition" stator assembly and armature normally located within the distributor body is non-existent. Instead, a new crankshaft position sensor (CPS) mounted on the front engine cover by the damper pulley is used to signal the EEC-III computer of crankshaft position. The distributor, therefore, serves only to distribute the high voltage generated by the ignition coil. Because of this, the relationship of the distributor rotor to the cap is of special importance for proper high voltage distribution in the Duraspark III system incorporated on all engines except the V6. For this reason, the distributor is secured to the engine and the distributor rotor, rather than the distributor body, is adjustable.

5   Duraspark III application on V6 engines so equipped use a modified Duraspark II type distributor assembly. The typical "breakerless ignition" stator assembly and armature are used for crankshaft position sensing (CPS) instead of the remote mounted crankshaft position sensor used on all other Duraspark III systems. Because the timing is electronically controlled by the EEC-III computer, the distributor's centrifugal weights have been removed and very strong centrifugal springs are used to keep the sleeve and plate assembly stationary with respect to the distributor shaft. The vacuum diaphragm assembly has been replaced by a special clip that prevents movement of the stator assembly. Rotor alignment is not adjustable on this distributor and the only serviceable parts are the cap, rotor and adapter. If the distributor assembly is found to be inoperative, the distributor housing and stator assembly must be replaced as a single unit.

6   The latest ignition system is the TFI-IV (Thick-Film Integrated - EEC-IV controlled) as used initially on some feedback control carburetors but is more typically associated with electronic fuel-injected vehicles. The operation of the TFI-IV system is very similar to the EEC-III controlled Duraspark III system, however, the electronics and components are different. Ignition timing is determined by the EEC-IV systems Powertrain Control Module (PCM) which controls the primary circuit switching duties of the new Thick-Film Integration Process Ignition Control Module (ICM). The module can be located directly on the distributor (ICM module with open bowl or universal distributor) or remotely mounted (ICM with closed bowl distributor). In addition, the TFI-IV system switched from the remote mounted CPS (EEC-III) back to a distributor mounted CPS, replacing the then typical "breakerless ignition" armature and stator assembly with a new "Hall Effect" type sensor for more accurate and reliable crankshaft position sensing. The TFI-IV system was later renamed the Distributor Ignition system (DI).

7   Duraspark systems use a conventional oil filled coil, while the TFI-IV system uses a special E-core type coil. All other secondary components such as the coil high tension lead, distributor cap and spark plug wires are of standard design.

8   Due to their relative limited usage, the Duraspark II with MCU control and Duraspark III systems will not be addressed in detail in this manual.

3   Ignition systems - general checks

Refer to illustration 3.6

Warning: *Because of the very high secondary (spark plug) voltage generated by the ignition system, extreme care should be taken when this check is done. This not only includes the distributor, coil, control module and spark plug wires, but related items that are connected to the system as well, such as the plug connectors, tachometer and testing equipment.*

General checks

1   Check all ignition wiring connections for tightness, cuts, corrosion or any signs of bad connections. Repair as needed.

2   Check for poor spark plug wire connections at plugs and distributor cap, and for

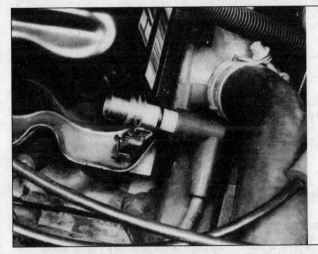

3.6 To use a calibrated ignition tester, simply disconnect a spark plug (or coil) wire, attach the wire to the tester, clip the tester to a good ground and operate the starter - if there's enough power to fire the tester, sparks will be visible

carbon deposits inside the spark plug boots.

3   If necessary, remove the spark plug wires and measure their resistance, each should be less than 30,000 ohms. Replace bad wires as required (see Chapter 1).

4   If necessary, remove and check the coil-to-distributor wire and compare it to this Chapter's Specifications. Replace the wire if required.

Calibrated ignition tester method

5   If the engine turns over but won't start, disconnect the spark plug lead from any spark plug and attach it to a calibrated ignition tester (available at most auto parts stores). Make sure the tester is designed for these ignition systems if a universal tester isn't available.

6   Connect the clip on the tester to a bolt or metal bracket on the engine **(see illustration)**, crank the engine and watch the end of the tester to see if bright blue, well-defined sparks occur.

7   If sparks occur, sufficient voltage is reaching the plug to fire it (repeat the check at the remaining plug wires to verify that the distributor cap and rotor are OK). However, the plugs themselves may be fouled, so remove and check them as described in Chapter 1 or install new ones.

8   If no sparks or intermittent sparks occur, remove the distributor cap and check the cap and rotor as described in Chapter 1. If moisture is present, dry out the cap and rotor, then reinstall the cap and repeat the spark test.

9   If there's still no spark, detach the coil wire from the distributor cap and hook it up to the tester (reattach the plug wire to the spark plug), then repeat the spark check.

10   If sparks now occur, the distributor cap, rotor, plug wire(s) or spark plug(s) or any combination may be defective. Replace as required (see Chapter 1). If the problem is a result of recent distributor removal, improper distributor installation may also be the cause (see Section 9).

11   If no sparks occur, check the primary (small) wire connections at the coil to make sure they're clean and tight.

12   If a no spark situation still occurs, review system operation information (see Section 4 or 6) and perform system checks (see Section 5 or 7). If harness repairs are necessary, see Chapter 12. If necessary, replace faulty ignition components (see Section 8), then repeat the check again.

4   Duraspark system - general description

1   The Duraspark II ignition system consists of a primary and a secondary circuit. Included in the primary circuit are the battery, ignition switch, ballast resistor, coil primary winding, ignition module and distributor stator assembly. The secondary circuit consists of the coil secondary winding, distributor rotor, distributor cap, ignition wires and spark plugs.

2   When the ignition switch is in the RUN position, primary circuit current flows from the battery, through the ignition switch, the coil primary windings, the ignition module switching circuit and back to the battery through the ignition system ground in the distributor. This current flow causes a magnetic field to be built up in the ignition coil primary circuit. It is this field, that when collapsed (current interrupted abruptly) cuts across the many windings of the secondary circuit of the coil and produces the very high voltages necessary for ignition.

3   To provide interruption of the primary circuit at the appropriate moment, the Duraspark system uses a distributor shaft mounted armature and stationary stator signal pick-up assembly. When the distributor's armature "teeth" or "spokes" approach the magnetic coil assembly (stator), a voltage is induced which signals the remotely mounted "ignition module" to turn off (open) the coil primary current. The collapsing field induces a high voltage in the coil secondary winding and the coil wire conducts the high voltage to the distributor, where the cap and rotor distribute it to the appropriate spark plug. A timing circuit in the ignition module turns the primary current back on after a short time for the next cycle.

4   The actual timing of the spark is a consequence of the position of the crankshaft (degrees before top dead center) when the armature and stator are in alignment. This relationship is influenced by only three factors, initial timing setting plus the affects of centrifugal and vacuum advance upon the initial setting. Initial timing is set by conventional means and procedure by rotation of the distributor housing. Centrifugal and vacuum advance mechanisms control the actual point of ignition based on engine speed and load. As engine speed increases, two weights move out and alter the position of the armature in relation to the distributor shaft, advancing the ignition timing. As engine load increases (when climbing hills or accelerating, for example), a drop in intake manifold vacuum causes the base plate to move slightly in the opposite direction under the action of the spring in the vacuum unit, retarding the timing and counteracting the centrifugal advance. Under light loads (moderate steady speeds, for example), the comparatively high intake manifold vacuum acting on the vacuum advance diaphragm causes the base plate assembly to move in a direction which provides a greater amount of timing advance.

5   Later models using Duraspark II with MCU control are essentially the same as the system described above except for the additional interface between the MCU and the ignition module (known as the Universal Ignition Module, UIM). This interface allows very limited electronic influence over timing.

6   On both modules, the red ignition module wire provides operating voltage for the ignition module's electronic components in the RUN mode. The white wire provides voltage for the ignition module during the START mode, while the bypass provides increased voltage for the coil during the START mode. The ballast resistor is actually a specific length of special wire, used to limit the primary ignition circuit current in the RUN mode. It is part of the vehicle wiring harness inside the passenger compartment and under no circumstances should it be cut, spliced or replaced by any other type of non-resistance wire.

7   The Duraspark III system operates very similarly to the Duraspark II system except for the primary circuit. The only operational difference is that in the Duraspark III, the distributor stator assembly (V6 only) or remote CPS (all others) signal is sent to the EEC-III computer instead of directly to the ignition module. Assuming the original timing was set correctly, this signals the EEC-III of the relative position of the crankshaft so the EEC-III can determine proper spark advance based on engine demand and calibration. The EEC-III will then signal the ignition module to interrupt primary circuit current. In all other respects, system operation of the Duraspark II and III is the same.

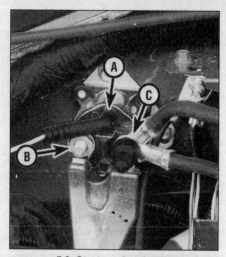

5.2 Starter relay details

A　Signal wire from ignition switch (S)
B　B+ terminal
C　Ignition enable terminal (I)

WIRE/TERMINAL	CIRCUIT	IGNITION SWITCH TEST POSITION
Red	Run	Run
White	Start	Start
"BATT" terminal of ignition coil	Ballast resistor bypass	Start

36058-5-5.6 HAYNES

5.6 Check the supply voltage circuits at the indicated locations with the ignition switch in the listed test positions

5　Duraspark system - checks

Caution: *The ignition module is a delicate and relatively expensive electronic component. The following tests must be done with the right equipment by someone that knows how to use it properly. Failure to follow the step-by-step procedures could result in damage to the module and possibly other electronic devices.* **Note:** *Perform general ignition checks (see Section 3) before entering into specific component checks.*

Module and coil bypass (START) supply voltage

Refer to illustrations 5.2 and 5.6

1　If you've been referred to this Section from the preliminary ignition system check in Section 3, remove the spark tester if you have not already done so and reconnect the coil wire to the distributor cap.

2　If the starter relay has a terminal labeled I, detach the cable from the starter relay to the starter motor **(see illustration)**. **Note:** *This disables the starter motor during ignition START tests but allows voltage bypass of ballast resistor to ignition module through the I circuit.*

3　If the starter relay doesn't have a terminal labeled I, detach the wire to the S terminal of the relay. **Note:** *This disables the starter motor during ignition START tests. Voltage bypass of ballast resistor is done at the ignition switch on these models.*

4　Check the battery voltage with a voltmeter and record it for reference later.

5　Carefully insert small straight pins into the red and white module wires **Caution:** *Don't allow the pins to ground on anything.*

6　Check the voltage at the points indicated with the ignition switch in various positions **(see illustration)**. **Note:** *Attach the negative lead of the voltmeter to the distributor base and wiggle the wires in the wiring harness*

when performing the voltage checks to test for intermittent failures.

7　If the indicated voltage readings are 90-percent of battery voltage, the supply voltage circuit is okay. Refer to Step 12.

8　If the indicated voltage readings are less than 90-percent of battery voltage, check the wiring harness and connector(s) for possible high resistance or shorts (refer to the wiring diagrams at the end of this book). Inspect the ignition switch for wear and/or damage (see Chapter 12).

9　Turn the ignition switch to the OFF position.

10　Remove the straight pins.

11　Reattach any cables/wires removed from the starter relay.

Component checks

Ignition coil (RUN) supply voltage

12　Attach the negative lead of a voltmeter to the distributor base.

13　Turn the ignition switch to the RUN position.

14　Attach the positive lead of the voltmeter to the BATT terminal on the ignition coil.

15　If the indicated voltage is between 6 to 8 volts, the circuit is okay. Proceed to Step 50.

16　If the indicated voltage is less than 6 or greater than 8 volts, check for high or low resistance in the ballast resistor.

17　Turn the ignition switch to the OFF position.

Ballast resistor

18　Separate and inspect the ignition module two-wire connector with the red and white wires.

19　Unplug and inspect the ignition coil connector.

20　Attach the leads of an ohmmeter to the BATT terminal of the ignition coil and the red wire in the module connector.

21　If the indicated resistance is the same as specified, the resistor is okay. Check for high or low primary coil resistance (see Step 24).

22　If the indicated resistance is less or more than the specified primary resistance, replace the ballast resistor and recheck ignition coil supply voltage (see Step 12).

23　Reconnect the module plug.

Ignition coil primary resistance

24　Detach the ignition coil wires.

25　Measure the primary resistance between the BATT and TACH terminals. Compare your reading with the value listed in this Chapter's Specifications.

26　If the resistance is as specified, the ignition coil primary resistance is normal. Check the primary circuit continuity (see Step 29).

27　If the indicated resistance is less or more than the specified resistance, replace the ignition coil (see Section 8) and recheck the ignition coil supply voltage (see Step 12).

28　Reconnect the ignition coil wires.

Primary circuit continuity

29　Carefully insert a small straight pin into the ignition module green wire. **Caution:** *Don't allow the straight pin to ground against anything.*

30　Attach the negative lead of the voltmeter to the distributor base.

31　Turn the ignition switch to the RUN position.

32　Measure the voltage at the green module wire.

33　If the indicated voltage is greater than 1.5 volts, the circuit is not being properly grounded by the module or the module ground circuit is faulty. To isolate, check the ignition module ground circuit (see Step 37).

34　If the indicated voltage is less than 1.5 volts, inspect the wiring harness and the connectors between the ignition module and the coil for a short circuit. After repair, repeat the ignition coil supply voltage check (see Step 12).

35　Turn the ignition switch to the OFF position.

36　Remove the straight pin.

Ignition module ground circuit

37　Carefully insert a small straight pin into the black module wire. **Caution:** *Don't allow the straight pin to ground against anything.*

38　Attach the negative lead of a voltmeter to the distributor base.

39　Turn the ignition switch to the RUN position.

40　Measure the voltage at the black wire.

41　If the voltage is greater than 0.5 volt,

check the distributor ground circuit (see Step 45).

42   If the voltage is less than 0.5 volt, circuit is okay. Since all previous checks pass, failure must be in the module - replace the ignition module (see Section 8).

43   Turn the ignition switch to the OFF position.

44   Remove the straight pin and detach the voltmeter.

Distributor ground circuit check

45   Unplug the distributor connector from the wiring harness and inspect it for dirt, corrosion and damage.

46   Attach one lead of an ohmmeter to the distributor base.

47   Attach the other lead to the black wire in the distributor connector. Measure the resistance in the distributor ground circuit. **Note:** *Wiggle the distributor grommet when making this check.*

48   If the resistance is less than 1 ohm, the distributor ground circuit is okay. Inspect the wiring harness and the connectors between the distributor and the ignition module for open. After repair, connect distributor connector and recheck ignition coil supply voltage (see Step 12).

49   If the resistance is greater than 1 ohm, check the ground screw in the distributor. After repair, plug in the distributor connector and recheck ignition coil supply voltage (see Step 12).

Stator assembly and wiring harness check

50   Unplug the ignition module four-wire connector. Inspect it for dirt, corrosion and/or damage.

51   Attach the leads of an ohmmeter to the wiring harness terminals of the orange and purple wires.

52   Measure the combined stator and harness resistance value. **Note:** *Wiggle the wires in the harness when making the check.*

53   Next, check the stator and wiring isolation to ground as follows:

54   Attach one lead of an ohmmeter to the distributor base.

55   Attach the second lead of an ohmmeter to the wiring harness terminals of the orange and purple wires one at a time.

56   If combined stator and harness resistance is as specified and stator and harness isolation is greater than 70,000 ohms, the components are okay. Check the ignition coil secondary resistance (see Step 65).

57   If stator resistance is less or more than the specified resistance and/or stator isolation resistance is less than 70,000 ohms, problem could be in harness or stator. Check the stator at the distributor connector to determine the exact problem source (see Step 58).

Stator check

58   Unplug the distributor wire harness connector. Inspect it for dirt, corrosion and damage.

59   Attach the leads of an ohmmeter to the wiring harness terminals of the orange and purple wires and record reading.

60   Next, check the stator and wiring isolation to ground as follows:

61   Attach one lead of an ohmmeter to the distributor base.

62   Attach the second lead of an ohmmeter to the wiring harness terminals of the orange and purple wires one at a time.

63   If stator resistance is less or more than the specified resistance and/or stator isolation resistance is less than 70,000 ohms, replace the stator assembly (see Section 8).

64   If the resistance is as specified, the distributor stator is okay. Inspect the wiring harness between the distributor and the ignition module for open or shorts.

Ignition coil secondary resistance check

65   Disconnect and inspect the ignition coil wires and connector.

66   Check the resistance between the BATT terminal and the center terminal of the coil.

67   If the resistance is as specified, the coil secondary circuit is normal. Check the coil TACH lead for a short to ground (see Step 70).

68   If the indicated resistance is less or more than the specified resistance, replace the ignition coil (see Section 8).

69   Reconnect the coil wires.

Ignition module-to-coil wire short check

70   Unplug and inspect the four-wire ignition module electrical connector and the ignition coil connector.

71   Connect one lead of an ohmmeter to the distributor base and the other lead to the TACH terminal of the ignition coil connector.

72   Measure the resistance between the TACH terminal of the ignition coil connector and ground.

73   If the resistance is more than 100 ohms, circuit is not shorted. Since all previous checks pass, the failure must be in the module. Replace the ignition module (see Section 8).

74   If the resistance is less than 100 ohms, the harness is shorted. Inspect the wiring harness between the ignition module and the coil. Repair as required.

75   Reattach the ignition module and coil connectors.

6   TFI-IV or DI system - general description

1   The TFI-IV ignition system (sometimes referred to as the Distributor Ignition [DI] system) consists of a primary and a secondary circuit. Included in the primary circuit are the battery, ignition switch, coil primary winding, ignition module, EEC-IV PCM (Powertrain Control Module) and the PIP (Profile Ignition Pick-up, or Hall Effect) sensor. The secondary circuit consists of the coil secondary winding, distributor rotor, distributor cap, ignition wires and spark plugs.

2   When the ignition switch is in the RUN position, primary circuit current flows from the battery, through the ignition switch, the coil primary windings, the ignition module switching circuit and back to the battery through the ignition system ground in the distributor. This current flow causes a magnetic field to be built up in the ignition coil primary circuit. It is this field, that when collapsed (current interrupted abruptly) cuts across the many windings of the secondary circuit of the coil and produces the very high voltages necessary for ignition. The ignition switch also provides operating power to the TFI-IV module (distributor mounted module systems) or to both PIP sensor and ICM (remote mounted module systems). In addition, when in the START position, the ignition switch will provide voltage to the "start" circuit of the ignition module. This signals the module to ignore PCM timing commands and revert to START mode timing. The PCM monitors the primary circuit for proper operation by tapping into and sensing the circuit between the coil and the ignition module. The Ignition Diagnostic Module portion of the PCM performs the monitoring and generates EEC-IV system trouble codes if a failure is noted.

3   The chain of events leading to the interruption of the primary circuit begins at the TFI-IV distributor. The operation of the TFI-IV distributor is accomplished through the Hall Effect vane switch stator assembly. The vane switch unit consists of a distributor shaft mounted rotary vane with a stationary Hall sensor on one side of the vane and a magnet on the other. The vane is made of ferrous material with small symmetrically positioned windows cut out. Each window represents a cylinder in the engine, therefore, a six-cylinder engine will have six windows. When a vane passes through the gap between the Hall sensor and the magnet, the magnetic field produced by the magnet is shunted (magnetically shorted). The Hall device is very sensitive to magnetic fields and senses this change and switches the supply voltage circuit on. This voltage is constantly being monitored by the PCM. When a window appears (as when the distributor turns the rotary vane) the magnetic field is again subjected to the hall sensor. The sensor reacts by switching the supply voltage off. Assuming the original timing was set correctly, this voltage drop signals the PCM of the relative position of the crankshaft. In effect, the Hall effect sensor (or PIP sensor) acts as a electronic crankshaft position sensor by producing a (PIP) Profile Ignition Pick-up signal to the PCM. In addition to providing crankshaft position information, the PCM counts the number of PIP signals in a given time interval to determine engine RPM.

4   With this information, the PCM can determine proper spark advance based on engine demand and calibration. After processing PIP and other sensor input, the PCM returns a Spark Output (SPOUT) signal to the ignition module. The ignition control module

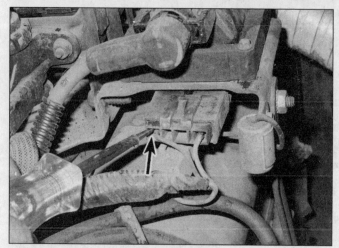

7.3 To determine an initial diagnosis, connect a test light to the coil negative (TACH) lead and ground other end, crank the engine and observe the light - it should flash as the primary circuit is alternately grounding and opening

7.10 Measuring the ignition coil primary resistance (TFI-IV or DI)

(ICM) promptly responds by electronically interrupting the primary coil circuit voltage. The high voltage distribution from the coil is accomplished through a conventional rotor, cap and ignition wires. If no SPOUT signal is received from the PCM, the ignition module will revert to a fail-safe mode and use the unconditioned PIP signal as the timing signal. Therefore, the PIP signal is wired to the PCM and ignition module. No timing advance beyond the initial timing setting is possible while in fail-safe mode.

5   All TFI-IV distributors are equipped with a gear-driven distributor with a die-cast base housing a "Hall Effect" vane switch stator assembly and a device for fixed octane adjustment. The original Thick Film Integrated IV (TFI-IV) ignition module is housed in a molded thermoplastic box mounted on the base of the distributor. Later model modules are housed in an aluminum-bodied heat sink assembly and mounted to the fender. These new modules were renamed to Ignition Control Module (ICM). In addition, the TFI-IV/EEC-IV type distributor has neither a centrifugal nor a vacuum advance mechanism (advance is handled by the computer instead).

7   TFI-IV or DI system - checks

Caution: *The ignition module is a delicate and relatively expensive electronic component. The following tests must be done with the right equipment by someone that knows how to use it properly. Failure to follow the step-by-step procedures could result in damage to the module and/or other electronic devices, including the EEC-IV microprocessor itself. Additionally, many ignition systems components are covered by a Federally mandated extended warranty (5 years or 50,000 miles at the time of this writing). Check with your dealer service department before attempting to diagnose them yourself to see if your vehicle qualifies.*

Preliminary checks

EEC-IV voltage supply check

Caution: *To assure accurate diagnosis and prevent component damage, review Chapter 4, Section 16 for general check and measurement procedures that are applicable.*
Note: *Perform general ignition checks (see Section 3) before entering into specific component checks.*
1   Turn key to RUN position and listen carefully for the fuel pump - it should run for about one or two seconds and then shut off. If the fuel pump is heard, the EEC-IV PCM is getting voltage. If no sound is heard, see Chapter 4 for the EEC-IV power check procedure.

Ignition problem symptoms

Refer to illustration 7.3
2   Unplug the electrical connector from the ignition control module (ICM). Inspect it for dirt, corrosion and damage, then plug it back in.
3   Attach a 12 volt DC test light between the coil TACH terminal and a good engine ground **(see illustration)**. Crank the engine and observe the test light.
4   Remove the test light.

Symptom 1
5   If the light flashes brightly (primary circuit operating okay) but there is still no spark at the coil wire, the problem is probably a bad coil (shorted primary or open/shorted secondary). Check the coil resistance (see Steps 8 and 13).

Symptom 2
6   If light comes on brightly but doesn't flash, the problem is in the primary circuit (open from TACH to module) or ignition control module (stuck open transistor). Check primary circuit harness continuity from TACH to ignition module first (see Step 16).

Symptom 3
7   If the light stays off or is very dim, the problem is either a voltage supply problem, short or open harness circuits, or electronics (no electronic switching). Electronic problems could be bad ICM, no PIP signal (PIP sensor), or no SPOUT signal (EEC-IV PCM). Check coil supply voltage first (see Step 21).

Ignition systems checks

Note: *Unless otherwise specified, use the distributor housing for all ground measurements.*

Ignition coil primary resistance
Refer to illustration 7.10
8   Turn the ignition switch to Off.
9   Unplug the ignition coil wire harness connector. Inspect it for dirt, corrosion and damage.
10   Measure the resistance between the primary terminals of the ignition coil **(see illustration)**.
11   If the indicated resistance is within the specified limits, primary side of coil is okay. Reconnect ignition coil connector and proceed to secondary resistance check (see Step 13).
12   If the indicated resistance is less or more than specified, replace the ignition coil (see Section 8) and perform general ignition checks (see Section 3).

Ignition coil secondary resistance check
Refer to illustration 7.13
13   Measure the resistance from the negative primary terminal to the secondary terminal of the ignition coil **(see illustration)**.
14   If the indicated resistance is within the specified limits, secondary side of coil is okay. Proceed as follows:

a)   *If checking for symptom 1, reconnect the ignition coil connector and return to general ignition checks for closer examination of checks (see Section 3).*

7.13 Measuring the ignition coil secondary resistance (TFI-IV or DI)

36058-5-7.12 HAYNES

7.17 Use this diagram for determining the location of pins when checking circuits going into the ignition control module - view is looking into the harness side connector for the ICM (TFI-IV or DI)

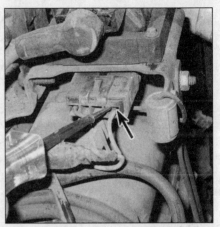

7.23 Checking ignition coil supply voltage with a test light (TFI-IV or DI)

b) *If checking for symptom 3, proceed to primary circuit continuity check (see Step 16).*

15   If the indicated resistance is less or more than the specified resistance, replace the ignition coil (see Section 8) and perform general ignition checks (see Section 3).

Primary circuit continuity check

Refer to illustration 7.17

16   Unplug the wiring harness connector from the ignition module and unplug the ignition coil wire harness. Inspect both connectors for dirt, corrosion and damage.

17   Check resistance from coil harness connector terminal TACH (coil negative) to module harness connector pin 2 (**see illustration**). Measurement should be less than 5 ohms. If greater, service open circuit in harness and perform general ignition checks (see Section 3).

18   Check resistance between coil harness connector terminal TACH (coil negative) to ground. Measurement should be greater than 10,000 ohms. If the resistance is lower, repair the short in the harness and perform the general ignition system checks (see Section 3).

19   Check for stray voltage at module harness connector pin 2. No voltage should be indicated. If voltage is indicated, service short to power in harness and perform general ignition checks (see Section 3).

20   If all continuity checks pass, proceed as follows;

a) *If checking for symptom 2, replace the ignition module (see Section 8) and perform the general ignition system checks (see Section 3).*

b) *If checking for symptom 3, proceed to the ignition control module supply voltage checks (see Step 25).*

Ignition coil supply voltage

Refer to illustration 7.23

21   This check can be performed with a test light, although a more accurate check can be made with a voltmeter.

22   Turn the ignition switch to the RUN position.

23   Measure the voltage at the positive terminal (coil +) of the ignition coil (**see illustration**). Voltage should be 90-percent of battery voltage. If correct voltage is indicated, check coil primary circuit (see Step 8).

24   If the indicated voltage is less than 90-percent of battery voltage, repair the circuit between the ignition coil and the ignition switch (refer to the wiring diagrams at the end of the book) and perform the general ignition system checks (see Section 3).

Ignition control module supply voltage check

Refer to illustration 7.32

25   Unplug the wiring harness connector from the ignition module. Inspect it for dirt, corrosion and damage.

26   Attach the negative lead of a voltmeter to the distributor base.

27   Turn the ignition switch to the RUN position and measure the voltage at connector pin 2 and 3 vehicle harness side (**see illustration 7.17**).

28   Disconnect S wire on the starter relay (disable the starter motor) (**see illustration 5.2**), turn the ignition switch to the START position and measure the voltage at pin 3 again.

29   Turn the ignition switch to START and

measure for voltage this time at connector pin 4 (**see illustration 7.17**).

30   Turn the ignition switch to the OFF position.

31   Reconnect the S wire at the starter relay and reconnect the module connector.

32   If the voltages are 90% of battery voltage in positions indicated (**see illustration**), circuits are okay. Proceed as follows:

a) *If system is remote mounted ICM, proceed to ignition control module ground check (remote mounted only) (see Step 34).*

b) *If systems is distributor mounted ICM, proceed to PIP check (distributor mounted ICM) (see Step 41).*

33   If any voltage is less than 90-percent of battery voltage, service ICM power circuits to the ignition switch for opens/shorts and perform general ignition checks (see Section 3).

Ignition control module ground check (remote mounted only)

Refer to illustration 7.38

34   Unplug the wiring harness connector from the ignition module. Inspect it for dirt, corrosion and damage.

35   Measure the resistance from pin 1 of the module electrical connector (**see illustration 7.17**) to a good ground on the distributor housing. **Note:** *The grounding end of this circuit is not attached directly to ground, but*

Connector Terminal	Wire/Circuit	Ignition Switch Test Position
Number 2	To ignition coil (–) terminal	Run
Number 3	Run circuit	Run and Start
Number 4	Start circuit	Start

36074-5-7.29 HAYNES

7.32 Check the supply voltage circuits at the designated ignition module connector locations with the ignition switch in the indicated positions (TFI-IV or DI)

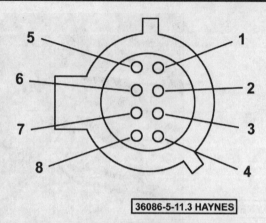

36086-5-11.3 HAYNES

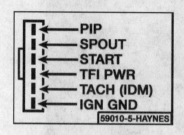

59010-5-HAYNES

7.38 On TFI-IV systems with a remote mounted ICM, use this diagram for determining the location of pins when checking circuits going into the distributor - view is looking into the harness side connector for the distributor PIP sensor

7.41 On the distributor-mounted ICM system, use a small pin to penetrate the insulation and tap into the wire from the PIP out terminal from the ICM - don't allow the pin to accidentally ground out to anything

rather through the PIP sensor stator assembly (in the distributor) and then to ground.

36   If the measured resistance is less than 5 ohms, the circuit is okay. Proceed to the PIP sensor check (remote mounted ICM) (see Step 44).

37   If the resistance is significantly greater than 5 ohms, there is a high resistance somewhere in the module-to-distributor harness (ICM pin 1-to-PIP pin 6), or within the distributor where the PIP sensor is attached (grounded) to the distributor housing.

38   To isolate the problem, disconnect the PIP connector at the distributor and check the resistance from the distributor pin 6 **(see illustration)** to the distributor housing.

39   If resistance is greater than 5 ohms, check the PIP sensor screws for tightness. If the screws are clean and tight, the PIP sensor has an open ground circuit - replace the PIP sensor (see Section 8) and perform the general ignition system checks (see Section 3).

40   If the resistance is less than 5 ohms, the problem is in the harness. Repair the cause of high resistance in the harness. After repair, perform the general ignition system checks (see Section 3).

PIP stator sensor checks (distributor mounted ICM)

Refer to illustration 7.41

Note: *The following procedure begins with a direct measurement for presence of the PIP signal. An alternative method is to perform the EEC-IV self-checks as outlined in Chap-ter 4, Section 14. Continuous trouble codes 14 or 211 indicate a failure in the PIP circuit. If a code is present, follow the remaining part of this procedure to isolate problem area.*

41   Verify all ignition systems connectors are installed. Near the ignition module connector, tap into PIP signal wire by using a small tailors pin to penetrate the insulation of the wire coming out of connector pin 6 of the module connector (PIP out signal) **(see illustration)**. Do

not allow the pin to ground on anything.

42   Prepare to measure the PIP sensor alternating current (AC) output voltage from wire tap to the battery negative post.

43   Crank the engine and observe the AC voltage. Voltage should indicate between 3.0 to 8.5 volts AC. If the voltage is within limits, proceed to the PCM module check (SPOUT).

PIP stator sensor checks (remote mounted ICM)

Note: *The following procedure performs a direct measurement for presence of the PIP signal. An alternative method is to perform the EEC-IV self-checks as outlined in Chapter 4, Section 14. Continuous trouble codes 14 or 211 indicate a failure in the PIP circuit. If a code is present, follow the remaining part of this procedure to isolate the problem area.*

44   Disconnect the distributor electrical connector and check for PIP sensor supply voltage at pin 8 **(see illustration 7.38)** with the key in the RUN position. Battery voltage should be indicated.

45   Disconnect the S wire on the starter relay (disable the starter motor) and again check for PIP sensor supply voltage at pin 8 with the key in the START position. Battery voltage should be indicated.

46   If no voltage or low voltage is indicated, repair the circuit to the ignition switch for opens or shorts and perform the general ignition system checks (see Section 3). If the checks pass, reconnect the S wire on the relay and proceed to the next step.

47   Verify all ignition systems connectors are installed. Near the distributor connector, tap into the PIP signal wire by using a small pin to penetrate the insulation of the wire coming out of connector pin 1 **(see illustration 7.38)** of distributor connector (PIP out signal). Do not allow the pin to short to anything.

48   Prepare to measure PIP sensor AC output voltage from the wire tap to the battery negative post.

49   Crank the engine and observe the volt-

age - it should indicate between 3.0 to 8.5 volts AC.

50   To help isolate the problem, disconnect the EEC-IV PCM connector at the PCM (see Chapter 4, Section 16 if required) and repeat the test.

51   If the voltage is now within limits, the PCM is shorting the PIP signal and probably should be replaced. At this point it would be a good idea to have your dealer service department check the vehicle, since they can try a new PCM module (which may or not be the problem) without having to buy one yourself.

52   If voltage is still not within limits, disconnect the ignition module connector and repeat the test.

53   If voltage is now within limits, the ICM is shorting the PIP signal. Replace the ICM (see Section 8) and perform the general ignition system checks (see Section 3).

54   If the voltage is still not within limits, proceed with the harness checks as follows:

55   Measure the resistance between module pin 6 **(see illustration 7.17)** and distributor pin 1 **(see illustration 7.38)**. Resistance should be less than 5 ohms.

56   Measure the resistance between module pin 6 and ground. Resistance should be greater than 10,000 ohms.

57   If any resistance measurements fail, repair the appropriate circuits for shorts or opens and perform the general ignition system checks (see Section 3).

58   If no problems can be found, and voltage is still not within limits, replace the PIP sensor stator assembly (see Section 8) and perform the general ignition system checks (see Section 3).

Ignition control module checks (distributor-mounted only)

Refer to illustration 7.60

Note: *This check only verifies PIP sensor circuit continuity through the module and is not a complete test of the electronic function of the module. Since the remote mounted mod-*

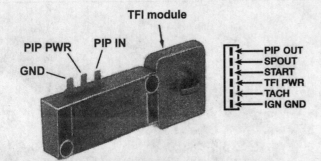

Measure between:	Resistance should be:
PIP IN and PIP OUT	Less than 150 ohms
PIP PWR and TFI PWR	Less than 150 ohms
GND and PIP IN	Greater than 500 ohms
GND and IGN GND	Less than 5 ohms
PIP PWR and PIP IN	Between 900 and 1.5k ohms

36058-5-7.60 HAYNES

7.60 On the distributor mounted ICM, test ICM module-to-PIP continuity by performing resistance measurements as shown - if out of specification, replace the module

ule has no PIP throughput signals, no checks are required.
59   Remove module from distributor (see Section 8).
60   Perform the module pin-to-pin resistance measurements **(see illustration)**.
61   If the module fails any test, install a new module on the distributor (see Section 8) and perform the general ignition system checks (see Section 3).
62   If the module passes, the PIP sensor must not be generating a signal (see the PIP sensor checks). Check the PIP sensor screws for tightness. If the screws are clean and tight, replace the PIP sensor stator assembly and reinstall the original ignition module (see Section 8).

PCM module check (SPOUT)

Note: *The following procedure begins with a direct measurement for presence of the SPOUT signal. An alternative method is to perform EEC-IV self-checks as outlined in Chapter 4, Section 14. Continuous trouble codes 18 and 212 or running codes 18 or 213 indicate a failure in the SPOUT circuit. If a code is present, follow the remaining part of this procedure to isolate the problem area.*
63   Verify all ignition systems connectors are installed. Near the ignition module connector, tap into the SPOUT signal wire by using a small pin to penetrate the insulation of the wire coming out of pin 5 **(see illustration 7.17)** of the module connector (PIP out signal). Do not allow the pin to short to anything.
64   Prepare to measure the SPOUT sensor AC output voltage from the wire tap to the battery negative post.
65   Crank the engine and observe the voltage - the meter should indicate between 3.0 to 8.5 volts AC.
66   If voltage is within limits, the ignition control module must be faulty by process of elimination. Replace the ICM (see Section 8) and perform the general ignition system checks (see Section 3).
67   If voltage is not within limits, isolate the problem as follows:
68   Locate the SPOUT single wire connector near the ignition module and disconnect it (see Section 10). Prepare to measure the (AC) output voltage from the PCM side of the harness at the SPOUT connector and repeat the test.

69   If voltage is now within limits, the ICM is shorting the SPOUT signal. Replace the ICM (see Section 8) and perform the general ignition system checks (see Section 3).
70   If no problems could be found and the voltage is still out of range, the problem is probably the PCM module itself. At this point it would be a good idea to have your dealer service department check the vehicle, since they can try a new PCM module (which may or not be the problem) without having to buy one yourself.

8   Ignition system components - replacement

Note: *Many ignition systems components are covered by a Federally mandated extended warranty (5 years or 50,000 miles at the time of this writing). Check with your dealer service department before replacing components to see if your vehicle qualifies. Also, on vehicles with Electronic Engine Control (EEC), when the battery is disconnected, the Powertrain Control Module (PCM) loses it's memory and some abnormal driving symptoms may result for the first 10 miles or so until the PCM relearns its adaptive strategy.*

Duraspark Ignition coil
1   Disconnect the negative battery cable from the battery.
2   Using coded strips of tape, mark each of the wires at the coil to help return the wires to their original positions during reinstallation.
3   Remove the coil-to-distributor high-tension lead.
4   Remove the connections at the coil. On electronic ignitions, these connections may be of the push-lock connector type. Separate them from the coil by releasing the tab at the bottom of the connector.
5   Remove the retaining bolt(s) holding the coil bracket to the cylinder head or intake manifold.
6   Remove the coil from the coil bracket by loosening the clamp bolt.
7   Installation is the reverse of removal. Apply a thin layer of silicone grease to the inside of the coil-to-distributor high-tension lead boot.

Duraspark ignition module
8   Detach the cable from the negative terminal of the battery.
9   Vehicles equipped with a Duraspark II system may have either the standard Duraspark II module or the universal ignition module. If your vehicle is equipped with the standard module, unplug both connectors. If your vehicle is equipped with the UIM module, unplug all three connectors. **Note:** *Modules are not interchangeable.*
10   Remove the mounting screws and detach the module.
11   Installation is the reverse of removal.

Duraspark, stator assembly
V8 engines
Removal
12   Remove the cable from the negative battery terminal.
13   Disconnect the spring clips retaining the distributor cap to the adapter and place the cap and wires aside.
14   Remove the rotor from the distributor shaft.
15   Disconnect the distributor connector from the wiring harness.
16   Disconnect the spring clips retaining the distributor cap adapter to the distributor body and remove the cap adjuster.
17   Using a small gear puller or two screwdrivers, remove the armature from the sleeve and plate assembly.
18   Remove the E-clip retaining the diaphragm rod to the stator assembly, then lift the diaphragm rod off the stator assembly pin.
19   Remove the screw retaining the ground strap at the stator assembly grommet.
20   Remove the wire retaining clip securing the stator assembly to the lower plate assembly.
21   Remove the grommet from the distributor base and lift the stator assembly off the lower plate assembly.

Installation
22   If the lower plate assembly is to be reused, clean the bushing to remove any accumulated dirt and grease.
23   Install the stator assembly by reversing the removal procedure. Note when installing the armature that there are two locating notches in it. Install the armature on the

8.47 To remove the TFI-IV ICM from the distributor, remove the two screws (arrows) . . .

8.48 . . . then pull the module straight down to detach the spade terminals from the PIP stator assembly - if room permits, this operation can be done with distributor still attached to the engine

sleeve and plate assembly employing the unused notch and a new roll pin.

24   Check the initial timing (see Section 10).

V6 engines

Removal

25   Disconnect the cable from the negative battery terminal.

26   Disconnect the spring clips retaining the distributor cap and place the cap and wires aside.

27   Remove the rotor from the distributor shaft.

28   Unplug the distributor connector from the wiring harness.

29   Using a small gear puller or two screwdrivers as levers, remove the armature sleeve and plate assembly.

30   Remove the two screws retaining the lower plate assembly and stator assembly to the distributor base, noting that there are two different size screws employed.

31   Remove the lower plate assembly and stator assembly from the distributor.

32   Remove the E-clip, flat washer and wave washer securing the stator assembly to the lower plate assembly, then separate the stator from the lower plate. Note the installation of the wave washer.

Installation

33   Before installing the stator, remove any accumulated dirt or grease from parts that are to be re-used.

34   Place the stator assembly on the lower plate assembly and install the wave washer (outer edges up), flat washer and E-clip.

35   Install the stator assembly/lower plate assembly on the distributor base, making sure to engage the pin on the stator assembly in the diaphragm rod.

36   Attach the lower plate assembly and stator assembly to the distributor base, making sure to install the different size screws in their proper locations.

37   When installing the armature, note that there are two notches in it. Install the armature on the sleeve and plate assembly employing

the unused notch and a new roll pin.

38   Connect the distributor connector to the wiring harness.

39   Reinstall the rotor and distributor cap, making sure that the ignition wires are securely connected to the cap and spark plugs.

40   Connect the cable to the negative battery terminal.

41   Check the initial timing (see Section 10).

TFI-IV ignition coil

42   Locate the coil assembly (usually above the valve cover or next to the distributor).

43   Unplug the electrical connector and coil wire.

44   Remove the coil retaining screws and detach the coil.

45   Installation is the reverse of removal.

TFI-IV ignition control module (distributor-mounted)

Refer to illustrations 8.47, 8.48 and 8.49

46   If necessary to gain access to remove the module, remove the distributor from the engine (see Section 9). **Note:** *On some mod-*

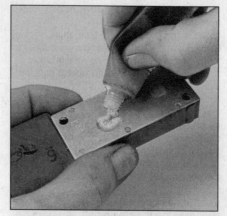

8.49 Be sure to wipe back of the ignition module clean and apply a film of dielectric grease (essential for cool operation of module) - DO NOT use any other type of grease!

els the distributor must be removed before the module can be detached because other components interfere with an on-vehicle removal.

47   Remove the two module mounting screws **(see illustration)**.

48   Pull straight down on the module to disconnect the spade connectors from the stator connector **(see illustration)**.

49   Whether you are installing the old module or a new one, wipe the back of the module clean and apply a film of silicone dielectric grease **(see illustration)**.

50   Installation is the reverse of removal. When plugging in the module, make sure that the three terminals are inserted all the way into the stator connector.

TFI-IV ignition control module (remote-mounted)

51   Locate the Ignition Control Module (ICM) in the engine compartment against the left fender apron.

52   Disconnect the electrical connector from the module.

53   Remove the heatsink-to-inner fender panel screws and remove the heatsink/module assembly.

54   Remove the two module-to-heatsink mounting screws and remove module.

55   Whether you are installing the old module or a new one, wipe the back of the module clean with a soft, clean shop rag and apply a film of silicone dielectric grease to the back side of the module **(see illustration 8.49)** .

56   Installation is the reverse of removal.

TFI-IV or DI distributor stator (PIP sensor)

Refer to illustrations 8.64, 8.66, 8.67, 8.68, 8.69, 8.70, 8.74, 8.83a and 8.83b

57   Remove the distributor cap and position it out of the way with the wires attached.

58   On distributor mounted modules, disconnect the module from the wire harness and remove module (see Steps 46 through 48).

59   Remove the distributor (see Section 9).

8.64 With the distributor housing locked securely in a vise lined with shop rags, drive out the roll pin with a 5/32-inch pin punch

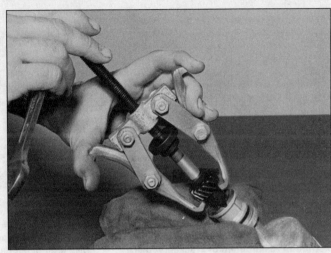

8.66 Use a small puller to separate the drivegear from the shaft

60   Remove the rotor.
61   Mark the rotary vane-to-shaft orientation and remove the screws retaining the rotary vane to the shaft. Remove the rotary vane.
62   Clamp the lower end of the distributor housing in a vise. Place a shop rag in the vise jaws to prevent damage to the distributor and don't over-tighten the vise.

63   Before removing the drivegear, note that the roll pin is slightly offset. When the distributor is reassembled, the roll pin cannot be reinstalled through the drivegear and distributor shaft holes unless the holes are perfectly lined up. Mark the orientation of the gear to the shaft for reassembly.
64   With an assistant holding the distributor

steady in the vise, use a 5/32-inch diameter pin punch to drive the roll pin out of the shaft (see illustration).
65   Loosen the vise and reposition the distributor with the drivegear facing up.
66   Remove the drivegear with a small puller (see illustration).
67   Before removing it from the distributor, check the shaft for burrs or built up residue, particularly around the drivegear roll pin hole (see illustration). If burrs or residue are evident, polish the shaft with emery cloth and wipe it clean to prevent damage to the seal and bushing in the distributor base.
68   After removing any burrs/residue, remove the shaft by gently pulling on the plate. Note the relationship of the spacer washer to the distributor base before removing the washer (see illustration).
69   Remove the octane rod retaining screw (see illustration).
70   Lift the inner end of the rod off the retaining post (see illustration) and pull the octane

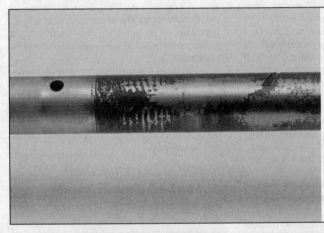

8.67 Inspect the distributor shaft for burrs or residue like this in the vicinity of the drivegear and remove it with emery cloth to prevent damage to the distributor bushings when the shaft is removed

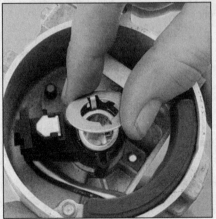

8.68 As soon as you remove the distributor shaft, note how the washer is installed before removing it (it could easily fall out and get lost)

8.69 Remove the octane rod by first removing the retaining screw then . . .

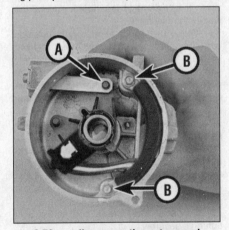

8.70 . . . disengage the octane rod (A) from the post and pull it out of the distributor - to remove the stator assembly (PIP sensor), remove both mounting screws (B) and lift the stator assembly out of the distributor (distributor-mounted module shown)

8.74 If the O-ring at the base of the distributor is hardened or cracked, replace it with a new one

8.83a If the drivegear and the shaft roll pin holes are not aligned, the roll pin cannot be installed - the drivegear will have to be pulled off the shaft and realigned

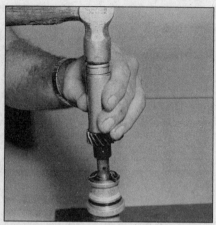

8.83b Secure the distributor in a vise, align the drivegear pin hole with the shaft hole and tap the gear onto the shaft using a deep socket and a hammer

rod from the distributor base. **Note:** *Don't lose the grommet installed in the octane rod hole. The grommet protects the electronic components of the distributor from moisture. Check the grommet for a good seal to the rod and the distributor body.*

71   Remove the stator screw(s) **(see illustration 8.70)**.

72   On distributor-mounted modules, gently lift the stator assembly straight up and remove the stator assembly from the distributor. On remote-mounted module systems, lift the stator assembly and wiring harness out as one unit.

73   Check the shaft bushing in the distributor base for wear or signs of excessive heat buildup. If signs of wear and/or damage are evident, replace the complete distributor assembly.

74   Inspect the O-ring at the base of the distributor. If it is damaged or worn, remove it and install a new one **(see illustration)**.

75   Inspect the base casting for cracks and wear. If any damage is evident, replace the distributor assembly.

76   Place the stator assembly in position over the shaft bushing and press it down onto the distributor base until it's completely seated on the posts. On stator assembly with wire harness, make sure harness grommet is properly positioned in distributor housing slot.

77   Install the stator screws and tighten them securely.

78   Insert the octane rod through the hole in the distributor base and push the inner end of the rod onto the post. **Note:** *Make sure that the octane rod hole is properly sealed by the grommet.*

79   Reinstall the octane rod screw and tighten it securely.

80   Apply a light coat of engine oil to the distributor shaft and insert the shaft through the bushing.

81   Mount the distributor in the vise with the lower end up. Be sure to line the vise jaws with a few clean shop rags to protect the dis-

tributor base. Place a block of wood under the distributor shaft to support it and prevent it from falling out while the drivegear is being installed.

82   Since the holes in the drivegear and distributor shaft are drilled off center, the gear can only be installed one way with the holes lined up.

83   Using a deep socket and hammer, carefully tap the drivegear back onto the distributor shaft **(see illustration)**. Make sure the hole in the drivegear and the hole in the shaft are lined up. Because the holes were drilled off center by the factory, they must be perfectly aligned or the roll pin cannot be installed **(see illustration)**.

84   Once the drivegear is seated and the holes are lined up, turn the distributor sideways in the vise and, with an assistant steadying it, drive a new roll pin into the drivegear. Make sure that neither end of the roll pin protrudes from the drivegear.

85   Check the distributor shaft for smooth rotation, then remove the distributor assembly from the vise.

86   On distributor-mounted ignition module systems, reinstall the TFI-IV module (see Steps 49 and 50).

87   Reinstall the rotary vane assembly.

88   Install the rotor.

89   Install the distributor (see Section 9).

90   Set the initial timing (see Section 10).

EEC-IV (PCM) module

91   See Chapter 4, Section 17 (EFI fuel system component replacement) for procedure.

---

9   Distributor - removal and installation

Refer to illustration 9.4

Removal

1   Detach the cable from the negative terminal of the battery.

2   Detach the coil secondary lead from the coil and the wires from the plugs, then remove the distributor cap from the distributor.

3   Unplug the module electrical connector. Mark and remove any vacuum lines if equipped.

4   Make a mark on the edge of the distributor housing directly below the rotor tip and in line with it. Also, mark the base of the distributor to the engine block or intake manifold to ensure that the distributor is positioned correctly upon re-installation **(see illustration)**.

5   Remove the distributor bolt and clamp, then pull the distributor straight up to remove it. Be careful not to disturb the intermediate driveshaft. **Caution:** *If the crankshaft is turned while the distributor is removed, or if a new distributor is required, the alignment marks will be useless.*

Installation (crankshaft not turned after distributor removal)

6   Insert the distributor into the engine so its mark lines up with the corresponding engine block or intake manifold mark. Due to the helical gears involved, upon initial insertion it will be necessary to position the rotor in such a way that it leads its alignment mark on the distributor housing slightly. The distributor shaft will rotate as the gears mesh, bringing the rotor and housing marks into alignment. This process may take several attempts until the correct "lead" is found.

7   If the distributor doesn't seat completely, the hex shaped recess in the lower end of the distributor shaft is not mating properly with the oil pump shaft. If this is the case, remove the distributor and use a long screwdriver (or special pump priming tool) to rotate the oil pump shaft. It shouldn't take much. Repeat Step 6 until the distributor seats properly and both distributor to engine and rotor to distributor marks are correctly aligned. Proceed to Step 12.

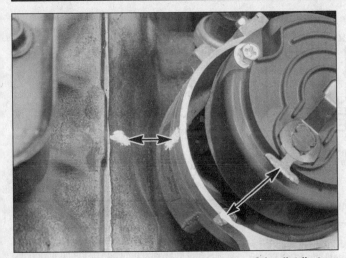

9.4 Mark the position of the rotor on the edge of the distributor housing (arrow) and make a second mark between the distributor base and engine block or intake manifold (arrow) to ensure proper reinstallation of the distributor

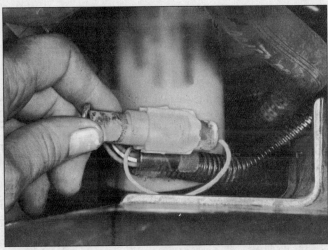

10.5 On EEC controlled ignitions (TFI-IV), locate the single wire SPOUT connector and unplug it prior to checking ignition timing - this is mandatory for accurate timing measurement

Installation (crankshaft turned after distributor removal, or new distributor)

8   See Chapter 2A or 2B and position the number one piston at TDC on the compression stroke.

9   Temporarily install the cap onto distributor and note the location of the number one spark plug wire (trace the correct wire back from the number one spark plug if necessary). Make a mark on the side of the distributor directly under the number one wire and as close to the cap as possible. Remove the cap.

10   If a new distributor is being installed, use the old distributor base mark as a reference and create a new mark in approximately the same location on the new distributor.

11   Perform Steps 6 and 7 using the new reference mark(s).

Final installation

12   With the distributor marks aligned, the rotor should be pointing at the alignment mark you made on the distributor housing, and the distributor base-to-engine block or manifold marks should be in alignment as they were before removal.

13   Place the clamp in position and loosely install the bolt.

14   Install the distributor cap and tighten the cap screws securely.

15   Plug in the module electrical connector.

16   Reattach any vacuum hoses.

17   Connect the cable to the negative terminal of the battery.

18   On Duraspark III systems (except on the V6 engine), check rotor alignment (see Section 11). If the sleeve/adapter slots cannot be aligned, pull the distributor out of the engine enough to disengage the distributor gear and rotate the shaft to engage a different distribu-

tor gear tooth with the cam gear, then reinstall the distributor.

19   Check the ignition timing (see Section 10) and tighten the distributor clamp bolt securely.

10   Ignition timing and advance - check and adjustment

Refer to illustrations 10.5 and 10.7.

Note 1: *On EEC controlled ignition systems (TFI-IV and Duraspark III) the PCM is programmed to assume the crankshaft is at specific location (degrees before top dead center) each time a PIP pulse is received from the PIP sensor. This assumed location is listed on the emissions control label for each model. All subsequent electronic control over timing is based on this assumed crankshaft position information. The following procedure can be somewhat misleading in that its purpose is not to set actual timing, but is intended to set the actual crankshaft position equal to the PCMs assumed crankshaft position. All further conditioning of the actual timing signal should therefore fall within design limits. Due to this critical requirement, Duraspark III ignition systems were designed without any capacity for timing adjustment. Later (TFI-IV) systems recognized the need to make baseline adjustments due to manufacturing tolerances.*

Note 2: *On all models, make sure to check the Vehicle Emission Control Information label on your vehicle to see if a different procedure is specified.*

Initial timing check and adjustment

1   Apply the parking brake and block the wheels. Place the transmission in PARK

(automatic) or NEUTRAL (manual). Turn off all accessories (heater, air conditioner, etc.).

2   Start the engine and warm it up. Once it has reached operating temperature, turn it off.

3   If the vehicle is an early model equipped with a Duraspark II ignition system, mark and disconnect the vacuum hose(s) from the distributor vacuum advance or combined advance/retard unit and plug the hose(s).

4   If the vehicle is an early California model with an inline six-cylinder engine with MCU-controlled Duraspark, disconnect the vacuum advance hoses and plug the hoses. Locate the Duraspark module and disconnect the Yellow and Black wire connector. Jumper the Yellow and Black wires together on the module side of the harness. **Note:** *Jumping the pins overrides the MCU-controlled timing retard circuit within the ignition module. Accurate timing measurements can only be made in this mode.*

5   If the vehicle is equipped with TFI-IV ignition system, unplug the single wire SPOUT (Spark Output) signal connector where it goes into the TFI/ICM module harness connector **(see illustration)**. Vehicles equipped with a double wire SPOUT connector incorporate a special shorting bar into the connector. If this is the case, remove the shorting bar. **Note:** *This operation disconnects the PCM's SPOUT signal to the number 5 terminal on the module. When no signal is received, the TFI-IV or ICM module reverts to a internal back-up timing mode. Accurate timing measurements can only be made in this mode.*

6   Connect an inductive timing light and a tachometer in accordance with the manufacturer's instructions. **Caution:** *Make sure that the timing light and tachometer wires don't hang anywhere near the cooling fan or they may become entangled.*

7   Locate the timing marks on the crankshaft vibration damper and timing chain

cover **(see illustration)**. Clean the marks of dirt or grease if necessary for easy identification.

8   Start the engine again and verify engine rpm is at or below timing rpm as specified on the *Vehicle Emission Control Information* label.

9   Point the light down toward the timing scale and compare your reading to the specification listed on the *Vehicle Emissions Control Information* label located in the engine compartment.

10   If the mark isn't aligned with the correct mark on the scale, loosen the distributor clamp bolt. Turn the distributor slightly clockwise or counterclockwise until the timing mark is aligned with the correct number on the timing scale. Tighten the distributor clamp bolt securely when the timing is correct and recheck it to make sure it didn't change when the bolt was tightened.

Mechanical and vacuum advance check (Duraspark II only)

11   While watching timing marks with light, increase engine speed to about 2500 rpm. Timing should advance. If not, remove the stator assembly and service stuck mechanical advance mechanism in distributor.

12   While engine is at idle, use a hand-held vacuum pump to pull vacuum on distributor vacuum advance diaphragm. Engine should speed up. Verify advanced timing with timing light. If the timing does not advance, but the diaphragm holds vacuum, service stuck distributor stator plate. If the diaphragm will not hold vacuum, replace the diaphragm. **Note:** *Dual vacuum diaphragms with timing retard port can be checked in the same manner, except engine speed should decrease when vacuum is applied to the port.*

13   Typically, with the engine at operating temperature, vacuum for advance is available at part throttle opening and vacuum for retard is available at closed throttle. Check your emissions control label for specific vacuum control details before checking.

Advance check (EEC controlled)

14   Turn off engine and reconnect the single wire SPOUT connector or install the SPOUT shorting bar.

15   Start engine and while watching timing marks, increase engine speed to about 2500 rpm. Timing should advance. If not, check the SPOUT connector for a good connection. If there's still no advance, the EEC-IV Powertrain Control Module may be malfunctioning. Take the vehicle to a dealer service department or other repair shop for further testing.

All models

16   Turn off the engine.

17   On Duraspark ignition systems, if not already done, reattach the vacuum hose(s) to the distributor advance diaphragm.

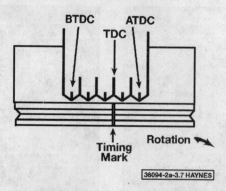

10.7 Ignition timing marks (typical)

18   On EEC controlled ignition systems, if not already done, reconnect the SPOUT connector.

19   On MCU controlled Duraspark ignition systems, remove the jumper and reconnect the electrical connector to the ignition module.

20   Restart the engine and check the idle speed. **Note:** *EEC controlled systems are equipped with automatic idle speed control - idle rpm is not adjustable. If the idle rpm is not within the specified range, review Chapter 4 for possible troubleshooting procedures or take the vehicle to a dealer service department or other repair shop.*

21   Turn off the engine.

22   Remove the timing light and tachometer.

23   Refer to Chapter 4, Section 14, and clear any trouble codes that may have been set during the procedure.

11   Duraspark III - rotor alignment

Note: *This procedure does not apply to the Duraspark III system used on V6 engines.*

1   Disconnect the spring clips retaining the distributor cap to the adapter and position the cap and wires to one side.

2   Remove the rotor from the sleeve assembly.

3   Rotate the engine until the number 1 piston is on the compression stroke (see Chapter 2, if required).

4   Slowly rotate the engine until a rotor alignment tool can be inserted in the alignment slots in the sleeve assembly and adapter.

5   Read the timing mark on the crankshaft damper indicated by the timing pointer **(see illustration 10.7)**.

6   If the timing mark reading is 0-degrees, plus or minus 4-degrees, alignment is acceptable.

7   If the timing mark reading is beyond the acceptable limit stated in Step 6, make sure the number 1 piston is on the compression stroke.

8   Slowly rotate the engine until the timing pointer aligns with the 0-degree timing mark on the crankshaft damper.

9   Loosen the two sleeve assembly adjust-

ment screws and insert the rotor alignment tool into the alignment slots in the sleeve assembly and adapter.

10   Tighten the sleeve assembly adjustment screws and remove the alignment tool.

11   Attach the rotor to the sleeve assembly.

12   Install the distributor cap and ignition wires, making sure that the ignition wires are securely connected to the cap and to the spark plugs.

12   Charging system - general information and precautions

1   The charging system includes the alternator, either an internal or an external voltage regulator, a charge indicator, the battery, a fusible link and the wiring between all the components. The charging system supplies electrical power for the ignition system, the lights, the radio, etc. The purpose of the voltage regulator is to limit the alternator's voltage to a preset value. This prevents power surges, circuit overloads, etc., during peak voltage output. The fusible link is a short length of insulated wire integral with the engine compartment wiring harness. The link is several wire gauges smaller in diameter than the circuit it protects. The alternator is driven by a drivebelt at the front of the engine.

2   The basic operation of an alternator is quite simple. The alternator consists of five main components, the stationary stator windings, the rectifier (diode) assembly, the rotating field windings (rotor), rotor brushes and the regulator. On external regulator systems (EVR), the regulator supplies voltage to the rotor windings. On later integral regulators alternators (IAR), the rotor windings are supplied voltage at one end from the battery and is shorted to ground on the other end by the voltage regulator which completes the circuit. Since the rotor must spin about its shaft, the field voltage must be applied and grounded through two shaft mounted slip rings and two isolated (housing mounted) brushes. This operation of the regulator causes current to flow through the rotors windings (field) which produces a strong magnetic field. It is the rotors magnetic field that, when rotated (alternator is turned by engine) cuts across the many windings of the stationary stator assembly, inducing a current in the stator windings. This induced current is A/C in nature and must be rectified (turned into D/C) by the rectifier assembly before being supplied to the battery. The strength of the rotor's field, and the resulting stator output current, is directly related to the relative amount of time the regulator supplies voltage (EVR) or shorts (IAR) the field circuit Verses the amount of time the regulator opens the circuit. The regulator is designed to sense the output voltage of the alternator and maintain a field current sufficient to keep the voltage output within specifications under all normal operating conditions.

3   The F-series and Bronco vehicles have utilized four different alternators over the years

covered by this manual, depending on the model and options installed. Early models used a basic external fan, rear or side terminal alternator in conjunction with a remote electronic voltage regulator. This alternator is recognizable by the EVR (external voltage regulator) being mounted on the right fender apron of the vehicle.

4   The IAR (integral alternator/regulator) external fan design followed shortly. This alternator features a built-in (integral) modular electronic regulator and modular rectifier assembly. This type can be recognized by its rear externally mounted regulator module and two plug in connectors (one into the regulator and one into the side of the alternator for the rectifier module).

5   The second IAR alternator was introduced to handle increased electrical load demands. This alternator can be most easily recognized by its internal fan design. Unfortunately, only the regulator and brush assembly can be serviced, further disassembly is not possible. Other problems (such as a diode failure) require that the entire alternator assembly be replaced. Due to this constraint, the regulator and brush holder are easily accessible from the outside of the unit.

6   The charging system doesn't ordinarily require periodic maintenance. However, the drivebelt, battery and wires and connections should be inspected at the intervals outlined in Chapter 1. Be very careful when making electrical circuit connections to a vehicle equipped with an alternator and note the following:

a) *When reconnecting wires to the alternator from the battery, be sure to note the polarity.*

b) *Before using arc welding equipment to repair any part of the vehicle, disconnect the wires from the alternator and the battery terminals.*

c) *Never start the engine with a battery charger connected.*

d) *Always disconnect both battery leads before using a battery charger.*

13 Charging system - check

1   If a malfunction occurs in the charging circuit, don't automatically assume the alternator is causing the problem. First check the following items:

a) *Check the drivebelt tension and condition (see Chapter 1). Replace it if it's worn or deteriorated.*

b) *Make sure the alternator mounting and adjustment bolts are tight.*

c) *Inspect the alternator wiring harness and the connectors at the alternator and voltage regulator. They must be in good condition and tight.*

d) *Check the fusible link (if equipped) located between the starter solenoid and the alternator. If it's burned, determine the cause, repair the circuit and replace the link (the vehicle won't start and/or the accessories won't work if the fusible link blows). Sometimes a fusible link may look*

good, but still be bad. If in doubt, remove it and check it for continuity.

e) *Start the engine and check the alternator for abnormal noises (a shrieking or squealing sound indicates a bad bearing).*

f) *Check the specific gravity of the battery electrolyte. If it's low, charge the battery (doesn't apply to maintenance free batteries).*

g) *Make sure the battery is fully charged (one bad cell in a battery can cause overcharging by the alternator).*

h) *Disconnect the battery cables (negative first, then positive). Inspect the battery posts and the cable clamps for corrosion. Clean them thoroughly if necessary (see Chapter 1). Reconnect the cable to the positive terminal.*

i) *With the key off, connect a test light between the negative battery post and the disconnected negative cable clamp.*

1) *If the test light does not come on, reattach the clamp and proceed to the next Step.*

2) *If the test light comes on, there is a short (drain) in the electrical system of the vehicle. The short must be repaired before the charging system can be checked.*

3) *Disconnect the alternator wiring harness.*

   a) *If the light goes out, the alternator is bad.*

   b) *If the light stays on, pull each fuse until the light goes out (this will tell you which component is shorted).*

2   Using a voltmeter, check the battery voltage with the engine off. It should be approximately 12-volts.

3   Start the engine and check the battery voltage again. It should now be approximately 14 to 15-volts.

4   Turn on the headlights. The voltage should drop, and then come back up, if the charging system is working properly.

5   If the voltage reading is more than the specified charging voltage, the voltage regulator is faulty (see Section 15).

6   If the voltage reading is less than the specified voltage, the alternator diode(s), stator or rectifier may be bad or the voltage regulator may be malfunctioning.

14 Alternator - removal and installation

1   Disconnect the negative battery cable.

2   Carefully note the terminal connections at the rear or side of the alternator and disconnect them. **Note:** *If there is any doubt as to where the wires go, mark them with pieces of numbered tape before disconnecting them.* Some connections will have a retaining nut and washer on them and some connections may have a plastic snap-fit connector with a retaining clip. If a terminal is covered by a slip-on plastic cover, be careful when pulling the cover back so as not to

damage the terminal or connector.

3   Remove the drivebelt (see Chapter 1).

4   Remove the alternator pivot and adjusting bolts (watch for spacers if equipped) and carefully lift the alternator up and out of the engine compartment. **Note:** *If you are purchasing a new or rebuilt alternator, take the original one with you to the dealer or parts store so the two can be compared side-by-side. Also, some replacement alternators don't come equipped with a pulley. Many auto parts stores are equipped to remove the pulley from the old alternator and install it on the new one.*

5   Installation is the reverse of removal. Be careful when connecting all terminals at the rear or side of the alternator. Make sure they are clean and tight and that all terminal ends are tight on the wires. If you find any loose terminal ends, make sure you install new ones, as any arcing or shorting at the wires or terminals can damage the alternator and could even start a fire.

6   Install alternator belt and check or adjust tension (see Chapter 1).

15 Alternator components - replacement

Note: *If an overhaul is indicated, explore all options before beginning the job. New and rebuilt alternators are available on an exchange basis, which makes the job quite easy. If it is decided to rebuild the alternator, make sure parts are available before proceeding.*

Rear terminal, external regulator alternator

Refer to illustrations 15.2, 15.5 and 15.7

Disassembly

1   Remove the alternator as described in Section 14.

2   Scribe a line across the length of the alternator housing to ensure correct reassembly **(see illustration)**.

3   Remove the housing through-bolts and the nuts and insulators from the rear housing.

15.2 Scribe a line across the alternator housing that can be used for alignment during reassembly

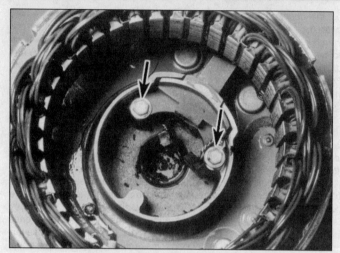

15.5 Remove the nuts securing the brush holder and remove the holder and the one brush within it

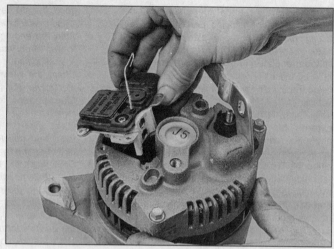

15.7 Use a piece of stiff wire inserted through the brush holder to hold the brushes in the retracted position

Make a careful note of all insulator locations.

4   Withdraw the rear housing section from the stator, rotor and front housing assembly.

Brush replacement

5   Remove the brush holder assembly from the rear housing and remove the brushes and springs **(see illustration)**.

6   Check the length of the brushes against the wear dimensions given in Specifications at the beginning of the Chapter and replace the brushes with new ones if necessary.

7   Position the rear brush wiring eyelet over the rear terminal and install the brush terminal insulator. Install the springs and brushes in the holder assembly and retain them in place by inserting a piece of stiff wire (paper clip) through the rear housing and brush terminal insulator **(see illustration)**. Make sure enough wire protrudes through the rear housing so it can be withdrawn at a later stage.

8   Position the brush holder in the rear housing and install the screws, making sure the ground brush wiring eyelet is positioned under its screw before tightening. **Note:** *Verify the brush retaining wire is accessible from the outside of the housing.* If only the brushes are being replaced, proceed to Step 14.

Rectifier or stator replacement

9   Remove the stator/rectifier assembly from the front housing and remove the radio suppression capacitor from rectifier terminals.

10   Using a soldering iron, remove the stator leads from the rectifier (if the rectifier is to be saved, be careful not to overheat it). Remove the stator phase lead by either pushing the stator terminal screw out of the rectifier (cast rectifier) or by turning the stator terminal screw 1/4-turn and removing it (fabricated rectifier).

11   Solder the new rectifier/stator together using electrical solder (do not overheat the rectifier).

12   Reinstall stator phase lead to rectifier and install radio suppression capacitor

between rectifier terminals.

13   Install the stator/rectifier assembly into the rear housing.

Reassembly

14   Attach the rear housing rotor and front housing assembly to the stator, making sure the scribed marks are aligned.

15   Install the housing through-bolts and rear end insulators and nuts but do not tighten the nuts at this time.

16   Carefully extract the piece of wire from the rear housing and make sure that the brushes are seated on the slip ring. Tighten the through-bolts and rear housing nuts.

17   Install the alternator as described in Section 14.

Side terminal, external regulator alternator

Disassembly

18   Remove the alternator as described in Section 14 and scribe a mark on both end housings and the stator for ease of reassembly.

19   Remove the through-bolts and separate the front housing and rotor from the rear housing and stator. Be careful that you do not separate the rear housing and stator.

Brush replacement

20   Use a soldering iron to unsolder and disengage the brush holder from the rear housing. Remove the brushes and springs from the brush holders.

21   Remove the two brush holder attaching screws and lift the brush holder from the rear housing.

22   Remove any sealing compound from the brush holder and rear housing.

23   Inspect the brushes for damage and check their dimensions against the Specifications. If they are worn out, replace them with new ones.

24   To reassemble, install the springs and brushes in the brush holders, inserting a piece

of stiff wire (paper clip) to hold them in place **(see illustration 15.7)**.

25   Place the brush holder in position in the rear housing, using the wire to retract the brushes through the hole in the rear housing.

26   Install the brush holder attaching screws and push the holder toward the shaft opening as you tighten the screws. If brush replacement is the only repair, proceed to Step 33.

Rectifier or stator replacement

27   Unsolder the three stator lead-to-rectifier connections (if rectifier is to be saved, do not overheat the rectifier).

28   Lift the stator windings out of the rear housing.

29   Remove the capacitor screw and four rectifier to housing screws. Remove the two external rectifier terminal nuts and isolators and lift rectifier out of rear housing. Watch for loose insulators from inside the housing.

30   Install the rectifier insulators over the mounting bosses on the inside of the rear housing and place an insulator over the large BAT terminal of the new rectifier. Install the new rectifier into rear housing. Place the outside insulator over the BAT terminal and tighten both BAT and GRD terminal nuts finger tight.

31   Install the four internal rectifier to housing screws along with the capacitor wire screw and tighten them securely.

32   Position the stator winding assembly into the rear housing and align the marks. Solder the three stator leads to the rectifier pins (do not overheat the rectifier).

Reassembly

33   Press the brush holder lead onto the rectifier pin and solder it securely (do not overheat the rectifier).

34   Place the rotor and front housing in position in the stator and rear housing. After aligning the scribe marks, install the through-bolts. Turn the fan and pulley to check for binding in the alternator.

35   Withdraw the wire that is retracting the brushes and seal the hole with waterproof

15.39 To detach the voltage regulator/brush holder assembly, remove the four screws (arrows) and withdraw the regulator from the alternator housing (IAR alternator)

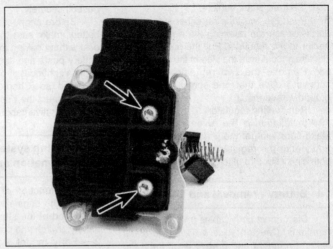

15.41 To remove the voltage regulator from the brush holder, detach the two rubber plugs (or in some cases metal tab) from the regulator and remove the two screws (arrows)

cement. **Note:** *Do not use RTV-type sealant on the hole.*

36   Install the alternator (see Section 14).

External fan, Integral regulator type alternator

Refer to illustrations 15.39, 15.41, and 15.45

Regulator or brush replacement

37   Remove the alternator (see Section 14).
38   Set the alternator on a clean workbench.
39   Remove the four voltage regulator mounting screws **(see illustration)**. **Note:** *Screws have Torx heads and require a special screwdriver.*
40   Detach the voltage regulator. If only the rectifier is to be replaced, proceed to Step 46.
41   Detach the rubber plugs and remove the brush lead retaining screws and nuts to separate the brush leads from the holder **(see illustration)**. **Note:** *These screws have Torx heads and require a special screwdriver.*
42   After noting the relationship of the brushes to the brush holder assembly, remove

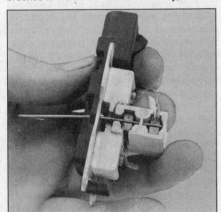

15.45 Before installing the voltage regulator/brush holder assembly, insert a paper clip as shown to hold the brushes in place during installation - after installation, remove the paper clip (IAR alternator)

both brushes. Don't lose the springs.
43   If you're installing a new voltage regulator, insert the old brushes into the brush holder of the new regulator. If you're installing new brushes, insert them into the brush holder of the old regulator. Make sure the springs are properly compressed and the brushes are properly inserted into the recesses in the brush holder.
44   Install the brush lead retaining screws and nuts.
45   Insert a short section of wire, like a paper clip, through the hole in the voltage regulator **(see illustration)** to hold the brushes in the retracted position during regulator installation. If only the voltage regulator is to be replaced, proceed to Step 55. If the rectifier needs to be replaced, continue.

Rectifier or stator replacement

46   Scribe a line across the end housings and stator laminated core for alignment reference during reassembly.
47   Remove the three through bolts.
48   Separate the front housing and rotor assembly from the stator and rear housing. It may be necessary to gently tap the front housing with a plastic mallet to aid in parting the assemblies.
49   Using a soldering iron, remove the solder from the rectifier and the stator leads. **Caution:** *If the rectifier is to be re-used, do not place the soldering iron on an individual lead for more than five seconds at a time - otherwise, the rectifier may be damaged if it's overheated.*
50   Some rectifier/stator assemblies use a spade-type connector block instead of solder. If this is the case, carefully pry the connector block from the rectifier.
51   Remove the four TORX-type rectifier attach screws and remove the rectifier from the rear housing.
52   Wipe the rear housing where the rectifier is will be located with a clean cloth and apply a 3/32-inch wide by 3/4-inch long strip of

Heat Sink Compound or equivalent dielectric grease across the base plate. **Warning:** *Failure to apply Heat Sink Compound will result in premature component failure.*
53   Clean the replacement rectifier mounting surface and seat the rectifier into the recessed mounting area and install the attach screws.
54   Reassembly up to regulator installation is reverse of removal. **Note:** *Remember to line up the scribe marks, use good electrical solder and don't overheat the rectifier leads.*

Reassembly

55   Carefully install the regulator. Make sure the brushes don't hang up on the rotor.
56   Install the voltage regulator screws and tighten them securely.
57   Remove the wire or paper clip.
58   Install the alternator (see Section 14).

Internal fan, integral regulator type alternator

Regulator or brush replacement

59   Remove the alternator (see Section 14).
60   Remove the four voltage regulator mounting screws. **Note:** *The screws have Torx heads and require a special screwdriver.*
61   Detach the voltage regulator.
62   Pry the insulating caps off of the countersunk holes containing the two regulator-to-brush block screws and remove the screws. **Note:** *The screws have Torx heads and require a special screwdriver.*
63   Install a new brush holder assembly to the regulator (or new regulator to the original brush holder). Tighten the screws securely.
64   The remaining reassembly is the reverse of removal.

External regulator replacement

65   Remove the negative battery cable from the battery.
66   Locate the voltage regulator. It will usually be positioned on the radiator wall or along the side of the engine compartment

near the front of the vehicle.

67   Push the two tabs on either side of the quick-release clip retaining the electrical connector to the regulator. Pull the quick-release clip straight out from the side of the regulator.

68   Remove the two regulator retaining screws. Notice that one screw locates the ground wire terminal.

69   Remove the regulator.

70   Installation is the reverse of removal. Make sure you get the wiring clip positioned firmly onto the regulator terminals and that both clips click into place.

16   Battery - removal and installation

1   Disconnect both cables from the battery terminals. **Caution:** *Use a battery terminal puller if required and always disconnect the negative cable first and hook it up last or the battery may be shorted by the tool being used to loosen the cable clamps.*

2   Loosen the two battery hold-down clamp nuts enough to disengage the hold-down legs from the battery tray. Remove the hold-down clamp as an assembly.

3   Lift out the battery. Special straps or clamps that attach to the battery are available - lifting and moving the battery is much easier if you use one.

4   Installation is the reverse of removal. Make sure the battery cables and battery posts are free of corrosion. Clean or replace them if necessary (see Section 17).

17   Battery cables - check and replacement

1   Periodically inspect the entire length of each battery cable for damage, cracked or burned insulation and corrosion. Poor battery cable connections can cause starting problems and decreased engine performance.

2   Check the cable-to-terminal connections at the ends of the cables for cracks, loose wire strands and corrosion. The presence of white, fluffy deposits under the insulation at the cable terminal connection is a sign that the cable is corroded and should be replaced. Check the terminals for distortion, missing mounting bolts and corrosion.

3   When replacing the cables, always disconnect the negative cable first and hook it up last or the battery may be shorted by the tool used to loosen the cable clamps. Even if only the positive cable is being replaced, be sure to disconnect the negative cable from the battery first.

4   Disconnect and remove the cable. Make sure the replacement cable is the same length and wire gauge (diameter).

5   Clean the threads of the starter relay or ground connection with a wire brush to remove rust and corrosion. Apply a light coat of petroleum jelly to the threads to prevent future corrosion.

6   Attach the cable to the starter relay or ground connection and tighten the mounting

nut/bolt securely.

7   Before connecting the new cable to the battery, make sure that it reaches the battery post without having to be stretched. Clean the battery posts and cable ends thoroughly and apply a light coat of petroleum jelly to prevent corrosion (see Chapter I).

8   Connect the positive cable first, followed by the negative cable.

18   Starting system - general information and precautions

1   The function of the starting system is to crank the engine to start it. The system is composed of the starter motor, starter relay, battery, switch and connecting wires.

2   Early model starters used a positive engagement drive mechanism and a moveable pole shoe activated by the field coils of the motor to engage the drive. Turning the ignition key to the START position actuates a fender-mounted, high-amperage starter relay through the starter control circuit. The starter relay then connects the battery to the starter. The battery supplies the electrical energy to the starter motor, which does the actual work of cranking the engine.

3   Later models followed with the industry standard by incorporating the high amperage relay into a more conventional starter motor solenoid/relay design. Although the remote relay is retained, it acts only as 1) a simple relay connecting battery voltage to the starter solenoid when the key is turned to start, and 2) as a terminal block for various connectors. Once actuated, the starter motor solenoid physically drives the high amperage relay contacts together and completes the starter motor circuit as well as engage the drive. The fender mounted relay does make the job of remote starting or "bumping" much easier, however.

4   Vehicles equipped with an automatic transmission have a Neutral Start switch in the Starter control circuit, which prevents operation of the starter unless the shift lever is in NEUTRAL or Park. The circuit on vehicles with a manual transmission prevents operation of the starter motor unless the clutch pedal is depressed.

5   Never operate the starter motor for more than 15 seconds at a time without pausing to allow it to cool for at least two minutes. Excessive cranking can cause overheating, which can seriously damage the starter.

19   Starter motor and circuit - checks

Refer to illustrations 19.3 and 19.4

1   If a malfunction occurs in the starting circuit, do not immediately assume that the starter is causing the problem. First, check the following items:

a)   *Make sure that the battery cable clamps are clean and tight where they connect to the battery.*

b)   *Check the condition of the battery cables*

19.3 To use an inductive ammeter, simply hold the ammeter over the positive or negative battery cable (whichever cable has better clearance)

(see Section 4). Replace any defective battery cables with new parts.

c)   *Test the condition of the battery (see Section 3). If it does not pass all the tests, replace it with a new battery.*

d)   *Check the starter solenoid wiring and connections. Refer to the wiring diagrams at the end of Chapter 12.*

e)   *Check the starter mounting bolts for tightness.*

f)   *Make sure that the shift lever is in PARK or NEUTRAL (automatic transaxle) or the clutch pedal is pressed (manual transaxle). Make sure that the Neutral start switch is correctly adjusted.*

g)   *Check the operation of the starter relay. Refer to Chapter 12 for the relay testing procedure.*

2   If the starter does not actuate when the ignition switch is turned to the start position, check for battery voltage to the solenoid. This will determine if the solenoid is receiving the correct voltage signal from the ignition switch. Connect a test light or voltmeter to the starter solenoid positive terminal and while an assistant turns the ignition switch to the start position. If voltage is not available, refer to the wiring diagrams in Chapter 12 and check all the fuses and relays in series with the starting system. If voltage is available but the starter motor does not operate, remove the starter from the engine compartment (see Section 13) and bench test the starter (see Step 4).

3   If the starter turns over slowly, check the starter cranking voltage and the current draw from the battery. This test must be performed with the starter assembly on the engine. Crank the engine over (for 10 seconds or less) and observe the battery voltage. It should not drop below 8.0 volts on manual transaxle models or 8.5 volts on automatic transaxle models. Also, observe the current draw using an ammeter **(see illustration)**. It should not exceed 400 amps or drop below 250 amps. **Caution:** *The battery cables might overheat because of the large amount of current being drawn from the battery. Discon-*

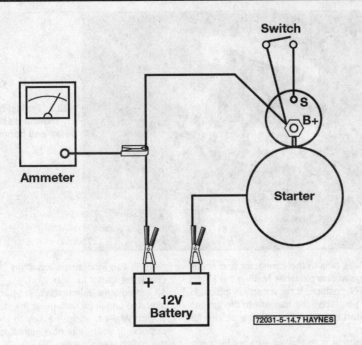

19.4 Starter motor bench testing details

tinue the testing until the starting system has cooled down. If the starter motor cranking amp values are not within the correct range, replace it with a new unit. There are several conditions that may affect the starter cranking potential. The battery must be in good condition and the battery cold-cranking rating must not be under-rated for the particular application. Be sure to check the battery specifications carefully. The battery terminals and cables must be clean and not corroded. Also, in cases of extreme cold temperatures, make sure the battery and/or engine block is warmed before performing the tests.

4   If the starter is receiving voltage but does not activate, remove and check the starter/solenoid assembly on the bench. Most likely the solenoid is defective. In some rare cases, the engine may be seized so be sure to try and rotate the crankshaft

pulley (see Chapter 2) before proceeding. With the starter/solenoid assembly mounted in a vise on the bench, install one jumper cable from the negative battery terminal to the body of the starter. Install the other jumper cable from the positive battery terminal to the B+ terminal on the starter. Install a starter switch and apply battery voltage to the solenoid S terminal (for 10 seconds or less) and see if the solenoid plunger, shift lever and overrunning clutch extends and rotates the pinion drive **(see illustration)**. If the pinion drive extends but does not rotate, the solenoid is operating but the starter motor is defective. If there is no movement but the solenoid clicks, the solenoid and/or the starter motor is defective. If the solenoid plunger extends and rotates the pinion drive, the starter/solenoid assembly is working properly.

20   Starter - removal and installation

Refer to illustrations 20.3, 20.4 and 20.5

1   Disconnect the negative battery cable from the battery.
2   Raise the vehicle and support it securely on jackstands.
3   Disconnect the battery cable from the starter motor and the starter relay wire, if equipped **(see illustration)**.
4   Remove the retaining bolts securing the starter to the bellhousing **(see illustration)**.
5   Pull the starter out and lower it from the vehicle **(see illustration)**.
6   Installation is the reverse of removal. When inserting the starter into its opening of the bellhousing, make sure it is situated squarely and the mating faces are flush. Make sure solenoid heat shield is reinstalled, if equipped. Tighten the retaining bolts securely.

21   Neutral safety switches - check and replacement

1   The purpose of the Neutral safety switch is to prevent accidental starting of the engine while the vehicle is in gear. The switch interrupts the Start circuit between the ignition key and the starter relay. Manual transmission switches are actuated (closed) by the clutch pedal assembly only when the clutch if fully depressed. Automatic transmission switches are actuated (closed) by the shift selector lever only when the lever is in the PARK or NEUTRAL position. There are two types of manual switches; clutch pedal mounted (early models) and clutch master cylinder mounted (later models). There are three types of automatic transmissions switches, one type for the E4OD transmission, a second type for the C-series transmissions and a third for the AOD transmission. The AOD switch is non-adjustable as is the later model manual switch. All other switch adjustments are documented in Chapter 7A or 7C. **Note:** *The following checks assume that a no-volt situation exists at starter relay S wire when key is turned to START position and battery is fully charged.*

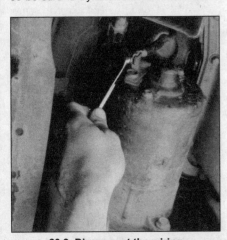

20.3 Disconnect the wiring from the starter . . .

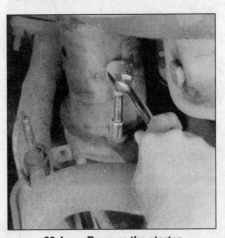

20.4 . . . Remove the starter mounting bolts . . .

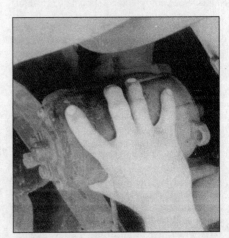

20.5 . . . and guide the starter out; be careful - it's heavy!

Manual transmission

Early models

2   Locate the switch on the clutch pedal (see Chapter 7A if necessary). Disconnect the electrical connector and check for voltage at one pin while holding the key in the START position. If no voltage is indicated at either pin, repair the harness to the ignition switch Start circuit and check the starter for operation.

3   If voltage is indicated, jumper between pins and check for voltage at the starter relay S wire while the holding the key in the START position. If voltage is now indicated, replace the switch and adjust it (see Chapter 7A).

Later models

4   From inside the cab, locate the switch on the clutch master cylinder actuator shaft. Disconnect the electrical connector and check for voltage at one of the R/LB colored wires while holding the key in the START position. If no voltage is indicated at either R/LB wire pins, repair the harness to the ignition switch Start circuit and check the starter for operation.

5   If voltage is indicated, jumper between pins and check for voltage at starter relay S wire while holding the key in the START position. If voltage is now indicated, replace the switch (see Chapter 7A).

Automatic transmission

C-Series and E4OD transmissions

6   Raise the vehicle and support securely on jackstands.

7   Locate the PARK/NEUTRAL position switch on the drivers side of the transmission (see Chapter 7B if necessary) and disconnect the electrical connector.

8   Locate the two R/LB or W/PK and R/LB

22.2 Typical fender-mounted starter relay and connections

colored wire pins in the connector and check for voltage at one pin while holding the key in the START position. If no voltage is indicated at either pin, repair the harness to the ignition switch Start circuit and check the starter for operation.

9   If voltage is indicated, jumper between pins and check for voltage at the starter relay S wire while holding the key in the START position. If voltage is now indicated, replace the switch and adjust it (see Chapter 7B).

AOD transmission

10   Raise the vehicle and support it securely on jackstands.

11   Locate the switch on the drivers side of the transmission above the selector lever (see Chapter 7B if necessary) and disconnect the electrical connector.

12   Check for voltage at one pin while the holding key in the START position. If no voltage is indicated at either pin, service the har-

ness to the ignition switch Start circuit and check the starter for operation.

13   If voltage is indicated, jumper between pins and check for voltage at the starter relay S wire while holding the key in the START position. If voltage is now indicated, replace the switch (see Chapter 7B).

22 Starter relay - replacement

Refer to illustration 22.2

1   Detach the cable from the negative terminal of the battery.

2   Label the wires and the terminals, then disconnect the Neutral safety switch wire (automatics only), the battery cable, the fusible link and the starter cable from the relay terminals **(see illustration)**.

3   Remove the mounting bolts and detach the relay.

4   Installation is the reverse of removal.

Chapter 6
Emissions control systems

Contents

Specifications

Torque specifications
Ft-lbs (unless otherwise indicated)

Note: *One foot-pound (ft-lb) of torque is equivalent to 12 inch-pounds (in-lbs) of torque. Torque values below approximately 15 ft-lbs are expressed in inch-pounds, since most foot-pound torque wrenches are not accurate at these smaller values.*

Air pump pulley bolts	120 to 150 in-lbs
Air pump mounting bolt	25
EGR valve mounting bolts	15 to 22
EGR tube to EGR valve	26 to 48

1 General information

Refer to illustrations 1.1 and 1.10

1   To prevent pollution of the atmosphere from incompletely burned and evaporating gases, and to maintain good driveability and fuel economy, a number of emission control systems are incorporated **(see illustration)**. The systems can be divided into two types, passive and active.

2   Passive systems operate without any outside control. Passive systems include:

Positive Crankcase Ventilation (PCV) system
Catalytic converter
Intake manifold heating system

3   The operation of active systems is under some form of open or closed-loop control. Active systems include:

Exhaust Gas Recirculation (EGR) system
Thermactor systems (secondary air injection)
Fuel evaporative emission control system
Inlet air temperature control system
Deceleration throttle control system
Spark control system
Fuel delivery system (refer to Chapter 4)

4   Depending on the year, the control of active systems may function autonomously or be linked, directly or indirectly, to an Electronic Engine Control system. Carbureted models without feedback control utilize active systems

that operate independent of any electronic control. Each has its own set of mechanical or electromechanical devices which, under a very limited set of conditions, control the operation of that particular emission control system without regard to the others.

5   Increasingly tighter pollution control standards demanded emission control systems which were much more responsive to the many specific emissions producing operating conditions that the vehicle would experience. In addition, due to the effects of one system upon another, an integrated architecture and control system was required to properly consolidate and manage the operation of all the systems. The solution was the introduction of Electronic Engine Control (EEC).

EMISSIONS AND ELECTRONIC ENGINE CONTROLS - 1990 5.0L ENGINE SHOWN

1. Manifold Absolute Pressure (MAP) sensor
2. Thermactor Air Bypass (TAB) solenoid
3. EGR Valve Position (EVP) sensor
4. Throttle Position Sensor (TPS)

5. Idle air bypass valve
6. Engine Coolant Temperature (ECT) sensor
7. Thermactor Air Diverter (TAD) solenoid
8. Canister purge solenoid

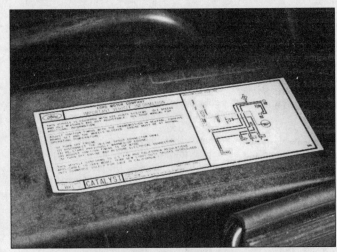

1.10 When servicing the engine or emissions systems, the VECI label in your particular vehicle should always be checked for up-to-date information.

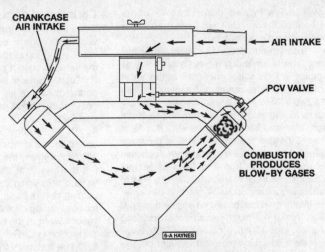

2.2 Gas flow in a typical Positive Crankcase Ventilation (PCV) system

6   On vehicles covered by this manual, the first attempt at EEC was with the MCU system (Microprocessor Control Unit). The MCU controls the secondary air and evaporative systems only. In addition, the MCU controls the carburetor feedback control solenoid and to a limited degree, ignition timing. The next generation EEC was the EEC-III system. The EEC-III system controls all active emission systems but is based around the feedback carburetor system. The final and present EEC system also controls all active emissions systems as first introduced on feedback carburetors and then Electronic Fuel Injected (EFI) vehicles to a degree unobtainable in earlier electronic versions.

7   Luckily, conditions can be simulated and checks made that allow diagnosis of the various systems regardless of the type of electronic control. The Sections in this Chapter include general descriptions and checking procedures within the scope of the home mechanic along with component replacement procedures (when possible) for each of the systems listed above.

8   Before assuming that an emissions control system is malfunctioning, check the fuel and ignition systems carefully (see Chapters 4 and 5). The diagnosis of some emission control devices requires specialized tools, equipment and training. If checking and servicing become too difficult or if a procedure is beyond your ability, consult a dealer service department. This doesn't mean, however, that emission control systems are particularly difficult to maintain and repair. You can quickly and easily perform many checks and do most (if not all) of the regular maintenance at home with common tune-up and hand tools. **Caution:** *The most frequent cause of emissions problems is simply a loose or broken vacuum hose or wire, so always check the hose and wiring connections first.*

9   Pay close attention to any special precautions outlined in this Chapter. It should be noted that the illustrations of the various

systems may not exactly match the system installed on your vehicle because of changes made by the manufacturer during production or from year-to-year.

10   A *Vehicle Emissions Control Information* (VECI) label is located in the engine compartment **(see illustration)**. This label contains important emissions specifications and adjustment information, as well as a vacuum hose schematic with emissions components identified. When servicing the engine or emissions systems, the VECI label in your particular vehicle should always be checked for up-to-date information.

2   Positive Crankcase Ventilation (PCV) system

Refer to illustrations 2.2 and 2.3

General description

1   During engine operation, the oil within the crankcase is agitated quite vigorously, producing a fine oil mist or vapor. In addition, combustion pressure which sneaks past the piston rings (blow-by) pressurizes the crankcase with partially unburned hydrocarbons and other exhaust components. This crankcase pressure must be relieved to protect various engine seals from blowing out. Simply venting the pressure to atmosphere would release these pollutants and is unacceptable, therefore the Positive Crankcase Ventilation (PCV) system was developed.

2   The PCV system simply relieves crankcase pressure by routing crankcase vapors and combustion blow-by gases into the intake manifold, where they mix with the normal air/fuel charge and are burned in the combustion process. However, the engine can only accept small amounts of these vapors at idle or it will misfire. On the other hand, the engine can accept large amounts of crankcase vapors at higher loads (where most of the pressure

is created anyway). Because of this, it is necessary to regulate the amount of ventilation occurring depending on operating conditions. The PCV valve serves this purpose. In operation, vapors travel from the crankcase, through the PCV valve and into the intake manifold **(see illustration)**.

3   For the PVC system to operate effectively, it needs to create a flow of air through the crankcase to help flush vapors out. There are many different fresh air supply configurations depending on the model, year and destination. However, all systems share the same common goal. Provide a source of fresh (filtered), unrestricted air for circulation into the crankcase. The air must be clean since it will eventually end up in the combustion chambers. In addition, under heavy load, large volumes of air will be required to flow through the crankcase, so the air supply system can't be restrictive. Most models provide air through a small air filter installed in the regular air cleaner housing. A large hose routes the air to the valve cover oil filer cap, which on some models incorporates a filter of its own **(see illustration)**. Other versions use a dedicated fresh air hose or cap on the valve

2.3 PCV fresh (clean) air hose from the air cleaner housing to oil filler cap - typical of early carbureted models

cover. A few models draw clean air down-stream of the air cleaner, from the throttle body or the air intake tube.

4   The various vapor/air-to-intake manifold subsystems are much more similar. They all employ a PCV valve mounted in the valve cover or, in some cases intake manifold, with a sizable vacuum hose connecting the PCV valve to the main intake manifold vacuum port. Manifold vacuum on the engine side of the PCV valve creates a negative pressure differential within the crankcase which causes the air to flow in from the fresh air supply system. The PCV valve regulates the flow of ventilating air and blow-by gas that can enter the intake manifold based on engine demand. High intake manifold vacuum characteristic of a low load situation causes the PCV valve to restrict flow. Low manifold vacuum causes the PCV valve to open fully, allowing full flow through the PCV valve and complete flushing of blow-by gasses and vapors.

Check

5   Checking procedures for the PCV system components are included in Chapter 1.

Component replacement

6   Refer to Section 10 for the PCV system component replacement procedures.

---

3   Fuel evaporative emissions control system - description and checks

---

General description

1   This system is designed to prevent raw fuel vapors (hydrocarbons) from being released into the atmosphere during both engine on and engine off conditions. To provide containment of the vapors when the vehicle is not being operated, the entire fuel system must be closed. This is done through the use of a check valve fuel tank filler cap on the supply end and a sealed carburetor bowl on the delivery end. If left in this closed condition, fuel vapor pressure could increase to damaging levels. To prevent this, each vapor source is connected to a single vapor absorbing charcoal canister, which under normal conditions keeps vapor pressure to reasonable limits. If exceeded, a vapor relief valve is built into the fuel tank to momentarily relieve trapped vapor pressure.

2   At some point, the canister will become saturated and must be evacuated (purged) of vapor to be useful again. To accomplish this, vapors are fed to the engine for consumption each time the engine reaches operating conditions. This completes the cycle. Although simple in theory, actual execution of this operation requires several control devices. The devices and techniques depend on the vehicle, year and destination. However, in general they can be classified into two types, carbureted systems and fuel-injected systems.

Carbureted engines

3   First, vapor trapped in the gas tank is vented through a one way (rollover) check valve in the top of the tank. The vapor leaves the valve through a single line and is routed to a charcoal canister located in the engine compartment, where it's stored. **Caution:** *Some heavy duty models may be equipped with two canisters.*

4   Next, sealed carburetor vapors are routed to the charcoal canister through two different valves, the bowl vent solenoid and the thermal vent valve. The vent solenoid valve closes when the ignition is in RUN, preventing reverse vapor flow into the carburetor bowl during normal operation, but allowing vapor flow from the bowl to the canister when the ignition is OFF.

5   The thermal vent valve is a temperature activated off/on valve and is closed when the engine compartment is cold. This prevents reverse flow of fuel tank vapor into the carburetor float bowl during non-operating conditions when the vapor pressure in the fuel tank is higher than normal. This condition usually occurs when sunlight strikes a vehicle that has been sitting out all night and begins to warm the fuel tank. As the engine compartment warms up during normal engine operation, the thermal vent valve opens. When the engine is again turned off, the thermal vent valve (now open because underhood temperature is above 120-degrees F) allows fuel vapor generated in the carburetor float bowl to pass through the valve and be stored in the charcoal canister. As the thermal vent valve cools, it closes and the cycle begins again.

6   On later models, the vent solenoid valve and thermal vent valve were combined into one device called the thermal vent solenoid valve. Operation is identical.

7   Finally, all the stored vapor must find its way into the intake manifold for burning in the combustion process. The canister purge control valve manages this operation. Although there are several styles of purge valves, their operation is similar. Located in the vapor hose linking the intake manifold and the carbon canister, the purge valve allows vapor flow only when activated by ported vacuum. Ported vacuum is only generated when the engine is running and is not available at idle. Therefore all purging is done off idle to avoid idle misfire. The purge hose is usually connected to the vacuum side of the PCV hose or to a large vacuum fitting under the carburetor. Some models insert a vacuum temperature valve in the vacuum line to further delay purging until the engine is warm, again avoiding potential misfire.

Fuel-injected engines

8   First, vapor trapped in the gas tank is vented through a one way (rollover) check valve in the top of the tank. The vapor leaves the valve through a single line and is routed to a charcoal canister located in the engine compartment, where it's stored. **Caution:** *Some heavy duty models may be equipped with two canisters.*

9   On all fuel-injected models, the canister outlet is connected to an electrically activated canister purge solenoid which is, in turn, connected to the intake manifold. The canister purge solenoid valve is normally closed when the engine is not at operating conditions, forcing vapors to the charcoal canister. The purge solenoid is controlled by the EEC PCM, which energizes (opens) the valve only when the proper operating conditions are met. When open, vapors travel through the valve into the intake tract where they are consumed in the combustion process. The purge hose is usually connected to the throttle body purge port(s) or to the vacuum side of the PCV hose. Purge solenoids can be found either free floating between canister and engine purge hoses or mounted to the throttle body.

Check

Charcoal canister

10   There are no moving parts and nothing to wear in the canister. Check for loose, missing, cracked or broken fittings and inspect the canister for cracks and other damage. If the canister is damaged, replace it.

Canister purge valve (carbureted models)

11   Clearly label all vacuum hoses and ports, then detach the hoses from the valve.
12   Remove the valve.
13   Apply vacuum to port B. The valve should be closed (no air flows through it). If air flows through it, the valve is open. Replace it with a new one.
14   After applying and maintaining 16 in-Hg of vacuum to port A, apply vacuum to port B again. Air should pass through (the valve should open). If no air flows, the valve is closed. Replace it. **Caution:** *Never apply vacuum to port C. Doing so may dislodge the internal diaphragm and the valve will be permanently damaged.*

Canister purge solenoid valve (fuel-injected models)

15   Remove the valve from the purge hoses and mounting bracket if equipped.
16   With the valve de-energized, apply 5 in-Hg of vacuum to the vacuum source port. The valve should not pass air. If it does, replace the valve.
17   Apply 9-to-14 volts to the valve electrical connector terminals with jumper wires. The valve should open and pass air. If it doesn't, replace the valve.

Carburetor fuel bowl solenoid vent valve

18   Remove the valve from the canister hoses.
19   Apply 9-to-14 volts to the valve electrical connector terminals with jumper wires. The valve should close, preventing air from passing through. If the valve doesn't close, replace it.

Carburetor fuel bowl thermal vent valve

20   Remove the valve from the canister hoses.

21   The vent should be fully closed at 90-degrees F and below, and fully open at 120-degrees F and above. If it isn't, replace it.

Combination thermal vent solenoid valve

22   Perform the checks described in Steps 18 through 21.

Component replacement

23   Refer to Section 10 for the component replacement procedures.

---

4   Exhaust Gas Recirculation (EGR) systems - description

General description

1   In the search for better gas mileage, designers have continuously leaned air/fuel ratios in the cruise mode. Lean mixtures burn very violently, resulting in high combustion temperatures. One natural consequence of high temperature combustion is the production of nitrogen oxides (NOx)which are considered pollutants. To reduce these oxides during lean cruise modes, the combustion temperatures must be reduced. The reduction of these temperatures is accomplished by the Exhaust Gas Recirculation system.

2   The EGR system is designed to reintroduce small metered amounts of exhaust gas back into the intake manifold during part throttle and cruise conditions, where it combines with the air/fuel mixture prior to the combustion process. The chemical composition of the exhaust being mostly inert, allows combustion to take place but in a less heat producing manner, thus reducing the generation of NOx emissions.

3   The actual EGR valve is responsible for providing the physical connection and flow between the exhaust system and the intake manifold. To operate, the EGR valve requires a source of spent exhaust gas and an unrestricted path into the intake manifold. Some early carbureted models took advantage of the intake manifold exhaust heat crossover as the exhaust gas source. On these models, the EGR valve is mounted directly to a cast-in location on the intake manifold which provides both feed exhaust and intake plenum passages. Other engines designed a special adapter plate between the carburetor and the manifold to mount the EGR valve. Passages in the plate allowed exhaust gases from the intake crossover to go through the valve and into the intake manifold. Still other engines provide exhaust gas externally through a tube connected to the exhaust manifold to an adapter plate-mounted EGR valve. With the advent of Electronic Fuel Injection, the need for intake manifold heating was eliminated. Therefore, all fuel-injected model EGR valves require an external source of exhaust gas. Typically, fuel-injected engines use upper intake manifold-mounted EGR valves for easy access to the intake tract.

4   In construction, the EGR valve is fairly simple, with two ports being physically connected through some type of poppet (off or on) or pintle (off or metered) valve. The operation of the valve is controlled by a vacuum-activated diaphragm built into the valve. The exact design of the EGR valve and the system for controlling its vacuum signal, is dependent on the model and year of the vehicle.

5   Three types of EGR systems have been used on F-series and Bronco vehicles covered by this manual; conventional ported vacuum (early non-US. models only), the integral backpressure valve as used on early models, and the Electronic EGR (EEGR) system (also called the Sonic system) as used on later models.

Ported vacuum valve

6   Early non-U.S. models utilize the ported vacuum valve and control system. This EGR valve is operated by a vacuum signal from the carburetor (ported vacuum). As the vacuum increases, the valve opens allowing EGR flow. The amount of flow is directly related to the amount of vacuum applied (more vacuum, more flow). This system is very basic, and was discontinued in U.S. models prior to 1980 due to its inability to conform to tighter emissions standards of the time.

Integral Backpressure (BP) transducer valve

7   Early U.S. carbureted models utilized the Integral Backpressure valve (BP) for more precise control over EGR flow. These valves were a first attempt at rudimentary closed loop control. Internal EGR valving controls EGR flow in response to both engine demands and emission requirements. The BP system was discontinued due to the introduction of Electronic Engine Control EEC systems and their associated EEGR system.

Electronic EGR (EEGR)

8   Electronic Engine Control (EEC-III and -IV) offered opportunity for true closed-loop feedback control of the EGR system. The EEGR system is the result. The EGR valve is operated in direct response to the EEC PCM computer, which uses its engine sensors and preprogrammed routines to determine the optimum duty cycles in concert with engine operating conditions and other emission control devices, to minimize pollutants and maximize driveability. The amount of exhaust gas reintroduced is dependent on many factors such as engine speed, altitude, manifold vacuum, exhaust system backpressure, coolant temperature and throttle angle.

---

5   Exhaust Gas Recirculation (EGR) systems - operation and checks

Ported vacuum valve - operation

1   As its name implies, the ported vacuum valve is operated by ported vacuum. Ported vacuum is provided by a small sensing pas-

5.3a Typical coolant temperature controlled thermal vacuum switch - two-port style

1   Vacuum present when hot
2   To vacuum source

sage just above the throttle plate. In the closed throttle position, the passage is exposed to ambient pressure (no vacuum). However, at part throttle, the port is exposed to manifold vacuum and begins to signal manifold vacuum. As the throttle is open further, ported vacuum will increase rapidly, then continue to decrease to zero at wide open throttle. This vacuum signal is ideal for EGR since it produces a signal only during part throttle and cruise conditions.

2   The ported vacuum EGR valve simply opens and closes in response to the ported vacuum signal, allowing exhaust flow into the intake manifold. No EGR flow should occur at idle or under conditions of heavy load. In addition, to aid cold driveability, the entire vacuum signal is interrupted by a coolant Ported Vacuum Switch or Temperature Vacuum Switch (PVS or TVS) until the engine warms to operating temperature. In some cases, a delay valve (a small restriction) is inserted in the vacuum line to help smooth the vacuum signal to the EGR valve during rapid vacuum transitions.

Integral back pressure transducer valve (BP) - operation

Refer to illustrations 5.3a and 5.3b

3   The BP valve also uses ported vacuum, however, this EGR valve (poppet or pintle type) cannot be opened by carburetor vacuum (ported vacuum) until its internal vacuum bleed hole is closed by exhaust back pressure. Once the initial amount of backpressure and vacuum is sensed, the valve will open and seek a position dependent upon the exhaust back pressure flowing through the orifice, and in so doing the vacuum oscillates at that level. The higher the signal vacuum and exhaust back pressure, the more the valve opens. In addition, to aid cold driveability, the entire vacuum signal is interrupted by either a coolant temperature thermal vacuum switch (TVS) **(see illustration)** or an air tem-

5.3b Typical air temperature controlled vacuum valve

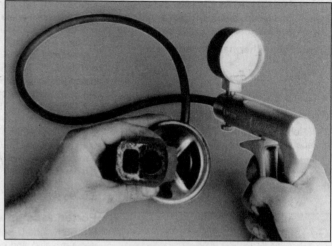

**5.11 Checking an EGR valve with a vacuum pump
(valve removed for clarity)**

perature TVS **(see illustration)** until the engine warms to operating temperature. In some cases, a delay valve (a small restriction) is inserted in the vacuum line to help smooth the vacuum signal to the EGR valve during rapid vacuum transitions.

Electronic EGR (EEGR) - operation

4   The electronic EGR valve controls EGR flow through a closed-loop electronically controlled system. In operation, the EGR Valve Position (EVP) sensor (attached to the top of the EGR valve) continuously signals the PCM of the position of the EGR valve. The PCM uses this data to indirectly calculate the flow through the EGR valve. This information, plus other sensor input is then processed in the PCM and if required, a more optimum EGR valve position is calculated.

5   On feedback carburetor models (EEC-III), this new valve position is directed by the PCM to either the EGR Control (EGRC) or EGR Vent (EGRV) solenoids. These solenoids provide vacuum control over the EGR valve, and supply or bleed vacuum to adjust the EGR valve to the position determined by the PCM.

6   On fuel-injected models, the new valve position is directed to the EGR Vacuum Regulator (EVR) which serves the same purpose. On either system, as supply vacuum overcomes the spring load, the EGR diaphragm is activated, lifting the pintle off the seat and allowing exhaust gas to recirculate. The actual amount of flow is proportional to the pintle position, however, the EVP sensor responds to the new position by sending an updated position signal to the PCM and the process repeats, thus closing the loop.

7   On some feedback carburetor models, an engine coolant heatsink is mounted between the EGR valve and intake manifold to allow better EGR flow and protect the EVP sensor from excessive heat. In some cases, a vacuum reservoir is used to guarantee an adequate supply of control vacuum under all conditions.

Troubleshooting options

8   There are typically three situations which might bring attention to EGR system performance.

 a) *Driveability problems such as rough idle, surge, hesitation or general poor performance.*
 b) *Failed state smog certification check.*
 c) *Indicator light comes on (EEC systems only).*

9   All the above conditions can be caused by problems other then the EGR system, and therefore can be difficult to diagnose. For this reason, the system incorporates a self-check function that monitors the EGR system during actual operating conditions. If a problem is noted, the computer will light up the dash mounted "check engine" or "service engine" indicator light and a specific Diagnostic Trouble Code (DTC) indicating the nature of the problem is generated and stored in the EEC memory.

10   If a concern is raised or if vehicle fails state smog certification, early EGR systems must be diagnosed in the time-honored "process of elimination" fashion as outlined in this Section. With this system, a second choice is available. The stored trouble codes can be retrieved to aid the technician in troubleshooting several EGR problems and avoid wasted time spent checking good components and circuits. If you wish to use them, refer to Section 9 for procedures in obtaining and utilizing trouble codes. Otherwise, use operating symptoms to help guide you through the following step by step procedures.

EGR Valve Checks

Ported valve

11   Remove the ported vacuum hose from the valve and using hand-held vacuum pump, apply vacuum to the valve while observing the diaphragm shaft **(see illustration)**.

12   The diaphragm should hold vacuum and the shaft should move up. If not, replace the valve. Release vacuum.

13   Start the engine and warm it to operating temperature.

14   Using the hand-held vacuum pump, apply vacuum to the valve and observe the engine idle. Idle speed should drop and roughen. If not, remove the valve and check the intake manifold (or adapter plate) for carbon buildup in the exhaust and intake passages. Clean as required to re-establish free flow. If unobstructed, check the EGR valve for the carbon buildup and clean as required. Reinstall the valve and repeat the test to verify proper operation.

15   If still no idle change is noticed, replace the EGR valve, then continue to the next Step.

16   With the engine at idle and at operating temperature, remove the ported vacuum hose and check for vacuum. No vacuum should be indicated. If it is, check the vacuum hose routing, verify the hose is connected to carburetor (ported) vacuum, not manifold vacuum. Make repairs as required and retest.

17   With the engine at operating temperature, increase engine speed to approximately 3500 rpm while checking for vacuum at the EGR vacuum hose. Vacuum should be indicated. If not, check the hose routing and condition back to the temperature switch and then to the carburetor ported vacuum fitting. **Caution:** *Some systems may use a delay valve in this line - if present, remove and retest.* If attached and in good condition, check for hose blockage. If no obstruction is found, replace the temperature switch and repeat the test to verify repair.

Integral backpressure transducer valve

18   Start engine and warm to operating temperature.

19   With engine running, disconnect vacuum hose to EGR valve and using hand held vacuum pump, apply vacuum to EGR valve. Vacuum **should** bleed off. If vacuum holds or if engine idle roughens, replace valve and repeat test to verify repair.

20   To completely test the valve under idle

conditions, unusually high exhaust backpressure must be produced to simulate operating conditions. proceed as follows:

a) *Start the engine and allow it to warm to operating temperature. Turn the engine off.*

b) *Obtain a socket approximately 1/16-inch less in diameter then the exhaust tailpipe. Plug the socket drive hole and insert into tailpipe drive end first. Using a small C-clamp or vise-grips, clamp the socket securely to the tailpipe (edge of socket to edge of tailpipe).* **Warning:** *The pipe may be hot. Wear gloves.*

c) *With the engine at idle, disconnect the vacuum hose from the EGR valve and using a hand-held vacuum pump, apply vacuum to the EGR valve. Engine idle should now roughen and vacuum should bleed slowly (approx. 1 inch Hg every 30 seconds). If not, remove the valve and check the intake manifold (or adapter plate) for carbon buildup in both exhaust and intake passages. Clean as required to re-establish free flow. If unobstructed, check the EGR valve for carbon buildup and clean as required. Reinstall the valve and repeat the test to verify repair.* **Caution:** *Do not operate the engine at above idle speed for extended periods with the exhaust plugged - remove the socket from the tailpipe after the test before continuing to the next Step.*

21   If still no idle change is noticed, replace the EGR valve, then continue to the next Step.

22   With the engine running and at operating temperature, remove the ported vacuum hose and check for vacuum at the hose. No vacuum should be indicated. If it is, check the vacuum hose routing, verify that the hose is connected to the carburetor (ported) vacuum, not manifold vacuum. Make repairs as required and retest.

23   With the engine at operating temperature, increase engine speed to approximately 3500 rpm while observing for vacuum at EGR vacuum hose. Vacuum should be indicated. If not, check the hose routing and condition back to the temperature switch and then to the carburetor ported vacuum fitting. **Caution:** *Some systems may use a delay valve in this line - if present, remove it and retest.* If attached and in good condition, check for hose blockage. If no obstruction is found, replace the temperature switch and repeat the test to verify proper operation.

Electronic EGR valve

24   To perform a leakage test, connect a hand-held vacuum pump to the EGR valve and apply 5-to-6 in-Hg of vacuum to the valve.

25   Vacuum should not drop more than 1 in-Hg in 30 seconds.

26   If the specified condition is not met, the EGR valve diaphragm, O-ring or EVP sensor is leaking. Check the EVP screws for tightness and retest.

27   If vacuum still leaks, remove the EVP

sensor and seal the EVP opening on the EGR valve. Retest the valve. If vacuum still leaks, replace the EGR valve. If vacuum holds, inspect the O-ring for possible damage. If acceptable, the EVP sensor is probably leaking. Replace the EVP sensor. Proceed to the next Step.

28   To perform functional tests, release the vacuum to the EGR valve but keep the pump connected.

29   Disconnect the Idle Air Control (IAR) solenoid. **Caution:** *If this is not done, the IAC will automatically attempt to increase the idle speed to normal during engine running vacuum test.*

30   Restart the engine and allow it to idle. Have an assistant hold the throttle steady at normal idle speed if necessary. Note the idle rpm.

31   Apply vacuum to the EGR valve and observe the engine idle speed. Idle speed should slow (more than 100 rpm) and roughen. Upon release of vacuum, the idle speed should return to normal. If acceptable, reconnect the IAC connector and proceed to Step 33.

32   If no change is noted, remove the valve and check the intake manifold and EGR valve for carbon buildup. Clean as required to re-establish free flow. If unobstructed, replace the EGR valve and repeat the test to verify proper operation. Continue to the next Step.

33   Start the engine and warm it to operating temperature.

34   With the engine running, check for vacuum at the EGR vacuum hose at idle. Vacuum should be below 1 inch-Hg. **Caution:** *EGR vacuum control valve will have slight internal leakage, therefore a small amount of residual vacuum is acceptable.* If acceptable, proceed to the next Step. If above 1 inch-Hg, disconnect the vacuum control solenoid (EVR or EGRC) electrical connector and check the vacuum. **Caution:** *On EGRC/EGRV solenoid sets, EGRC is the solenoid with the manifold vacuum supply hose.* If vacuum is now within limits, proceed to the circuit checks (improper signal). If the vacuum is still above limit, replace the solenoid valve(s) (leaking to manifold vacuum).

35   Install a vacuum gauge to the EGR valve vacuum hose.

36   With the engine at operating temperature, increase the engine speed to approximately 3500 rpm while observing for vacuum at the EGR vacuum hose. Vacuum should be indicated. If vacuum is indicated, proceed to Step 38. If not, check for manifold supply vacuum at the EVR or EGRC inlet vacuum hoses. If no vacuum is indicated, check vacuum hose from the solenoid valve to the intake manifold for leaks or blockage. If vacuum is indicated, continue to the next operation.

37   With the engine running, initiate Engine Running Self-Check (refer to Chapter 4, Section 14) and observe gauge. Vacuum should increase above 1 inch Hg at some point in the test as the self test actuates the EVR or EGRC solenoid. If proper signal is not indicated, problem can be electrical (no signal to

EVR/EGRC) or bad solenoid (open winding, stuck). Proceed to solenoid checks.

38   If all checks pass, the system is probably operating properly. If in doubt, clear the trouble codes, and repeat self-test. If no EGR codes are generated, the system is operating correctly. If EGR codes are present, see *Troubleshooting options* near the beginning of this Section.

Solenoid checks (EVR, EGRC and EGRV)

Feedback carburetor systems - operation and checks

39   Feedback control carburetor EGR systems use two EEC controlled solenoid valves to control the vacuum signal to the EEGR valve, the EGR control (EGRC) and EGR Vent (EGRV). In operation, the EGRC is supplied a continuous source of manifold vacuum at its inlet port. When directed (energized) by the PCM, it will open from its normal closed position and allow vacuum to the EGR valve. When the EGR valve opens to the proper position (EVP sensor indicates position to PCM), the PCM will turn the EGRC off and the solenoid closes. Vacuum is now trapped between the EGR valve and the EGRC solenoid valve, maintaining the EGR in the desired (Hold) position. If the PCM desires a less open EGR valve position, it will direct (de-energize) the normally open EGRV solenoid valve. When de-energized, the EGRV will open and vent the trapped (Hold) vacuum to atmosphere, allowing the EGR valve to move to a more closed position. This fluctuating action occurs continuously, maintaining the EGR valve at the desired position. EGRC and EGRV solenoids are provided continuous voltage in RUN position, the PCM completes the circuit on ground side by alternately grounding and opening circuit. **Note:** *A small leakage during valve closed tests is considered acceptable.*

40   Here are the conditions for the next check: Engine not running, key off, EGRC and EGRV solenoid electrical connectors disconnected.

41   Remove the vacuum supply line at EGRC/EGRV solenoid set. Install a vacuum gauge to the EGRC outlet port (on EGRC/EGRV solenoid sets, the EGRC is the solenoid with the manifold vacuum supply hose) and cap the EGRV outlet port. Using the vacuum pump, apply vacuum to the manifold vacuum supply inlet port. Vacuum should hold and no vacuum should be indicated at the gauge. If not, replace the valve set.

42   Move the gauge to the EGRV outlet port and repeat the test. Vacuum should now be indicated on the gauge and should hold. If not, replace the valve set.

43   Install a ground jumper to one EGRV solenoid terminal and a 12-volt source jumper to the other to close the valve. Release trapped vacuum if required and repeat the EGRV vacuum pump test. Vacuum should hold and no vacuum should be indicated on the gauge. If not, replace the valve set. **Cau-**

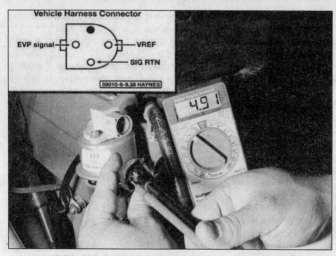

5.55 Checking the reference voltage to the EVP

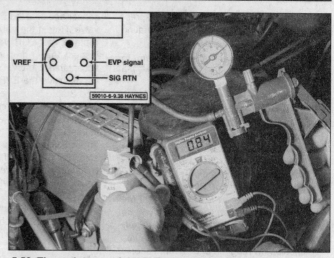

5.58 The resistance of the EVP sensor should drop as vacuum is applied to the EGR valve

tion: *Do not leave the hot (battery) jumper wire installed any longer than necessary.*
44   Install gauge to EGRC outlet and cap EGRV outlet port. Install jumpers to EGRC solenoid to open valve. Repeat EGRC vacuum pump check. Vacuum should now be indicated on the gauge and vacuum should hold. If not, replace the valve set. **Caution:** *Do not leave the hot (battery) jumper installed any longer than necessary.*
45   Measure the resistance of each solenoid valve at its electrical terminals. Each solenoid should indicate between 30 and 70 ohms. If not, replace the valve set.
46   If all checks pass, the EGRC and EGRV solenoid valves are operational - proceed to the circuit checks.

Electronic fuel injected systems - operation and checks

47   Vehicles with EFI use only one solenoid valve to control vacuum to the EGR valve, the Exhaust Valve Regulator (EVR). In operation, the EVR is supplied a continuous source of manifold vacuum at its inlet port. When directed (energized) by the PCM, it will open from its normal closed position and allow vacuum to the EGR valve. When the EGR valve opens to the proper position (EVP sensor indicates position to PCM), the PCM will turn the EVR off and the solenoid closes. Vacuum between the EGR valve and the EVR solenoid valve now vents through the EVR valve, allowing the EGR valve to move to a more closed position. To maintain the EGR in desired (Hold) position, the PCM must again direct (energize) the EVR to open, and the cycle continuously repeats. To change EGR valve position, the PCM simply holds the EVR open longer (opens EGR further) or closed longer (closes EGR valve further). This duty cycle occurs continuously, maintaining the EGR valve at the desired position. The EVR solenoid is provided continuous voltage in RUN position, the PCM completes the circuit on ground side by alternately grounding and opening circuit. **Caution:** *A small leakage dur-*

ing valve closed tests is considered acceptable.
48   The conditions for testing are as follows: Engine not running, key off, EVR electrical connector disconnected.
49   Remove the vacuum supply line from the EVR solenoid. Install a vacuum gauge to the EVR outlet port and using a hand-held vacuum pump, apply vacuum to the manifold vacuum supply inlet port. Vacuum should not hold and no vacuum should be indicated at gauge. If not, replace valve.
50   Install ground jumper to one EVR solenoid terminal and a 12-volt source jumper to the other to open valve. Release trapped vacuum if required and repeat the vacuum pump test. Vacuum should now be indicated on the gauge and vacuum should hold. If not, replace the valve set. **Caution:** *Do not leave the hot (battery) jumper installed any longer than necessary.*
51   Remove the jumpers to close the valve and connect the vacuum pump to the EVR outlet port. Apply vacuum to the port to test venting. Vacuum should bleed. If not, replace the valve.
52   Measure the resistance of the solenoid valve at its electrical terminals. Resistance should be between 20 to 70 ohms except for 7.5L engine, which should be between 100 to 135 ohms. If not, replace the valve.
53   If all checks pass, the EVR solenoid valve is operational.

EVP circuit checks

Refer to illustration 5.55
54   Disconnect the EVP electrical connector at the EGR valve.
55   With the ignition in RUN position, check for reference voltage at EVP harness electrical connector pin (VREF) and pin SIG RTN **(see illustration)**. Voltage should be between 4 and 6 volts. If not, move probe from SIG RTN to a good ground source and recheck. If proper voltage is now indicated, service SIG

RTN circuit to PCM for open. If voltage is still out of limit, proceed to Chapter 4 Section 15 and perform VREF checks to obtain proper voltage.

EVP sensor - operation and checks

Refer to illustration 5.58
56   The EVP sensor is a variable resistance type device. Located on top of the EGR valve, its sensing plunger extends down through the valve and contacts the EGR diaphragm. As the diaphragm responds to vacuum signals to open or close the EGR valve, the plunger follows this movement and the EVP sensor translates the instantaneous position of the valve into a specific resistance reading. At idle, the EVP sensor signal should be approximately 5,000 ohms (EGR valve closed), reducing to 100 ohms when the EGR valve is fully open. The PCM measures the changing voltage drop across this variable resistance, and therefore, knows the EGR valve position at any time.
57   Disconnect the EVP electrical connector at the EGR valve.
58   Check resistance of EVP sensor between sensor pin VREF and sensor pin EVP **(see illustration)**. Resistance can be slightly less than, but no greater than 5000 ohms.
59   Check the resistance of the EVP sensor between sensor pin SIG RTN and sensor pin EVP. Resistance can be slightly greater than, but no lower than 100 ohms.
60   Connect a vacuum pump to the EGR valve and slowly pull the vacuum from zero to 10 inches-Hg to actuate the sensor while observing the resistance at pins VREF to EVP. Resistance should change smoothly (no jumps or flat spots) from 5000 to 100 ohms. **Caution:** *Vacuum should hold - if not, replace the EGR valve.*
61   If any of the above tests fail, remove the EVP sensor and check it using the same procedure as in Step 60, but resistance values should be between no greater than 5,500 ohms (sensor shaft extended) to no less than

100 ohms (sensor shaft retracted). If not, replace the EVP sensor.

62 If the sensor is acceptable, the EGR valve must be keeping the sensor from its proper idle and/or full open position. This could be caused by improper EGR seating, EGR stuck, EGR damaged, carbon buildup, etc. Perform the EGR valve check procedure as outlined in this section and replace the valve if necessary.

63 If all EVP sensor checks pass, the EGR system malfunction is probably the PCM module itself. At this point it would be a good idea to have further diagnosis performed by a dealer service department or other repair shop, since they can try a new PCM module (which may or not be the problem) without the risk of you having to buy one.

Component replacement

64 Refer to Section 9 for the component replacement procedures.

---

6 Spark control system (carbureted models)

Caution: *The information in this Section is applicable only to vehicles equipped with the Duraspark II ignition system. Because spark advance and retard functions on EEC vehicles is controlled by the EEC microprocessor, checks and tests involving proper emission spark control must be performed by a dealer service department or other repair shop.*

General description

1 The spark control system is designed to reduce hydrocarbon and oxides of nitrogen (NOx) emissions by advancing the ignition timing only when the engine is cold.

2 These systems are fairly complex and have many valves, relays, amplifiers and other components built into them. Each vehicle will have a system peculiar to the model year, geographic region and gross vehicle weight rating. A schematic diagram located on the underside of the hood will detail the exact components and vacuum line routing of the particular system on your vehicle.

3 Depending on engine coolant temperature, altitude and the position of the throttle, vacuum is applied to either one or both of the diaphragms in the distributor vacuum unit and the ignition timing is changed to reduce emissions and improve cold engine driveability.

Checking

4 Visually check all vacuum hoses for cracks, splits or hardening. Next, remove the distributor cap and rotor. Apply a vacuum to the distributor advance port (and retard port, if so equipped) and see if the breaker or relay plate inside of the distributor moves. The plate should move opposite the distributor direction of rotation when vacuum is applied to the advance port and should move in the direction of rotation if vacuum is applied to the retard port (if so equipped).

5 Checking of the temperature relays, delay valves or other modifiers of the spark timing system is beyond the scope of the average home mechanic. Consult an expert if you suspect that you have other problems within the spark advance system.

Component replacement

6 When replacing any vacuum hoses, remove only one hose at a time and make sure that the replacement hose is of the same quality and size as the hose being replaced.

7 If it is determined that a malfunction in the spark control system is due to a faulty distributor, refer to Chapter 5 for the replacement procedure.

---

7 Thermactor systems - description

General description

1 Thermactor systems are employed to reduce carbon monoxide and hydrocarbon emissions, both a result of incomplete combustion. The thermactor air injection system functions by continuing combustion of unburned gasses after they leave the combustion chamber by injecting fresh air (from the engine-driven air pump) into the hot exhaust gases at some point after they exit the exhaust ports.

Conventional Thermactor (CT)

2 Early Conventional Thermactor (CT) systems introduced the injected air directly into the exhaust manifold at each exhaust port. At this point, the fresh air mixed with hot exhaust gas to promote further oxidation of both hydrocarbons and carbon monoxide, thereby reducing their concentration and converting some of them into harmless carbon dioxide and water. However, it was found that during extended periods of fuel rich operation, the heat produced by the secondary combustion process would raise the temperature of the exhaust manifold significantly, causing other emission related problems. Therefore, during some modes of operation, such as extended idle or deceleration, the thermactor pump air must bypass the exhaust manifold and be "dumped" into the atmosphere. To manage the injected air under these conditions, the extended idle timer and vacuum switch control operation of an air bypass valve. The air bypass valve then "dumps" the injected air to prevent overheating of the exhaust system. Collectively, the control system is known as the Idle Air Bypass system. Considering its simplicity, the CT system worked reasonable well except during cruise conditions where the additional air injected at the exhaust manifold would dilute the EGR supply, causing a lean air fuel condition. This condition lead to some driveability problems such as surging and pre-ignition.

Managed Thermactor Air (MTA) (non-EEC controlled)

3 With stiffening pollution control standards, additional help was needed in the control of carbon monoxide and hydrocarbon emissions. The catalytic converter was the answer. However, for the converter to operate effectively, it requires an oxygen-rich environment to maintain the heated chemical reaction necessary for oxidation (burning) of pollutants. Therefore, on later models, in addition to providing exhaust manifold air (known as upstream air), the secondary air injection system also provides air to the catalytic converter (known as downstream air). The catalytic converter system is very effective in all conditions except cold start (converter not up to temperature).

4 Because the converter can also be easily overheated if supplied a fuel-rich exhaust supply for an extended period, a slightly different bypass valve and modified control circuit provides the same protection as with the CT system under conditions of extended idle. Also, since the converter system was so effective, additional air injection at the manifold (and the associated poor driveability side effects at cruise) was no longer required under most conditions. However, injected air at the manifold was still required at cold start (converter not effective) and hot restarts (to burn off excessively rich start mixtures before they can overheat the converter). To manage the injected air under these conditions, the thermactor air timer and vacuum switch control operation of the new air diverter valve. The air diverter valve switches the air to either upstream (manifold) or downstream (converter) locations depending on the basic operating conditions. Collectively, the two separate air control systems are known as Managed Thermactor Air (MTA). Some models employ a combination bypass and diverter valve which performs both functions in one unit.

Managed Thermactor Air (MTA) (EEC controlled)

5 With the introduction of Electronic Engine Control, the control of the secondary air supply system became totally electronic. Operationally, the air bypass and diverter valves perform the same function as with the previous non-EEC controlled MTA system. The difference being that the operation of the valve is no longer limited by relatively simple control circuits and devices. Instead, they are controlled by the EEC computer which, through the various engine sensors, can determine their optimum duty cycles in concert with engine operating conditions and other emission control devices to minimize pollutants and maximize component life. After sensing engine demand and operating conditions, the EEC Powertrain Control Module will determine the proper status (vacuum applied or not) for both air bypass and diverter valves and issue the appropriate commands. The integrity of

the electrical portion of the control system is constantly monitored by the EEC self-checking system.

8   Thermactor systems - operation and checks

Operation

CT bypass valve operation (non-Managed Thermactor Air [MTA] carbureted models)

1   The extended idle air bypass control system consists of the engine-driven air pump, idle tracking switch, timer/relay, solenoid vacuum valve and the air bypass valve. Under all conditions except idle, the carbureted mounted idle tracking switch provides voltage to the timer/relay. The relay portion of the timer/relay then supplies voltage to the normally open solenoid vacuum valve, which in turn interrupts the vacuum path to the bypass valve. Without vacuum applied, the normally open bypass valve routes air from the pump to the exhaust manifold. When the throttle returns to its idle position the relationship between it and idle tracking switch causes the tracking switch to open, cutting off the voltage to the timer/relay. The timer portion of the relay then kicks in, allowing voltage to the solenoid vacuum valve for only 100 to 180 additional seconds, after which point it cuts off the voltage. With no voltage applied, the normally open solenoid vacuum valve will then allow vacuum to the bypass valve, which responds by "dumping" pump air to the atmosphere. On vented bypass valves (two vacuum ports), air is also dumped during deceleration to prevent the fuel rich mixture from backfiring in the exhaust manifold.

2   The valve will continue to provide bypass air for periods longer than the allotted time during engine warm-up since the fast idle cam holds the throttle off the idle tracking switch until warm. Since the bypass valve used on the CT system is of the normally open design, unrestricted flow is obtained even under heavy loads. This was necessary to control emission prior to the introduction of catalytic converters.

Early MTA bypass valve operation (carbureted models)

3   The operation of the early non-EEC controlled (no feedback carburetor) vehicles is similar to the CT system except for the following:

a) *The bypass valve now directs air to the diverter valve where it is routed to either upstream (exhaust manifold) or downstream (converter).*

b) *The bypass valve is now normally closed (dumps unless provided medium to high vacuum) so that under conditions of heavy load (low manifold vacuum) the catalytic converter will be protected from overheating.*

c) *The vacuum solenoid switch changed to a normally closed design to correspond with the change in the bypass valve.*

Early MTA diverter valve operation (carbureted models)

4   The Thermactor Air Timer control system consists of the engine driven air pump, timer relay, timer, solenoid vacuum switch, and coolant temperature Vacuum Control Valve (VCV). Under all conditions except warm start and cold engine warming, the manifold vacuum supply to the diverter valve is interrupted by both of its two control sources. When no vacuum is applied to the diverter valve, it will route pump air downstream to the converter. During engine warming, manifold vacuum is routed to the Vacuum Control Valve (VCV) which routes the signal to the diverter valve only until the engine coolant reaches about 128-degrees. With vacuum applied, the diverter valve routes pump air upstream (exhaust manifold). The second vacuum control source is the solenoid vacuum switch. During warm engine starts, the timer/relay opens the ground circuit between it and the timer. The timer then kicks in, allowing voltage to the solenoid vacuum valve for 100 to 180 seconds. When energized, the solenoid valve connects manifold vacuum to the diverter valve, which responds by routing pump air upstream (exhaust manifold) until the voltage signal from the timer elapses.

EEC controlled bypass and diverter valve operation

5   The EEC controlled secondary air injection systems uses essentially the same valves and air pump plumbing as the earlier version. And in fact, in addition to its own unique set of operating conditions, incorporates the same basic operating restraints as the other systems as follows:

a) *Proper dumping of air during periods of heavy load, extended idle or rapid deceleration. **Caution:** EEC models with fuel injection are much more tolerant to extended idle and deceleration conditions, air is not dumped unless the engine coolant temperature exceeds normal range.*

b) *Proper diverting of air to the exhaust manifold during cold start, warming, and warm start conditions or to the converter in all other conditions by the diverter valve.*

6   Under all conditions, manifold vacuum to the bypass and diverter valves is controlled by the EEC computer (PCM) through two normal closed solenoid vacuum valves. The Thermactor Air Bypass (TAB) solenoid controls vacuum to the bypass valve and the Thermactor Air Diverter (TAD) solenoid controls vacuum to the diverter valve. The solenoid vacuum switches are supplied continuous power through the EEC-IV power relay. When certain operating conditions are met, the PCM will exercise control over the normally closed vacuum switches by grounding the power return circuit of the solenoid

internally within the PCM. When grounded, the solenoids open, allowing vacuum to be applied to the applicable air control valve. Later models renamed the solenoid vacuum switches as the AIR Diverter (AIRD) solenoid and AIR Bypass (AIRB) solenoid. Their function is identical.

Troubleshooting options

7   The proper operation of thermactor systems can be difficult to judge since in some cases a failure can exist with no outward symptoms or signs. This is particularly true in the case of EEC controlled systems where many functions occur in response to conditions impossible to duplicate during a test situation. For this reason, the system incorporates a self-check function that monitors the thermactor system during actual operating conditions. If a problem is noted, the computer will light up the dash mounted "check engine" or "service engine" indicator light and a specific trouble code (DTC) indicating the nature of the problem is generated and stored in the EEC memory.

8   If a concern is raised or if vehicle fails state smog certification, early thermactor systems must be diagnosed in the time honored step by step "process of elimination" fashion as outlined in this section. With this system a second choice is available. The stored trouble codes can be retrieved to aid the technician in troubleshooting several thermactor problems and avoid wasted time spent checking good components and circuits. If you wish to use them, refer to Section 9 for procedures in obtaining and utilizing trouble codes. Otherwise, use operating symptoms to help guide you through the following step by step procedures.

Pump and control valve checks

Air supply pump check

9   Check and adjust the drivebelt tension if necessary and applicable (see Chapter 1).

10   Disconnect the air supply hose at the air bypass valve inlet or air pump outlet.

11   The pump is operating satisfactorily if airflow is felt at the pump outlet with the engine running at idle, increasing as the engine speed is increased.

12   If the air pump does not successfully pass the above tests, check inlet filter or hose for obstruction. If inlet tract is free of restrictions, replace pump with a new or rebuilt unit.

Air bypass valve check (normally closed)

13   **Caution:** *The majority of bypass valves will be normally closed types recognizable by the top mounted vacuum port. If you have an early normally open valve (vacuum port on side), simply reverse the expected value.*

14   Remove the vacuum line from the bypass valve and disconnect the outlet hose to the exhaust manifold (CT) or diverter valve (MTA).

15 Start the engine and check for airflow at bypass valve dump outlet (or ports) while in default state. If no flow is indicated, replace the valve.

16 Using a hand-held vacuum pump (or convenient source of manifold vacuum), apply vacuum to the valve and check the bypass valve at the outlet for airflow. If no flow is indicated or the valve will not hold vacuum, replace the valve.

17 If operating properly, reconnect the hoses and continue to the diverter valve test (MTA only).

Air diverter valve check (normally closed)

18 Remove the vacuum hose from the diverter valve and disconnect the upstream (exhaust manifold) and downstream (converter) outlet hoses.

19 Start engine and check for airflow at downstream (converter) outlet while in default state. If no flow is indicated, verify input air from the bypass valve is available. If not proceed to bypass valve check or vacuum control check. If input air is available, replace diverter valve.

20 Using hand held vacuum pump (or convenient source of manifold vacuum), apply vacuum to valve and check valve upstream (exhaust manifold) outlet for airflow in active state. If no flow is indicated or the valve will not hold vacuum, replace the valve.

21 If operating properly, reconnect the hoses and continue to vacuum control checks.

Combined air bypass and diverter valve

22 Mark and remove both vacuum hoses from the valve and disconnect upstream (exhaust manifold) and downstream (converter) outlet hoses.

23 Start the engine and check for airflow at the dump outlet (or ports) while in default state. If no flow is indicated, replace the valve. **Caution:** *Airflow should be restricted from both upstream and downstream outlets during this test. If flow is indicated, replace the valve.*

24 Using a hand-held vacuum pump (or convenient source of manifold vacuum), apply vacuum to the bypass vacuum port and check the valve at the downstream (converter) outlet for airflow. If no flow is indicated or the valve will not hold vacuum, replace the valve.

25 Tee vacuum line from the hand pump (or manifold vacuum line) and simultaneously apply vacuum to both vacuum ports on valve.

26 Check for airflow at upstream (exhaust manifold) outlet. If no flow is indicated, replace the valve. **Caution:** *Air flow should be restricted from the downstream outlet during this test. If flow is indicated, replace the valve.*

27 If operating properly, reconnect the hoses and continue to vacuum control checks.

Vacuum control checks

Caution: *The following checks assume that the bypass and diverter valve are themselves functional. If in doubt, perform valve checks before proceeding.*

Bypass valve vacuum check (except EFI models)

28 Warm engine to operating temperature.

29 Rev the engine for approximately 30 seconds, then allow the engine to return to idle.

30 Begin timing as soon as engine throttle returns to idle stop and listen for thermactor bypass valve to "dump" air.

31 If sometime after 100 and before approximately 180 seconds the bypass valve begins dumping air to the atmosphere, the system is operating properly.

32 If dumping occurs immediately, the valve is not seeing the proper vacuum signal. On early normally open valves, the valve is seeing vacuum when it shouldn't and on normally closed valves, vacuum is absent when it should be present.

33 If dumping does not occur at all, the situation is the exact reverse of above.

34 Check all vacuum hoses for leaks or obstructions, then check for vacuum with the engine running at the manifold side of solenoid valve. Repair any vacuum supply problems if found. If the hoses are okay and vacuum is present, the problem could be the vacuum solenoid switch or electrical circuits. Proceed to the solenoid checks to isolate.

Bypass valve vacuum check (EFI vehicles)

35 Warm the engine to operating temperature.

36 With the engine running, remove and check for vacuum at the bypass valve vacuum hose (on combination valves, remove the hose at bypass port). Vacuum should be indicated at the hose.

37 If no vacuum is indicted, check all vacuum hoses for leaks or obstructions, then check for vacuum with the engine running at the manifold side of the solenoid valve. Repair any vacuum supply problems if found. If hoses are okay and vacuum is present, the problem could be a vacuum solenoid switch or the electrical circuits. Proceed to the solenoid checks to isolate.

Diverter valve vacuum check (all models)

38 Warm the engine to operating temperature. Turn the engine off and prepare to check vacuum at the diverter valve vacuum hose (on combination valves, at diverter port vacuum hose).

39 Start the engine and begin timing as soon as the engine starts. Observe the vacuum gauge.

40 If the gauge indicates vacuum upon initial start, then sometime after 100 and before approximately 180 seconds drops to zero, the system is operating properly.

41 If no vacuum is indicated, check all vacuum hoses for leaks or obstructions, then check for vacuum with engine running at manifold side of solenoid valve. Vacuum should be indicated.

42 If no manifold vacuum is indicated, on non-EEC MTA system, check the Vacuum Temperature Valve for free flow (over 128 ohms only) between the solenoid valve and the bypass valve. On EEC systems, trace the hose to the manifold source and eliminate blockage.

43 Repair any vacuum supply problems if found. If the hoses are okay, manifold vacuum is present, or if bypass vacuum stays high, the problem could be the vacuum solenoid switch or electrical circuits. Proceed to the solenoid checks to isolate.

Solenoid valve checks (TAD/ TAB, AIRD/AIRB)

44 Solenoid vacuum valve problems can be physical (blocked, stuck, leaking to atmosphere or internally) or electrical (open/ shorted windings). Solenoid valves used in this application are normally closed with a vented outlet (vacuum bleeds from the air control valve when solenoid is closed). The quickest way to check the solenoid valve is to perform a combination test to each solenoid valve as follows:

45 Disconnect electrical connector(s) from the solenoid valve(s).

46 Connect a vacuum source on one port and a vacuum gauge on the other.

47 Jumper one solenoid electrical terminal to ground and the other to a known 12 volt source. **Caution:** *Do not leave the hot (battery) jumper on any longer than necessary.*

48 Apply vacuum and observe the gauge. Release the vacuum, remove the power to the solenoid, and repeat the vacuum test - observe the gauge.

49 The gauge should indicate and hold vacuum in one test but not the other if the valve is operating properly. Replace the solenoid vacuum valve if a failed condition is found. **Caution:** *A very small leakage rate is acceptable.*

50 Apply vacuum to the outlet port of the valve to check venting. Vacuum should bleed. If not, replace the valve. If each solenoid valve passes, the problem must be in the control circuitry. Proceed to *Circuit checks*.

Circuit checks

Bypass control (Non-EEC vehicles)

51 Using the operation description in this section, check the following:

a) *Disconnect Idle Tracking Switch (ITS) at the timer/relay on the carburetor and check the ITS switch continuity. Switch should show continuity when the throttle is open and no continuity with the throttle in the idle position. If the switch is always open (no continuity), replace it. If the switch is always on (continuity) check the mechanical linkage between the throttle and the switch - make sure the switch is being activated at idle. If the mechanical check passes, replace the switch.*

b) Check for voltage at the timer/relay with the ignition in the RUN position. Battery voltage should be present. If not, service the circuit to the ignition switch for an open (fuse) or shorts.

c) Check the continuity of the circuit between the timer/relay and the solenoid vacuum valve positive terminal. Resistance should be less than 5 ohms. If not, service the circuit for an open. Check the continuity between the solenoid valve positive terminal and ground. Resistance should be greater than 10,000 ohms. If not, service the circuit for a short to ground.

d) Check the continuity between the solenoid vacuum valve negative terminal and ground. Resistance should be less than 5 ohms. If not, service the circuit for an open.

e) If all checks pass, replace the timer/relay and retest.

Diverter control (non-EEC vehicles)

52   Using the operation description in this section, check the following:

a) Remove the timer electrical connector and check continuity at power relay ground circuit pin and ground, key off. Resistance should be less than 5 ohms. If not, replace the power relay. Next, turn ignition switch to the RUN position and repeat the check. Resistance should be greater than 10,000 ohms. If not, service the ignition switch to the power relay circuit for an open or replace the power relay.

b) Check for voltage to the timer in the RUN position. Battery voltage should be indicated. If not, service the circuit to ignition switch.

c) Check the continuity of the circuit between the timer and the solenoid vacuum valve positive terminal. Resistance should be less than 5 ohms. If not, service the circuit for an open. Check the continuity between the solenoid valve positive terminal and ground. Resistance should be greater than 10,000 ohms. If not, service the circuit for a short to ground.

d) Check the continuity between the solenoid vacuum valve negative terminal and ground. Resistance should be less than 5 ohms. If not, service the circuit for an open.

e) If all checks pass, replace the timer and retest.

Bypass and diverter control (EEC-IV vehicles)

Caution: *Review Chapter 4, Section 16 on proper circuit check procedures and cautions. Because of their limited application, MCU and EEC-III systems are not addressed in this procedure.*

53   Disconnect the applicable solenoid valve electrical connector and check for voltage at the electrical connectors Vehicle Power (VPWR) terminal with the ignition in RUN position engine off. Voltage should be greater than 10.5 volts. If not, check EEC power relay (refer to Chapter 4 Section 15) and service as required to obtain the required voltage.

54   If problem was found and repaired, repeat vacuum control checks for verification of repair. If using trouble codes, clear memory and repeat self-check.

55   If a problem was found and repaired, repeat the vacuum control checks for verification of repair. If using trouble codes, clear the memory and repeat the self-check. If proper resistance was indicated, continue to next operation.

56   If all checks pass and the problem still exists, the cause is probably the PCM module itself. At this point it may be a good idea to have your dealer (or other repair shop) service the vehicle, since they can try a new PCM module (which may or not be the problem) without having to buy one yourself.

Reverse flow check valve - check

57   Disconnect the hoses from both ends of the check valve.

58   Blow through both ends of the check valve, verifying that air flows in one direction only.

59   If air flows in both directions or not at all, replace the check valve with a new one.

60   When reconnecting the valve, make sure it is installed in the proper direction.

Thermactor system noise test

61   The thermactor system is not completely noiseless. Under normal conditions, noise rises in pitch as the engine speed increases. To determine if noise is the fault of the air injection system, detach the drivebelt (after verifying that the belt tension is correct) and run the engine. If the noise disappears, proceed with the following checks. **Caution:** *The pump must accumulate 500 miles (vehicle miles) before the following check is valid.*

a) Check for seized pump and replace if required.

b) Check for loose or broken mounting brackets or bolts, replace and/or tighten securely if required.

c) Check for overtightened mounting bolts (may warp or bind pump).

d) Check for leaky, pinched, kinked, or damaged hoses and rework or replace as required.

e) Check that the bypass and diverter valves are operating correctly, reference this Section. Repair as required.

Component replacement

62   Refer to Section 10 for component replacement procedures.

9   EEC-IV trouble codes - descriptions and procedures

Trouble codes - general information

Note: *To access the code information on 1996 models, it is necessary to use a scan tool. See Chapter 4 for the trouble code chart for these models.*

1   The Electronic Engine Control (EEC) is a complicated electromechanical system. As with any such system, problem diagnosis would be very difficult. With this in mind, the designers of the EEC-IV systems incorporated a self-testing and self-diagnosing feature into the system. At start up and during normal operation, most of the main functions and sensors of the system are being constantly monitored for proper operation. If a function or component fails to respond or operate within design limits, several things automatically happen depending on the severity of the anomaly. First, a specific trouble code (DTC) indicating the nature of the problem is generated and stored in the EEC memory. Second, the EEC-IV will light up the dash mounted "check engine" or "service engine" indicator light. The light will stay illuminated as long as the problem still exists.

2   The stored trouble codes can be retrieved to aid the technician in troubleshooting many EEC problems. The following section is intended to give the reader the ability to retrieve and interpret trouble codes applicable to the emissions control system. Although a great help, trouble codes are still only guides to problem areas.

3   Refer to Chapter 4, Section 14 and review the procedure for accessing trouble codes. Listed below are the trouble codes pertaining to the emissions control system, their description and suggested procedure. If no emission control codes are present and the specific system is still suspect, proceed with step-by-step procedures in the applicable section of this Chapter. If other (non-emissions) codes are present, proceed to Chapter 4 for descriptions and procedures.

Additional circuit check aids and check procedure

Caution: *When working with the PCM (also known as the EEC-IV module) or associated harness while still attached to module, avoid direct contact with input-output pins. Static electricity generated by normal activity and stored on the surface of the skin can discharge and damage delicate electronic components inside the PCM. It is best to always wear a static discharging wrist strap (available at electronic stores) and avoid working on electronics when the relative humidity is under 25-percent.*

4   Follow the suggested procedure in order top to bottom making note of the following:

a) Harness continuity checks are always done at electrical connectors at both ends of the harness (not component har-

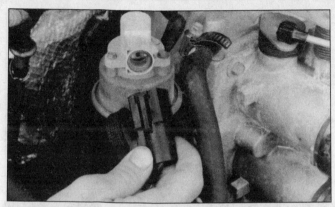

10.2 The EVP sensor is located on top of the EGR valve; to remove it, unplug the electrical connector and remove the three bolts

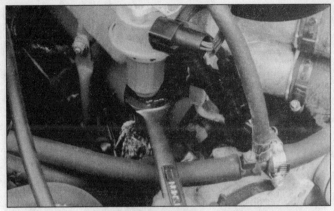

10.19 Unscrew the pipe from the bottom of the EGR valve, if so equipped

ness electrical connector) unless specified otherwise.

b) *Component checks are done at the component electrical connector unless specified otherwise.*

c) *Make sure all connections are tight and clean and fuses intact prior to troubleshooting as most problems are as a result of these simple causes. Remember, some circuits will fail if only a few extra ohms of unwanted resistance is present. Also, certain components may be diagnosed as failed when in reality it is simply a poor connection in the circuit.*

d) *Avoid direct probing of electrical connector pins by purchasing appropriately sized male and female pins and sockets which can be inserted into or over the harness electrical connector pin. This avoids potential damage to vehicle pins and helps maintain proper pin retention (engagement) forces.*

e) *Resistance checks must be made with a high quality meter capable of accurate measurement down to only a few ohms, otherwise, erroneous diagnoses and component replacement will result.*

f) *Note some procedures outlined in this Chapter can themselves result in a "check engine" light and corresponding trouble code. Do not panic, after the repair is made the light should go out the next time the vehicle is started. If not, check codes for direction. Remember, all codes, even those produced during diagnostic routines, will remain in continuous memory for up to 80 driving cycles unless manually erased. See Chapter 4, Section 14 for continuous memory erase procedures.*

EGR system trouble codes

5   For suggested check procedures, refer to Section 5.

   KOEO and Continuous codes:
   31 and 327, EVP circuit below minimum voltage - Perform EVP circuit check.
   35 and 337, EVP circuit above maximum voltage - Perform EVP circuit check.
   KOEO, Running and Continuous codes:
   32 and 328, EVP voltage below closed

limit - Perform EGR valve, EVP sensor and EVP circuit check.
34 and 334, EVP voltage above closed limit - Perform EGR valve, EVR vacuum, EVR circuit, EVP circuit and EVP sensor check.
Running and Continuous code:
33 and 332, EGR valve not opening - Perform EGR valve and EVR vacuum checks.
KOEO codes only:
84 and 558, EVR (or EGRV) circuit failure.
83, EGRC circuit failure.

Secondary Air trouble codes

6   For suggested check procedures, Refer to Section 8.
   Running codes:
   44 and 311, Secondary air inoperative - Perform pump, valve, valve vacuum and solenoid checks.
   45 and 312, Air not properly diverting - Perform diverter valve, diverter vacuum and TAD (ARID) solenoid checks.
   46 and 313, Air not properly bypassing - Perform bypass valve, bypass vacuum and TAB (AIRB) solenoid checks.
   KOEO codes:
   81 and 553, TAD (AIRD) circuit failure - Perform TAD (AIRD) circuit checks.
   82 and 552, TAB (AIRB) circuit failure - Perform TAB (AIRB) circuit checks.

Evaporative control system trouble code

7   For check procedures, refer to Section 3.
   KOEO code:
   85 and 565, Purge solenoid valve circuit failure.

10   Emission related components - removal and installation

Refer to illustrations 10.2, 10.19, 10.20, 10.21, 10.31 and 10.35

EGR system components

EGR Valve Position (EVP) sensor

1   Detach the cable from the negative ter-

minal of the battery.
2   Locate the EVP sensor on the EGR valve **(see illustration)**.
3   Unplug the electrical connector from the sensor.
4   Remove the three mounting bolts and detach the sensor.
5   Installation is the reverse of removal except use new O-ring.

EGR Control (EGRC) or EGR Vent (EGRV) Solenoid

6   Detach the cable from the negative terminal of the battery.
7   Locate the vacuum control solenoid(s) on the firewall, fender apron or engine mounted solenoid bracket assembly.
8   Unplug the electrical electrical connector from the solenoid(s).
9   Label the vacuum hoses and ports, then detach the hoses.
10   Remove the solenoid/bracket screws and detach the solenoid(s).
11   Installation is the reverse of removal.

EGR Vacuum Regulator (EVR) solenoid

12   Detach the cable from the negative terminal of the battery.
13   Locate the EVR on the engine mounted solenoid bracket assembly.
14   Detach the sensor harness electrical connector and vacuum hose.
15   Remove the sensor screw and remove the solenoid.
16   Installation is the reverse of removal.

EGR valve

17   Detach the cable from the negative terminal of the battery.
18   On vehicles with EEGR, unplug the electrical connector from the EGR valve position sensor **(see illustration 10.2)**.
19   On vehicles with external exhaust supply tube, unscrew the threaded fitting that attaches the EGR pipe to the EGR valve **(see illustration)**.
20   Remove the vacuum line and two mounting bolts, then detach the valve **(see illustration)**.

10.20 Unscrew the EGR valve bolts and remove the valve

10.21 Carefully remove all traces of the old gasket

21 Remove the old gasket **(see illustration)**.

22 On vehicles with EEGR, If you're replacing the EGR valve but not the position sensor, remove the sensor from the old valve and install it on the new valve with a new O-ring.

23 Installation is the reverse of removal.

Thermactor system components

Thermactor Air By-Pass (TAB/AIRB) or Thermactor Air Diverter (TAD/AIRD) solenoid

24 Detach the cable from the negative terminal of the battery.

25 Locate the vacuum control solenoid(s) on the rear firewall, fender apron, or engine mounted solenoid bracket assembly.

26 Unplug the electrical electrical connector from the solenoid(s).

27 Label the vacuum hoses and ports, then detach the hoses.

28 Remove the solenoid/bracket screws and detach the solenoid(s).

29 Installation is the reverse of removal.

Air pump and control valves

30 On MTA systems, to replace the air bypass valve, air supply control valve, check valve, combination air bypass/air control valve or the silencer, label and disconnect the hoses leading to them, replace the faulty component and reattach the hoses to the proper ports. Make sure the hoses are in good condition. If not, replace them with new ones.

31 To replace the MTA air supply pump, first loosen the appropriate engine drivebelts (refer to Chapter 1), then remove the faulty pump from the mounting bracket **(see illustration)**. Label all hoses as they're removed to facilitate installation of the new unit.

32 After the new pump is installed, adjust the drivebelts to the specified tension (refer to Chapter 1).

33 If you're replacing either of the check valves, be sure to use a back-up wrench if connected to a steel air tube.

Evaporative systems component

Charcoal canister

34 Locate the canister in the engine compartment.

35 Reach up above the canister and remove the single mounting bolt **(see illustration)**.

36 Lower the canister, detach the hose from the purge valve, or purge solenoid valve, and remove the canister.

37 Installation is the reverse of removal.

All other components

38 Referring to the appropriate vacuum hose and vacuum valve schematics in this Section and on the VECI label of your vehicle, locate the component to be replaced.

39 Label the hoses and fittings, then detach the hoses and remove the component.

40 Installation is the reverse of removal.

Air inlet control components

41 Replacement of the thermal vacuum valves and vacuum motor is straightforward and is accomplished either unsnapping or unbolting the faulty component, removing the vacuum lines leading to it (where appropriate) and installing the new component.

Deceleration throttle control system components

42 Replacement of the throttle positioner, solenoid valve and/or sensing switch is straightforward, accomplished by disconnecting the attached wires and/or hoses, removing the faulty component and replacing it with a new one.

10.31 Location of thermactor system air pump on early carbureted vehicles - V8 shown, others similar

10.35 To remove the charcoal canister, detach the vacuum hose and remove the mounting bolt (arrows)

11.3a The bi-metal vacuum control sensor for the heated air intake system is mounted inside the air cleaner housing. To remove it, detach the hoses and pry the clip off the ports

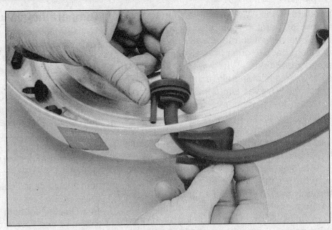

11.3b The heated intake air Cold Weather Modulator (CWM) is mounted inside the air cleaner housing and is retained by a spring clip

Intake manifold heating system components

43   The replacement of the exhaust heat control valve is straightforward, accomplished by unbolting the faulty valve from its location, cleaning the mating surfaces on the exhaust manifold and head pipe and installing a new valve.

PCV system components

44   Component replacement involves simply installing a new valve, hose, or filter in place of the one removed during the checking procedure.

Catalytic converter

45   Do not attempt to remove the catalytic converter until the complete exhaust system is cool. Raise the vehicle and support it securely on jackstands. Apply some penetrating oil to the clamp bolts and allow it to soak in.
46   Remove the bolts and the rubber hangers, then separate the converter from the exhaust pipes. Remove the old gaskets if they are stuck to the pipes.

47   Installation of the converter is the reverse of removal. Use new exhaust pipe gaskets and tighten the clamp bolts to the specified torque (refer to the Chapter 4 Specifications). Replace the rubber hangers with new ones if the originals are deteriorated. Start the engine and check carefully for exhaust leaks.

11   Inlet air control system (carbureted models) - description and checks

Refer to illustrations 11.3a, 11.3b, 11.4a, and 11.4b

General description

1   The air cleaner temperature control system is used to keep the air entering the carburetor at a warm and consistent temperature. The carburetor can then be calibrated much leaner for emissions reduction, improved warm-up and better driveability.
2   When the underhood temperature is cold, air is drawn through a shroud which fits

over the exhaust manifold, up through the heat riser tube and into the air cleaner. This provides warm air for the carburetor, resulting in better driveability and faster warm-up. As the under-hood temperature rises, some means of redirecting incoming air away from the heat tube to normal air is necessary for best performance. This is accomplished by a vacuum motor duct valve and by two temperature sensitive vacuum control valves, the bi-metal sensor and the Cold Weather Modulator (CWM) valve. **Caution:** *Some vehicles may not use CWM valve.*
3   The bi-metal sensor allows manifold vacuum to pass through it only if the average temperature of the air inside the air cleaner housing is under a certain temperature **(see illustration)**. When warm, the bi-metal sensor closes, shutting of the supply vacuum and venting the control line. When open, the vacuum passing through the bi-metal sensor is routed to the CWM valve. The CWM is also installed in the air cleaner housing very close to the hot air inlet **(see illustration)**. This allows the CWM to sense incoming air tem-

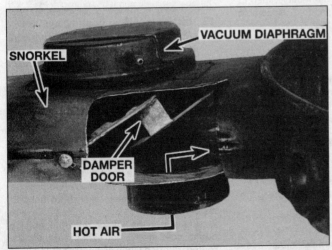

11.4a When the engine is cold, the damper door is raised and hot air is admitted to the carburetor

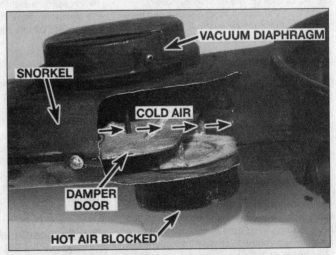

11.4b When the engine reaches operating temperature, the vacuum diaphragm receives no vacuum and the damper door shuts, allowing cool air into the carburetor

perature. The CWM allows vacuum to pass at low temperatures but also incorporates a check valve function to prevent reverse flow (venting) back through the valve under these same conditions. When warm, the CWM valve opens allowing air/vacuum flow in both directions. The vacuum from the CWM valve is routed to the vacuum-activated duct valve motor. The duct valve is a simple flap-type valve controlling the path of incoming air (heated or normal). It is moved by the vacuum motor and a mechanical link.

4   In operation, when cold, manifold vacuum travels through the bi-metal sensor and through the CWM valve to the duct valve vacuum motor. With vacuum applied, the duct valve will route the incoming air through the heated air supply **(see illustrations)**. The CWM effectively traps the vacuum between the motor and itself to maintain the duct position even if manifold vacuum should decrease (such as when the vehicle is accelerated). For the duct valve to move to its normal spring loaded position (normal incoming air) the bi-metal sensor must be warmed to its closing position and the CWM valve must be warmed to its opening temperature. Only then will the trapped motor vacuum be allowed to vent through the open CWM to the vented port of the closed bi-metal sensor.

Check
General
5   Checking of this system should be done while the engine is cold.
6   Remove the clamp retaining the air hose to the rear of the metal duct and valve assembly. Looking through the rear of the duct and valve assembly, observe that the duct valve (heat control door) is positioned to allow normal air entry from the air intake snorkel into the air cleaner housing.
7   Start the engine and as the engine warms up, the vacuum motor should pull the valve towards the heat riser tube and allow heated air to enter the air cleaner housing.
8   When the vehicle reaches operating temperature, the duct valve (heat control door) should again be positioned to allow normal air entry from the air intake snorkel into the air cleaner housing.

Duct valve
9   If the duct valve does not perform as indicated, check that it is not rusted in an open or closed position by attempting to move it by hand. If it is rusted, it can usually be freed by cleaning and oiling it, otherwise replace it with a new unit.

Vacuum motor
10   If the vacuum motor fails to perform as indicated, check carefully for a leak in the hose leading to it. If no leak is found, use a hand vacuum pump to check motor operation. Motor should hold vacuum and move duct valve from the spring loaded position. If not, replace vacuum motor.

Temperature vacuum valves
11   Check vacuum at bi-metal sensor inlet port. Vacuum should be present with engine running. If not, trace hose to source and/or remove any blockages until vacuum is indicated.
12   Check for vacuum at outlet port of bi-metal sensor with engine cold and warm. Vacuum should be indicated at cold only. if not, replace sensor. Reconnect bi-metal sensor hoses for next check.
13   Disconnect CWM outlet (to motor) hose and check for vacuum with engine cold. Vacuum should be indicated. If not, replace CWM valve.
14   Disconnect both CWM valve hoses and check for free flow through valve when warm. Flow should be indicated. If not, replace CWM valve.

12   Deceleration throttle control system (carbureted models) - description and checks

General description
1   This system reduces the hydrocarbon and carbon monoxide content of exhaust gasses by opening the throttle slightly during deceleration.
2   The system consists of a throttle positioner, a vacuum solenoid valve, a vacuum sensing switch and electrical linkups to an electronic speed sensor/governor module, although not all components are included in all systems.
3   On those models without a vacuum sensing switch, when the engine speed is higher than a predetermined rpm, a signal is sent to the solenoid, which allows manifold vacuum to activate the throttle positioner.
4   On those models with a vacuum sensing switch, when the engine speed is higher than a predetermined rpm and manifold vacuum is at a certain value, the signal from the vacuum switch sends a signal to the module, then to the solenoid, allowing manifold vacuum to activate the throttle positioner.

Check
General
5   All of the following checks are to be made with the engine at full operating temperature and with all accessories off unless otherwise noted.
6   With the engine at idle, accelerate to 2000 rpm or more, then let the engine fall back to idle while watching to see if the vacuum diaphragm plunger extends and retracts. If the plunger performs as indicated, the system is functioning normally. If not, check the throttle positioner.

Throttle positioner
7   Remove the hose from the throttle positioner and, using a hand-operated vacuum pump, apply a 19 in.Hg vacuum to the diaphragm and trap it. If the diaphragm does not

respond or will not hold vacuum, replace the throttle positioner with a new one.
8   Remove the vacuum pump from the diaphragm and see if the diaphragm returns within five seconds. If not, replace the throttle positioner with a new one.

Vacuum solenoid valve
9   With the engine at idle, disconnect the vacuum supply hose from the solenoid valve and verify that the hose is supplying vacuum.
10   Disconnect the wires from the solenoid and apply battery voltage to both terminals, verifying that there is no increase in engine speed.
11   With battery voltage supplied to one terminal, ground the other terminal and verify that engine speed increases.
12   Remove the ground and verify that the engine returns to idle rpm.
13   If the solenoid fails to pass any of the above tests, replace it with a new one.

Vacuum sensing switch (if so equipped)
14   Disconnect the hose from the vacuum fitting on the switch.
15   Hook up a hand-operated vacuum pump to the fitting.
16   Using an ohmmeter, verify that the switch is open (no continuity) while applying a 19.4 in.Hg vacuum or less to the switch.
17   Increase the vacuum to 20.6 in.Hg or more and verify that the switch is closed (continuity).
18   If the switch fails to pass either of the above tests, replace it with a new one.

Electronic speed sensor/governor module (if so equipped)
19   If a fault is suspected in the module, it must be checked by a dealer service department or other repair shop.

Component replacement
20   Refer to Section 10 for component replacement procedures.

13   Intake manifold heating system (carbureted models) - description and checks

Refer to illustrations 13.4 and 13.7

General description
1   This system is employed to eliminate any condensation of fuel on the cold surfaces of the intake system during cold engine operation and to provide better evaporation and distribution of the air/fuel mixture. The result is better driveability, faster warm-up and a reduction in the release of hydrocarbons to the atmosphere.
2   To warm the intake manifold quickly during cold starts, hot exhaust gases are routed through special heat riser or heat crossover passages in the intake manifold. After the intake manifold is warm, these hot

13.4 Typical temperature-controlled heat control valve

ACTUATOR ASSEMBLY

13.7 Typical vacuum-controlled heat control valve

gases must be redirected away from the intake manifold for best performance. Therefore, a control system is required to properly manage the exhaust flow into the intake crossover. The component of this system is the exhaust heat control valve, which is controlled by either a bi-metal thermostat or a temperature activated vacuum motor.

3   The heat control valve is mounted between the exhaust manifold and one branch of the exhaust pipe. The valve operates by remaining closed when the engine is cold which forces hot exhaust gasses to the intake manifold area through the heat riser (crossover) passage. The bi-metal thermostat heat valve uses a heat sensitive spring to keep the valve closed when cold, and opens the valve when warm. The vacuum motor heat valve uses a coolant temperature Vacuum Control Valve (VCV) which allows manifold vacuum to the motor when cold, but closes vacuum off when warm. When vacuum is applied to the motor, the valve is closed. When vacuum is released, the motor returns to its normal spring-loaded open condition.

Checking

Bi-metal thermostat valve

4   With the engine cold, manually rotate the valve shaft **(see illustration)**. It must move freely and return to the closed position as long as the engine is cold. If it's stuck, spray it with penetrating oil until free. If unsuccessful in freeing, replace it.

5   Start the engine and, as it warms up, make sure that the valve shaft has rotated to the open position. **Caution:** *Valve will be hot!*

6   If the valve fails to operate as described, replace it with a new one.

Vacuum operated valve

7   With the engine cold, the vacuum motor must be in the extended (valve open) condition. Manually rotate the shaft and verify free movement of the shaft and vacuum motor mechanical linkage **(see illustration)**. If stuck, spray with penetrating oil until free. If unsuccessful in freeing, replace valve.

8   Using hand held vacuum pump, apply vacuum to motor and observe motor linkage. Vacuum should hold and valve should move to closed position. If not, replace vacuum motor or entire heat control valve.

9   Start up the engine and verify that there is vacuum at the motor vacuum hose. If not, check the vacuum line, VCV (should be open) and manifold vacuum source.

10   Reconnect the vacuum line at the valve and verify the heat valve closes. After it has warmed, verify the heat valve has opened (motor has no vacuum and has fully extended). **Caution:** *Valve will be hot!* If the motor has vacuum when hot, replace the VCV.

Component replacement

11   Refer to Section 10 for component replacement procedures.

---

14   Catalytic converter - description and checks

General description

1   The catalytic converter is designed to reduce emissions of unburned hydrocarbons (HC), carbon monoxide (CO) and, in the case of newer converters, nitrogen oxides (NOx) as well. The converter oxidizes these components and converts them to water and carbon dioxide. The converter is a post combustion device, in that it does all its work after the engine has expelled the exhaust but before the exhaust leaves the vehicle. The converter assembly closely resembles a muffler, however its internal construction is completely different. The converter assembly consists of a monolithic honeycomb structure filled will ceramic "pellets" which have been impregnated with a catalytically active metal. The spaces between the pellets allow free flow of exhaust gasses through the converter while allowing the greatest exposed active surface area.

2   To operate most effectively, the converter requires a secondary source of injected air (see thermactor operation) to initiate the oxidation (burning) process of the incoming pollutants. Once begun, the catalytic action of the pellets greatly increases the rate of oxidation (burning) and the corresponding internal temperature inside the converter. The high temperatures further reduce the amount of pollutants in the exhaust gases.

3   The converter is located in the exhaust system between the engine and the muffler. Some models have two converters, a light-off catalyst type, mounted just past the exhaust manifold pipe, and a conventional oxidation catalyst or three-way catalyst type mounted farther downstream. **Caution:** *If large amounts of unburned gasoline enter the catalyst, it may overheat and cause a fire. Always observe the following precautions: Use only unleaded gasoline, avoid prolonged idling, do not perform prolonged engine compression checks, do not run the engine with a nearly empty fuel tank, avoid coasting with the ignition turned Off, and do not dispose of a used catalytic converter along with oily or gasoline soaked parts as a reaction may take place.*

Physical checks

4   The catalytic converter requires little if any maintenance and servicing at regular intervals. However, the system should be inspected whenever the vehicle is raised on a lift or if the exhaust system is checked or serviced.

5   Check all connections in the exhaust pipe assembly for looseness or damage. Also check all the clamps for damage, cracks, or missing fasteners. Check the rubber hangers for cracks.

6   The converter itself should be checked for damage or dents which could affect its performance and/or be hazardous to your health. At the same time the converter is inspected, check the metal protector plate under it as well as the heat insulator above it for damage or loose fasteners.

Functional checks

7   Potential converter problems can be associated with two situations, vehicle fails state smog certification check or poor engine power. Both situations can be caused by a converter that has been overheated and is either non-functional or restrictive.

8   A non-functional converter is difficult to diagnose. If all other engine systems are operating properly, and the converter is relatively cold (this is a judgment call, no specifications exist, **do not** check by feeling converter) the converter is probably bad.

9   A restricted converter can be checked. if a performance issue is in question, proceed to backpressure check.

Backpressure check

10   Attach a vacuum gauge to a source of manifold vacuum and attach tachometer (if none in dash).

11   Set the parking brake and put the transmission in Neutral (manual transmission) or Park (automatic transmission).

12   Start engine and warm to operating temperature. Turn engine off and wait for a few minutes (allows any backpressure to escape).

13   Start engine and observe vacuum gauge. Vacuum should be 16 inch Hg or greater on engine in good tune.

14   Let engine idle for a few minutes while watching gauge. Vacuum should hold fairly steady.

15   Increase engine speed and hold for one minute at 2000 rpm while observing vacuum gauge. Vacuum gauge should read continuously high vacuum at the end of one minute with no additional throttle required to maintain rpm. If vacuum gauge dropped significantly or if more throttle was required to maintain rpm, converter restriction is suspect. Turn engine off and proceed to next operation to isolate.

16   Let exhaust system cool, then remove the exhaust pipe at the exhaust manifold(s).

17   Repeat test. If vacuum is now steady and high in engine running test, the converter is restrictive. Replace the converter. **Caution:** *Although rare, if a restricted muffler is suspected, reconnect the converter, disconnect the muffler and repeat the test to determine if the muffler is the cause.*

Component replacement

18   Refer to Section 10 for the component replacement procedures.

Chapter 7 Part A
Manual transmission

Contents

Specifications

Torque specifications

Ft-lbs (unless otherwise indicated)

Note: *One foot-pound (ft-lb) of torque is equivalent to 12 inch-pounds (in-lbs) of torque. Torque values below approximately 15 ft-lbs are expressed in inch-pounds, since most foot-pound torque wrenches are not accurate at these smaller values.*

Gearshift linkage adjusting nuts (3.03 3-speed)	12 to 18
Transmission-to-clutch housing bolts	
3.03 3-speed	42 to 50
T-18 4-speed	35 to 50
T-19B 4-speed	37 to 42
New process 435 4-speed	70 to 110
Single rail 4-speed overdrive	35 to 45
Transmission-to-engine bolts	50
Shift lever-to-shift housing stub shaft	
T-18-4 speed (later model)	16 to 24
Mazda M5OD 5-speed	12 to 18
ZF S5-42 and ZF S5-47 5-speed	16 to 24
Transmission mounting	
Lower absorber assemblies (early 4WD)	30 to 50
Mount-to-transmission	45 to 60
Mount-to-crossmember	60 to 80
Crossmember and gussets to frame	45 to 55
Speedometer cable retaining bolt	60 to 84 in-lbs
Rear output shaft yoke retaining nut (if equipped)	
ZF S5-42 5-speed	184
ZF S5-47 5-speed	200
All others	75 to 110

1   Manual transmission - general information

1   Many manually shifted transmissions have been available on F-series and Bronco vehicles over the years. From 1980 through 1987 these include the 3.03 3-speed, the Warner T-18 4-speed, the Warner T-19 4-speed, the New Process 435 4-speed, the single-rail 4-speed overdrive (SROD) and the top mounted shifter 4-speed overdrive (TOD). Transmissions available from 1988 include the Mazda M5OD 5-speed, the S5-42 ZF 5-speed light and heavy duty and the T-18 4-speed.

2   Regardless of year, all transmissions are fully synchronized with all gears, except the reverse sliding gear, which is in constant mesh. The 3 and 4-speed models utilize a bolt-on clutch housing (bell housing) while the 5-speed models incorporate the clutch housing and transmission into a single casting. The 3-speed model is a side shifter with external shift levers and mechanism allowing the use of a steering column shift lever. The remaining transmissions contain the shift mechanisms internally allowing direct-shifting from a simple top mounted shift lever which extends through the floor of the cab. The S5-42 ZF 5-speed is available in two case configurations; concentric slave cylinder design (light duty) or external slave cylinder design (heavy duty).

3   Application of the transmissions depends on the year, engine and model of the vehicle in which it is installed. If you are in doubt as to which transmission is in your particular vehicle, check with your local Ford dealer or automotive transmission facility.

4   Due to the complexity of transmissions and because of the special tools and expertise required to perform an overhaul, it is not advised that it be undertaken by the home mechanic. Therefore, the procedures in this Chapter are limited to routine adjustments, and removal and installation procedures.

5   Depending upon the expense involved in having a faulty transmission overhauled, it may be of advantage to consider replacing the unit with either a new or rebuilt one. Your local dealer or transmission specialty shop should be able to supply you with information concerning these units as to their cost, availability and exchange policy. Regardless of how you decide to remedy a faulty transmission problem, however, you can still save considerable expense by removing it and installing it yourself.

2   Shift linkage adjustment (column mounted shifter)

1   The 3.03 3-speed transmission has provisions for adjustment of the shifting linkage. The other transmissions applicable to vehicles covered by this manual are of the direct-shifting, non-adjustable type.

2   Find the shift levers at the base of the steering column, in the engine compartment. Install a steel pin of 3/16-inch diameter through the locating hole and plastic spacer in the steering column shift levers with the levers in Neutral.

3   Working under the vehicle, locate the two shift lever locknuts at the transmission. Loosen the locknuts and position the transmission shift levers in the Neutral detent positions.

4   Tighten the locknuts, using care to prevent movement between the studs and rods as the nuts are tightened.

5   Remove the gauge pin from the steering column shift levers.

6   Check the linkage operation.

7   **Note:** *Always use new retaining rings and insulators when making linkage adjustments.*

3   Shift lever - removal and installation

Note: *Removal of the shift lever is a prerequisite to removing the transmission from the vehicle. Although the shift lever is part of a much more complicated gear shift housing mechanism, only the removal steps necessary to allow transmission removal will be outlined in this section. See the overhaul section for further information on the internal shifting mechanisms.*

Top-mounted (floor) shifters

1   Depending on model, from inside cab, remove floor carpet, shift lever boot, pad, floor plate and or transmission cover to gain access to top of gear shift housing. **Note:** *The shift lever dust boot can be simply slid up the shift lever shaft, total removal is not necessary.*

2   Follow the steps as applicable to your transmission to remove shift lever from gear shift housing:

a)   *On early model T-18, T-19, NP 435 and TOD transmissions, using large adjustable pliers unscrew lever cap from top of gear shift housing and lift lever up and out of transmission.* **Caution:** *Avoid marring the cap with the jaw teeth if possible.*

b)   *On later model T-18 and all S5-42 ZF transmissions, remove the two screws securing shift lever to gear shift housing stub shaft and remove lever.*

c)   *On the SROD transmission, remove the bolts securing the shift lever pivot assembly into the gear housing turret and lift lever up and out of transmission.*

d)   *On the Mazda M5OD, remove the lock nut from the tapered bolt securing shift lever to gear shift housing stub shaft. Install the locknut on the other end of the tapered bolt and tighten to break loose the interference fit of the bolt. Remove the bolt and lift the shift lever*

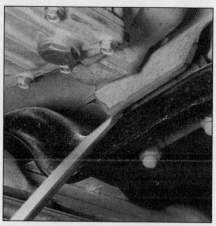

4.2 Pry up on the transmission mount and check for excessive looseness

out of the stub shaft.

3   Installation is reverse of removal with the following additions as applicable:

a)   *On early model T-18, T-19, NP 435 and TOD transmissions, align the slots in the shift lever pivot "half ball" with the pins in the gear housing.*

b)   *On SROD transmission, make sure slot in bottom of shift lever aligns with tab in gear housing turret.*

c)   *On Mazda M5OD, align flat in tapered bolt with flat in gear housing stub shaft.*

4   Tighten the fasteners to the torque listed in this Chapter's Specifications.

3-speed side-mounted (column) shifter

5   Raise the vehicle and support it securely on jackstands.

6   Remove the shift linkage at the transmission shift levers.

7   Installation is reverse of removal, except be sure to adjust the shift linkage prior to tightening the linkage-to-shift lever nuts to the torque listed in this Chapter's Specifications.

4   Transmission mounts - check and replacement

Refer to illustration 4.2

Check

1   Raise the vehicle and support it securely on jackstands.

2   Insert a large screwdriver or prybar into the space between the transmission extension housing and the frame crossmember and pry up **(see illustration)**.

3   The transmission should not move significantly away from the insulator. If it does, the mount should be replaced - proceed to Step 5 or 10.

4   If the mount is okay, remove the jackstands and lower vehicle.

Replacement

Early 4WD models

5   Remove the two lower insulator retainers and insulators, then remove the two insulator bolts.

6   Place a jack under the transmission and raise it enough to allow removal of the two upper insulators between the transmission bracket and crossmember.

7   Install new upper insulators with the protruding shoulder facing down through the crossmember.

8   Lower transmission and install the insulator bolts. Tighten two new lower insulator retainer assemblies to the torque listed in this Chapter's Specifications.

9   Remove the jackstands and lower the vehicle. Test drive the vehicle to confirm proper operation.

All other models

10   Remove the two mount-to-crossmember nuts and the two mount-to-transmission bolts.

11   Place a jack under the transmission and raise enough to allow removal of the mount.

12   Install a new mount and lower the transmission enough to start all fasteners hand tight.

13   Remove the jack and tighten the mount fasteners to the torque listed in this Chapter's Specifications.

14   Remove the jackstands and lower the vehicle.

5   Manual transmission - removal and installation

Removal

1   Disconnect the battery negative cable.

2   Drain the transmission lubricant into a suitable container.

3   Raise the vehicle and support it securely on jackstands.

4   On vehicles equipped with direct-shifting (no external linkage arms) transmissions, remove the shift lever (see Section 3)

5   On vehicles equipped with a column shift, detach the shift linkage at the transmission (see Section 3).

6   Disconnect the electrical connector from the back-up light switch.

7   On 1991 and earlier 2WD models, remove the speedometer cable retaining bolt and remove the speedometer cable and gear assembly. On vehicles equipped with cruise control, disconnect the speed sensor electrical connector. Position the cable out of the way to avoid damage or contamination. **Note:** *1992 and later models do not use a mechanical speedometer cable.*

8   On vehicles with a concentric slave cylinder, disconnect the clutch hydraulic line from slave cylinder (see Chapter 8).

9   On 5-speed models equipped with a 7.5L engine, remove the external slave cyl-

inder from transmission housing (see Chapter 8). **Note:** *It is not necessary to disconnect the hydraulic line from slave cylinder. Also, it's a good idea to detach the pushrod from the clutch pedal to prevent damage to the slave cylinder just in case the clutch pedal is accidentally depressed.*

10   On 2WD models, disconnect the driveshaft (see Chapter 8).

11   If the vehicle is a 4WD, remove the transfer case shift lever assembly from the transmission extension housing and remove transfer case (see Chapter 7C).

12   On 5 speed models, remove the bolts retaining the starter motor from the transmission (see Chapter 5).

13   Support the transmission with a transmission jack. Make sure the transmission is securely fastened to the jack.

14   Remove the transmission rear mount (see Section 4). If the right and left gussets are installed between the crossmember and frame rails, remove the gusset attaching nuts and bolts and remove the gussets. Remove any harness ties on crossmember and remove the crossmember.

15   On 3 and 4-speed transmissions, remove the transmission retaining bolts from the rear of the clutch housing. On 5-speed models, remove the transmission case-to-engine block retaining bolts.

16   Slowly withdraw the transmission straight back to disengage the input shaft from the clutch disc, making sure not to put unnecessary pressure on the transmission input shaft. Once the input shaft has cleared the clutch housing (3 and 4-speed models) or clutch disc (5-speed models), lower the transmission and remove it from beneath the vehicle.

Installation

17   Check all clutch related components and replace worn parts as required prior to transmission installation (see Chapter 8).

18   Prepare the release bearing for reinstallation (see Chapter 8).

19   Install the clutch housing if removed on vehicles so equipped and make sure the clutch release bearing and hub are properly positioned on the release lever fork (see Chapter 8).

20   Secure the transmission to the transmission jack and raise it up so that the input shaft is in line with the clutch disc splines.

21   Verify that the dowel pins are installed in the engine block.

22   On models with a separate clutch housing, wiggle the transmission forwards, inserting the input shaft through the release bearing hub and into the clutch disc splines until the transmission mates with the clutch housing. **Note:** *If difficulty is encountered, rotate the output shaft with the transmission in gear to help engage the splines, and make sure the transmission centerline is in alignment with crankshaft centerline. Wiggle the release lever if the release bearing is having difficulty sliding over the transmission input shaft bearing retainer.*

23   On models with one piece transmission/clutch housings, wiggle the transmission forwards, inserting the input shaft into the clutch disc splines until the transmission mates with the engine block. **Note:** *If difficulty is encountered, rotate the output shaft with the transmission in gear to help engage the splines, and make sure the transmission centerline is in alignment with the crankshaft centerline.*

24   Install the retaining bolts, tightening them to the torque listed in this Chapter's Specifications.

25   The remainder of installation is the reverse of removal.

26   After connecting the line to the concentric slave cylinder on models so equipped, bleed the clutch hydraulic system (see Chapter 8).

6   Speedometer pinion gear and seal - replacement

Refer to illustrations 6.5 and 6.6

Note: *1992 and later models use an electronic speedometer which gets its speed signal from the rear anti-lock brake speed sensor. Therefore, no mechanical speedometer cable is required.*

1   Raise the vehicle and support it securely on jackstands.

2   Remove the bolt securing the speedometer cable retaining bracket and remove the bracket and bolt as an assembly.

3   Pull the speedometer cable and pinion gear straight out of the transmission or transfer case.

4   On vehicles equipped with cruise control, disconnect the speed sensor electrical connector.

5   Use a small screwdriver to remove the retaining clip from the pinion gear, then slide the gear off the cable **(see illustration)**.

6   If necessary, use a small screwdriver to remove the O-ring from the retaining groove **(see illustration)**. Discard the O-ring.

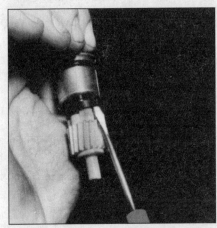

6.5 Pry the retaining clip from the pinion gear and slide the gear off of the cable

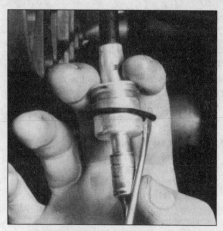

6.6 Pry off the old O-ring with a small screwdriver

7   Lubricate the new O-ring with transmission lubricant and install it in the retaining groove. Make sure it's seated correctly and not twisted.

8   Install the pinion gear on the cable and install the retaining clip. Make sure the clip is properly seated in the groove.

9   Install the speedometer pinion gear and cable in the transfer case or transmission and secure it with the bolt and bracket.

10   Connect the speed sensor electrical connector if equipped.

---

7   Extension housing oil seal - replacement

Note: *This procedure applies only to 2WD models.*

1   Raise the vehicle and support it securely on jackstands.

2   The extension housing oil seal is located at the extreme rear of the transmission, where the driveshaft is attached. If leakage at the seal is suspected, raise the vehicle and support it securely on jackstands. If the seal is leaking, transmission lubricant will be built up on the front of the driveshaft and may be dripping from the rear of the transmission.

3   Refer to Chapter 8 and remove the driveshaft.

4   On circular flange or yoke type rear output shafts, remove the flange/yoke nut and washer and remove flange/yoke.

5   Using a soft-faced hammer, carefully tap the dust shield (if equipped) to the rear and remove it from the transmission. Be careful not to distort it.

6   Using a screwdriver or prybar, carefully pry the oil seal and bushing (if equipped) out of the rear of the transmission. Do not damage the splines on the transmission output shaft.

7   If the oil seal and bushing cannot be removed with a screwdriver or prybar, a special oil seal removal tool (available at auto parts stores) will be required.

8   Using a large section of pipe or a very large deep socket as a drift, install the new oil seal. Drive it into the bore squarely and make sure it's completely seated.

9   Reinstall the dust shield, if equipped, by carefully tapping it into place.

10   On circular flange or yoke type output shafts, clean the yoke splines and lightly lubricate them with multi-purpose grease, then slip the flange/yoke over the output shaft and carefully past the new seal until it bottoms. Coat the nut with a thread locking compound. Install the washer and nut and tighten the nut to the torque listed in this Chapter's Specifications.

11   Lubricate the splines of the transmission output shaft and the outside of the driveshaft sleeve yoke with lightweight grease, then install the driveshaft. Be careful not to damage the lip of the new seal.

12   On circular flange or yoke type output shaft, install the yoke, washer and retaining nut.

13   Install the rear driveshaft (see Chapter 8).

14   Check/refill the transmission with lubricant (see Chapter 1).

15   Remove the jackstands and lower the vehicle.

---

8   Manual transmission overhaul - general information

1   Overhauling a manual transmission is a difficult job for the do-it-your-selfer. It involves the disassembly and reassembly of many small parts. Numerous clearances must be precisely measured and, if necessary, changed with select fit spacers and snap-rings. As a result, if transmission problems arise, it can be removed and installed by a competent do-it-your-selfer, but overhaul should be left to a transmission repair shop. Rebuilt transmissions may be available - check with your dealer parts department and auto parts stores. At any rate, the time and money involved in an overhaul is almost sure to exceed the cost of a rebuilt unit.

2   Nevertheless, it's not impossible for an inexperienced mechanic to rebuild a transmission if the special tools are available and the job is done in a deliberate step-by-step manner so nothing is overlooked. The tools necessary for an overhaul include internal and external snap-ring pliers, bearing puller, slide hammer, set of pin punches, dial indicator and possibly a hydraulic press. In addition, a large, sturdy work-bench and a large vise or

transmission stand will be required.

3   Before taking the transmission apart for repair, it will help if you have some idea what area of the transmission is malfunctioning. Certain problems can be closely tied to specific areas in the transmission, which can make component examination and replacement easier. Refer to the *Troubleshooting* section at the front of this manual for information regarding possible sources of trouble.

4   If you choose to overhaul the transmission yourself, try to obtain exploded-view drawings of your particular transmission. Several suggestions can be made to assist you in your efforts:

a)   *It is very helpful to draw your own simple diagram, take instant photos or video tape during the disassembly process. Laying each part out in the order in which it was removed also helps.*

b)   *If a case half or component will not remove easily, look closely for any missed bolts, snap rings or other source of interference before moderate force is used. Excessive force is not required and is a sure sign something in the disassembly/reassembly sequence was missed.*

c)   *Try to anticipate which parts may have to be replaced and have them available before beginning. Regardless of broken or badly worn components, there are certain items which must be replaced as a matter of course when the transmission is reassembled. These include gaskets, snap-rings, oil seals and sometimes bearings. You will also need some multi-purpose grease and a silicone-type gasket sealer to properly reassemble the transmission.*

d)   *Cleanliness is extremely important when working on a precision piece of equipment such as a transmission. The work area should be kept as clean and free of dirt and dust as possible. Also, adequate space should be available to lay out the various parts as they are removed.*

e)   *Prelubricate all parts prior to assembly with the appropriate type of fluid. Use assembly lube to hold loose needle bearings, thrust washers and other small difficult-to-handle items into position during assembly.*

f)   *Prior to reinstallation into vehicle, rotate the input shaft and shift the case through its gears observing for any binding, excessive resistance or lock-up. If any anomalous behavior is exhibited, resolve the problem before further damage is done by trying to apply engine power.*

g)   *Remember to fill the case with the appropriate type and quantity of fluid.*

Chapter 7 Part B
Automatic transmission

Contents

Specifications

Torque specifications
Note: *One foot-pound (ft-lb) of torque is equivalent to 12 inch-pounds (in-lbs) of torque. Torque values below approximately 15 ft-lbs are expressed in inch-pounds, since most foot-pound torque wrenches are not accurate at these smaller values.*

Ft-lbs (unless otherwise indicated)

Torque converter-to-driveplate nuts	20 to 30
Fluid pan bolts	See Chapter 1
Converter housing-to-transmission case	28 to 40
E4OD solenoid body fasteners	80 to 100 in-lbs
Transmission-to-engine bolts	38 to 52

---

1 Automatic transmission - general information

Since the F-series and Bronco introduction, several automatic transmissions have been available. Early options included the automatic overdrive (AOD) 4-speed and the C4, C5 and C6 3-speed transmissions. In 1988, the electronically controlled E4OD 4-speed transmission supplemented the C6 and AOD models.

Other than the number of forward speeds, the main differences between the transmissions are in their maximum torque carrying capacity and their speed and load sensing mechanisms which determine shift points. The C-series automatic transmissions utilize a governor for speed sensing and a vacuum diaphragm throttle valve to sense engine load. A throttle kickdown rod is incorporated for operator-forced downshifts upon application of wide open throttle. The AOD transmission uses a governor for speed and throttle valve rod (early year) or cable (later year) for load sensing. The throttle valve mechanism translates the full range of throttle positions into throttle valve lever movement at the transmission. The E4OD transmission

uses various engine and drivetrain sensors and special programming within the electronic engine control (EEC) computer to calculate speed and load conditions, then commands actuators within the transmission to initiate a shift.

Due to the complexity of automatic transmissions, if performance is not up to par and overhaul is necessary, repairs should be performed by a dealership or other shop with the qualified personnel and special equipment necessary. The Sections which follow in this Chapter are designed to provide the home mechanic with service information and instructions for operations that he may perform without specialized equipment and training.

Depending upon the expense involved in having a faulty transmission overhauled, it may be of advantage to consider replacing the unit with either a new or rebuilt one. Your local dealer or transmission specialty shop should be able to supply you with information concerning these units as to their cost, availability and exchange policy. Regardless of how you decide to remedy a faulty transmission problem, however, you can still save considerable expense by removing it and installing it yourself.

Note: *All automatic transmissions supplied as original equipment on vehicles covered by this manual are equipped with high-temperature-resistant seals. This includes those seals used on the manual and kickdown levers, the O-rings and oil pan gasket. Under no circumstances should older design seals be used on the transmission.*

2 Diagnosis - general

Note: *Automatic transmission malfunctions may be caused by five general conditions: poor engine performance, improper adjustments, hydraulic malfunctions, mechanical malfunctions or malfunctions in the computer or its signal network. Diagnosis of these problems should always begin with a check of the easily repaired items: fluid level and condition (see Chapter 1), shift linkage adjustment and throttle valve (TV) linkage adjustment. Next, perform a road test to determine if the problem has been corrected or if more diagnosis is necessary. If the problem persists after the preliminary tests and corrections are completed, additional diagnosis should be done by a dealer service department or transmission repair shop. Refer to the Troubleshooting section at the front of this manual for information on symptoms of transmission problems.*

Preliminary checks

1   Drive the vehicle to warm the transmission to normal operating temperature.
2   Check the fluid level as described in Chapter 1:

a) *If the fluid level is unusually low, add enough fluid to bring the level within the designated area of the dipstick (see Chapter 1), then check for external leaks (see below).*
b) *If the fluid level is abnormally high, drain off the excess, then check the drained fluid for contamination by coolant. The presence of engine coolant in the automatic transmission fluid indicates that a failure has occurred in the internal radiator walls that separate the coolant from the transmission fluid (see Chapter 3).*
c) *If the fluid is foaming, drain it and refill the transmission (see Chapter 1), then check for coolant in the fluid or a high fluid level.*

3   Check the engine idle speed and general operating performance. **Note:** *If the engine is malfunctioning, do not proceed with the preliminary checks until it has been repaired and runs normally.*
4   Inspect the manual shift control linkage (see Section 3). Make sure that it's properly adjusted and that the linkage operates smoothly.
5   On AOD transmissions, check the throttle valve rod or cable for freedom of movement. Adjust it if necessary (see Section 4). **Note:** *The throttle valve mechanism may function properly when the engine is shut off and cold, but it may malfunction once the engine is hot. Check it cold and at normal engine operating temperature.*
7   On C-series transmissions, check the kickdown rod for freedom of movement and proper adjustment (see Section 5).
6   On C-series transmissions, check the vacuum diaphragm throttle valve for proper operation and vacuum signal from engine (see Section 6).
8   On C-series transmissions, adjust bands as required (see Section 7).

Fluid leak diagnosis

9   Most fluid leaks are easy to locate visually. Repair usually consists of replacing a seal or gasket. If a leak is difficult to find, the following procedure may help.
10   Identify the fluid. Make sure it's transmission fluid and not engine oil or brake fluid (automatic transmission fluid is a deep red color).
11   Try to pinpoint the source of the leak. Drive the vehicle several miles, then park it over a large sheet of cardboard. After a minute or two, you should be able to locate the leak by determining the source of the fluid dripping onto the cardboard.
12   Make a careful visual inspection of the suspected component and the area immediately around it. Pay particular attention to gasket mating surfaces. A mirror is often helpful for finding leaks in areas that are hard to see.

13   If the leak still cannot be found, clean the suspected area thoroughly with a degreaser or solvent, then dry it.
14   Drive the vehicle for several miles at normal operating temperature and varying speeds. After driving the vehicle, visually inspect the suspected component again.
15   Once the leak has been located, the cause must be determined before it can be properly repaired. If a gasket is replaced but the sealing flange is bent, the new gasket will not stop the leak. The bent flange must be straightened.
16   Before attempting to repair a leak, check to make sure that the following conditions are corrected or they may cause another leak. **Note:** *Some of the following conditions cannot be fixed without highly specialized tools and expertise. Such problems must be referred to a transmission repair shop or a dealer service department.*

Gasket leaks

17   Check the pan periodically. Make sure the bolts are tight, no bolts are missing, the gasket is in good condition and the pan is flat (dents in the pan may indicate damage to the valve body inside).
18   If the pan gasket is leaking, the fluid level or the fluid pressure may be too high, the vent may be plugged, the pan bolts may be too tight, the pan sealing flange may be warped, the sealing surface of the transmission housing may be damaged, the gasket may be damaged or the transmission casting may be cracked or porous. If sealant instead of gasket material has been used to form a seal between the pan and the transmission housing, it may be the wrong sealant.

Seal leaks

19   If a transmission seal is leaking, the fluid level or pressure may be too high, the vent may be plugged, the seal bore may be damaged, the seal itself may be damaged or improperly installed, the surface of the shaft protruding through the seal may be damaged or a loose bearing may be causing excessive shaft movement.
20   Make sure the dipstick tube seal is in good condition and the tube is properly seated. Periodically check the area around the speedometer gear or sensor for leakage. If transmission fluid is evident, check the O-ring for damage.

Case leaks

21   If the case itself appears to be leaking, the casting is porous and will have to be repaired or replaced.
22   Make sure the oil cooler hose fittings are tight and in good condition.

Fluid comes out vent pipe or fill tube

23   If this condition occurs, the transmission is overfilled, there is coolant in the fluid, the case is porous, the dipstick is incorrect, the vent is plugged or the drain-back holes are plugged.

3   Manual shift linkage - inspection, removal, installation and adjustment

Note: *Removal of the shift linkage is a prerequisite to removing the transmission from the vehicle. Although the shift linkage is part of a more complicated steering column shift mechanism, only the linkage removal steps necessary to allow transmission removal will be outlined in this section. In addition, adjustment procedures are provided for use after re-installation of linkage or for correction of possible performance related problems.*

Inspection

1   Raise the vehicle and support it securely on jackstands.
2   On models with bellcrank linkages, locate the shift linkage on the driver's side of the transmission and inspect it for loose pivot bracket hardware and worn bellcrank and rod grommets.
3   On models with a cable shift linkage, inspect the cable for kinks, dents, thermal damage or any other condition that may hinder smooth operation. Check for a loose transmission cable bracket. Inspect the remaining cable inside the cab under the dash panel for similar problems.
4   Correct any problems found prior to adjustment.

Bellcrank shift linkage (1991 and earlier models)

Removal

5   Remove the shift rod-to-bellcrank lever retaining nut, located on top of the frame rail, on the driver's side. The shift rod is the slotted rod coming from above. Secure the shift rod out of the way.
6   Carefully pry the shift control rod out of its grommet in the manual control lever. Don't distort the control lever while doing this.
7   Remove the outer bellcrank pivot bracket bolts from the frame rail, slide the bellcrank shaft out of the inner transmission pivot bracket and remove the bellcrank assembly.

Installation

8   Installation is reverse of removal, but be sure to install a new grommet in the transmission shift lever prior to installing the control rod. Don't tighten the shift rod-to-bellcrank nut until after adjustment.

Cable shift linkage (1992 and later models)

Removal

9   Remove the shift cable end from the transmission lever ballstud.
10   Remove the shift cable from the transmission bracket by releasing the cable body retaining tabs and pulling it out of the bracket. Secure the cable out of the way.

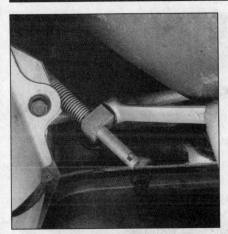

4.16 Loosen the set bolt on the TV trunnion block to free it from the rod for adjustment (early AOD models only)

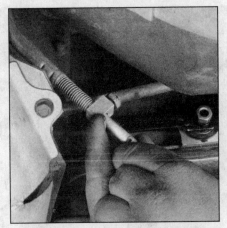

4.17 Hold the rod down and push the trunnion block up until the transmission lever bottoms against its internal stop (early AOD models only)

Installation

11   Installation is the reverse of removal, but don't install the shift cable to the transmission lever ball stud until adjustment.

Adjustment

12   With the engine off and the parking brake applied, place the transmission selector lever at the steering column in the Drive (C4, C5, C6) or Overdrive (AOD and E4OD) position.
13   Have an assistant hold the selector lever against it stop by applying a bit of downward pressure on the lever.
14   If not already done, loosen the shift rod adjusting nut (bellcrank) or remove the shift cable end from transmission lever ballstud (cable).
15   On AOD and E4OD transmissions, pull down the cable freeplay locking tab on the lower cable body end.
16   Shift the manual lever at the transmission into the Drive position by moving the lever all the way to the rear, then forward two (2) detents.

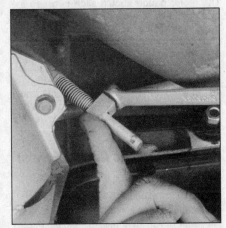

4.18 While holding the lever in position, tighten the set bolt

17   On C4, C5 and C6 transmissions, with the selector lever and transmission manual lever both in the Drive position, tighten the nut at the bellcrank securely, using care to prevent movement between the stud and rod.
18   On AOD and E4OD transmissions, with the selector lever and transmission manual lever both in the Overdrive position, snap the shift cable onto the transmission lever ballstud and re-lock the cable freeplay locking tab by pushing the tab back into the cable body.
19   Have your assistant remove pressure from the shift lever knob and check the operation of the shift lever in all positions to make certain the manual lever at the transmission is in full detent in all gear ranges. Readjust the linkage as required.

---

4   Throttle valve (TV) mechanisms (AOD only) - removal, installation and adjustment

TV control rod (early model 5.0L only)

Refer to illustrations 4.16, 4.17 and 4.18

Removal

1   Raise the vehicle and support it securely on jackstands.
2   Remove the upper end of the TV control rod from the carburetor lever pin.
3   Locate the transmission TV lever and loosen the control rod trunnion block set bolt to free the rod from the transmission. Lift the TV control rod from the vehicle.

Installation

4   Installation is the reverse of removal, but don't tighten the trunnion block set bolt until adjustment is performed.

Adjustment at carburetor

5   If the throttle rod has not been removed and the lower rod-to-transmission lever rela-

tionship has not been disturbed, a minor adjustment at the carburetor TV rod adjustment screw should be attempted prior to trying to adjust at the transmission.
6   Check that the engine idle speed has been properly set. **Note:** *Idle speed adjustments of 50 rpm or greater (either higher or lower) subsequent to TV adjustment require that the rod adjustment be checked and readjusted if required.*
7   With the engine at normal operating temperature, verify that the choke plate is open and the carburetor throttle lever is resting on its idle stop.
8   Place the transmission in N (neutral) and set the parking brake.
9   Back out the throttle linkage TV adjusting screw until it's flush with the outside face of the lever. The adjusting screw is directly opposite of the dashpot, on the driver's side of the carburetor.
10   Insert a 0.005-inch feeler gauge between the adjusting screw and the throttle lever and turn the adjusting screw in until the feeler gauge fits snugly between the pieces. Remove feeler gauge and push the adjusting screw linkage forwards (tending to close the gap) and release it to remove any residual friction, then check the gap again. **Note:** *When checking the gap, do not apply any load on the levers, as this will give a false gap measurement.* Re-adjust if necessary to get the proper gap.
11   After gap has been successfully set, turn the adjusting screw in (clockwise) an additional four complete turns to complete the procedure. **Note:** *If it is not possible to obtain at least two turns or if the initial gap is too wide for the adjust screw to bridge, perform linkage adjustment at transmission.*

Adjustment at transmission

12   The linkage lever adjusting screw has limited capability. If adjust screw procedure fails, the length of the TV rod assembly must be adjusted as follows:
13   Raise vehicle and place securely on jackstands.
14   Perform Steps 6 through 8.
15   Set the TV linkage lever adjustment screw at approximately mid-point.
16   Locate the transmission TV lever and loosen the control rod trunnion block set bolt to free the rod **(see illustration)**. Remove any corrosion or dirt that might prevent free movement of the block along the rod.
17   Push up on the control rod to seat the upper lever adjusting screw against the throttle lever, then release it **(see illustration)**.
18   Push the transmission's TV lever and trunnion block up until the transmission lever firmly bottoms against its internal stops. Hold the lever in this position and tighten the trunnion block set screw securely **(see illustration)**.
19   Perform adjustment at carburetor procedure and fine tune adjust screw if necessary.
20   Remove the jackstands and lower vehicle.

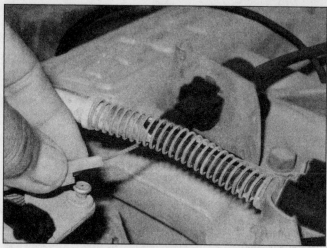

5.12a Disconnect the kickdown cable at the engine throttle lever . . .

5.12b . . . and at the transmission, then disconnect the cable from its brackets

TV control cable (all except early 5.0L)

Removal

Note: *Removal of the throttle valve cable is a prerequisite to removing the transmission from the vehicle and only those cable removal steps necessary to allow transmission removal will be outlined in this section. In addition, adjustment procedures are provided for use after re-installation of linkage or for correction of possible performance related problems.*

21   Disconnect the shift cable end from the transmission lever ballstud.

22   Remove shift cable from transmission bracket by releasing the cable body retaining tabs and pulling it out of the bracket. Secure the cable out of the way.

Installation

23   Installation is the reverse of removal. Proceed to step 24 to adjust the cable.

Adjustment

24   On non-EFI engines, check that the engine idle speed has been properly set. **Note:** *Idle speed adjustments of 150 rpm or greater (either higher or lower) subsequent to TV adjustment require that the cable adjustment be checked and readjusted if required. Do not attempt to adjust the idle set screw on EFI models.*

25   Verify that the cable routing is free of sharp bends and that the cable operates freely.

26   On non-EFI engines equipped with idle positioning solenoids, make sure solenoids are in the retracted (anti-diesel) position.

27   On carbureted engines (non-variable venturi), if the engine is cold, decam the fast idle cam by first wedging the choke plate fully open, then open the throttle all the way and let it return to the idle stop. Verify that the carburetor throttle lever is resting on its normal idle stop.

28   On variable venturi carbureted models, if the engine is cold, decam the fast idle cam by

retracting the choke control diaphragm linkage against choke spring tension and open the throttle to allow cam to rotate to normal idle position. Release throttle and verify that throttle is resting on it's normal idle stop.

29   Place the transmission in N (neutral) and set the parking brake.

30   At the carburetor or throttle housing (EFI), unlock the TV control cable self-adjusting lock mechanism at the end of the cable housing body by releasing the clamp tabs in the housing window and prying the clamp out from the top with a small screwdriver. Verify that the cable housing can be pushed freely towards the cable bracket against the spring tension.

31   From under the vehicle, have an assistant hold the transmission TV lever against it's idle position stop (clockwise as far to the rear as possible) and hold. The cable slack take-up spring will then set the proper cable length automatically. An alternative method is to install a suitable spring (or springs) to hold the lever rewards with about 10-pounds of force.

32   While still holding transmission lever against idle stop, lock upper cable clamp in place by pushing the clamp back into the cable body until it's flush. **Note:** *Prior to re-locking cable, verify that the throttle lever is resting on it's normal idle stop.*

33   If used, remove the transmission lever retention springs.

34   Remove the jackstands and lower the vehicle.

---

5   Kickdown mechanisms (C4, C5 and C6 only) - removal, installation and adjustment

Kickdown rod (early years)

Removal

1   Raise the vehicle and support it securely on jackstands.

2   Remove the upper end of the kickdown control rod from the carburetor lever pin.

3   Locate the transmission kickdown lever and remove the C-clip securing the control rod to lever. Lift the kickdown control rod out of the vehicle.

Installation

4   Installation is the reverse of removal except adjust after installation.

Adjustment

5   Raise the vehicle and support it securely on jackstands.

6   Have an assistant hold the transmission kickdown lever in the wide open throttle (WOT) position (counterclockwise as far to the rear as possible). An alternative method is to hang approximately six pounds of weight onto the transmission kickdown lever to hold it against the WOT stop.

7   From the engine compartment, hold the carburetor or throttle housing (EFI) throttle lever to the wide open position and insert a 0.060 feeler gauge between the throttle lever and adjusting screw and check for proper fit. The feeler gauge should slide between the pieces with some resistance.

8   If necessary, adjust the screw until the proper feeler gauge resistance if obtained.

9   Remove the feeler gauge and recheck the gap. Gaps from 0.030 to 0.070 are acceptable.

10   If used, remove the weight at the transmission kickdown lever.

11   Remove the jackstands and lower the vehicle.

Kickdown cable (later models)

Removal

Refer to illustrations 5.12a and 5.12b

12   Remove the kickdown cable end from the transmission lever ballstud and the throttle lever on the engine **(see illustrations)**.

13   Remove the kickdown cable from the transmission bracket by releasing the cable

6.2 On "C"-series transmissions, the vacuum modulator is located on the right side or rear of the transmission, as shown here. To replace it, remove the vacuum hose and bracket, then slide the modulator out

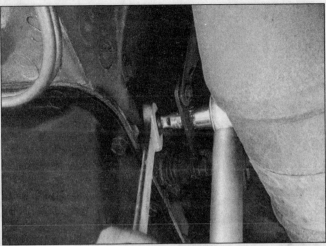

7.2 Adjusting the intermediate band ("C"-series transmissions)

body retaining tabs and pulling it out of the bracket. Secure the cable out of the way.

Installation

14   Installation is the reverse of removal. Proceed to adjust the cable.

Adjustment

15   Ratchet the cable self-adjusting mechanism to obtain maximum outer conduit length.
16   Insert a 0.060 feeler gauge between the upper cable conduit body and the cable bracket on the conduit side of the bracket.
17   Set the cable length by opening the throttle to the wide open position. The self adjuster should ratchet as the cable outer conduit shortens in length.
18   Remove the feeler gauge to gain proper cable freeplay.
19   Remove the jackstands and lower the vehicle.

---

6   Vacuum modulator (C4, C5 and C6 only) - check and replacement

---

Refer to illustration 6.2

Check

1   Raise vehicle and support securely on jackstands.
2   Locate the vacuum modulator on rear or side of transmission (**see illustration**).
3   Detach the vacuum hose from the modulator.
4   Connect a vacuum gauge to the vacuum hose and start the engine. If the gauge does not indicate manifold vacuum, trace the vacuum hose back to the engine to locate the leak or restriction. Repair as required.
5   Remove the bolt from the modulator bracket and remove the valve from the transmission.
6   Using a magnet, remove the control rod

from the bore in the transmission.
7   Place the control rod into modulator.
8   Using a hand-held vacuum pump, apply vacuum to the modulator and observe the rod and the vacuum gauge. The modulator should hold a steady vacuum and the control rod should retract. As vacuum is released, the rod should extend back to its static position. If the modulator fails either check, replace it.

Replacement

9   Check the O-ring on the modulator. If it's cracked, hardened or shows any other signs of wear, replace it with a new one. Lubricate the O-ring with clean automatic transmission fluid before installation.
10   Installation is the reverse of removal. Don't forget to install the control rod prior to modulator installation. Tighten the bracket bolt securely.

---

7   Band adjustment (C4, C5 and C6 only)

Refer to illustration 7.2

Intermediate band (C4, C5 and C6)

1   The intermediate or front band is used to hold the sun gear stationary to produce Second gear. If it is not correctly adjusted, there will be noticeable slip during the First-to-Second gear shift or on the downshift from the High to Second gear. The first symptoms of these problems will be very sluggish shifts.
2   To adjust the intermediate band, loosen, remove and discard the locknut on the band adjustment screw (located on the left-hand side of the case). Tighten the adjusting screw to 120 inch-pounds, then loosen it exactly 1-1/2 turns (C4 and C6) or 4-1/4 turns (C5) (**see illustration**). Install a new locknut and

tighten it securely while holding the adjustment screw to keep it from turning.

Low and reverse band (C4 and C5)

3   The low and reverse band is operational when the selector lever is placed in the Low or Reverse positions. If it is not correctly adjusted, there will be no drive with the selector lever in Reverse (also associated with no engine braking with the selector lever in Low).
4   To adjust this band, remove the adjusting screw locknut from the screw (located on the right-hand side of the transmission, at the rear, near the vacuum modulator) and discard it. Tighten the adjusting screw to 120 inch-pounds, then loosen it exactly three turns. Install a new locknut and tighten it securely while holding the adjusting screw to keep it from turning.

---

8   Automatic transmission - removal and installation

Refer to illustrations 8.2 and 8.5

Removal

1   Disconnect the cable from the negative battery terminal.
2   If possible, raise the vehicle on a hoist. Alternatively, raise the vehicle to obtain the maximum possible amount of working room underneath, and support it securely on jackstands. Familiarize yourself with the applicable components (**see illustration**).
3   Drain the transmission fluid (see Chapter 1). After draining, temporarily install the pan with four bolts to hold it in place.
4   Remove the torque converter access cover and adapter plate bolts from the front lower end of the converter housing.
5   Remove the driveplate-to-converter attaching nuts, turning the engine as neces-

8.2 Bottom view of automatic transmission (C6 shown) and transfer case (Borg-Warner 1345 shown)

1   Front heat shield
2   Rear transmission mount-to-crossmember insulator
3   Rear transmission support bracket bolt
4   Transmission oil pan
5   Neutral safety switch
6   Transmission shift linkage
7   Front driveshaft
8   Crossmember
9   Transfer case
10   Rear driveshaft universal joint
11   Rear heat shield

sary to gain access by means of a socket on the crankshaft pulley attaching bolt **(see illustration). Caution:** *Do not rotate the engine backwards.*

6   Rotate the engine until the converter drain plug is accessible, then remove the plug, catching the fluid in the drain pan. Install and tighten the drain plug securely.

7   On 2WD models, remove the driveshaft (see Chapter 8). Place a polyethylene bag over the end of the transmission to prevent dirt from entering.

8   On 4WD models, remove the transfer case (see Chapter 7C).

9   On 2WD models prior to 1992, detach

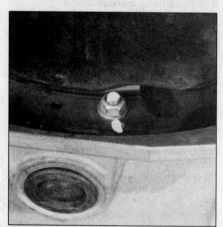

8.5 Before removing the driveplate-to-converter nuts, mark the relationship of a stud to the driveplate, as shown here. This will keep the assembly in balance

the speedometer cable from the extension housing by removing the hold-down bolt and withdrawing the cable and gear.

10   Remove the manual shift linkage (see Section 3)

11   Remove the TV control rod or cable if equipped (see Section 4, AOD only).

12   Remove the kickdown rod or cable if equipped (see Section 5, C-series only).

13   Remove the vacuum modulator hose, if equipped (see Section 6, C-series only).

14   Disconnect the Neutral safety switch electrical connector (C-series and AOD).

15   Disconnect the manual lever position sensor electrical connector (E4OD only).

16   Remove the two bolts retaining the solenoid body connector heat shield and remove the shield. Disconnect the solenoid body electrical connector (E4OD only).

17   Remove the transmission fluid filler tube retaining bolt and lift the filler tube and dipstick out of transmission housing.

18   Remove the starter (see Chapter 5).

19   Disconnect the oil cooler lines at the transmission and plug them to prevent dirt from entering. Use a flare nut wrench to avoid rounding off the nuts.

20   Position a transmission jack beneath the transmission and raise it so that it *just begins* to lift the transmission weight.

21   Remove the nuts and bolts securing the rear mount and insulators to the crossmember (see Section 12).

22   If right and left gussets are installed between the crossmember and frame rails, remove the gusset attaching nuts and bolts and remove the gussets.

23   Remove any harness ties on crossmember and the nuts and bolts securing the crossmember to the frame rails, raise the transmission slightly and remove the crossmember.

24   Disconnect the inlet pipe flange(s) from the exhaust manifold(s) (see Chapter 4).

25   Support the rear of the engine using a jack or blocks of wood.

26   Make sure that the transmission is securely mounted on the jack and remove the transmission housing-to-engine bolts.

27   Carefully move the transmission to the rear, down and away from the vehicle. Make sure the converter stays with the transmission.

Installation

28   Installing the transmission is essentially the reverse of the removal procedure, but the following points should be noted:

a) *Push in on the converter and turn it to ensure that it's completely engaged with the front pump of the transmission.*

b) *Rotate the converter to align the bolt drive lugs and drain plug with their holes in the driveplate.*

c) *Do not allow the transmission to take a "nose-down" attitude as the converter will move forward and disengage from the pump gear.*

d) *If the torque converter is fastened to the driveplate with bolts, position the driveplate so one bolt hole is in the six o'clock position. Install one bolt, then rotate the engine (clockwise only) and install the other bolts. Don't tighten any bolts until all of them have been installed.*

10.4 Before adjustment, loosen the two bolts on the Manual Lever Position Sensor (E4OD only)

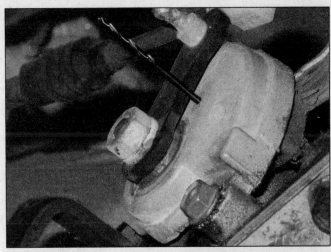

11.3 Loosen the bolts securing the neutral start switch, then rotate it until the drill bit passes through all three holes in the switch ("C"-series transmissions only)

e) Adjust the kickdown rod/cable (see Section 5) or TV rod/cable (see Section 4) and manual selector linkage (see Section 3) as necessary.

f) When the vehicle has been lowered to the ground, add sufficient fluid to bring the level up to the Max mark on the dipstick with the engine not running. Having done this, start the engine and check and top-up the fluid level as described in Chapter 1.

9 E4OD electronic shift transmission - general information

The E4OD transmission is a fully automatic, electronically controlled, four speed unit with locking torque converter. Transmission gear selection and converter clutch operation in the Overdrive range is controlled by the Electronic Engine Control system. Operating conditions are relayed to the Powertrain Control Module (PCM) by various sensors throughout the vehicle and transmission. The computer compares these conditions with stored parameters and logically determines the state in which the transmission should operate. The computer sends the appropriate commands to the internal solenoid body. Five solenoids within the assembly actuate the hydraulic circuits which control gear selection, gear change harshness (control pressure) and torque converter lock-up or coast operation.

10 Manual lever position sensor (E4OD only) - adjustment

Refer to illustration 10.4

1   Raise the vehicle and support it securely on jackstands.
2   Check the manual shift linkage (see Section 3).
3   Place the transmission in the Neutral position.
4   Loosen the two MLPS retaining bolts **(see illustration)**.
5   Using the MLPS adjusting tool position MLPS and tighten the retaining bolts securely.
6   Remove the jackstands and lower the vehicle.

11 Neutral start switch (C4, C5 and C6 only) - adjustment

Refer to illustration 11.3

1   With the automatic transmission linkage properly adjusted (see Section 3), loosen the two Neutral start switch retaining bolts.
2   Place the transmission selector lever in Neutral.
3   Rotate the switch and insert a No. 43 drill bit (shank end) into the gauge pin holes of the switch **(see illustration)**. **Note:** *The drill shank must be inserted a full 31/64 inch through all three holes of the switch.*
4   Tighten the switch retaining bolts securely, then remove the drill bit from the switch.
5   Check the operation of the switch. The back-up lights should come on only when the transmission is in Reverse and the engine should start only with the transmission lever in Park and Neutral.

Notes

Chapter 7 Part C
Transfer case

Contents

Specifications

Torque specifications

Ft-lbs (unless otherwise indicated)

Note: *One foot-pound (ft-lb) of torque is equivalent to 12 inch-pounds (in-lbs) of torque. Torque values below approximately 15 ft-lbs are expressed in inch-pounds, since most foot-pound torque wrenches are not accurate at these smaller values.*

New Process 208 transfer case

4-wheel-drive indicator switch	15 to 20
Drain and filler plugs	30 to 40
Assembly-to-assembly shift lever mounting bolts (for vehicles equipped with SROD transmission only)	25 to 43
Shift lever assembly to transmission bracket bolts (for vehicles equipped with SROD transmission only)	14 to 20
Shift lever assembly to transmission bracket bolt	70 to 90
Yoke nuts-to-transfer case	90 to 130
Transfer case-to-transmission adapter	25 to 43
Heat shield-to-transfer case	
Upper bolt	40 to 45
Lower bolt	11 to 16
Skid plate-to-frame	11 to 16

Borg-Warner 13-45 transfer case

4-wheel drive indicator switch	96 to 144 in-lbs
Yoke nuts-to-transfer case	100 to 130
Drain plug	72 to 168 in-lbs
Fill plug	15 to 25
Transfer case-to-transmission adapter	25 to 43
Heat shield-to-transfer case	
Upper bolt	40 to 45
Lower bolt	11 to 16
Skid plate-to-frame	11 to 16
Shift lever assembly to transmission bracket bolt (early models)	70 to 90
Shift handle to control lever assembly bolts (later models)	96 to 132 in-lbs
Control assembly to transmission bolts (later models)	70 to 90

Borg-Warner 13-56 transfer case

4-wheel drive indicator switch (manual shift only)	25 to 35
Yoke nuts-to-transfer case	120 to 150
Drain plug	7 to 17
Fill plug	7 to 17
Transfer case-to-transmission adapter	25 to 43
Heat shield-to-transfer case	
Upper bolt	40 to 45
Lower bolt	11 to 16
Skid plate-to-frame	15 to 20
Shift handle to control lever assembly bolts (early and mid year models)	96 to 132 in-lbs

Torque specifications (continued)   Ft-lbs

Note: *One foot-pound (ft-lb) of torque is equivalent to 12 inch-pounds (in-lbs) of torque. Torque values below approximately 15 ft-lbs are expressed in inch-pounds, since most foot-pound torque wrenches are not accurate at these smaller values.*

Borg-Warner 13-56 transfer case (continued)
Control assembly to transmission bolts
(early and mid year models).. 70 to 90
Shift Handle pinch bolt (later models)............................. 20 to 28
Control lever pivot bolt (later models)............................ 70 to 90
Detent plate to transmission (later models)..................... 70 to 90

Borg-Warner 44-07 transfer case
Four-wheel drive indicator switch .... 25 to 35
Yoke nut-to-transfer case .... 150 to 180
Drain plug .... 7 to 17
Fill plug .... 7 to 17
Transfer case-to-extension housing .... 30 to 40
Transfer case half retaining bolts .... 22 to 36
Skid plate-to-frame .... 16 to 20
Control assembly-to-transmission extension housing bolts.... 71 to 90
Shift handle pinch bolt .... 20 to 28
Control lever assembly-to-control rod pivot bolt .... 68 to 92

Electronic shift models only
Shift motor to transfer case .... 72 to 96 in-lbs
Rear bearing (extension) housing to transfer case.......... 22 to 36

1   Transfer case - general information

1   Operationally, all the transfer cases mentioned perform the same function. In 2WD mode, power is transferred from the transmission to the input shaft of the transfer case where it in turn drives the output shaft through the essentially non-functional (no gear reduction) planetary gear set. Shifting into 4WD mode locks a previously free wheeling gear onto the 2WD output shaft. This gear connects a second transfer case output shaft (for the front driveshaft) to the first (2WD) output shaft via a multi-row chain, thus completing the transfer of power to the front wheels. Shifting into 4WD low causes the power entering the transfer case via the input shaft to be routed through the now functional transfer case planetary gears for gear reduction of the 2WD output shaft. Since the 2WD output shaft drives the 4WD front output shaft (4WD mode only) both axles receive the reduced gearing. Where the transfer cases differ is in the various mechanical means devised to implement the planetary gear reduction and shift mode mechanisms.
2   All transfer cases include an oil pump for internal lubrication of critical components. The pump is driven from the rear output shaft to maintain pressure anytime the rear driveshaft is rotating (during normal operation and towing). **Warning:** *Consult your owners manual before towing any 4WD, as there are speed and distance restrictions that vary from vehicle to vehicle.*

2   Transfer case - removal and installation

Removal

1   Raise the vehicle and support it securely on jackstands.
2   If transfer case disassembly will be required, drain the transfer case fluid into a suitable container (see Chapter 1).
3   On manual shift models, disconnect the 4WD drive indicator switch electrical connector at the transfer case (see Section 8). On electronic shift models, disconnect the shift motor harness electrical connector (see Section 11).
4   On 1991 and earlier 4WD vehicles, remove the speedometer cable retaining bolt and remove the speedometer cable and gear assembly from the transfer case rear bearing retainer. On vehicles equipped with speed control, disconnect the speed sensor electrical connector. Position the cable out of the way to avoid damage or contamination. **Note:** *1992 and later models do not use a mechanical speedometer cable.*
5   Disconnect the vent hose from the transfer case.
6   On manual shift models, disconnect the transfer case shift rod link from the shift lever or transfer case lever (see Section 7).
7   If equipped, unbolt and remove the skid plate from the frame.
8   Unbolt the heat shield from the transfer case. **Note:** *The catalytic converter is located beside the heat shield. Be careful when work-*

ing in this area, since the converter generates extremely high temperatures.
9   Disconnect the front and rear driveshafts and tie them securely out of the way (see Chapter 8).
10   Support the transfer case with a transmission jack.
11   Remove the bolts retaining the transfer case to the transmission adapter.
12   Carefully move the transfer case to the rear, until the input shaft clears the adapter and lower the assembly from the vehicle, then remove the gasket between the transfer case and adapter.

Installation

13   Installation is the reverse of the removal procedure. Be sure to check and fill the transfer case with the correct grade and quantity of lubricant (see Chapter 1). Tighten the fasteners to the torque listed this Chapter's Specifications and any referenced Chapter's Specifications.

3   Transfer case - overhaul

Note: *Prior to condemning the transfer case as the source of a 4WD related problem, first absolve the following components of any contributory effects: engine, clutch or transmission, front or rear driveline, front or rear driveaxles, front or rear brakes, front locking hubs and front or rear tires and wheels. Remember that normal driveline windup produced in the 4WD mode can produce hop, skips, bounces and with electronic shifting can cause delayed shifts out of 4WD mode.*

This condition is aggravated by the affects of slightly different tire sizes, wear and loading.

1   Overhaul of a transfer case is considered a major repair and beyond the scope of this manual. If a major overhaul is required, it may be a good idea to consider replacing the faulty unit with either a new or rebuilt one. Your dealer or local transmission specialty shop should be able to supply you with information as to the cost, availability and exchange policy concerning these units. However, if you decide to do the work yourself, several suggestions can be made to assist you in your efforts:

a) It is very helpful to draw your own simple diagram, take instant photos or video tape during the disassembly process. Laying each part out in the order in which it was removed also helps.

b) Remove all peripheral components, then work from the rearmost (output) case forward as certain components will prevent case splitting otherwise.

c) If a case half or component will not remove easily, look closely for any missed bolts, snap rings or other source of interference before moderate force is used. Excessive force is not required and is a sure sign something in the disassembly or reassembly sequence was missed.

d) Pay particular attention to critical components such as oil pumps and shifting mechanisms.

e) Try to anticipate which parts may have to be replaced and have them available before beginning. Regardless of broken or badly worn components, there are certain items which must be replaced as a matter of course when the transfer case is reassembled. These include gaskets, snap-rings, oil seals and sometimes bearings. You will also need multipurpose grease and a silicone-type gasket sealant to properly reassemble the transfer case.

f) Cleanliness is extremely important when working on a precision piece of equipment such as a transfer case. The work area should be kept as clean and free of dirt and dust as possible. Also, adequate space should be available to lay out the various parts as they are removed.

g) Prelubricate all parts prior to assembly with the appropriate type of fluid. Use assembly lube to hold loose needle bearings, thrust washers and other small difficult-to-handle items into position during assembly.

h) Prior to reinstallation into the vehicle, rotate the input shaft and shift the case through its modes observing for any binding, excessive resistance or lock-up. **Note:** On electronic shift cases, rotate the shift drum shaft prior to installing shift motor. If any abnormal behavior is exhibited, resolve the problem before further damage is done by trying to apply engine power.

i) Remember to fill the case with the appropriate type and quantity of fluid.

j) Do not test the transfer case operation in 4WD mode on the street as torsional windup stress will occur. Testing is best done on dirt, sand or mud where torsional driveline windup can be released as harmless wheel spin.

4   Front output shaft oil seal - removal and replacement

Removal

1   Raise the vehicle and support it securely on jackstands.

2   Drain the transaxle if the filler plug is higher then the lowest part of the seal to prevent fluid loss during seal removal.

3   Mark the front driveshaft to transfer case yoke orientation, remove the driveshaft and swing it out of the way (see Chapter 8).

4   Holding the yoke with a suitable tool, remove the yoke retaining nut. **Note:** An alternative method is to put the transfer case in 4WD mode and set the parking brake to keep the output shaft from turning during nut removal. If equipped with an automatic transmission, make sure transfer case is in neutral or the transmission is in neutral as this process can place excess stress on the parking pawl.

5   Remove the front output shaft yoke nut and washer. On 13-56 models, also remove the rubber seal. Remove the yoke and slinger from the transfer case output shaft.

6   Remove the early model non-flanged seal with a slide-hammer and adapter. An alternative method is to carefully pry the seal out of the case bore with a blunt screwdriver. **Caution**: Do not damage the output shaft threads or nick the case bore.

7   Remove later model flanged seals using a slide-hammer and adapter. An alternative method is to tap out an edge of the seal using a dull screwdriver avoiding contact with the output shaft or threads. Using vise-grips or other similar clamping pliers, grip the exposed edge and tap out the seal.

8   Inspect the oil seal contact surface on the case for scoring or burrs that will damage the new oil seal. If found, remove them with emery cloth or fine sandpaper. Clean any residue left from the deburring process.

Replacement

9   Apply multi-purpose grease to the oil seal and position it squarely into the case bore with any markings facing outwards.

10 Drive the seal squarely into the bore using an appropriately sized seal driver, large socket or pipe section of equivalent dimensions. Drive non-flanged seals flush with the case and flanged seals until the flange bottoms against the bore face.

11 Clean the yoke splines and lubricate lightly with multi-purpose grease, then slip the slinger and yoke over the output shaft and carefully past the new seal until it bottoms.

12 On all except 13-56 models, coat the face of the yoke retaining nut with RTV sealant and apply thread locking compound to the threads.

13 Install the rubber seal (13-56 models only), washer and yoke retaining nut onto the output shaft. Tighten the retaining nut to the torque listed in this Chapters Specifications.

14 Install the front driveshaft (see Chapter 8).

15 Refill the transfer case lubricant (see Chapter 1).

16 Remove the jackstands and lower the vehicle.

17 If necessary, remember to shift out of 4WD mode before returning the vehicle to normal service.

5   Rear output shaft oil seal - removal and replacement

Remove

1   Raise the vehicle and support it securely on jackstands.

2   Drain the transaxle fluid (see Chapter 1) if the filler plug is higher then the lowest part of the seal to prevent fluid loss during seal removal.

3   On a yoke type output shaft, mark the rear driveshaft to transfer case yoke orientation, remove the driveshaft from the yoke and swing it out of the way (see Chapter 8). On a slip spline type extension housing, remove the driveshaft at the rear axle (and center bearing assembly if equipped) and slide the driveshaft out of transfer case extension housing.

4   On yoke type output shaft, hold the rear yoke with a suitable tool and remove the center retaining nut. **Note:** An alternative method is to put the transfer case in 4WD mode, lock the front hubs and have an assistant apply the brakes to keep the output shaft from turning during nut removal. If equipped with automatic transmission, make sure the transfer case or transmission is in neutral as this process can place excess stress on the parking pawl. On vehicles equipped with automatic hubs, the output shaft may have to be rotated through several revolutions to engage the hubs.

5   On yoke type rear output shaft, remove the yoke nut and washer. On 13-56 models, also remove the rubber seal. Remove the yoke and slinger from the transfer case rear output shaft.

6   Remove early model non-flanged seals with a slide-hammer and adapter. An alternative method is to carefully pry the seal out of the case bore with a blunt screwdriver. **Caution:** Do not damage the output shaft threads or nick the case bore.

7   Remove later model flanged seals using a seal remover and slide hammer. If a special tool is not available, an alternative method is to tap out an edge of the seal using a dull screwdriver avoiding contact with the output shaft and threads. Using vise-grips or other similar clamping pliers, grip the exposed

edge and tap out the seal.

8   Inspect the oil seal contact surface on the case for scoring or burrs that will damage the new oil seal. If found, remove them with emery cloth or fine sandpaper. Clean any residue left from the deburring process.

Replacement

9   Apply multi-purpose grease to the oil seal. On yoke type rear output shafts, position the seal squarely into the case bore with any markings facing outwards. On slip spline type rear output shafts, position the seal with the vent hole facing down and any markings facing outwards.

10   Drive the seal squarely into the bore using an appropriately sized seal driver, large socket or pipe section of equivalent dimensions. Drive the non-flanged seals flush with the case and flanged seals until the flange bottoms against the bore face.

11   On a yoke type output shaft, clean the yoke splines and lubricate lightly with multi-purpose grease, then slip the slinger and yoke over the output shaft and carefully past the new seal until it bottoms.

12   On a yoke type output shaft (all except 13-56 models), coat the face of the yoke retaining nut with RTV sealant and apply thread locking compound to the threads.

13   On a yoke type output shaft, install the rubber seal (13-56 models only), washer and yoke retaining nut onto the output shaft. Tighten the retaining nut to the torque listed in this Chapter's Specifications.

14   Install the rear driveshaft (see Chapter 8).

15   Check and refill the transfer case lubricant as necessary (see Chapter 1).

16   Remove the jackstands and lower the vehicle.

17   If necessary, remember to shift out of 4WD and unlock hubs before returning the vehicle to normal service.

---

6   Rear extension housing bushing (slip spline type) - removal and replacement

Removal

1   Raise the vehicle and support it securely on jackstands.

2   Drain the transaxle fluid (see Chapter 1).

3   Remove the driveshaft at the rear axle (and center bearing assembly if equipped) and slide the driveshaft out of the transfer case extension housing.

4   Remove the seal using a seal remover and slide hammer. If a special tool is not available, an alternative method is to tap out an edge of the seal using a dull screwdriver avoiding contact with the output shaft or threads. Using vise-grips or other similar clamping pliers, grip the exposed edge and tap out the seal.

5   Remove the bushing from the extension housing using a bushing removal tool, available at auto parts stores.

Replacement

6   Drive the new bushing squarely into the extension housing bore using a bushing driver, until the tool bottoms against the bore face.

7   Inspect the oil seal contact surface on the case for scoring or burrs that will damage the new oil seal. If found, remove them with emery cloth or fine sandpaper. Clean any residue left from the deburring process.

8   Apply multi-purpose grease to the oil seal and position it squarely into the case bore with the vent hole pointing down and any markings facing outwards.

9   Drive the seal squarely into the bore using an appropriately sized seal driver, large socket or pipe section of equivalent dimensions. Drive the non-flanged seals flush with the case and flanged seals until the flange bottoms against the bore face.

10   Install the rear driveshaft (see Chapter 8).

11   Refill the transfer case lubricant (see Chapter 1).

12   Remove the jackstands and lower the vehicle.

---

7   Manual shift lever assembly - removal and installation

NP 208 and early model Borg Warner 13-45 transfer cases

1   From inside the cab, remove the shift floor pan cover.

2   On early SROD transmissions, remove the two screws holding the two shift lever halves together.

3   Raise the vehicle and support it securely on jackstands.

4   Remove the vent hose from the shift handle.

5   Disconnect the shift rod link from the shift lever.

6   Remove the shift lever-to-transmission bracket bushing bolt and remove shift lever. On early SROD transmissions, remove the two shift lever half bushing bolts and remove the shift levers.

7   Installation is the reverse of removal. Tighten the fasteners to the torque listed in this Chapters Specifications.

8   Remove the jackstands and lower the vehicle.

9   Check the transfer case for proper shifting and operation before returning the vehicle to normal service.

Borg Warner 13-56 transfer case (early models)

10   From inside cab, remove the rubber boot and floor pan cover.

11   Disconnect the vent hose from the shift lever handle.

12   Remove the two shift handle to shift control lever bolts and remove the shift handle.

13   Raise the vehicle and support it securely on jackstands.

14   Remove the two shift lever assembly-to-transmission case bolts.

15   Slide the shift lever assembly off of the transfer case shift lever bushing and remove the assembly.

16   Prior to installation, move the transfer case shift lever into 4WD low position.

17   Slide the shifter assembly over the transfer case lever bushing and install the assembly-to-transmission bolts finger tight.

18   From inside the cab, position the shift selector cam plate rearwards until the plate neutral safety lug just contacts the forward edge of the shift control lever.

19   While holding the shift control lever in this position, have an assistant tighten the shift assembly-to-transmission bolts. Tighten the fasteners to the torque listed in this Chapters Specifications.

20   Check the transfer case for proper shifting and positive engagement and verify that there is a slight end clearance between the shift lever and the cam plate at both 2WD high and 4WD low positions.

21   Installation is the reverse of removal. Tighten the fasteners to the torque listed in this Chapters Specifications.

22   Remove the jackstands and lower the vehicle.

23   Check the transfer case for proper shifting and operation before returning the vehicle to normal service.

Borg Warner 13-56 transfer case (1988 through 1991) and later model 13-45 cases

24   Raise the vehicle and support it securely on jackstands.

25   Remove the two bolts attaching the shift lever to the control lever assembly.

26   Disconnect the vent hose from the control lever assembly.

27   Disconnect the shift rod link between the transfer case shaft lever and the control lever assembly.

28   Remove the two bolts retaining the control lever assembly to the transmission extension housing and remove the shift lever assembly.

29   Installation is the reverse of removal. Tighten the fasteners to the torque listed in this Chapters Specifications.

30   Remove the jackstands and lower the vehicle.

31   Check the transfer case for proper shifting and operation before returning the vehicle to normal service.

Borg Warner 13-56 transfer case (1992 and later)

32   Place the transfer case in 2WD high gear.

33   Raise the vehicle and support it securely on jackstands.

34   Loosen but do not remove the shift handle pinch bolt and slip the handle out of the control lever assembly.

35   Remove the vent hose from the detent plate.

36   Disconnect the shift rod link from the control lever assembly.

37   Loosen the control lever assembly pivot bolt but do not remove.

38   Swing the control lever assembly to gain access to the detent plate retaining bolts and remove the bolts.

39   Remove the control lever from the transmission.

40   Installation is the reverse of removal. Tighten the fasteners to the torque listed in this Chapters Specifications.

41   Remove the jackstands and lower the vehicle.

42   Check the transfer case for proper shifting and operation before returning the vehicle to normal service.

8   4WD indicator switch (manual shift models only) - removal and replacement

1   Raise the vehicle and support it securely on jackstands.

2   locate the 4WD indicator switch on the transfer case housing.

3   Remove the harness electrical connec-tor from the switch.

4   Remove the switch from the housing not-ing any washers under switch.

5   Installation is the reverse of removal. **Note:** *Make sure any washers present under the switch prior to removal are reinstalled. Tighten the switch to the torque listed in this Chapters Specifications.*

6   Remove the jackstands and lower the vehicle.

9   Electronic shift (shift on the fly) transfer case - general information

1   The Borg Warner 13-56 Electronic Shift system is composed of the following com-ponents; electronic control module, 4WD selection switch, wire harness, neutral safety switch, transfer case mounted speed sensor, shift motor with integral shift position sensor, electromagnetically actuated front drive gear spin-up clutch, rotary shift cam (drum) and an otherwise conventional transfer case.

2   When the 4WD selection switch is depressed, the electronic module will look at input from the shift position sensor to verify that the case is presently in 2WD mode and at the speed sensor to verify that the maxi-mum vehicle speed for shift on the fly has not been exceeded. If both conditions are met, the electronic module will command the spin-up clutch to energize and synchronize the front drive line to the rear. Almost simul-taneously, the module will command the shift motor to rotate its shift drum to the 4WD posi-tion. This rotation causes the 4WD in/out shift fork and lock hub to physically engage the front drive gear to the rear drive output shaft. After the shift has been made, the module will again quarry its sensors to verify shift mode and will then illuminate the shift indicator light on the selection switch.

3   When the 4WD low selection is made, the module will verify that the vehicle is not moving (less then 3 mph) and that the trans-mission is in neutral prior to commanding the shift motor to rotate the shift drum tc the 4WD low position. This is required since the shift to 4WD low is a non-synchronized shift. The shift drum rotation causes the 4WD low/high shift fork to engage the planetary gear sys-tem resulting in reduced gearing of the output shaft.

Notes

Chapter 8
Clutch and driveline

Contents

Specifications

Clutch release bearing travel

External slave cylinders
All 1980 through 1989 models .... 0.53 inch
1990 and later models
7.5L engine .... 0.425 inch
All others... 0.67 inch
Concentric slave cylinders... 0.425 inch

Rear axle

Types covered .... Ford semi-floating with integral carrier (8.8 in ring gear);
Ford semi-floating with removable carrier (9.0 in ring gear);
Ford semi-floating and full floating with integral carrier (10.25 in ring gear);
Dana semi-floating and full-floating with integral carrier.
Ratio .... Varies; ratio is stamped on metal tag attached to rear cover bolt

Front axle

Type... Dana standard and heavy-duty (IFS) and Monobeam.
Ratio .... Varies; ratio is stamped on metal tag attached to rear cover bolt

Driveshaft

Type... One-piece or two-piece depending on wheelbase of vehicle

Torque specifications

Note: *One foot-pound (ft-lb) of torque is equivalent to 12 inch-pounds (in-lbs) of torque. Torque values below approximately 15 ft-lbs are expressed in inch-pounds, since most foot-pound torque wrenches are not accurate at these smaller values.*

Ft-lbs (unless otherwise indicated)

Clutch
Pressure plate-to-flywheel bolts

10 inch disc	15 to 20
11 inch disc	20 to 29
12 inch disc	15 to 20
Clutch housing to transmission (if equipped)	40 to 50

Clutch master cylinder nuts

ZF S5-47 5-speed	89 to 124 in-lbs
All others	15 to 20
Concentric slave cylinder bolts	14 to 19
Cross-shaft to lever nut	50 to 70
Pedal to cross-shaft nut	50 to 70

Rear axle

Dana

Drive pinion nut minimum torque	250 to 270*
Drive pinion rotation preload (used bearings)	15 to 20 in-lbs
Pinion shaft lockpin	20 to 25
Cover-to-housing bolts	30 to 40
Axleshaft retaining bolts (full-floating axle)	40 to 50
Wheel bearing adjusting nut (full-floating axle)	120 to 140 (back off 1/8 to 3/8 turn)*

Ford 8.8 inch ring gear (integral carrier axle)

Drive pinion nut minimum torque	160*
Drive pinion rotation preload (used bearings)	8 to 14 in-lbs
Pinion shaft lock bolt (using Loctite or equivalent)	15 to 30
Rear cover screw	25 to 35

Ford 9.0 inch ring gear (removable carrier axle)

Drive pinion nut minimum torque	160*
Drive pinion rotation preload (used bearings)	8 to 14 in-lbs
Axleshaft bearing retainer nuts (bearing retainer plate)	20 to 40
Carrier-to-housing nuts	25 to 40

Ford 10.25 inch ring gear (integral carrier axle)

Drive pinion nut minimum torque	160*
Drive pinion rotation preload (used bearings)	8 to 14 in-lbs
Pinion shaft lock bolt (using Loctite or equivalent)	15 to 30
Rear cover screw	25 to 35
Axleshaft retaining bolts (full-floating models)	60 to 80
Wheel bearing adjusting nut (full-floating models only)	55 to 65 (back off 5 [new] or 8 [used] clicks)*
Lubricant fill plug	15 to 30

Front axle

Dana (Independent Front Suspension)

Axle assembly pivot bolt	120 to 150
Drive pinion nut minimum torque	200 to 220*
Drive pinion rotation preload (used bearings)	15 to 20 in-lbs
Carrier-to-housing bolts	30 to 40
Wheel bearing adjusting nut	See Section 28
Lubricant fill plug	20 to 30
Spindle to knuckle (model 44)	35 to 40
Spindle to knuckle (model 50)	50 to 60
Manual locking hub capscrews	35 to 55 in-lbs
Automatic locking hub capscrews	40 to 50 in-lbs

Dana Monobeam

Drive pinion nut minimum torque	220 to 280*
Drive pinion rotation preload (used bearings)	15 to 20 in-lbs
Wheel bearing adjusting nut	See Section 28
Lubricant fill plug	20 to 30
Spindle to knuckle	50 to 60
Hub lock cap	36 to 48 in-lbs
Manual locking hub cap screws	35 to 55 in-lbs
Automatic locking hub cap screws	40 to 50 in-lbs

*See text in this Chapter for details of the procedure

Driveshafts

Single snap-ring type U-joint

Coupling shaft center bearing bracket-to-support	37 to 54
Driveshaft U-joint-to-rear yoke bolt	90 to 110
U-joint adapter-to-rear axle bolt and nut	60 to 70

Double cardan type U-joint

Driveshaft-to-transfer case bolts...	20 to 28
Driveshaft-to-front and rear axle U-bolts.................................	96 to 180 in-lbs

1 Clutch - general information and checks

General information

1   All models with a manual transmission use a single dry plate, diaphragm spring type clutch. The clutch disc has a splined hub which allows it to slide along the splines of the transmission input shaft. The clutch and pressure plate are held in contact by spring pressure exerted by the diaphragm in the pressure plate. All models equipped with three and four speed transmissions use a separate clutch housing (bellhousing) attached to the engine block which requires removal after the transmission is withdrawn to gain access to the clutch. Five speed transmissions are a one piece design (clutch housing integral with transmission).

2   Early models (1980 through 1983) utilized a mechanical release system of levers and actuating rods to transmit force from the clutch pedal to the clutch release bearing. These early designs were soon replaced with more efficient and lower maintenance release systems employing hydraulic pressure. The original hydraulic release system consists of the clutch pedal, a master cylinder and fluid reservoir, the hydraulic line, release cylinder, release lever and the clutch release (or throwout) bearing. When pressure is applied to the clutch pedal to release the clutch, hydraulic pressure is exerted against the outer end of the clutch release lever. As the lever pivots, its forked end pushes against the release bearing. This pressure pushes against the diaphragm spring of the pressure plate assembly, which in turn releases the clutch plate.

3   With the later addition of a new five speed transmission, a second hydraulic system was added. This system is essentially identical to the original hydraulic system except it utilizes an internal (concentric) slave cylinder for clutch release instead of the conventional forked release lever. Centered around the input shaft of the transmission, the concentric slave cylinder actuates the release bearing directly and uses larger internal surface area as opposed to the leverage principle to multiply the input line pressure to the extent necessary to counteract the clutch diaphragm spring force. This pressure pushes against the diaphragm spring of the pressure plate assembly, which in turn releases the clutch plate.

4   Early hydraulic systems were not serviceable and required that the complete system (clutch cylinder to slave cylinder) be replaced if air entered the system or if a failure (leak) was encountered. All later hydraulic systems allow for individual component replacement and system bleeding. Consult an auto parts store or a dealer service department as to the specifics regarding your vehicle.

5   Terminology can be a problem when discussing the clutch components because common names are in some cases different from those used by the manufacturer. For example, the driven plate is also called the clutch plate or disc, the clutch release bearing is sometimes called a throwout bearing, the release cylinder is sometimes called the operating or slave cylinder.

Checks

6   Other than to replace components with obvious damage, some preliminary checks should be performed to diagnose clutch problems.

7   On early mechanical linkages, check the various pivot bushings and brackets, actuating bars and rods and the pedal shaft and lever for excess play, binding and deflection/bending under load (see Section 9). Adjust the release lever rod freeplay if necessary (see Section 8).

8   On hydraulic systems, first check the fluid level in the clutch master cylinder. If the fluid level is low, add fluid as necessary and inspect the hydraulic system for leaks. If the master cylinder reservoir has run dry, bleed the system (see Section 6) and retest the clutch operation.

9   To check "clutch spin down time," run the engine at normal idle speed with the transmission in Neutral (clutch pedal up engaged). Disengage the clutch (pedal down), wait several seconds and shift the transmission into Reverse. No grinding noise should be heard.

10   To check for complete clutch release, run the engine (with the parking brake applied to prevent movement) and hold the clutch pedal approximately 1/2-inch from the floor. Shift the transmission between first gear and Reverse several times. If the shift is hard or the transmission grinds, component failure is indicated. Check the release cylinder pushrod travel or the release bearing travel (see Section 7). Also check the pedal cross-shaft lever to clutch cylinder pushrod interface and re-spline lever to shaft if necessary (see Section 8).

11   Inspect the pivot bushing at the top of the clutch pedal to make sure there is no binding or excessive play (see Section 10).

12   Except on concentric slave cylinder models, crawl under the vehicle and make sure the clutch release lever is solidly mounted on the ball stud (see Section 4).

13   Some vehicles are equipped with a removable inspection plate on the bottom of the clutch housing, observable from under the vehicle. If your vehicle is so equipped, be sure to raise the vehicle and place it securely on jackstands before attempting to remove the plate.

14   Remove the bolts retaining the plate to the housing, then remove the plate.

15   Inspect the clutch assembly from the bottom of the housing. Look for any broken, loose or worn parts. If no apparent defect is revealed, compare the thickness of the clutch disc (sandwiched between the pressure plate and the flywheel) to a new disc. This comparison will give you some idea of the clutch disc life left in your vehicle and the need for replacement.

16   Reinstall the plates and bolts.

17   Remove the jackstands and lower the vehicle.

2 Clutch components - removal, inspection and installation

Refer to illustrations 2.6, 2.8, 2.12 and 2.14

Removal

Warning: *Dust produced by clutch wear and deposited on clutch components is hazardous to your health. DO NOT blow it out with compressed air and DO NOT inhale it. DO NOT use gasoline or petroleum-based solvents to remove the dust. Brake system cleaner should be used to flush the dust into a drain pan. After the clutch components are wiped clean with a rag, dispose of the contaminated rags and cleaner in a covered, marked container.*

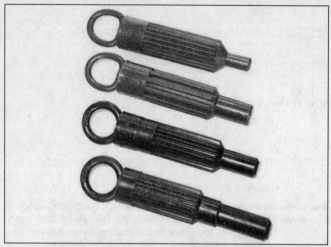

2.6 A clutch alignment tool can be purchased at most auto parts stores and eliminates all guesswork when centering the clutch disc in the pressure plate

2.8 Loosen the pressure plate bolts (arrows) a little at a time in a criss-cross pattern

Note 1: *When the battery is disconnected on later year models with a Powertrain Control Unit (PCM), the PCM loses it's memory and some abnormal driving symptoms may result for the first 10 miles or so until the PCM relearns it's adaptive strategy.*

Note 2: *Access to the clutch components is normally accomplished by removing the transmission (and transfer case on 4WD models), leaving the engine in the vehicle. If, of course, the engine is being removed for major overhaul, then check the clutch for wear and replace worn components as necessary. However, the relatively low cost of the clutch components compared to the time and trouble spent gaining access to them warrants their replacement anytime the engine or transmission is removed, unless they are new or in near perfect condition. The following procedures are based on the assumption the engine will stay in place.*

1   On early models with mechanical linkages, remove the clutch rod and equalizer bar from the transmission (see Section 9).

2   On models with an external slave cylinder, remove the slave cylinder and tie up out of the way (see Section 5). **Note:** *It is not necessary to disconnect the hydraulic line.* On models with a concentric (internal) slave cylinder, detach the clutch line at the slave cylinder inlet port (see Section 5).

3   If the vehicle is a 4WD model, remove the transfer case from the vehicle (see Chapter 7C).

4   Remove the transmission from the vehicle (see Chapter 7A).

5   On 3 and 4-speed models with a separate clutch housing, perform the following:

a) *Disconnect the negative battery cable.*

b) *Remove the bolts retaining the starter motor to the clutch housing (see Chapter 5).*

c) *Remove the bolts retaining the clutch housing to the engine block.* **Note:** *When removing the clutch housing,*

watch for the presence of shims between the engine block and housing at the bolt hole locations. Be sure to install them in their original locations during reassembly.

6   To support the clutch disc during removal, install a clutch alignment tool through the clutch disc hub **(see illustration)**.

7   Carefully inspect the flywheel and pressure plate for indexing marks. The marks are usually an X, an O or a white letter. If they cannot be found, scribe marks yourself so the pressure plate and the flywheel will be in the same alignment during installation.

8   Turning each bolt only 1/4-turn at a time, loosen the pressure plate-to-flywheel bolts **(see illustration)**. Work in a criss-cross pattern until all spring pressure is relieved evenly. Then hold the pressure plate securely and completely remove the bolts, followed by the pressure plate and clutch disc.

Inspection

9   Ordinarily, when a problem occurs in the clutch, it can be attributed to wear of the

clutch driven plate assembly (clutch disc). However, all components should be inspected at this time.

10   Inspect the flywheel for cracks, heat checking, grooves and other obvious defects. If the imperfections are slight, a machine shop can machine the surface flat and smooth, which is highly recommended regardless of the surface appearance. Refer to Chapter 2 for the flywheel removal and installation procedure.

11   Inspect the pilot bearing and replace if necessary (see Section 3).

12   Inspect the lining on the clutch disc. There should be at least 1/16-inch of lining above the rivet heads. Check for loose rivets, distortion, cracks, broken springs and other obvious damage **(see illustration)**. As mentioned above, ordinarily the clutch disc is routinely replaced, so if in doubt about the condition, replace it with a new one.

13   Inspect the release bearing and replace if necessary (see Section 4). **Note:** *The release bearing is a relatively inexpensive part compared to the time and effort required to replace it, therefore, it is wise to replace it*

2.12 The clutch disc

1   *Lining - this will wear down in use*

2   *Rivets - these secure the lining and will damage the flywheel or pressure plate if allowed to contact the surfaces*

3   *Marks - "flywheel side" or similar*

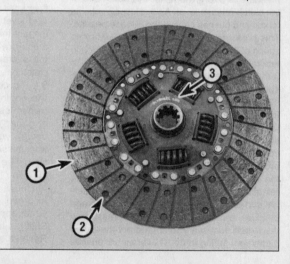

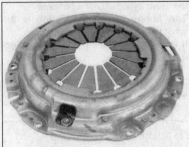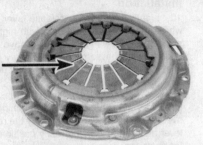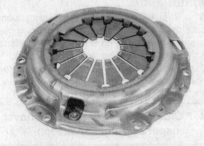

NORMAL FINGER WEAR   **EXCESSIVE FINGER WEAR**   **BROKEN OR BENT FINGERS**

2.14 **Replace the pressure plate if excessive or abnormal wear is noted**

regardless of condition.

14   Check the machined surfaces and the diaphragm spring fingers of the pressure plate **(see illustration)**. If the surface is grooved or otherwise damaged, replace the pressure plate. Also check for obvious damage, distortion, cracking, etc. Light glazing can be removed with sandpaper or emery cloth. If a new pressure plate is required, new and factory rebuilt units are available. **Note:** *The release bearing should be replaced along with the pressure plate.*

Installation

15   If the pilot bearing was removed for replacement, install a new bearing at this time (see Section 3).

16   Before installation, clean the flywheel and pressure plate machined surfaces with lacquer thinner, acetone or brake system cleaner. It's important that no oil or grease is on these surfaces or the lining of the clutch disc. Handle the parts only with clean hands.

17   Position the clutch disc and pressure plate against the flywheel with the clutch held in place with an alignment tool **(see illustration 2.6)**. Make sure it's installed properly (most replacement clutch plates will be marked "flywheel side" or something similar - if not marked, install the clutch disc with the flat side of the hub toward the flywheel).

18   Tighten the pressure plate-to-flywheel bolts only finger tight, working around the pressure plate.

19   Center the clutch disc by ensuring the alignment tool extends through the splined hub and into the pilot bearing in the crankshaft. Wiggle the tool up, down or side-to-side as needed to bottom the tool in the pilot bearing. Tighten the pressure plate-to-flywheel bolts a little at a time, working in a criss-cross pattern to prevent distorting the cover. After all of the bolts are snug, tighten them to the torque listed in this Chapter's Specifications. Remove the alignment tool.

20   If removed from transmission or clutch housing, install the clutch release bearing and release lever or concentric slave cylinder and release bearing if so equipped (see Section 4).

21   Install the clutch housing on vehicles so equipped. **Note:** *Don't forget to reinstall the*

shims between block and housing if any were present when the housing was removed. Be careful not to dislodge the release bearing from the lever. Tighten the bolts to the torque listed in this Chapter's Specifications.

22   Install the transmission (see Chapter 7A) and transfer case if equipped (see Chapter 7C).

23   On external slave cylinder models, install the slave cylinder (see Section 5). On models with a concentric (internal) slave cylinder, connect the clutch line to the slave cylinder inlet port (see Section 5).

24   If the clutch hydraulics require bleeding, see Section 6.

25   On early model mechanical linkages, install the clutch rod and equalizer bar to the transmission (see Section 9) and adjust linkage (see Section 8).

3   Pilot bearing - inspection, removal and installation

Refer to illustration 3.4

Warning: *Dust produced by clutch wear and deposited on clutch components is hazardous to your health. DO NOT blow it out with compressed air and DO NOT inhale it. DO NOT use gasoline or petroleum-based solvents to remove the dust. Brake system cleaner should be used to flush the dust into a drain pan. After the clutch components are wiped clean with a rag, dispose of the contaminated rags and cleaner in a covered, marked container.*

Inspection

1   The clutch pilot bearing is a needle roller type bearing which is pressed into the rear of the crankshaft. It is greased at the factory and does not require additional lubrication. Its primary purpose is to support the front of the transmission input shaft. The pilot bearing should be inspected whenever the clutch components are removed from the engine. Due to its inaccessibility, if you are in doubt as to its condition, replace it with a new one. **Note:** *Some early models may be equipped with a single piece, oil-impregnated bronze bushing instead of a bearing. A puller is usually required to remove this bushing.*

2   Remove the clutch assembly (see Section 2).

3   Inspect for any excessive wear, scoring, lack of grease, dryness or obvious damage. If any of these conditions are noted, the bearing should be replaced. A flashlight will be helpful to direct light into the recess.

Removal

4   Removal can be accomplished with a special puller and slide hammer **(see illustration)**, but an alternative method also works very well.

a) *Find a solid steel bar which is slightly smaller in diameter than the bearing. Alternatives to a solid bar would be a wood dowel or a socket with a bolt fixed in place to make it solid.*

b) *Check the bar for fit, it should just slip into the bearing with very little clearance.*

c) *Pack the bearing and the area behind it (in the crankshaft recess) with heavy grease. Pack it tightly trying to eliminate as much air as possible.*

d) *Insert the bar into the bearing bore and strike the bar sharply with a hammer which will force the grease to the back side of the bearing and push it out. Remove the bearing and clean all grease from the crankshaft recess.*

3.4 **One method of removing the pilot bearing requires a puller connected to a slide hammer**

Installation

5   To install the new bearing, lightly lubricate the outside surface with multi-purpose grease, then drive it into the recess with a soft-face hammer. The seal must face out.
6   The remainder of installation is the reverse of removal.

4   Clutch release bearing - removal, inspection and installation

Warning: *Dust produced by clutch wear and deposited on clutch components is hazardous to your health. DO NOT blow it out with compressed air and DO NOT inhale it. DO NOT use gasoline or petroleum-based solvents to remove the dust. Brake system cleaner should be used to flush the dust into a drain pan. After the clutch components are wiped clean with a rag, dispose of the contaminated rags and cleaner in a covered, marked container.*

Release lever type

Removal

1   On early models with mechanical linkages, remove the clutch rod and equalizer bar from the transmission (see Section 9).
2   If the vehicle is equipped with an external slave cylinder, remove the cylinder (see Section 5). **Note:** *It is not necessary to remove the hydraulic lines.*
3   If the vehicle is a 4WD model, remove the transfer case from the vehicle (see Chapter 7C).
4   Remove the transmission (see Chapter 7A) from the vehicle.
5   Remove the bolts retaining the clutch housing to the engine block on vehicles so equipped. **Note:** *When removing the clutch housing, watch for the presence of shims between the engine block and the housing at the bolt hole locations. If present, mark each by location for reinstallation during reassembly.*
6   On early models, remove the clutch housing and slide the release bearing and hub assembly away from lever to release its retaining clips from the lever seat.
7   On later models with a separate clutch housing, remove the clutch housing and simply slide the release bearing away from lever.
8   On later models with a one piece transmission/clutch housing, withdraw the clutch release lever from the transmission by pulling the lever out to disengage it from the ball stud just far enough to allow removal of the hub and bearing assembly. Remove the bearing from the input shaft tube.

Inspection

9   Hold the center of the bearing and rotate the outer portion while applying pressure. If the bearing doesn't turn smoothly or if it's noisy, replace it with a new one. Wipe the bearing with a clean rag and inspect it for damage, wear and cracks. Don't immerse the bearing in solvent - it's sealed for life and to do so would ruin it. Also check the release lever for cracks and other damage.

Installation

10   Lightly lubricate the release lever crown where it contacts the bearing with high-temperature grease. Fill the inner groove of the bearing with the same grease. Apply a light coat over the transmission input shaft bearing retainer plate tube.
11   On early models, within clutch housing, insert the two bearing hub retaining clips over the release lever forks. Verify the release lever pivot and clip is correctly positioned on the lever seat.
12   On later models with a separate clutch housing, within clutch housing simply engage the hub and release bearing channel with the release lever fork trunnions. Verify the release lever ball stud retaining clip is correctly positioned under ball of stud.
13   On later models with a one piece transmission/clutch housing, install the bearing over the transmission input shaft tube, lubricate the clutch release lever ball socket with high-temperature grease and push the lever onto the ball stud and simultaneously into the bearing fork channel until it's firmly seated. Verify release lever ball stud retaining clip is correctly positioned under ball of stud and forked end trunnions centered within the bearing hub channel. Move the release lever back and forth and check that the bearing slides easily on the input shaft tube.
14   Apply a light coat of high-temperature grease to the face of the release bearing where it contacts the pressure plate diaphragm fingers.
15   Install the clutch housing and tighten the bolts to the torque listed in this Chapter's Specifications. **Note:** *Don't forget to reinstall shims between block and housing if required.*
16   The remainder of installation is the reverse of the removal Steps.

Concentric slave cylinder type

Removal

17   Disconnect the hydraulic line from the concentric slave cylinder inlet (see Section 5).
18   If the vehicle is a 4WD model, remove transfer case from the vehicle (see Chapter 7C).
19   Remove the transmission from the vehicle (see Chapter 7A).
20   Within the clutch housing, twist the release bearing and carrier assembly until resistance is felt. Continue to turn the assembly further and the preload spring will push the release bearing off the slave cylinder.

Inspection

21   Inspect the bearing (see Step 9) and replace it if necessary.

Installation

22   Apply a light coat of high-temperature lithium-based grease to the face of the release bearing, where it contacts the pressure plate diaphragm fingers.
23   Lubricate the inner bore of the bearing and bearing carrier with the same grease.
24   Push the release bearing and carrier

onto the slave cylinder until it bottoms out.
25   The remainder of installation is the reverse of the removal Steps.
26   If the clutch requires bleeding, see Section 6.

5   Clutch slave cylinder - inspection, removal and installation

Refer to illustrations 5.32 and 5.36
Caution: *Prior to any vehicle service that requires removal of the* **external** *slave cylinder, (transmission and clutch housing removal), the master cylinder push rod should be disconnected from the clutch pedal. If not disconnected, permanent damage to the slave cylinder will occur if the clutch pedal is depressed while the slave cylinder is disconnected.*

Inspection

1   Raise vehicle and place securely on jackstands
2   On models with external slave cylinders, peel back the dust boot and look for evidence of excessive trapped fluid. **Note:** *Some light wetting of the boot is normal.*
3   On models with concentric slave cylinders, look for evidence of fluid leakage around the transmission bellhousing lower vent hole or look for evidence through the side inspection port in the clutch housing. **Note:** *Do not mistake transmission fluid for brake fluid.*
4   Any signs of leakage indicate replacement of the slave cylinder (or entire system on certain models) is in order.

External slave cylinder (1987 and earlier models)

Note: *The slave cylinder on 1987 and earlier models is removed and installed as a complete unit with the master cylinder and hydraulic line. The slave cylinder itself is not available separately.*

Removal

5   From the inside of the cab, carefully pry the clutch cylinder pushrod and retainer bushing from the pedal cross-shaft lever pin (see Section 10).
6   If the slave cylinder is to be replaced, the entire system must be replaced. Remove the two nuts retaining the clutch master cylinder assembly to the firewall and remove the master cylinder. **Note:** *Removal of the clutch master cylinder assembly is unnecessary if the slave cylinder is only being detached from the transmission for service other then replacement of the clutch hydraulic components. If this is the case, proceed to Step 9.*
7   Note the routing of the hydraulic line and the location of the line to firewall clips. Remove the clips.
8   Raise the vehicle and place it securely on jackstands.
9   On 7.5L engines, use a screwdriver or a similar tool and lift the two retaining tabs of the slave cylinder retaining bracket. Disengage the tabs from the cast clutch housing

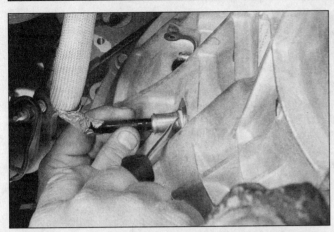

5.32 To disconnect the hydraulic line, use a special tool to press the white sleeve toward the transmission while pulling gently on the line. If the special tool is not available, you can sometimes release the line by pressing the sleeve gently with a screwdriver, as shown here

5.36 Locations of the mounting bolts for the concentric slave cylinder - upper right arrow is to the bleeder screw

lugs and then slide the cylinder out to remove. On 4.9/5.0/5.8L engine vehicles, remove the C-clip from the slave cylinder and slide the cylinder out of the clutch housing bracket. Disengage the pushrod from the release lever as the slave cylinder is removed.

10   If component replacement is necessary, remove the entire clutch hydraulic system from the vehicle at this time.

Installation

11   Position the clutch master cylinder assembly onto the firewall and install the two nuts, tightening them securely. **Note:** *Installation of the clutch master cylinder assembly is unnecessary if the slave cylinder was only being detached from the transmission for service other than replacement of the clutch hydraulic components. If this is the case, proceed to Step 14.*

12   Correctly route the clutch tubing and slave cylinder to the bellhousing. **Note:** *Care must be taken during routing of the nylon line to keep away from engine exhaust system components.*

13   Reinstall the clutch tube to firewall retaining clips.

14   Install the slave cylinder by first pushing the slave cylinder push rod into the cylinder. On 7.5L engines, engage the push rod into the release lever and slide the slave cylinder into the clutch housing lugs. Seat the cylinder into the recess in the lugs. On 4.9/5.0/5.8L engine vehicles, slide the slave cylinder into the clutch housing bracket and attach the retaining C-clip. **Note:** *When installing a new hydraulic system, the slave cylinder contains a shipping strap that pre-positions the pushrod for installation and also provides a bearing insert. Following installation of the new slave cylinder, the first actuation of the clutch pedal will break the shipping strap and give normal system operation.*

15   Clean and apply a light film of SAE 30 engine oil or equivalent to the master cylinder push rod bushing.

16   From inside the cab, press the master cylinder pushrod and retainer bushing onto

the cross-shaft lever pin until the bushing tabs snap into position in the groove.

17   Check the clutch reservoir and add fluid if required. Depress the clutch pedal at least ten times to verify smooth operation and proper release. **Note:** *The proper fluid level is indicated by a step on the reservoir. Do not overfill. The upper portion of the reservoir must accept fluid that is displaced from the slave cylinder as the clutch wears.*

18   Remove jackstands and lower vehicle.

External slave cylinder (1988 and later)

Removal

19   From the inside of the cab, carefully pry the clutch cylinder pushrod and retainer bushing from the pedal cross-shaft lever pin to prevent possible damage to slave cylinder in the event the clutch pedal is depressed while the slave cylinder is disconnected (see Section 10).

20   Raise the vehicle and place it securely on jackstands.

21   On 7.5L engines, use a screwdriver or a similar tool and lift the two retaining tabs of the slave cylinder retaining bracket. Disengage the tabs from the transmission lugs and then slide the cylinder out. On 4.9/5.0/5.8L engine vehicles, remove the C-clip from the slave cylinder and slide the cylinder out of the clutch housing bracket. Disengage the pushrod from the release lever as the slave cylinder is removed.

22   If replacement is necessary, use a 3/32-inch punch and drive out the tube retaining pin from the slave cylinder.

23   Cap the clutch line to prevent excess fluid loss.

Installation

24   If the slave cylinder was replaced or removed from the hydraulic line, bench bleed the slave cylinder prior to installation (see Section 6).

25   Install the slave cylinder by first pushing the slave cylinder push rod into the cylinder.

On 7.5L engines, engage the push rod into the release lever and slide the slave cylinder into the transmission lugs. Seat the cylinder into the recess in the lugs. On 4.9/5.0/5.8L engine vehicles, slide the slave cylinder into the clutch housing bracket and attach the retaining C-clip.

26   If the slave cylinder was replaced or removed from the hydraulic line, bleed the clutch master cylinder hydraulic line (see Section 6), then install the line into the slave cylinder and install the line retaining pin.

27   Clean and apply a light film of SAE 30 engine oil or equivalent to the master cylinder push rod bushing.

28   From inside the cab, press the master cylinder pushrod with the retainer bushing onto the cross-shaft lever pin until the bushing tabs snap into position in the groove.

29   Check the clutch reservoir and add fluid if required. Depress the clutch pedal at least ten times to verify smooth operation and proper release. **Note:** *The proper fluid level is indicated by a step on the reservoir. Do not overfill. The upper portion of the reservoir must accept fluid that is displaced from the slave cylinder as the clutch wears.*

30   Remove jackstands and lower vehicle.

Concentric slave cylinder

Removal

31   Raise vehicle and support securely on jackstands.

32   Disconnect the clutch fluid hydraulic line from the transmission **(see illustration).** Have rags handy, as some fluid will be lost as the line is removed.

33   If the vehicle is a 4WD model, remove the transfer case (see Chapter 7C).

34   Remove the transmission from the vehicle (see Chapter 7A)

35   Remove the clutch release bearing (see Section 4).

36   Remove the slave cylinder-to-transmission bolts and remove the slave cylinder **(see illustration).**

6.15a The bleeder valve for concentric slave cylinders looks just like the bleeder on a brake caliper or wheel cylinder and is loosened the same way

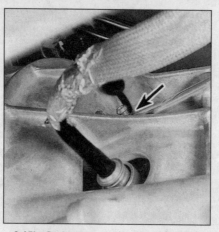

6.15b On later models with concentric slave cylinders, locate the bleeder screw (arrow) above the release cylinder hydraulic line fitting on the left side of the transmission

Installation

37   Install the slave cylinder over the transmission input shaft with the bleed screw and line coupling facing the left side of the transmission. Tighten the fasteners to the torque listed in this Chapter's Specifications.

38   Installation is the reverse of the removal Steps with the following additions:

a) *When connecting the hydraulic line to the release cylinder, simply insert male coupling into female coupling and check for secure engagement.*

b) *Bleed the clutch hydraulic system if necessary (see Section 6).*

6   Clutch system - bleeding

Refer to illustrations 6.15a and 6.15b

External slave cylinder (1983 through 1987)

Note: *The hydraulic clutch systems on 1983 to 1987 models are bled and sealed at the factory as a complete system. Therefore, if air has entered this type of system, the entire system must be replaced (see Section 5).*

External slave cylinder systems (1988 and later)

1   Clean the reservoir cap and slave cylinder in the area of the tube connection.

2   Remove the slave cylinder from the transmission and detach the hydraulic line (see Section 5).

3   Place the tube end into a container of brake fluid and tighten the reservoir cap securely to minimize loss of fluid.

4   Hold the slave cylinder so the connector port is at the highest point, by tipping cylinder to approximately 30-degrees. Fill the cylinder with brake fluid through the connector port. **Note:** *It may be necessary to "rock" the slave cylinder around or push gently on the pushrod*

to expel all the air. Pushing on the pushrod too hard will cause fluid to spray out of the connector hole.

5   When all the air is expelled from the slave cylinder and no more bubbles come out of the port hole, while holding the slave cylinder in such a way as to avoid fluid loss or air entrance, install the slave cylinder back onto the transmission housing (see Section 6).

6   Remove the reservoir cap and diaphragm - fluid should begin flowing out the slave cylinder end of the tube. Watch the reservoir and keep it full.

7   When fluid is flowing out in a steady, uninterrupted flow (no bubbles), top off the reservoir and install the diaphragm and cap to slow the flow.

8   From under the vehicle, insert the clutch line quickly into the slave cylinder and replace the retaining pin.

9   The system should be bled and functioning properly.

10   Top off the clutch reservoir and lower the vehicle.

11   Check for proper operation of the clutch (see Section 1).

Concentric slave cylinder system

12   Remove the cap and fill the reservoir to the top with brake fluid.

13   Raise the vehicle and support it securely on jackstands.

14   To keep brake fluid from entering the clutch housing, route a suitable rubber tube of the appropriate inside diameter from the bleed screw to a clear container partially filled with clean brake fluid.

15   Loosen the bleed screw located in the slave cylinder body next to the inlet connection **(see illustrations)**. Fluid will flow from the master cylinder down the tube to the slave cylinder and into the container. **Note:** *The reservoir must be kept full at all times so no*

additional air enters the system. Bubbles will appear at the bleed screw outlet, meaning air is being expelled.

16   When the slave is full, a steady flow of fluid will come from the slave outlet. Tighten the bleed screw.

17   Depress the clutch pedal to the floor and hold for a couple of seconds. Release the pedal as rapidly as possible. The pedal must be released completely. Pause for a couple of seconds. Repeat this procedure ten times.

18   Check the fluid level in the reservoir. The fluid should be level with the indicator step when the diaphragm is removed.

19   Repeat Steps 17 and 18 five times.

20   Replace the reservoir diaphragm and cap.

21   Apply moderate pressure to the pedal and have an assistant loosen the bleed screw just a crack to expel additional air. **Note:** *If the bleed screw is opened too far, fluid will spray out.* Tighten the bleed screw and release the pedal.

22   Check the fluid level. The hydraulic system should now be fully bled.

23   Check proper operation of clutch (see Section 1).

7   Clutch release bearing - travel measurement

External slave cylinders

1   Raise vehicle and support securely on jackstands.

2   Measure the distance from the edge of the slave cylinder to the clutch bearing release lever parallel to the pushrod.

3   Have an assistant depress the clutch pedal completely and perform the same measurement to the same points.

4   The release bearing travel measurement is the difference between the two measurements. Compare your results with the specifications listed in this Chapter for your transmission.

5   If the results are less than specified, several possibilities exists (assuming a clutch release problem "grinding" is occurring). These include low fluid level, a leaking slave cylinder, leaking clutch master cylinder, misadjusted clutch or pedal, air in the system, or a combination of items. Refer to the appropriate Section in this Chapter for proper resolution of the problem.

6   If the measurement is equal to or greater then specified, the hydraulic system is operating correctly.

7   Remove the jackstands and lower the vehicle.

Concentric slave cylinder

8   Raise the vehicle and support it securely on jackstands.

9   Remove the rubber plug from the inspection port in the side or bottom of the transmission.

8.1 The distance the pedal travels before beginning to release the clutch is called "freeplay"

10.3 To disengage the clutch master cylinder pushrod from the cross-shaft lever pin, carefully pry the pushrod and bushing from the pin

10   Position a shortened steel ruler through the inspection port and against the slave cylinder.

11   Using the black plastic bearing retainer rear edge as a reference point, take a measurement with the clutch pedal fully up.

12   Have an assistant depress the clutch pedal completely and perform the same measurement to the same points.

13   The release bearing travel measurement is the difference between the two measurements. Compare your results with the specifications listed in this Chapter for your transmission.

14   If the results are less than specified several possibilities exist (assuming a clutch release problem "grinding" is occurring). These include low fluid level, a leaking slave cylinder, leaking clutch master cylinder, misadjusted clutch or pedal, air in the system, or a combination of items. Refer to the appropriate section in this Chapter for proper resolution of the problem.

15   If the measurement is equal to or greater than specified, the hydraulic system is operating correctly.

16   Remove the jackstands and lower the vehicle.

8   Clutch linkage - check and adjustment

Refer to illustration 8.1

Mechanical linkages

1   From inside the cab, measure the clutch pedal freeplay at the pedal **(see illustration)**. Freeplay should be between 1/2 to 2 inches. If the freeplay is less than or greater than specified, adjust the clutch as follows.

2   Raise the vehicle and support it securely on jackstands.

3   Locate the clutch release lever actuating rod and loosen the locknuts. The actuating rod is the short rod that pushes directly against the release lever on the left side of

the transmission bellhousing. Move the outer locknut freely down the threaded rod.

4   To gain more freeplay, reduce the length of the actuating rod by turning the locknut in contact with the rod extension in the appropriate direction. To reduce the freeplay, increase the length of the actuating rod.

5   Verify correct freeplay at pedal and tighten the free locknut against the adjusting locknut.

6   Remove the jackstands and lower the vehicle.

7   Check for proper operation of the clutch (see Section 1).

Hydraulic systems

8   From the inside of the cab, carefully pry the clutch master cylinder pushrod and retainer bushing from the pedal cross-shaft lever pin (see Section 10).

9   Making sure that the clutch pedal is in the full up position (against the rubber stop). Try to reassemble the pushrod and cross-shaft lever pin, particularly noting if they are in alignment or not.

10   If the clutch pedal must be depressed off its stop slightly to align, or if the clutch master cylinder pushrod must be pushed in slightly to align, then the cross-lever must be re-splined to the cross-lever shaft. If the pin and pushrod align, no adjustment is necessary.

11   To re-spline, first remove the cross-lever to pedal shaft retaining nut and pry lever from shaft.

12   Raise the pedal up fully to its stop and secure (a block of wood to the floor works well).

13   Insert the lever pin into the clutch cylinder pushrod and place the other end of the lever over the cross shaft.

14   Verify the pedal is in the full up position and loosely install the cross-lever retaining nut while holding the cross lever centered on the cross shaft splines. Do not exert any pressure that might alter the clutch cylinder pushrod from its nominal (static) position.

15   Without inducing any movement in the set-up, tighten the cross-lever retaining nut. **Note:** *Tightening the nut pushes the lever onto the cross shaft splines and should cut new corresponding splines in the lever.* Tighten the nut to the torque listed in this Chapter's Specifications.

16   Repeat Steps 8 through 10 to verify proper adjustment. Repeat the adjustment procedure if necessary. **Note:** *In some cases a new cross-lever which has never been cut might be necessary for successful adjustment.*

17   From inside the cab, press the master cylinder pushrod and retainer bushing onto the cross-shaft lever pin until the bushing tabs snap into position in the groove.

18   Check for proper operation of the clutch (see Section 1)

9   Clutch linkage (mechanical) - removal and installation

Removal

1   The most likely source of wear in the clutch linkage is the equalizer bar bushings.

2   To replace the bushings, first raise the front of the vehicle and support it securely on jackstands.

3   Disconnect the clutch release lever retracting spring.

4   Remove the retainer spring clip and disconnect the clutch pedal-to-equalizer bar rod and bushing from the equalizer outer arm.

5   Remove the clutch adjuster assembly from the equalizer bar swivel.

6   Remove the bolts attaching the outer equalizer bar pivot bracket to the chassis and remove the bracket and equalizer bar.

7   Remove the snap-rings holding the equalizer bar bushings to the inner and outer pivot brackets and remove the bushings and washers.

Installation

8   Installation is the reverse of the removal procedure. Lubricate all bushings and pivot points with multi-purpose grease.

10   Clutch and brake pedal assembly - removal and installation

Refer to illustration 10.3

Removal

1   On mechanical linkage systems, remove the retracting spring from the clutch release lever (see Section 9).

2   On mechanical linkage systems, pull the upper retaining pin and disconnect the clutch rod from pedal cross-shaft lever (see Section 9).

3   On hydraulic systems, carefully pry the clutch master cylinder pushrod and retainer bushing from the pedal cross-shaft lever pin **(see illustration)**.

4   Working under the dash, temporarily wire the spring coil to prevent it from expanding beyond its normal installed length.

5   Carefully push the clutch pedal to the floor and remove the spring.

6   Remove the locknut attaching the clutch cross-shaft lever to the clutch pedal cross-shaft and remove the lever.

7   Remove the starter interlock switch from the clutch pedal assembly, if equipped (see Section 12).

8   Remove the locknut attaching the clutch pedal to the clutch pedal cross-shaft and remove the pedal.

9   Pull the clutch pedal cross-shaft out of the bushings. **Note:** *The brake pedal shares the same cross-shaft for support and will "hang loose" when the cross-shaft is removed.* If the brake pedal requires removal, detach the master cylinder pushrod retainer from the pedal pin and disconnect the pedal mounted brake switch if equipped. Remove the brake pedal.

10   Right and left hand clutch cross-shaft bushings can now be replaced if necessary.

Installation

11   Installation is basically the reverse of the removal procedure. Lubricate all bushings and pivot points with multi-purpose grease.

12   When installing a new assist spring, first compress the spring in a vise and temporarily wire the spring to maintain a compressed length. Do not compress the spring solid, as spring damage will occur and clutch pedal effort will be increased. Don't forget to clip and remove the coil retaining wires after spring installation is complete.

13   When the installation is complete, check the clutch linkage and adjust it if necessary (see Section 8) and check the operation of the pedal mounted starter interlock switch, if equipped (see Section 12).

11   Clutch master cylinder - inspection, removal and installation

Inspection

1   From inside of cab, locate clutch master cylinder pushrod on the right side of the pedal support assembly under the dash.

2   Peel back dust boot from master cylinder and look for evidence of excessive trapped fluid. **Note:** *Some light wetting of the boot is normal.*

3   Any signs of leakage indicate replacement of the slave cylinder (or entire system on certain models) is in order.

Removal

1987 and earlier models

Note: *The clutch master cylinder on 1987 and earlier models is removed and installed as a complete unit with the slave cylinder and*

hydraulic line. The master cylinder itself is not available separately.

4   See Section 5 for slave cylinder replacement for these models, as it describes the removal and installation of a complete hydraulic system as required due to the lack of individual replacement components.

1988 and later models

5   From inside the cab, carefully pry the clutch master cylinder pushrod and retainer bushing from the pedal cross-shaft lever pin (see Section 10).

6   Disconnect and remove the interlock switch (see Section 12).

7   Remove as much fluid from the reservoir as possible and place shop rags under the master cylinder to catch leaking fluid.

8   Disconnect the hydraulic line from the master cylinder and plug the line and outlet to avoid contamination and excessive fluid loss.

9   Remove the two nuts retaining the clutch master cylinder to the firewall and remove master cylinder.

Installation

10   Installation is the reverse of removal except after installation, bleed the system (see Section 6).

11   Check the system for proper operation (see Section 1).

12   Clutch/starter interlock switch - check, adjustment, removal and installation

Clutch pedal mounted switch (1985 through 1987 models)

1   1985 and later manual transmission models are equipped with a clutch/starter interlock switch, which requires that the clutch pedal be fully depressed in order to start the engine.

2   Working inside the vehicle, disconnect the electrical connector at the switch located on upper part of the clutch pedal.

3   Use a test light or ohmmeter and test the switch continuity. With the pedal up (clutch engaged), the switch contacts should be open. The test light should not illuminate or the ohmmeter should indicate no continuity. With the clutch pedal pressed to the floor, the switch contacts should be closed (the test light should come on or the ohmmeter should indicate continuity).

4   If the switch passes, install the connector.

5   If the switch doesn't work, remove the clip and reposition the clip closer to the switch.

6   Depress the clutch pedal to the floor to automatically reset the switch clip.

7   Repeat Step 3. If the switch still fails, replace it.

8   If not already done, disconnect switch wire harness connector.

9   Remove switch pushrod to pedal retaining clip.

10   Remove the switch to pedal support fasteners and remove the switch.

11   Installation is reverse of removal.

12   Check the operation of the switch and adjust if necessary.

Clutch master cylinder mounted switch (1988 and later)

13   The three way switch on 1988 and later models is designed to be non-adjustable and should work properly if installed correctly.

14   From inside the vehicle, disconnect the electrical connector from the switch located on the clutch master cylinder pushrod.

15   Using small screwdriver, bend lower orientation retaining tab down to release switch and rotate switch sideways to gain access to upper retainer.

16   Push upper retainer tabs together and disengage retainer from switch by sliding the retainer rearwards (away from the firewall).

17   Pull the switch free from the clutch cylinder pushrod and remove it.

18   Installation is the reverse of removal.

19   Check the switch for proper operation.

13   Rear axle - general information

1   The rear axle assembly consists of a straight, hollow housing enclosing a differential assembly and axleshafts. These assemblies support the vehicle's 'sprung' weight components through leaf or coil springs attached between the axle housings and the vehicle's frame rails.

2   The rear axle assemblies employed on vehicles covered by this manual are of two designs: those with semi-floating axleshafts and those with heavy duty full-floating axleshafts. Full-floating axleshafts do not themselves bear any of the vehicle's weight, can be removed independent of the tapered roller wheel bearings and are designed only to transfer power to the rear wheels. Semi-floating axleshafts are themselves an integral part of the rear wheel support system, bearing vehicle weight as well as transferring power to the rear wheels. Both types of rear end designs use hypoid gears with the pinion gear centerline below the axle-shaft centerline.

3   Due to the need for special tools and equipment, it is recommended that operations on these models be limited to those described in this Chapter. Where repair or overhaul is required, remove the axle assembly and take it to a rebuilder, or exchange it for a new or reconditioned unit. It is becoming increasingly rare to find individual axle components for local repair work as it is generally recognized that dismantling and rebuilding this unit is an "in plant" job requiring special equipment and techniques.

14.3a A slide-hammer with an adapter like this can be used to remove the axle bearing

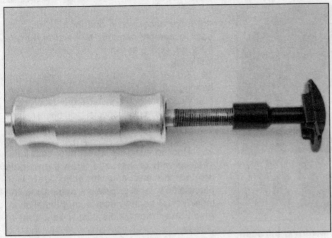

14.3b Here's the tool in use. The adapter grips the bearing from behind

4 Always make sure that an axle unit is changed for one of identical type and gear ratio.

14 Rear axleshaft oil seal and bearing (semi-floating, ball bearing type) - replacement

Refer to illustrations 14.3a, 14.3b and 14.5

1 Remove the axleshaft (see Section 17).
2 Remove the axleshaft seal using special slide hammer type puller. If seal replacement is all that is required, proceed to Step 4.
3 If both bearing and seal require removal, both can be removed at the same time. Use the slide hammer in combination with a bearing removal tool (manufacturer no. T85T-1225-A or equivalent). Pivot the jaws of the tool sideways and insert behind bearing **(see illustrations)**. Let jaws pivot out to engage the bearing and remove the bearing and seal using the slide hammer.

14.5 Installing a rear axle bearing into the axle tube using a bearing driver - semi-floating ball bearing axle

4 Inspect the inner surface of the housing for any conditions that would prevent the new seal or bearing from fitting into its seat correctly. Remedy any problems of this type such as burrs, galling or rust before attempting to install the new bearing or seal.
5 If replaced, lubricate the new bearing with rear axle lube and install squarely into axle housing bore. Using appropriate bearing/seal driver, tap bearing into housing until it bottoms in the bore **(see illustration)**. **Caution:** *Continuously verify that the bearing is being pressed squarely and not being cocked in the bore during this process.*
6 Prior to seal installation, smear a small amount of RTV sealant on the outer edge of the seal (do not allow the sealant to touch the sealing lip) and coat the inner sealing lip with multi-purpose grease.
7 Using an appropriate seal driver, tap the new seal into its bore. The seal must receive even pressure around its circumference, thus a tubular drift, large socket or special tool should be used for this. Drive the seal into the housing until it seats.
8 Install the axleshaft(s) (see Section 17).

15 Rear axleshaft oil seal and bearing (semi-floating tapered bearing type) - replacement

Refer to illustration 15.4
Warning: *This procedure is potentially dangerous and is best done by an automotive machine shop.*

Removal

1 Remove the axleshaft (see Section 17).
2 When it is determined that the wheel bearing is to be replaced, the bearing cup, which normally remains in the axle housing when the axleshaft is removed, must also be replaced. Use a slide hammer-type puller to remove it from the housing.
3 Before the wheel bearing and/or seal can be replaced, the inner retainer ring must first be removed. Never use heat to remove the ring as this would damage the axleshaft. Use the procedure which follows.
4 Using a drill of 1/4 to 1/2-inch diameter, drill a hole in the outside diameter of the inner retainer approximating 3/4 of the thickness of the retainer ring **(see illustration)**. Do not drill

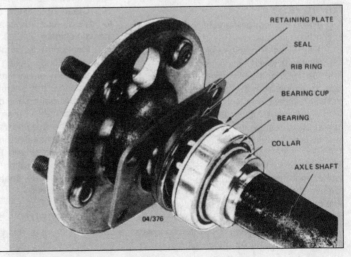

15.4 Components of the axleshaft bearing assembly. The collar (retainer ring) must first be drilled, then cracked with a hammer and chisel

RETAINING PLATE

SEAL

RIB RING

BEARING CUP

BEARING

COLLAR

AXLE SHAFT

04/376

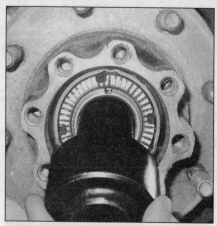

16.4 A special hub locknut wrench is required to turn the hub nut on late model Ford full-floating axles - the drive tangs must fit into the hub nut slots

17.6 Position a large screwdriver between the rear axle case and a ring gear bolt to keep the differential case from turning when removing the pinion shaft lockpin

all the way through the retainer ring, as the drill would damage the axleshaft.

5   After drilling the hole in the retainer ring, use a chisel positioned across the drilled hole and strike it sharply to split the retainer ring.

6   Due to the need for a hydraulic press and various adapters to remove the wheel bearing, you must take the axleshaft(s) to an automotive machine shop or parts store with the equipment required for the work. **Note:** *On vehicles with tapered roller axle bearings, the axleshaft retaining plate and seal must be installed prior to pressing the new bearing and retainer ring on the shaft.*

Replacement

7   After the new bearing has been pressed onto the axleshaft reinstall the axleshaft (see Section 17).

---

16   Rear wheel hub bearings and grease seal (full-floating type) - replacement

Refer to illustration 16.4

Removal

1   Raise the rear of the vehicle and place it securely on jackstands.

2   Remove the rear wheels, then remove the axleshafts (see Section 18).

3   On 1986 and earlier models, remove the locking wedge from the adjusting nut keyway slot with a screwdriver. **Note:** *This must be done before the adjusting nut is removed or even turned.* Next, remove the wheel bearing adjusting nut using the correct size large socket.

4   On 1987 and later models, install a hub wrench so that the drive tangs of the tool engage the four slots in the hub nut and remove the nut **(see illustration)**. **Caution:** *The hub nuts are right-hand thread (right hub) and left-hand thread (left hub). Remove the right hub nut by rotating it counterclockwise and the left hub nut by rotating it clockwise.*

Note: *During the loosening process, the hub nut will ratchet. Also, each hub nut is stamped "LH" for left and "RH" for right. Note these markings for proper reassembly.*

5   On 1986 and earlier models, pull the brake drum/wheel hub assembly off the axle spindle. The entire assembly should pull off by hand. If the assembly seems loose but wont come off, it may be necessary to retract the brake shoes slightly (see Chapter 9).

6   1987 and later models allow separate removal of the brake drum from the wheel hub assembly, allowing easier removal of the wheel hub. To remove the brake drum, remove the push-on drum retainers, if equipped, and simply pull drum from hub. If the brake drum won't come off easily, it may be necessary to retract the brake shoes slightly (see Chapter 9).

7   On 1987 and later models, a large two-jaw puller is required to remove the wheel hub assembly from the axle spindle. Be sure to use any necessary adapters to perform this job safely and without damaging components.

8   Remove the outer bearing from the hub.

9   Use a brass drift to drive the inner bearing cone and inner seal out through the back of the wheel hub.

10   Clean the inside of the wheel hub to remove all axle lubricant and grease. Clean the axle spindle.

11   Inspect the bearing assemblies for signs of wear, pitting, galling and other damage. Replace the bearings if any of these conditions exist. Inspect the bearing races for signs of erratic wear, galling and other damage.

12   If the outer races need replacement, drive out the bearing races from the wheel hub with a brass drift. Install the new races with a bearing driver. Never use a drift or punch for this operation as these races must be driven squarely, seated correctly and can be damaged easily.

Replacement

13   Prior to installation, pack the inner and outer wheel bearing assemblies with high

temperature grease or equivalent. If you do not have access to a bearing packer, pack each assembly carefully by hand and make sure the entire assembly is penetrated with lubricant.

14   Install the newly packed inner wheel bearing into the brake drum hub. Install a new hub inner seal with a suitable drive tool (tubular drift, large socket, special tool) being careful not to damage the seal. **Note:** *Install seal with logo facing up.*

15   Prior to installing wheel hub, coat inner seal lip with grease and wrap the spindle around the end and threaded area with electrician's tape to prevent damage to the inner wheel bearing seal during installation. Also, cover the spindle with a light coat of grease.

16   Carefully slide the hub and drum assembly over the spindle, being very careful to keep it straight so as not to contact the spindle with the seal (which would damage it). Remove the electrician's tape.

17   Install the newly packed outer wheel bearing over the spindle and into the wheel hub.

18   Install the hub nut and adjust wheel bearing preload (see Section 19). **Caution:** *When installing the hub nut on 1987 and later models, make sure the tab is located in the keyway with the identification markings facing out.*

19   Install the axleshaft (see Section 18) and brake drum (1987 and later models only). Tighten the fasteners to the torque listed in this Chapter's Specifications. **Note:** *Push-on retainers for 1987 and later brake drums do not require re-installation.*

20   Adjust the brakes if they were retracted for removal purposes (see Chapter 9).

21   Install the wheel, remove the jackstands and lower the vehicle.

22   Recheck the torque on the axleshaft bolts (see Section 18).

---

17   Rear axleshaft (semi-floating type) - removal and installation

Refer to illustrations 17.6, 17.7 and 17.8

Ford 10.25 inch, 8.8 inch and Dana (ball bearing type)

Removal

1   Raise the rear of the vehicle and place it securely on jackstands.

2   Remove the wheel(s) (see Chapter 1).

3   Release the parking brake and remove the brake drum(s) (see Chapter 9).

4   Drain the rear axle lubricant into a suitable container by removing the rear axle housing cover (see Chapter 1).

5   If still in place, discard the gasket.

6   Remove the differential pinion shaft lockpin and discard it **(see illustration)**. **Note:** *It is possible for some Dana semi-floating axles to be equipped with lockpins coated with*

17.7 Rotate the differential case 180-degrees and slide the pinion shaft out of the case until the stepped part of the shaft contacts the ring gear

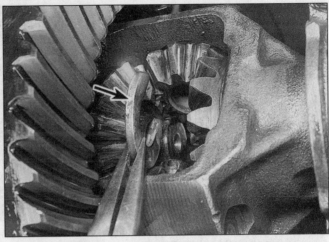

17.8 Push in on the axle flange and remove the C-lock (arrow) from the inner end of the axleshaft

Loctite (or equivalent), or with lockpins with torque-prevailing threads. The Loctite-treated lockpins have a 5/32-inch hexagonal socket head, and the torque-prevailing lockpin has a 12-point drive head. If the axle is equipped with a Loctite-treated lockpin, it must not be re-used. If the lockpin is of the torque-prevailing type, it may be re-used up to four times (four removals and installations). When in doubt as to the number of times the torque-prevailing pin has been used, replace it with a new one.

7   Lift out the differential pinion shaft to gain access to the axleshaft C-locks **(see illustration).**

8   Push the flanged end of the axleshaft toward the center of the vehicle and remove the C-lock from the end of the shaft **(see illustration).** Note: *Make sure not to lose or damage the rubber O-ring which is in the axleshaft groove under the C-clip.*

9   Pull the axleshaft from the housing, making sure not to damage the oil seals.

Installation

10   Installation is basically the reverse of the removal procedure. Make sure not to damage the axle seal when reinstalling the axleshaft (the splines on the end of the shaft are sharp). Apply a thread locking compound to a new pinion shaft lockpin and tighten it to the torque listed in this Chapter's Specifications. **Caution:** *Failure to correctly install the axleshaft C-locks or lockpin can result in loss of wheel/axle assembly or rear wheel lockup.*

11   Most axle housing covers are sealed with RTV sealant rather than a gasket. Before applying this sealant, make sure the machined surfaces on both cover and carrier are clean and free of oil. When cleaning the surfaces, cover the inside of the axle with a clean lint-free cloth to prevent contamination. Apply a continuous bead of the sealant to the carrier casting face, inboard of the cover bolt holes. Install the cover

within 15 minutes of the application of the sealant and tighten the bolts in a criss-cross pattern to the torque listed in this Chapter's Specifications.

12   Install the brake drum(s) and adjust if required (see Chapter 9).

13   Install the wheel(s) (see Chapter 1).

14   Fill the rear axle with lubricant (see Chapter 1).

15   Remove jackstands and lower vehicle. Test drive and check for leaks.

Early model Ford 9.0 inch axle assembly (tapered bearing type)

Removal

16   Perform Steps 1 through 3 of this Section.

17   Loosen the axleshaft retaining nuts by inserting a socket and extension through the hole provided in the outer axle flange (wheel interface). Rotate the axleshaft to allow access to all four nuts. Remove the nuts.

18   Remove the axleshaft by pulling on the flange. If the axle is stuck it can sometimes be removed by reinstalling the wheel assembly and using the greater leverage of the wheel to pull it out. When pulling out the axle, be careful not to damage the seal if you are reusing it although seals should always be replaced whenever an axle is removed (see Section 15). Secure the brake backing plate to the housing with one nut to make sure it doesn't fall off while you are performing other operations on the axleshaft or housing.

Installation

19   Installation is the reverse of removal. Install a new gasket between the brake backing plate and the axle housing flange. Be careful not to damage the inner lips of the axle seal when you are inserting the axleshaft into the housing (the splines on the end of the shaft are sharp). Install the axleshaft retaining

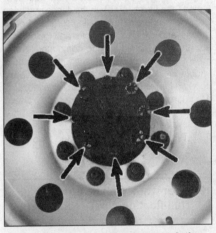

18.1 Remove the bolts that attach the axleshaft flange to the hub

nuts. Tighten to the torque listed in this Chapter's Specifications.

20   Install the wheel(s).

21   Check the differential lubricant level and fill if required (see Chapter 1).

22   Lower the vehicle and test drive. Check for fluid leaks.

18   Rear axleshaft (full-floating type) - removal and installation

Refer to illustrations 18.1 and 18.3

1   Unscrew and remove the bolts which attach the axleshaft flange to the hub **(see illustration).** There is no need to remove the wheel or jack up the vehicle.

2   Tap the flange with a soft-faced hammer to loosen the shaft and then grip the rib of the face of the flange with a pair of locking pliers; twist the shaft slightly in both directions and withdraw it from the axle tube.

3   Installation is the reverse of removal but hold the axleshaft level in order to engage the

18.3 Install a new gasket or O-ring prior to installing the axleshaft

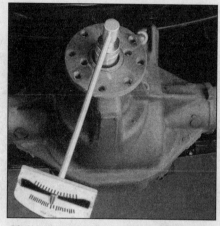

20.4 Using an inch-pound torque wrench (scale from 0 to 40 in-lbs) on the drive pinion nut, measure and record the torque necessary to rotate the drive pinion in a load-free state

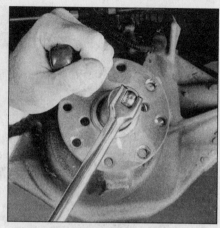

20.6 Securing the companion flange while loosening the pinion nut

splines at its inner end with those in the differential side gear. Always use a new gasket or O-ring **(see illustration)** on the flange and keep both the flange and hub mating surfaces free of grease and oil. Use new bolts and lock washers and/or a thread locking compound. **Note:** *Final tightening of the axleshaft retaining bolts should be done after the wheel lug nuts have been tightened (if the wheel was removed).*

4   If a loss of fluid is observed, check the differential lubricant level and refill if required (see Chapter 1).

5   Test drive the vehicle and check for leaks.

19   Rear wheel hub bearings (full-floating type) - adjustment

1987 and earlier models (Dana axle)

1   Raise the rear of the vehicle and place it securely on jackstands.

2   Remove the axleshafts (see Section 18).

3   Remove the locking wedge from the adjusting nut keyway slot with a screwdriver. **Note:** *This must be done before the adjusting nut is removed or even turned.*

4   Loosen the wheel bearing adjusting nut using the correct size large socket.

5   While rotating the hub/drum assembly, tighten the adjusting nut to 120 to 140 ft-lbs. Back off the nut enough to get 0.001 to 0.010 inch endplay. This should require about 1/8 to 3/8 of a turn.

6   Position the locking wedge in the keyway and hammer it into position. **Note:** *It must be bottomed against the shoulder of the adjusting nut when fully installed.* The locking wedge and adjusting nut can be used over, providing the locking wedge cuts a new groove in the nylon retainer material within 1/8 to 3/8 of a turn. The wedge must not be pressed into a previously cut groove. If it is not possible to align uncut nylon in which to press the locking wedge, discard the nut and wedge and replace them with new ones. Also discard the nut and/

or wedge if there is any evidence of damage.

7   Install the axleshaft (see Section 18).

8   If any lubrication was lost, check the lubricant level in the differential and add if necessary (see Chapter 1).

9   Test drive the vehicle and check for leaks.

1987 and later models (Ford axle)

10   Install a hub nut wrench so the drive tangs of the tool engage the four slots in the hub nut and loosen nut **(see illustration 16.4)**. **Caution:** *The hub nuts are right-hand thread (right hub) and left-hand thread (left hub). loosen right hub nut by rotating counterclockwise and left hub nut by rotating clockwise.* **Note:** *During the loosening process, the hub nut will ratchet.*

11   Tighten the hub nut to 55 to 65 ft-lbs, rotating the hub while tightening. Then back off the hub nut, listening for clicking from the hub nut. For new bearings, back off the nut five clicks. For used bearings, back off the nut 8 clicks.

12   Install axleshaft (see Section 18).

13   If any lubrication was lost, check the lubricant level in the differential and add if necessary (see Chapter 1).

14   Test drive the vehicle and check for leaks.

20   Rear differential pinion bearing seal - replacement

Refer to illustrations 20.4, 20.6, 20.7 and 20.10

Note: *This procedure is not recommended by the factory and should only be used if a proper repair facility is not available and circumstances warrant it. In several cases no factory specification exists for used bearing preload rotation torque, therefore, specifications listed are estimates.*

Removal

1   Raise the rear of the vehicle and place it securely on jackstands.

2   Remove the axleshafts (see Section 17 or 18). **Note:** *The removal of the axleshafts is advisable to eliminated the added pinion shaft rotation resistance that otherwise might contribute to a false pinion shaft rotation preload torque value.*

3   Remove the driveshaft (see Section 36).

4   Using an inch-pound torque wrench (scale from approximately 0 to 40 inch-pounds) on the drive pinion nut, measure and record the torque necessary to rotate the drive pinion in a load free state **(see illustration)**.

5   Mark the drive pinion to companion flange orientation for proper location of flange to pinion upon reassembly (see Section 36).

6   Using a suitable holding tool **(see illustration)** secure the companion flange while removing the pinion nut.

7   Using a two-jaw puller, remove the companion flange from the drive pinion shaft **(see illustration)**. **Note:** *Some fluid loss may occur.*

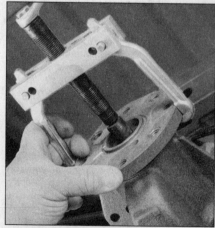

20.7 Using a puller to remove the companion flange from the drive pinion

8   Avoiding contact with the pinion shaft/threads, tap out an edge of the seal using a dull screwdriver. Using Vise-grips or other similar clamping pliers, grip the exposed edge and tap out the seal.

Replacement

9   Prior to installing the new seal, coat the housing mating surface with RTV sealant and lubricate the seal lip with clean differential lubricant.

10   Clean the seal mating surface and install a new seal squarely in the housing bore. Using an appropriate seal driver if available, drive the seal squarely into the housing until it bottoms **(see illustration)**. If a seal driver isn't available, a large deep socket or section of pipe can be used.

11   Align the companion flange to the pinion marks and gently tap the flange onto the shaft far enough to get several pinion nut threads started. **Note:** *Do not tap on the flange any more than necessary - allow the pinion nut to press the flange onto the shaft.*

12   Using a suitable holding tool, secure the companion flange while tightening the pinion nut to the minimum torque listed in this Chapter's Specifications. While tightening, take frequent measurements of rotation torque using an inch-pound torque wrench (see Step 4) until the original free loaded rotation torque is obtained. **Note:** *If the original recorded reading was less than the specified rotation preload torque, continue tightening the drive pinion nut above the minimum torque value (in small increments) to obtain the specified rotation torque. If the rotation reading was higher than specification, stop tightening pinion nut when the original rotation torque value is obtained again. In no case should the drive pinion nut be backed off to reduce rotation torque, so increase nut torque in small increments and check rotation torque after each increase.*

13   Install the driveshaft (see Section 36).

14   Install the axleshafts (see Section 17 or 18).

15   Install the wheels (see Chapter 1).

16   Check the differential lubricant level and add if required (see Chapter 1).

17   Test drive the vehicle and check for leaks.

21   Rear differential assembly (removable carrier type) - removal and installation

Removal

1   The differential assembly used in the early light-duty axle housing is of the removable type. This unit must be removed for service operations including pinion seal replacement and gear lash preload to correct for noise or wear. This type of differential is used in conjunction with semi-floating axles.

2   Raise the vehicle and support the rear axle housing or frame securely.

3   Drain the rear axle housing using the

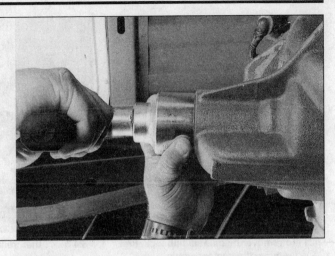

20.10 Drive a new pinion seal into the housing using a seal driver or deep socket to clear the drive pinion

plug under the center section.

4   Remove the axleshafts (see Section 17, Ford 9 inch). It is not necessary to remove them totally but pull them out a few inches to clear the differential side gears.

5   Remove the driveshaft (see Section 36).

6   Remove the carrier housing retaining nuts and washers around the entire circumference of the housing. Be careful not to lose the identification tag retained by one of these nuts as it contains valuable information about the differential assembly.

7   Clean the area around the mating surfaces of the differential carrier housing.

8   Support the unit (a transmission jack is ideal) and remove the differential assembly.

Installation

9   Clean the mating surface on the carrier housing and remove any old gasket material from the housing or the carrier assembly.

10   Installation is the reverse of removal. Make sure you use a new gasket and that the mating faces of the housing and the carrier assembly are clean. Tighten the fasteners to the torque listed in this Chapter's Specifications.

11   Fill the differential with the correct type and grade of lubricant (see Chapter 1).

22   Rear axle assembly - removal and installation

1   Chock the front wheels, raise the rear of the vehicle and support it on jackstands placed under the rear frame member.

2   Remove the wheels, brake drums and axleshafts (see Section 17 or 18).

3   Remove the driveshaft (see Section 36).

4   Disconnect the lower end of the shock absorbers from the axle housing and disconnect the rear stabilizer bar if so equipped (see Chapter 10).

5   Remove the brake vent tube (if equipped) from the brake line junction and retaining clamp.

6   Remove the brake lines from the clips that retain them to the axle but do not disconnect any of the line fittings.

7   Remove the brake shoes and backing plates and support them with wire to avoid straining the hydraulic brake lines which are still attached. On vehicles with rear anti-lock brakes (RABS), be sure to unplug the brake sensor electrical connector (see Chapter 9).

8   Support the weight of the axle on a floor jack and remove the nuts from the spring U-bolts. Remove the bottom clamping plates (see Chapter 10).

9   Lower the axle assembly on the jack and withdraw it from the rear of the vehicle.

10   The axle assembly is installed by reversing the removal procedure. Tighten all fasteners to the torque values listed in this Chapter's Specifications and Chapter 10 Specifications.

23   Front drive axle assembly (4x4) - general information

1   Four types of Dana front-drive axles are available for 4x4 truck application. The Dana 44-IFS (independent front suspension) is available on Bronco and F150 4x4s. The Dana 44-IFS-HD (heavy duty) is available on F250 4x4s. The Dana 50-IFS was available on F250 and F350 4x4s and is now an option on the F250 only. Finally, the Dana model 60 Monobeam axle is now standard on F350 4x4. If there is a question about which axle is on your vehicle, consult the rating plate located in the engine compartment and your owners manual.

2   All IFS axles are basically alike with only minor differences among the three. The 44-IFS is on vehicles equipped with coil front springs. The 44-IFS-HD and 50-IFS are on models equipped with leaf front springs. The model 60 Monobeam is a solid axle design mechanically identical to the model 60 rear axle.

3   Manual or automatic locking hubs are available as either standard or options on most axles. Consult your owner's manual for your particular vehicle if there is a question.

24.1 To remove the manual hub lock, first remove the cap assembly . . .

24.3 . . . then remove the hub lock ring

24.4 Remove the stop screw, then slide the inner portion of the hub out

24 Manual locking hubs - removal and installation

Refer to illustrations 24.1, 24.3, 24.4, 24.5 and 24.6

1   Remove the cap screws attaching the cap assembly to the body assembly **(see illustration)**. **Note:** *Later models are equipped with Torx head screws and require a Torx driver to remove them.*

2   Remove the cap assembly.

3   Using screwdriver, remove the lock ring seated in the groove of the wheel hub **(see illustration)**.

4   Remove the stop screw in the outer portion of the hub body **(see illustration)**, then slide the inner portion out.

5   On models so equipped, using snap-ring pliers, remove the snap-ring from the end of the axleshaft **(see illustration)**.

6   Slide the body assembly out of the wheel hub. If necessary. use an appropriate puller or two cap screws to remove the body assembly **(see illustration)**.

7   Installation is the reverse of the removal procedure. Be sure to apply a *light* coat of high-temperature wheel bearing grease to the splines of the axleshaft and the components of the locking hub. Tighten the fasteners to the torque listed in this Chapter's Specifications.

25 Automatic locking hubs - removal and installation

Removal

1   Remove the cap screws attaching the cap assembly to the body assembly. **Note:** *Later models are equipped with Torx head screws and require a Torx driver to remove them.*

2   Remove the cap, making sure not to drop the ball bearing, bearing race or spring. Remove the sealing ring.

3   On 1994 and earlier models, remove the seal bridge retainer (small metal stamping) from the retainer ring. Remove the retainer ring

by closing the ends with needle-nose pliers.

4   On 1995 and later models, remove the lock-ring from the groove in the wheel hub.

5   Pull the hub body assembly from the wheel hub.

6   If the wheel hub and spindle are to be removed, follow Steps 7 through 9. **Note:** *The automatic locking hubs are unique. To avoid mixing up parts, service one hub assembly at a time.*

7   Remove the snap-ring from the stub shaft groove.

8   On 1994 and earlier models, remove the splined spacer from the shaft. On 1995 and later models, remove the thrust washers and cam assembly.

9   Remove the wheel bearing locknuts and lock washer.

Installation

1994 and earlier models

10   If the wheel bearing and lock washer were removed, adjust wheel bearing nut (see Section 28) then install the splined spacer and C-washer on the axleshaft.

11   Remove any excessive grease from the hub lock and hub splines.

24.5 On models so equipped, remove the axleshaft snap-ring . . .

12   Start the hub lock assembly into the hub, making sure the large tangs are lined up with the lock washer and that the outside-diameter and inside-diameter splines are in line with the hub and axleshaft splines.

13   Install the retainer ring by closing the ends with needle-nose pliers and at the same time push the hub lock assembly into the hub.

1995 and later models

14   Align the cam retaining spring with the keyway and install the cam assembly. Press the assembly onto the wheel bearing retainer nut.

15   Install the metal thrust washer, then the plastic thrust washer, followed by the splined thrust washer. The thrust washers must be installed in the correct order or excessive wear will result.

16   Install the snap-ring on the stub shaft. If necessary, push the axle out from the backside and make sure the snap-ring is seated in the groove.

17   Before installing the hub body, position one of the cam stops at the one-o'clock position in relation the cam retaining key. Install the hub body into the hub, aligning the legs on the hub body with the pockets in the cam assembly.

24.6 . . . and pull the hub body out of the wheel hub

18 Press the hub body into the hub and install the large lock-ring. **Caution:** *Do not force the hub body into the hub. If it will not seat far enough into the hub to install the lock-ring, remove the body and recheck the alignment.*

All models

19 The remaining installation steps are the reverse of the removal procedures. Be sure to apply a light coat of high-temperature wheel bearing grease to the splines of the axleshaft and to the components of the locking hub. Tighten the cap screws to the torque listed in this Chapter's Specifications.

26 Front wheel grease seal and bearing (4x4) - replacement

Note: *Before disassembling your vehicle, purchase or rent the tool necessary to remove the locknut and adjusting nut from the spindle. Also obtain the parts necessary to replace the inner bearing seal, as it should always be replaced whenever the entire front hub assembly is dismantled. If you can't obtain the special tool necessary for the locknut and adjusting nut, this operation would be best handled by a dealer service department or shop specializing in this type of work.*

1 Raise the front of the vehicle and place it securely on jackstands.
2 Remove the wheel(s) and brake caliper(s) (see Chapter 9).
3 Remove the manual or automatic locking hubs (see Section 24 or 25).
4 On all axles except model 44 with manual hub locks, remove the wheel bearing locknut, lock ring and adjusting nut using the special lockwrench tool. Check with your local auto parts store for the availability of the proper tool.
5 On model 44 axles with manual hub locks, remove the adjusting nut with a special locknut tool by applying inward pressure on the wrench to disengage the self-locking mechanism. Check with your local auto parts store for the availability of the proper tool. Continue to apply pressure as the nut is loosened and removed.
6 Pull the hub and disc assembly off the spindle. The outer wheel-bearing assembly will slide out as the hub is removed.
7 Remove the inner bearing and grease seal from the hub using an appropriate puller and slide hammer.
8 Using solvent, clean all the old grease from the bearings and Inspect for pits, cracks, score marks and flat spots. Replace if excessive wear is observed.
9 Clean the bearing outer races within the hub and inspect for same criteria. If the outer races need replacement, drive out the bearing races from the wheel hub with a brass drift. Install the new races with a bearing driver. Never use a drift or punch for installing the races, as they must be driven in squarely, seated correctly and can be damaged easily.
10 Lubricate the bearings with high temperature wheel bearing grease. If a bearing packer is not available, work as much lubricant as possible between the rollers and cages.

11 Clean all old grease from the hub.
12 Position the inner bearing in the inner cup and install a new grease seal using an appropriate seal driver.
13 Carefully position the hub and disc assembly on the spindle.
14 Install the outer bearing and the adjusting nut.
15 Adjust the wheel bearing (see Section 28).
16 Install the locking hubs (see Section 24 or 25).
17 Install the caliper(s) (see Chapter 9) and wheel(s).
18 Lower the vehicle and tighten the lug nuts to the torque listed in the Chapter 1 Specifications.

27 Front axleshaft spindle bearing and seal (4x4) - replacement

1 Remove the front wheel hub assembly to gain access to the spindle (see Section 26).
2 Remove the spindle retaining nuts, then carefully remove the spindle from the knuckle studs and axleshaft.
3 Remove the spindle seal and needle bearing from the spindle using a slide hammer and internal bearing puller attachment. **Note:** *Prior to bearing removal, note and record the depth of the bearing in the spindle bore for reassembly.*
4 Using solvent, clean all old grease from the bearings and spindle bore seal. Blow the bearings dry with compressed air, if available. **Warning:** *Do not allow the bearings to spin - they could fly apart with great force. Also, be sure to wear eye protection whenever using compressed air.*
5 Inspect the bearing and spindle for corrosion, pitting or score marks and replace with new ones if signs of excessive wear are noted.
6 Using high temperature grease, thoroughly lubricate the needle bearing and pack the spindle bore.
7 Using an appropriate bearing driver, install the greased bearing into the spindle bore with any writing (on the bearing) facing out to the proper depth as recorded in Step 3.
8 Install a new bearing seal using a seal driver.
9 Lightly coat the face of the seal with high temperature lubricant.
10 Install the spindle over the axleshaft onto the knuckle studs. Tighten the nuts to the torque listed in this Chapter's Specifications.
11 Install the wheel hub (see Section 26).
12 The remainder of installation is the reverse of removal.

28 Front wheel bearing (4x4) - adjustment

Note: *Special tools are required for tightening and loosening the bearing adjusting nut and locknut.*

1 Raise the vehicle and place it securely on jackstands.

2 Remove the hub lock assembly (see Section 24 or 25).

1980 through 1994 models
Early model Bronco and F150 with Dana 44-IFS/44-IFS-HD front axle

3 If not already done, remove outer locknut and washer using a locknut spanner. Check with your local auto parts store for the availability of the proper tool.
4 Using the locknut spanner and a torque wrench, tighten the inner bearing adjusting nut to 50 ft-lbs while rotating the wheel back-and-forth to seat the bearing.
5 Back off the adjusting nut approximately 45-degrees.
6 Assemble the lock washer by turning the inner locknut to align the pin with the nearest hole in the lock washer. To lock it, install the outer locknut and tighten it to 150 ft-lbs.
7 Grab the top of the tire with one hand and the bottom of the tire with the other. Move the tire in and out on the spindle. Endplay should be less than 0.006-inch.
8 Install the hub lock assembly (see Section 24 or 25).
9 Remove the jackstands and lower the vehicle.

Early model F250 and F350 with Dana 50-IFS front axle

10 If not already done, bend the locking tab ear from the outer locknut slot and remove the outer locknut and lock washer using a locknut spanner. Check with your local auto parts store for the availability of the proper tool.
11 Using the locknut spanner and a torque wrench, tighten the inner locknut to 50 ft-lbs to seat the bearing.
12 Back off the inner locknut and retighten it to 30 to 40 ft-lbs.
13 While rotating the hub, back off the inner locknut 135 to 150-degrees.
14 Assemble the outer lock washer and locknut and tighten to 65 ft-lbs.
15 Bend one ear of the lock washer over the inner nut and the other ear of the lock washer over the outer nut.
16 Check the endplay as described in Step 7. Endplay should be 0.001 to 0.009-inch.
17 Install the locking hub assembly (see Section 24 or 25).
18 Remove the jackstands and lower the vehicle.

Later models (except Dana 44-IFS/44-IFS-HD front axle with manual locking hubs)

19 If not already done, remove the outer locknut and lock washer using a locknut spanner (manufacturer no. D85T-1197-A) or equivalent.
20 Using the locknut spanner and a torque wrench, tighten the inner locknut to 50 ft-lbs to seat the bearing.
21 Back off the inner locknut and retighten it to 30 to 40 ft-lbs
22 While rotating the hub, back off the inner locknut 90-degrees.

23   Install the lockwasher so that the key is positioned in the spindle groove.
24   Continue to tighten the inner locknut until the inner locknut pin aligns with the nearest lockwasher hole.
25   Install the outer locknut and torque to 160 to 205 ft-lbs.
26   Check that the hub assembly has no endplay.
27   Install the locking hub assembly (see Section 24 or 25).
28   Remove the jackstands and lower the vehicle.

Later model Dana 44-IFS front axle (with manual locking hubs)

29   Using a torque wrench and a spanner locknut wrench (check with your local auto parts store for the availability of the proper tool), apply inward pressure to unlock the adjusting nut locking splines and turn the nut clockwise to tighten the nut to 70 ft-lbs while rotating the wheel back and forth to seat the bearing.
30   Apply inward pressure on the locknut wrench to disengage the adjusting nut locking splines and back off the adjusting nut approximately 90-degrees.
31   Retighten the adjusting nut to 15 to 20 ft-lbs. Remove the tool and torque wrench.
32   Check that the hub assembly has no endplay.
33   Install the hub lock assembly (see Section 24 or 25).
34   Remove the jackstands and lower the vehicle.

1995 and later models

Model Dana 44-IFS, Dana 50-IFS, Dana 60 Monobeam (with automatic locking hubs)

35   Remove the outer C-ring or retaining ring and the three piece thrust washers from the spindle. **Note:** *Keep the splined thrust washer, the plastic thrust washer and the steel thrust washer in the correct order as you remove them from the spindle assembly.*
36   Remove the cam assembly and the wheel nut retainer key (spring clip).
37   Loosen the inner wheel bearing nut using a special tool (manufacturer number T95T-1197A for F-150 models, or T95T-1197B for F-250 and F-350 models) or equivalent. Retighten the inner wheel bearing nut to 50 ft-lbs to reseat the assembly.
38   While rotating the brake disc and hub, back-off the inner nut 90 degrees.
39   Tighten the inner locknut to 16 inch pounds. Tighten the inner nut to the next slot to allow the installation of the retainer key.
40   Install the retaining key into the spindle keyway by inserting the short leg into the aligned slot in the nut. Make sure the retaining key is pressed in all the way and the curved portion of the key is seated into the counterbore of the wheel retainer nut.
41   Install the cam assembly.
42   Install the three thrust washers in the correct order; steel washer first, the plastic washer second and the splined washer last.

43   Install the outer C-ring or retaining ring.
44   Check that hub assembly endplay is 0.002 inch or less. The front disc/hub assembly should rotate with a torque of 20 inch pounds or less.
45   Install the locking hub assembly (see Section 24 or 25).
46   Remove the jackstands and lower the vehicle.

Model Dana 44-IFS, Dana 50-IFS, Dana 60 Monobeam (with manual locking hubs)

47   If not already done, remove the outer locknut and washer using a special tool (manufacturer number D85T-1197A) or equivalent. This tool has 4 locating tabs that lock into the four recess holes in the outer lock nut.
48   Remove the lockwasher and loosen the inner locknut using the same special tool. Retighten the inner locknut to 50 ft-lbs.
49   While rotating the brake disc and hub, back-off the inner locknut 90 degrees.
50   Install the lockwasher so the key is positioned in the spindle groove.
51   Continue to tighten the inner locknut until the inner locknut pin aligns with the nearest lockwasher hole.
52   Install the outer locknut and torque to 160 to 205 ft-lbs using the special tool.
53   Check that hub assembly endplay is 0.002 inch or less. The front disc/hub assembly should rotate with a torque of 20 inch pounds or less.
54   Install the locking hub assembly (see Section 24 or 25).
55   Remove the jackstands and lower the vehicle.

---

29   Front axleshaft (4x4) - removal and installation

Axleshafts

1   Loosen the wheel lug nuts. Raise the front of the vehicle and support it securely on jackstands. Remove the wheels
2   Remove the front wheel hub(s) and the spindle assembly (see Sections 26 and 27).
3   On independent front suspensions, the left side axle assembly can be simply pulled out of the differential case. Pull the axleshaft assembly from the axle housing, being very cautious as you pull the universal joint through the knuckle bore. On F350 Monobeam front ends, both axle assemblies can simply be pulled out of the axle tube.
4   On late model independent front suspensions, to remove the right side axle assembly, first remove the stub axle slip joint boot clamps. Slide the boot over the stub axle and pull the drive axle from the stub axle slip joint and out through the knuckle bore. On early models the right axleshaft can be slid out of the slip joint/grease seal. **Note:** *The stub axle and its universal joint will remain in the differential case and thus cannot be serviced in this configuration.*
5   At this point the axle assembly can be serviced as required.

6   Prior to installation, make sure all axle components are in good, serviceable condition. If not, replace them with new ones.
7   To install the left side axleshaft on IFS systems and both axles on monobeam axle, carefully insert it through the knuckle bore being careful not to damage the axle or seals. Engage the axle spline with the side gears of the differential and push the axle into its correct position. Install a new RDS seal on the knuckle end of the axle shaft with the lip of the seal facing towards the spindle. Coat the seal face with grease.
8   To install the right side axle on IFS systems, carefully insert it through the knuckle bore being careful not to damage the axle or seals. Engage the axle spline with the stub axle slip joint spline and push the axle into its correct position. **Note:** *The axle splines are keyed and can only be installed with the key splines aligned.* Install a new RDS seal on the knuckle end of the axle shaft with the lip of the seal facing towards the spindle. Coat the seal face with grease.
9   The remaining installation steps are the reverse of the removal procedure. Tighten all fasteners to the torque values listed in this Chapter's Specifications.

Right stub axle shaft (early model, externally retained), IFS systems

10   Remove the right side axleshaft.
11   Remove the stub axle bearing retainer bolts.
12   Pull the stub axle, seal and bearing as an assembly out of the axle housing. **Note:** *A slide hammer may be required if the axle assembly does not easily detach from the housing.*
13   The stub axle universal joint, seal and bearing can now be serviced.
14   Prior to stub axle installation, verify that it's components are in proper working order.
15   Install the stub axle assembly into the axle housing and engage the differential side gear splines.
16   Gently tap the assembly into the case until the bearing bottoms in the bore.
17   Carefully tap the seal into the case until it seats evenly around the bore.
18   Install the bearing retainer plate and bolts, tightening them to the torque listed in this Chapter's Specifications.
19   The remainder of installation is the reverse of removal.
20   Check the lubricant level and add if necessary (see Chapter 1). Test drive the vehicle and check for leaks and proper operation.

Right stub axle shaft (later model, internally retained), IFS systems

21   Remove the right and left side axleshafts.
22   Mark the orientation of the transfer case driveshaft to the differential yoke for proper location during reassembly.

23 Remove the driveshaft (see Section 36).
24 Position a drain pan under the differential to catch fluid.
25 Support the differential carrier with a floor jack and remove the bolts retaining the carrier to the axle case.
26 Separate the carrier from the axle case.
27 Rotate the stub axle shaft assembly until the open side of the axle-to-side gear snap-ring is exposed. Remove the snap-ring from the stub axle shaft and pull stub axle out of carrier.
28 The stub axle shaft universal joint and or seal/bearing can now be serviced.
29 Prior to stub axle installation, verify that it's components are in proper working order.
30 Install the stub axle into the right side of the carrier, engage the splines of the side gear and install the new snap-ring.
31 Clean all traces of sealant from the surfaces of the carrier and axle case.
32 Apply a bead of RTV sealant approximately 1/4-inch wide around the carrier sealing surface. Do not route the bead around the outside of, or through, the fastener holes.
33 Position carrier on the jack and install it in the axle case. Tighten the fasteners to the torque listed in this Chapter's Specifications.
34 The remainder of installation is the reverse of removal
35 Refill the case with the recommended lubricant (see Chapter 1) and check for leaks. Test drive the vehicle and check for proper operation.

30 Front axleshaft oil seal and bearing (4x4) - replacement

Independent Front Suspension (IFS) models

1 Loosen the wheel lug nuts. Raise the front of the vehicle and place it on jackstands, then remove the wheel.
2 Remove the front wheel hub(s) and the spindle assembly(s) (see Sections 26 and 27).
3 If the left side seal/bearing needs replacement, remove the left axleshaft only (see Section 29).
4 If the stub axle (right side) seal/bearing needs replacement, first remove both axleshafts (see Section 29). In addition, if the stub axle is an early externally retained type, remove the stub axle (see Section 29). If the stub axle is a later internally (C-clip) retained type, remove the axle carrier and the right side stub axle assembly from the axle carrier (see Section 29).
5 Early externally retained stub axle assemblies must be taken to a repair facility with the appropriate press to remove the pressed on bearing retainer ring, replace the bearing and seal and press a new bearing retainer ring back on the shaft. All other seals and bearings can be removed directly from housing using a slide hammer with a collet-type adapter.
6 Install a new bearing into the carrier bore with the part number facing out and drive the bearing squarely into the housing until it bot-

toms using an appropriate bearing driver.
7 Verify that the seal surface is clean and free of nicks and burrs. Coat the outer mating surface of the seal with RTV sealant and the inner lip with multi-purpose grease.
8 Place the seal squarely into the carrier bore and drive it into the housing until it bottoms, using a suitable seal driver.
9 Install the stub axle and carrier if applicable (see Section 29).
10 Install the axleshaft(s) as required (see Section 29).
11 Install the front wheel spindle and hub assemblies (see Section 26 and 27).
12 Install the calipers (see Chapter 9) and wheels (see Chapter 1).
13 Fill axle with the recommended lubricant and check for leaks.
14 Remove jackstands and lower vehicle. Test drive the vehicle and check for proper operation.

F350 (4WD) Monobeam

15 The axleshaft seals for the monobeam front axle are located in the differential case and require removal of the differential/ring gear assembly. This process requires tools and techniques beyond the scope of this manual and therefore should be left to a professional repair facility or dealer service department.

31 Front differential pinion seal (4WD) - replacement

Note: *This procedure is not recommended by the factory and should only be used if a proper repair facility is not available and circumstances warrant it. In several cases no factory specification exists for used bearing preload rotation torque, therefore, specifications listed are estimates.*

1 Raise the front of the vehicle and place it securely on jackstands.
2 Remove the axleshafts (see Section 29). **Note:** *The removal of the axleshafts is advisable to eliminate the added pinion shaft rotation resistance that otherwise might contribute to a false pinion shaft rotation torque value.*
3 The remainder of this procedure is similar to that of the rear axle pinion seal (see Section 20, Steps 3 through 12).
4 Install the driveshaft (see Section 36).
5 Install the axleshafts (see Section 29).
6 Install the wheels.
7 Check the differential lubricant level and add if required (see Chapter 1).
8 Remove the jackstands and lower the vehicle. Test drive and check for leaks.

32 Front drive axle assembly (4x4) - removal and installation

IFS vehicles
Removal
1 Raise the front of the vehicle and support it by placing jackstands under the radius arm brackets.

2 Remove the wheels.
3 Remove the brake calipers (see Chapter 9). **Note:** *Secure the brake calipers on the frame after removal, in a manner that will prevent suspending the caliper from the hose at any time during the axle removal and installation procedures. These precautions are necessary to prevent damage to the tube portion of the caliper hose assembly.*
4 On Broncos with four wheel anti-lock brakes, disconnect the sensor electrical connectors at the knuckles (see Chapter 9).
5 Detach the stabilizer bar from the axle housing assemblies (see Chapter 10).
6 Remove the steering tie-rod ends from the knuckles (see Chapter 10).
7 On coil spring models, remove the shock absorbers (see Chapter 10)
8 On coil spring models, remove the coil springs, retainers, insulators and seats (see Chapter 10). On leaf spring models, detach the leaf springs U-bolts from the axle housing assemblies (see Chapter 10).
9 On coil spring models, detach the radius arms from the axle housing assemblies (see Chapter 10).
10 Disconnect the vent tube at the differential housing and discard the hose clamps.
11 Remove the vent fitting and install a 1/8-inch pipe plug to prevent contamination. **Note:** *Failure to remove plug upon reassembly can result in seal failure and fluid loss.*
12 Disconnect the front driveshaft at the flange and suspend it out of the way (see Section 36). Secure the universal joint caps so that they do not fall off.
13 Position a floor jack under the right-hand axle arm assembly.
14 Remove the right axleshaft-to-stub axle boot clamps and pull the boot over the stub axle (see Section 29).
15 Remove the pivot bolt securing the right-hand axle arm assembly to the crossmember (see Chapter 10). **Caution:** *The axle is detached at this point - make sure it is well supported.*
16 Remove the axle assembly free from vehicle by simultaneously lowering and sliding out to disengage the right-hand axleshaft from the stub axle slip joint.
17 Position a floor jack under the differential housing.
18 Remove the bolt securing the left-hand axle assembly to the crossmember (see Chapter 10). **Caution:** *The axle is detached at this point, make sure it is well supported.*
19 Remove the left-hand drive axle assembly from under the vehicle.

Installation
20 Installation is basically the reverse of the removal procedure. Tighten all nuts and bolts to the torque values listed in this Chapter's Specifications and in the Specifications of any referenced Chapter.
21 After work on the front axle assembly has been completed, the caster and camber should be checked by an alignment technician.

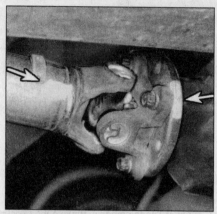

36.2 Mark the driveshaft-to-companion flange relationship for proper reassembly

F350 Monobeam

Removal

22 Raise the vehicle and support it by placing jackstands under the frame members.
23 Remove the wheels.
24 Remove the brake calipers (see Chapter 9). **Note:** *Position the brake calipers on the frame after removal in a manner that will prevent suspending the caliper from the hose at any time during the axle removal and installation procedures. These precautions are necessary to prevent damage to the tube portion of the caliper hose assembly.*
25 Remove the stabilizer bar link nuts (if equipped) and the U-bolts retaining the stabilizer bar to the axle housing (see Chapter 10).
26 Remove the steering tie-rod ends from both knuckles (see Chapter 10).
27 Position a jack under the axle assembly.
28 Mark the orientation of and disconnect the front driveshaft at the flange and suspend it out of the way (see Section 36). Secure the universal joint caps so that they do not fall off.
29 Disconnect the vent tube at the differential housing and plug the vent to prevent contamination. **Note:** *Failure to remove the plug upon reinstallation can result in seal failure and fluid loss.*
30 Detach the tracking bar from the axle assembly (see Chapter 10).
31 Detach the leaf spring U-bolts from the tube and yoke assembly (see Chapter 10). **Caution:** *The axle is detached at this point - make sure it is well supported.*
32 Carefully lower the axle assembly and remove it from under the vehicle.

Installation

33 Installation is the reverse of the removal procedure. Tighten all nuts and bolts to the torque values listed in this Chapter's Specifications and the Specifications in any referenced Chapter.
34 After work on the front axle is complete, the caster, camber and toe-in should be checked by an alignment technician.

33 Front drive axle assembly pivot bushing (IFS) - replacement

1 Remove appropriate drive axle housing assembly (see Section 32)
2 Using a forcing screw, bushing remover and receiver cup, press the old bushing out of the axle housing. This is known as a "draw-bolt-type" bushing removal and installation tool, and can be obtained at many auto parts stores and specialty tool retailers.
3 Using the forcing screw, bushing installer and receiver cup, install the new bushing into the axle housing.
4 Install axle housing assembly (see Section 32).

34 Driveshaft(s) - general information

The driveshaft is of tubular construction and may be of a one or two-section type according to the wheelbase of the vehicle.

On 4-wheel-drive models, the rear wheel driveline is very similar to that described above, but in order to drive the front wheels a driveshaft is incorporated between the transfer case and the front axle. This shaft is basically similar to the shafts used to drive the rear axle.

All driveshafts used to drive the rear wheels have needle bearing type universal joints. Single-section shafts have a splined sliding sleeve at the front end connecting it to the output shaft of the transmission, while two-section shafts have a central slip joint. The purpose of these devices is to accommodate, by retraction or extension, the varying shaft length caused by the movement of the rear axle as the rear suspension deflects. On some 4-wheel-drive models, due to the extent of the front driveshaft angle, a constant velocity joint is used at the transfer case end of the driveshaft.

Where a two-section shaft is used, the shaft is supported near its forward end on a ball bearing which is flexibly mounted in a bracket attached to the frame crossmember.

The attachment of the rear end of the driveshaft to the rear axle pinion flange (or the attachment of the front driveshaft to the front axle pinion flange) may be by U-bolt or bolted flange, according to the date of production and model.

The driveshaft is finely balanced during manufacture and it is recommended that care be used when universal joints are replaced to help maintain this balance. It is sometimes better to have the universal joints replaced by a dealership or shop specializing in this type of work. If you replace the joints yourself, mark each individual yoke in relation to the one opposite in order to maintain the balance. Do not drop the assembly during servicing operations.

35 Driveshaft(s) - balancing

1 Vibration of the driveshaft at certain speeds may be caused by any of the following:

Undercoating or mud on the shaft
Loose attachment bolts
Worn universal joints
Bent or dented driveshaft

2 Vibrations which are thought to be emanating from the driveshaft are sometimes caused by improper tire balance. This should be one of your first checks.
3 If the shaft is in a good, clean, undamaged condition, it is worth disconnecting the rear end attachment straps and turning the shaft 180 degrees to see if an improvement is noticed. Be sure to mark the original position of each component before disassembly so the shaft can be returned to the same location.
4 If the vibration persists after checking for obvious causes and changing the position of the shaft, the entire assembly should be checked out by a professional shop that has the proper equipment, or replaced.

36 Driveshaft(s) - removal and installation

Refer to illustration 36.2

Note: *Where two-piece driveshafts are involved, the rear shaft must be removed before the front shaft.*

Removal

1 Raise the vehicle and support it securely on jackstands.
2 Use chalk or a scribe to "index" the relationship of the driveshaft(s) to the differential axle assembly mating flange. This ensures correct alignment when the driveshaft is reinstalled **(see illustration)**.
3 Remove the nuts or bolts securing the universal joint clamps to the flange. If the driveshaft has a splined slip joint on one end (either to the transmission or the center carrier bearing) be sure to place marks on the mating flange or shaft to retain proper alignment during reinstallation.
4 Remove the nuts or bolts retaining the straps or universal joint to the flange on the opposite end of the driveshaft (if so equipped).
5 Pry the universal joint away from its mating flange and remove the shaft from the flange. Be careful not to let the caps fall off of the universal joint (which would cause contamination and loss of the needle bearings).
6 Repeat this process for the opposite end if it is equipped with a universal joint coupled to a flange.
7 If the opposite end is equipped with a sliding joint (spline), simply slide the yoke off the splined shaft.
8 If the shaft being removed is the front shaft of a two-piece unit, the rear is released by unbolting the two bolts securing the cen-

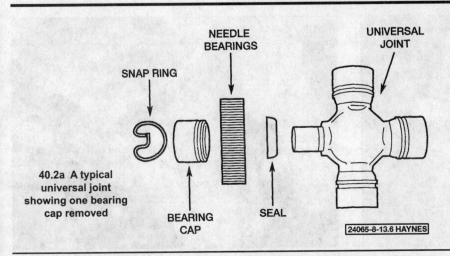

40.2a A typical universal joint showing one bearing cap removed

SNAP RING

NEEDLE BEARINGS

UNIVERSAL JOINT

BEARING CAP

SEAL

24065-8-13.6 HAYNES

40.2b Removing a snap-ring from the bearing cup

ter bearing assembly. Again, make sure both ends of the shaft have been marked for installation purposes.

Installation

9   Installation is the reverse of removal. If the shaft cannot be lined up due to the components of the differential or transmission having been rotated, put the vehicle in Neutral or rotate one wheel to allow the original alignment to be achieved. Make sure the universal joint caps are properly placed in the flange seat. Tighten the fasteners to the torque specifications listed in this Chapter.

37   Driveshaft carrier bearing - check and replacement

1   The carrier bearing can be checked in a similar manner as the universal joints are examined. Check for looseness or deterioration of the flexible rubber mounting.
2   Further examination of the carrier bearing can be made by running the vehicle in gear with the rear wheels raised in the air. However, this should be done only by an authorized dealer who can perform the tests safely.
3   Remove the driveshaft assembly (see Section 36).
4   With the driveshaft removed from the vehicle and the shaft sections separated at the center bearing, remove the bearing dust shield.
5   Remove the strap which retains the rubber cushion to the bearing support bracket.
6   Separate the cushion, bracket and bearing.
7   Pull the bearing assembly from the driveshaft.
8   Replace any worn components with new ones and reassemble. If the inner deflector was removed, install it to the shaft and stake it at two opposite points to ensure that it is a tight fit.
9   Pack the space between the inner dust deflector and the bearing with lithium-base grease.

10   Carefully tap the bearing and slinger assembly onto the driveshaft journal until the components are tight against the shoulder on the shaft. Use a suitable piece of tubing to do this, taking care not to damage the shaft splines.
11   Install the dust shield (small diameter first) and press it up against the outer slinger.
12   Install the bearing rubber cushion, bracket and strap.
13   Reconnect the driveshafts, making sure the previously made marks are aligned (see Section 36).

38   Universal joints - general information

Universal joints are mechanical couplings which connect two rotating components that meet each other at different angles.
These joints are composed of a yoke on each side connected by a crosspiece called a trunnion. Cups at each end of the trunnion contain needle bearings which provide smooth transfer of the torque load. Snap-rings, either inside or outside of the bearing cups, hold the assembly together.
Two main types of universal joints are used, with small differences in retention providing further variation. The first type of universal joint is constructed with a single joint retained to its yoke with either internal or external snap-rings. The second type referred to as a "double cardan," has two universal joints, a centering socket yoke and a center yoke. This type of coupling must be used in 4x4 models where high torque loads and steep drive-line angles are encountered (Broncos and some pick-ups).

39   Universal joints, driveshafts and axleshafts - lubrication and check

1   Refer to Chapter 1 for details on universal joint lubrication. Also see the routine

maintenance schedule at the beginning of Chapter 1.
2   Wear in the needle roller bearings is characterized by vibration in the driveline, noise during acceleration, and in extreme cases of lack of lubrication, metallic squeaking and ultimately grating and shrieking sounds as the bearings disintegrate.
3   It is easy to check if the needle bearings are worn with the driveshaft in position, by trying to turn the shaft with one hand, the other hand holding the rear axle flange when the rear universal joint is being checked, and the front half coupling when the front universal joint is being checked. Any movement between the driveshaft and the front half couplings, and around the rear half couplings, is indicative of considerable wear. Another method of checking for universal joint wear is to use a pry bar inserted into the gap between the universal joint and the driveshaft or flange. Leave the vehicle in gear and try to pry the joint both radially and axially. Any looseness should be apparent with this method. A final test for wear is to attempt to lift the shaft and note any movement between the yokes of the joints.
4   If any of the above conditions exist, replace the universal joints with new ones.

40   Universal joints (driveshafts and axleshafts) - overhaul

Refer to illustrations 40.2a, 40.2b, 40.3a and 40.3b

Outer snap-ring type
1   With the driveshaft removed, mark the location of the joint yokes in relation to each other.
2   Extract the snap-rings from the ends of the bearing cups **(see illustrations)**.
3   Using sockets or pieces of pipe of suitable diameter, use a vise to press on the end of one cup and to displace the opposite one into the larger socket wrench or pipe. The bearing cup will not be fully ejected and it should be gripped with pliers and twisted completely out of the

40.3a Removing the bearing cups from the yoke using different size sockets on either side of the cup

40.3b Pliers are used to twist the cup completely out of the yoke

yoke **(see illustrations)**.

4   Remove the first bearing cup by pressing the trunnion in the opposite direction, then repeat the operations on the other two cups.

5   Clean the yoke and inspect for damage or cracks.

6   Obtain the appropriate repair kit which will include trunnion, cups, needle rollers, seals, washers and snap-rings.

7   Before beginning reassembly, pack the reservoirs in the ends of the trunnion with grease and work some into the needle bearings taking care not to displace them from their location around the inside of the bearing cups.

8   Position the trunnion in the yoke, partially install one cup into the yoke and insert the trunnion a little way into it. Partially install the opposite cup, center the trunnion, then, using the vise, press both cups into position using sockets of diameter slightly less than that of the bearing cups. Make sure that the needle bearings are not displaced and trapped during this operation.

9   Install the snap-rings.

10   Align the shaft yokes and install the other bearing cups in the same way.

Injected plastic (inner snap-ring) type

11   This type of universal joint may be found on some vehicles covered in this manual. Repair can be carried out after destroying the production line plastic retainers and fitting conventional snap-ring type repair kits.

12   Support the joint yoke in a press so that, using a suitable forked pressing tool, pressure can be applied to two eyes of the yoke to eject a bearing cup partially into a socket wrench of adequate diameter.

13   Repeat on all the cups and then twist the cups out of the yokes with a vise.

14   Clean away all trace of the plastic bearing cup retainers. This can be facilitated by probing through the plastic injection holes.

15   Obtain the appropriate repair kit which will include one prelubricated trunnion assembly, bearing cups, seals and other components.

16   Assemble the universal joint as described in paragraphs 8, 9 and 10 of this Section. Note that the snap-rings are installed on the inside of the yokes on this type of joint.

17   When reassembly is complete, and the joint is stiff to move, apply some hammer blows to the yoke which will free the bearing cups from the snap-rings.

Double cardan type constant velocity joint

18   An inspection kit containing two bearing cups and two retainers is available to permit the joint to be dismantled to the stage where the joint can be inspected. Before any dismantling is started, mark the flange yoke and coupling yoke to permit reassembly in the same position, then follow the procedure given previously for the snap-ring or injected plastic type, as applicable.

19   Disengage the flange yoke and trunnion

from the centering ball. Pry the seal from the ball socket and remove the washers, spring and the three ball seats.

20   Clean the ball seat insert bushing and inspect for wear. If evident, the flange yoke and trunnion assembly must be replaced.

21   Clean the seal, ball seats, spring and washers and inspect for wear. If excessive wear is evident or parts are broken, a repair kit must be used.

22   Remove all plastic material from the groove of the coupling yoke (if applicable).

23   Inspect the centering ball - if damaged it must be replaced with a new one.

24   Withdraw the centering ball from the stud using a suitable extractor.

25   Press a new ball onto the stud until it seats firmly on the stud shoulder. It is extremely important that no damage to the ball occurs during this stage.

26   Using the grease provided in the repair kit, lubricate all the parts and insert them into the ball seat cavity in the following order: spring washer (small o.d.), three ball seats (largest opening out to receive the ball), washer (large o.d.) and the seal.

27   Lubricate the seal lips and press it (lip in) into the cavity. Fill the cavity with the grease provided.

28   Install the flange yoke to the centering ball, ensuring that the alignment marks are correctly positioned.

29   Install the trunnion caps as described previously for the snap-ring or injected plastic types.

Chapter 9 Brakes

Contents

Specifications

General
Brake fluid type .... DOT type 3 heavy duty

Drum brakes
Drum wear limit	Specified on drum
Lining wear limit	1/16 inch above rivet head or metal shoe

Disc brakes
Rotor minimum thickness	Specified on disc
Rotor maximum runout	
Integral hub and rotor	0.003 inch
Two-piece hub and rotor	0.005 inch
Rotor thickness max variation	
Integral hub and rotor	0.0005 inch
Two-piece hub and rotor	0.0007 inch
Pad lining wear limit	1/8 inch above rivet head or metal backing plate

Torque specifications
Ft-lbs (unless otherwise indicated)

Note: *One foot-pound (ft-lb) of torque is equivalent to 12 inch-pounds (in-lbs) of torque. Torque values below approximately 15 ft-lbs are expressed in inch-pounds, since most foot-pound torque wrenches are not accurate at these smaller values.*

Drum brake adjustable anchor pin nut	80 to 100
Master cylinder-to-firewall or vacuum booster nuts	13 to 25
Vacuum booster mounting bracket-to-firewall nuts	13 to 25
Key retaining bolt (light duty)	12 to 20
Key retaining bolt (heavy duty)	14 to 22
Anchor plate-to-spindle	74 to 102
Caliper anchor bracket bolts (pin slider type)	141 to 191
Caliper mounting bolts (pin slider type)	22 to 26
Brake hose-to-caliper attaching bolt	17 to 25
Wheel cylinder bolts to backing plate	10 to 20
ABS and RABS hydraulic control valve (HCV) mounting bolts	15 to 18
ABS front wheel speed sensors-to-knuckle hold down bolt	40 to 80 in-lbs
ABS and RABS rear speed sensor hold down bolt	25 to 30
ABS electronic control unit mounting bolts	
Rear ABS systems	19 to 25 in-lbs
4 wheel ABS systems	40 to 80 in-lbs

1   General information

The models covered in this manual are equipped with hydraulically activated front disc brakes and rear drum brakes.

The hydraulic system has a dual master cylinder and separate front and rear brake line circuits. The master cylinder contains two hydraulic pistons (primary and secondary) fed by separate fluid reservoirs. On early systems, a pressure differential valve assembly is incorporated into the hydraulic system. Later models incorporate a master cylinder-mounted proportioning valve. These valves provide a higher percentage of braking force to the front wheels to compensate for weight transfer when the brakes are applied. Early models incorporate a pressure differential valve warning switch and a dash light which indicates to the vehicle's operator when a failure has occurred in one of the braking circuits. Later models utilize a fluid level indicator switch within the master cylinder reservoir and dash light to warn the operator of low fluid level and possible system failure. In addition,

an anti-lock brake system warning light is also standard on vehicles so equipped. On all systems, if a failure in one of the circuits occurs, the other one will continue to operate the brakes, although total braking efficiency will be half or less of normal.

On some early models and all later model vehicles, the hydraulic brake system is assisted by a vacuum booster. The booster unit for all but F350 vehicles is a single-diaphragm, dash-mounted model. The F350 unit is similar but operates through a tandem diaphragm.

A parking brake system is provided and operates independently of the normal hydraulic brake system. A pedal on the driver's side of the cab operates a system of cables to activate the rear brake shoes only.

Precautions

There are some general precautions involving the brake system on this vehicle:

a) *Use only brake fluid conforming to DOT 3 specifications.*

b) *The brake pads and linings may contain fibers which are hazardous to your health if inhaled. Whenever you work on*

the brake system components, clean all parts with brake system cleaner or denatured alcohol. Do not allow the fine dust to become airborne.

c) *Safety should be paramount whenever any servicing of the brake components is performed. Do not use parts or fasteners which are not in perfect condition, and be sure to follow all torque specifications. If you are uncertain about a procedure, seek professional advice. Upon completion of brake system work, test the brakes carefully in a controlled area before putting the vehicle into normal service. If a problem is suspected in the brake system, don't drive the vehicle until it's fixed.*

2   Rear brake shoes (light duty) - replacement

Refer to illustrations 2.2, 2.5a through 2.5y and 2.6

Warning: *Brake shoes must be replaced on both rear wheels at the same time - never replace the shoes on only one wheel. Also, the dust created by the brake system is harmful to your health. Never blow it out with compressed air and don't inhale any of it. An approved filtering mask should be worn when working on the brakes. Do not, under any circumstances, use petroleum-based solvents to clean brake parts. Use brake system cleaner only! When servicing the brakes, use only high quality, nationally recognized brand name parts.*

Caution: *Whenever the brake shoes are replaced, the retractor and hold-down springs should also be replaced. Due to the continuous heating/cooling cycle that the springs are subjected to, they lose their tension over a period of time and may allow the shoes to drag on the drum and wear at a much faster rate than normal.*

1   The brakes on F100, F150 and F250 (standard) vehicles are considered light duty. In addition, the above models equipped with 4WD and Bronco models are classed as light duty.

2   To ease installation of the brake assembly, during the removal procedures lay out all parts in an assembled order on a rag near the work area **(see illustration)**. Note: *It is advisable to service the brakes on one side of the vehicle at a time, leaving the other side fully assembled for reference if necessary.*

3   Loosen the wheel lug nuts, raise the rear of the vehicle and support it securely on jackstands. Block the front wheels to keep the vehicle from rolling.

4   Release the parking brake.

5   Follow the accompanying photos **(see illustrations 2.5a through 2.5y)** for replacement of the brake shoes. Be sure to stay in order and read the caption under each illustration. Prior to reassembly, inspect the wheel cylinder for early signs of leakage and overhaul or replace a leaking wheel cylinder as required (see

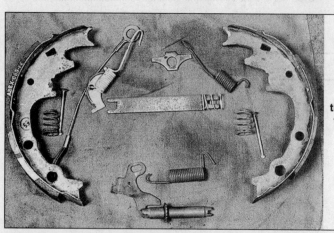

2.2 During removal lay the parts out in their order of removal to keep from getting confused

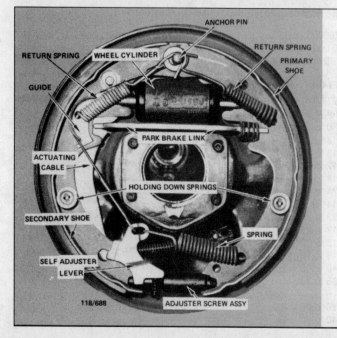

2.5a Components of a typical light duty rear brake assembly (right side shown)

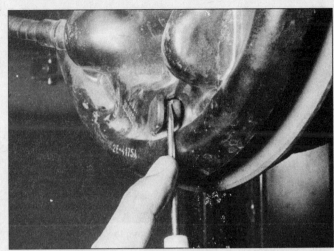

2.5b If, after releasing the parking brake, the drum will not slide off the shoes, remove the rubber plug from the backing plate . . .

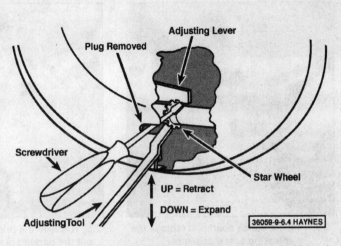

2.5c . . . then, using a narrow-bladed screwdriver, push the adjusting lever away from the star wheel so you can turn the star wheel with a brake tool to retract the shoes - note the direction of rotation for loosening or tightening the shoes

2.5d Slide the drum off the shoes

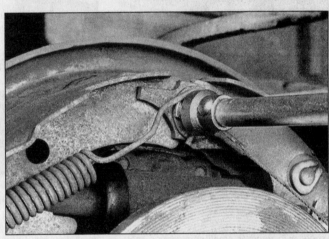

2.5e Use a spring removal tool to remove the retracting springs

Section 4). **Note:** *If the brake drum cannot be easily pulled off the axle and shoe assembly, make sure that the parking brake is completely released, then apply some penetrating oil at the* hub-to-drum joint. Allow the oil to soak in and try to pull the drum off. If the drum seems loose on the axle flange but still can't be pulled off, the brake shoes will have to be retracted. This is accomplished by first removing the plug from the backing plate. With the plug removed, push the lever off the adjusting star wheel with one small screwdriver while turning the adjusting

2.5f Pull up on the adjusting cable and disconnect the cable eye from the anchor pin

2.5g Remove the anchor pin plate

2.5h Remove the shoe retaining springs and pins - one on each shoe

2.5i Pull the shoes apart and remove the adjusting screw assembly

2.5j Remove the primary shoe, then slide out the parking brake strut and spring

2.5k Remove the adjusting pawl

2.5l Pull the secondary shoes away from the backing plate

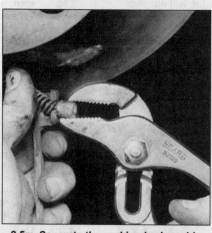

2.5m Separate the parking brake cable and spring from the actuating lever

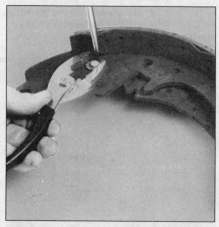

2.5n Remove the retaining clip that holds the parking brake actuating lever to the brake shoes

wheel with another small screwdriver, moving the shoes away from the drum. The drum should now come off.

6   Before reinstalling the drum it should be checked for cracks, score marks, deep scratches and hard spots, which will appear as

small discolored areas. If the hard spots cannot be removed with fine emery cloth or if any of the other conditions listed above exist, the drum must be taken to an automotive machine shop to have it resurfaced. **Note:** *Professionals recommend resurfacing the drums when-*

ever a brake job is done. Resurfacing will eliminate the possibility of out-of-round drums. If the drums are worn so much that they can't be resurfaced without exceeding the maximum allowable diameter (cast into the drum), then new ones will be required (see

2.5o Install the parking brake actuating lever onto the new shoes and install the clip

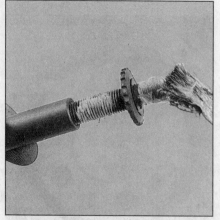

2.5p Clean the adjusting screw assembly, then lubricate the threads and the star wheel end with high-temperature brake grease

2.5q Lightly coat the shoe guide pads on the backing plate with high-temperature brake grease

2.5r Position the shoes on the backing plate, insert the retaining pins through the backing plate and put the springs over them. Install the parking brake strut.

2.5s Install the retaining spring caps

2.5t Make sure the slots in the wheel cylinder plungers and parking brake actuating lever properly engage the brake shoes

2.5u install the adjusting screw with the long end pointing towards the front of the vehicle

2.5v Install the adjusting pawl

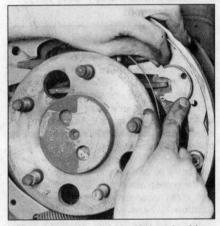

2.5w Install the cable guide and cable

illustration). *At the very least, if you elect not to have the drums resurfaced, remove the glazing from the surface with sandpaper or emery cloth using a swirling motion.*
7   Install the brake drum on the axle flange.

8   Install the wheels and lower the vehicle to the ground. Tighten the lug nuts to the torque specifications listed in Chapter 1.
9   Check the brakes by applying them several times before attempting to drive the

vehicle. Verify master cylinder fluid level then adjust the brakes by backing up and applying the brakes several times.
10   Check brake operation before driving the vehicle in traffic.

2.5x Install the shoe guide and adjusting cable eye to the anchor pin, then install the shoe retracting springs

2.5y Connect the cable and spring to the lever, then install the drum and adjust the brake shoe-to-drum clearance

2.6 Location of the maximum inside diameter markings on a typical brake drum

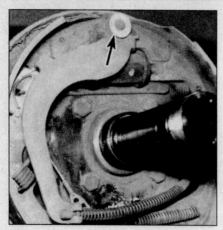

3.4 The parking brake lever is secured in place by the pivot bolt at the top

3.7 Remove the brake shoe hold-down springs

3.20 Make sure the adjusting lever contacts the adjusting screw as shown

3   Rear brake shoes (heavy duty) - replacement

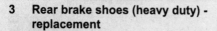

Refer to illustration 3.4, 3.7 and 3.20

Warning: *Brake shoes must be replaced on both rear wheels at the same time - never replace the shoes on only one wheel. Also, the dust created by the brake system is harmful to your health. Never blow it out with compressed air and don't inhale any of it. An approved filtering mask should be worn when working on the brakes. Do not, under any circumstances, use petroleum-based solvents to clean brake parts. Use brake system cleaner only! When servicing the brakes, use only high-quality, nationally recognized brand-name parts.*

Caution: *Whenever the brake shoes are replaced, the retractor and hold-down springs should also be replaced. Due to the continuous heating/cooling cycle that the springs are subjected to, they lose their tension over a period of time and may allow the shoes to drag on the drum and wear at a much faster rate than normal.*

1   Heavy duty drum brakes are found on F250 models with full-floating axle and F350 series vehicles, both 2WD and 4WD.
2   Remove the wheel(s) from the vehicle after raising and supporting it securely. Remove the axle and wheel hub and drum assembly (refer to Chapter 8).
3   If the drum will not come off after removing the proper retaining components, refer to Section 2 for brake releasing instructions.
4   Remove the parking brake lever assembly retaining nut from the rear of the backing plate. Remove the parking brake lever assembly **(see illustration)**. **Note:** *It is advisable to service the brakes on one side of the vehicle at a time, leaving the other side fully assembled for reference if necessary.*
5   Remove the adjusting cable assembly from the anchor pin. Unthread it from the cable guide and disconnect the other end from the adjusting lever.
6   Remove the brake shoe retracting springs from both the primary and secondary brake shoes. Use a brake spring tool for

this operation.
7   Remove the brake shoe hold-down springs from both the primary and secondary brake shoes **(see illustration)**.
8   Remove the brake shoes. The adjusting screw assembly will fall loose at this time. Keep all parts of this assembly together.
9   Clean all of the springs and adjusting components with brake system cleaner. **Warning:** *Never use petroleum-based solvents and never blow the parts clean with compressed air, as fine asbestos dust is a serious health hazard if inhaled.*
10   Clean the brake backing plate and hub components left on the vehicle. If the six ledge pads on the backing plate are corroded or rusty, sand them lightly to bare metal. **Note:** *Prior to reassembly, inspect the wheel cylinder for signs of leakage and overhaul or replace a leaking wheel cylinder as required (refer to Section 4).*
11   Apply a light coat of brake lube to the ledge pads. Apply a coating of lube to the retracting and hold-down spring contact points on the brake shoes and backing plate.
12   Dismantle and clean the pivot nut, adjusting screw, washer and socket. Take care not to mix these adjusting components from side-to-side as they are built for left-side or right-side installation only. If these components become mixed, the adjusting lever and the socket end of the adjusting screw are stamped with the letter L (left) or R (right).
13   Lubricate the threads of the adjusting screw components with brake lube and retract the adjustment to the smallest dimension.
14   Install the upper brake retracting spring between the two brake shoes and make sure you have the shoes positioned correctly.
15   Place the shoes and spring assembly into position on the backing plate and position the wheel cylinder pushrods into their proper slots on the brake shoe webbing.
16   Install both brake shoe hold-down springs.
17   Position the brake shoe adjusting screw assembly into place between the bottom of the brake shoes with the slot in the head of the adjusting screw pointed toward the pri-

mary shoe.
18   Install the lower brake shoe retracting spring.
19   Install the adjusting lever spring and the cable assembly to the adjusting lever. Position the adjusting lever onto the proper pin of the secondary shoe.
20   Place the adjusting lever cable into its proper position around the cable guide and hook the cable end to the anchor pin. Make sure the adjusting lever is engaged in the teeth of the adjusting screw **(see illustration)**.
21   Install the parking brake lever and retaining nut.
22   Before reinstalling the drum and hub assembly, the drum should be checked for cracks, score marks, deep scratches and hard spots, which will appear as small discolored areas. If the hard spots cannot be removed with fine emery cloth or if any of the other conditions listed above exist, the drum must be taken to an automotive machine shop to have it resurfaced. **Note:** *Professionals recommend resurfacing the drums whenever a brake job is done. Resurfacing will eliminate the possibility of out-of-round drums. If the drums are worn so much that they can't be resurfaced without exceeding the maximum allowable diameter (cast into the drum), then new ones will be required* **(see illustration 2.6)**. *At the very least, if you elect not to have the drums resurfaced, remove the glazing from the surface with sandpaper or emery cloth using a swirling motion.*
23   Install the hub and drum assembly and adjust the bearing preload (refer to Chapter 8).
24   Manually adjust the brakes (by turning the adjustment screw) until there is a slight drag on the brake drum **(see illustration 2.5c)**.
25   Lower the vehicle from the stands or supports.
26   Check the brakes by applying them several times before attempting to drive the vehicle. Verify master cylinder fluid level then adjust the brakes by backing up and applying the brakes several times.
27   Check brake operation before driving the vehicle in traffic.

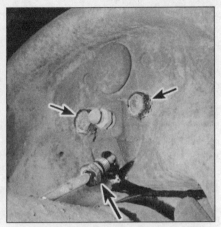

4.6 Disconnect the brake line fitting, then remove the mounting bolts (arrows)

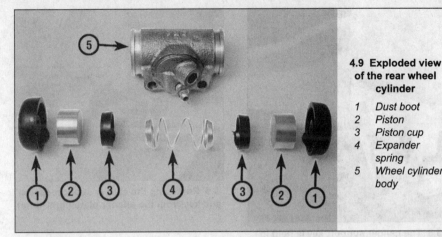

4.9 Exploded view of the rear wheel cylinder

1   Dust boot
2   Piston
3   Piston cup
4   Expander spring
5   Wheel cylinder body

4   Rear brake wheel cylinders- inspection, removal, overhaul and installation

Refer to illustrations 4.6 and 4.9

Note: *If an overhaul is indicated (usually because of fluid leakage or sticky operation) explore all options before beginning the job. New wheel cylinders are available, which makes this job quite easy. If it's decided to rebuild the wheel cylinder; make sure that a rebuild kit is available before proceeding. Never overhaul only one wheel cylinder - always rebuild both sides at the same time.*

Inspection

1   Loosen the wheel lug nuts, raise the rear of the vehicle and support it securely on jackstands. Block the front wheels to keep the vehicle from rolling.
2   Remove the brake drum (see Section 2 or 3).
3   Insert a suitable blunt instrument between the wheel cylinder and it's rubber boots and peel back slightly. If the wheel cylinder is leaking, a small amount of brake fluid will be trapped in the cylinder cavity and should now be observed as it leaks past the boot. **Note:** *A slight wetting of the inside surface of the boot is normal.*

Removal

4   If the cylinder is leaking or must be removed for other reasons, remove the brake shoe assembly (see Section 2 or 3).
5   Remove all dirt and foreign material from around the wheel cylinder.
6   Unscrew the brake line fitting **(see illustration)**. Don't pull the brake line away from the wheel cylinder.
7   Remove the wheel cylinder mounting bolts.
8   Detach the wheel cylinder from the brake backing plate and place it on a clean workbench. Immediately plug the brake line to prevent fluid loss and contamination. **Note:** *If the brake shoe linings are contaminated with brake fluid, install new brake shoes.*

Overhaul

9   Remove the bleeder screw, cups, pistons, boots and spring assembly from the wheel cylinder body **(see illustration)**.
10   Clean the wheel cylinder with brake fluid, denatured alcohol or brake system cleaner. **Warning:** *Do not, under any circumstances, use petroleum-based solvents to clean brake parts!*
11   Use compressed air to remove excess fluid from the wheel cylinder and to blow out the passages.
12   Check the cylinder bore for corrosion and score marks. Crocus cloth or a wheel cylinder hone can be used to remove light corrosion and stains, but the cylinder must be replaced with a new one if the defects cannot be removed easily, or if the bore is scored.
13   Lubricate the new cups with brake fluid.
14   Assemble the wheel cylinder components. Make sure the cup lips face in.

Installation

15   Place the wheel cylinder in position and install the bolts finger tight.
16   Connect the brake line by hand, being careful not to cross-thread the fitting. Tighten the wheel cylinder mounting bolts to the torque listed in this Chapter's Specifications, then tighten the brake line fitting. Install the brake shoe and drum assembly (see Section 2 or 3).
17   Bleed the brakes (see Section 11).
18   Check brake operation before driving the vehicle in traffic.

5   Front disc brake pads - replacement

Warning: *Disc brake pads must be replaced on both front wheels at the same time - never replace the pads on only one wheel. Also, the dust created by the brake system is harmful to your health. Never blow it out with compressed air and don't inhale any of it. An approved filtering mask should be worn when working on the brakes. Do not, under any circumstances, use petroleum-based solvents to clean brake parts. Use brake system cleaner only! When servicing the disc brakes, use*

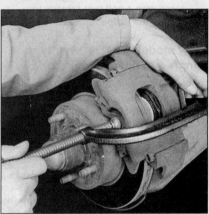

5.7 Using a large C-clamp, push the piston back into the caliper bore - note that one end of the C-clamp is on the flat area of the inner side of the caliper and the other end is pressing on the outer pad

only high-quality, nationally recognized brand-name parts.

Removal

All models

Refer to illustration 5.7

1   To avoid fluid overflow when the caliper piston is pressed into the caliper cylinder bore, remove about one-third of the brake fluid out of the larger master cylinder reservoir (connected to the front disc brakes) and discard the removed fluid.
2   Loosen the lug nuts on the front wheels but do not remove them yet.
3   Chock the rear wheels.
4   Set the parking brake.
5   Raise the front of the vehicle and support it securely on jackstands.
6   Remove the wheels.
7   Place a large C-clamp between the back of the caliper and the exposed portion of the outer brake pad **(see illustration)**. Tighten the clamp to bottom the caliper piston in the cylinder bore, then remove the clamp. **Caution:** *If the opposite caliper has been removed or previously retracted, secure the piston from possible accidental expulsion using a second C-clamp or wedge.*

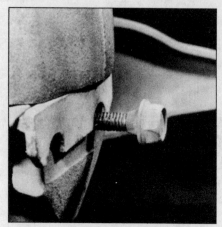

5.8 The caliper support key is held in place with a bolt that threads into the caliper bracket

5.9 Removing the caliper support spring and key from the anchor plate (light-duty)

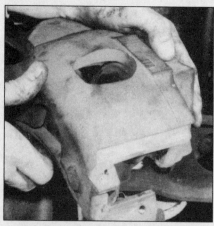

5.10 Pivot the caliper up for removal

Early model "key" retainer type (single and dual piston)

Refer to illustrations 5.8, 5.9, 5.10 and 5.11

8 Remove the retaining bolt from the caliper retaining key (see illustration).

9 Use a hammer and a soft drift to carefully tap the caliper retaining key and spring either in or out of the anchor plate (see illustration). Use care so as not to damage the key.

10 Press the caliper assembly in and up against the caliper support springs and pivot the caliper off the rotor (see illustration). Once the bottom of the caliper has cleared the anchor plate, pull it straight off the plate. **Note:** *On single-piston calipers, the inner brake pad will remain in the caliper support and the outer pad will remain in the caliper assembly. Both pads will remain in the caliper in dual piston calipers.*

11 Use caution not to stretch or kink the flexible brake hose and use wire to suspend the caliper from an upper suspension component out of the way (see illustration).

12 Inspect the rotor for possible resurfacing or replacement (see Section 7).

Late model "rail slider" retainer type (single and dual-piston)

Refer to illustrations 5.13a and 5.13b

13 Using pliers, squeeze the outer retaining tab on the upper caliper pin flush with the side of the pin while simultaneously prying the pin in using a screwdriver wedged against the spindle and the inner pin retaining tab. Continue prying until the leading edge of the squeezed tab just enters the support groove (see illustration). Repeat this process on the adjacent outer tab on the same pin. Once both tabs are disengaged, drive the pin in through the caliper/spindle groove until it is free using a suitable punch (see illustration). Repeat this procedure on the lower caliper pin. Lift the caliper assembly away from the spindle. **Note:** *On single piston calipers, the inner brake pad will remain in the caliper support and the outer pad will remain in the caliper assembly. Both pads will remain in the caliper in dual-piston calipers.* Use caution not to stretch or kink the flexible brake hose and use wire to suspend the caliper from an upper suspension component out of the way (see illustration 5.11).

14 Inspect the rotor for possible resurfacing or replacement (refer to section 7).

Late model "pin slider" retainer type (single and dual piston)

Refer to illustration 5.15

15 Remove the two caliper mounting bolts and remove the caliper from the brake disc (see illustration). Suspend the caliper from

5.11 If the caliper isn't going to be removed for service, suspend it with a length of wire to relieve any strain on the brake hose

5.13a Use pliers and squeeze the caliper retaining pin while prying the other end until the tabs enter the pin groove

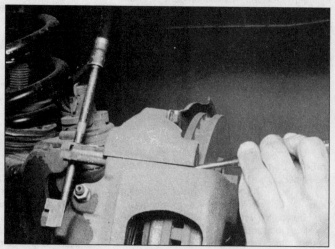

5.13b Drive out the pin with a punch and hammer

5.15 Remove the two caliper mounting bolts, check them for thread damage and replace as necessary

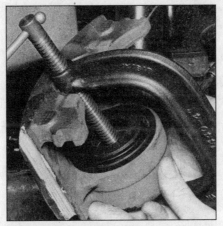

5.19 Use a C-clamp to depress the piston into the caliper until it bottoms out

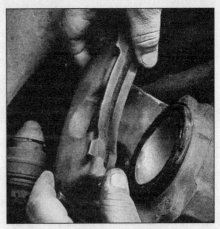

5.21 Install the new outer brake pad on the caliper

an upper suspension component.

16 Inspect the rotor for possible resurfacing or replacement (refer Section 7). On a heavy-duty dual-piston caliper, remove the two bolts and the caliper anchor bracket, if necessary.

Pad replacement (single-piston calipers)

Refer to illustrations 5.19, 5.21, 5.22a, 5.22b and 5.22c

17 If the pads are being re-used, mark them for position so they can be installed in their original location (drivers vs. passenger side).

18 Remove the inner pad and anti-rattle clip from the anchor plate. Detach the early style outer pad from the caliper by forcing the pad towards the piston to disengage the pad flanges. Detach the later style outer pad by pressing the pad in against the retaining spring tension to disengage the torque buttons and then slide the pad down and out of the caliper.

19 If not already accomplished, using a C-clamp, retract the caliper piston completely into it's bore until it bottoms out **(see illustration)**.

20 Clean the caliper support, caliper and pads (if they are being re-used) with brake system cleaner. Replace the pads if they measure less than the minimum thickness listed in this Chapters Specifications.

21 To install the early style outer pads, position the pad on the caliper and use your fingers to press the shoe flanges into place **(see**

illustration). If the shoe cannot be pressed into place by hand, use a C-clamp. Be careful not to damage the lining with the clamp. To install later style outer pads, engage the retaining spring and press the pad in against the spring tension, then slide the pad up into the caliper and engage the torque buttons to the caliper retention notches. **Warning:** *Failure to properly engage torque buttons solidly in the notches may result in loss of braking function.*

22 To install the inner pad, Install the anti-rattle clip to the pad and install the pad/clip onto the spindle anchor plate **(see illustrations)**. If the old pads are being reinstalled, make sure they're in their original position. **Warning:** *Verify that the pad linings are facing the correct way (against the rotor).*

Pad replacement dual-piston calipers)

Refer to illustration 5.24

23 Remove the large anti-rattle spring and both pads from the caliper.

24 If not already accomplished, using a C-clamp and old pad, retract the caliper pistons completely into their bores until they bottom out **(see illustration)**.

5.22a Insert a new anti-rattle clip on the lower end of the inner pad

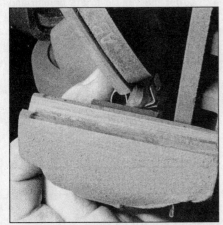

5.22b Make sure the tabs on the spring clip are positioned correctly and the clip is fully seated on the inner pad

5.22c Compress the anti-rattle clip and slide the upper end of the inner pad into position

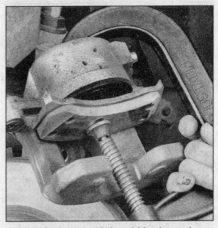

5.24 A C-clamp and the old brake pad can be used to retract the caliper piston(s)

5.28 Prior to installing the caliper, lightly lubricate the V-grooves where the caliper slides into the anchor plate with disc brake caliper grease

25   Clean the caliper support, caliper and pads (if they are being re-used) with brake cleaning solvent. Replace the pads if they measure less than the minimum thickness listed in this Chapter's Specifications.

26   Install the pads into the caliper and install the anti-rattle spring. **Note:** *The notches on the ends of the pads should interface with the caliper only one way, but verify that the pad lining is facing the correct way (against the rotor) just to be sure.*

Installation

Early model "key" retainer type (single and dual-piston

Refer to illustration 5.28, 5.32a and 5.32b

27   If removed for resurfacing, install the rotor and hub assembly and adjust the wheel bearings (refer to Section 7).

28   Lubricate the caliper to spindle sliding (contact) surfaces with caliper grease **(see illustration)**.

29   Detach the caliper from its supporting wire and position it against the spindle with the lower beveled edge on top of the rear caliper support. Make sure the pads and clips

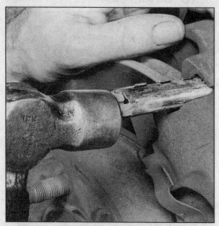

5.37a Place the caliper and outer pad assembly over disc and inner pad, then drive the caliper pins into their grooves

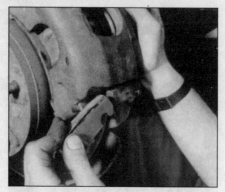

5.32a Insert the caliper support spring and key . . .

remain in their correct position.

30   Carefully slide the caliper over the rotor with a pivoting motion until the caliper upper beveled edge can be pushed over and engage the forward caliper support.

31   Use a large screwdriver or similar tool to hold the caliper over the upper caliper support spring and against the anchor plate.

32   Carefully install the caliper retaining key and spring. Remove the screwdriver and carefully tap the caliper key into its correct position **(see illustrations)**.

33   Install the caliper key retaining bolt and tighten it to the torque listed in this Chapter's Specifications.

Late model "rail slider" retainer type (single and dual-piston)

Refer to illustrations 5.37a and 5.37b

34   If removed for resurfacing, install the rotor and hub assembly and adjust the wheel bearings (see Section 7).

35   Lubricate the caliper pin grooves in both caliper and spindle with caliper grease or equivalent **(see illustration 5.28)**.

36   Detach the caliper from its supporting wire and slide the caliper over the rotor and align the caliper pin grooves. Make sure the pads and clips remain in their correct position.

37   Position the upper caliper pin with the

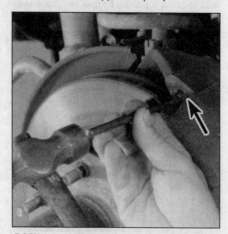

5.37b . . . until the tabs on the pin contact the spindle flank

5.32b . . . then drive it into place and install the retaining bolt

retention tabs oriented adjacent to the spindle groove side and tap the pin through the groove until the outer retention tabs contact the spindle face **(see illustration)**. Verify that both inner and outer pin tabs are clear of the groove, have sprung out and are free to catch the spindle faces (not the face of the caliper) **(see illustration)**. Repeat the procedure for the lower caliper pin. **Caution:** *Failure to properly orient the caliper pin retention tabs can result in a potentially hazardous condition.*

Late model "pin slider" retainer type (single and dual piston)

38   If removed for resurfacing, install the rotor and hub assembly (see Section 7). On a heavy-duty dual-piston caliper models, install the caliper anchor bracket and tighten the bolts to the torque listed in this Chapter's Specifications.

39   Install the caliper onto the rotor. On light duty single piston models, pull the slide pins back and slide the caliper into the outer brake pad clip. Make sure the brake pad clips are seated in the holes on the caliper.

40   Install the caliper mounting bolts and tighten the bolts to the torque listed in this Chapter's Specifications.

All models

41   Install the wheel and lug nuts.

42   Lower the vehicle to the ground and tighten the lug nuts to the torque listed in the Chapter 1 Specifications.

43   Press the brake pedal several times before attempting to drive it. It will take several strokes of the brakes to bring the pads into contact with the rotor. If the brake hose was not disconnected, bleeding will not be necessary.

44   Check the master cylinder fluid level. Test drive the vehicle and make the first several stops gentle ones to seat the brake pads.

---

6   Disc brake caliper - overhaul

Refer to illustrations 6.5, 6.7, 6.8, 6.11, 6.12, 6.13a, 6.13b and 6.13c

Warning: *The dust created by the brake system is harmful to your health. Never blow it out*

6.5 With caliper padded to catch the piston, use compressed air to force the piston out of its bore - make sure your hands or fingers are not between the caliper and piston

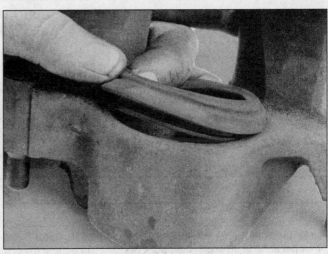

6.7 Remove the dust boot from the caliper bore groove

with compressed air and don't inhale any of it. An approved filtering mask should be worn when working on the brakes. Do not, under any circumstances, use petroleum-based solvents to clean brake parts. Use brake system cleaner only! When servicing the disc brakes, use only high-quality, nationally recognized brand-name parts.

Note: If an overhaul is indicated, explore all options before beginning the job. New and rebuilt calipers are available on an exchange basis, which makes the job quite easy. If it is decided to rebuild the calipers, make sure a rebuild kit is available before proceeding. Always rebuild the calipers in pairs, never rebuild just one of them.

1 A leaking caliper seal is usually indicated when the level in the master cylinder drops excessively. Brake fluid may be found running down the inside of one wheel, or you may notice that a pool of fluid forms alongside a wheel.

2 Refer to Section 5 and remove the caliper and brake pads.

3 Unscrew the caliper from the flexible hose and plug the hose to prevent fluid loss or contamination.

4 Clean the exterior of the caliper with brake system cleaner.

5 Position a wood block or several shop rags in the caliper as a cushion, then using compressed air at the fluid port, carefully apply air pressure to eject the piston(s) **(see illustration).Warning:** Wear eye protection!

6 If the piston(s) has seized in the bore, carefully tap around the piston while applying air pressure. **Warning:** The piston will come out with force - make sure your hands and fingers are not between the caliper and piston.

7 Remove the rubber dust boot from the caliper assembly **(see illustration).** Repeat the process for the second piston on dual-piston calipers.

8 Carefully remove the rubber piston seal from the cylinder bore with a soft wood or plastic tool. Do not use a screwdriver as it could damage the bore **(see illustration).**

Repeat process for the second piston on dual piston calipers.

9 Thoroughly wash all parts in brake system cleaner.

10 Inspect the piston and bore for signs of wear, score marks or other damage; if evident, a new caliper assembly will be necessary.

11 To reassemble, first lubricate a new piston seal with clean brake fluid and place the new piston seal into the caliper bore groove. The seal must not become twisted **(see illustration).** Repeat the process for the second piston on dual piston calipers.

12 Install a new dust boot and ensure that the flange seats correctly in the outer groove of the caliper bore **(see illustration).** Repeat the process for the second piston on dual piston calipers.

13 Coat the piston with clean brake fluid, stretch the lips of the dust boot over the bottom of the piston and carefully insert the piston into the bore **(see illustration).** Push the piston fully into the bore, then seat the lip of the boot into the groove in the piston **(see il-**

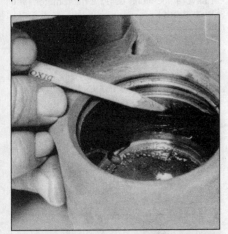

6.8 The piston seal should be removed with a plastic or wooden tool to avoid damage to the bore and seal groove (a pencil will do the job)

6.11 Push the new seal into the groove with your fingers, then check to see that it isn't twisted of kinked

6.12 Install the dust boot in the upper groove in the caliper bore, making sure it's completely seated

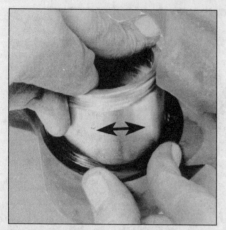

6.13a Insert the piston into the dust boot (not the bore) at an angle, then work the piston completely into the dust boot using a rotating motion

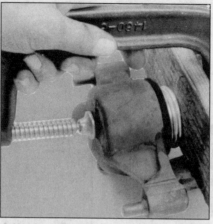

6.13b Use a C-clamp and a block of wood to bottom the piston in the caliper bore - make sure it goes in perfectly straight, as the caliper or piston may be damaged otherwise

6.13c Install the lip of the dust boot in the groove in the caliper piston

lustrations). Repeat the process for the second piston on dual-piston calipers.

14   Reassembly is now complete and the unit is ready for installation on the vehicle as described in Section 5.

15   After installing the caliper and pads in the vehicle, bleed the brakes as described in Section 11.

16   Install the wheel(s) and lower the vehicle to the ground. Tighten the lug nuts to the torque listed in the Chapter 1 Specifications. Check the operation of the brakes carefully before returning the vehicle to normal service.

7   Disc brake rotor - inspection

Refer to illustrations 7.3a, 7.3b, 7.4a and 7.4b

1   Remove the front caliper assembly (see Section 5). It's not necessary to disconnect the brake hose.

2   Inspect both sides of the rotor for deep scratches and scoring (over 0.015-inch deep) and signs of cracking or breakage. If any of these conditions exist, the rotor must be removed for refinishing at a shop equipped

for this type of machining work, or replaced. Light scratches and shallow grooves are normal and are not always detrimental to brake operation. If any signs of wobble such as a pulsating pedal exist, measure the runout.

3   Runout is measured with a dial indicator. These are available as rentals or they can be purchased. Attach the base of the indicator to a stable part of the suspension so that the indicator's stylus touches the rotor surface approximately 1/2-inch from the rotor's outer edge **(see illustration)**. Starting with the indicator set at zero, slowly rotate the disc through one revolution. Note the high and low readings on the dial as the rotor revolves. The difference between the high and low readings is the total rotor runout. If the rotor exceeds the maximum specification for runout, it will have to be removed for machining or replacement.

Note: *Professionals recommend resurfacing of brake rotors regardless of runout or appearance to eliminate brake pulsation and other undesirable symptoms related to questionable rotors. At the very least, if you elect not to resurface, deglaze the rotor with sandpaper or emery cloth using a swirling motion to ensure*

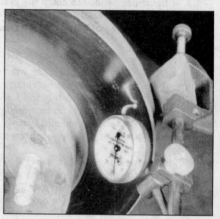

7.3a Use a dial indicator to check disc runout - if the reading exceeds the maximum allowable runout limit, the disc will have to be resurfaced or replaced

a non-directional finish **(see illustration)**.

4   The rotor must not be machined to a thickness less than the minimum refinish thickness dimension cast into the inner surface of the disk. Check the rotor thickness at several locations using a micrometer **(see illustrations)**.

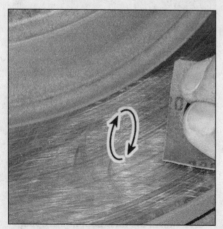

7.3b Using a swirling motion, remove the glaze from the disc surface with emery cloth or sandpaper

7.4a The minimum thickness limit is cast into the disc (typical)

7.4b Use a micrometer to measure the disc thickness at several points near the edge

8.9 Removing the master cylinder from the power booster - early model shown, later models similar

5   For removal and installation of the rotor for resurfacing on 2WD vehicles, refer to Chapter 1. On 4WD vehicles with a two piece hub and rotor, simply slide the rotor off and on the hub assembly. On 4WD vehicles with an integral rotor and hub, refer to Chapter 8 for hub removal, installation and bearing adjustment.

6   Install the brake caliper and brake pads (see Section 5).

7   Install the wheel(s) and lug nuts, then lower the vehicle to the ground. Tighten the lug nuts to the torque listed in the Chapter 1 Specifications. Check the operation of the brakes carefully before returning the vehicle to normal service.

8   Master cylinder - removal, overhaul and installation

Refer to illustrations 8.9, 8.13a, 8.13b, 8.14, 8.17, 8.19a, 8.19b and 8.23

Removal

1   Disconnect the cable from the negative battery terminal.

2   If the vehicle is equipped with a power brake booster system, push the brake pedal

8.13a Use a Phillips screwdriver to push the primary piston into the bore, then remove the snap-ring

down to expel the vacuum.

3   If equipped with manual (not power) brakes, disconnect the wires from the brake light switch (located adjacent to the brake pedal) and remove the nut and shoulder bolt securing the master cylinder pushrod to the brake pedal.

4   On later models, disconnect the fluid level indicator connector at the reservoir.

5   Place newspapers, rags, etc. under the master cylinder to catch leaking brake fluid. Brake fluid will ruin paint.

6   Using a suitable suction device, remove as much brake fluid from the reservoir as possible. Discard the fluid.

7   Unscrew the brake lines from the primary and secondary outlets of the master cylinder. Plug the ends of the lines to prevent any dirt from entering.

8   Remove the fasteners securing the master cylinder to the firewall or power booster.

9   Pull the master cylinder forward and lift it up and out of the vehicle **(see illustration)**. **Caution:** *Do not allow fluid to contact any paint as it will damage it.*

Overhaul

Note: *It should be noted that new and rebuilt master cylinders are commonly available for*

these vehicles. If one of these is purchased, skip to Step 23 for installation instructions. If it is decided to overhaul the original unit, obtain an overhaul kit, which will contain all necessary parts, and then proceed as follows.

10   Clean the exterior of the master cylinder with brake system cleaner.

11   Remove the reservoir cover or cap and pour any remaining brake fluid into a suitable container.

12   Remove the secondary piston stop bolt from the bottom of the master cylinder body.

13   Depress the primary piston and remove the snap-ring from the groove at the rear of the master cylinder bore **(see illustration)**. Remove the primary piston assembly **(see illustration)**. Consult your overhaul kit instructions and determine which parts (if any) will need to be saved for later reassembly. Discard any replaced parts and rework the primary piston assembly per overhaul kit instructions, if required. **Note:** *Some kits will include a complete primary piston assembly.*

14   Remove the secondary piston assembly by inverting the cylinder and tapping it against a wood block **(see illustration)**. Consult your overhaul kit instructions and determine which parts (if any) will need to be saved for later reassembly. Discard any replaced parts and rework the secondary piston assembly per overhaul kit instructions, if required. **Note:** *Some kits will include a complete secondary piston assembly.*

15   *Do not* remove the outlet line seats, outlet check valves and outlet check valve springs from the master cylinder body.

16   Examine the bore of the cylinder carefully for signs of corrosion, scoring or damage. On early cast iron master cylinders, if imperfections are slight, a hone can be used to smooth the surface of the bore. On later year aluminum alloy master cylinders, if imperfections are noted the entire master cylinder body will require replacement. **Warning:** *Do not attempt to hone aluminum master cylinders.*

17   On later models, if the plastic reservoir is damaged or if the grommets are leaking, pry the reservoir off the cylinder with a large screwdriver, remove and discard the grommets **(see illustration)**. Lubricate new grom-

8.13b Remove the primary piston assembly from the cylinder

8.14 Tap the master cylinder against a block of wood to dislodge the secondary piston assembly

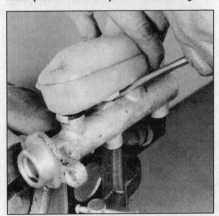

8.17 If you must remove the fluid reservoir, gently pry it off with a screwdriver (later models only)

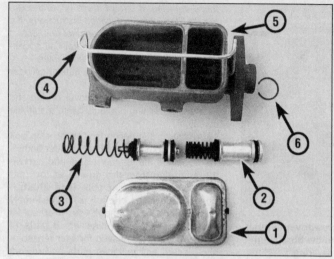

8.19a Exploded view of an early model master cylinder

1	Reservoir cover	4	Bail
2	Primary piston and spring	5	Master cylinder body
3	Secondary piston and spring	6	Snap-ring

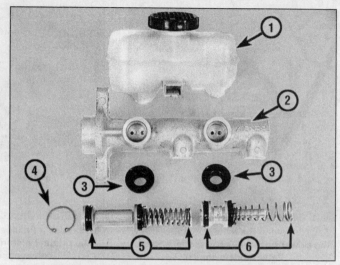

8.19b Exploded view of a later model master cylinder

1	Reservoir	4	Snap-ring
2	Master cylinder body	5	Primary piston assembly
3	Reservoir-to-master cylinder grommets	6	Secondary piston assembly

mets with brake fluid and insert them into the master cylinder and press the reservoir into the grommets by hand.

18   Thoroughly clean all parts with brake system cleaner. Ensure that the ports are clear. **Warning:** *DO NOT use petroleum based solvents.*

19   Dip the new or overhauled secondary piston assembly into clean brake fluid and install it into the cylinder bore, spring first **(see illustrations)**. Take care that the seals do not roll over.

20   Dip the new or overhauled primary piston assembly into clean brake fluid and install it into the cylinder bore, spring first. Take care that the seals do not roll over.

21   Depress the primary piston and install the snap-ring.

22   Push in the primary piston, then install and tighten the secondary piston stop screw.

Installation

23   Whenever the master cylinder is removed, the entire system must be bled. The time required to bleed the system can be reduced by first bench bleeding the master cylinder prior to installation as follows:

a) *Support the master cylinder in a vise, or other device, in such a manner as to allow fluid filling and piston stroking.* **Note:** *Do not clamp the cylinder in such a manner that the cylinder bore becomes distorted.*

b) *Locate two master cylinder outlet port plugs and place them conveniently next to the master cylinder for use later in the procedure.*

c) *Place a container and/or several rags under the master cylinder to catch the expelled brake fluid.*

d) *Fill the reservoir full of brake fluid.*

e) *Place two fingers over the master cylinder outlet ports with slight pressure* **(see illustration).**

f) *Using a Phillips screwdriver, or other suitable tool, slowly stroke the primary piston in, until bottoming resistance is felt, while allowing fluid to escape past your fingers. Maintain finger pressure to seal the ports (to keep air from entering) and allow the pistons to return slowly back to the extended position.*

g) *Stroke the piston several more times using the above procedure to ensure all air is expelled.* **Note:** *Make sure the fluid level does not go below the minimum level.*

h) *After the final stroke, quickly place the outlet port plugs into the master cylinder while trying to minimize fluid loss.*

24 If equipped with a power brake booster system, check the pushrod-to-mounting-face

distance. It may be necessary to turn the adjusting screw to achieve the correct dimension (see Section 12).

25 Installation of the master cylinder is the reverse of the removal procedure. After the cylinder is installed, bleed the hydraulic system as described in Section 11.

9   Brake pressure differential valve (early models) - resetting and replacement

Resetting

1   If the light for the brake warning system comes on, a leak or problem has been detected by the pressure differential valve causing the valve piston to shift from it's centered position. This shift causes the brake warning light circuit to be completed and the light to

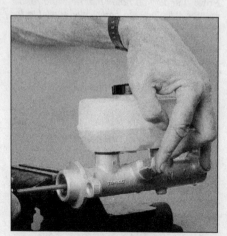

8.23 When bench bleeding the master cylinder, start with the rear outlet port

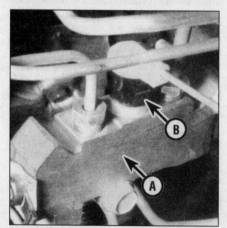

9.1 Typical pressure differential valve (A). B is the brake warning lamp switch

glow. Once the leak or problem has been repaired or if the hydraulic system has been opened up for brake cylinder overhaul or a similar repair, the pressure differential valve must be centered. Once the valve is centered, the brake light on the dash will go out.

2   To center the valve, first fill the master cylinder reservoir and make sure the hydraulic system has been bled (see Section 11).

3   Block the wheels from rolling while the parking brake is released.

4   Turn the ignition switch to On or Accessory and release the parking brake. The warning light should be on at this point if the valve is not centered.

5   Place rags under the master cylinder outlet lines to catch bleed brake fluid.

6   Crack open one of the outlet lines of the master cylinder (usually the line opposite of the failed or repaired circuit) using a flare-nut wrench.

7   Have the person assisting you sit in the driver's seat of the vehicle and have the assistant push the brake pedal down slowly while watching the warning light. As the pedal is pushed, the pressure differential within the valve created by cracking the one line should force the valve to it's centered position and the light should go out. **Note:** *Immediately stop pushing the pedal and hold it as soon as the light goes out or you may force the piston to shift to the opposite side of the valve and the process will have to be repeated on the other outlet line.* Do not release the brake pedal at this point.

8   Once the light has gone out, tighten the outlet line fitting securely and have your assistant release the brake pedal only after you have closed the valve tightly.

9   If this first process fails to center the valve, try the same procedure on the other outlet line.

10   Check the brake pedal for firmness and correct operation.

11   Replenish the brake fluid as required.

Replacement

12   If the pressure differential valve has been determined to be defective or if it is leaking, it must be replaced. It is a non-serviceable unit and no repair operations are possible.

13   Disconnect the brake warning light connector from the warning light switch.

14   Disconnect the front inlet and rear outlet pipe unions from the valve assembly. Plug the ends of the lines to prevent loss of brake fluid and the entry of dirt.

15   Remove the bolts and nuts securing the valve assembly to the chassis member.

16   Remove the valve assembly and bracket, taking care not to allow any brake fluid to contact the paint as it will damage it.

17   Installation is the reverse of removal.

18   Bleed the system after the replacement valve has been installed.

19   Center the valve as described in Steps 1 through 11 above.

10 Brake hoses and lines - inspection and replacement

Inspection

1   Brake hoses and lines should be inspected when recommended in the maintenance schedule. See Chapter 1 for inspection intervals and procedures.

Replacement

Front brake hose

2   Using a flare-nut wrench and a back-up wrench, disconnect the brake line from the hose fitting, being careful not to bend the frame bracket or brake line.

3   Use a pair of pliers to remove the U-clip from the female fitting at the bracket, then detach the hose from the bracket.

4   Unscrew the brake hose from the caliper.

5   To install the hose, first thread it into the caliper, tightening it securely.

6   Without twisting the hose, install the female fitting in the hose bracket. It will fit the bracket in only one position.

7   Install the U-clip retaining the female fitting to the frame bracket.

8   Using a flare-nut wrench and a back-up wrench, attach the brake line to the hose fitting.

9   When the brake hose installation is complete, there should be no kinks in the hose. Make sure the hose doesn't contact any part of the suspension. Check this by turning the wheels to the extreme left and right positions. If the hose makes contact, remove it and correct the installation as necessary. Bleed the system (see Section 11).

Rear brake hose

10   Using a flare-nut wrench and a back-up wrench, disconnect the hose at the frame bracket, being careful not to bend the bracket or steel lines. Plug the line to prevent fluid loss and contamination.

11   Remove the U-clip with a pair of pliers and separate the female fitting from the bracket.

12   Disconnect the two hydraulic lines at the junction block, then unbolt and remove the hose.

13   Bolt the junction block to the axle housing and connect the lines, tightening them securely. Without twisting the hose, install the female end of the hose in the frame bracket.

14   Install the U-clips retaining the female end to the bracket.

15   Using a flare-nut wrench and a back-up wrench, attach the steel line fittings to the female fittings. Again, be careful not to bend the bracket or steel line.

16   Make sure the hose installation did not loosen the frame bracket. Tighten the bracket if necessary.

17   Fill the master cylinder reservoir and bleed the system (see Section 11).

Metal brake lines

18   When replacing brake lines be sure to use the correct parts. Don't use copper tubing for any brake system components. Purchase steel brake lines from a dealer or auto parts store.

19   Prefabricated brake line, with the tube ends already flared and fittings installed, are available at auto parts stores and dealers. These lines will have to be bent to the proper shapes. Use the proper tubing bending tools, follow the manufactures instructions and be sure you do not kink the line.

20   When installing the new line make sure it's securely supported in the brackets and has plenty of clearance from moving or hot components.

21   After installation, check the master cylinder fluid level and add fluid as necessary. Bleed the brake system (see Section 11) and test the brakes carefully before driving the vehicle in traffic.

11 Brake hydraulic system - bleeding

Refer to illustration 11.4

Warning: *Wear eye protection when bleeding the brake system. If the fluid comes into contact with your eyes, immediately rinse them with water and seek medical attention.*

Note: *When any part of the brake hydraulic system has been removed or disconnected for repair or servicing, the system must be bled to purge it of any air which may have entered. It will probably be necessary to bleed both front and rear circuits if air has entered the system due to low fluid level or replacement of the master cylinder. Only the affected circuit will need be bleed if air has entered at only that particular wheel cylinder, caliper or brake line.*

1   The system may be bled with either a pressure bleeder or manually, utilizing two people. Follow the instructions of the pressure bleeder manufacturer if you are using that system. If the entire system must be bled, begin with the rear circuit first. The manual bleeding procedure is as follows:

2   Fill the master cylinder with fluid to within 1/4 inch of the top of the reservoirs (cast-iron reservoir) or to the MAX mark (plastic reservoirs). Keep the cylinders filled during the bleeding process. Cover the cylinder with a lint-free shop towel to prevent brake fluid from splashing on the painted surfaces.

3   It may be necessary to raise the vehicle to gain access to the bleeder screws located at each wheel cylinder or caliper. If this is necessary, support it securely before attempting this procedure.

Rear circuit bleeding

4   Start with the wheel cylinder farthest from the master cylinder (right rear). Wipe the bleeder screw clean and install a tight-fitting section of rubber tubing over the fitting. The other end of the tubing should be placed into a container of new brake fluid. (Glass jars work well for this as they allow the person operating the bleeder to see any air bubbles coming

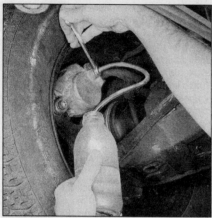

11.4 When bleeding the brakes, one end of the hose is connected to the bleeder valve at the caliper or wheel cylinder and the other end submerged in brake fluid - air bubbles will be seen in the container which must be expelled before moving to the next wheel

from the hose) **(see illustration)**.

5   Have the person assisting you sit in the driver's seat of the vehicle. Open the bleeder screw using a box-end or flare nut wrench and have the assistant push the brake pedal down, Once the pedal reaches the bottom of its travel, have him hold the pedal down while you close the bleeder valve. Have him release the brake pedal only after you have closed the valve tightly. Continue this sequence until only brake fluid and no air bubbles are being pushed from the hose into the container. It may be necessary to stop and fill the master cylinder reservoir from time to time as it must *not* be allowed to run dry.

6   Repeat this process at the next farthest brake cylinder from the master cylinder (left rear).

7   On vehicles equipped with anti-lock rear brakes using the RABS I or II system, bleed the RABS valve at the valve itself using the same procedure as the rear brake cylinders. If necessary, continue to the front calipers.

8   If the front circuit does not require bleeding, 'feel' the brake pedal at this time. It should be firm with no sponginess. Top off the master cylinder for the last time and replace the lid.

Front circuit bleeding

9   If you're working on an early model with a pressure differential valve (see Section 9) and you're using a pressure bleeding kit to bleed the brakes, a bleeder pin located on the pressure differential valve must be released to allow fluid to run to the front calipers. On all early vehicles except F350 models, the bleeder pin must be pulled out. On early F350 vehicles, the bleeder pin must be pushed in. **Caution:** *When the bleeding procedure is complete, be sure to restore the pin to its original position.*

10   Working the right front caliper first, bleed the circuit using the procedure outlined in operation 5 this section.

11   Repeat this process at the left front caliper.

12   At this time, the 'feel' at the brake pedal should be firm with no sponginess. Top off the master cylinder for the last time and replace the lid.

13   Once you have ascertained that the brake hydraulic system is free of air, release the differential valve bleeder pin (if equipped, and if you used a pressure bleeder) and lower the vehicle to the ground.

14   If the brake warning light is on, verify that the parking brake is fully released. If the light is still on, center the differential valve as described in Section 9 (early models only) or check the low brake fluid indicator switch in the master cylinder reservoir (later models).

15   Check the brake pedal once again for feel before road testing the vehicle. Make the first few brake applications at low speeds to make certain the system is working properly and all valves and connections are tight.

Warning: *Do not operate the vehicle if you are in doubt about the effectiveness of the brake system. On models with ABS it is possible for air to become trapped in the ABS hydraulic unit, so, if the pedal feels spongy after repeated bleedings or the BRAKE or ANTI-LOCK light stays on, have the vehicle towed to a dealer service department or other qualified shop to have the system bled with the aid of a scan tool.*

---

12   Power brake booster unit - removal, installation and adjustment

Refer to illustration 12.12

1   The power brake booster unit requires no special maintenance apart from periodic inspection of the vacuum hose and the case. Dismantling of the power unit requires special tools and is not ordinarily performed. If a problem develops, install a new or factory rebuilt unit.

Removal

2   Remove the fasteners attaching the master cylinder to the booster and carefully pull the master cylinder forward until it clears the mounting studs. Don't bend or kink the brake lines.

3   Loosen the clamp and disconnect the vacuum hose where it attaches to the check valve on the power brake booster. Detach the hose from the booster.

4   From inside the passenger compartment, disconnect the electrical connector from the brake light switch.

5   Also from the passenger compartment, disconnect the retaining pin, then slide the brake light switch, booster pushrod, spacers and bushings off the brake pedal arm.

6   Also from this location, remove the bolts securing the booster to the firewall.

7   Carefully lift the booster unit away from the firewall and out of the engine compartment.

Installation

8   Installation is the reverse of the removal Steps with the following additions:

9   Check the pushrod length as described at the end of this section.

10   Make sure the booster rubber reaction disc is properly installed if the master cylinder pushrod has been removed or accidentally pulled out. A dislodged disc may cause excessive pedal travel and extreme operation sensitivity. The disc is black, compared to the silver colored valve plunger that will be exposed after the pushrod and front seal are removed. The booster is serviced as a unit and the entire unit must be replaced if the disc cannot be properly installed and aligned, or the disc cannot be located within the booster unit.

11   Carefully test the operation of the brakes before placing the vehicle in normal service.

Adjustment

12   Boosters feature an adjustable pushrod. They are matched to the booster at the factory and most likely will not require adjustment, but if a misadjusted pushrod is suspected, a gauge can be fabricated out of a piece of heavy-gauge sheet metal **(see illustration)**.

13   Some common symptoms caused by a misadjusted pushrod include dragging brakes (if the pushrod is too long) or excessive brake pedal travel accompanied by a groaning sound from the brake booster (if the pushrod is too short).

14   To check the pushrod length, unbolt the master cylinder from the booster and position it to one side. It isn't necessary to disconnect the hydraulic lines, but be careful not to bend them.

15   Block the front wheels, apply the parking brake and place the transmission in Park (automatic) or Neutral (manual).

16   Start the engine and place the pushrod gauge against the end of the pushrod **(see illustration 12.12)**. The rod should touch the end of the notch in the gauge. If not, adjust the rod by turning the adjusting screw in or out to obtain the correct length.

17   When adjustment is complete, reinstall

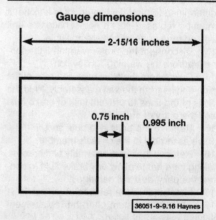

Gauge dimensions

2-15/16 inches

0.75 inch   0.995 inch

36051-9-9.16 Haynes

12.12 Dimensions of the pushrod-to-booster mounting face measurement

the master cylinder and check for proper operation before driving the vehicle in traffic.

13 Anti-lock brakes - general information

Two types of anti-lock brake systems are pertinent to this manual. When originally available, F-series vehicles and Broncos utilized a rear wheel only anti-lock system (RABS I). In 1993, all F-series vehicles incorporated a slightly improved rear wheel only anti-lock system (RABS II) and Broncos converted to a completely new all (four) wheel anti-lock brake system (ABS).

The RAB system is composed of the RAB computer module, Hydraulic Control Valve (HCV), rear axle speed sensor and test connector, RAB system failure warning light and the diagnostic test connector. When the brake pedal is applied, the RABS module senses the drop in rear wheel speed via the speed sensor located in the rear differential. If the rate of deceleration is too great, indicating that wheel lockup is going to occur, the RABS module activates the electro-hydraulic valve (HCV) causing the isolation valve to close. With the isolation valve closed, the rear wheel cylinders are isolated from the master cylinder and the rear brake pressure cannot increase. If the rate of deceleration is still too great, the RABS module will energize the dump solenoid with a series of rapid pulses to bleed off rear wheel cylinder fluid into an accumulator built into the RABS HCV. This will reduce the rear wheel cylinder pressure and allow the rear wheels to spin back up to vehicle speed.

The ABS system is composed of the Electronic Control Unit (ECU), Hydraulic Control Unit (HCU), rear axle speed sensor, front wheel speed sensors and deceleration sensor. When the brakes are applied, fluid is forced from the master cylinder outlet ports to the Hydraulic Control Unit (HCU) inlet ports. This pressure is transmitted through three normally open solenoid valves (two front and one rear) contained inside the HCU, then through the outlet ports of the HCU to the wheels. If the Electronic Control Unit (ECU) senses that a wheel is about to lock, based on wheel speed sensor data, it pulses the normally open solenoid valve closed for that circuit. This prevents any more fluid from entering that circuit. The ECU then looks at the sensor signal from the affected wheel again. If that wheel is still decelerating, it opens the normally closed solenoid valve for that circuit. This dumps any pressure that is trapped between the normally open valve and the brake back to the reservoir. The deceleration sensor provides information on the rate (magnitude) of vehicle slowing affecting the signature of the pulses based on several preprogrammed "typical braking scenarios". Once the affected wheel comes back up to speed, the ECU returns the valves to their normal condition allowing fluid flow to the affected brake.

Both systems perform system tests dur-

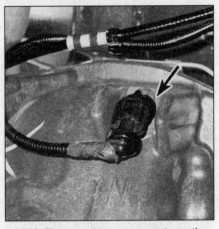

14.16 The speed sensor mounts on the rear axle housing

ing start-up and constantly during normal operation. All systems components and sensors plus fluid level are monitored for proper operation. If a concern is found, the system will be deactivated and the dash warning will be illuminated. Depending on the system, the diagnostic trouble code (DTC) can be obtained under certain conditions allowing the technician to better troubleshoot anti-lock systems problems.

14 Anti-lock brake components - removal and installation

Refer to illustrations 14.16 and 14.35

RABS I and II
RABS Modules

1   Disconnect the cable from the negative battery terminal.
2   On RABS I systems, locate the module in the cab to the right of the brake pedal and under the upper dash panel. On RABS II systems, locate the module in the cab directly behind the glove box.
3   Disconnect the wiring harness from the module by depressing the plastic tab on the connector and pulling the connector off.
4   Remove the two screws that retain the module to the dash and remove the module.
5   Installation is the reverse of removal.
6   Verify that the warning light is indicating proper operation of the system.

RABS Hydraulic Control Valve (HCV)

7   Locate the RABS Valve on the left frame rail just behind the crossmember.
8   Disconnect the inlet and outlet brake lines and plug the lines to prevent excess fluid loss and line contamination.
9   Disconnect the wiring harness.
10 Remove the three nuts (or screws on some models) retaining the valve to the frame rail and remove the valve.
11 Installation is the reverse of removal. Tighten the fasteners to the torque listed in

this Chapter's Specifications.
12 Bleed the hydraulic system (see Section 11).
13 Verify that the warning light is indicating proper operation of the system.

RABS Speed Sensor

14 Locate the sensor in the upper part of the rear differential housing.
15 Disconnect the sensor electrical connector.
16 Remove the sensor hold-down bolt and remove the sensor from the axle housing **(see illustration)**.
17 If the sensor is to be reinstalled, inspect and clean the magnetized sensor pole piece and inspect the O-ring. Replace the defective parts, if required.
18 Installation is the reverse of removal. Tighten the fasteners to the torque listed in this Chapter's Specifications.
19 Verify that the warning light is indicating proper operation of the system.

RABS Speed Sensor Ring

20 The sensor ring is part or the rear axle ring gear assembly and requires complete disassembly of the differential to replace. If the ring has damaged teeth, take the vehicle to a professional repair facility.

Four wheel ABS system (Bronco only)
Hydraulic Control Unit (HCU)

Warning: *Special Test equipment to actuate the internal valves is required to bleed the HCU if it is removed. Therefore, if you decide to replace the HCU the braking system will not be safe to drive after installation. It will be necessary to have the vehicle towed to a facility which can properly bleed the HCU.*

21 Disconnect the cable from the negative battery terminal.
22 Locate the HCU in the front of the engine compartment on the left frame rail.
23 Disconnect the electrical connectors (8 pin and 4 pin connectors).
24 Remove the two inlet and three outlet lines and plug the lines to prevent excess fluid loss and line contamination.
25 Remove the three nuts retaining the HCU to the mounting bracket and remove the HCU.
26 Installation is the reverse of removal. Tighten all fasteners to the torque listed in this Chapter's Specifications.
27 Have the vehicle towed to a dealer service department or other repair shop for HCU bleeding.
28 Verify that the warning light is indicating proper operation of the system.

ECU Module

29 Disconnect the cable from the negative battery terminal.
30 Locate the ECU at the left front fender apron.
31 Disconnect the ECU electrical connector.
32 Remove the ECU-to-retaining bracket

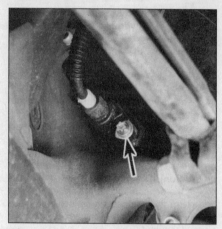

14.35 The ABS front wheel speed sensors are mounted on the steering knuckles

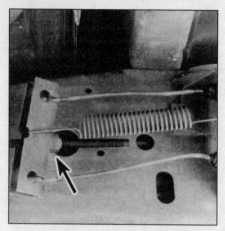

15.6 Turn the equalizer nut to adjust the parking brake cable

9   Lower the vehicle and check for proper operation of the parking brake.

Auto tensioned systems (1992 and later)

10   Late model vehicles utilize a system that maintains a constant and proper preload tension on the parking brake cable while in the non-applied state. This static tension allows the driver to always be able to set the proper parking brake pressure in the normal range of travel of the parking brake pedal assembly. It eliminates the need for any adjustment but leaves the ultimate parking brake holding power up to the individuals "feel". The tension is maintained by a clock spring and cam built into the parking brake pedal assembly.
11   No adjustment is provided for. Check the cables, parking pedal assembly and adjust the rear brakes (see Section 2 or 3) if problems are encountered.

screws and slide the ECU out of the bracket.
33   Installation is the reverse of removal.
34   Verify that the warning light is indicating proper operation of the system.

Wheel Speed Sensors (front)

35   Locate the right or left sensor mounted on the steering knuckle(s) **(see illustration)**.
36   Locate the sensor harness connector inside the engine compartment and disconnect the electrical connector. Also separate the sensor harness from the brake hose clips.
37   Remove the sensor hold-down bolt from the knuckle and slide the sensor out.
38   Installation is the reverse of removal. Tighten the fasteners to the torque listed in this Chapter's Specifications.
39   Verify that the warning light is indicating proper operation of the system.

Wheel Speed Sensor (rear)

40   The rear sensor is similar to the one on the RABS system. Refer to Steps 14 through 19 in this section

Speed Sensor Ring (front)

41   Remove the affected front wheel (see Chapter 1).
42   Remove the caliper, rotor and hub assembly (see Chapters 9 and 8).
43   Using a three-jaw puller, remove the speed ring from the hub.
44   Position a new ring on the hub and press the ring onto the hub using an appropriately sized driver. Seat the ring against the hub shoulder.
45   Installation is the reverse of removal. Tighten the fasteners to the torque listed in this Chapters Specifications and any other referenced Chapters.
46   Verify that the warning light is indicating proper operation of the system.

Speed Sensor Ring (rear)

47   The sensor ring is part or the rear axle ring gear assembly and requires complete disassembly of the differential to replace. If the ring has damaged teeth, take the vehicle to a professional repair facility.

15   Parking brake - adjustment

Refer to illustration 15.6

Tension limiter systems (1980 through 1991)

1   The parking brakes employ a cable system that incorporates a tension limiter. If the parking brake system is in normal operating condition, depressing the parking brake pedal to the floor will automatically set the proper tension and pedal feel. The system relies on a special cinch strap hook (part of the tension limiter) made of a malleable material that will deform at a given tensile load. This deformation is what sets the upper limit of cable tension after each parking brake adjustment is made. Therefore, adjustment should only be done when necessary, because the limiter is a perishable item and must be replaced if deformed to its safety stop.
2   Raise vehicle and support it securely on jackstands.
3   Make sure the rear brakes are cold and properly adjusted (see Section 2 or 3).
4   Depress the parking brake pedal all the way to the floor.
5   Locate the tension limiter and observe the cinch strap hook. If the stop at the end of the cinch strap hook is in contact with the limiter housing, a new limiter must be installed before proceeding.
6   Grip the limiter housing and tighten the equalizer nut about six turns on the threaded rod or until the cinch strap hook begins to slip (deform) around the housing **(see illustration)**. This indicates that the parking cable tension has been automatically set.
7   Inspect the cinch strap hook again. If the stop at the end of the cinch strap hook is in contact with the limiter housing, a new limiter must be installed and the parking brake adjusted again.
8   Release the parking brake and check for rear wheel drag. If drag is excessive, readjust the parking brake as required.

16   Brake pedal assembly - removal and installation

1   On vehicles equipped with a manual transmission, the brake pedal pivots on the clutch pedal shaft, and both pedals are removed as described in Chapter 7. On automatic transmission models, remove the retaining clip and slide the shaft to the right until the brake pedal and pedal bushings can be removed.
2   Disconnect the master cylinder pushrod and brake switch assembly and remove the pedal.
3   Replace the bushings if worn and install the pedal and pushrod using the reverse of the removal procedure.

17   Brake light switch - adjustment

1   The brake light switch is located under the dashboard directly above the brake pedal. It is activated by the pedal traveling away from its bottomed position, which releases the plunger and closes an electrical circuit in the system. The switch is mounted in a metal bracket which can be bent to vary its position.
2   Make sure the switch is fully seated in its bracket. Use an assistant or a mirror to determine when the brake light circuit is activated. A test light connected to the two terminals of the switch would also provide you with this information.
3   The switch should activate the brake circuit within the first 1/4-inch of brake pedal travel.
4   If the switch does not perform in this manner, bend the mounting bracket up or down to obtain the desired results. Do not bend the bracket down to the point where it is preventing the pedal from returning fully.
5   The factory suggests that a 25-pound or less pull up on the pedal is sufficient to adjust the switch. Again, make sure the brake lights are off when the pedal is at rest.

Chapter 10
Steering and suspension systems

Contents

Specifications

Front suspension type
2WD ... Forged or stamped twin I-beam axles with coil springs and telescoping shock absorbers
4WD ... Independent front suspension (IFS) with two-piece front drive axle assembly, leaf or coil springs and telescoping shock absorbers, except F350 monobeam (F350 monobeam has springs and telescoping shock absorbers)

Rear suspension type (all) ... Leaf spring with telescoping shock absorbers

Steering systems
Manual
  Type ... Recirculating ball
  Ratio ... 24:1
  Lock-to-lock turns (not attached to Pitman arm) ... 6
  Worm bearing preload ... 5 to 8 in-lbs
  Sector shaft backlash (torque required to rotate input shaft and worm assembly past the center high point) ... 10 to 16 in-lbs
  Total steering meshload on center ... 16 in-lbs

Steering systems (continued)

Power assisted type	Ford integral worm and sector, torsion-bar feedback
Ratio	17:1
Lock-to-lock turns (not attached to Pitman arm)	4
Pump fluid	Type F (ESW-M2C33-F) or equivalent
Power assisted over-center meshload	10 to 14 in-lbs

Torque specifications

Ft-lbs (unless otherwise indicated)

Note: *One foot pound (ft-lb) of torque is equivalent to 12 inch-pounds (in-lbs) of torque. Torque values below approximately 15 ft-lbs are expressed in inch-pounds, since most foot pound torque wrenches are not accurate at these smaller values.*

Front suspension (2WD)

Spring upper retainer-to-spring upper seat...............................	13 to 18
Spring upper seat-to-frame (early stamped axle, left side only)..............	52 to 73
Shock absorber stud-to-spring upper seat	25 to 35
Shock absorber-to-lower bracket bolt/nut	
1980 through 1993	
2WD models	29 to 41
4WD models	52 to 74
1994 through 1996	52 to 74
1997	44 to 59
Shock lower bracket-to-radius arm...............................	27 to 37
Spring lower retainer-to-spring lower seat	
Early forged axle	30 to 70
Early stamped axle...	70 to 100
Later forged axle	70 to 100
Radius arm-to-front axle and bracket	
Early forged axle	240 to 320
Early stamped axle...	269 to 329
Later forged axle	269 to 329
Radius arm-to-bracket	80 to 120
Radius arm bracket-to-frame	77 to 110
Front axle-to-pivot bracket/crossmember	120 to 150
Front axle pivot bracket to crossmember (left axle only)........................	76 to 109
Stabilizer bar link-to-bracket...	52 to 74
Stabilizer bar link-to-stabilizer bar	52 to 74
Stabilizer bar retainer-to-frame crossmember mounting bracket	24 to 35
Stabilizer bar bracket-to-frame (early F250 and F350	
with stamped axle only)...	52 to 74
Wheel spindle pin lock pin nut (early forged axle only)	38 to 62
Wheel spindle plug (early forged axle only)........................	35 to 50
Wheel spindle steering arm to steering rod-and-link ball joint	
Early forged axle	70 to 100
Early stamped axle...	52 to 73
Later forged axle	52 to 73
Upper balljoint nut (early stamped axle only)	85 to 110
Lower balljoint nut (early stamped axle only)	
Manufacturer part no. 388981	140 to 180
Manufacturer part no. 33850.............................	104 to 146
Lower balljoint to axle nut (later forged axle).............................	95 to 110*
Upper balljoint axle clamp pinch bolt (later forged axle)........................	48 to 65*

* Follow special installation procedure to prevent binding when torquing (see Section 4).

Front suspension (4WD)

Coil spring (F100, F150, Bronco)

Radius arm-to-rear bracket...	80 to 120
Radius arm to axle upper stud bolt	240 to 260
Radius arm to axle lower bolt...	320 to 340
Radius arm pivot bracket-to-frame...	76 to 114
Radius arm/axle front bracket bolts...	20 to 26
Radius arm/axle front shock bracket (quad shocks only)..................	20 to 26
Front axle pivot to bracket/crossmember	120 to 150
Front axle pivot bracket to crossmember (left axle only)..................	76 to 109
Spring retainer-to-upper spring seat	13 to 18
Lower spring retainer-to-radius arm stud	70 to 100
Front shock-to-shock bracket (lower)...	52 to 74
Front shock absorber stud (upper)...	25 to 35

Front shock bracket to radius arm	25 to 35
Upper balljoint stud nut	85 to 100**
Lower balljoint stud nut	95 to 110**
Leaf spring (F250/F350)	
Front axle pivot bracket to crossmember (right & left, F250 only)	77 to 110
Front axle pivot to bracket (right & left, F250 only)	120 to 150
Front spring-to-axle U-bolt	85 to 120
Front spring assembly-to-rear hanger bracket	120 to 150
Front spring rear hanger bracket-to-frame (non riveted)	35 to 50
Front spring shackle-to-shackle bracket	150 to 210
Front spring-to-shackle	120 to 150
Front shock bracket-to-frame	52 to 74
Front shock absorber upper (stud mounted models)	25 to 35
Front shock absorber upper (bolt mounted models)	52 to 74
Front shock-to-front spring plate spacer	52 to 74
Kingpin - upper (early F350 monobeam)	500 to 600
Kingpin - upper spindle cap (early F350 monobeam)	70 to 90
Kingpin - lower (early F350 monobeam)	70 to 90
Tracking bar to lower U bolt spacer plate (F350 monobeam)	120 to 150
Tracking bar to mounting bracket (F350 monobeam)	120 to 150
Tracking bar bracket to crossmember (F350 monobeam)	77 to 110
Upper balljoint stud nut	85 to 100**
Lower balljoint stud nut	95 to 110**

**Follow special installation procedure to prevent binding when torquing (see Section 5).*

Rear suspension

Lower shock mount	52 to 74
Upper shock mount	40 to 60
Spring-to-axle U-bolt mounting nuts	
F100, F150, F250, Lighting, Bronco	75 to 100
F250 over 8500 GVW and F350	150 to 210
Spring-to-front hanger	
F100, F150 (2WDs), Lighting	75 to 115
F250, F350 (2WDs) and Bronco	150 to 177
F150, F250, F350 (4WDs)	150 to 210
Spring-to-rear shackle	
All vehicles except F250/350 (2WD) Chassis Cab	75 to 115
F250/350 (2WD) Chassis Cab	150 to 210
Rear shackle-to-shackle bracket	
All vehicles except F250/350 (2WD, 4WD) Chassis Cab	75 to 115
F250/350 (2WD, 4WD) Chassis Cab	150 to 210

Steering

Steering rod and link assembly-to-Pitman arm	52 to 73
Steering gearbox-to-frame	54 to 66
Flex coupling-to-worm (input) shaft	25 to 34
Drag link/tie-rod end studs	52 to 74
Linkage adjusting sleeve clamp	30 to 42
Flange and insulator assembly-to-steering gearbox	30 to 42
Flange and insulator assembly-to-coupling shaft	14 to 21
Coupling shaft-to-steering shaft	45 to 59
Steering wheel-to-steering shaft	30 to 42
Modulator assembly-to-steering gearbox	28 to 35
Steering column-to-support bracket bolts	120 to 156 in-lbs
Steering column lower mounting bracket bolts	62 to 97 in-lbs
Sector shaft cover	
Manual steering	30
Power steering	55 to 70
Worm bearing (preload) adjuster locknut	85
Sector shaft backlash adjuster screw locknut	
Manual steering	25
Power steering	35 to 45
Pitman arm-to-steering gear	
Manual steering	170 to 230
Power steering	190 to 230
Power steering support and mounting brackets	30 to 45

1   General information

Refer to illustrations 1.4, 1.5 and 1.6

Warning: *Whenever any of the suspension or steering fasteners are loosened or removed, they must be inspected and, if necessary, replaced with new ones of the same part number or of original equipment quality and design. Torque specifications must be followed for proper reassembly and component retention.*

Front suspension

2WD models

1   The front suspension system of these light duty trucks is unusual in design with its patented twin I-beam layout. This design, using two independent I-beam axles (one for each side) suspended by coil springs, has a number of advantages. The I-beam axles provide high strength and durability while the independent feature allows each side to absorb bumps and provide a smoother ride for passengers and cargo.

2   Several versions of the twin I-beam layout are employed on the 2WD models covered by this manual: A stamped I-beam (and, on later models, forged) axle employing pressed-in balljoints with stud mounted spindles on early F100 and F150 pick-ups, a forged axle employing spindle pins (kingpin) on early F250 and F350 pick-ups, and the latest forged I-beam design which utilizes a spindle which houses pressed-in balljoints with their studs attached to the I-beam on all models.

3   The I-beam of each axle on all designs is located by a radius arm mounted in rubber and damped by a hydraulic telescoping shock absorber. The inner ends of the I-beam are attached to a pivot bracket on the opposite side of the vehicle. This design provides for good suspension compliance and long spring travel.

4WD models

4   The 4WD Bronco and F150 independent front suspension system (IFS) comprises a two-piece front driving axle assembly (see Chapter 8), two coil springs, and two radius arms **(see illustration)**. One end of each axle assembly is anchored to the frame, with the other end supported by the coil spring and radius arm.

5   All models of F250 and early model F350 IFS employs the same type of two-piece driving axle as the Bronco and F150, but is attached to the frame with two semi-elliptic leaf-type springs **(see illustration)**. Each spring is clamped to the axle arm assembly with two U-bolts at the spring center. The rear eye of the leaf spring is attached to the frame by a hanger bracket, with the front eye attached via a shackle bracket. Later model F350s utilize the monobeam type solid front axle assembly. The monobeam axle is supported by both leaf springs and a transversely

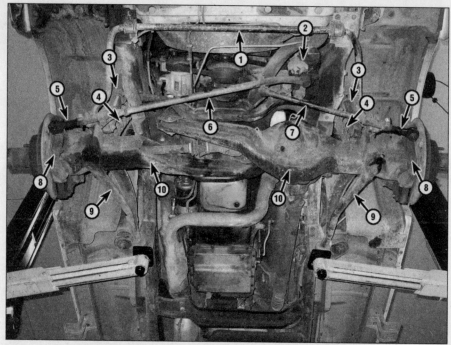

1.4 Front suspension and steering components - 4WD Bronco

1	Stabilizer bar	6	Drag link
2	Steering gear	7	Tie-rod
3	Shock absorber	8	Spindle (knuckle)
4	Coil spring	9	Radius arm
5	Tie-rod end	10	Axle assembly

mounted tracking bar. The first monobeam axles used upper and lower kingpins to secure the steering knuckle. Later monobeam axles utilize balljoints similar to the F250.

Rear suspension (all models)

6   The rear suspension consists of leaf-type springs mounted to the axle with U-bolts. The springs are mounted to the frame

1.5 Front suspension and steering components - 4WD F250 model

1	Shock absorber	5	Tie-rod	9	Adjusting sleeve
2	Drag link	6	Tie-rod ballstud	10	Spindle pin
3	Steering damper	7	Spring/axle U-bolt	11	Spindle
4	Pitman arm	8	Leaf spring		

1.6 Rear suspension components

1	Leaf spring	4	Shock absorber
2	Spring plate	5	U-bolts
3	Rear axle assembly		

by brackets and shackles and telescoping shock absorbers are used for damping **(see illustration)**.

Steering (all models)

7   Several types of manual and power assisted steering gear boxes are used and the steering wheel is connected through a collapsible shaft and flexible coupling. Some models incorporate a hydraulic damper in the steering linkage to reduce road shock at the steering wheel.

8   Due to the special techniques and tools required, several procedures involving complicated assemblies such as power steering pumps and the front axle on 4-wheel-drive vehicles are beyond the scope of the home

mechanic. Consequently, only tasks which can be accomplished with standard tools and limited experience are described in this Chapter.

2   Front coil spring - removal and installation

Refer to illustrations 2.4 and 2.6

Warning: *Coil springs should always be replaced in pairs to maintain proper ride height and handling characteristics. As an additional safety precaution, use a chain to secure the spring to the axle during removal and installation. This will prevent the spring from flying out of position during the procedures.*

Removal

1   Loosen the front wheel lug nuts. Raise the front of the vehicle and support it securely on jackstands. Remove the wheels.

2   Support the bottom of the axle being worked on with a floor jack. **Note:** *The axle must be supported on the jack throughout the spring removal and installation, and must not be permitted to hang by the brake hose. If the brake hose is not long enough to provide clearance for removal and installation of the spring, the disc brake caliper must be removed (see Chapter 9). After removing the caliper, it must be placed on the frame or otherwise supported to prevent suspending the caliper by the brake hose.*

3   Detach the stabilizer bar at the link if equipped (see Section 10) and disconnect the lower end of the shock absorber(s) (see Section 7) while using the jack to compress the spring and support the axle.

4   Remove the bolt holding the upper spring retainer to the frame. Remove the upper spring retainer **(see illustration)**.

5   Carefully lower the axle until the open end of the spring is exposed. Drop the axle/spring assembly slowly as the coil spring could spring out slightly as the axle is moved.

6   Use a socket and a long extension to unfasten the lower spring retaining nut through the open end of the top of the spring **(see illustration)**. Remove the nut, washer, chain and spring from the axle. **Warning:** *Verify that the chain is loose prior to removal.*

Installation

7   To install, place the spring in position on the lower seat. Position it so that the end of the spring fits correctly into the recess of the upper spring cup. The spring can fit into a number of different positions, but the flat surface of the spring end must fit into the area where it is retained by the upper spring retainer.

8   Install the lower spring retainer washer and nut. Tighten the nut to the torque listed in this Chapter's Specifications.

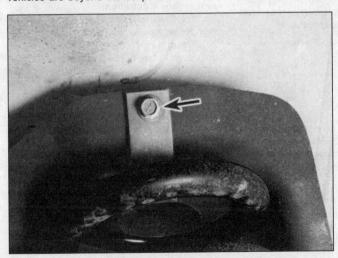

2.4 Remove the bolt and the retainer holding the spring to the frame

2.6 Remove the lower spring retaining nut

9   Raise the spring/axle combination until the spring top fits snugly against the upper spring cup. Work slowly and carefully to ensure that the spring is properly seated.
10   Install the upper spring retainer and retaining bolt. Tighten the bolt to the torque listed in this Chapter's Specifications.
11   Connect the lower end of the shock absorber(s) (see Section 7) and reattach the stabilizer bar to the link if equipped (see Section 10).
12   If the brake caliper was removed, reinstall it (see Chapter 9).
13   Install the wheel (see Chapter 1). Lower the vehicle and tighten the lug nuts to the torque listed in the Chapter 1 Specifications.

3   Front leaf spring - removal and installation

Removal

1   Loosen the wheel lug nuts, raise the vehicle and support it securely on jackstands. Remove the wheel.
2   Support the axle with a floor jack and raise it just enough to take the weight of the axle off the spring.
3   Disconnect the lower end of the shock absorber from the front spring plate spacer (see Section 7).
4   If required, on F350 monobeam remove the tracking bar to lower spring plate bolt.
5   Remove the spring to axle U-bolt nuts, U-bolt and spacer.
6   Remove the nut from the hanger bolt retaining the rear of the spring.
7   Drive the hanger bolt out of the spring eye. If the bolt is to be reused, use a soft brass drift so the bolt is not damaged.
8   Remove the nut connecting the front shackle and spring eye.
9   Remove the bolt in the same manner as in Step 6.
10   Remove the spring from under the vehicle.
11   If the spring eye bushings are worn or damaged, they must be replaced by an automotive repair shop with the necessary hydrau-

lic press and associated tools.

Installation

12   To install the spring, position it on the axle spring seat and install the front lower shackle bolt through the shackle and spring. Tighten the bolt to the torque listed in this Chapter's Specifications.
13   Position the rear of the spring and install the hanger bolt through the hanger and spring. Tighten the bolt to the torque listed in this Chapter's Specifications.
14   Install the front spring plate spacer and install the axle U-bolts through the holes in the U-bolt spacer. Finger tighten the U-bolt nuts.
15   Connect the lower end of the shock absorber to the front spring plate spacer.
16   Install the wheel, lower the vehicle to the ground and tighten the U-bolt nuts to the torque listed in this Chapter's Specifications. Tighten the lugnuts to the torque listed in the Chapter 1 Specifications.

4   Front spindle (2WD) - removal and installation

Refer to illustration 4.21

Removal

All vehicles

1   Raise the front of the vehicle and support it securely on jackstands.
2   Remove the wheel.
3   Remove the brake caliper (see Chapter 9) and support it out of the way with wire. **Note:** *Do not disconnect the brake line from the caliper.*
4   Remove the dust cap, cotter pin, nut retainer, nut, washer and outer bearing (see Chapter 1, *Wheel bearing check, repack and adjustment*).
5   Remove the disc from the spindle (see Chapter 1 if necessary).
6   Remove the inner bearing cone and seal, and discard the seal. **Note:** *This step is unnecessary for spindle removal, but bearing packing and seal replacement is recommended anytime the front hub/disc is removed.*

7   Remove the brake dust shield.
8   Disconnect the steering linkage from the spindle arms by removing the cotter pin and nut (see Section 20).
9   Remove the tie-rod end from the spindle arm (see Section 20).

Early model axles (kingpin)

10   Remove the nut and lock washer from the spindle pin lock pin, then remove the lock pin with a brass drift.
11   Remove the upper and lower spindle pin plugs.
12   Drive the spindle pin out of the top of the axle with a brass drift.
13   Remove the spindle from the axle.
14   Remove the spindle pin seal and thrust bearing from the axle.

Early model axles (balljoints integral to I-beam)

15   Mark the orientation of the upper balljoint camber adjuster sleeve (located in the spindle) for proper positioning upon reassembly.
16   Remove the cotter pins from the upper and lower balljoint studs.
17   Remove the nuts from the upper and lower balljoint studs.
18   Using a brass hammer, strike the inside of the spindle at the tapered bosses to pop the balljoints loose from the spindle. Remove the spindle. If this procedure fails to loosen the balljoints, strike the outside of the upper portion of the spindle. **Caution:** *Do not use a pickle fork type tool to separate the balljoint from the spindle as this will damage the seal and the balljoint socket.*

Later model axles (balljoints integral with spindle)

19   Remove lower balljoint cotter pin and loosen the stud nut.
20   Remove the nut from the upper balljoint stud pinch bolt and remove the pinch bolt from the spindle.
21   Mark the orientation of the upper balljoint camber/caster adjuster sleeve (located in axle assembly) for proper positioning upon reassembly **(see illustration)**.
22   Remove adjuster sleeve from I-beam axle. **Note:** *A puller may be required.*
23   Using a brass hammer, strike the inside area of the I-beam axle by the lower balljoint stud to pop the stud loose. **Caution:** *If the lower balljoint stud nut is removed, the spindle will be free to fall and possibly injure you.*
24   Remove the lower stud nut and detach the spindle from the I-beam axle.

Installation

Early model axles (kingpin)

25   Check the spindle pin hole in the axle for nicks, burrs, corrosion and foreign matter. Clean up the bore as necessary and lightly coat the surface with grease.
26   Install a new spindle pin seal with the metal backing facing up, toward the bushing. Carefully press the seal into position, taking care not to distort the casing.
27   Install a new thrust bearing with the lip

4.21 Marking the camber adjusting sleeve - 2WD models

flange facing down, toward the lower bushing. Press the bearing until it is firmly seated against the surface of the spindle.

28   Lightly coat the bushing surfaces with grease and position the spindle on the axle.

29   Install the spindle pin with the end stamped with a **T** toward the top and the notch in the pin aligned with the lock pin hole in the axle.

30   Drive the pin through the bushings and the axle from the top until the spindle pin notch and the axle lock pin hole are aligned.

31   Install the lock pin with the threads pointing forward and the wedge groove facing the spindle pin notch. Drive the lock pin into position and install the lock washer and nut. Tighten the nut to the torque listed in this Chapter's Specifications.

32   Install the spindle pin plugs in the threads at the top and bottom of the spindle. Tighten the plugs to the torque listed in this Chapter's Specifications.

33   Using multi-purpose grease, lubricate the spindle pin and bushings through both fittings until grease is seen seeping past the upper seal at the top and from the thrust bearing slip joint at the bottom. If grease does not appear, recheck the installation procedure. **Caution:** *Lack of proper lubrication will result in rapid failure of the spindle components.*

Early model axles (balljoints integral to I-beam)

34   Before installing the spindle, make sure the upper and lower balljoint rubber seals are in place.

35   Place the spindle over the balljoints.

36   Install the nut on the lower balljoint stud and partially tighten it to about 30 ft-lbs. **Note:** *The lower nut must be installed first.*

37   Position and align the camber adjuster in the spindle over the upper balljoint stud. Install the nut on the upper balljoint and tighten it to the torque listed in this Chapter's Specifications. Hold the camber adapter with a wrench to keep the ballstud from turning. Continue tightening the castle nut until the cotter pin can be inserted through the hole in the stud.

38   Tighten the lower nut to the torque listed in this Chapter's Specifications, then advance the castle nut until the cotter pin can be inserted through the hole in the stud.

Later model axles (balljoints integral with spindle)

39   Install the spindle balljoint studs into the I-beam.

40   Install the lower balljoint stud nut and tighten it to 95 to 110 ft lbs. After this initial torque, continue tightening the nut until the nearest cotter pin hole aligns with the nut, then install the pin.

41   Install the camber/caster adjuster over the balljoint stud and into the I-beam axle until it bottoms out. Re-align the orientation marks for proper alignment.

42   Install the upper balljoint pinch bolt and nut. Tighten the nut to the torque listed in this Chapter's Specifications.

5.8 Marking the camber adjusting sleeve - 4WD models

All models

43   Install the brake dust shield.

44   If the bearings and seal were removed, repack the bearings and install a new seal (see Chapter 1).

45   Install the front hub/disc and adjust the front wheel bearing assembly (see Chapter 1).

46   Install the brake caliper (see Chapter 9).

47   Connect the tie-rod end to the spindle and tighten the nut to the torque listed in this Chapter's Specifications, then advance the castle nut as required for installation of the cotter pin (see Section 10).

48   Install the wheel and lug nuts and lower the vehicle. Tighten the lug nuts to the torque listed in the Chapter 1 Specifications.

49   Drive the vehicle to an alignment shop and have the front end alignment checked, and if necessary, adjusted.

5   Front knuckle/spindle (4WD) - removal and installation

Refer to illustration 5.8

Balljoint models

Removal

1   Raise the front of the vehicle and place it securely on jackstands.

2   Remove the wheel (see Chapter 1).

3   Remove the brake caliper and ABS speed sensor connectors, if equipped (see Chapter 9). Support the caliper out of the way with wire. **Note:** *Do not disconnect the brake line from the caliper.*

4   Remove the front wheel drive hub locking mechanism and the disc/hub assembly (see Chapter 8).

5   Remove the spindle from the knuckle and remove the drive axle (see Chapter 8).

6   Remove the steering arm from the knuckle (see Section 10).

7   Remove the cotter pin from the upper balljoint and remove the upper stud nut. Loosen but do not remove the lower balljoint nut.

8   Mark the relationship of the camber/caster adjuster sleeve (if equipped) for re-

assembly reference **(see illustration)**.

9   Using a plastic mallet or equivalent, hit upper balljoint stud sharply downwards to free it from axle/monobeam. **Caution:** *If the lower balljoint stud nut is removed, the spindle will be free to fall and possibly injure you.* **Note:** *If the lower balljoint stud refuses to pop loose, hit the axle housing in the area of the stud to help free it.*

10   Remove the knuckle from the axle/monobeam assembly.

Installation

11   Install the upper and lower knuckle balljoint studs into the axle/monobeam.

12   If removed, install the camber/caster adjuster over the balljoint stud and into the I-beam axle until it bottoms out. Re-align the matchmarks for proper alignment.

13   Install the lower balljoint stud nut using Loctite 242 or equivalent, then tighten it to 35 to 40 ft-lbs.

14   Install a new upper balljoint stud nut and tighten it to 85 to 100 ft-lbs. After this initial torque, continue tightening the nut until the nearest cotter pin hole aligns with nut. Install a new cotter pin.

15   Tighten the lower balljoint stud nut to 95 to 110 ft lbs. **Caution:** *Failure to follow this procedure may result in excessive balljoint wear and steering effort.*

16   Install the axleshaft and spindle (see Chapter 8).

17   Install the hub/disc and locking hub mechanism (see Chapter 8).

18   Install the brake caliper (see Chapter 9).

19   Install the steering arm (see Section 20).

20   Install the wheel. Lower the vehicle and tighten the lug nuts to the torque listed in this Chapter's Specifications.

21   Have the front end alignment checked, and if necessary, adjusted.

Early model Monobeam models (kingpins)

Removal

22   Raise the front of the vehicle and place it securely on jackstands.

23   Remove the wheel and tire (see Chapter 1).

24   Remove the brake caliper (see Chapter 9) and support it out of the way with wire. **Note:** *Do not disconnect the brake line from caliper.*

25   Remove the front wheel drive hub locking mechanism and the disc/hub assembly (see Chapter 8).

26   Remove the spindle from the knuckle and remove the drive axle (see Chapter 8).

27   Remove the steering arm from the knuckle (see Section 10).

28   Alternately and evenly loosen the four bolts retaining the spindle cap (upper kingpin cap) to the knuckle and remove the cap, spring and retainer. **Warning:** *The cap is under spring pressure.*

29   Remove the four lower kingpin retainer bolts and remove the retainer/kingpin from the knuckle.

30   Remove the upper kingpin tapered bushing from the upper knuckle bore.

31   Remove the knuckle from the axle yoke.

32   If required for servicing, remove the upper kingpin and kingpin seal from the yoke with a 7/8-inch hex socket. **Note:** *The kingpin is tightened to 500 to 600 ft-lbs and will require a 3/4 or 1-inch drive breaker bar and cheater bar for sufficient leverage.* **Warning:** *If it is necessary to remove the kingpins, be extremely careful not to allow the vehicle to topple off the jackstands as they are loosened or tightened.*

33   If required for servicing, press the lower kingpin bearing, bearing cup and grease seals from the knuckle using a two-jaw puller.

Installation

34   If removed, install a new lower kingpin grease retainer cap into the knuckle, followed by a new bearing cup. Drive the bearing into the axle bore with an appropriate bearing driver.

35   If removed, pack the new lower kingpin bearing with high-temperature grease and install it into the lower bearing cup.

36   If removed, install a new lower kingpin seal with an appropriate seal driver.

37   If removed, install a new upper kingpin seal and kingpin onto the axle yoke. Tighten it to the torque listed in this Chapter's Specifications.

38   Install the knuckle onto the axle yoke and place the upper kingpin tapered bushing into the knuckle bore and over the upper kingpin.

39   Install the lower kingpin and retainer. Tighten the bolts to the torque listed in this Chapter's Specifications.

40   Install the upper spring retainer, spring, new gasket and spindle cap onto the knuckle, tightening the bolts alternately and evenly to compress the spring. Tighten the bolts to the torque listed in this Chapter's Specifications.

41   Grease the upper kingpin through the grease fitting.

42   Install the axleshaft and spindle (see Chapter 8).

43   Install the hub/disc and locking mechanism (see Chapter 8).

44   Install the brake caliper (see Chapter 9).

7.2a Remove the nut from the stud at the upper end of the shock absorber (arrow) (hidden from view in this photo) . . .

45   Install the steering arm (see Section 20).

46   Install the wheel.

47   Lower the vehicle and tighten the lug nuts to the torque listed in the Chapter 1 Specifications.

48   Have the front end alignment checked, and if necessary, adjusted.

6   Balljoints - replacement

Note: *This procedure requires the use of a balljoint removal/installation tool.*

Early model axles (balljoints integral to I-beam)

1   Remove the spindle (see Section 4).

2   Remove the snap-ring from both balljoints, using snap-ring pliers.

3   Using a balljoint removal tool, install the press and receiver cup over the upper balljoint and turn the forcing screw on the press clockwise until the balljoint is removed from the axle. **Note:** *Always remove the upper balljoint first.*

4   Repeat the procedure on the lower balljoint.

5   **Caution:** *Do not heat the axle to aid in removal - it will remove the temper from the axle.*

6   To install the lower balljoint, assemble the balljoint press and the appropriate adapters over the new balljoint and turn the forcing screw on the clamp until the balljoint is seated. Install the snap-ring. **Note:** *Always install the lower balljoint first.*

7   Repeat the procedure on the upper balljoint. Install the snap-ring.

8   **Caution:** *Do not heat the axle to aid in installation.*

9   Reinstall the spindle (see Section 4).

Late model axles (balljoints integral to spindle/knuckle)

10   Remove the spindle (2WD) or the spindle/knuckle (4WD) (see Section 4 or 5).

11   Place the spindle/knuckle securely in a vise.

7.2b . . . then remove the lower shock absorber mounting nut

12   Remove the lower balljoint snap ring from the spindle/knuckle.

13   Using a balljoint press and the appropriate adapters, press out the lower balljoint. **Note:** *The lower balljoint must be removed first and installed last.*

14   Repeat the procedure on the upper balljoint.

15   Install the new upper balljoint into the spindle/knuckle using the press and the appropriate adapters.

16   Repeat the procedure on the lower balljoint.

17   Install lower balljoint snap-ring.

18   Reinstall the spindle (2WD) or the spindle/knuckle (4WD) (see Section 4 or 5).

7   Front shock absorbers - removal, inspection and installation

Refer to illustrations 7.2a and 7.2b

Removal

1   Block the rear wheels, apply the parking brake, loosen the front wheel lugs nuts, raise the front of the vehicle and support it securely on jackstands. Remove the wheel.

2   On coil spring models, remove the nut and washer from the top end of the shock absorber **(see illustrations)**. If necessary, use a backup wrench on the hex provided on the lower part of the stud mount. On later leaf spring models, simply remove the upper shock mount bolt and nut.

3   Remove the nut and bolt securing the bottom end of the shock absorber to the lower bracket (coil spring) or spacer plate (leaf spring). Remove the shock absorber and insulators.

Inspection

4   Remove and examine the shock absorber for signs of damage to the body, distorted piston rod, loose mounting or hydraulic fluid leakage which, if evident, means a new unit should be installed. Inspect the upper frame mounted shock insulators on coil spring models for signs of wear. Replace if required.

9.7 Radius arm-to-frame nut

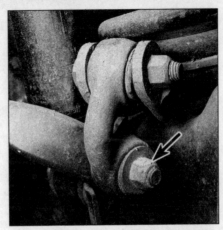

10.2 Remove this nut and bolt (arrow) from each side of the stabilizer bar (some models use a link nut, similar to the one shown in illustration) . . .

10.3 . . . then support the stabilizer bar and remove the nuts (arrows) from the two stabilizer bar brackets

5   To test for shock absorber efficiency, hold the unit in a vertical position. Completely extend the piston rod and then invert the unit and completely compress it. Perform this sequence several times to work out any trapped air bubbles. Mount the bottom end of the shock absorber in a soft-jawed vise. Grasp the upper rod of the shock absorber, extend it fully and then contract it fully as rapidly as possible. The resistance should be smooth and uniform throughout the entire stroke in both directions. The resistance should be greater during the extension stroke than during the compression stroke. If there is erratic or notchy resistance during either stroke, or if the resistance is the same (or less) during the extension stroke, the shock absorbers should be replaced. The shock absorbers on each axle should have identical action and shock absorbers should always be replaced in pairs (on the same axle).

Installation

6   Installation is the reverse of removal. If old shock absorbers are being reinstalled (after being checked for correct operating action), the bushings should be replaced if there are any signs of deterioration or wear. New shock absorbers always come equipped with new bushings. When installing new bushings, never compress them beyond the diameter of the steel washers retaining them.

8   Steering damper - removal and installation

1   The steering damper is attached to the steering linkage on some 4-wheel-drive models. It is a specially calibrated shock absorber mounted horizontally and fastened to the frame on one end and the steering cross linkage on the other end.
2   The removal and installation procedure is the same as for a shock absorber with the exception of the location. When testing the damper, it should have the same resistance to compression as it does to extension. All other test and inspection procedures are the same as for a normal suspension shock absorber.

Replace any worn or deteriorated grommets and tighten all mounting nuts and bolts securely.

9   Radius arm - removal and installation

Refer to illustration 9.7

Removal

1   Raise the front of the vehicle and support it securely on jackstands.
2   Place a jack beneath the outer end of the axle and remove the wheel.
3   Disconnect the lower end of the shock absorber (see Section 7). Detach the front stabilizer bar (if equipped) at the link (see Section 10).
4   Remove the coil spring (see Section 2). Remove the lower spring seat from the radius arm.
5   On 2WD models, remove the nut and long bolt securing the front of the radius arm to the axle.
6   On 4WD models, remove the two self-tapping screws that retain the front axle-to-radius arm bracket to the axle tube and then remove the lower bolt and upper stud retaining the radius arm to the axle **(see illustration 1.4)**. **Note:** *Do not disturb the caster adjuster cam retaining screw on vehicles so equipped.*
7   Remove the nut, washer, heat shield (if equipped), rubber insulator and spacer (if equipped) from the rear end of the radius arm **(see illustration)**.
8   Push the front of the radius arm away from the front axle and withdraw it from the rear support bracket.
10   Remove the front retainer and rubber insulator from the rear of the radius arm and retrieve any shims that may be present.

Installation

11   Install the radius arm by reversing the procedure, ensuring that the rubber insulators are in good condition and installed in the cor-

rect order. Replace worn insulators if required. **Note:** *On 4WD models, a new stud and bolt are required because of the adhesive coating on the original part. If new fasteners are not available, thoroughly clean the old parts and apply Loctite No. 242 (or equivalent) to the threads of the fasteners.* **Caution:** *It is important that the shock absorber-to-lower bracket retaining bolt is installed with the bolt head toward the tire to maximize clearance to the brake system components.*
12   Have the front wheel alignment checked and, if necessary, adjusted.

10   Front stabilizer bar - removal and installation

Refer to illustrations 10.2 and 10.3

1   Raise the front of the vehicle and place it securely on jackstands.
2   Disconnect the right and left ends of the stabilizer bar from the link assembly attached to the axle beam bracket **(see illustration)**.
3   Disconnect the stabilizer bar bracket bolts and remove the stabilizer bar **(see illustration)**.
4   Check the bracket bushings and linkage bushings for wear, cracking and other signs of deterioration. Replace parts as necessary.
5   To install the bar, loosely assemble all stabilizer bar components, with both link assemblies outboard of the stabilizer bar. **Note:** *To help identify the left and right link assemblies, an R or L is stamped on the shaft of the link.* Force the stabilizer bar to the rear to connect the bar ends to the link assemblies.
6   Tighten the nuts and bolts retaining the link assemblies to the stabilizer bar and axle brackets.
7   Check to be sure the insulators are seated in the retainers and that the stabilizer bar is centered in the assembly.
8   Tighten the stabilizer bar bracket fasteners securely.
9   Remove the jackstands and lower the vehicle.

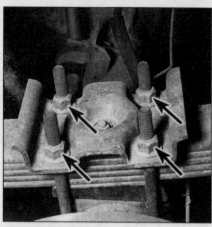

12.3　Remove the four U-bolt nuts (arrows)

12.5　Remove the nut and drive the spring hanger bolt out of the spring and bracket

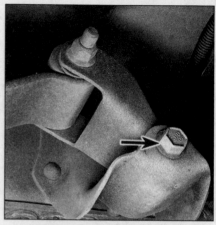

12.6　Remove the spring shackle bolt (arrow)

11　Front I-beam axle - removal, bushing replacement and installation

Note: The following procedure is for 2WD models. The procedure for 4WD model front axle removal and installation is described in Chapter 8.

Removal

1　Raise the vehicle and support the frame securely on jackstands.
2　Remove the front wheel spindle from the axle (see Section 4). **Note:** *If only the pivot bushing is to be replaced, it can be done with the I-beam still attached to the vehicle with the proper tool, and therefore removal of the spindle is not required.*
3　Remove the front spring (see Section 2).
4　Remove the stabilizer bar (if equipped) (see Section 10).
5　Remove the lower spring seat from the radius arm and remove the nut and long bolt securing the front of the radius arm to the axle. **Note:** *If only the pivot bushing is to be replaced, it can be done with the I-beam still attached to the vehicle with the proper tool, and therefore removal of the radius arm is not required.*
6　Remove the nut and bolt securing the end of the axle to the pivot bracket. If total removal is required, withdraw the axle from beneath the vehicle. If only the pivot bushing is to be replaced, simply pull the pivot end of the axle down until the bushing is exposed.

Bushing replacement

7　Examine the bushings and pivot bolt for wear and replace if required. The bushing can be removed using forcing screw, bushing remover and cup. As an alternative to these tools, two appropriately sized sockets and a long bolt and nut can be used. After pressing the old bushing out, press the new bushing into the I-beam leaving 0.210 to 0.290-inch gap between shoulder of bushing and face of the I-beam. **Note:** *Do not use grease on the bushing to aid in installation.*

Installation

8　Install the axle by reversing the removal procedure. Don't tighten the fasteners completely yet. The remainder of installation is the reverse of removal.
9　Lower the vehicle. Tighten the nuts to the torque listed in this Chapter's Specifications.
10　Have the front end alignment checked, and if necessary, adjusted.

12　Rear leaf spring - removal and installation

Refer to illustrations 12.3, 12.5 and 12.6

Removal

1　Raise the vehicle until the weight is off the rear spring being worked on, but the tire is still touching the ground.
2　Place the frame securely on jackstands.
3　Remove the nuts from the spring U-bolts and drive the U-bolts from the U-bolt plate **(see illustration)**.
4　If so equipped, remove the auxiliary spring and spacer. On 4WD models, remove the ride height spacer between spring and axle. **Note:** *Take note of the orientation of the wedged-shaped spacer for proper reinstallation (Bronco models only).*
5　Remove the spring-to-bracket nut at the front of the spring and drive the bolt out of the spring eye bushing **(see illustration)**. If the bolt is to be reused, use a soft brass drift so that the bolt is not damaged.
6　Remove the spring shackle bolt, holding the nut on the other side with a back-up wrench **(see illustration)**.
7　Remove the spring and shackle assembly from the rear shackle bracket.
8　Remove the spring from under the vehicle.
9　If the spring eye bushings are worn or damaged, they must be replaced by an automotive repair shop with the necessary hydraulic press and associated tools.

Installation

10　To install the spring, position the rear of the spring in the shackle and install the upper shackle-to-spring bolt and nut with the bolt head facing out. Finger tighten the nut. On 4WD models, install ride height spacers between spring and axle. **Note:** *On Bronco models, the sharper edge portion of the wedge must face forward.*
11　Position the front of the spring in the bracket and install the bolt and nut. Finger tighten the nut.
12　Position the shackle in the rear bracket and install the bolt and nut.
13　Position the spring on top of the axle with the spring tie bolt centered in the hole in the seat.
14　If so equipped, install the auxiliary spring and spacer.
15　Install the spring U-bolts, U-bolt plate and nuts, Finger tighten the nuts.
16　Lower the vehicle to the ground, then, in order, tighten the U-bolt nuts, the front spring nut and bolt and the rear shackle bolts and nuts to the torque listed in this Chapter's Specifications.

13　Rear shock absorbers - removal, inspection and installation

Refer to illustrations 13.2 and 13.3

1　Block the front wheels. Raise the rear of the vehicle and support it securely on jackstands. Support the axle with a floor jack near the shock absorber to be removed.
2　Remove the shock absorber lower attaching nut and pull it free of the mounting bracket **(see illustration)**.
3　Remove the securing nut from the upper mounting stud **(see illustration)** and withdraw the shock absorber from the vehicle.
4　Inspection of the rear shock absorber is similar to that for the front shock absorber (see Section 7).
5　Installation of the rear shock absorber is the reverse of removal.

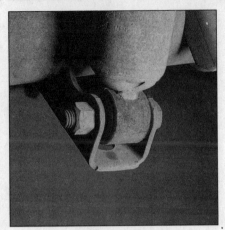

13.2 Remove this lower nut . . .

13.3 . . . and this upper nut, then remove the shock absorber

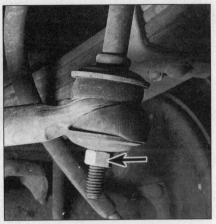

14.2 Remove the two stabilizer bar link nuts (arrow)

14   Rear stabilizer bar - removal and installation

Refer to illustrations 14.2 and 14.6

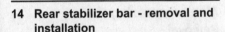

1   Raise the rear of the vehicle and place it securely on jackstands.

2   Remove the nut from the lower end of the stabilizer bar link **(see illustration)**.

3   Remove the outer washer and insulator.

4   Disconnect the stabilizer bar from the link.

5   Remove the inner insulators and washers and disconnect the link from the frame by removing the retaining nuts and bolts.

6   Remove the nuts which attach the retainer and bracket to the U-bolt **(see illustration)**, then remove the U-bolt and stabilizer bar.

7   Installation is the reverse of the removal procedure. Tighten the nuts and bolts securely.

15   Steering system - general information

The manual steering gear for all vehicles covered by this manual is a recirculating ball-nut type, with the steering shaft, worm shaft and ball nut all in line.

The steering shaft and worm shaft are separated by a flexible coupling which permits removal of the gearbox assembly or steering shaft (with column) independent of one another.

The mechanical element of the steering gearbox is a low-friction, high-efficiency, recirculating ball system in which steel balls act as a rolling thread between the steering worm and ball nut. The one-piece ball nut is geared to the sector shaft and the lash between the sector shaft and rack of the ball nut is controlled by an adjusting screw through the sector cover which is retained in the end of the sector shaft.

The power steering system installed in all vehicles with which this manual is concerned employs a Ford Coil pump, which is a belt-driven slipper type with a fiberglass

nylon reservoir attached to the rear side of the pump housing front plate. The pump body is encased within the housing and reservoir. The pressure hose is attached with a quick-connect fitting, located below the filler neck at the outboard side of the reservoir, which allows the line to swivel. This is normal and does not indicate a loose fitting.

The pump supplies fluid under pressure to an integral power steering gearbox of the torsion-bar feedback type. This gearbox is designed with a one-piece rack piston, with the worm and sector shaft in one housing and the rotary valve assembly in an attached housing. This makes possible internal fluid passages between the valve and the power cylinder, eliminating all external hoses except the pressure and return lines between the pump and the gearbox.

Due to the complexity of the power steering system and the special tools required to work on its components, servicing and adjustments described here are limited to those operations that can readily be performed by the home mechanic. Any other work should be referred to a dealership or other reputable automotive repair shop specializing in this type of work.

14.6 The stabilizer bar is attached to the rear axle by two brackets and U-bolts like this

16   Steering gearbox - check and adjustment

Refer to illustrations 16.4, 16.12 and 16.27

1   Check the reservoir fluid level (if so equipped).

2   Check the steering linkage for wear if there is looseness present in the steering.

3   If the looseness is traceable to wear in the steering box, check and adjust it as follows:

Manual steering

4   Remove the Pitman arm from the steering gear sector shaft using an appropriate puller **(see illustration)**. **Caution:** *Do not hammer on the end of the sector shaft.*

5   Lubricate the worm shaft seal with a drop of power steering fluid.

6   Remove the horn pad to gain access to the steering wheel retaining nut (see Section 21).

7   Be sure the steering column is properly aligned, so that no resistance to turning is induced by column binding.

8   Turn the steering wheel all the way to one side.

16.4 Use a puller like this to remove the Pitman arm

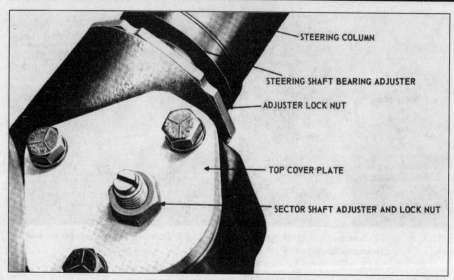

16.12 Manual steering gear details

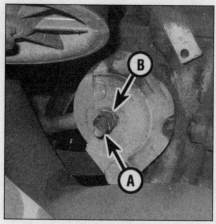

16.27 Power steering gear sector shaft adjusting screw (A) and locknut (B)

9   Place an inch-pound torque wrench on the steering wheel nut and measure the lowest torque required to turn the wheel at a constant rate. This is the worm bearing preload.
10   Check that the torque is within the range listed in this Chapter's Specifications. If not, remove the steering gear from the vehicle (see Section 17).
11   Be sure that the sector cover bolts are tightened to the torque listed in this Chapter's Specifications.
12   Loosen the preload adjuster locknut and tighten the worm bearing adjuster nut until all endplay has been removed **(see illustration)**.
13   Using an 11/16-inch socket and an inch-pound torque wrench, carefully turn the worm shaft all the way to the right and then turn it back about one-half turn.
14   Tighten the adjuster nut until the specified worm bearing preload is obtained:
15   Tighten the adjuster nut locknut to the torque listed in this Chapter's Specifications.
16   Rotate the worm shaft from stop-to-stop, counting the total number of turns, then turn the shaft back half way, placing the gear on center.
17   Loosen the sector shaft adjuster locknut by turning it in a counterclockwise direction.
18   Turn the sector shaft adjuster screw clockwise to remove all lash between the ball nut and the sector teeth, then tighten the sector shaft locknut to the torque listed in this Chapter's Specifications.
19   Using an 11/16-inch, 12 point socket and an inch-pound torque wrench, observe the highest reading while the gear is turned through the center position. This is the backlash measurement.
20   Check that the backlash is within the range listed in this Chapter's Specifications.
21   If necessary, repeat Steps 17 through 19 until the proper backlash is obtained.
22   Reinstall the steering gear.
23   Reinstall the Pitman arm and tighten the retaining nut to the torque listed in this Chapter's Specifications.

Power steering

24   Remove the Pitman arm **(see illustration 16.4)** and remove the horn pad to gain access to the steering wheel retaining nut (see Section 21). Disconnect and plug the fluid return line at the reservoir.
25   Place the fluid return line in a suitable container and turn the steering wheel lock-to-lock several times to discharge all of the fluid from the steering gear.
26   Turn the shaft back 45-degrees from the left stop and attach a torque wrench calibrated in inch-pounds to the steering wheel nut.
27   Rotate the steering gear about one-eighth of a turn and then move it back across the center position several times. Loosen the adjuster locknut and turn the adjuster screw until the specified torque reading is reached when the steering gear is rotated through the over-center position **(see illustration)**.
28   Hold the screw and tighten the nut.
29   Install the Pitman arm and steering wheel center cover. Reconnect the fluid return line and refill the reservoir. Be sure the Pitman arm retaining nut is tightened to the torque listed in this Chapter's Specifications.

17   Steering gearbox - removal and installation

Refer to illustration 17.27
Warning: *On models equipped with airbags, make sure the steering shaft is not turned while the steering gear or box is removed or you could damage the airbag system. To prevent the shaft from turning, turn the ignition key to the lock position before beginning work or run the seat belt through the steering wheel and clip the seat belt into place. Due to possible damage to the airbag system, we recommend only experienced mechanics attempt this procedure.*

Manual steering
Removal

1   Raise the front of the vehicle and place it securely on jackstands.
2   Disengage the flex coupling shield from the steering gear input shaft shield and slide it up the intermediate shaft.
3   Disconnect the flex coupling from the intermediate steering shaft flange by removing the attaching bolts.
4   Using an appropriate tie-rod end remover, disconnect the drag link from the Pitman arm.
5   Remove the Pitman arm-to-sector shaft attaching nut and washer.
6   Using an appropriate puller, remove the Pitman arm from the steering gear sector shaft. **Caution:** *Do not hammer on the end of the sector shaft or on the tool*
7   While supporting the steering gear, remove the bolts and washers that attach the steering gear to the frame rail.
8   Lower the steering gear assembly out of the vehicle.
9   Remove the coupling-to-gear attaching bolt from the lower half of the flex coupling and remove the coupling from the assembly.

Installation

10   To install the gearbox, position the flex coupling on the input shaft of the steering gear. **Note:** *Be sure to use a new coupling-to-gear attaching bolt and tighten it to the torque listed in this Chapter's Specifications.*
11   Center the input shaft (the center position is approximately three turns from either stop).
12   Position the steering gear assembly so that the stud bolts on the flex coupling enter the bolt holes in the steering shaft flange and the holes in the mounting bosses of the gearbox match the bolt holes in the frame rail.
13   While supporting the gearbox in the proper position, install the gearbox-to-frame rail attaching bolts and washers and tighten the bolts to the torque listed in this Chapter's Specifications. **Note:** *If new bolts and washers are required, be sure that they are Grade 9.*
14   Connect the drag link to the Pitman arm,

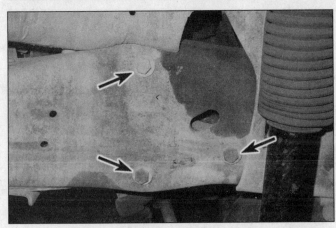

17.27 Steering gear mounting bolts

19.9 This special tool, designed for removing power steering pulleys, is available at tool stores and some auto parts stores

install the drag link ball stud nut and tighten the nut to the torque listed in this Chapter's Specifications. Install a new cotter pin.
15   Place the Pitman arm on the sector shaft, pointing down. Install the attaching nut and washer and tighten the nut to the torque listed in this Chapter's Specifications.
16   Attach the flex coupling to the steering shaft flange with the two attaching nuts and tighten the nuts to the torque listed in this Chapter's Specifications.
17   Snap the flex coupling shield to the steering gear input shaft shield.
18   Remove the jackstands and lower the vehicle.

Power steering

Removal

19   Place a drain pan under the steering gearbox.
20   Disconnect the pressure and return lines from the gearbox and plug the lines and the ports in the gearbox to prevent contamination.
21   Disengage the flex coupling shield from the splash shield.
22   Disconnect the flex coupling at the steering gearbox by removing the retaining bolt.
23   Raise the front of the vehicle and place it securely on jackstands.
24   Using an appropriate tie-rod end remover, disconnect the tie-rod from the Pitman arm.
25   Remove the nut and washer attaching the Pitman arm to the sector shaft.
26   Using an appropriate puller, remove the Pitman arm from the sector shaft **(see illustration 16.4)**. **Caution:** *Be very careful not to damage the seals.*
27   Support the steering gearbox and remove the steering gearbox-to-frame rail attaching bolts **(see illustration)**.
28   Work the steering gearbox free of the flex coupling and remove the steering gearbox from the vehicle.
29   Remove the splash shield from the retaining lugs on the steering gearbox.

Installation
30   To install the gearbox, position the splash shield over the gearbox lugs.
31   Turn the steering wheel so that the spokes are in the horizontal position.
32   Slide the flex coupling into position on the steering shaft assembly.
33   Center the steering gear input shaft with the index flat facing down (the center position is approximately three turns from either stop).
34   Slide the steering gear input shaft into the flex coupling and the gearbox into place on the frame rail.
35   Install the flex coupling attaching bolt and tighten it to the torque listed in this Chapter's Specifications.
36   Install the gearbox-to-frame rail attaching bolts and tighten them to the torque listed in this Chapter's Specifications.
37   Be sure that the wheels are in the straight ahead position, then install the Pitman arm on the sector shaft.
38   Install the Pitman arm attaching washer and nut and tighten the nut to the torque listed in this Chapter's Specifications.
39   Attach the drag link to the Pitman arm, install the retaining nut and tighten it to the torque listed in this Chapter's Specifications. Install a new cotter pin.
40   Remove the jackstands and lower the vehicle.
41   Install and tighten the pressure and return lines. Be sure you have removed the plugs from the lines and ports.
42   Snap the flex coupling shield over the hose fittings and the splash shield.
43   Disconnect the coil wire from the distributor.
44   Fill the power steering fluid reservoir, then crank the engine and turn the steering wheel from lock-to-lock to distribute the fluid.
45   Recheck the fluid level and add more if necessary.
46   Connect the coil wire, start the engine and turn the steering wheel from side-to-side.
47   Inspect for leaks.

18   Power steering system - bleeding

1   If bubbles are visible in the power steering fluid, the air in the system should be bled off.
2   Fill the reservoir (see Chapter 1).
3   Run the engine until the fluid reaches normal operating temperature (165 to 175-degrees F).
4   Turn the steering wheel lock-to-lock several times. **Note:** *Do not hold the wheel all the way to the left or right for more than five seconds or you may damage the pump.*
5   Recheck the fluid level and add more as necessary.

19   Power steering pump - removal and installation

Refer to illustrations 19.9 and 19.12

Removal
1   Remove the power steering fluid from the pump reservoir by disconnecting the fluid return hose at the reservoir and draining the fluid into a suitable container.
2   Disconnect the pressure hose from the pump.
3   Remove the bolts from the pump adjustment bracket.
4   On early models, loosen the pump enough to allow removal of the belt from the pulley. On later models with an auto tensioner, place a 5/8-inch wrench on the tensioner pulley bolt and rotate against spring tension enough to loosen and remove belt.
5   Remove the pump (still attached to the adjustment bracket) from the support bracket and from the vehicle.
6   If the pulley and adjustment bracket are to be removed from the pump, follow Steps 7 through 14.
7   Drain as much fluid as possible from the pump through the filler pipe.
8   Place the pump in a bench vise.
9   Install a pulley removal tool **(see illustration)**.

19.12 This special tool, designed for installing the power steering pulley, is available at tool stores and some auto parts stores

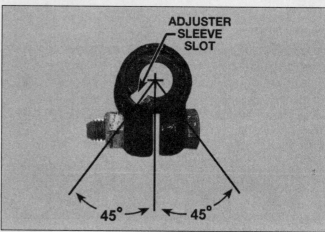

20.6 Position the steering linkage clamps within a limit of 45-degrees as shown - the threaded portion of the bolts on the right (passenger's) side must face the rear, and the threaded portion of the bolts on the left (driver's) side must face the front of the vehicle

10   Rotate the tool bolt counterclockwise to remove the pulley, then remove the bolts attaching the adjustment bracket to the pump and remove the bracket.

Installation

11   To install the pump, place the adjustment bracket on the pump and install and tighten the retaining bolts to the torque listed in this Chapter's Specifications.

12   Thread a pulley installation into the steering pump shaft **(see illustration)**.

13   Rotate the tool nut clockwise to install the pulley on the shaft. **Caution:** *Do not apply in-and-out pressure on the shaft as such pressure will damage the internal pump components. When properly installed, the pulley hub face must be flush within plus or minus 0.010 inch of the end of the pump shaft.*

14   Place the pump with the attached pulley and adjustment bracket on the support bracket.

15   Install the bolts connecting the support bracket to the adjustment bracket and tighten

them securely.

16   Place the belt on the pulley and adjust the belt tension as described in Chapter 1. **Note:** *Do not pry against the reservoir. Pressure on the fiberglass reservoir will cause it to crack.*

17   Attach the pressure hose to the pump fitting.

18   Connect the return hose to the pump and tighten the clamp.

19   Fill the reservoir and bleed the system (see Section 18).

20   Check for leaks and recheck the fluid level, adding fluid if necessary.

20   Steering linkage - removal and installation

Refer to illustration 20.6

Warning: *All fasteners in the steering system are important as they could affect the safety of the system. They must be replaced with*

fasteners of the same part number if replacement is necessary. Never substitute with a replacement part of lesser quality.

Removal

1   Steering linkages for these vehicles come in many configurations and combinations, depending on driveaxle, suspension type and load carrying capabilities. They are all of a common type and consist of a connecting link with either two ball-type links on either end or one ball-type link and a male or female thread.

2   If a linkage is bent or if the balljoint end is excessively worn, it must be replaced.

3   Any balljoint end can be removed after the cotter pin and retaining nut are first withdrawn. A "pickle fork" designed for this job is the quickest and easiest method for removing this type of connection. However, the rubber dust seat is usually damaged with this type of tool and the seal should be replaced (even if the joint is being reused). A balljoint end can also be removed with a puller. Use

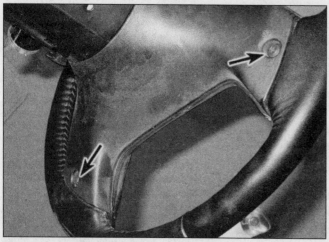

21.3 Horn pad mounting screws (typical)

21.4 If equipped, disconnect the cruise-control system ground terminal with needle-nose pliers

21.5 Disconnect the horn wiring

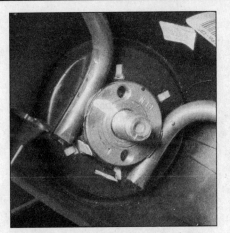

21.7 Remove the steering wheel nut, then mark the relationship of the steering wheel to the shaft

21.8 Use a puller to remove the steering wheel from the steering shaft - DON'T beat on the shaft

the jaws of the puller to grasp the housing of the component (Pitman arm, sector shaft, spindle arm, etc.). Situate the point of the screw on the center of the balljoint bolt. Tighten the puller to put tension on it and lightly tap the housing with a brass hammer to help break the joint free. Be careful not to damage either the joint or the housing.

4   If the threaded end of a linkage component is being removed, first mark the component so that the threads can be reinserted to the same exact depth. The vehicle will still need an alignment, but the setting will be close to original so the vehicle can be driven to the alignment facility.

5   Unscrew the component after releasing the bolts and nuts of the clamps.

Installation

6   Install the new component to a depth matching the original part and install a retaining nut and new cotter pin. Tighten the bolts and nuts on any clamps to the torque listed in this Chapter's Specifications and have the vehicle's front end alignment checked. Align the clamps as shown **(see illustration)**.

21   Steering wheel - removal and installation

Refer to illustrations 21.3, 21.4, 21.5, 21.7 and 21.8

Warning: *Some later models are equipped with airbags. If your vehicle is equipped with an airbag, DO NOT attempt to remove the steering wheel. Have the procedure performed by a dealer service department or other qualified repair shop.*

1   Park the vehicle with the front wheels in the straight ahead position.

2   Disconnect the cable from the negative battery terminal.

3   Remove one screw from the underside of each steering wheel spoke and lift the horn switch assembly (steering wheel pad) off the steering wheel to gain access to the wires beneath **(see illustration)**. Do not remove the horn assembly at this time.

4   On models with cruise control, pinch the

J-clip ground wire terminal firmly and pull it out of the hole in the steering wheel **(see illustration)**. **Note:** *Do not pull the ground terminal out of the threaded hole without pinching the terminal clip to relieve the spring retention of the terminal in the threaded hole.*

5   Disconnect the horn switch wiring **(see illustration)**.

6   Remove the horn switch assembly.

7   Remove the steering wheel retaining nut **(see illustration)**. Mark the relationship of the steering wheel to the shaft to ensure correct positioning of the steering wheel upon installation.

8   Using a steering wheel puller, remove the steering wheel **(see illustration)**. **Caution:** *Do not beat on the shaft in an attempt to remove the wheel.*

9   Installation is the reverse of the removal procedure. When attaching the steering wheel to the steering column shaft, place it on the shaft so that the mark and the flat on the wheel are in line with the mark and the flat on the shaft. Tighten the steering wheel retaining nut to the torque listed in this Chapter's Specifications.

22   Wheel alignment - general information

Refer to illustration 22.1

Note: *Since wheel alignment is generally out of the reach of the home mechanic, this section is intended only to familiarize the reader with the basic terms used and procedures followed during a typical wheel alignment job. In the event that your vehicle needs a wheel alignment check or adjustment, we recommend that the work be done by a reputable wheel alignment shop.*

1   The three basic adjustments made when aligning a vehicle's front end are toe-in, caster and camber **(see illustration)**.

2   Toe-in is the amount the front wheels are angled in relationship to the centerline of the vehicle. For example, in a vehicle with zero toe-in, the distance measured between

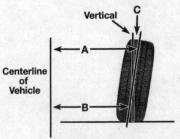

CAMBER ANGLE (FRONT VIEW)

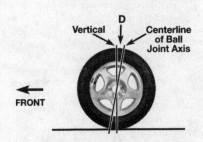

CASTER ANGLE (SIDE VIEW)

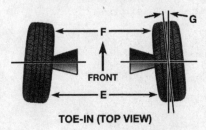

TOE-IN (TOP VIEW)

22.1 Typical alignment details

A minus B = C (degrees camber)
D = caster (measured in degrees)
E minus F = toe-in (measured in inches)
G = toe-in (expressed in degrees)

the front edges of the wheels is the same as the distance measured between the rear edges of the wheels. The wheels are running parallel with the centerline of the vehicle. Toe-in is adjusted by lengthening or shortening the tie-rods. Incorrect toe-in will cause tires to wear improperly by making them "scrub" against the road surface.

3　Camber and caster are the angles at which the wheel and suspension upright are inclined to the vertical. Camber is the angle of the wheel in the lateral (side-to-side) plane, while caster is the angle of the wheel and upright in the longitudinal (fore-and-aft) plane. Camber angle affects the amount of tire tread which contacts the road and compensates for change in the suspension geometry when the vehicle is traveling around curves or over an undulating surface. Caster angle affects the self-centering action of the steering, which governs straight-line stability.

4　Some vehicles covered in this manual have caster and camber angles designed into the front suspension and no provision is available to change them. On other vehicles, provision is made for camber adjustment, but not for caster adjustment. Still others have provisions for adjustment to both caster and camber. For those vehicles with no provision for these adjustments, in extreme cases, certain components may be bent by a shop with the proper equipment in order to correct the caster and camber. In all cases, however, steering alignment work should always be performed by a facility with the proper equipment and experienced personnel.

Chapter 11 Body

Contents

Specifications

Torque specifications

Ft lbs (unless otherwise indicated)

Note: *One foot-pound (ft-lb) of torque is equivalent to 12 inch-pounds (in-lbs) of torque. Torque values below approximately 15 ft-lbs are expressed in inch-pounds, since most foot-pound torque wrenches are not accurate at these smaller values.*

Door hinge to pillar	17 to 25
Fiberglass roof to body (long screws) (Bronco)	84 to 120 in-lbs
Fiberglass roof to body (short screws) (Bronco)	13 to 20
Front bumper to frame	65 to 87
Hood hinge to fender	13 to 19
Hood hinge to hood	13 to 19
Hood latch to radiator support	84 to 120 in-lbs
Hood link assembly to fender	13 to 19
Hood link assembly to hood	13 to 19
Rear bumper to bumper bracket (inner)	72 to 105
Rear bumper to bumper bracket (outer)	16 to 21
Rear bumper to bumper bracket (Styleside)	72 to 98
Striker to post	24 to 32
Tailgate support straps	20 to 30
Tailgate torsion bar (Bronco)	20 to 30

1 General information

The covered pick-ups are built with body-on-separate frame construction. The frame is ladder-type, consisting of two C-section steel side rails joined by a variable number of cross-members. All crossmembers are riveted, with the exception of the one under the transmission, which is bolted in to facilitate transmission removal and installation. The number of crossmembers in the frame depends on the vehicle wheelbase and load rating.

Pick-up body styles available range from standard cabs to super cabs and crew cab models. All cabs are of single welded unit construction. The cabs are bolted to the frame and use rubber mounts for noise and vibration isolation.

Front fenders, hood, inner fender panels and grills are bolted to the cab and the radiator support at the front of the vehicle. The radiator support is attached to the front frame rails and insulated with rubber 'donuts'. Bolts retain the support.

Bumpers are bolted to the frame horns at the front and to the frame rails at the rear via mounting brackets. Doors, seats, and dashboard are all bolted to the cab and are individually replaceable.

2   Body - maintenance

1   The condition of your vehicle's body is very important, because it determines the secondhand value. It is much more difficult to repair a neglected or damaged body than it is to repair mechanical components. The hidden areas of the body, such as the fender wells, the frame, and the engine compartment, are equally important, although obviously not requiring as frequent attention as the rest of the body.

2   Once a year, or every 12,000 miles, it is a good idea to have the underside of the body and the frame steam cleaned. All traces of dirt and oil will be removed and the underside can then be inspected carefully for rust, damaged brake lines, frayed electrical wiring, damaged cables, and other problems. The suspension components should be greased upon completion of this job.

3   At the same time, clean the engine and the engine compartment using either a steam cleaner or a water soluble degreaser.

4   The fender wells should be given extra attention, as undercoating can peel away and stones and dirt thrown up by the tires can cause the paint to chip and flake, allowing rust to set in. If rust is found, clean down to the bare metal and apply an anti-rust paint.

5   The body should be washed once a week (or when dirty). Thoroughly wet the vehicle to soften the dirt, then wash it down with a soft sponge and plenty of clean soapy water. If the surplus dirt is not washed off very carefully, it will in time wear down the paint.

6   Spots of tar or asphalt coating thrown from the road surfaces should be removed with a cloth soaked in solvent.

7   Once every six months, give the body and chrome trim a thorough wax job. If a chrome cleaner is used to remove rust on any of the vehicle's plated parts, remember that the cleaner also removes part of the chrome, so use it sparingly.

3   Vinyl trim - maintenance

1   Don't clean vinyl trim with detergents, caustic soap or petroleum based cleaners. Plain soap and water works just fine, with a soft brush to clean dirt that may be ingrained. Wash the vinyl as frequently as the rest of the vehicle.

2   After cleaning, application of a high quality rubber and vinyl protection will help prevent oxidation and cracks. The protection can also be applied to weather-stripping, vacuum lines and rubber hoses, which often fail as a result of chemical degradation, and to the tires.

4   Upholstery and carpets - maintenance

1   Every three months remove the carpets or mats and clean the interior of the vehicle (more frequently if necessary). Vacuum the upholstery and carpets to remove loose dirt and dust.

2   Leather upholstery requires special care. Stains should be removed with warm water and a very mild soap solution. Use a clean, damp cloth to remove the soap, then wipe again with a dry cloth. Never use alcohol, gasoline, nail polish remover or thinner to clean leather upholstery.

3   After cleaning, regularly treat leather upholstery with a leather wax. Never use car wax on leather upholstery.

4   In areas where the interior of the vehicle is subject to bright sunlight, cover leather seats with a sheet if the vehicle is to be left out for any length of time.

5   Body repair - minor damage

See photo sequence

Repair of minor scratches

1   If the scratch is superficial and does not penetrate to the metal of the body, repair is very simple. Lightly rub the scratched area with a fine rubbing compound to remove loose paint and built up wax. Rinse the area with clean water.

2   Apply touch-up paint to the scratch, using a small brush. Continue to apply thin layers of paint until the surface of the paint in the scratch is level with the surrounding paint. Allow the new paint at least two weeks to harden, then blend it into the surrounding paint by rubbing with a very fine rubbing compound. Finally, apply a coat of wax to the scratch area.

3   If the scratch has penetrated the paint and exposed the metal of the body, causing the metal to rust, a different repair technique is required. Remove all loose rust from the bottom of the scratch with a pocket knife, then apply rust inhibiting paint to prevent the formation of rust in the future. Using a rubber or nylon applicator, coat the scratched area with glaze-type filler. If required, the filler can be mixed with thinner to provide a very thin paste, which is ideal for filling narrow scratches. Before the glaze filler in the scratch hardens, wrap a piece of smooth cotton cloth around the tip of a finger. Dip the cloth in thinner and then quickly wipe it along the surface of the scratch. This will ensure that the surface of the filler is slightly hollow. The scratch can now be painted over as described earlier in this section.

Repair of dents

4   When repairing dents, the first job is to pull the dent out until the affected area is as close as possible to its original shape. There is no point in trying to restore the original shape completely as the metal in the damaged area will have stretched on impact and cannot be restored to its original contours. It is better to bring the level of the dent up to a point which is about 1/8 inch below the level of the surrounding metal. In cases where the dent is very shallow, it is not worth trying to pull it out at all.

5   If the back side of the dent is accessible, it can be hammered out gently from behind using a soft-face hammer. While doing this, hold a block of wood firmly against the opposite side of the metal to absorb the hammer blows and prevent the metal from being stretched.

6   If the dent is in a section of the body which has double layers, or some other factor makes it inaccessible from behind, a different technique is required. Drill several small holes through the metal inside the damaged area, particularly in the deeper sections. Screw long, self tapping screws into the holes just enough for them to get a good grip in the metal. Now the dent can be pulled out by pulling on the protruding heads of the screws with locking pliers.

7   The next stage of repair is the removal of paint from the damaged area and from an inch or so of the surrounding metal. This is easily done with a wire brush or sanding disk in a drill motor, although it can be done just as effectively by hand with sandpaper. To complete the preparation for filling, score the surface of the bare metal with a screwdriver or the tang of a file or drill small holes in the affected area. This will provide a good grip for the filler material. To complete the repair, see the subsection on filling and painting.

Repair of rust holes or gashes

8   Remove all paint from the affected area and from an inch or so of the surrounding metal using a sanding disk or wire brush mounted in a drill motor. If these are not available, a few sheets of sandpaper will do the job just as effectively.

9   With the paint removed, you will be able to determine the severity of the corrosion and decide whether to replace the whole panel, if possible, or repair the affected area. New body panels are not as expensive as most people think and it is often quicker to install a new panel than to repair large areas of rust.

10   Remove all trim pieces from the affected area (except those which will act as a guide to the original shape of the damaged body, such as headlight shells, etc.). Using metal snips or a hacksaw blade, remove all loose metal and any other metal that is badly affected by rust. Hammer the edges of the hole in to create a slight depression for the filler material.

11   Wire brush the affected area to remove the powdery rust from the surface of the metal. If the back of the rusted area is accessible, treat it with rust inhibiting paint.

12   Before filling is done, block the hole in some way. This can be done with sheet metal riveted or screwed into place, or by stuffing the hole with wire mesh.

13   Once the hole is blocked off, the affected area can be filled and painted. See the following subsection on filling and painting.

Filling and painting

14 Many types of body fillers are available. Generally speaking, body repair kits which contain filler paste and a tube of resin hardener are best for this type of repair work. A wide, flexible plastic or nylon applicator will be necessary for imparting a smooth and contoured finish to the surface of the filler material. Mix-up a small amount of filler on a clean piece of wood or cardboard (use the hardener sparingly). Follow the manufacturer's instructions on the package, otherwise the filler will set incorrectly.

15 Using the applicator, apply the filler paste to the prepared area. Draw the applicator across the surface of the filler to achieve the desired contour and to level the filler surface. As soon as a contour that approximates the original one is achieved, stop working the paste. If you continue, the paste will begin to stick to the applicator. Continue to add thin layers of paste at 20 minute intervals until the level of the filler is just above the surrounding metal.

16 Once the filler has hardened, the excess can be removed with a body file. From then on, progressively finer grades of sandpaper should be used, starting with a 180-grit paper and finishing with 600-grit wet-or-dry paper. Always wrap the sandpaper around a flat rubber or wooden block, otherwise the surface of the filler will not be completely flat. During the sanding of the filler surface, the wet-or-dry paper should be periodically rinsed in water. This will ensure that a very smooth finish is produced in the final stage.

17 At this point, the repair area should be surrounded by a ring of bare metal, which in turn should be encircled by the finely feathered edge of good paint. Rinse the repair area with clean water until all of the dust produced by the sanding operation is gone.

18 Spray the entire area with a light coat of primer. This will reveal any imperfections in the surface of the filler. Repair the imperfections with fresh filler paste or glaze filler and once more smooth the surface with sandpaper. Repeat this spray-and-repair procedure until you are satisfied that the surface of the filler and the feathered edge of the paint are perfect. Rinse the area with clean water and allow it to dry completely.

19 The repair area is now ready for painting. Spray painting must be carried out in a warm, dry, windless and dust-free atmosphere. These conditions can be created if you have access to a large indoor work area, but if you are forced to work in the open, you will have to pick the day very carefully. If you are working indoors, dousing the floor in the work area with water will help settle the dust which would otherwise be in the air. If the repair area is confined to one body panel, mask off the surrounding panels. This will help minimize the effects of a slight mismatch in paint color. Trim pieces such as chrome strips, door handles, etc., will also need to be masked off or removed. Use masking tape and several thicknesses of newspaper for the masking operations.

20 Before spraying, shake the paint can thoroughly, then spray a test area until the spray painting technique is mastered. Cover the repair area with a thick coat of primer. The thickness should be built-up using several thin layers of primer rather than one thick one. Using 600-grit wet-or-dry sandpaper, rub down the surface of the primer until it is very smooth. While doing this, the work area should be thoroughly rinsed with water and the wet-or-dry sandpaper periodically rinsed as well. Allow the primer to dry before spraying additional coats.

21 Spray on the top coat, again building up the thickness by using several thin layers of paint. Begin spraying in the center of the repair area and then, using a circular motion, work out until the whole repair area and about two inches of the surrounding original paint is covered. Remove all masking material 10 to 15 minutes after spraying on the final coat of paint. Allow the new paint at least two weeks to harden, then use a very fine rubbing compound to blend the edges of the new paint into the existing paint. Finally, apply a coat of wax.

6 Body repair - major damage

1 Major damage must be repaired by an auto body shop specifically equipped to perform body and frame repairs. These shops have the specialized equipment available that is required to do the job properly.

2 If the damage is extensive, the body must be checked for proper alignment or the vehicle's handling characteristics may be adversely affected and other components may wear at an accelerated rate.

3 Due to the fact that all of the major body components (hood, fenders, etc.) are separate and replaceable units, any seriously damaged components should be replaced rather than repaired. Sometimes the components can be found in a wrecking yard that specializes in used vehicle components, often at considerable savings over the cost of new parts.

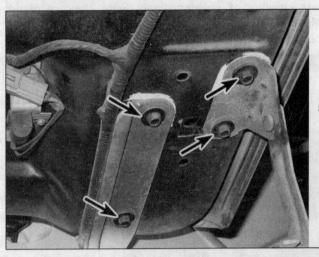

8.4 Mark the hinge and hinge link positions on the hood, then support the hood and remove the bolts

7 Hinges and locks - maintenance

Once every 3000 miles, or every three months, the hinges, locks and latch assemblies on the doors, hood and trunk should be given a few drops of light oil or lock lubricant. The door latch strikers should also be lubricated with a thin coat of grease to reduce wear and ensure free movement.

8 Hood - removal, installation and alignment

Refer to illustrations 8.4, 8.11 and 8.15

Removal

1 This procedure must be performed with two people to avoid personal injury and to avoid damage to the hood and surrounding body components.

2 With the hood open, carefully mark the position of the hood in relationship to the link assemblies and hinges.

3 If the vehicle is equipped with an underhood light, disconnect it.

4 With one person situated on either side of the hood, loosen and remove the link assembly and hood-to-hinge bolts on both sides **(see illustration)**.

5 Pivot the nose of the hood down slowly until the assembly is level and remove it toward the front of the vehicle.

Installation

6 Installation is the reverse of removal. Be sure to position the hood carefully and align it with the previously made marks. Tighten all bolts securely and check the hood for proper operation and fit.

Alignment (hood)

7 If necessary, adjust the hood for proper fit by shifting the hood on the hinges using the following procedure.

8 Loosen the hinge-to-fender inner screws enough to allow the hood/hinge to move with some resistance on the fender mount.

These photos illustrate a method of repairing simple dents. They are intended to supplement *Body repair - minor damage* in this Chapter and should not be used as the sole instructions for body repair on these vehicles.

1 If you can't access the backside of the body panel to hammer out the dent, pull it out with a slide-hammer-type dent puller. In the deepest portion of the dent or along the crease line, drill or punch hole(s) at least one inch apart . . .

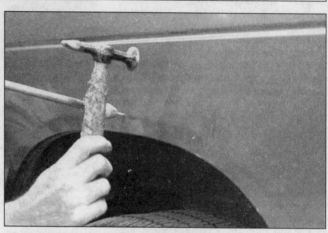

2 . . . then screw the slide-hammer into the hole and operate it. Tap with a hammer near the edge of the dent to help 'pop' the metal back to its original shape. When you're finished, the dent area should be close to its original contour and about 1/8-inch below the surface of the surrounding metal

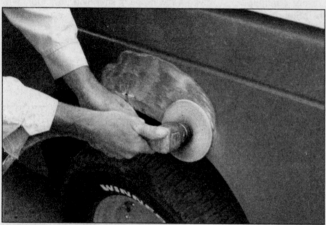

3 Using coarse-grit sandpaper, remove the paint down to the bare metal. Hand sanding works fine, but the disc sander shown here makes the job faster. Use finer (about 320-grit) sandpaper to feather-edge the paint at least one inch around the dent area

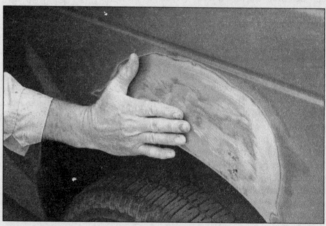

4 When the paint is removed, touch will probably be more helpful than sight for telling if the metal is straight. Hammer down the high spots or raise the low spots as necessary. Clean the repair area with wax/silicone remover

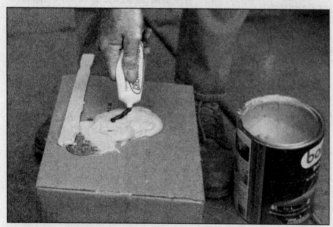

5 Following label instructions, mix up a batch of plastic filler and hardener. The ratio of filler to hardener is critical, and, if you mix it incorrectly, it will either not cure properly or cure too quickly (you won't have time to file and sand it into shape)

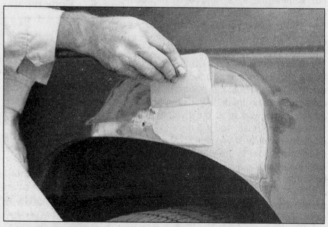

6 Working quickly so the filler doesn't harden, use a plastic applicator to press the body filler firmly into the metal, assuring it bonds completely. Work the filler until it matches the original contour and is slightly above the surrounding metal

7 Let the filler harden until you can just dent it with your fingernail. Use a body file or Surform tool (shown here) to rough-shape the filler

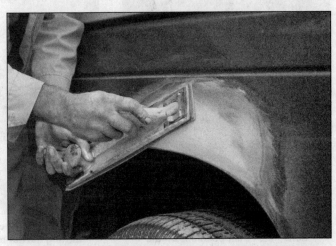

8 Use coarse-grit sandpaper and a sanding board or block to work the filler down until it's smooth and even. Work down to finer grits of sandpaper - always using a board or block - ending up with 360 or 400 grit

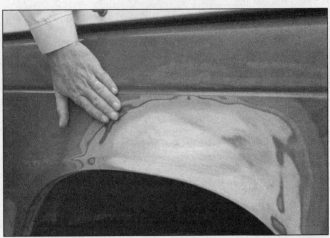

9 You shouldn't be able to feel any ridge at the transition from the filler to the bare metal or from the bare metal to the old paint. As soon as the repair is flat and uniform, remove the dust and mask off the adjacent panels or trim pieces

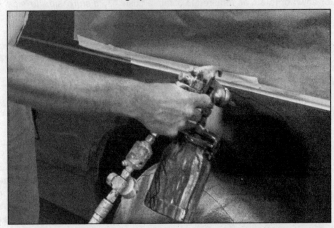

10 Apply several layers of primer to the area. Don't spray the primer on too heavy, so it sags or runs, and make sure each coat is dry before you spray on the next one. A professional-type spray gun is being used here, but aerosol spray primer is available inexpensively from auto parts stores

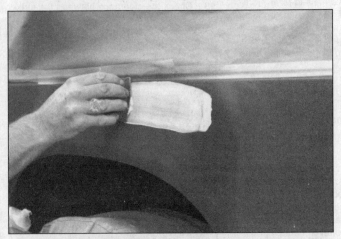

11 The primer will help reveal imperfections or scratches. Fill these with glazing compound. Follow the label instructions and sand it with 360 or 400-grit sandpaper until it's smooth. Repeat the glazing, sanding and respraying until the primer reveals a perfectly smooth surface

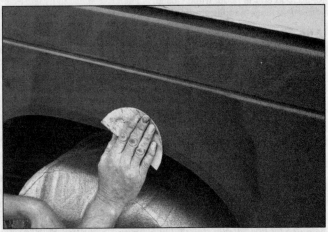

12 Finish sand the primer with very fine sandpaper (400 or 600-grit) to remove the primer overspray. Clean the area with water and allow it to dry. Use a tack rag to remove any dust, then apply the finish coat. Don't attempt to rub out or wax the repair area until the paint has dried completely (at least two weeks)

8.11 Before loosening the hood latch bolts, mark their positions on the radiator support

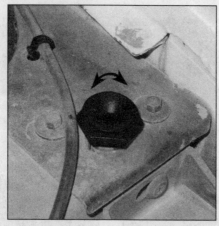

8.15 Adjust the hood closed height by turning the hood bumpers in or out

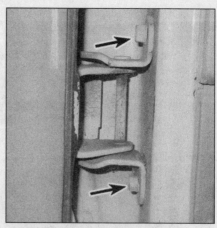

9.11 Door hinge-to-body bolts (loosening these bolts will allow up-and-down and back-and-forth adjustment; loosening the hinge-to-door bolts will allow in-and-out adjustment)

9   Lower the hood and adjust the hinge up or down or rotate as required to obtain a flush fit between the hood and the top of the cowling.

10   Have an assistant raise the hood only enough to allow access to the hinge-to-fender screws and tighten. **Note:** *To maintain alignment, try not to disturb the hinge to fender positioning prior to tightening screws.*

11   Loosen the two latch assembly screws from the front radiator support **(see illustration)**.

12   Loosen the hinge-to-hood screws enough to allow the hood to move with some resistance on the hinge.

13   Lower hood and adjust the hood forward or rearward and from side to side as required for proper hood to fender fit.

14   Have an assistant raise the hood only enough to allow access to the hinge-to-hood screws and tighten. **Note:** *To maintain alignment, try not to disturb the hinge to hood positioning prior to tightening the screws.*

15   Adjust the hood bumpers on the radiator support so the hood, when closed, is flush with the fenders **(see illustration)**.

Alignment (hood latch)

16   If not already done, loosen the two latch assembly screws at the front radiator support.

17   Lower the hood to an almost closed position and move the latch assembly until it is properly aligned with the hood striker.

18   Raise the hood and tighten the latch assembly screws.

19   Close the hood and check for proper latch engagement.

20   If the hood latches, but moves slightly up and down, the latch assembly is probably too high. Carefully loosen the latch assembly screws and tap the assembly down slightly. Tighten the screws. **Note:** *Try not to disturb side to side adjustment.* Repeat the engagement check.

21   If the hood refuses to latch or must be slammed to properly latch, the latch assembly is probably to low. Carefully loosen the latch assembly screws and tap the assembly up

slightly. Tighten the screws. **Note:** *Try not to disturb side to side adjustment.* Repeat the engagement check.

---

9   Door - removal, installation and alignment

Refer to illustrations 9.11 and 9.17

Removal

1   Disconnect the cable at the negative battery terminal.

2   If the door is to be replaced, removal all usable hardware, trim and glass parts.

3   Remove the upper and lower hinge access hole cover plates, if equipped. Mark the location of the hinges on the door and door pillar by scribing a line around the hinges.

4   Inside the cab, remove the lower side kick panel on the door to be removed. Disconnect the door harness electrical connectors from the vehicle harness.

5   Remove the door harness-to-pillar grommet and pull the harness free from the body.

6   Open and support the door so that it doesn't fall after the hinges are removed.

7   Remove the door to hinge retaining bolts and remove the door.

Installation

8   Installation is the reverse of removal except align the door if necessary.

Alignment

Hinges

9   The door hinges provide sufficient adjustment to correct most door misalignment conditions. The holes in the hinge and/or hinge attaching points are enlarged or elongated to provide for hinge and door alignment.

10   Close the door and check the fit, the door to cab outer panels should be flush and all gaps equal.

11   If the door needs alignment, determine which hinge bolts must be loosened to move

the door in the desired direction **(see illustration)**.

12   Open the door and loosen the hinge bolts enough to allow movement of the door with a padded pry bar.

13   With the door open and supported, move the door the distance estimated to obtain the desired fit by prying at the hinges, then tighten the hinge bolts.

14   Carefully close the door while checking for binding and interference with the adjacent panels.

15   Once closed and latched, check the door for proper fit. Repeat the sequence as needed to get the desired fit.

16   Adjust the door latch and striker plate if necessary.

Latch and striker

17   The striker pin can be adjusted laterally and vertically as well as forward and rearward **(see illustration)**.

18   Check the clearance between the striker and latch as shown.

9.17 Once loosened, the striker can be moved up, down, in or out, as necessary, to mate properly with the door latch

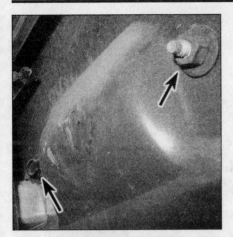

10.2 Outside door handle mounting fasteners

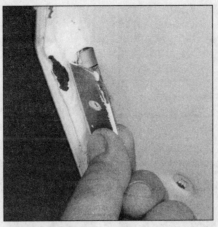

10.10 From the end of the door, pull out the lock cylinder retaining clip

careful when reinstalling the watershield to ensure that it fits tightly to the door and is not torn or deformed in any way. If this shield is not watertight, it can cause an accumulation of water inside of the door and eventual rusting. It is sometimes necessary to re-glue the lip of the seal, using contact cement.

11 Door trim panel - removal and installation

Refer to illustrations 11.4a, 11.4b, 11.9a, 11.9b and 11.9c

Removal

1   Remove the screw retaining the armrest section of the trim panel to the door inner panel and remove the armrest pad.
2   Remove the screw retaining the inside door handle and remove the handle.
3   On vehicles with manually operated window cranks, remove the screws retaining the crank, then remove the crank and washer.
4   On vehicles with power windows, remove the power window switch panel by inserting a thin-blade screwdriver between the bezel and the trim panel, at either side of the bezel. Then carefully pry the bezel from the trim panel and the housing assembly will snap out **(see illustration)**. Remove the retaining screws from the bottom side of the connector and remove the switch assembly from the connector **(see illustration)**.
5   On models so equipped, remove the door lock control knob.
6   On models with power door locks, remove the switch housing assembly from the panel by inserting a thin-blade screwdriver into the spring tab slot located at the top and bottom of the switch housing. Apply pressure and the assembly will pop out. Disconnect the housing from the wiring assembly connector by separating the locking fingers.
7   If equipped with a power outside rear view mirror, remove the switch housing bezel by removing the two retaining bezel nuts and the bezel.

19   If required, remove the striker and shim the striker-to-door pillar to obtain the proper clearance between the striker and latch as shown. **Note:** *A special TORX drive socket will be required to loosen and tighten the striker.*
20   Move the striker as required to provide a flush fit between the door and body panels.
21   Tighten the striker and check the door for proper fit. Repeat the sequence as needed to obtain the desired fit.

10 Door handle (outside) and lock cylinder - removal and installation

Refer to illustrations 10.2 and 10.10

Door handle

1   Remove the inner door trim panel as described in Section 11. Remove the plastic watershield from the inside of the door.
2   Disconnect the latch actuator rod from the door handle assembly **(see illustration)**.
3   Using a socket and small ratchet, remove the nut and the screw retaining the door han-

dle assembly.
4   Remove the door handle assembly and the pads from the door.
5   If the handle is being replaced, transfer the pads and the actuator rod clip to the new handle assembly.
6   Installation is the reverse of removal. Check the handle assembly for correct operation before installing the inner door watershield and panel.

Lock cylinder

Note: *If a lock cylinder is being replaced, it should be replaced in both doors and the ignition cylinder. These cylinders come in sets and allow the vehicle to be unlocked and driven with one key.*
7   Roll the window all the way up.
8   Remove the inner door trim panel and watershield as described in Section 11.
9   Disconnect the lock actuating rod from the lock cylinder.
10   Slide the lock cylinder retaining clip out of the groove in the lock cylinder. Remove the lock cylinder from the outside of the door **(see illustration)**.
11   Installation is the reverse of removal. Be

11.4a Carefully pry out the switch . . .

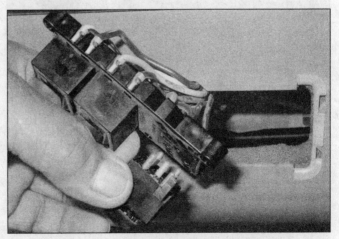

11.4b . . . then remove the screws and disconnect the electrical connector

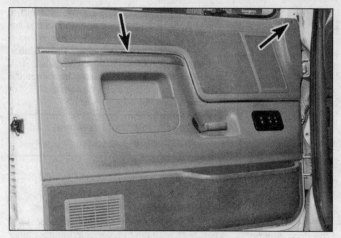

11.9a Remove the screw at the top front corner of the door panel, and also from the pull handle

11.9b Use a trim panel tool to carefully pry out the retaining clips

8   On early models, using a thin-blade screwdriver or putty knife, insert it at each of the door panel retaining clip locations and carefully pry the clips from the door. **Note:** *Do not use the panel itself to pull the clips from the door, as damage to the panel may occur.*
9   On later models, remove the door panel retaining screws first **(see illustration)**. Then, using a thin-blade screwdriver or putty knife, insert it at each of the retaining clip locations and carefully pry the clips from the door **(see illustrations)**.

Installation

10   Replace any damaged or missing clips with new ones.
11   Position the trim panel on the inner door panel, locating the clips properly in the countersunk holes and firmly push the trim panel by hand at each clip location to seat the panel. Do not use a hammer or other tool, as damage to the trim panel may occur.
12   The remaining installation steps are the reverse of the removal procedure.

12   Door glass - replacement and adjustment

Replacement

1   Remove the door trim panel (refer to Section 11).
2   Remove the vent window assembly (refer to Section 14).
3   Rotate the front edge of the door glass down, then lift the glass and channel assembly from the door.
4   If the glass is to be replaced, it must be removed and new glass installed in the glass channel by a glass shop with the special tools required for the job.
5   Installation is the reverse of the removal procedure. When inserting the glass and channel into the door, be sure that the regulator roller arm is positioned correctly in the glass bracket channel. If necessary, before installing the door trim, adjust the window for proper fit.

Adjustment

6   The front door window glass can be adjusted forward and rearward by loosening the front division bar lower attaching screws and the rear retainer lower attaching screws. After proper fit is obtained, tighten the screws.

13   Door window regulator - replacement

Refer to illustration 13.3

1   Remove the door trim panel (refer to Section 11).
2   Support the window glass in the full up position.
3   To remove the regulator, remove the center pin from the regulator attaching rivets using a drift punch. Using a 1/4 inch drill, remove the head from each rivet and remove the rivet. Be careful not to enlarge the sheet metal holes during the drilling procedure **(see illustration)**.

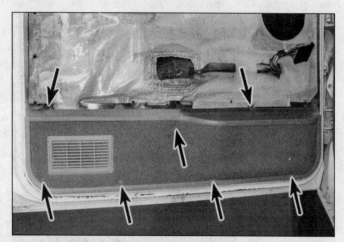

11.9c After the top portion of the door panel has been removed, remove the screws and take off the lower part

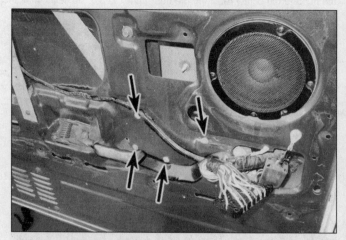

13.3 To remove the window regulator rivets, knock the center pin out with a hammer and punch, then carefully drill off the heads (don't enlarge the hole in the door)

4   Disengage the regulator arm from the glass bracket and remove the regulator.

5   If rivets are not available when installing the regulator, a 1/4-20 x 1/2 inch screw and washer assembly, and a 1/4-20 nut and washer assembly may be used instead.

6   All window regulator rollers, shafts and the entire length of the roller guides should be lubricated with polyethylene grease before installation.

7   Remaining installation is the reverse of removal.

14   Vent window assembly - removal and installation

1   Refer to Section 11 and remove the door trim panel.

2   Remove the screw retaining the division bar to the inner door panel.

3   Remove the screws retaining the vent window assembly to the leading edge of the door.

4   Lower the door glass to the bottom of its travel.

5   Pull the glass run out of the upper run retainer next to the vent window division bar. Pull the glass run out just far enough to allow the vent window assembly to be removed.

6   Tilt the vent window and the division bar assembly toward the rear of the door. Carefully guide the assembly up and out of the door.

7   Remove the two upper pivot-to-vent frame screws.

8   Remove the retaining nut and tension spring from the vent window lower pivot.

9   Separate the vent glass retainer and the pivot stops from the vent frame and weatherstripping assembly.

10   Installation is the reverse of the removal procedure. The pivot tension spring should be adjusted so the vent will remain open at highway speeds. Be sure the front door window spacer is in place when installing the vent window and division bar assembly.

15   Rear window - removal and installation

Removal

1   Remove the molding from around the rear window, then, using a screwdriver from the inside of the cab, pry carefully around the weatherstrip lip forcing the weatherstripping out. Have an assistant pull on the window assembly to remove it, with the weatherstripping attached.

2   On sliding type rear windows, using a screwdriver and pliers, remove the sliding glass stopper from the channel.

3   From the channel track, remove the four screws holding the two fixed frame divider bars.

4   With the window assembly standing vertically on its lower edge, place a folded rag near the center of the window frame to protect the channel.

5   Stand on the rag with one foot and gently lift the top edge of the frame and remove the sliding windows and fixed frame divider bars.

6   Move the rag toward either end of the channel frame and remove the two non-sliding windows in the same manner.

Installation

7   Clean all old sealer from the body recess and from the glass.

8   Inspect the body sheet metal flange for straightness. Remove waves and dents as required.

9   Reassemble the sliding window fixed glass, division bars, and moveable glass into the frame and install the screws. **Note:** *Apply silicone lubricant to window weatherstrip and track to make glass installation easier.*

10   Install the body to window weatherstripping (fixed glass) or body to window assembly weatherstripping (movable glass). **Note:** *It is probable that the old weatherstripping has become weather-hardened and may develop water leaks. Replace the weather-stripping with new material if any such deterioration is indicated.*

11   Once the rear window is assembled, insert a draw cord along the weatherstripping groove.

12   Apply liquid Butyl sealer (available at most auto parts stores) to the back of window openings.

13   Position the glass with weatherstripping to the window opening.

14   Begin the installation in the center of the lower part of the glass.

15   Attach the window assembly to the body by pulling on the cord from the inside while an assistant pushes along the weatherstripping from the outside.

16   Seat the window assembly by tapping around the circumference of the glass with your open hand, then install the molding.

16   Tailgate - removal and installation

Note: *To facilitate tailgate removal, a helper should assist in the procedure.*

Styleside pick-up

1   Remove the screws retaining the left and right tailgate support straps at the upper attachment points.

2   Lift the tailgate off at the right-hand lower hinge. Then remove the tailgate from the left-hand hinge. Be careful not to lose the hinge inserts.

3   If a new tailgate is being installed, transfer all moldings, latches, hinges, brackets, links, clips and washers from the old tailgate to the new one.

4   Installation is the reverse of the removal procedure.

Flareside pick-up

5   Unhook the tailgate chains from the tailgate.

6   Remove the two bolts retaining the removable pivot to the body on the right side, then remove the pivot.

7   Slide the tailgate off the stationary pivot on the left.

8   If a new tailgate is being installed, transfer all moldings, latches, hinges, brackets, links, clips and washers from the old tailgate to the new one.

9   Installation is the reverse of the removal procedure.

Bronco

10   Unlatch the tailgate handle and lower the tailgate.

11   Disconnect the left and right cable assemblies at the tailgate.

12   Disconnect the tailgate window motor wire at the connector. Pull the lead wire from the tailgate body rail.

13   Support the tailgate while slightly open, and remove the torsion bar retainer from the body.

14   Remove the three left and right hinge assemblies to the body.

15   Remove the tailgate from the vehicle.

16   If a new tailgate is being installed, transfer all moldings, latches, hinges, brackets, links, clips and washers from the old tailgate to the new one.

17   Installation is the reverse of removal.

17   Tailgate glass and regulator (Bronco only) - removal and installation

Regulator

1   Lower the tailgate and remove the access panel, water shield and panel support. If the tailgate will not lower because the glass will not go down, remove the access panel and depress the safety lockout rod located in the bottom center of the tailgate.

2   Raise the glass using a jumper wire to the motor or manually close the latches and use the switch. If the glass will not go up it must be removed first.

3   Remove the regulator screws and washers and remove the regulator.

4   If equipped with an electric motor, disconnect the wiring harness and remove the motor from the tailgate. **Warning:** *The counterbalance spring is under tension. To prevent personal injury, clamp or lock the gear sectors together before removing the motor.*

5   Installation is the reverse of removal.

Glass

6   Lower the tailgate and remove the access panel, water shield and panel support.

7   Manually close the latches and raise the glass to gain access to the nuts retaining the glass and bracket to the window regulator. If the glass will not go up, drill 5/8 inch access holes in the panel directly above each of the retaining nuts. **Note:** *A template is available from your local dealer to aid you in drilling the*

holes in the proper location. Cover the glass with a protective cover before drilling the holes.

8   Remove the glass bracket-to-window regulator retaining nuts.

9   Grind the heads off of the rivets retaining the glass to the bracket and using a punch, remove the rivets, retainers and spacers.

10   Remove the protective cover and disconnect the rear window defogger terminals, if equipped.

11   Remove the corner seals and inside weatherstrip. Slide the glass out of the tailgate.

12   Clean up the metal filings and apply touch up paint to any drilled hole surfaces before reassembly.

13   Installation is the reverse of removal. Cycle the window up and down several times to assure smooth operation.

18   Bumpers - removal and installation

Refer to illustrations 18.2 and 18.5

Front

1   On early models with bumper guards, first remove the upper attachment nuts from the bumper guards, then remove the screws retaining the bumper guard brackets to the bumper and remove the bumper guards.

2   On early models with the bumper bolted directly to the frame and all later models, remove the two bolts on each side and lift the bumper off the frame **(see illustration)**.

3   Remove the two lower bumper bolts and remove the bumper from the vehicle.

4   Installation is the reverse of the removal procedure.

Rear

5   Remove the bumper bracket-to-frame retaining bolts **(see illustration)**.

6   Remove the bumper and brackets from the vehicle.

7   If a new bumper and/or brackets are being installed, transfer any undamaged components from the old assembly to the new component.

8   Installation is the reverse of the removal procedure.

19   Fiberglass roof (Bronco only) - removal and installation

Caution: *The tailgate window must always remain closed to prevent breakage when the roof is removed.*

1   Lower the tailgate window to the full down position and lower the tailgate.

2   Remove the screws attaching the trim molding and remove the plastic trim from around the side window openings and the cab opening to gain access to the roof retaining bolts.

3   Scribe the location of the molding brackets on the fiberglass roof's surface and num-

18.2 Front bumper bracket-to-frame bolts

ber each bracket as it is removed for reinstallation in their original positions.

4   Remove all the roof retaining bolts and molding brackets.

5   With the help of several assistants, carefully lift the roof off the vehicle to prevent tearing or separating the weatherstrip from the fiberglass roof. **Note:** *The roof weighs about 120 pounds.*

6   To prevent deformation of the roof and weatherstrip, store the roof right side up on a level surface at least six inches above the ground.

7   Installation is the reverse of removal.

20   Grille assembly - removal and installation

Early models

Radiator grille

1   Remove the screws retaining the grille to the support assembly.

2   Remove the grille.

3   Installation is the reverse of removal.

Upper grille molding

4   Remove the radiator grille.

5   Remove the right and left-hand headlight door assemblies.

6   Remove the screws which fasten the upper grille molding to the retainer assembly.

7   Remove the molding.

8   Installation is the reverse of removal.

Lower grille molding

9   **Note:** *It is not necessary to remove the radiator grille in order to remove the lower molding*. Remove the right and left-hand headlight door assemblies.

10   Remove the screw at the hood latch support brace and center of the lower molding, then remove the screws at the right and left ends of the molding where it attaches to the radiator grille support.

11   Remove the molding.

12   Installation is the reverse of removal.

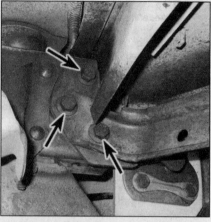

18.5 Rear bumper bracket-to-frame bolts

Later models

13   Remove the screws retaining the grille assembly to the grille opening reinforcement.

14   Remove the grille.

15   Installation is the reverse of removal.

21   Floor carpet/mat - removal and installation

1   Remove the seat(s).

2   If equipped, remove the shift boot bezel.

3   Grasp the carpet or mat around the shifter boot edge and pull up and out away from the shift boot.

4   Remove the screws retaining the right and left cowl side trim panels.

5   Remove the screws retaining the right and left door sill scuff plates. Remove the plates and side cowl panels.

6   Remove all carpet or mat retaining screws and remove the carpet.

7   Installation is the reverse of removal.

22   Glove box - removal and installation

1   Depress both tabs on the sides of the glove box. Rotate the door and bin assembly down until the keepers engage. Hold the assembly in the full open position.

2   Pull down and out on the door and bin assembly. Wedge the blade of a flat-head screwdriver between each hinge and rotate the tension tab.

3   Remove the glove box.

4   Installation is the reverse of removal.

23   Windshield and fixed glass - replacement

Due to the possibility of glass breakage when installing a new windshield and/or possible damage to the surrounding body panels and paint, it is recommended that a damaged windshield be replaced by a dealership or auto glass shop.

Chapter 12
Chassis electrical system

Contents

1 General information

The electrical system is of the 12 volt, negative ground type. Power for the lighting system and all electrical accessories is supplied by a lead/acid battery which is charged by an alternator.

This Chapter covers repair and service procedures for the various lighting and electrical components not associated with the engine. Information on the battery, alternator, voltage regulator and starter motor can be found in Chapter 5.

It should be noted that whenever portions of the electrical system are worked on, the negative battery cable should be disconnected to prevent electrical shorts and/or fires.

2 Electrical troubleshooting - general information

1   A typical electrical circuit consists of an electrical component, any switches, relays, motors, fuses, fusible links or circuit breakers, etc. related to that component and the wiring and connectors that link the component to both the battery and the chassis. To help you pinpoint an electrical circuit problem, wiring diagrams are included at the end of this book.

2   Before tackling any troublesome electrical circuit, first study the appropriate wiring diagrams to get a complete understanding of what makes up that individual circuit. Trouble spots, for instance, can often be isolated by noting if other components related to that circuit are operating properly. If several components or circuits fail at one time, chances are the problem is in a fuse or ground connection because several circuits are often routed through the same fuse and ground connections.

3   Electrical problems usually stem from simple causes such as loose or corroded connectors, a blown fuse, a melted fusible link or a bad relay. Visually inspect the condition of all fuses, wires and connectors in a problem circuit before troubleshooting it.

4   The basic tools needed for electrical troubleshooting include a circuit tester, a high impedance (10 K-ohm) digital multi-meter, a continuity tester and a jumper wire with an inline circuit breaker for bypassing electrical components. Before attempting to locate or define a problem with electrical test instruments, use the wiring diagrams to decide where to make the necessary connections.

Voltage checks

5   Perform a voltage check first when a circuit is not functioning properly. Connect one lead of a circuit tester to either the negative battery terminal or a known good ground. Connect the other lead to a connector in the circuit being tested, preferably nearest to the battery or fuse. If the bulb of the tester lights up, voltage is present, which means that the part of the circuit between the connector and the battery is problem free. Continue checking the rest of the circuit in the same fashion. When you reach a point at which no voltage is present, the problem lies between that point and the last test point with voltage. Most of the time the problem can be traced to a loose or corroded connection. **Note:** *Keep in mind that some circuits receive voltage only when the ignition key is in the Accessory or Run position.*

3.3 When checking continuity or voltage with a circuit testing device, insert the test probe from the wire harness side if possible - this avoids possible pin damage and poor pin retention force due to direct probing

4.1 Location of the fuse panel under the dashboard - early models

Finding a short circuit

6   One method of finding shorts in a circuit is to remove the fuse and connect a test light or voltmeter in its place. There should be no voltage present in the circuit. Move the wiring harness from side-to-side while watching the test light. If the bulb goes on, there is a short to ground somewhere in that area, probably where the insulation has rubbed through. The same test can be performed on each component in the circuit, even a switch.

Ground check

7   Perform a ground test to check whether a component is properly grounded. Disconnect the battery and connect one lead of a self-powered test light, known as a continuity tester, to a known good ground. Connect the other lead to the wire or ground connection being tested. If the bulb goes on, the ground is good. If the bulb does not go on, the ground is not good.

Continuity check

8   A continuity check determines if there are any breaks in a circuit if it is conducting electricity properly. With the circuit off (no power in the circuit), a self-powered continuity tester can be used to check the circuit. Connect the test leads to both ends of the circuit, and if the test light comes on the circuit is passing current properly. If the light doesn't come on, there is a break somewhere in the circuit. The same procedure can be used to test a switch, by connecting the continuity tester to the power in and power out sides of the switch. With the switch turned on, the test light should come on.

Resistance check

9   Some troubleshooting procedures within this manual require resistance measurements. Performing a resistance measurement is similar to checking continuity except that an exact

value of the electrical resistance (ohms) in the circuit between the test leads is required. This necessitates the use of a self powered ohmmeter or multi-meter (combined volt/ohmmeter).

10   Resistance checks must be made with a high quality meter capable of accurate measurement down to only a few ohms, otherwise, erroneous diagnoses and component replacement will result. Digital meters are preferred for testing most circuits.

11   Make sure all connections are tight and clean and fuses are intact prior to troubleshooting as most problems are as a result of these simple causes. Remember, some circuits will fail if only a few extra ohms of unwanted resistance is present. Also, certain components may be diagnosed as failed when in reality it is simply a poor connection in the circuit.

Finding an open circuit

12   When diagnosing for possible open circuits it is often difficult to locate them by sight because oxidation or terminal misalignment are hidden by the connectors. Merely wiggling a connector on a sensor or in the wiring harness may correct the open circuit condition. Remember this if an open circuit is indicated when troubleshooting a circuit. Intermittent problems may also be caused by oxidized or loose connections.

13   Electrical troubleshooting is simple if you keep in mind that all electrical circuits are basically electricity running from the battery, through the wires, switches, relays, fuses and fusible links to each electrical component (light bulb, motor, etc.) and then to ground, from which it is passed back to the battery. Any electrical problem is an interruption in the flow of electricity to and from the battery.

Circuit check precautions

14   **Caution:** *When working with electronic components such as the PCM or associated*

harness when still attached to module, avoid direct contact with input-output pins. Static electricity generated by normal activity and stored on the surface of the skin can discharge and damage delicate electronic components inside the PCM. It is best to always wear a static discharging wrist strap (available at electronic stores) and avoid working on electronics when the relative humidity is under 25%.

3   Connectors - general information

Refer to illustration 3.3

1   Always release the lock lever(s) before attempting to unplug electrical connectors. Although nothing more than a finger is usually necessary to pry lock levers open, a small pocket screwdriver is effective for hard torelease levers. Once the lock levers are released, try to pull on the connectors themselves, not the wires, when unplugging two connector halves (there are times, however, when this is not possible - use good judgment).

2   It is usually necessary to know which side, male or female, of the connector you're checking. Male connectors are easily distinguished from females by the shape of their internal pins.

3   When checking continuity or voltage with a circuit tester, insertion of the test probe into the receptacle may open the fitting to the connector and result in poor contact. Instead, insert the test probe from the wire harness side of the connector **(see illustration)**.

4   If contact probing is necessary, avoid direct probing of connector pins by purchasing appropriately sized male and female pins and sockets which can be inserted into or over the harness or component connector pin. This avoids potential damage to vehicle pins and helps maintain proper pin retention (engagement) forces.

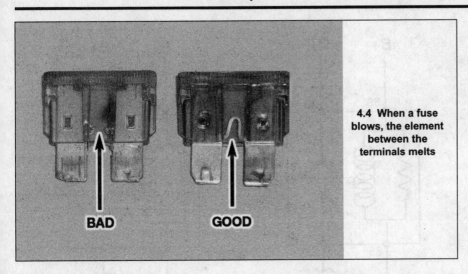

4.4 When a fuse blows, the element between the terminals melts

4 Fuses - general information

Refer to illustrations 4.1 and 4.4

1   The electrical circuits of this vehicle are protected by a combination of fuses, fusible links and circuit breakers. On later models, the various protection devices are located in two separate fuse blocks, the fuse panel and the power distribution box. The fuse panel is located under the dash behind an access door on the left side of the steering column **(see illustration)**. The power distribution box is located in the engine compartment on the left side fender apron.

2   Each fuse block is equipped with miniaturized fuses because their compact dimensions and convenient blade-type terminal design allow fingertip removal and installation. Each fuse protects one or more circuits. The protected circuit is identified on the face of the fuse panel cover above each fuse.

3   If an electrical component fails, always check the fuse first.

4   The best way to check a fuse is with a test light. Check for power at the exposed terminal tips of each fuse. If power is present on one side of the fuse but not the other, the fuse is blown. A blown fuse can also be confirmed by visually inspecting it **(see illustration)**.

5   Remove and insert fuses straight in and out without twisting. Twisting could force the terminals open too far, resulting in a bad connection.

6   Be sure to replace blown fuses with the correct type and amp rating. Fuses of different ratings are physically interchangeable, but replacing a fuse with one of a higher or lower value than specified is not recommended. Each electrical circuit needs a specific amount of protection. The amperage value of each fuse is usually molded into the fuse body. **Caution:** *Always turn off all electrical components and the ignition switch before replacing a fuse. Never bypass a fuse with pieces of metal or foil. Serious damage to the electrical system could result.*

7   If the replacement fuse immediately fails, do not replace it again until the cause of the problem is isolated and corrected. In most cases, this will be a short circuit in the wiring caused by a broken or deteriorated wire.

5 Fusible links - general information

1   Some circuits are protected by fusible links. These links are used in circuits which are not ordinarily fused, such as the ignition circuit. If a circuit protected by a fusible link becomes inoperative, inspect for a blown fusible link.

2   Although fusible links appear to be of heavier gauge than the wire they are protecting, their appearance is due to thicker insulation. All fusible links are several wire gauges smaller than the wire they are designed to protect.

3   Fusible links cannot be repaired, they must be replaced. If you must replace one, make sure that the new fusible link is a duplicate of the one removed with respect to gauge, length and insulation. Replacement fusible links have insulation that is flame proof. Do not fabricate a fusible link from ordinary wire - the insulation may not be flame proof. **Warning:** *Do not mistake a resistor wire for a fusible link. The resistor wire is generally longer and is identified by a label that says "Resistor - don't cut or splice."*

Charging system fusible link

4   To replace the fusible link in the charging system, proceed as follows:

a) *Disconnect the negative cable at the battery.*

b) *Disconnect the fusible link from the wiring harness or the fusible link eyelet terminal from the battery terminal of the starter relay (on some vehicle applications, the fusible link is looped outside the wire harness).*

c) *Cut the damaged fusible link and the splices from the wires to which it is attached. Disconnect the feed wire part of the wiring and cut out the damaged portion as closely as possible behind the splice in the harness. If the fusible link wire insulation is burned or opened, disconnect the feed as close as possible behind the splice in the harness. If the damaged fusible link is between two splices (the weld points in the harness), cut out the damaged portion as close as possible to the weld points.*

d) *Strip the insulation back approximately 1/2-inch.*

e) *Splice and solder the new fusible link to the wires from which the old link was cut. Use rosin core solder at each end of the new link to obtain a good solder joint.*

f) *Wrap the splices completely with vinyl electrical tape around the soldered joint. No wires should be exposed.*

g) *Securely connect the eyelet terminals (if any) to the battery stud on the starter relay.* **Note:** *Some fusible links have an eyelet terminal for a 5/16-inch stud on one end. When the terminal is not required, use one of the fusible links shown with the insulation stripped from both ends.*

h) *Install the repaired wiring as before, using existing clips, if provided.*

i) *Connect the battery ground cable.*

j) *Test the circuit for proper operation.*

All other fusible links

5   To service any other blown fusible link, use the following procedure:

a) *Determine which circuit is damaged, its location and the cause of the open fusible link. If the damaged fusible link is one of three fed by a common 10 or 12 gauge feed wire, determine the specific affected circuit.*

b) *Disconnect the negative battery cable.*

c) *Cut the damaged fusible link from the wiring harness and discard it. If the fusible link is one of three circuits fed by a single wire, cut it out of the harness at each splice and discard it.*

d) *Identify and procure the proper fusible link and butt connectors for attaching the fusible link to the harness.*

6   To service any fusible link in a three-link group with one feed:

a) *After cutting the open link out of the harness, cut each of the remaining undamaged fusible links close to the feed wire weld.*

b) *Strip approximately 1/2-inch of insulation from the detached ends of the two good fusible links. Insert two wire ends into one end of a butt connector and carefully push one stripped end of the replacement fusible link into the same end of the butt connector and crimp all three firmly together.* **Note:** *Be very careful when fitting the three fusible links into the butt connector - the internal diameter is a snug fit for three wires. Be sure to use a proper crimping tool. Pliers, side cutters, etc. will not apply the proper crimp to retain the wires.*

c) After crimping the butt connector to the three fusible links, cut the weld portion from the feed wire and strip about 1/2-inch of insulation from the cut end. Insert the stripped end into the open end of the butt connector and crimp very firmly.

d) To attach the remaining end of the replacement fusible link, strip about 1/2-inch of insulation from the wire end of the circuit from which the blown fusible link was removed and firmly crimp a butt connector to the stripped wire. Insert the end of the replacement link into the other end of the butt connector and crimp firmly.

e) Using rosin core solder with a consistency of 60 percent tin and 40 percent lead, solder the connectors and the wires at the repairs and insulate with electrical tape.

7   To replace any fusible link on a single circuit in a harness, cut out the damaged portion, strip about 1/2-inch of insulation from the two wire ends and attach the appropriate replacement fusible link to the stripped wire ends with two proper size butt connectors. Solder the connectors and wires and insulate with tape.

8   To service any fusible link which has an eyelet terminal on one end (like the charging circuit), cut off the open fusible link behind the weld, strip about 1/2-inch of insulation from the cut end and attach the appropriate new eyelet fusible link to the stripped wire with an appropriate size butt connector. Solder the connectors and wires at the point of service and insulate with tape.

9   Connect the cable to the negative terminal of the battery.

10   Test the system for proper operation.

6   Circuit breakers - general information

1   Circuit breakers protect accessories such as power windows, power door locks, the windshield wiper, windshield wiper pump, electronic shift motor (4X4), etc. Circuit breakers are located in the fuse panel. Refer to the fuse panel guide in your owner's manual for the location of the circuit breakers used in your vehicle.

2   Because a circuit breaker resets itself automatically, an electrical overload in a circuit breaker protected system will cause the circuit to fail momentarily, then come back on. If the circuit does not come back on, check it immediately.

a) Remove the circuit breaker from the fuse panel.

b) Using an ohmmeter, verify that there is continuity between both terminals of the circuit breaker. If there is no continuity, replace the circuit breaker.

c) Install the old or new circuit breaker. If it continues to cut out, a short circuit is indicated. Troubleshoot the appropriate circuit (see the wiring diagrams at the

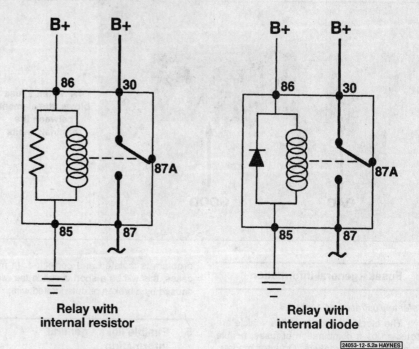

Relay with internal resistor   **Relay with internal diode**

24053-12-5.2a HAYNES

7.2a Typical ISO relay designs, terminal numbering and circuit connections

back of this book) or have the system checked by a professional mechanic.

7   Relays - general information and testing

General information

1   Several electrical accessories in the vehicle, such as the fuel injection system, horns, starter, and fog lamps use relays to transmit the electrical signal to the component. Relays use a low-current circuit (the control circuit) to open and close a high-current circuit (the power circuit). If the relay is defective, that component will not operate properly. Refer to the guide in your owner's manual for the exact location and function of the relays used in your vehicle. If a faulty relay is suspected, it can be removed and tested using the procedure below or by a dealer service department or a repair shop. Defective relays must be replaced as a unit.

Testing

Refer to illustrations 7.2a and 7.2b

2   Most of the relays used in these vehicles are of a type often called "ISO" relays, which refers to the International Standards Organization. The terminals of ISO relays are numbered to indicate their usual circuit connections and functions. There are two basic layouts of terminals on the relays used in these vehicles (see illustrations).

3   Refer to the wiring diagram for the circuit to determine the proper connections for the

relay you're testing. If you can't determine the correct connection from the wiring diagrams, however, you may be able to determine the test connections from the information that follows.

4   Two of the terminals are the relay control circuit and connect to the relay coil. The other relay terminals are the power circuit. When the relay is energized, the coil creates a magnetic field that closes the larger contacts of the power circuit to provide power to the circuit loads.

5   Terminals 85 and 86 are normally the control circuit. If the relay contains a diode, terminal 86 must be connected to battery positive (B+) voltage and terminal 85 to ground. If the relay contains a resistor, terminals 85 and 86 can be connected in either direction with respect to B+ and ground.

7.2b Most relays are marked on the outside to easily identify the control circuits and the power circuits - four terminal type shown

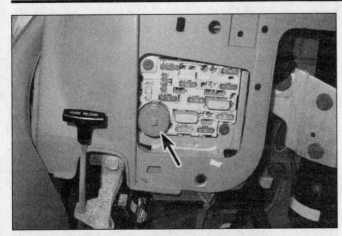

8.1 Location of the turn signal flasher

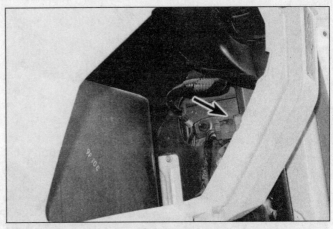

8.2 The hazard flasher on some models is located behind the right end of the instrument panel

6   Terminal 30 is normally connected to the battery voltage (B+) source for the circuit loads. Terminal 87 is connected to the ground side of the circuit, either directly or through a load. If the relay has several alternate terminals for load or ground connections, they usually are numbered 87A, 87B, 87C, and so on.
7   Use an ohmmeter to check continuity through the relay control coil.

a) *Connect the meter according to the polarity shown in* **illustration 7.2a** *for one check; then reverse the ohmmeter leads and check continuity in the other direction.*
b) *If the relay contains a resistor, resistance will be indicated on the meter, and should be the same value with the ohmmeter in either direction.*
c) *If the relay contains a diode, resistance should be higher with the ohmmeter in the forward polarity direction than with the meter leads reversed.*
d) *If the ohmmeter shows infinite resistance in both directions, replace the relay.*

8   Remove the relay from the vehicle and use the ohmmeter to check for continuity between the relay power circuit terminals. There should be no continuity between terminal 30 and 87 with the relay de-energized.
9   Connect a fused jumper wire to terminal 86 and the positive battery terminal. Connect another jumper wire between terminal 85 and ground. When the connections are made, the relay should click.
10   With the jumper wires connected, check for continuity between the power circuit terminals. Now, there should be continuity between terminals 30 and 87.
11   If the relay fails any of the above tests, replace it.

8   Turn signal and hazard flasher - check and replacement

Refer to illustrations 8.1 and 8.2
1   The turn signal flasher unit is located on

the front of the fuse panel **(see illustration)**.
2   The hazard flasher can be located in one of two places; it is either located on the rear of the fuse panel behind the turn signal flasher or mounted on a bracket at the right end of the instrument panel **(see illustration)**.
3   If either of the two flasher functions fail to blink, the problem may be due to a blown fuse, a faulty flasher unit, a broken switch, blown turn indicator bulb(s), or a loose or open connection. If a quick check of the fuse panel indicates that the turn indicator or hazard fuse has blown, check the wiring for a short before installing a new fuse.
4   If the fuse is good, locate and remove the suspect flasher unit.
5   Check for voltage at the flasher connector socket (red/white wire). Voltage should be indicated. If not, repair the open circuit to the battery.
6   Testing of the flasher can be done manually, however, their low cost dictates that replacement is the best option if failure is suspected.
7   Install a new flasher unit. If a new flasher fails to correct the problem, there is an open in the circuit between the flasher and the external lights.
8   Check and replace all of the turn indicator bulbs as required. If the bulbs are okay, the problem is probably in the turn signal/hazard switch or related wiring.
9   Check the turn signal/hazard switch as applicable (refer to Section 9).

9   Steering column switches - replacement

Turn signal/hazard switch (early models)
1   Disconnect the negative cable from the battery.
2   Remove the steering wheel (refer to Chapter 10). Be sure to heed the airbag warning in the steering wheel removal section.
3   Remove the turn signal switch lever from

the switch and remove the screws that retain the switch to the steering column.
4   Remove the steering column shroud and instrument panel opening cover.
5   Disconnect the turn signal switch harness connector at the base of the steering column.
6   Using a wire terminal removal tool, remove each individual wire from the turn signal harness connector. Record the color code and location of each wire as you remove them, so that they may be reinstalled in the correct location.
7   Wrap the loose wire ends with tape and tape a pull through wire to the end. Remove the protective wire cover and remove the switch, pulling the wire harness out of the steering column.
8   Remove the tape from the defective switch and tape the wires of the new switch to the pull wire. Gently pull the wire harness through the steering column while guiding the switch into position. Remove the pull wire.
9   Insert the wire terminals back into their proper location in the connector. If they do not snap securely into position, slightly bend the locking tabs out.
10   The remainder of installation is the reverse of removal. Check the operation of all the turn signal and warning flasher functions.

Multi-function switch (later models)
11   Remove the steering column shrouds.
12   Remove the screws securing the switch to the steering column casting and remove the switch.
13   Installation is the reverse of removal.

10   Ignition switch and key lock cylinder - check and replacement

Switch
Early models
1   Disconnect the negative cable from the battery.

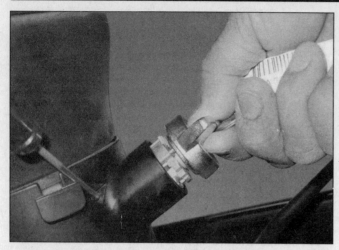

10.19 Depress the retaining pin and pull out the lock cylinder (later models)

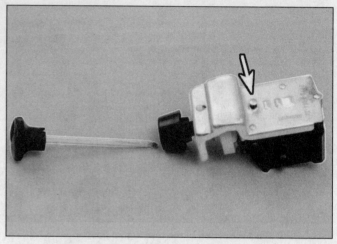

11.2 Reach under the dash and push this button to remove the knob and shaft from the headlight switch (early models)

2   Remove the bolts securing the steering column support bracket. Lower and support the steering column.
3   Remove the nuts securing the ignition switch to the steering column. Lift the switch up, unplug the electrical connector, disengage the actuator rod from the switch and remove the switch.
4   When installing the ignition switch, both the lock cylinder and the ignition switch must be in the LOCK position. Place the lock cylinder in LOCK and remove the key. Place the ignition switch in the LOCK position and insert a 5/64-inch drill bit into the locking pin hole on the side of the switch. **Note:** *New replacement switches will already be pinned in the LOCK position by a shipping pin.*
5   Install the switch by first engaging the actuator rod into the switch. Position the switch on the steering column and install the nuts finger tight.
6   Move the switch up and down along the steering column and when you locate the mid-point of rod lash, tighten the retaining nuts.
7   After removing the lock pin, the remainder of installation is the reverse of removal. Check the operation of the ignition switch in all the positions.

Later models

8   Place the ignition key in the RUN position.
9   Remove the ignition switch retaining screws (a special TORX type bit will be required).
10   Remove the switch from the steering column.
11   To install, align the switch pin with the slot in the lock/column assembly. **Note:** *Both the switch and the ignition key should be in the RUN position, the slot will align with the index mark in the steering column casting when positioned correctly.*
12   Install and tighten the switch retaining screws.
13   The remainder of installation is the reverse of removal.

Key lock cylinder
Check

14   Test the steering column ignition system mechanical operation by rotating the key through all switch positions. The movement should feel smooth with no sticking or binding. The ignition switch should return from the Start position to the Run position without assistance (spring return). If sticking or binding is encountered, remove the lock cylinder assembly and check for burrs on the key and for binding of the lock cylinder. If damage is evident, replace the lock cylinder assembly.

Replacement

Refer to illustration 10.19

Note: *The following procedure pertains only to functional lock cylinders for which keys are available or for which keys can be made when the lock cylinder number is known. If the ignition lock is inoperative and the lock cylinder cannot be turned due to a lost or broken key and the key number is not known, or the lock cylinder cap is damaged and/or broken to the extent that the lock cylinder cannot be turned, have the lock cylinder assembly replaced by a dealer service department or other repair shop. Replacement will likely involve installation not only of a new lock cylinder but a new lock cylinder housing as well, a procedure that requires disassembly of the steering column.*

15   Detach the cable from the negative terminal of the battery.
16   On early models, remove the steering wheel (refer to Chapter 10).
17   On later models, remove the steering column trim shrouds.
18   Turn the lock key to the Run position.
19   Place a 1/8-inch drill bit or a narrow screwdriver in the hole in the casting surrounding the lock cylinder (early models) or in the hole in the trim shroud (later models). Depress the retaining pin while pulling out on the lock cylinder to remove it from the column housing **(see illustration)**.
20   Install the lock cylinder by turning it to

the Run position and depressing the retaining pin. Insert the lock cylinder into the lock cylinder housing. Make sure that the cylinder is completely seated and aligned in the interlocking washer before turning the key to the Off position. This will permit the retaining pin to extend into the hole.
21   Turn the lock to ensure that the operation is correct in all positions.
22   The remainder of installation is the reverse of removal.

---

11   Headlight switch - replacement

Early models

Refer to illustration 11.2

1   Disconnect the cable from the negative battery terminal.
2   Remove the knob on the switch by reaching under the dash and pressing the shaft lock tab while pulling the knob and shaft away from the cluster panel **(see illustration)**.
3   Remove the steering column shroud.
4   Remove the screws securing the top of the instrument cluster finish panel to the dash and remove the finish panel (refer to Section 16).
5   Unscrew the headlight switch mounting nut.
6   Remove the switch from the panel, then disconnect the wiring connector from the switch.
7   Installation is the reverse of the removal procedure. It is not necessary to push the knob lock tabs when reinstalling the knobs.

Later models

Refer to illustration 11.10

8   Disconnect the cable from the negative battery terminal.
9   Unsnap the right and left moldings by carefully prying at the notches on the bottom of the moldings (refer to Section 16).
10   Using a hooked tool, remove the head-

light knob by depressing the spring inside the knob **(see illustration)**.

11 Remove the exposed screws that are under the right and left moldings.

12 Remove the instrument cluster finish panel by unsnapping it's retaining clips starting at the lower clips and then the upper clips.

13 Disconnect the wiring attached to the finish panel and remove the panel.

14 Remove the switch pushrod by inserting a punch or similar tool into the switch access hole while pulling the rod from the switch.

15 Unscrew the switch molding nut and pull the switch out through the rear of the dash.

16 Disconnect the switch wiring harness and remove the switch.

17 Installation is the reverse of removal.

12 Headlights - removal and installation

Sealed beam headlight (early models)

Refer to illustration 12.3

1 The headlights are replaceable sealed-beam units. The high-beam and low-beam filaments are contained in the same unit. If one fails, the entire unit must be replaced with a new one.

2 To replace the headlight unit, first remove the screws retaining the decorative trim ring surrounding the headlight. Be careful not to disturb the two headlight adjusting screws.

3 If the vehicle is equipped with a rectangular headlight unit, remove the four retaining ring screws **(see illustration)**. If the vehicle has a round headlight unit, loosen the retaining ring screws and rotate the ring counterclockwise to release it from the screws.

4 Pull the headlight unit out far enough to allow access to the rear and disconnect the plug from the unit.

5 Replace the headlight unit with one of the exact same size and type. Attach the plug to the prongs at the back of the unit. Place

11.10 To remove the headlight switch knob on later models, use a hooked tool to depress the spring inside the knob, then pull the knob from the shaft

the bulb into the bucket with the large number embossed on the lens at the top. Make sure the alignment lugs cast into the unit are positioned in the recesses of the bucket.

6 Install the retaining ring (if so equipped) and the trim ring.

Halogen bulb headlights (aerodynamically styled)

Refer to illustrations 12.8 and 12.10

Warning: *The replaceable halogen bulb contains gas under pressure. The bulb may shatter if the glass is scratched or the bulb is dropped. Handle the bulb carefully. Grasp the bulb only by it's plastic base to avoid touching the glass. If you do touch the glass, clean it off with rubbing alcohol.*

7 Make sure the headlamp switch is in the OFF position. Lift the hood and locate the bulb installed in the rear of the headlamp body.

8 Remove the bulb retaining ring by rotating it counterclockwise (when viewed from rear) and sliding the ring off of the housing **(see illustration)**. Keep the ring; it will be used again to retain the new bulb.

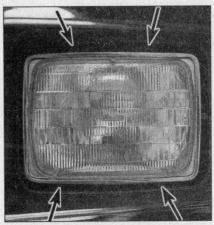

12.3 Location of the four headlight retaining ring screws - early models (note the adjusting screws on the outboard side and top center - DO NOT loosen these screws)

9 Carefully remove the headlamp bulb by gently pulling it straight out of the housing.

10 Unplug the bulb from its electrical connector **(see illustration)**. Plug the new bulb into the connector, being careful not to touch the glass with your fingers (oil from your skin can cause the bulb to overheat, causing premature failure).

11 With the flat side of the plastic bulb base facing upward, insert the bulb into the socket. Turn the base slightly to the left or right, if necessary, to align the grooves in the forward part of the plastic base with the corresponding locating the tabs inside the socket. When the grooves are aligned, push the bulb firmly into the socket until the mounting flange on the base contacts the rear face of the socket.

12 Slip the bulb retaining ring over the rear of the plastic base against the mounting flange. Lock the ring into the socket by rotating the ring clockwise. A stop will be felt when the retaining ring is fully engaged.

13 Turn the headlamps on and check for proper operation. **Note:** *A properly aimed*

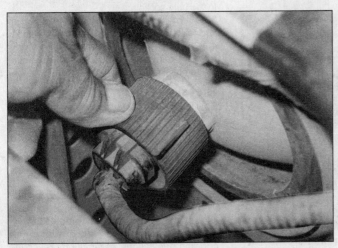

12.8 Unscrew the retaining ring . . .

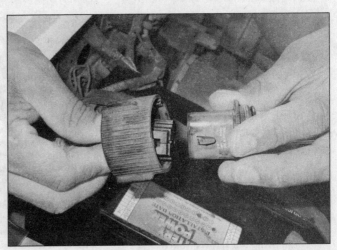

12.10 . . . then unplug the bulb from its electrical connector

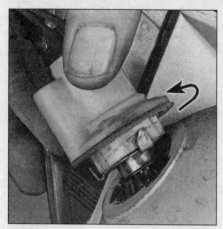

13.2 To remove the bulb holder from the side marker/turn signal lamp assembly, turn it counterclockwise and pull it out

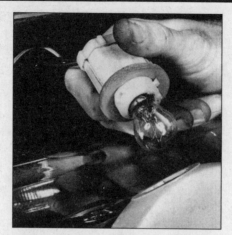

13.6 Rotate the socket while holding the lamp assembly to remove the socket/bulb for replacement

headlamp normally need not be re-aimed after installation of this bulb. A burned out bulb should not be removed from the headlamp reflector until just before a replacement bulb is to be installed. Removal of a bulb for an extended period of time may allow contaminants (dust, moisture, smoke) to enter the headlamp body and affect the performance of the headlamp. When servicing the headlamp bulb, energize the bulb only while it is contained within the headlamp body.

Headlight assembly replacement (aerodynamically styled)

Warning: *The replaceable halogen bulb contains gas under pressure. The bulb may shatter if the glass is scratched or the bulb is dropped. Handle the bulb carefully. Grasp the bulb only by it's plastic base to avoid touching the glass. If you do touch the glass, clean it off with rubbing alcohol.*

14   Remove the parking/turn/side indicator light assembly from the grill opening by removing the upper screws and lower nuts.
15   Pull the parking/turn/side indicator light assembly from the grill opening and unplug

the bulb connectors. Remove the assembly completely.
16   Remove the headlight bulb from the rear of the headlight housing as described in Steps 7 through 9 this Section.
17   Unsnap the upper headlight assembly retainers to release the assembly from the front grill.
18   Turn the horizontal adjuster completely out of the adjusting nut.
19   Remove the headlight assembly from the vehicle.
20   Installation is the reverse of removal. After installation the headlight must be properly adjusted (aimed) (refer to Section 17).

13   Front parking, turn and side marker lights - replacement

Early models

Refer to illustrations 13.2 and 13.6

Front parking lights

1   From inside the engine compartment, locate the bulb socket in the rear of the lamp housing.

2   Turn the socket counterclockwise and pull it out of the housing **(see illustration)**.
3   Replace the defective bulb with a new one and reinstall the socket in the housing.

Front side marker lights

4   Remove the two screws securing the side marker lens.
5   Pull the lamp assembly out of the fender.
6   Turn the socket counterclockwise and pull it out of the housing **(see illustration)**.
7   Replace the defective bulb with a new one and reinstall the assembly by reversing the removal procedure.

Later models (aerodynamically styled)

Note: *The parking, turn indicator and side marker lamps are all housed in a single lamp assembly.*

8   Remove the parking/turn/side indicator light lamp assembly from the grill opening by removing the upper screws and lower nuts.
9   Pull the assembly from the grill opening and remove the failed bulb socket from the lamp assembly by rotating the socket.
10   Remove the failed bulb from the socket and replace it with a new bulb.
11   Installation is the reverse of removal.

14   Rear brake, turn, back-up, parking and side marker lights - replacement

Tail light assembly bulbs

Note: *The rear tail light lamp assembly includes the combined brake, turn, and parking lamp plus the back-up lamp.*

Styleside pick-up and Bronco

Refer to illustrations 14.1 and 14.2

1   Remove the screws from the face of the tail light lens **(see illustration)**.
2   With the tailgate down, remove the screws from the rear of the lens **(see illustration)** and pull the lens and light assembly away from the body far enough to gain access to the bulb sockets.
3   Turn the socket with the failed bulb counterclockwise and pull it out of the light assembly.
4   Replace the defective bulb with a new one and reinstall the assembly by reversing the removal procedure.

Flareside pick-up

5   Remove the screws retaining the lens.
6   Replace the defective bulb with a new one and reinstall the lens.

Rear side marker lights

7   Remove the screws securing the side marker lens.
8   Pull the lamp assembly out of the fender.
9   Turn the socket counterclockwise and pull it out of the housing **(see illustration 13.6)**.
10   Replace the defective bulb with a new one and reinstall the assembly by reversing the removal procedure.

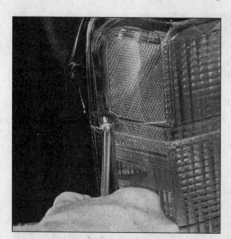

14.1 Removing the screws from the face of the tail light lens on a Styleside pick-up

14.2 Removing the screws from the rear of the tail light lens on a Styleside pick-up

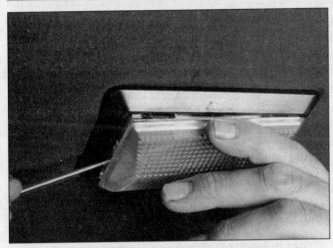

15.11 To replace the dome light bulb, pop the plastic lens loose with a small screwdriver

16.5a To remove the instrument cluster finish panel, remove these screws from the right side . . .

Hi-mounted brake light

11   Remove the two screws retaining the lamp assembly to the top.

12   Pull the lamp assembly away from the top.

13   Disconnect the lamp wiring connector from the vehicle wiring.

14   Remove the bulbs sockets from the lamp assembly by twisting, then replace the failed bulbs.

15   Installation is the reverse of removal.

15   License plate, dome, and cargo lights - replacement

License plate light (vehicles with rear bumper)

1   From the rear side of the light assembly, rotate the bulb socket turn and pull the socket out.

2   Remove the defective bulb and replace it with a new one, then reinstall the socket in the light assembly.

License plate light (vehicles without rear bumper)

Styleside pick-up

3   Remove the screws retaining the license plate light cover to the light assembly.

4   Remove the defective bulb and replace it with a new one.

5   Reinstall the light cover.

Flareside pick-up

6   Remove the two screws retaining the light assembly to the license plate bracket assembly.

7   Rotate the bulb socket and pull it out of the light assembly.

8   Remove the defective bulb and replace it with a new one.

9   Install the socket in the light assembly.

10   Install the light assembly.

Dome light

Refer to illustration 15.11

11   Using a screwdriver at the corners of the plastic lens, carefully pry it off the light assembly **(see illustration)**.

12   Replace the defective bulb with a new one and snap the plastic lens back into place.

Cargo area light

F100-F350

13   Remove the two screws retaining the lens and light assembly to the rear of the cab.

14   Replace the defective bulb with a new one and reinstall the lens and light assembly.

Bronco

15   Using a screwdriver at the corners of the light assembly in the cargo area, carefully pry it from the body.

16   Replace the defective bulb with a new one and snap the light assembly back into place.

16   Instrument cluster - removal, bulb replacement and installation

Early models

Refer to illustrations 16.5a, 16.5b and 16.6

1   Disconnect the cable from the negative battery terminal.

2   Using a hook tool to release each knob lock tab, remove the knobs from the wiper-washer, headlight and fog light (if so equipped) switches.

3   Remove the screws retaining the steering column shrouds. **Note:** *Caution should be taken not to damage the transmission control selector indicator on vehicles equipped with an automatic transmission.*

4   On vehicles with an automatic transmission, remove the loop on the indicator cable assembly from the retainer pin and open the cable retaining clips (two for tilt column-nequipped vehicles, one for non-tilt steering). Remove the bracket screw from the cable bracket and slide the bracket out of the slot in the column.

5   Remove the screws retaining the cluster finish panel to the dash and remove the finish panel **(see illustrations)**.

6   Remove the four instrument cluster

16.5b . . . and these screws from the left side

16.6 Instrument cluster mounting screws

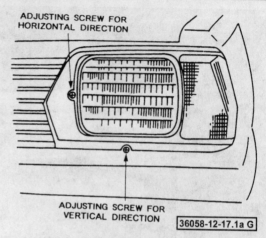

17.1a Headlight adjusting screws - sealed-beam headlights

retaining screws **(see illustration)** and pull the cluster out far enough to reach behind it and pry the retaining tab up to release the speedometer cable from the cluster. Disconnect the wire connector from the printed circuit, disconnect the 4x4 indicator light (if equipped) and remove the instrument cluster.

7   Replace the failed bulbs as required by simply twisting the socket from the back of the instrument cluster.

8   When installing the instrument cluster, reconnect the wire connector, cable and light (if equipped), then install the cluster and retaining screws.

9   On vehicles equipped with an automatic transmission, place the loop on the transmission indicator cable assembly over the retainer on the column.

10   Position the tab on the cable bracket in the slot in the column.

11   Align the pointer and attach the retaining screw.

12   Reposition the cable conduit in the retaining clip(s) and secure it.

13   With the parking brake applied, place the transmission selector at the steering column in the Drive position. Hold the lever against the Drive stop using a weight of approximately eight pounds attached to the selector lever knob.

14   Secure the cable to the column mounting clip(s) and adjust the bracket to position the pointer in the proper location.

15   Shift the transmission lever to each gear, checking the pointer position at each transmission shift position.

16   The remainder of the installation steps are the reverse of removal.

Later models (programmable speedometer/odometer)

17   Disconnect the cable from the negative battery terminal.

18   Unsnap the right and left moldings by carefully prying at the notches on the bottom of the moldings.

19   Using a hooked tool, remove the headlight knob by depressing the spring inside of the knob.

20   Remove the exposed screws that are under the right and left moldings.

21   Remove the instrument cluster finish panel by unsnapping it's retaining clips starting at the lower clips and then the upper clips.

22   Disconnect the wiring attached to the finish panel and remove the panel.

23   Remove the transmission indicator cable loop from the ball stud on the shift lever (automatic transmission only) **(see illustration)**.

24   Remove the thumbwheel bracket from the steering column by removing the thumbwheel bracket screws (automatic transmissions only).

25   Remove the screws attaching the instrument cluster assembly to the instrument panel and pull the cluster out of the panel **(see illustration 16.6)**. **Warning:** *Always store and place the instrument cluster in an upright (normal in dash) position. Failure to do so can result in loss of gauge anti-vibration fluid and contamination of the gauge face with fluid.*

26   Disconnect the electrical connectors and remove the instrument cluster assembly.

27   Replace the failed bulbs as required by simply twisting the socket from the back of the

instrument cluster.

28   The remainder of the installation is the reverse of removal.

17 Headlights - adjustment

Refer to illustrations 17.1a, 17.1b and 17.2

Note: *It is important that the headlights be aimed correctly. If adjusted incorrectly they could blind the driver of an oncoming vehicle and cause a serious accident or seriously reduce your ability to see the road. The headlights should be checked for proper aim every 12 months and any time a new headlight is installed or front end body work is performed. It should be emphasized that the following procedure is only an interim step which will provide temporary adjustment until the headlights can be adjusted by a properly equipped shop.*

1   Earlier model sealed beam type headlights have two spring loaded adjusting screws, one on the top, controlling up-and-down movement and one on the side, controlling left-and-right movement **(see illustration)**. Later year aerodynamically styled halo-

17.1b Headlight adjusting screws - aerodynamic headlights

A   *Turn this screw for right-and-left adjustments*

B   *Turn this screw for up-and-down adjustments*

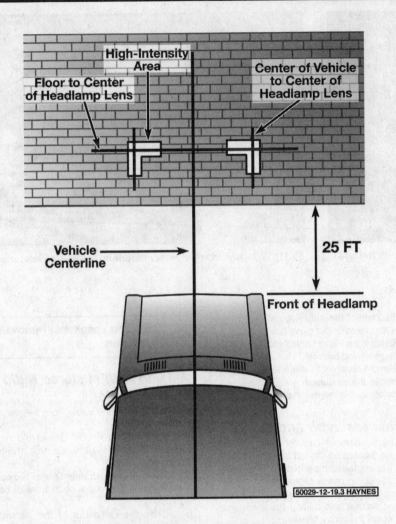

17.2 Headlight adjustment details

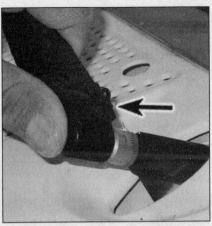

18.2 Pull the slide latch out and remove the wiper arm from its pivot shaft

gen headlights utilize one upper adjusting screw for left-and-right movement and one inner corner angle drive mechanism for up-and-down movement **(see illustration)**.

2   There are several methods of adjusting the headlights. The simplest method requires a blank wall 25 feet in front of the vehicle and a level floor **(see illustration)**.

3   Position masking tape vertically on the wall in reference to the vehicle centerline and the centerlines of both headlights.

4   Position a horizontal tape line in reference to the centerline of all the headlights. **Note:** *It may be easier to position the tape on the wall with the vehicle parked only a few inches away.*

5   Adjustment should be made with the vehicle sitting level, the gas tank half-full and no unusually heavy load in the vehicle.

6   Starting with the low beam adjustment, position the high intensity zone so it is two inches below the horizontal line and two inches to the side of the headlight vertical line, away from oncoming traffic. Adjustment is made by turning the appropriate adjusting screw (refer to Step 1) to raise or lower the beam or to move the beam left or right.

7   With the high beams on, the high intensity zone should be vertically centered with the exact center just below the horizontal line. **Note:** *It may not be possible to position the headlight aim exactly for both high and low beams. If a compromise must be made, keep in mind that the low beams are the most used and have the greatest effect on driver safety.*

8   Have the headlights adjusted by a dealer service department at the earliest opportunity.

18   Wiper and washer system - component replacement

Refer to illustrations 18.2, 18.11a and 18.11b

1   The windshield wiper/washer system on vehicles covered by this manual consists of a motor with dual speed capabilities (plus optional interval operations), linkages to convert rotary motion of the motor to oscillating movement at the blades and the wiper blades themselves. Windshield wiper blade replacement instructions can be found in Chapter 1.

In addition, washer chores are handled by a plastic reservoir equipped with a pump which distributes washing fluid to a nozzle on each side of the windshield. On early models, the functions are controlled by a single dash mounted switch. On late models, the functions are controlled by the multi-function switch (refer to Section 9).

Arm and blade assembly

2   Raise the blade end of the arm off the windshield and move the slide latch away from the pivot shaft **(see illustration)**.

3   The wiper arm can now be pulled off the pivot shaft without the aid of any tools.

4   Reinstall the arm and blade assembly by holding the main arm head on the pivot shaft while raising the blade end of the wiper arm and pushing the slide latch into the lock under the pivot head shaft. **Note:** *When reinstalling the wiper arms, make sure the motor is in the Parked position by allowing it to run a few cycles, then turning it off. The shafts will then come to rest in the parked position.*

Wiper motor

5   Disconnect the cable from the negative battery terminal.

6   Remove both wiper arm and blade assemblies from the pivot shafts.

7   Remove the cowl grille attaching screws and lift the grille slightly.

8   Disconnect the washer nozzle hose and remove the grille assembly.

9   Remove the wiper linkage clip from the motor output arm and disconnect the linkage from the arm.

10   Disconnect the wiper motor wiring connector.

11   Remove the three motor attaching screws and remove the motor **(see illustrations)**.

12   Installation is the reverse of the removal procedure.

Pivot shaft and linkage

13   Refer to and perform Steps 5 through 9.

14   Remove the pivot body-to-cowl screws, then remove the linkage and pivot shaft

18.11a Location of the windshield wiper motor beneath the cowl in the engine compartment - early models

18.11b Windshield wiper motor mounting fasteners - later models

assembly. The left and right pivots and linkage are independent and can be serviced separately.

15 Installation is the reverse of the removal procedure. Refer to the **Note** in Step 4.

Wiper/washer control switch (early models)

16 Remove the wiper switch knob using a hooked tool to release the clip.

17 Remove the bezel nut by unthreading it from the switch. Remove the switch bezel.

18 Pull the switch out from the rear of the instrument panel.

19 Disconnect the plug-in wire connector from the switch and remove the switch.

20 Installation is the reverse of the removal procedure.

Interval governor (if so equipped, early models)

21 Disconnect the wire connectors from the governor.

22 Remove the governor attaching screws and remove the governor. **Note:** *On models with an electric rear window, remove the electric device switch assembly to obtain tool clearance for the right-hand governor attaching screw.*

23 Installation is the reverse of the removal procedure.

Wiper/washer control switch (later models)

24 Operation is controlled by the multifunction switch (refer to Section 9).

Wiper control module (if so equipped, later models)

Note: *The wiper control module provides interval wiper operation and windshield washer pump control on vehicles so equipped.*

25 Disconnect the negative cable from the battery and remove the glove box.

26 Remove the wiper control module (WCM) from it's mounting bracket.

27 Remove the WCM electrical connector and remove the module.

28 Installation is the reverse of removal.

Washer reservoir and pump

29 The windshield washer reservoir and pump are located on the left inner fenderwell, inside the engine compartment. If the reservoir or the pump needs replacement, the reservoir may be removed by removing the three retaining screws and pulling the wiring connector out of the motor terminals.

30 Using a small screwdriver, pry out the retaining ring.

31 To remove the pump from the reservoir, grasp the wall of the pump near the electrical terminals with pliers and pull the pump out of the reservoir. If the impeller and/or the seal come off of the pump during this operation, they may be reassembled.

32 Installation is basically the reverse of the removal procedure. Lubricate the outside of the pump seal with a dry lubricant such as powdered graphite. Align the tang of the pump end cap with the slot in the reservoir before pushing the pump into the reservoir. Also, use a 1 inch socket (preferably 12 point) to hand press the retaining ring securely against the pump end plate.

19 Horn - removal and installation

1 Disconnect the cable from the negative terminal of the battery.

2 Locate the horns mounted on the back side of the radiator support.

3 Unplug the electrical connectors.

4 Remove the mounting bolt and remove the horns.

5 Installation is the reverse of removal.

20 Radio and speakers - removaland installation

AM and AM/FM stereo radio (early models)

1 Disconnect the cable from the negative battery terminal.

2 Remove the knobs, discs, and retaining nuts from the radio control shafts, if equipped.

3 Remove the instrument panel bezel.

4 Remove the rear support bracket bolt (if equipped).

5 Slide the radio out of the instrument panel and disconnect the antenna cable and wire connector(s).

6 Separate the radio chassis from the mounting plate.

7 Installation is the reverse of removal.

Electronic radio and stereo tape player (later models)

Refer to illustration 20.8

8 The procedure for removal and installation of the radio in later models is much simpler than for earlier units. However, you'll have to obtain a pair of special radio removal tools - available from a dealer or an automotive radio store **(see illustration)**.

9 Disconnect the cable from the negative battery terminal.

10 Insert the radio removal tools into each side of the radio faceplate. Press them in a full inch to release the radio retaining clips. Pull the radio out of the instrument panel using the tools as handles.

11 Unplug the wiring connectors and antenna cable from the rear of the radio.

12 If you're replacing the radio, switch the rear mounting bracket to the new radio.

13 Attach the wiring connectors and antenna cable to the radio.

20.8 Late model radios require special tools - the tools are inserted in holes provided in both sides of the radio to unlock the radio retaining springs and allow removal

14   Slide the radio into the instrument panel. Engage the rear mounting bracket in the track in the instrument panel.

15   Connect the cable to the negative battery terminal.

Speakers

Front speaker

16   Remove the instrument panel pad.

17   Remove the speaker wire connector.

18   Remove the screws retaining the speaker to the instrument panel and remove the speaker.

19   Installation is the reverse of removal.

Door speakers

20   Remove the door trim panel (see Chapter 11).

21   Remove the speaker mounting screws.

22   Pull the speaker from the mounting recess in the door and unplug the electrical connector.

23   Installation is the reverse of removal.

Rear speakers

24   Detach the cable from the negative terminal of the battery.

25   Remove the speaker screws and body-side trim panel grille.

26   On SuperCab and Bronco vehicles, the speaker trim cover must be removed to gain access to the speaker screws.

27   Remove the speaker and grille assembly and disconnect the wiring connector at the speaker.

28   Installation is reverse of removal.

21   Radio antenna - check and replacement

Note: *If you are replacing a worn or broken antenna mast, unscrew the old mast and install a new one. If, however, reception is poor (even though the antenna looks okay) perform the following tests and, if the antenna assembly fails either test, refer to the replacement part of this Section and replace the entire antenna base and cable assembly.*

Resistance check

Antenna cable-to-mast

1   With the antenna cable installed on the vehicle and the cable unplugged from the radio, check the resistance between the cable and the mast with an ohmmeter. The resistance should be less than five ohms.

2   If the indicated reading is correct, the antenna is okay. If not, check the antenna cable and base.

Antenna cable

3   With the antenna cable unplugged from the radio and antenna, check the resistance of the cable with an ohmmeter. Again, the resistance should be less than five ohms.

4   If the indicated reading is correct, the cable is okay. If not, replace the antenna cable.

Antenna

5   With the antenna cable unplugged, check the resistance of the antenna with an ohmmeter by contacting the probes of the meter between the mast and the probe in the center of the antenna socket.

6   If the indicated reading is less than five ohms, the antenna is okay. If not, replace the antenna.

Replacement

7   Detach the antenna cable from the radio. If you are unable to disconnect the cable this way, pull the radio out of the dashboard and disconnect the antenna cable from the back of the radio (see Section 20).

8   Detach all the antenna cable retaining clips along the bottom of the instrument panel. **Note:** *It may be necessary to remove glove box.*

9   Unscrew the antenna mast from it's base.

10   Pry the cap loose with a small screwdriver. **Caution:** *Do not damage the paint.*

11   Remove the base attaching screws.

12   Pull the antenna cable through the hole in the fender far enough to detach the base.

13   From inside the passenger compart-

ment, remove the antenna cable. The grommet in the inner cowl should come free. If it doesn't, from the engine compartment, pry it loose with a small screwdriver. Remove the antenna cable assembly from the vehicle.

14   Installation is the reverse of removal.

22   Cruise control - general information

Because of the complexity of the cruise control system and the special tools and techniques required for diagnosis, and the considerations of safety, repair should be left to a dealer service department or other repair shop. However, it is possible for the home mechanic to make simple checks of the wiring and vacuum connections for minor faults which can be easily repaired. These include:

a) *Inspect the cruise control actuating switches for broken wires and loose connections.*

b) *Check the cruise control fuse.*

c) *Except for later models, the cruise control system is operated by vacuum so it's critical that all vacuum switches, hoses and connections are secure. Check the hoses in the engine compartment for tight connections, cracks and obvious vacuum leaks.*

23   Power door lock system - general information

The power door lock system operates the door lock actuators mounted in each door. The system consists of the switches, actuators and associated wiring. Diagnosis can usually be limited to simple checks of the wiring connections and actuators for minor faults which can be easily repaired. These include:

a) *Check the system fuse and/or circuit-breaker.*

b) *Check the switch wires for damage and loose connections. Check the switches for continuity.*

c) *Remove the door panel(s) and check the actuator wiring connections to see if they're loose or damaged. Inspect the actuator rods (if equipped) to make sure they aren't bent or damaged. Inspect the actuator wiring for damaged or loose connections. The actuator can be checked by applying battery power momentarily. A discernible click indicates that the solenoid is operating properly.*

24   Power windows - general information

The power window system operates the electric motors mounted in the doors which lower and raise the windows. The system consists of the control switches, the motors (regulators), glass mechanisms and associated wiring.

Diagnosis can usually be limited to simple checks of the wiring connections and motors for minor faults which can be easily repaired. These include:

a) *Inspect the power window actuating-switches for broken wires and loose connections.*

b) *Check the power window fuse/and or circuit breaker.*

c) *Remove the door panel(s) and check the power window motor wires to see if they're loose or damaged. Inspect the glass mechanisms for damage which could cause binding.*

25 Wiring diagrams - general information

Since it isn't possible to include all wiring diagrams for every year covered by this manual, the following diagrams are those that are typical and most commonly needed.

Prior to troubleshooting any circuits, check the fuse and circuit breakers (if equipped) to make sure they're in good condition. Make sure the battery is properly charged and has clean, tight cable connections (Chapter 1).

When checking the wiring, make sure all connectors are clean, with no broken or loose pins. When unplugging a connector, don't pull on the wires, only on the connector housings themselves.

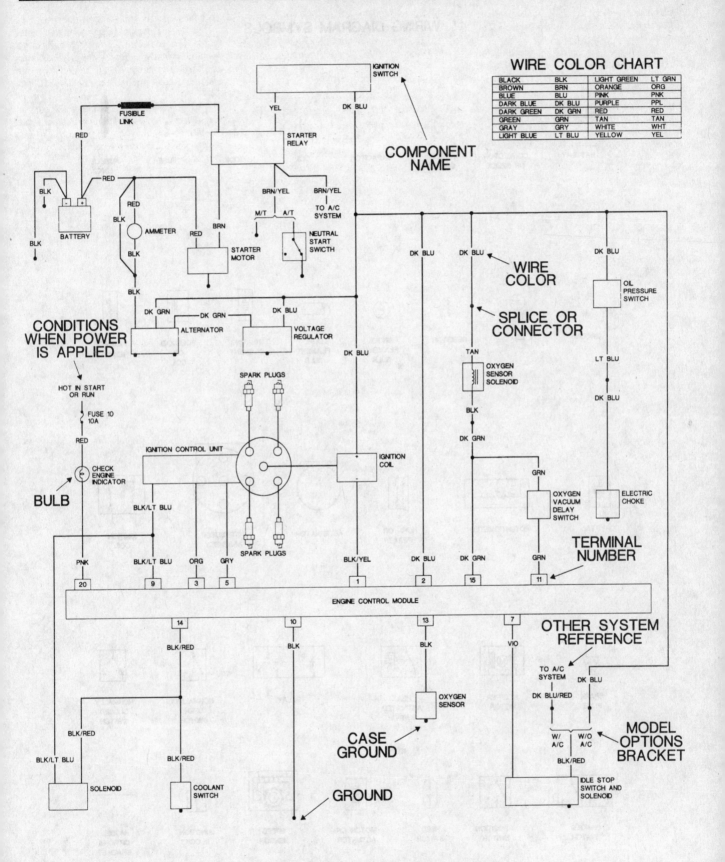

Sample diagram - how to read and interpret wiring

WIRING DIAGRAM SYMBOLS

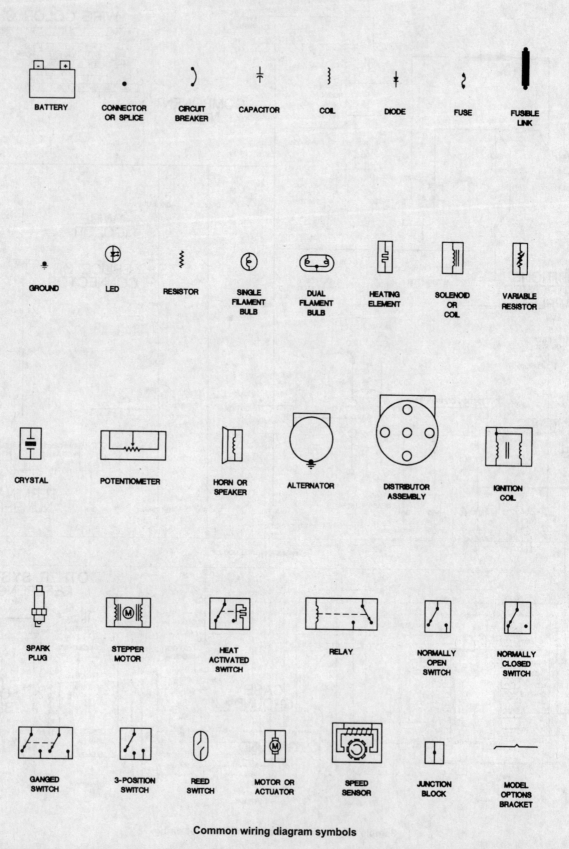

Common wiring diagram symbols

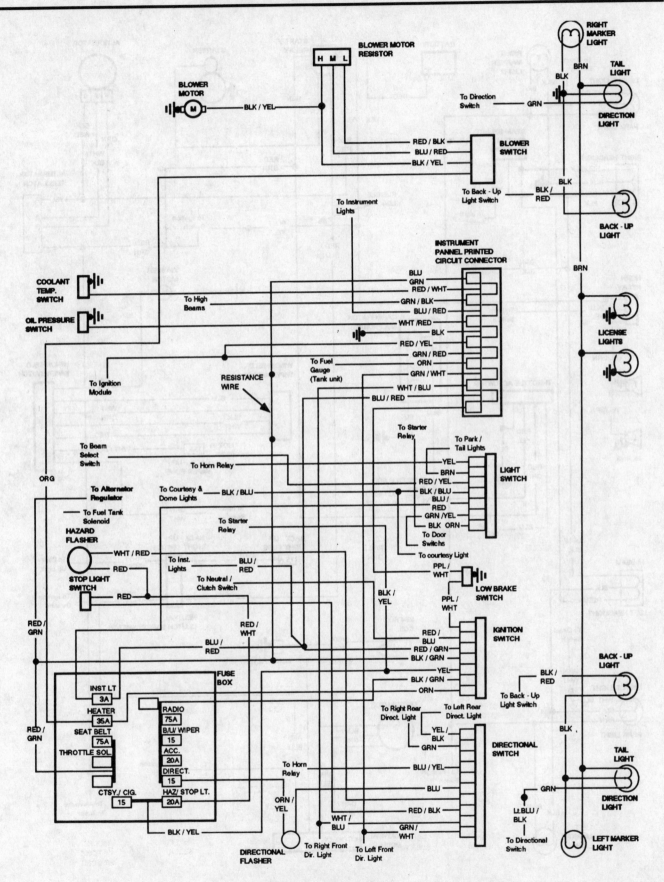

1980 F-Series Pick-up - Part 1

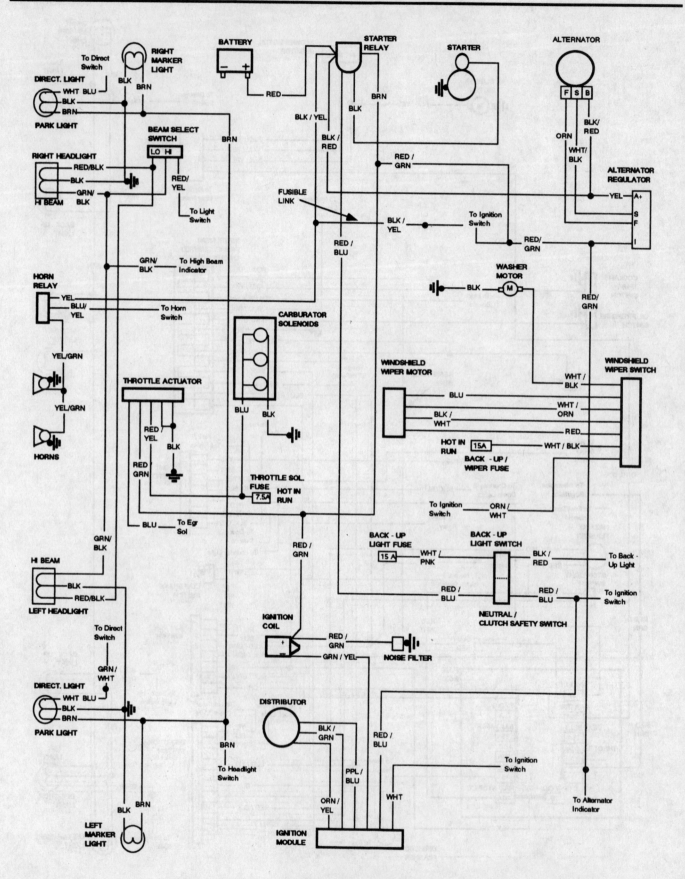

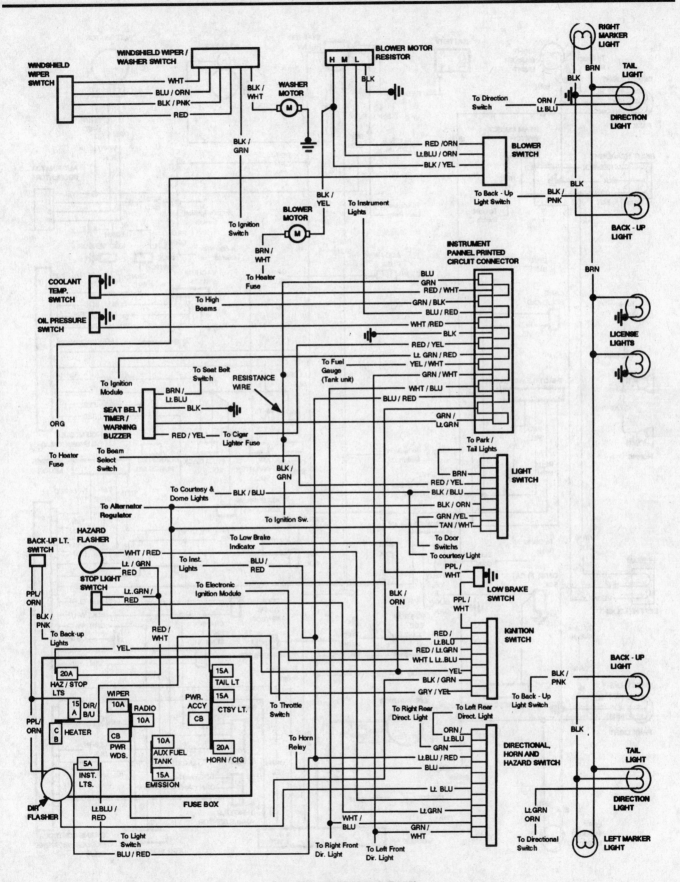

1981 F-Series Pick-up - Part 1

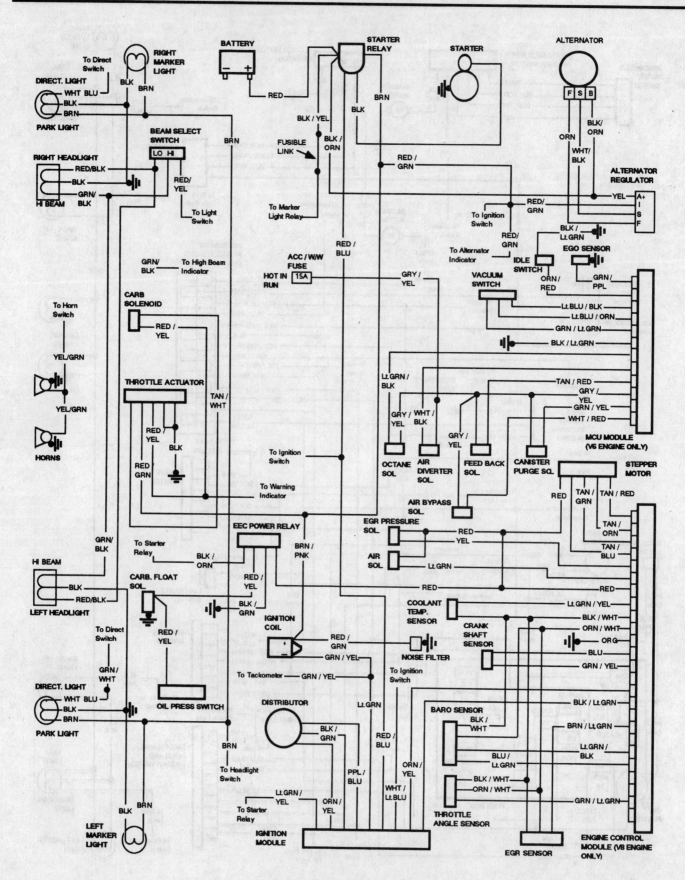

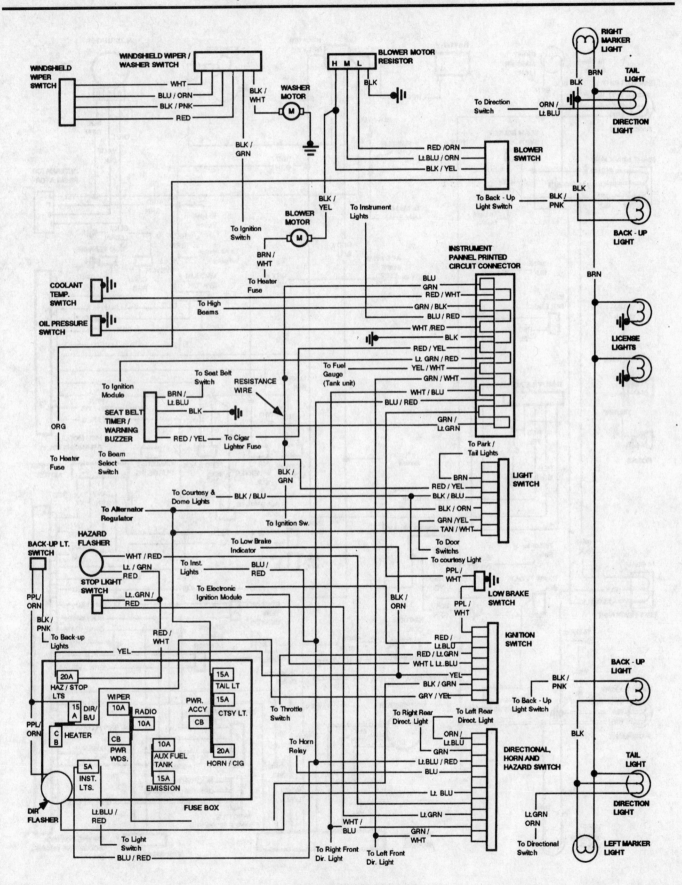

1982 F-Series Pick-up

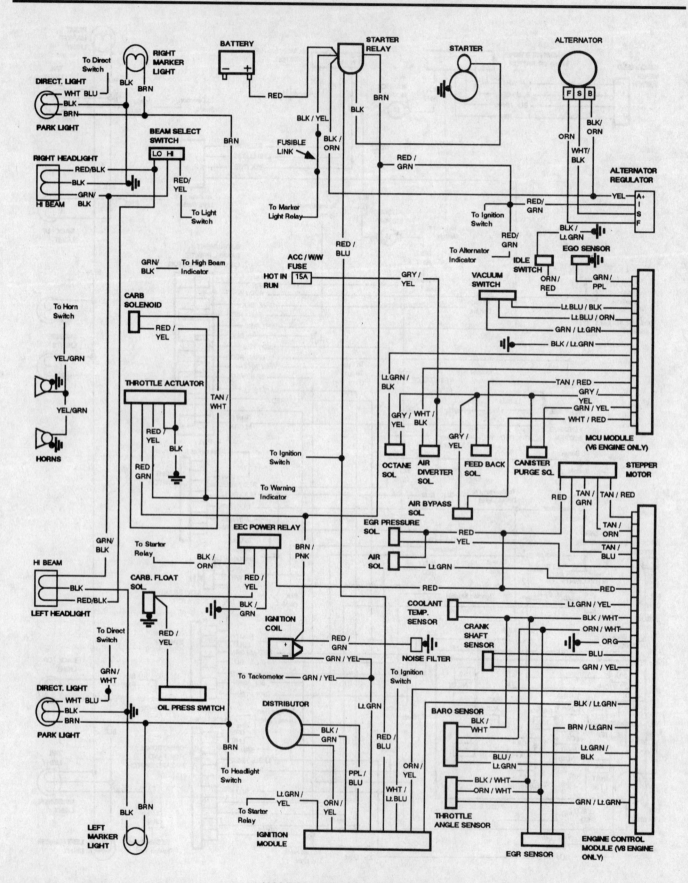

1982 F-Series Pick-up and Bronco

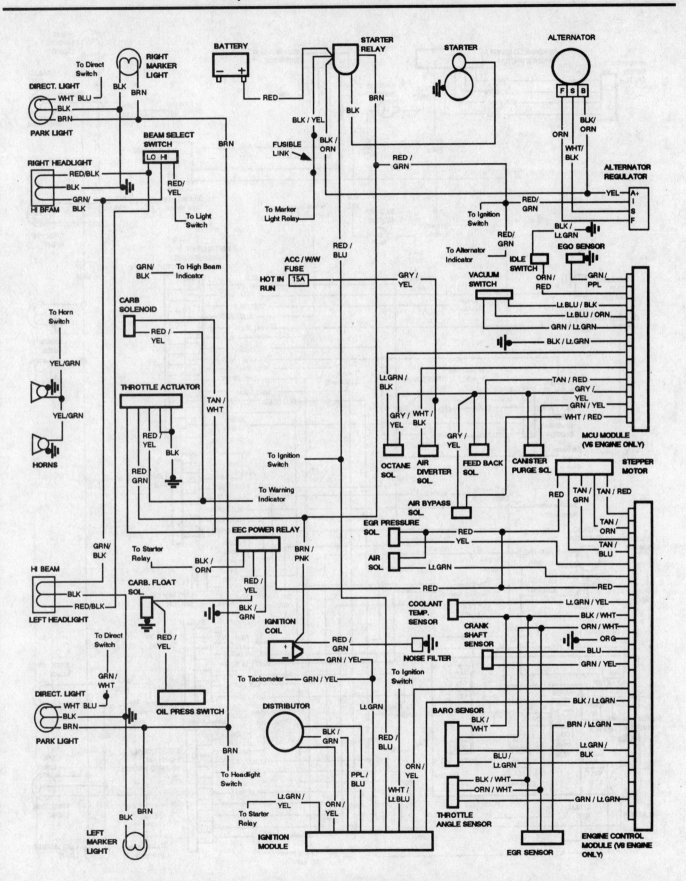

1983 F-Series Pick-up and Bronco

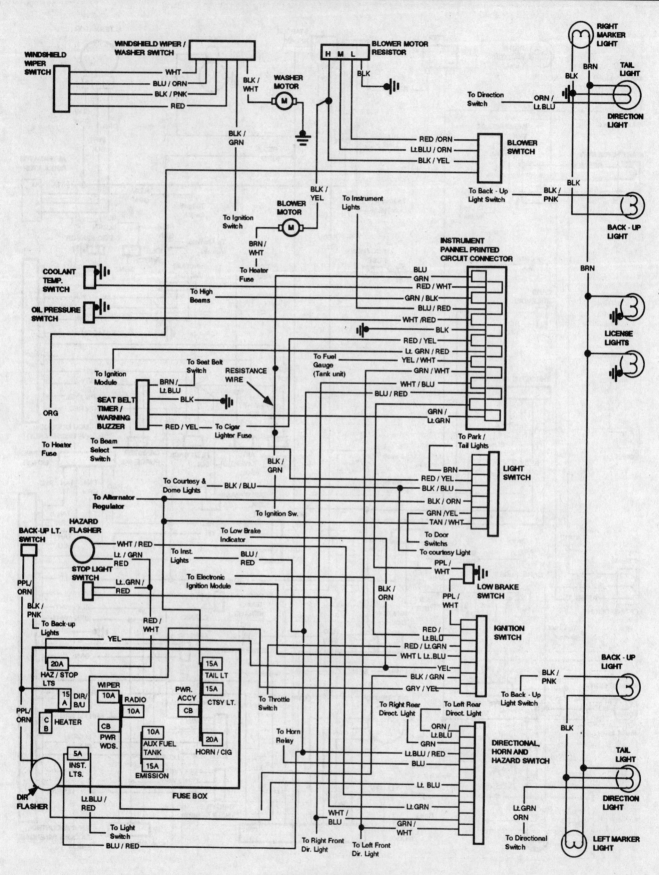

1983 F-Series Pick-up

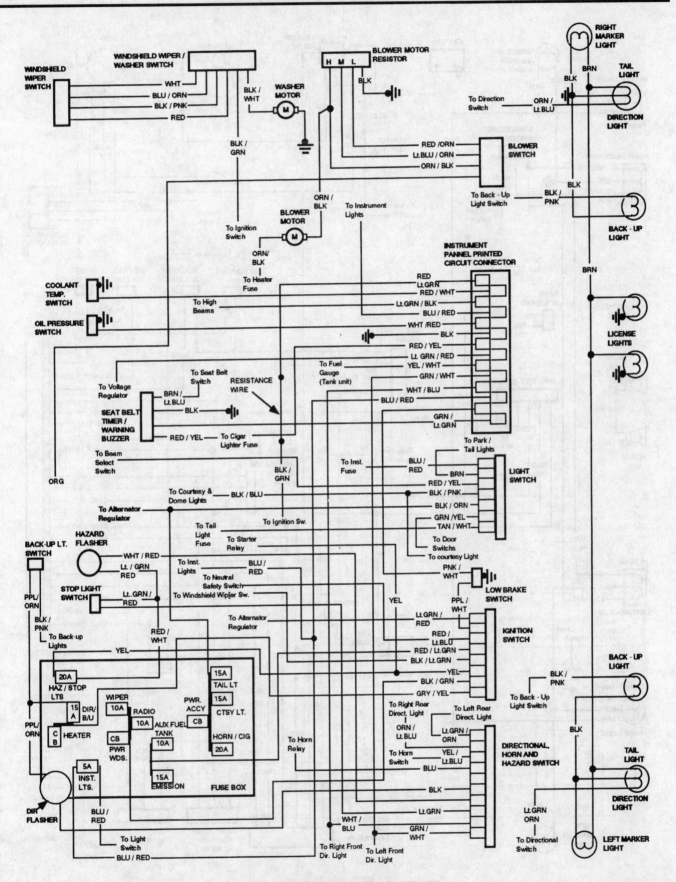

1984 F-Series Pick-up and Bronco - Part 1

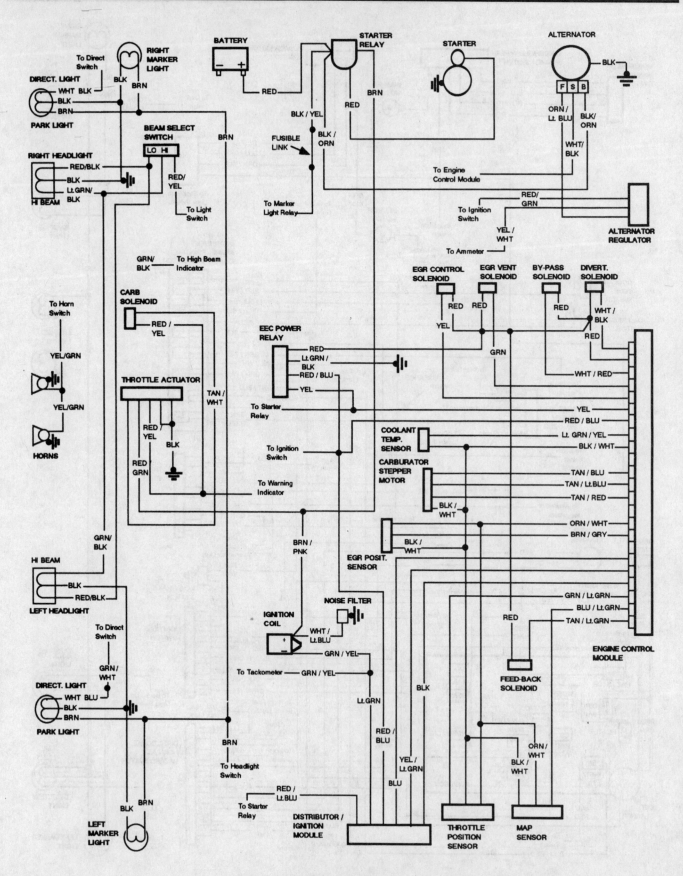

1984 F-Series Pick-up and Bronco - Part 2

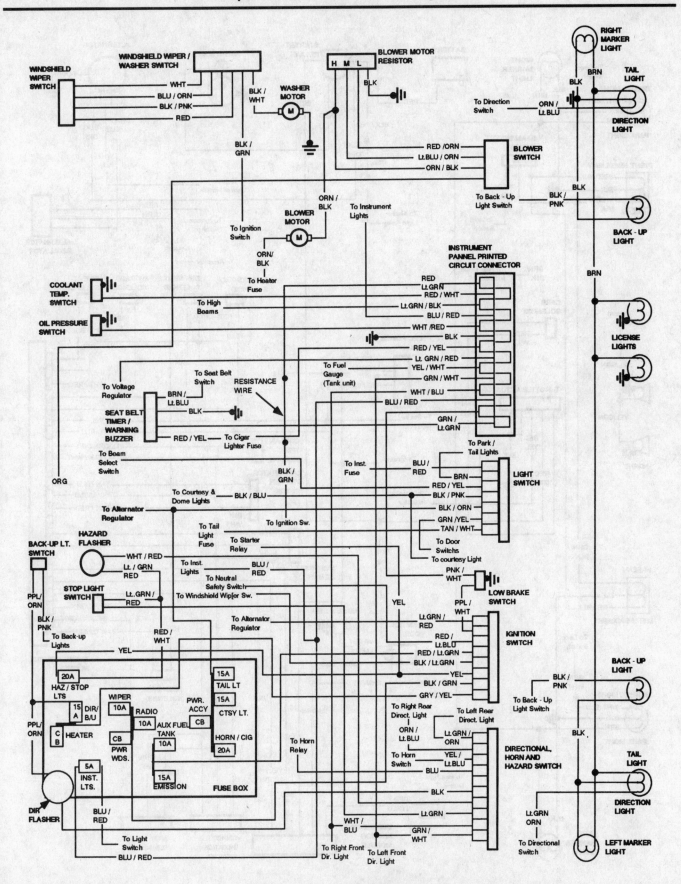

1985 F-Series Pick-up and Bronco - Part 1

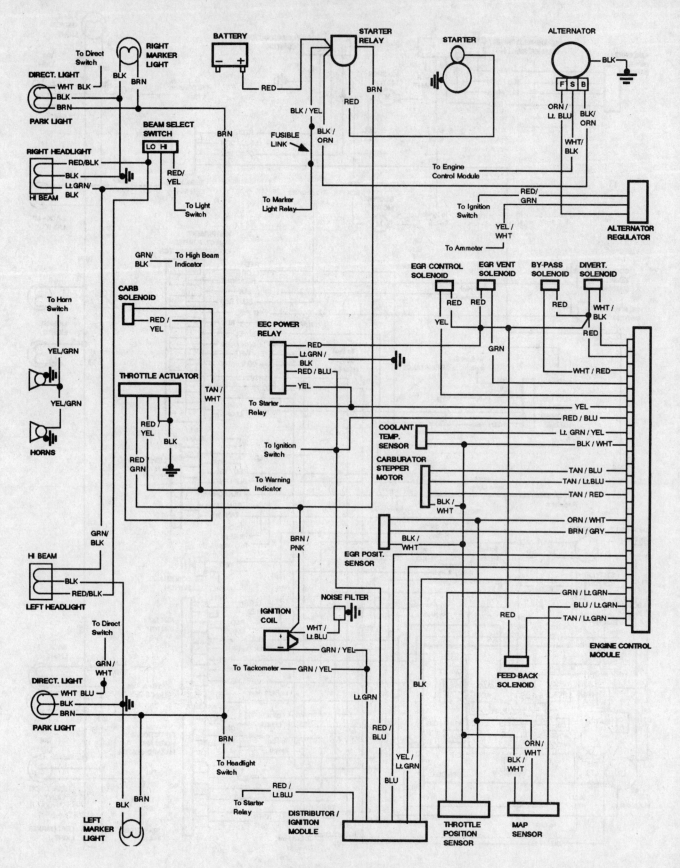

1985 F-Series Pick-up and Bronco - Part 2

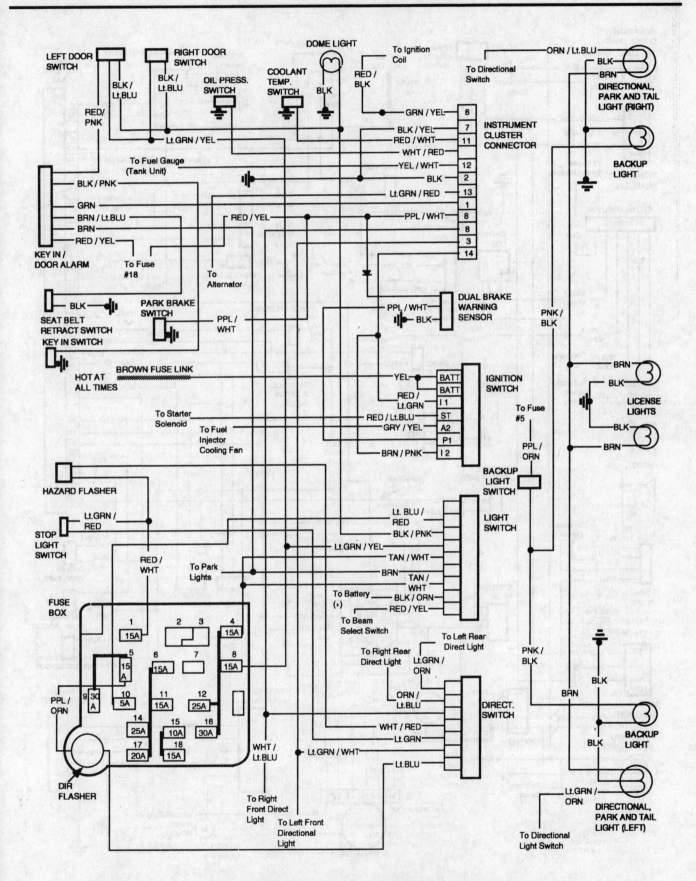

1986 F-Series Pick-up and Bronco - Part 1

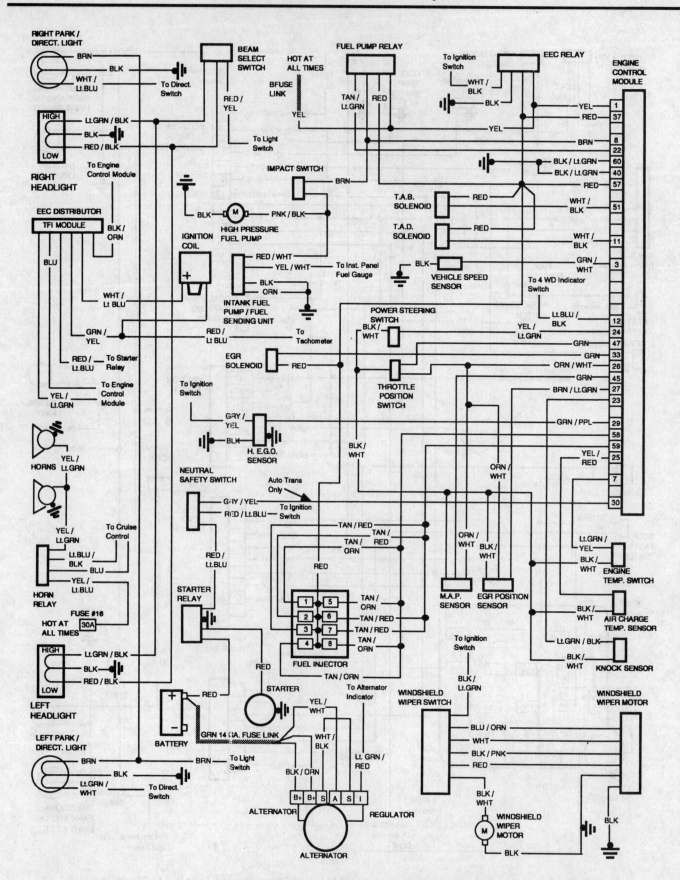

1986 F-Series Pick-up and Bronco - Part 2

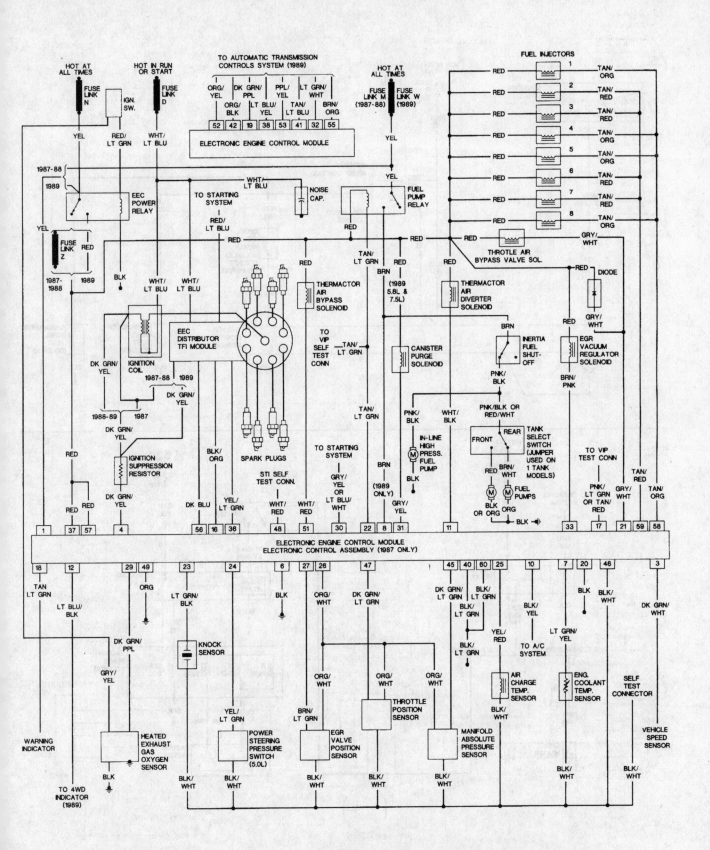

Engine wiring - 1987-89 F-Series and Bronco 5.0L (VIN N), 1988-89 F-Series and Bronco 5.8L (VIN H) and 1988-89 F-Series Pick-up 7.5L (VIN G) engines

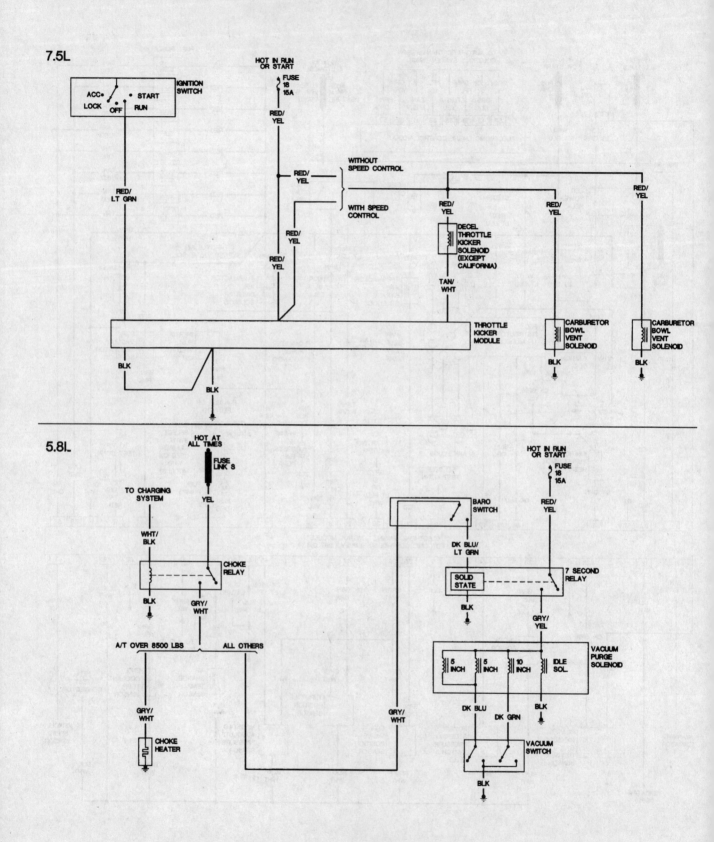

Engine wiring - 1987 F-Series Pick-up 7.5L (VIN G), 1987 F-Series and Bronco 5.8L (VIN H) engines

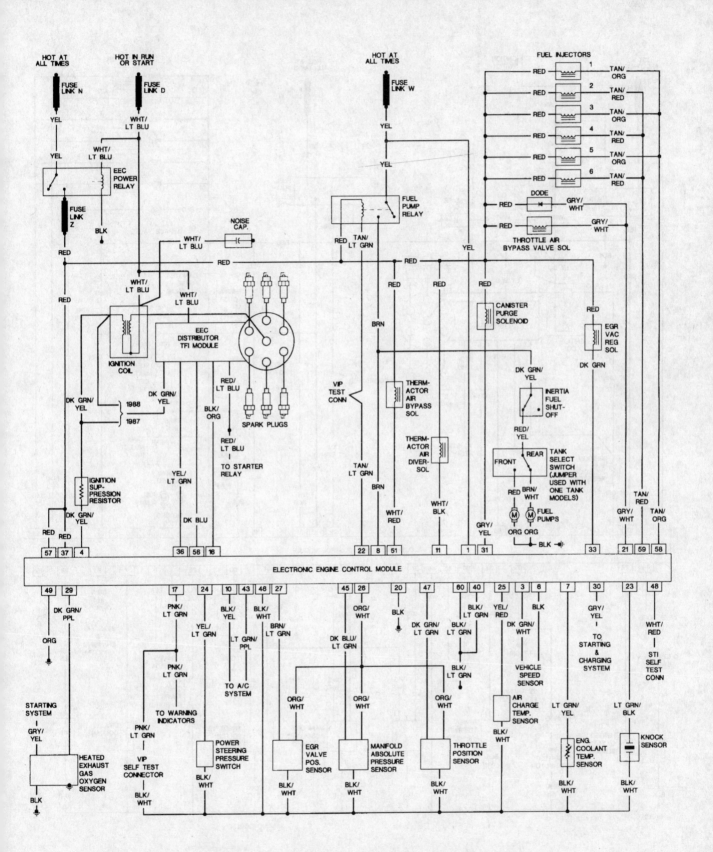

Engine wiring - 1987-88 F-Series Pick-up 4.9L (VIN Y) engine

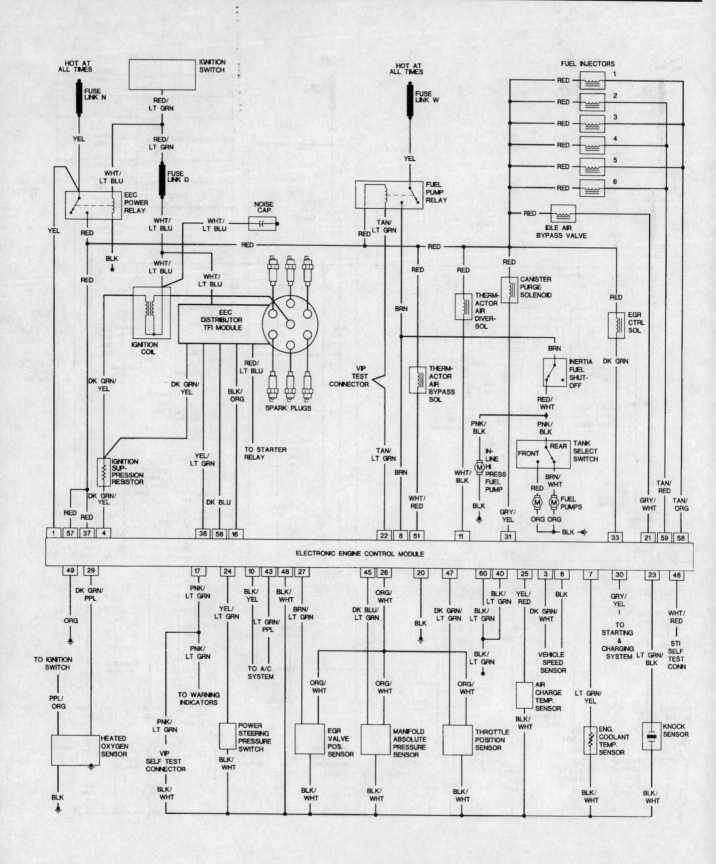

Engine wiring - 1989 F-Series Pick-up 4.9L (VIN Y) engine

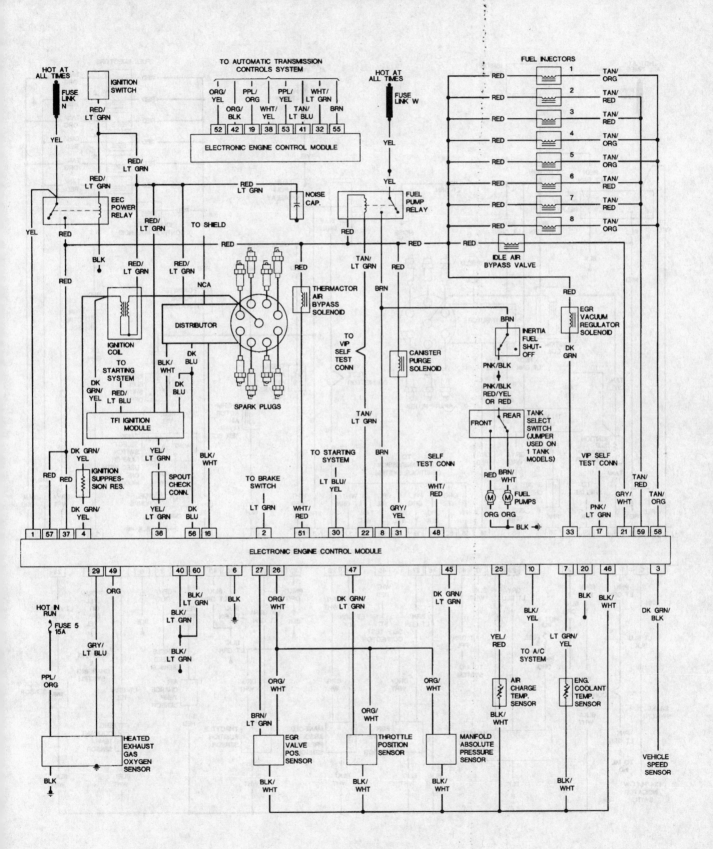

Engine wiring - 1990 F-Series Pick-up 7.5L (VIN G) engine

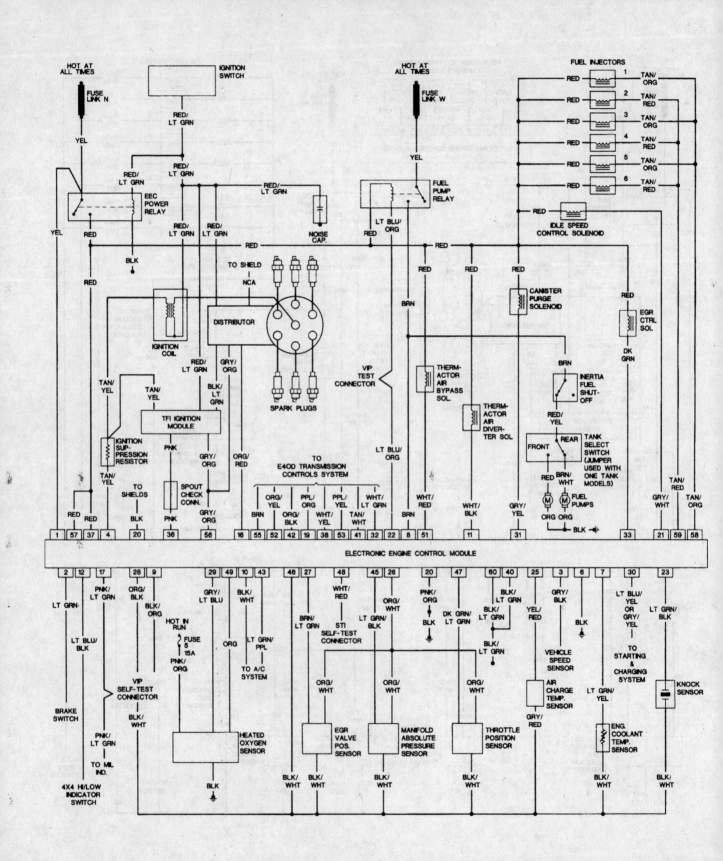

Engine wiring - 1990 F-Series Pick-up 4.9L (VIN Y) engine

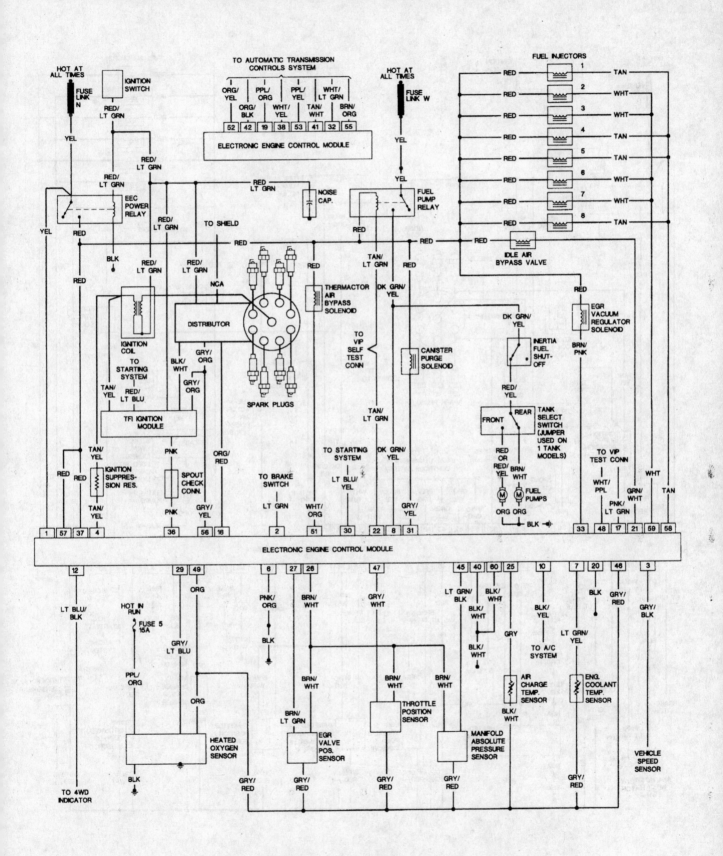

Engine wiring - 1991 F-Series Pick-up 7.5L (VIN G) engine

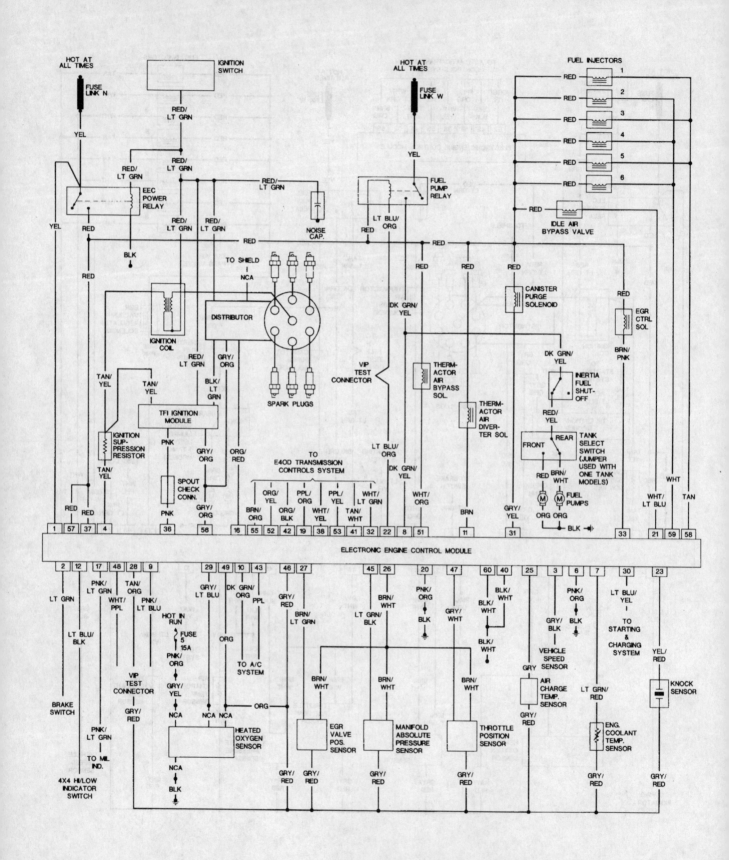

Engine wiring - 1991 F-Series Pick-up 4.9L (VIN Y) engine

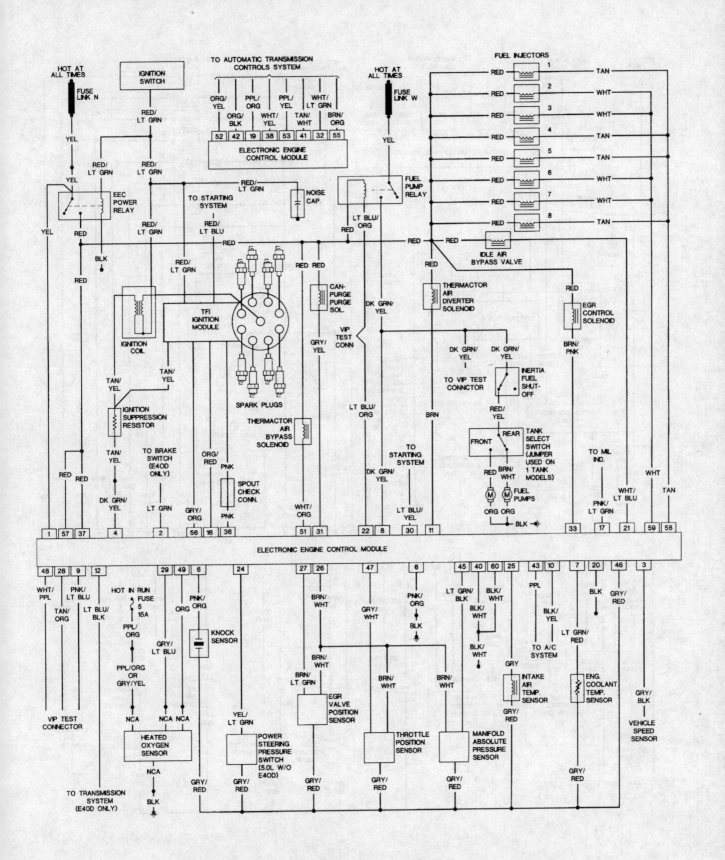

Engine wiring - 1991 F-Series and Bronco 5.0L (VIN N) and 5.8L (VIN H) (1990 similar)

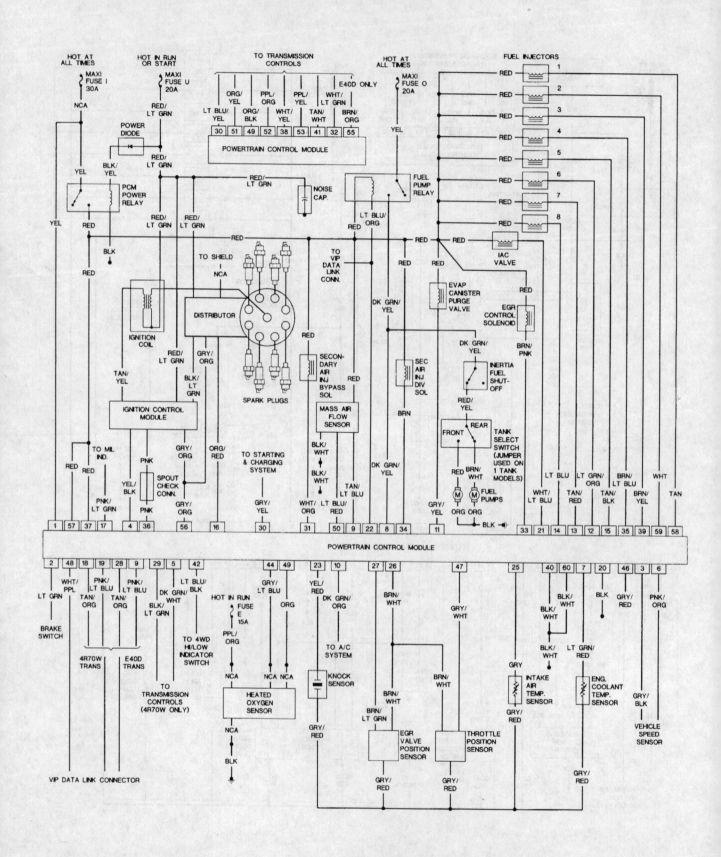

Engine wiring - 1994-95 F-Series and Bronco 5.0L Auto Transmission (VIN N) engine

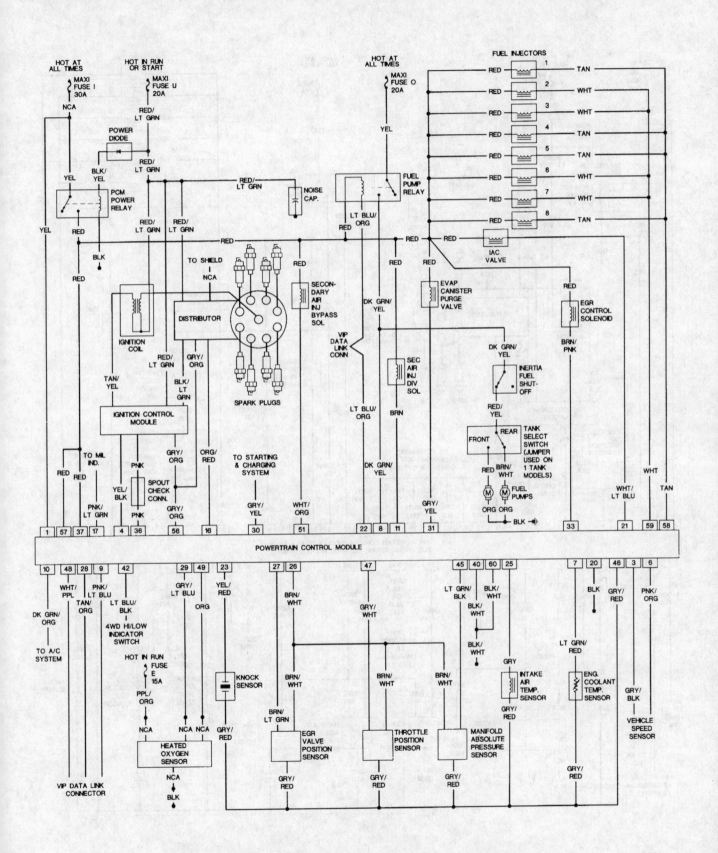

Engine wiring - 1994-95 F-Series and Bronco 5.0L Manual Transmission (VIN N) engine

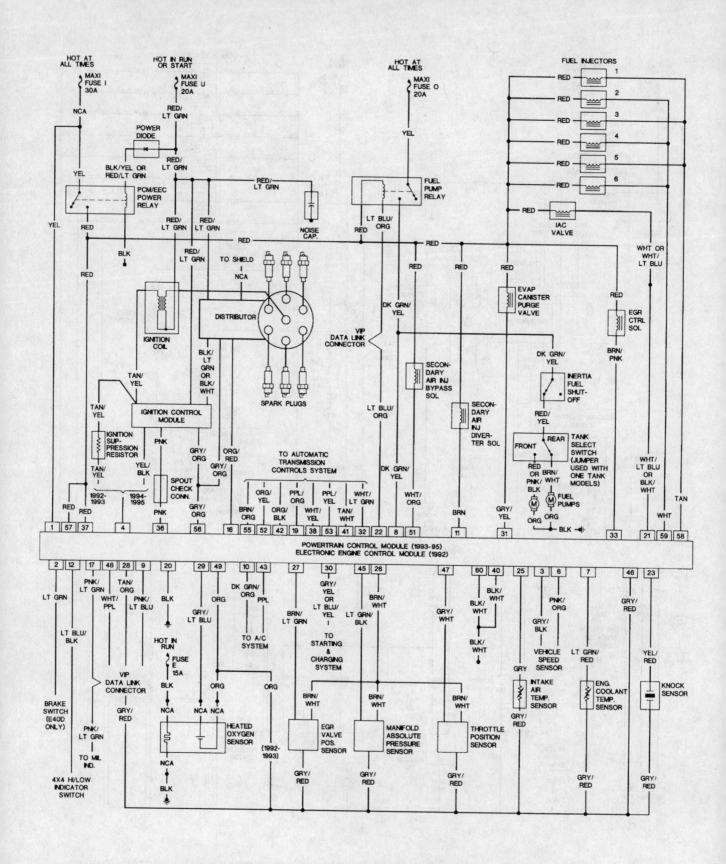

Engine wiring - 1992-94 F-Series 4.9L (VIN Y) and 1995 4.9L Federal (VIN Y) engines

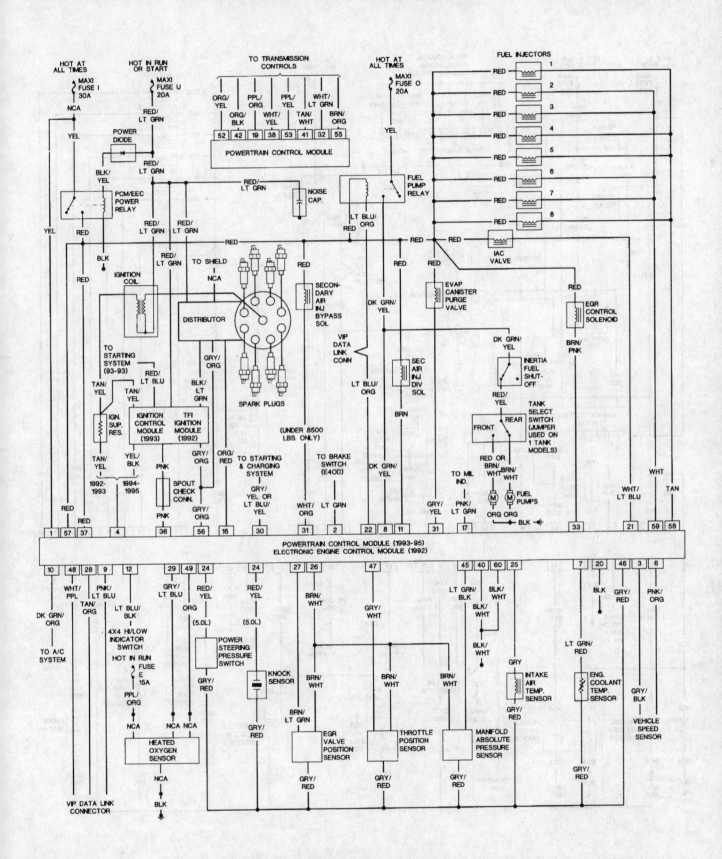

Engine wiring - 1992-93 F-Series and Bronco 5.0L (VIN N), 1992-94 F-Series and Bronco 5.8L (VIN H) and 1995 F-Series and Bronco 5.8L (VIN H) engine

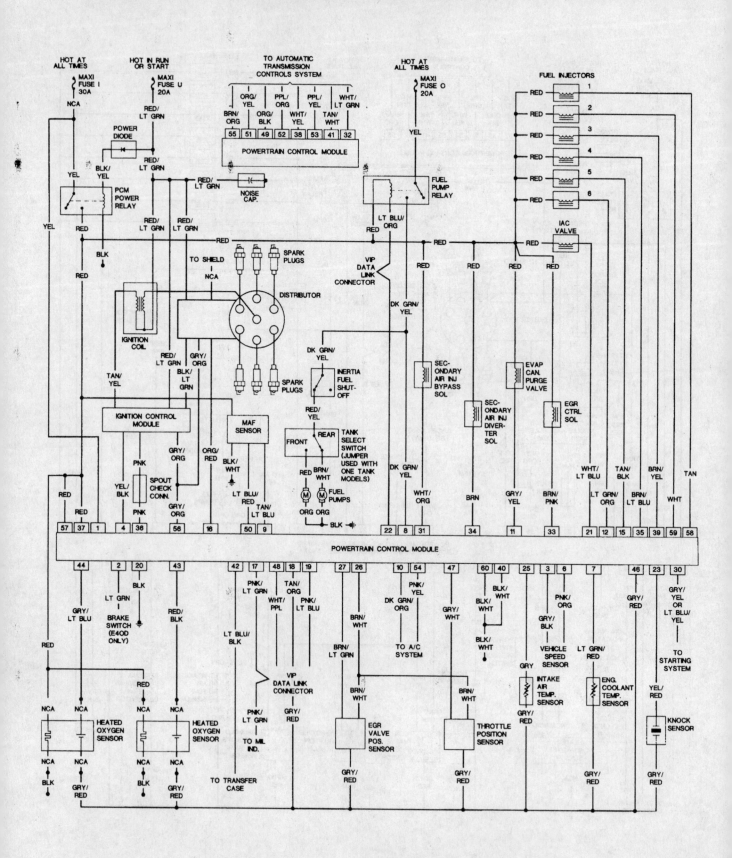

Engine wiring - 1995 F-Series 4.9L California (VIN Y) engine

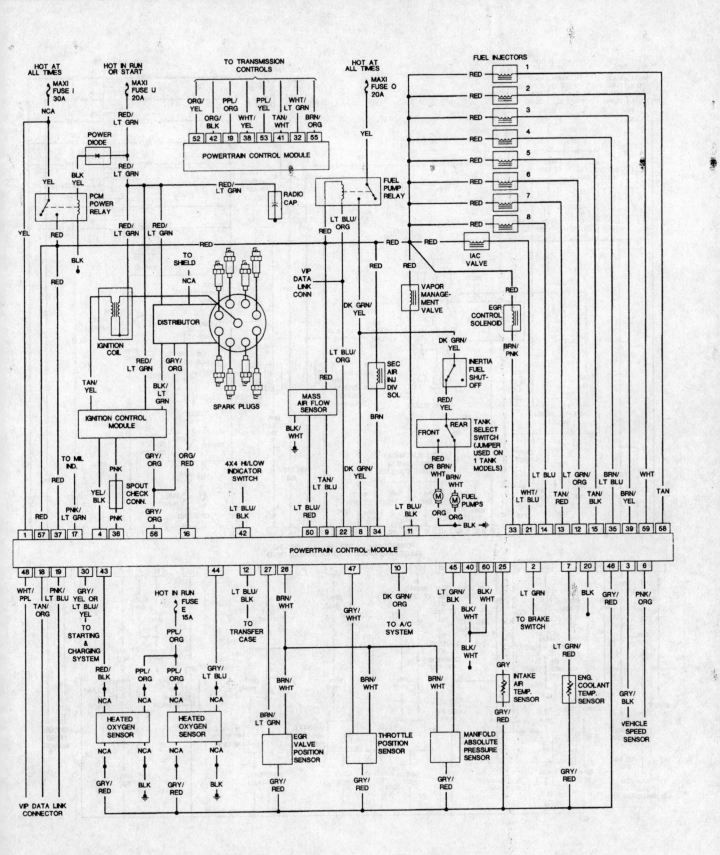

Engine wiring - 1995 F-Series and Bronco 5.8L California (VIN H) engine

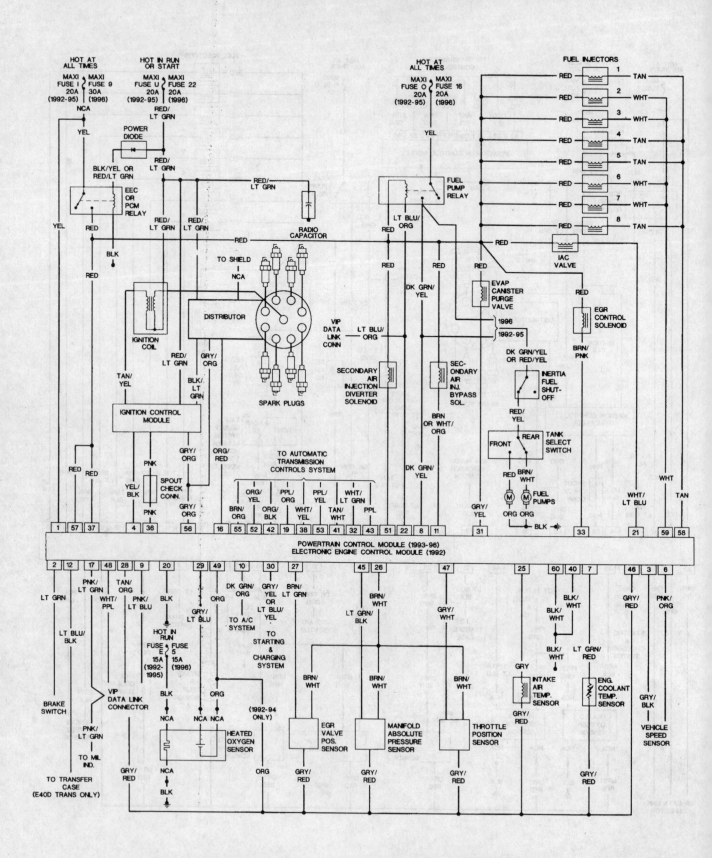

Engine wiring - 1992-95 F-Series 7.5L (VIN G), 1996 F-Series 7.5L Federal (VIN G) and
1996 F-Series Pick-up 5.8L (VIN H over 8500 GVW) engines

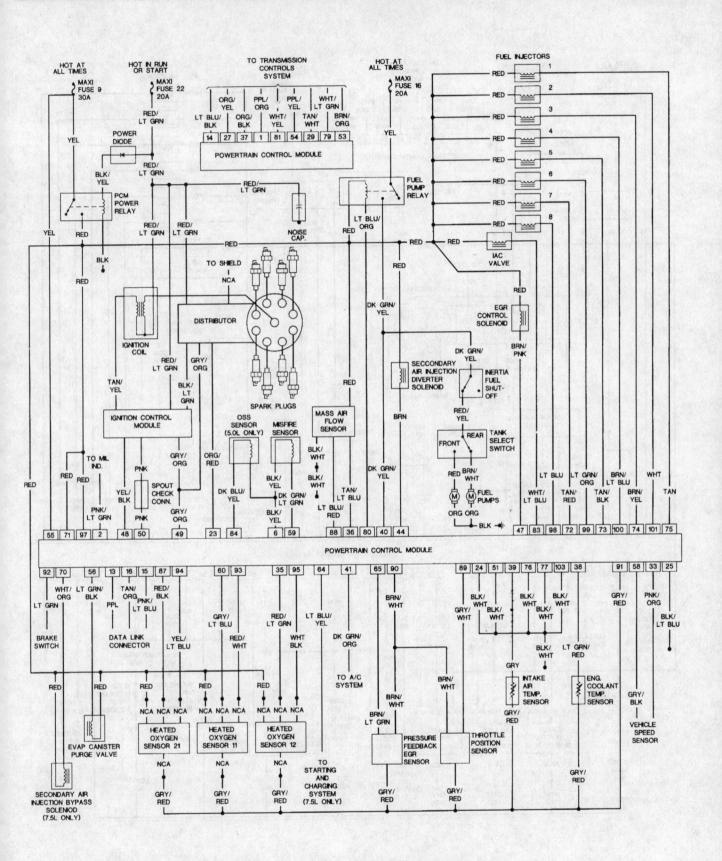

Engine wiring - 1996 F-Series and Bronco 5.0L (VIN N), 5.8L (VIN H under 8500 GVW), 7.5L California (VIN G) engines

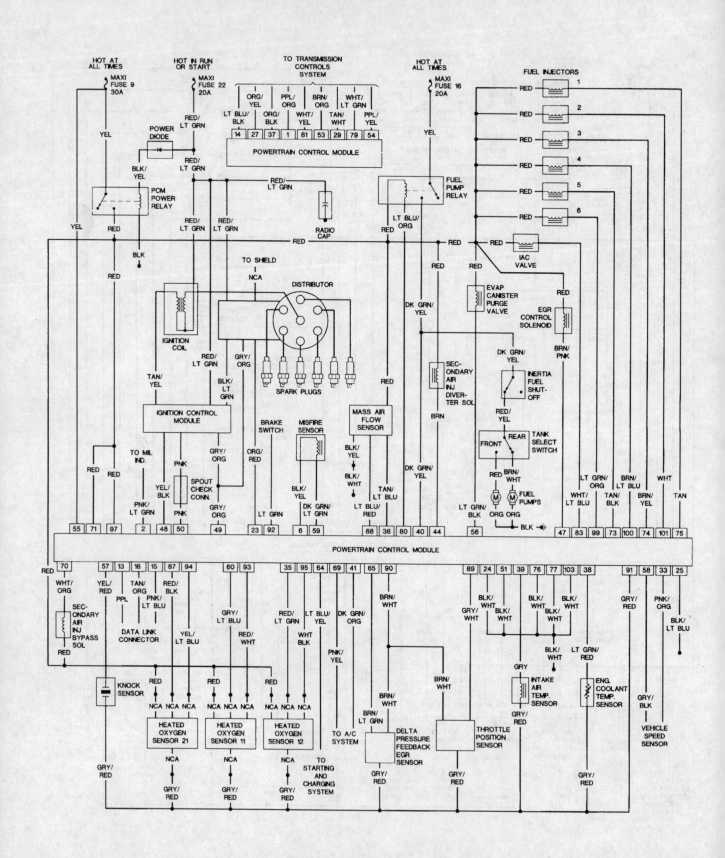

Engine wiring - 1996 F-Series 4.9L (VIN Y) engine

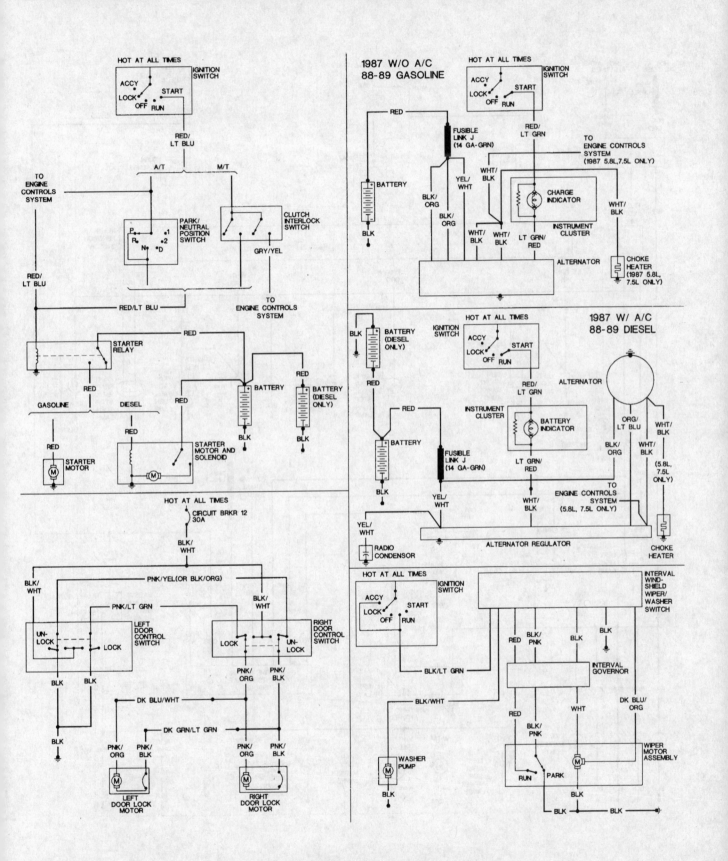

Chassis wiring - 1987-89 F-Series and Bronco

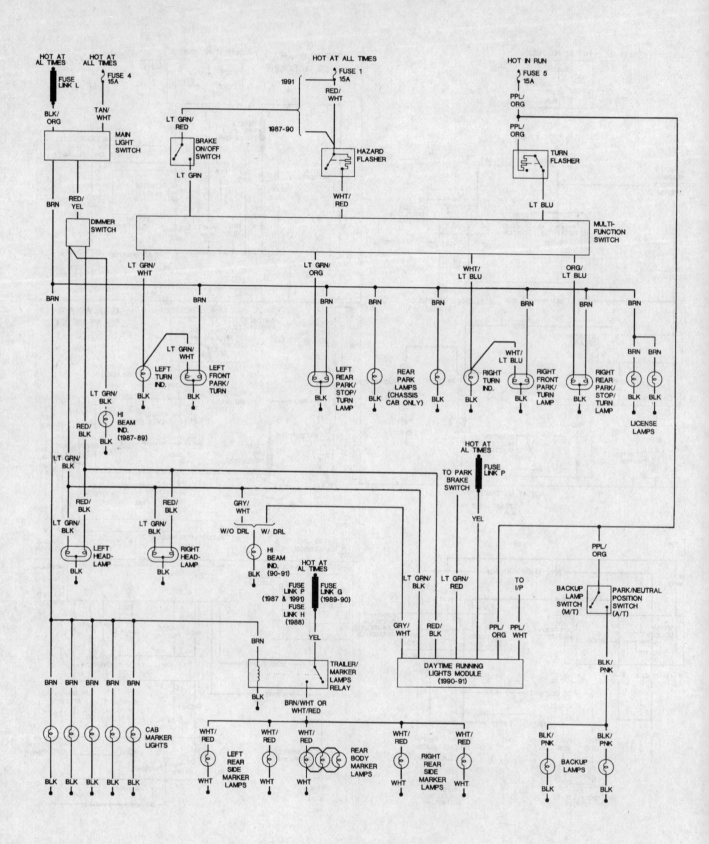

Chassis wiring - 1987-91 F-Series and Bronco

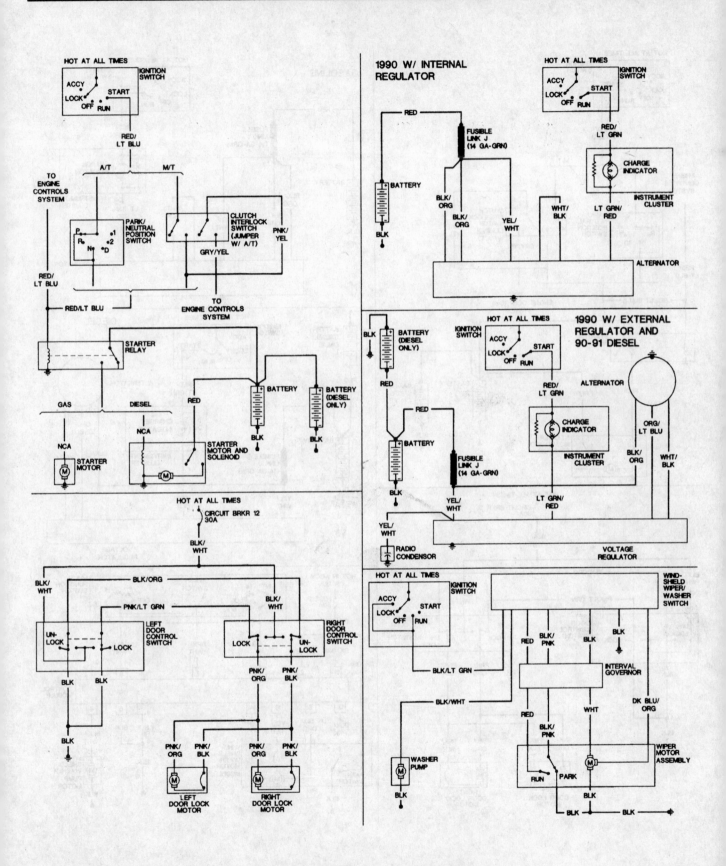

Chassis wiring - 1990-91 F-Series and Bronco

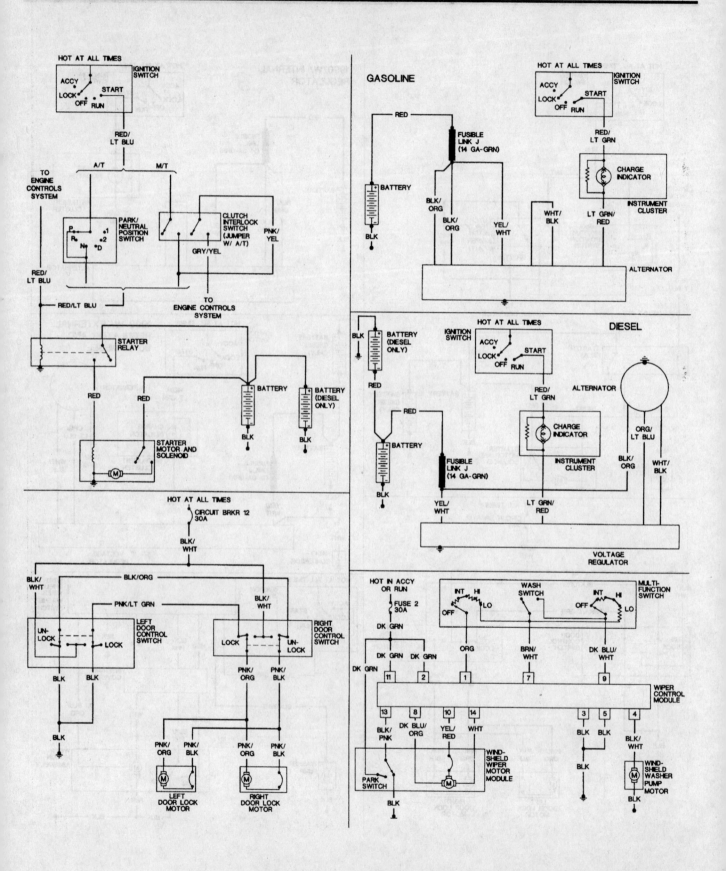

Chassis wiring - 1992 F-Series and Bronco

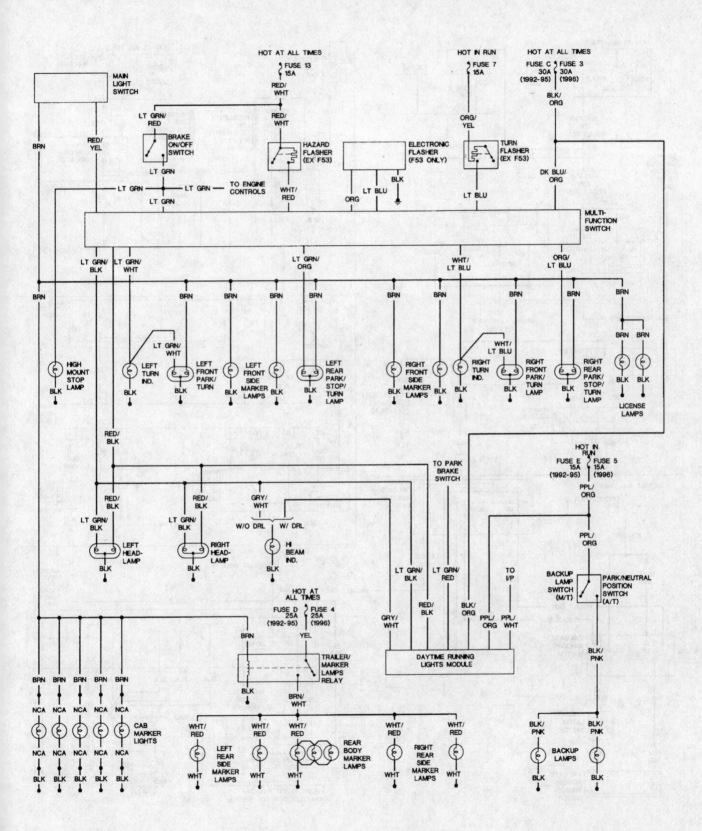

Chassis wiring - 1992-96 F-Series and Bronco

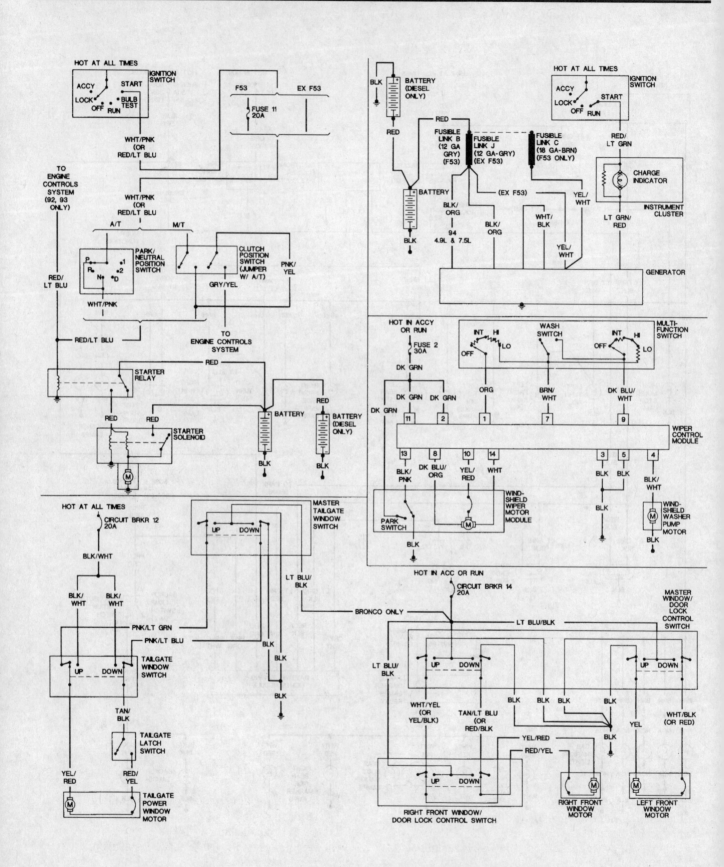

Chassis wiring - 1993-96 F-Series and Bronco

Index

Notes

Haynes Automotive Manuals

NOTE: If you do not see a listing for your vehicle, consult your local Haynes dealer for the latest product information.

Haynes North America, Inc., 861 Lawrence Drive, Newbury Park, CA 91320-1514 • (805) 498-6703 • http://www.haynes.com

Haynes Automotive Manuals (continued)

NOTE: If you do not see a listing for your vehicle, consult your local Haynes dealer for the latest product information.

42023 Civic all models '84 thru '91
42024 Civic & del Sol '92 thru '95
42025 Civic '96 thru '00, CR-V '97 thru '01, Acura Integra '94 thru '00
42026 Civic '01 thru '10, CR-V '02 thru '09
42035 Odyssey all models '99 thru '10
Passport - see ISUZU Rodeo (47017)
42037 Honda Pilot '03 thru '07, Acura MDX '01 thru '07
42040 Prelude CVCC all models '79 thru '89

HYUNDAI
43010 Elantra all models '96 thru '10
43015 Excel & Accent all models '86 thru '09
43050 Santa Fe all models '01 thru '06
43055 Sonata all models '99 thru '08

INFINITI
G35 '03 thru '08 - see NISSAN 350Z (72011)

ISUZU
Hombre - see CHEVROLET S-10 (24071)
47017 Rodeo, Amigo & Honda Passport '89 thru '02
47020 Trooper & Pick-up '81 thru '93

JAGUAR
49010 XJ6 all 6 cyl models '68 thru '86
49011 XJ6 all models '88 thru '94
49015 XJ12 & XJS all 12 cyl models '72 thru '85

JEEP
50010 Cherokee, Comanche & Wagoneer Limited all models '84 thru '01
50020 CJ all models '49 thru '86
50025 Grand Cherokee all models '93 thru '04
50026 Grand Cherokee '05 thru '09
50029 Grand Wagoneer & Pick-up '72 thru '91 Grand Wagoneer '84 thru '91, Cherokee & Wagoneer '72 thru '83, Pick-up '72 thru '88
50030 Wrangler all models '87 thru '11
50035 Liberty '02 thru '07

KIA
54050 Optima '01 thru '10
54070 Sephia '94 thru '01, Spectra '00 thru '09, Sportage '05 thru '10

LEXUS
ES 300/330 - see TOYOTA Camry (92007) (92008)
RX 330 - see TOYOTA Highlander (92095)

LINCOLN
Navigator - see FORD Pick-up (36059)
59010 Rear-Wheel Drive all models '70 thru '10

MAZDA
61010 GLC Hatchback (rear-wheel drive) '77 thru '83
61011 GLC (front-wheel drive) '81 thru '85
61012 Mazda3 '04 thru '11
61015 323 & Protegé '90 thru '03
61016 MX-5 Miata '90 thru '09
61020 MPV all models '89 thru '98
Navajo - see Ford Explorer (36024)
61030 Pick-ups '72 thru '93
Pick-ups '94 thru '00 - see Ford Ranger (36071)
61035 RX-7 all models '79 thru '85
61036 RX-7 all models '86 thru '91
61040 626 (rear-wheel drive) all models '79 thru '82
61041 626/MX-6 (front-wheel drive) '83 thru '92
61042 626, MX-6/Ford Probe '93 thru '02
61043 Mazda6 '03 thru '11

MERCEDES-BENZ
63012 123 Series Diesel '76 thru '85
63015 190 Series four-cyl models, '84 thru '88
63020 230/250/280 6 cyl sohc models '68 thru '72
63025 280 123 Series gasoline models '77 thru '81
63030 350 & 450 all models '71 thru '80
63040 C-Class: C230/C240/C280/C320/C350 '01 thru '07

MERCURY
64200 Villager & Nissan Quest '93 thru '01
All other titles, see FORD Listing.

MG
66010 MGB Roadster & GT Coupe '62 thru '80
66015 MG Midget, Austin Healey Sprite '58 thru '80

MINI
67020 Mini '02 thru '11

MITSUBISHI
68020 Cordia, Tredia, Galant, Precis & Mirage '83 thru '93
68030 Eclipse, Eagle Talon & Ply. Laser '90 thru '94
68031 Eclipse '95 thru '05, Eagle Talon '95 thru '98
68035 Galant '94 thru '10
68040 Pick-up '83 thru '96 & Montero '83 thru '93

NISSAN
72010 300ZX all models including Turbo '84 thru '89
72011 350Z & Infiniti G35 all models '03 thru '08
72015 Altima all models '93 thru '06
72016 Altima '07 thru '10
72020 Maxima all models '85 thru '92
72021 Maxima all models '93 thru '04
72025 Murano '03 thru '10
72030 Pick-ups '80 thru '97 Pathfinder '87 thru '95
72031 Frontier Pick-up, Xterra, Pathfinder '96 thru '04
72032 Frontier & Xterra '05 thru '11
72040 Pulsar all models '83 thru '86
Quest - see MERCURY Villager (64200)
72050 Sentra all models '82 thru '94
72051 Sentra & 200SX all models '95 thru '06
72060 Stanza all models '82 thru '90
72070 Titan pick-ups '04 thru '10 Armada '05 thru '10

OLDSMOBILE
73015 Cutlass V6 & V8 gas models '74 thru '88
For other OLDSMOBILE titles, see BUICK, CHEVROLET or GENERAL MOTORS listing.

PLYMOUTH
For PLYMOUTH titles, see DODGE listing.

PONTIAC
79008 Fiero all models '84 thru '88
79018 Firebird V8 models except Turbo '70 thru '81
79019 Firebird all models '82 thru '92
79025 G6 all models '05 thru '09
79040 Mid-size Rear-wheel Drive '70 thru '87
Vibe '03 thru '11 - see TOYOTA Matrix (92060)
For other PONTIAC titles, see BUICK, CHEVROLET or GENERAL MOTORS listing.

PORSCHE
80020 911 except Turbo & Carrera 4 '65 thru '89
80025 914 all 4 cyl models '69 thru '76
80030 924 all models including Turbo '76 thru '82
80035 944 all models including Turbo '83 thru '89

RENAULT
Alliance & Encore - see AMC (14020)

SAAB
84010 900 all models including Turbo '79 thru '88

SATURN
87010 Saturn all S-series models '91 thru '02
87011 Saturn Ion '03 thru '07
87020 Saturn all L-series models '00 thru '04
87040 Saturn VUE '02 thru '07

SUBARU
89002 1100, 1300, 1400 & 1600 '71 thru '79
89003 1600 & 1800 2WD & 4WD '80 thru '94
89100 Legacy all models '90 thru '99
89101 Legacy & Forester '00 thru '06

SUZUKI
90010 Samurai/Sidekick & Geo Tracker '86 thru '01

TOYOTA
92005 Camry all models '83 thru '91
92006 Camry all models '92 thru '96
92007 Camry, Avalon, Solara, Lexus ES 300 '97 thru '01
92008 Toyota Camry, Avalon and Solara and Lexus ES 300/330 all models '02 thru '06
92009 Camry '07 thru '11
92015 Celica Rear Wheel Drive '71 thru '85
92020 Celica Front Wheel Drive '86 thru '99
92025 Celica Supra all models '79 thru '92
92030 Corolla all models '75 thru '79
92032 Corolla all rear wheel drive models '80 thru '87
92035 Corolla all front wheel drive models '84 thru '92
92036 Corolla & Geo Prizm '93 thru '02
92037 Corolla all models '03 thru '11
92040 Corolla Tercel all models '80 thru '82
92045 Corona all models '74 thru '82
92050 Cressida all models '78 thru '82
92055 Land Cruiser FJ40, 43, 45, 55 '68 thru '82
92056 Land Cruiser FJ60, 62, 80, FZJ80 '80 thru '96
92060 Matrix & Pontiac Vibe '03 thru '11
92065 MR2 all models '85 thru '87
92070 Pick-up all models '69 thru '78
92075 Pick-up all models '79 thru '95
92076 Tacoma, 4Runner, & T100 '93 thru '04
92077 Tacoma '05 thru '09
92078 Tundra '00 thru '06 & Sequoia '01 thru '07
92079 4Runner all models '03 thru '09
92080 Previa all models '91 thru '95
92081 Prius all models '01 thru '08
92082 RAV4 all models '96 thru '10
92085 Tercel all models '87 thru '94
92090 Sienna all models '98 thru '09
92095 Highlander & Lexus RX-330 '99 thru '07

TRIUMPH
94007 Spitfire all models '62 thru '81
94010 TR7 all models '75 thru '81

VW
96008 Beetle & Karmann Ghia '54 thru '79
96009 New Beetle '98 thru '11
96016 Rabbit, Jetta, Scirocco & Pick-up gas models '75 thru '92 & Convertible '80 thru '92
96017 Golf, GTI & Jetta '93 thru '98, Cabrio '95 thru '02
96018 Golf, GTI, Jetta '99 thru '05
96019 Jetta, Rabbit, GTI & Golf '05 thru '11
96020 Rabbit, Jetta & Pick-up diesel '77 thru '84
96023 Passat '98 thru '05, Audi A4 '96 thru '01
96030 Transporter 1600 all models '68 thru '79
96035 Transporter 1700, 1800 & 2000 '72 thru '79
96040 Type 3 1500 & 1600 all models '63 thru '73
96045 Vanagon all air-cooled models '80 thru '83

VOLVO
97010 120, 130 Series & 1800 Sports '61 thru '73
97015 140 Series all models '66 thru '74
97020 240 Series all models '76 thru '93
97040 740 & 760 Series all models '82 thru '88
97050 850 Series all models '93 thru '97

TECHBOOK MANUALS
10205 Automotive Computer Codes
10206 OBD-II & Electronic Engine Management
10210 Automotive Emissions Control Manual
10215 Fuel Injection Manual '78 thru '85
10220 Fuel Injection Manual '86 thru '99
10225 Holley Carburetor Manual
10230 Rochester Carburetor Manual
10240 Weber/Zenith/Stromberg/SU Carburetors
10305 Chevrolet Engine Overhaul Manual
10310 Chrysler Engine Overhaul Manual
10320 Ford Engine Overhaul Manual
10330 GM and Ford Diesel Engine Repair Manual
10333 Engine Performance Manual
10340 Small Engine Repair Manual, 5 HP & Less
10341 Small Engine Repair Manual, 5.5 - 20 HP
10345 Suspension, Steering & Driveline Manual
10355 Ford Automatic Transmission Overhaul
10360 GM Automatic Transmission Overhaul
10405 Automotive Body Repair & Painting
10410 Automotive Brake Manual
10411 Automotive Anti-lock Brake (ABS) Systems
10415 Automotive Detailing Manual
10420 Automotive Electrical Manual
10425 Automotive Heating & Air Conditioning
10430 Automotive Reference Manual & Dictionary
10435 Automotive Tools Manual
10440 Used Car Buying Guide
10445 Welding Manual
10450 ATV Basics
10452 Scooters 50cc to 250cc

SPANISH MANUALS
98903 Reparación de Carrocería & Pintura
98904 Manual de Carburador Modelos Holley & Rochester
98905 Códigos Automotrices de la Computadora
98906 OBD-II & Sistemas de Control Electrónico del Motor
98910 Frenos Automotriz
98913 Electricidad Automotriz
98915 Inyección de Combustible '86 al '99
99040 Chevrolet & GMC Camionetas '67 al '87
99041 Chevrolet & GMC Camionetas '88 al '98
99042 Chevrolet & GMC Camionetas Cerradas '68 al '95
99043 Chevrolet/GMC Camionetas '94 al '04
99048 Chevrolet/GMC Camionetas '99 al '06
99055 Dodge Caravan & Plymouth Voyager '84 al '95
99075 Ford Camionetas y Bronco '80 al '94
99076 Ford F-150 '97 al '09
99077 Ford Camionetas Cerradas '69 al '91
99088 Ford Modelos de Tamaño Mediano '75 al '86
99089 Ford Camionetas Ranger '93 al '10
99091 Ford Taurus & Mercury Sable '86 al '95
99095 GM Modelos de Tamaño Grande '70 al '90
99100 GM Modelos de Tamaño Mediano '70 al '88
99106 Jeep Cherokee, Wagoneer & Comanche '84 al '00
99110 Nissan Camioneta '80 al '96, Pathfinder '87 al '95
99118 Nissan Sentra '82 al '94
99125 Toyota Camionetas y 4Runner '79 al '95

Over 100 Haynes motorcycle manuals also available

7-12